7.75N

INSTRUCTIONAL PROCESS
AND MEDIA INNOVATION

INSTRUCTIONAL PROCESS AND MEDIA INNOVATION

Edited by
ROBERT A. WEISGERBER, Ed. D.
American Institutes for Research
Palo Alto, California

RAND McNALLY & COMPANY · Chicago

Forethought

SOLEMN THOUGHTS
ON THE SECOND INDUSTRIAL REVOLUTION*

S. I. Hayakawa

In each insurance company, in every bank and store,
Are filing clerks and billing clerks and typists by the score;
The work that all these people do will one day disappear
In ERMA[1] systems tended by a lonely engineer.
   (But they'll never mechanize me — not me!
   Said Charlotte, the Louisville harlot.)

While former auto workers try to fill their empty days,
The automated auto-plant will turn out Chevrolets;
With automatic pilots landing jet planes on the strip,
The present men who guide them will not need to take the trip.
   (But how can they automate me? Goodness me!
   Asked Millie, the call girl from Philly.)

Who'll keep the inventory up, who'll order the supplies
Of paper towels, linens, iron pipe, or railroad ties?
Executives now do this with a steno and a phone,
But big computers soon will make decisions all alone.
   (They cannot cybernate me, tee hee!
   Laughed Alice, the hooker from Dallas.)

Machines will teach our children how to read and add and spell;
Because they've lots of patience, they will do it very well.
If business men and managers are not on the alert,
Their functions will be taken on by CPM[2] and PERT.[3]
   (I'll never be coded in FORTRAN[4] — wheee!
   Cried Susie, the Hackensack floozie.)

      Chorus of Charlotte, Millie, Alice, and Susie:
The future will be like the past despite all dire foreseeings;
We stoutly shall defend the human use of human beings.

*Reprinted by permission from *ETC.: A Review of General Semantics*, Vol. XXIII, No. 1; copyright 1966, by the International Society of General Semantics.
1Electronic Recording and Machine Accounting
2Critical Path Method
3Program Evaluation and Review Technique
4Formula Translation

Preface

Education is surrounded by technology. It has become commonplace to rely on technology for transportation, communication, manufacture, agriculture, business, entertainment, and even exploration. To some, education represents one of the few remaining bulwarks of singularly human endeavor, where the personal contact and discourse of lecture methods has reigned supreme for centuries and could continue to do so indefinitely. To others, education represents a frontier of our time: a frontier which, like others before it, will be pushed back by those individuals who are not content to settle for the status quo and who believe that better methods can be developed. Those who are concerned with the frontiers of education should read this book.

Much of the text material available today, which bears upon the instructional process, is narrow in scope. On the one hand, there have been numbers of books on audiovisual materials written especially for teacher trainees; there have been texts in programed instruction written for graduate P.I. courses; there have been texts in computer-based instruction written for researchers in the field; and, on the other hand, there have been texts written about curriculum development for administrators, subject matter disciplines for content specialists, and human behavior for those in psychology. It was felt that a broad view might be a refreshing and useful change . . . that instead of narrowly defining the scope of this text it might be rewarding *to examine the instructional process from a number of viewpoints.* It was further felt that a broad view might best be obtained not from a single writer but from many, each considering a different aspect of the instructional process, offering provocative thoughts and, in some cases, citing reports of applied experiences in fulfillment of those thoughts.

Many individuals have examined education from the standpoint of process, found it wanting, and as a result have, in one respect or another, become engaged in innovation through research, development, or critical analysis of the teaching/learning cycle. The individuals who have contributed chapters to this book are among those who so firmly believe that education *should* make human use of human resources that they are actively studying the instructional process to ascertain those elements which may be nonhuman in nature, or, to put it in a positive sense, are appropriate for technological implementation.

The tragic irony of a technologically sophisticated society that still misuses its human resources is sharply pointed out by my friend Dr. S. I. Hayakawa, the leading semanticist and teacher, in an opening forethought. The book is organized around generic principles in Part I, educational levels in Part II, curricular programs in Part III, the major media and evolving technologies in Part IV, and practical steps toward instructional implementation of media in Part V. Questions are posed before each chapter to provide continuity and give a partial insight into chapter content. Most chapters have been authored specifically for inclusion in this text. Some, being appropriate to the theme, are reprinted from other sources, as indicated on the first page of those chapters. The editor is aware that gaps remain, even as gaps remain in the field itself.

It is likely that the reader of these chapters will become aware of the exciting atmosphere of change that is growing throughout education, and he should become more cognizant of the variety of significant innovative approaches that are being explored on the educational frontier. Those who read the book for final solutions or simple formulae will not be likely to find them. Those who read the book with the intent of sampling the thoughts of a variety of educators, in order to ascertain probable directions in which instructional process may yet be further refined and developed, will most likely be rewarded.

Lastly, this book is intended to emphasize the *utilization* of technology in education — the consideration in depth of media production, facilities and environment, theory, administrative logistics, and research remain as emphases for further collaborative works.

R.A.W.

Acknowledgements

The editor has appreciated the many instances of helpful feedback from professional colleagues in review of the various chapters and on the content outline of the book. Most particularly, the early counsel and guidance of Dr. Chester Babcock, Assistant Superintendent for Curriculum and Instruction, State of Washington, was indispensable as a means of shaping the nature of the book and the selection of collaborating writers. While personal injury prevented his active involvement in the final stages it is truly said that his participation as a curriculum expert was extremely helpful. Others who have given freely of their time to discuss elements of the book include Nellene Smith and Frank Moakley, of San Francisco State College, and John Bertrand, of Shasta College, and the late Hilda Taba.

In secretarial respects the editor offers sincere thanks to Rosalie Martinez, Linda Spendow, Vickie Ruiz, Karen Tolui, Jerri Baker, Marguerite Mihailoff, and Norma Stead, all of whom have, at one time or another, contributed their talents to facilitate my task.

In contacts with Rand McNally I have found new friends simply through the good fortune of working with Tom LaMarre and Larry Hill. They are men who live and work in a world of books but who appreciate 'visuals' none the less.

In the last analysis, however, my real debt is to Adrienne, Laraine, and Scott, for they make it all worthwhile.

R.A.W.

TABLE OF CONTENTS

Part One

INDUCING CHANGE IN THE LEARNER

Chapter 1

What is effective teaching and how is learning accomplished?
*What innovations are occurring in curriculum development and
instructional strategy?*
*What respective values are derived from the inductive/deductive
approaches to learning?*
*What significant roles can the various media have in the
instructional process?*

RELATIONSHIPS OF
MEDIA AND THE CURRICULUM

W. C. MEIERHENRY, Assistant Dean and Professor of Education
Teachers College, University of Nebraska

Learning is a change in behavior brought about in an individual as a
result of experience. The outline and plan for presenting or making
available the experiences to the learner is the curriculum. The role of
the teacher is to plan and make available the experiences suggested or
specified in the curriculum designed to bring about the changes of behavior in the most efficient and permanent manner. Thus, media play
an integral role so far as the presentation of experiences are concerned.

VIEWS OF TEACHING.

One of the problems in teaching is to make decisions about the way in
which the changes in behavior of the pupils are to be accomplished. One
extreme position proposes that the student is a receptacle into which
facts and information can be crammed or poured. This view suggests
that there is someone in a position to determine the facts and information which the students should master, and further that the order and
sequence of them is determined best by the teacher.
   Another extreme view of teaching is to assume that the student him-

3

self is in the best position to determine his learning needs. This type of teaching takes its cue from the physiological phenomenon that most children will eventually adjust their eating habits so that they will select a balanced diet if all types of foods are made equally available to them. Those who propose making a rich environment of learning resources available argue that the individual learner is in the best position to make judgments about the type and order of experience which he needs in order to achieve objectives successfully. This view of learning requires that all types of resources including both print and non-print be readily available.

There have been a number of attempts to develop different types of teaching models so far as the use of materials are concerned. A recent attempt was that of Thelen when he indicated:

> There are several points of view about how materials work into the educative process, and I will mention four. The first is that the experience of the child is determined to a significant extent by the materials he uses. If you believe this is true, then you begin to have fantasies about building a self-contained program based on materials, with the teacher playing a minimum role – like motivating the child. . . .
>
> The second approach, I think, has been the traditional one. It is based on the sound proposition that materials can be made effective if the teacher knows what to do with them. . . . There are all sorts of wonderful ingenious things you can do if you have decent reference material – and I would call it reference material. And, if the aim is limited (as it usually is), to teaching the 'information,' any old method of teaching will work. . . .
>
> The third possibility lies between the first two. It makes room for the teacher, but it doesn't make him quite as important as does the second one. The third approach proposes that effective teaching is some kind of interaction between the teacher, the materials, and the students. That is, there are some peculiar combinations of teacher-skill plus appropriate materials that arrive at good educational results. . . .
>
> Here, then, are three common positions about the relation of materials to classroom teaching. I am now going to suggest a fourth approach which makes more sense than the other three: Instead of using materials to program the child, use them to program the class.[1]

Thelen then proceeds to identify three different ways of involving students in thinking and inquiry. Each example which he cites requires the learners and the teacher to be involved in experiences which encourage the students to solve problems presented by situations without being given the answers by the teacher.

Another attempt to identify teaching models has been developed by

[1] Herbert Thelen, "Materials That Promote Inquiry and Thinking," *Educational Screen and Audiovisual Guide*, XLIV, No. 12/452 (December 1965), p. 25.

Scheffler. He labels his three models "the impression model," "the insight model," and "the rule model." Each is described below:

The impression model is perhaps the simplest and most widespread of the three, picturing the mind essentially as sifting and storing the external impressions to which it is receptive. The desired end result of teaching is an accumulation in the learner of basic elements fed in from without, organized and processed in standard ways, but, in any event, not generated by the learner himself. In the empiricist variant of this model generally associated with John Locke, learning involves the input by experience of simple ideas of sensation and reflection, which are clustered, related, generalized, and retained by the mind. Blank at birth, the mind is thus formed by its particular experience which it keeps available for its future use. . . .

The next model I shall consider, the 'insight model,' represents a radically different approach. Where the impression model supposes the teacher to be conveying ideas or bits of knowledge into the student's mental treasury, the insight model denies the very possibility of such conveyance. Knowledge, it insists, is a matter of vision, and vision cannot be dissected into elementary sensory or verbal units that can be conveyed from one person to another. It can, at most, be stimulated or prompted by what the teacher does, and if it indeed occurs, it goes beyond what is thus done. Vision defines and organizes particular experiences and points up their significance. It is vision or insight into meaning which makes the crucial difference between simple storing and reproducing learned sentences, on the one hand, and understanding their basis and application on the other. . . .

The shortcoming of the insight model . . . is remedied in the 'rule model,' which I associate with Kant. For Kant, the primary philosophical emphasis is on reason, and reason is always a matter of abiding by general rules or principles. Reason stands always in contrast with inconsistency and with expediency in the judgment of particular issues. In the cognitive realm, reason is a kind of justice to the evidence, a fair treatment of the merits of the case, in the interests of truth. In the moral realm, reason is action on principle, action which therefore does not bend with the wind, nor lean to the side of advantage or power out of weakness or self-interest. Whether in the cognitive or the moral realm, reason is always a matter of treating equal reasons equally, and of judging the issues in the light of general principles to which one has bound oneself.[2]

INDUCTIVE APPROACH TO LEARNING.

A great deal of the recent curricular emphasis has been upon discovery or inquiry teaching (Thelen's fourth approach discussed above). It should be recognized that such teaching involves the inductive approach.

2 Israel Scheffler, "Philosophical Models of Teaching," *Harvard Educational Review*, XXXV, No. 2 (Spring 1965), pp. 132, 135, 139.

It requires that the sequence of learning begin with an exposure to concrete experiences. The concrete experiences which are chosen must be of such a nature that the learner can make use of them in such a way that he can discover the generalization, principle, or rule which the concrete experience contains and suggests. In this type of intellectual development the sequence is from the concrete experiences to the verbalization of the idea, principle, or concept, as the final intellectual act.

The process of discovery includes, therefore, the presentation of pertinent concrete experiences which are most likely to suggest to the learner certain principles, generalizations, or concepts. The role of the teacher is to raise questions in order to provoke mental activity on the part of the learner but without giving the answer so that the learner himself 'discovers' the desired response. There then follows the attaching of verbal symbols but with appropriate caution so that the desired name tag is not attached before the learner has had an opportunity to internalize and reorganize the experience.

Most of the newer curricular developments have placed heavy emphasis upon the 'inductive approach to learning. Science teaching has emphasized the inductive principle for a long time with the major concrete experience as the laboratory experiment. The theory behind the laboratory experiment has been that the learner will, from the series of observations performed in the laboratory, arrive at certain principles or laws which the experiment has been selected to demonstrate. In elementary school science a textbook approach of teaching facts has been replaced by simple laboratory equipment in order that the children themselves might perform various kinds of experiments. Philip Morrison, professor of physics, Cornell University, described this new approach to a group of elementary science teachers as follows:

> A. N. Whitehead, a man known for the mathematical density of his prose and formulae, nevertheless, late in life, in his book, *Science and the Modern World*, wrote the following: "My own criticism of traditional educational methods is that they are far too much occupied with intellectual analysis, with the acquirement of formularized information. What I mean is that we neglect to strengthen habits of concrete appreciation of individual facts, in their full interplay of emergent values; that we merely emphasize abstract formulations which ignore this aspect of the interplay of diverse values. We are too exclusively bookish in our scholastic routine. There should be some analysis, but only enough to illustrate the ways of thinking in diverse spheres. In the Garden of Eden, Adam saw the animals before he named them. In the traditional system, the children named animals before they saw them."
>
> Notice that *both* the seeing and the naming of the animals are held as valuable parts of educational activity. It is a question of priority. As a

simple example, you can look at a wristwatch under a microscope to see the minute hand move. If you magnify it a bit, it plainly moves. With a good microscope, you can even see the hour hand move; in fact, it usually moves five jumps a second, but to see its motion it must be much magnified. The extension of the perceptions by instrumentation here clearly fulfills the analytical understanding of the nature of motion. One has perception of its motion which is distinct from the analytical motion, in which the object successively occupies many places as a function of time. It is not the same thing. We see something move; but we can see the minute hand move only with a magnifier — just as we can see the sun move in a telescope. This mixture of direct experience, individual concrete experience, with analysis — is the sun really moving in the sky? is the shadow of the wall really moving across the courtyard? — this forms a mixture of the aesthetic and the analytic. The aesthetic, because it rests on an individual experience; it is certainly not the same when I merely tell you about it; that is something, but it is not as good as when you can see it for yourself.

We have a commitment which is shared by almost all the scientists and artists I have spoken with, that this direct experience is invaluable and cannot be fully replaced by the purely abstract. Of course, the abstract can enormously enrich and transform the concrete experience.

Our job then, has been largely to produce this sort of mixture, a very difficult mixture, and one which implies, of course, a great amount of attention to details, details of concept and of manipulation.

There is no use in designing a curriculum now which encompasses everything that is important, because you can be quite sure that thirty years from now many of those things are not going to be so important any more. You would do better to include something beyond your own judgment of what is important. This does not mean, of course, that we do not think there are important topics; but I think you cannot hope to span the entire body of useful, important knowledge with any set curriculum.

If I add the human time spent by all teachers per student in education, even for a well-educated person, it is three human years on the average. Let us compare that to the ten to thirty years of a realizable self-education. Thus, you cannot hope to cram much in through schools. There are two ways of going about this problem. One is to compress everything into the most formularized, the most compact method possible, and commit it all to memory, and then it cannot be wrong. I have given ample argument why that will not do. The other solution is to accept that you cannot hope to teach enough to make a really serious dent on stored information, so that what you should teach are those concrete experiences, those attitudes, those beginning abstract formulations, which have the maximum degree of importance for transferring, building upon, and continuing to learn. This is why we do not feel that it is necessary to pick out particularly large numbers of topics on which to concentrate.[3]

3 Philip Morrison, "Experimenters in the Schoolroom," *ESI Quarterly Report* (Winter–Spring 1964), pp. 64–65.

Morrison discusses the same problem but in a somewhat different fashion in the following statement:

. . . One of the differences between science and technology has been the essentially playful activities of the scientist. He has tried to see how bodies fall not only in order to design rockets or cannons, but, simply, to see. The suspicion that cannons would be improved thereby has often proved true. Still, the ability to suspend a goal for the sake of clarity and human delight is part and parcel of science. Play makes no pots, but playing with clay makes potters. The potter is his own clay, as the epigram tells us; and the scientist, or the child studying science, is also his own experiment. We would not forget this, nor would we forget that the tone of playfulness is not the tone of prescribed and demanding ends. The child who does something off the track is usually not wasting time and effort; what he changes is himself, if not the apparatus. School is an institution for changing children, and perhaps teachers, too. Our experimental directions ought not always to be efficient, clear, earnest and single-minded. Sometimes they have to be easy-going, ambiguous, laughable and rambling. No single attitude can properly span all of what we mean by science.

One mandate is imperative for our style of work: there must be personal involvement. The child must work with his own hands, mind and heart. It is not enough for him to watch the teacher demonstrate or stand in line to take a hurried glimpse of the reflection of his own eyelashes in the microscope eyepiece. It is not enough for him to watch the skillful classmate at work, not enough to follow the TV screen. He needs his own apparatus, simple, workable. This is not a peremptory command. Many matters are handled by film or in a group or, sometimes, by the teacher. But we must work hard to bring a more varied range of science into the child's own hands; where he may be potter and clay at once . . .

The final criterion of our curricular style is this: it takes time. What the textbook can summarize in a page of results — life is cellular, cells have water and carbon, cells divide to multiply — our methods with the childs' own work, with his own hands, with his own microscope and his own labored arithmetic may take six weeks of classroom effort. We do not begrudge this time. We are not disturbed by slowness, for what goes slow can run deep. And school hours are not all of life. To stroll into reality, the detail of it and the context, to unravel and to uncover it is a better thing than to sprint past, reading the billboards, of science.[4]

It should be noted that Morrison places considerable emphasis upon the need to study less material than often attempted and to deal with these fewer critical ideas and concepts in depth. This approach has often been referred to as postholing, which suggests that certain key points or structures which have significant implications for an understanding of the

[4] Philip Morrison, "The Curricular Triangle and Its Style," ESI *Quarterly Report,* III, No. 2 (Summer–Fall 1964), p. 70.

entire content area under consideration should be studied in depth but with the most careful examination of the individual parts so that the learner can induce the necessary generalizations.

Mathematics content as well as methods of teaching it have been undergoing tremendous changes recently. There are a number of factors which characterize the so-called new math, but among them is the involvement of the learner in the development of number manipulations and relationships as the result of experience. Rote learning of number facts has been replaced by the learners discovering for themselves the desired facts through the examination of materials and models. Some idea of the nature of these changes is suggested by the following:

> Finally, all new curriculum projects [in mathematics] must, of course, make assumptions about the nature of schools in general. A recent trend has appeared, among some but not all projects, to assume a background of a new kind of school. This 'new kind of school' would, in general, relate to such ideas as these: the increasing recognition of the role of *intrinsic motivation;* the emphasis on *learning how to learn;* the emphasis on *individualizing instruction;* the emphasis on *creativity* and *divergent thinking;* the increasing use of *digital computers* in relation to schools; the *scheduling of classes* to allow *greater flexibility,* and especially *longer periods,* when necessary, for laboratory experimentation: the present interest in *physical materials* such as Cuisenaire rods, Dienes blocks, and single-concept film loops; the interest in *small group* and *large group* instruction; a greater use of *field trips,* '*action assignments*' *outside of school, outside lecturers, television,* and *other community resources;* a tendency to '*ungrade*' the entire school program; a greater emphasis on the open-ended aspect of learning; and a growing concern over *inadequacies in our testing programs.* The newer approach also manifests itself in the concern for the structure of mathematics rather than for facts; and in the matter of *teaching the subject itself,* rather than some 'simplified' version of the subject which lacks authenticity. It is involved, also, in the growing concern about indoctrination.[5]

Zacharias, a scientist, describes very well the process of discovery in a presentation which he made to a group of English teachers. He suggested that the process of discovery in science likely also had some application to the field of language and literature.

> We, the scientists, take stuff from the bucket. When we let down our scientific buckets, we come up with some lovely stuff which we, as children, wanted, and which children today still seem to enjoy. Lovely pieces, crystal clear, that only come to the surface with dipping. And we think that we can help the children dip, until our children out-dip us.

5 Robert B. Davis, "Mathematics," *New Curriculum Developments.* Glenys G. Unruh, editor. Washington, D. C.: Association for Supervision and Curriculum Development, 1965, p. 52. © 1965 by the Association for Supervision and Curriculum Development.

Can you, too, dip in your buckets and help the children dip? I think you can. But you can't know until you try.

I should perhaps be required to give an example of dipping, in order to exhibit a piece of the science we love. Unfortunately, here I can use only words; with the pupils I could use things. One problem set before ten-year-olds is: how does a mealworm find its meal? The children go to work with mealworms and bran on a large board. They tile the board, illuminate the mealworm in various ways, heat it, cool it, twist it, turn it until they drop. The answer comes out, the mealworm gets to its meal by a random process, but when he is there, he knows he is there. This, of course, raises another question: "How does he know that he is under bran?" No easy scientific study. No trivial result. There are lessons to be learned, other tries to make — other worlds, other ways. . . .

The mealworm experiments may take six weeks of school work, but the children are captured by the problems, which are just the kind of problems that capture the scientists. It is never the teacher who has the answers to the students' questions. Nature, with the mealworm as spokesman, reveals the answers only when asked properly. It is the inventing of the questions and proposing ways for nature to answer that capture the pupils' interest and love. They are doing and learning and loving it. I believe that you might use a piece like the one from Huck Finn that I quoted to capture a child's sustained interest. But I would never know until I tried. The doing of that is the work of humanists. I believe that your involvement in some such exercise might need to be as time-consuming as ours. Many, many children and many teachers must be involved before you can feel confident that the topic or sequence of topics that you choose to try will survive. You must be careful not to be entrapped by the public stereotype of learning. For science, the public belief is that there are laws of science that the student must learn. He must be able to state them and to work with them. I believe that the children will learn the laws, at least the ones that we think we know, if they come to them from specific experience with specific events and observations. I believe, at least I am willing to bet, that this statement holds for literature and its languages. So when I plead with you to go to the schools, I mean that you go not with commas or spelling but with clear ideas and with love, patience, and the willingness to let the children carry the day, their way.[6]

As Zacharias suggested, the "discovery method" is being used in connection with some of the newer English curricular proposals. In Project English at the University of Nebraska (a federally supported center for the improvement of the teaching of English) heavy emphasis is placed from the first through the twelfth grades on the use of literature as a means of helping learners to discover the best ways of expressing them-

6 Jerrold R. Zacharias, "Research Scholars and Curriculum Development," ESI Quarterly Report, III, No. 3 (Summer–Fall 1965), pp. 103–104.

selves, modeled from the literature which they are asked to study. They are expected to discover the basic patterns of the language, and through reading and discussion be able to apply these patterns to their own writing and speaking. Under such a scheme there is a minimum of emphasis on memorization of rules of grammar. The learner is expected to arrive inductively at the principles through thoughtful consideration of good literature.

The social sciences are now undergoing a major revolution. A social studies program which has the support of a number of agencies, but which is being developed by Educational Services, Inc., has indicated the following purposes.

The basic aims of the elementary social studies program are:

To introduce children to the natural and cultural history of the human genus, from the time when it began to differentiate from other primates, until it reached the status of Homo Sapiens and the beginnings of what archaeologists now call "civilization."

To introduce children at the same time to one particular set of methods that contemporary Western man has developed to find out about the human past and the present human conditions: that is, the methodology of the social sciences, especially anthropology, archaeology, economics, psychology, sociology, and history.

To encourage children to study social science by giving them an opportunity to handle the raw data of social science, especially in the form of filmed sequences that bring into the classroom the lives of people all over the world, as well as sequences that show how social scientists work.

From the very outset of this program, the place of films has been central to all the planning. All of the proposed materials will include much written material, and many experiments and kits of artifacts to be studied and recreated, but a large portion of the data of the social scientists — especially of the archaeologist and the anthropologist — cannot be vividly or most efficiently presented in textual form.

Much of the data on the human past comes out of the ground in places remote from the American classroom. Although to some extent facsimiles of the bones and artifacts can be created for classroom use, it is hardly possible to take every American school child to the ancient Sumerian city of Nippur, to see for himself what lies beneath the earth, except by film. Similarly, it is difficult to communicate the actual operations of a dig, and the methodological approach of the archaeologist, except by letting the children actually see a large and complex dig in operation, from the beginning survey through the final analysis of the material in the laboratory, including processes of absolute and relative dating.

Similarly, almost all of the data of the ethnographer and ethnologist exist in their raw form in places not accessible to most American school children. While some such material can and should be presented in textual form, most American children can see people living their lives in non-Western and especially non-literate societies only through the medium of film. . . .

The films will be designed not to tell the students something but rather to present data which cannot be presented in any other fashion, or data that can best be presented on film. Some of the films will have the function of conveying in as inductive a manner as possible the concepts and generalizations around which contemporary social science is organized. Much will be left for students to piece together and figure out for themselves. Areas of dispute and ignorance will be left open.[7]

Thus, it is clear that the four basic academic areas—English, mathematics, science, and social science—are all undergoing major revolutions. Further, it is evident that much activity in these areas includes the inductive approach to learning. In order for the inductive approach to function it is necessary to have concrete materials in the form of motion pictures, filmstrips, recordings, field experiences, and other similar resources which can be studied by the learners and the appropriate outcomes discovered by them. A critical aspect of such approaches is to have available the pertinent experiences which contain the necessary elements from which the learners can draw ideas and generalizations and from which skillful teachers are able to pose questions and to carry on an inquiry process in such a way that the learners discover the answers. The final stage is one of relating language and narration to what has been discovered.

IS THE INDUCTIVE APPROACH BEST FOR ALL LEARNING?

Whether it is Thelen discussing four approaches to teaching or Scheffler presenting three models, each approach includes a place for a wide range of resources and the inductive as well as the deductive approach. It is interesting to note that Scheffler suggests all three models have a part to play depending upon the type of objective which the teacher has in mind.

I have intimated that I find something important in each of the models we have considered. The impression model reflects, as I have said, the cumulative growth of knowledge in its public sense. Our aim in teaching should surely be to preserve and extend this growth. But we cannot do this by storing it piecemeal within the learner. We preserve it, as the insight model stresses, only if we succeed in transmitting the live spark that keeps it growing, the insight which is a product of each learner's

[7] Kevin Smith and Evans Clinchy, "The Social Studies Curriculum Program and Its Films," *ESI Quarterly Report* (Winter–Spring 1964), pp. 88–89.

efforts to make sense of public knowledge in his own terms, and to confront it with reality. Finally as the rule model suggests, such confrontation involves deliberation and judgment, and hence presupposes general and impartial principles governing the assessment of reasons bearing on the issues.[8]

The position just expressed by Scheffler is also supported by Hilda Taba when she says:

Learning by discovery as pursued today pertains largely to cognitive aspects of learning: the development and organization of concepts, ideas, and insights, and the use of inference and other logical processes to control a situation. The content of these explorations is, furthermore, limited to science and mathematics.

Naturally, there are other types of learning such as mastering the skill of typing or memorizing a poem, in which the cognitive control of the situation is at a minimum. There are also other types of content in which cognition and valuing merge. To assume that the principles of learning by discovery apply to all varieties of learning or apply to all in a similar way leads to misapprehension.[9]

In part, the question about various approaches to teaching and learning rests upon certain learning theories. In spite of the fact that the inductive approach is being given considerable stress in the new curriculum developments, there are some voices being raised as to whether such an approach is the only one under all circumstances. The inductive approach has many elements in common with cognitive theories of learning which are being advanced by Bruner, Piaget, and many others. Anderson takes a rather critical view, particularly from the research point of view, as to whether the emphasis upon induction and cognition really merit the attention and support which they are receiving:

Attitudes toward cognitive psychology are currently more favorable than at any time in recent years. This resurgence in popularity need not be attributed to the irresistible cogency of the contemporary cognitive position. Sufficient cause is to be found in such factors as the high visibility and readability of cognitive theorists like Bruner and the increased believability of the information-processing model accompanying the rise of computer technology. The status of cognitive theory has undoubtedly received an indirect boost from scholars in other disciplines especially mathematics and the sciences, who have been involved in school curriculum reform. They have attempted to rationalize innovations with an appeal to psychology. The intuitive psychology of these persons is in-

---

[8] See Scheffler, *ESI Quarterly Report*, XXV, pp. 142–143.
[9] Hilda Taba, "Learning By Discovery: Psychological and Educational Rationale," *Elementary School Journal* LXIII, No. 6, (March 1963), p. 310. Copyright 1963 by the University of Chicago Press.

variably cognitive. If the cognitive position is inherently fruitful, the time is ripe for a demonstration of its fruitfulness.[10]

Some research studies conducted recently also raise questions about the superiority of the inductive approach for all types of learning outcomes. Some of the findings of a recent study by Krumboltz and Yabroff are as follows:

1. The inductive and deductive methods, as defined in this study, were about equally efficient in terms of the time required to teach a given body of information.

2. The two methods were about equally effective in producing accurate transfer of training.

3. Some increment of speed on the *Knowledge of Rules Subtest* was produced by the inductive method, but this advantage was offset by the dissatisfaction with that method expressed by the groups using it.[11]

DEDUCTIVE APPROACH TO LEARNING.

It is desirable, therefore, to give attention to the more traditional deductive approach. In the deductive method of teaching a rule or principle or law is stated first and then the learner is expected to deduce examples and applications from it. The teaching of rules of grammar first in the expectation that the learner can apply those to his own writing or speaking exemplifies the deductive approach. Similarly, in science the statement of a law in chemistry is to be followed with various applications of that law in the laboratory. An algebraic formula in mathematics is to be mastered so that the learner is able to apply the formula in actual situations.

In deductive reasoning, therefore, the use of media and other experiences follows after the statement of the principle which is generally in abstract or symbolic form. After the principle is mastered, opportunities must then be presented for applications of it in functional situations. The method presumes, for example, that the learning of the mathematics formula $a = lw$ must be followed by an opportunity to measure an actual figure on a piece of paper in order to demonstrate that he understands the application of the formula. In science it is expected that the formula $Na\ Cl + H_2SO_4 \rightarrow Na\ HSO_4 + HCl$ can be applied by the learner to a laboratory exercise in which he uses the appropriate chemicals and apparatus. Therefore, there is an essential place for media in the deductive process although it follows after the rules or laws have been formalized, stated, and mastered.

[10] Richard C. Anderson and David P. Ausubel (eds.) *Readings in the Psychology of Cognition,* "Introduction, Part Three: Concept Formation," by Richard C. Anderson, (New York: Holt, Rinehart and Winston, 1965) p. 403. Copyright © 1965 by Holt, Rinehart and Winston, Inc.

[11] John D. Krumboltz and William W. Yabroff, "The Comparative Effects of Inductive and Deductive Sequences in Programmed Instruction," *American Educational Research Journal,* II, No. 4 (November 1965), p. 232.

SEQUENTIAL DEVELOPMENT OF LEARNING EXPERIENCE.

There are a number of indications that learning proceeds according to a sequence which initially requires concrete experiences but which later involves more abstractions. Piaget, for example, has suggested that certain transformations take place from early childhood to adolescence. He states four factors as follow:

1. *Maturation of the nervous system.* — This first factor does not explain everything, but it should be remembered that the order of succession of the stages is constant, though the chronological ages will vary.

2. *Experience with objects of the physical world.* — Again, this factor does not explain everything for several reasons:

(a) Some notions, such as substance, are acquired at the beginning of the stage of concrete operations, and others, such as weight and volume, not until later on.

(b) There are two kinds of experience: (1) the physical experience, which is an action or an abstraction from the object; this kind of experience leads to such statements as "This watch is heavier than this pencil," and (2) the logical-mathematical experience, which is knowledge gathered from actions on the object. A good example is that of the child's counting pebbles, lining them up in one direction, then in the reverse direction, and finding that the sum is independent of the order. In this case the child himself introduces order.

3. *Educational transmission, such as language.* — The child can receive valuable information only if he is ready to understand it.

4. *Equilibration, or balance among the first three factors.* — There is a succession of levels of equilibration such that the attainment of level two is possible only when equilibration has been obtained on level one. For example, when the ball of clay is changed into a sausage, there are probably four successive levels: first, the child thinks just about one dimension such as length, without taking width into account. If the examiner continues to lengthen the sausage, the child at a given time says "It is getting too thin," and he thinks about the width. Then, on a third level, he wavers between the factors of length and width, he discovers their solidarity and says "When you make it longer it becomes thinner . . . consequently, it is the same thing," and this is his equilibration process coming into play.[12]

Taba, Levine, and Elzey suggest a somewhat similar spiral development of intellectual activities.

Another useful concept is that of a necessary sequence in the development of thought, such as that concrete or operational thinking must pre-

12 Lydia Muller-Willis, "Stages In The Child's Intellectual Development: Piaget's Views," *The Low Achiever in Mathematics.* Report of a Conference held in Washington, D. C. March 25–27, 1964 sponsored jointly by the U.S. Office of Education and the National Council of Teachers of Mathematics. (Washington, D. C.: U. S. Government Printing Office, 1965) Catalog No. FS 5.229:29061, pp. 19–20.

cede the abstract and formal thought. This idea of a sequential order of steps in the development of thought seemed to offer a fruitful model for conceptualizing the career of learning of the various modes of thinking during the school years.

Assuming a sequential order in the development of thought, there should also be a sequence in learning experiences so that each preceding step develops the skills which are prerequisite for the next step. For example, because the transition from concrete to operational thinking is of especial importance for school age children, the sequence of school experiences should begin with experiences with concrete objects, materials to facilitate description, analysis, and differentiation. The early years of school may need to concentrate on providing abundant experience in manipulation and combining matching and grouping objects in order to facilitate the mastery of concrete thinking. Opportunities for the active processing of information may provide the necessary conditions for the evolution and organization of abstract conceptual schemes. This preparation lays the groundwork for formal thinking, for manipulation of abstract symbols, and for the capacity to discover relationships between objects and events.[13]

If one follows this line of reasoning, it is evident that the early years of the child require a wide range of experiences. Since these experiences must be concrete, they would involve all kinds of media. It is necessary to involve language along with these experiences, but only when it is evident that the child has had realistic contacts with his environment.

TEACHER AS A LEARNER FROM MEDIA.

Emphasis has been placed thus far on the impact of media upon the learner. There is considerable evidence that the teacher needs to also be a learner in terms of new content and methods of teaching. One of the strengths of television is its contributions to teachers through their observation of superior teachers as well as an understanding of the new content which these teachers are presenting. In a study in the use of motion pictures in the teachings of physics, Wittich[14] found that the teachers made greater gains in the knowledge of physics content than did their students. This experiment and others like it suggests that teachers also learn through media in the very same way in which students learn from such kinds of experiences.

[13] Hilda Taba, Samuel Levine and Freeman F. Elzey, "The Premises and the Objective of the Study," *Thinking in Elementary School Children*. U. S. Office of Education Research Project No. 1574, (San Francisco State College, April, 1964), p. 22.

[14] *The Wisconsin Physics Film Evaluation Project*. A study of the influence of a new communication technique upon standard procedures currently in use in the teaching of high school physics. W. A. Wittich, chairman. The University of Wisconsin, 1961. 51 pages.

CONCLUSION.

The foregoing discussion indicates that the use of media makes possible the reaching of a much wider range of objectives than has previously been possible. In fact, the developments in the newer media really make feasible for the first time the widespread application of inductive reasoning to learning. The newer media are able equally to demonstrate and to clarify for learners the abstract statements which are a part of the deductive approach. Media also make possible the contact with reality which is necessary for young children to move to the stage of rich and extensive use of language in the adolescent and the adult years. The same or similar media also provide the teacher with opportunities for the continuous acquisition of the new understanding and skills which she needs to be a superior professional person.

Chapter 2

How can words and pictures bring about behavior change in the student?

What specific relationships exist between types of cues and forms of student response?

How have experiments involving media clarified the process of learning associative tasks and concepts?

What are the properties of words and pictures which will elicit and reinforce responses, leading to the development of principles and abstract ideas?

WORD-PICTURE RELATIONSHIPS IN AUDIO VISUAL PRESENTATIONS: THE ACQUISITION OF SKILLS, CONCEPTS AND UNDERSTANDINGS*

MARK A. MAY, Professor of Educational Psychology (Emeritus) Yale University

A. INTRODUCTION.

Words and pictures are stimuli. What is learned from them depends on the kinds of response that they elicit. For convenience of exposition they can be put into three major categories. In the first are all preparatory responses of attention, selective discrimination and perception which presumably have been learned previous to the presentation. Second are the responses involved in learning what the presentation purports to teach. These are called acquisition responses. In the third category are the responses involved in anchoring what has been learned so that it can be used on subsequent occasions. These are called consolidating

*This chapter is a part of a longer paper, "Word-Picture Relationships in Audio Visual Presentations," prepared for the USOE under contract OE-5-16 006. It is adapted and reproduced with the permission of the author.

responses. This chapter deals only with the responses involved in acquiring new information, skills, concepts and understandings.

1. Acquisition responses are specified by learning task.

All A-V presentations require close and sustained attention. Beyond this first stage, the particular responses made to the audio-visual stimuli are specified by the learning task. The cues on which attention is focused must be relevant to the learning task. The meanings attached to the relevant cues are also, in some respects, determined by the learning task.

If the task is to *reproduce* the materials verbatim from memory, the responses required to perform it are different from those that would be required to produce evidence that the substance of the material had been comprehended. If the task is to perform a sequence of acts, such as knot tying or assembling the parts of an automobile ignition distributor, the responses required by the demonstration are also different from those required by verbal learning tasks.

Before any useful statement can be made about the roles of visuals and verbals in motivating, cueing and reinforcing acquisition responses, it is necessary to know what kinds of responses are being considered and the conditions on which they depend. For example, if the task is to acquire a perceptual-motor skill, or to memorize a list of names or verses of poetry, or to form a new concept, a number of repetitions or amounts of practice may be required. But if the task is to understand an explanation, or to grasp a principle, a single presentation may be sufficient. As to the relative roles of words and pictures, it is rather obvious that a motion picture of a performance is much more helpful for cueing the correct manual responses than a verbal description of the performance or a set of verbal instructions. The relative values of words and pictures in teaching the binomial theorem or the second law of thermodynamics might be quite different.

2. A suggested taxonomy of learning tasks.

In order to proceed, there is need for a taxonomy of learning tasks, based on and related to a taxonomy of educational objectives, and articulated with the characteristics of audio-visual materials. One source of materials for such a taxonomy is the large number of evaluative studies that have been made in which A-V presentations have been compared with conventional methods of teaching. This has been done for practically every subject in the curriculum from the first grade through graduate and professional schools. The list of such studies is long.

A report on the number of studies initiated under Part A of Title VII of the NDEA, from 1958 to 1964, lists the following: in social studies and behavioral sciences 58; in the physical sciences 44; in the biological sciences 38; in mathematics 34; in the language arts 31; in foreign languages 31; and in the humanities 15. In practically all of these studies a criterion test was used. An examination of the items in the tests (if they have been preserved), might provide useful data for the construction of a taxonomy of the kinds of tasks which A-V materials attempt to teach.

Without the benefit of information that might be derived from such a study, a crude analysis of learning tasks is presented here. It is not claimed to be exhaustive. It will serve as a kind of map for guidance through a considerable amount of unexplored territory. The two main divisions into reproductive and productive tasks were suggested by Gagné (7).

I. Reproductive Tasks. Included in this category are all tasks in which the learner is required to reproduce or to recognize a reproduction of, the whole or a part, of the materials learned. Some are:

1. Verbal reproductions — illustrated by experiments on memorizing. Included here are such tasks as memorizing and reproducing lists of words, verses of poetry, paragraphs of prose. Also are included tasks of learning the vocabulary of a foreign language.
2. Manual reproductions — tasks involved in the acquisition of perceptual motor skills.
3. Pictorial reproductions — tasks of reproducing the materials learned by drawing and copying from a model.

II. Productive-Constructive Tasks. In this category are all the tasks that require evidence that the substance of the material was comprehended, and can be utilized in other situations. Examples are:

1. The task of recognizing an item of information or an idea when it is stated in terms different from those used in the learning situation.
2. Writing, in the student's own words, the substance of materials learned, as in the typical essay-type of examination.
3. Reproducing an explanation in the student's own words.
4. Giving examples of a concept.
5. Solving problems similar to those given in the presentation.
6. Translating a foreign language.

3. Processes and products of learning.

It will be noted that this classification is based on the *products* rather than the processes of learning. When we speak of learning by classical conditioning, operant conditioning, discrimination, assessing probabilities of reinforcement, memorizing, insight and problem solving, we are speaking of the processes, not the products of learning. At this point the problem arises as to how to match processes to products. Which of the various types of learning are required by, or best suited for, the achievement of types of learning tasks? In a recent volume edited by Melton (20) seven distinct categories of learning are recognized and discussed by fourteen authors. Gagné (8) has identified eight types of learning arranged in a hierarchial order. There is a considerable amount of overlap between Melton's seven categories and Gagné's eight types. All of them have been shaped out of laboratory experiments on animal and human learning.

Learning from an A-V presentation appears to involve a mixture of these types. The problem is to discover which of the various types best fulfill the conditions on which the achievement of different kinds of learning tasks depend. Such a discovery would greatly simplify the task of assessing the relative merits of words and pictures for motivating, cueing and reinforcing the responses required by different tasks. It would also enable us to apply to classroom learning many of the facts and principles derived from experiments on laboratory learning.

In the discussion of acquisition responses that follows, an effort will be made to relate them to the type of learning that seems most appropriate to each type of task.

B. RESPONSES REQUIRED BY REPRODUCTIVE TASKS.

Consideration will be given first to responses required by reproductive tasks, which include verbal, pictorial, and manual reproductions of the learned materials.

1. The role of words and pictures in the learning of verbal associations.

An illustration of this type of task is learning the vocabulary of a foreign language by the method of paired-associates. Pioneering research was done on the problem by Lumsdaine (16), by Kopstein and Roshal (15), Kale and Grosslight (13), Bern (2) and Asher (1). These studies are summarized by Hartman (11).

Lumsdaine (16) prepared a large number of pairs of unrelated words, pairs of unrelated pictures, pairs of pictures and words, and pairs of words and pictures. The pairs were presented in random order, 16 pairs to each list, to intermediate grade school children and to college students. The experimental conditions were varied in respect to rate of presentation and in other respects.

The members of each pair were selected to minimize previously learned associations. The learning task was mainly that of rote memorizing. It was found that under all conditions and for different grade levels of students, picture-word pairs were learned best, word-picture pairs least, with word-word and picture-picture in between.

The importance of this experiment lies in the theoretical reasons why pictures are better stimulus terms than words. One reason is based on the principle of temporal contiguity. While looking at a picture a person can simultaneously say a word out loud or silently, but while looking at a word it is difficult to say another word at the same instant of time. Furthermore, it is impossible to say two words at the same time. The response word to a picture can be practiced while looking at the picture, but to practice saying a name of a picture while looking at a word is much more difficult.

Words are poorer stimulus terms than pictures mainly because they are apt to have more than one meaning. The word "fence," for example, may mean a barrier, or a dealer in stolen goods. But the picture of a barrier is perceived as a fence and not as a dealer in stolen goods. Words are better response terms than pictures partly because most people have had a great deal more experience in seeing an object or picture, *before* hearing or seeing its name, than vice versa. Furthermore, in Lumsdaine's experiment the criterion task was always to name the response term when the stimulus term was presented. When a picture was presented it was necessary to recall the word associated with it, but when a word was presented the subjects were required to name the picture that had been associated with it.

In this connection it is noted that when Bern (2) changed the criterion task from recall to discrimination, presenting both words and pictures in the test situation, he found that for the performance of this task, picture-picture and word-picture were superior to word-word and to picture-word. Thus it would appear that when the criterion task is changed the associations that mediate the correct responses are different.

The role of mediators in paired-associate learning was investigated in an experiment by Davidson (5). The materials were pairs of pictures of objects familiar to second grade school children who served as subjects. They were divided into a high and low ability group based on the results of a preliminary experiment, in which they were tested for initial abilities to form associations between pairs of pictures. Each of the two groups was assigned at random to five experimental conditions. For each condition twenty pairs of pictures were exposed at the rate of a pair every five seconds. There followed two test trials during which only the stimulus picture was exposed and the task was to choose from four pictures in a workbook the one that belonged to the stimulus picture. On the second trial the order of presentation was changed.

For condition A no mediators were employed. For condition B the experimenter pronounced the names of the two pictures (e.g. "chair"–"shoe") on the presentation trials, but not on the test trials. Condition C was the same except the experimenter inserted a preposition between the pairs (e.g. "chair under shoe"). For condition D a mediating sentence was used such as "the chair doesn't look large under a big shoe." For condition E the picture showed a big shoe on a chair.

The mean scores (maximum 40) took a big jump beginning with condition C where connective mediators were introduced. For the high ability groups the jump was from a mean of about 13 to 33, and for the low ability groups it was from about 10 to 26. At the level of conditions D and E where sentences and pictures were the mediators the low ability groups had combined mean score almost as high as the combined means of the high ability groups. When pictures of relations (such as a big shoe on a chair) were added to sentences the combined mean score of both groups went up about five points.

Thus it would appear that when powerful mediators are introduced children of both high and low associational abilities can achieve almost perfect scores in two trials. Pictorial mediators added more scores to sentences, than sentences added to prepositions, and both added substantially more to the pronunciations of the names of the two pictures.

The role of words and pictures in paired-associate verbal learning has been further investigated by studies of learning the vocabulary of a foreign language which has an origin different from English. Two studies on the learning of Russian vocabulary have been reported. Kopstein and Roshal (15) found that picture-word combinations were superior to word-picture, confirming Lumsdaine's results. Kale and Grosslight (13) translated Russian nouns and verbs from the Cyrillic alphabet to English equivalents and presented paired lists in five versions of a film. In one version, pairs of words were presented with English words always in the stimulus position. In the second and third versions, English-Russian nouns were presented below a picture of the object denoted by each noun. Each pair of verbs was shown below a motion picture depicting the action denoted by the pair. The fourth version was the same except that the printed words were pronounced by the narrator. In the fifth version, the students repeated the pronunciations after the narrator.

Ten films were used, five for verbs and five for nouns. Each version contained twenty pairs. The procedure was to present the pairs in each list at a rate of 5 to 11 seconds each. After a preliminary presentation of each list, six test trials were run in which each English word was exposed briefly and the subjects required to write its Russian equivalent on a workform while blank film was exposed for 10 seconds, after which the correct word was flashed on the screen. The criterion was the number of Russian words spelled correctly or nearly so on each trial.

The main variables in the presentations were (a) words alone; (b) words with pictures; (c) words with pictures plus pronunciation; (d) audience vocalization of the words; (e) fixed vs. random order of pairs; (f) pictures and Russian words alone vs. pictures of English-Russian pairs. Under all of these conditions the presentations *with* pictures, both motion for verbs and stills for nouns, were more effective than presentations without pictures. Pictures shown in combinations with pairs were somewhat more effective than pictures with Russian words alone.

This result would seem to indicate that on the test trials where the English word was the stimulus and the task was to write the Russian equivalent the picture functioned to mediate the correct response. The order of associations could have been:

$$\text{English word} \underset{\downarrow}{\overset{(1)}{\ldots\ldots\ldots\ldots}} \text{Picture} \overset{(2)}{\ldots\ldots\ldots} \underset{\uparrow}{\text{Russian word.}}$$

$$\ldots\ldots\ldots\ldots\ldots(3)\ldots\ldots\ldots\ldots\ldots$$

It was easier to learn association (2) than association (3) provided association (1) had previously been learned. In terms of classical conditioning the picture functioned as the unconditioned stimulus which reinforced the power of the conditioned stimulus (the English word) to elicit the conditioned response (the Russian word).

The pronunciation of the pairs of words by the narrator tended to interfere with learning. In all comparisons of pronunciation *vs.* no pronunciation on tests of immediate recall, the mean learning scores were less when the pairs were pronounced. But this was not the case on tests of delayed recall. The authors conjectured that one of the reasons for the interference was that a transliterated Russian word is not necessarily pronounced according to the English rules of phonetics. In writing a Russian word in the English alphabet the subjects were perhaps guided by how it would sound in English.

The conditions of the foregoing experiments on the relations between words and pictures in rote verbal learning of paired-associates are different from those involved in associative learning from A-V presentations in two fundamental respects. First, associative learning from A-V material is more meaningful; second the words are usually presented orally instead of visually. Further experiments are needed in which the pairs are more meaningfully related and presented orally.

The interrelationships between aural and visual presentations have been investigated by Asher (1) in a series of three experiments on learning Spanish vocabulary. One group of college students learned lists of Spanish words visually and, after 48 hours, relearned the same lists aurally; another group learned the same list aurally and relearned them visually. There were ten lists of about 10 words in each list. After all lists had been learned and relearned, all subjects were given a story to translate that contained the words in all the lists.

In the first experiment, each English word was printed on a card with two Spanish words. Each subject was required to choose the correct one. The subjects who were learning visually were shown the three words and required to write the correct choice; the aural subjects heard the three words pronounced and were required to pronounce the correct one. Immediately after each response the subject was told whether he was right or wrong. After two correct responses the card was dropped from the list. The score for each list was the number of initial and perseveration errors. This same procedure was used in the relearning sessions.

In the second experiment, pairs of pictures and their Spanish names were presented at intervals of one second per pair for each list of ten pairs. On the test trials, only the pictures were presented and the subjects required to write or pronounce the correct Spanish word. The third experiment was the same except that English words were used instead of pictures.

Forty subjects participated in each of the experiments. Twenty learned aurally and relearned visually; and 20 learned visually and relearned aurally. All subjects were unfamiliar with the Spanish language.

All subjects were pretested for sensory dominance and for guessing ability. Sensory dominance was measured by requiring all subjects to learn an initial list visually, and another list aurally. Students who made the fewest errors on the first list were considered visually dominant; those who made the fewest on the second list were considered aurally dominant. Students who guessed the correct answer on the first presentation of a pair the most times on each list were considered to be the best guessers. Guessing ability was found to be highly correlated with all other measures of learning.

Under all conditions the students who learned visually and relearned aurally made fewer errors in learning than those who learned aurally and relearned visually. Among those who learned visually, the visually dominants learned somewhat better than the aurally dominants; and of those who learned aurally and relearned visually the aurals made fewer learning errors than the visually dominants. The correlations between guessing scores and learning and relearning scores were significantly positive; but significantly negative with scores on retention tests. Furthermore, the retention test scores of those who learned visually were not significantly better than for those who learned aurally.

This final result indicates an interesting relation between learning and retention. It supports the hypotheses that, regardless of the channel through which verbal materials are learned, retention is mediated by the sensory dominant channel. Visually dominant subjects recall materials learned aurally in terms of how they would look; and aurally dominant subjects recall visually learned materials in terms of how they would sound when pronounced. If this hypothesis is correct, it is of extreme importance for assessing the roles of visual and auditory stimuli in A-V presentations.

2. The Role of Visuals and Verbals in Learning to Perform Skilled Acts.

Two different kinds of learning tasks are immediately recognized. First are tasks performed with one's hands such as handwriting, drawing from a model, tying knots, assembling the parts of an instrument, playing golf, tennis, and so on. The second are tasks performed with one's speech apparatus, as illustrated by learning to pronounce words correctly, to speak fluently a foreign language, to sing, to whistle, and so on. In between are tasks that involve both the hands and the lips such as learning to play a musical wind instrument.

It is obvious that in learning to perform manual tasks visual or audio-visual presentation should be more effective than merely being told how to do it, or given printed instructions in how to perform it, as every American father on Christmas morning knows all too well. It is equally obvious that in learning vocal skills, auditory demonstrations are more effective than visual ones. It is true that deaf children can learn lip reading, and blind children can learn manual performances. But such learnings are very difficult and require a large amount of practice and patient teaching.

Most of the experiments on the roles of visuals and verbals in learning from demonstrations are found in studies on perceptual-motor learning, in studies of speech, and learning to speak a foreign language. Such experiments, unfortunately, were not designed to test the relative merits of words and pictures for performing the functions that are required by these learning tasks. Needed are some experiments designed to test hypotheses such as the following:

(1) The hypothesis is that visual demonstrations are more effective than verbal descriptions for defining the learning task, not only in respect to the end result, but also in relation to the steps required to achieve it. It is further hypothesized that a visual-demonstration of the performance plus a verbal description of the steps would be even more effective.

(2) Experiments performed thus far demonstrate that the function of cue identification by pointers, circles and labels is more effective than verbal directions alone. Would combinations of visual-verbal be even more effective?

(3) The hypothesis is that visuals in motion are more effective for the formulation of a "perceptual blue print" (Sheffield, [23]) from which the correct sequence of response in performing a skilled act can be read off than a verbal description of the sequence of movements. This hypothesis

should be checked against May's theory (see below) that verbals often do play a significant role in learning from a demonstration.

(4) The hypothesis advanced by Gropper (10) that seeing oneself perform a task correctly is more reinforcing than merely being told that it is correct on the ground that "seeing is believing" should be checked by further experimentation.

May's argument (18) is that covert verbal responses to a demonstration as it is being viewed perform a function similar to that of Sheffield's visual perceptual blueprints. If during a demonstration the viewer tells himself what responses are made at each step, or repeats to himself what the narrator tells him, this sequence of verbal responses will become conditioned to the sequence of visual stimuli, which in the test situation are similar to those in the learning situation, and hence will serve to cue the correct sequence of responses. As the performance becomes more practiced these verbal mediators will tend to drop out, and thereafter the cues that control the correct sequence of responses will be largely visual and proprioceptive. Eventually the visuals may drop out and the learner can perform the act with his eyes shut.

The model for this theory of learning from a demonstration is that of delayed imitation, described at length by Dollard and Miller (6). A driver finding his way through a maze of city streets by following a leader car, is a case of immediate imitation. But finding one's way later without the benefit of a leader depends on how many cues were noted and recalled as to where to make right and left turns. In this case the performance is guided by verbal recall of the cues. So in learning from a demonstration film, if the learner can verbalize self-directions for each step, and remember them in the test situation, he can successfully perform the task, provided these self-induced verbal directions have already acquired the power to elicit the correct responses. The verbal responses are elicited by the similarities between sequences of visual stimuli in the learning and in the test situations.

This section on associative responding may be concluded by noting that the formation of associations between stimuli and responses usually requires some sort of a mediating link. (See Gagné, [8] p. 99). As noted above, the association between visual stimuli presented by the steps in a demonstration and the responses required for its performance may be mediated effectively by words. The association between English words and the Russian equivalents may be mediated by pictures or by some other kind of linkage. Thus, for some learning tasks, words serve the function of mediators better than pictures; for other tasks, pictures or visual images are more effective than words. Psychological studies of the mechanisms involved in associative learning indicate that visual images are often used to link pairs of words (see Cofer, [4]). For example, the pair of words "bow-trousers" is apt to elicit a visual image of trousers on a bow-legged man; "spoon-mailbox" elicits an image of a spoon lying in a mailbox. Other linkages may be provided by a knowledge of the derivation of words, such as terra-earth (mediated by terrestrial) (from Gagné, [8] p. 101).

The more meaningful the terms to be associated, the easier it is to find linkages. The terms "terra" and "earth" have almost the same meaning. In contrast the syllables "Zok-bif" require much more inventiveness to construct a connecting link.[1] This illustrates the importance of perceptual learning as a prerequisite to associative learning.

A pair of associates may be regarded as a chain of three links. Learning lists of words or verses of poetry constitutes a chain of many links. Learning that Mt. McKinley in Alaska is 20,300 feet high, making it the highest mountain in the United States, is an example of verbal chaining that is characteristic of factual information learning. The conditions on which such verbal learning depend are discussed by Gagné ([8], p. 103-112). One of the conditions is that the meaning of each link in the chain must have been previously learned and discriminated from other links, and that the mediators between links must have been previously learned. Most of this previous learning is designated in this paper as perceptual learning.

C. RESPONSES REQUIRED BY CONSTRUCTIVE TASKS.

1. At this point we turn from the reproductive types of learning tasks to productive-constructive types.

Many A-V presentations require more than perceptual and associative learning. The tasks are, grasping an idea, understanding an explanation, comprehending a general principle, and solving a problem. Learning to perform these tasks from one or two presentations requires a considerable amount of previously acquired relevant knowledge which can be recalled and applied to the tasks. Lumsdaine (17) found that when filled by one presentation the size of the gap between previously acquired knowledge about the phenomena of osmosis, as measured by a pretest, and a perfect score on the posttest was considerably greater for students with the higher pretest scores than those with the lower scores. The more a subject already knew about the topic, the greater was the percentage of new knowledge gained from the film.

The question now arises as to what kinds of previously acquired knowledge are needed to understand an explanation or to grasp a new idea, or to comprehend the substance of a presentation. First of all, the

---

[1] Bugelski (3) found that some subjects connected a pair of nonsense syllables, *dup-tez* by translating it into "deputize."

student must be able to perceive correctly the new meanings of the words and sentences in the narration and in the visuals. To the extent that these meanings have not been acquired, an amount of perceptual learning will be required. Second, the learner should have acquired associations between objects, places, events and relationships. Mediational linkages between stimulus and response terms, or units, must have been acquired and retained. Third, previous conceptual learning may be very useful. Knowing the names of the classes or categories to which the verbals and visuals belong, and knowing what the cues *connote*, as well as what they *denote*, should be helpful. To the extent that the necessary concepts have not been formed, conceptual learning will become part of the new learning task.

These prerequisites to substance, or idea learning, may be viewed as types of prelearned instrumental responses that lead to the goal responses of correctly and fully comprehending the materials in the presentation. The better these instrumental responses have been learned, the easier it is for the learner to march straight ahead to the goal without hesitating, hemming-and-hawing, and trial and error. If these instrumental responses have not been learned, or learned but not applied, then a considerable part of the instruction in an A-V presentation is precisely that of telling, illustrating, and demonstrating the correct instrumental responses. (See Gagné [7].)

Assuming that students have already acquired the prerequisite kinds of knowledge, then what kinds of further responses must be made to the material in order to perform the criterion task successfully? What, for example, is required by a comprehension reading test beyond a knowledge of vocabulary and sentence structure? What responses must a student make to a paragraph in order to answer correctly the test questions about the idea or ideas that it conveys? What responses must a student make to an A-V presentation in order to "get" the new information that it conveys, or to comprehend its full meaning?

Many instructional films teach both facts and explanations. Students may learn the facts but fail to grasp the explanations. This point is illustrated in a study by May and Lumsdaine (18). They noted that students who had had previous instruction in the phenomena of osmosis made much greater gains on questions of facts about temporary osmosis than on questions about the explanations of these facts. But for explanations about permanent osmosis the results were reversed. This difference was traced to the fact that the animated diagrams illustrating the passage of molecules of different sizes through semipermeable membranes were much clearer and more easily comprehended for the phenomena of permanent than for temporary osmosis. . . . This illustrates the importance of animation that clearly depicts an explanation. The correct responses to questions about explanations were perhaps mediated by the retention of visual images of the animation. They aided the students in grasping the explanation.

2. The role of words and pictures in the construction of new concepts.

For the purposes of this paper a concept is any class or category of objects, events, relations or stimulus elements, that share one or more common properties, and which can be identified by a label or a definition. Most concepts are abstract because their identifying properties are abstracted from concrete percepts. The concepts of length, volume, velocity, position, tallness, squareness, nouns, verbs, etc. do not refer to any particular object or word. They are labels for definable categories.

From the standpoint of behavior, the label or definition of a class of objects, or relationships, can elicit a response of naming a member, or giving an example. Conversely, an example in the stimulus position can elicit the name of a label or a definition. Concepts are, therefore, of great importance for classifying and organizing knowledge so that it is retained and can be used. The fact that they are associations which function both as cues and responses is of signal importance (Kendler, [14]) (see also Goss on the acquisition of perceptual schemes, [9]).

New concepts may be formed either by discovery or by instruction, or both. In laboratory experiments, the learning task is that of discovering the features or properties which arrays of stimulus patterns have in common. A strategy often employed by experimental subjects is to make guesses or form hypotheses about possible key features from the initial presentation, and test them by observations of other examples. This is quite similar to the trial and check phase in perceptual learning. If the key cue is only one feature, such as size or shape or color, learning is fairly rapid; but if it is a particular size plus a particular color, in a particular position, learning is much more difficult. But once the key feature, or combination of features, is discovered a rule is formulated which controls the correct response to further examples.

Such rules can be taught without requiring the learner to go through the long and tedious process of discovery.[2] The rule can be communicated in the form of an operational definition. The students are simply told that if a pattern contains an element that is square and red it belongs to a class. If the class can be named by a common noun or nouns, such as "red squares," these words will then control the correct response to subsequent examples. But as Gagné (8) has pointed out, the new concept is composed of two previously acquired concepts of redness and squareness.

2 Homme and Glaser (12) developed a system for writing frames for a program of instruction in terms of rules and examples. It is called a *ruleg* system.

A-V presentations usually attempt to teach new concepts by definition and examples. The success of this procedure depends on a number of factors such as the choice of words by which the concept is defined, and the amount of previous perceptual and associative learning that is relevant to the task of comprehending the full meaning of the concept. Take for example a concept that may be new to some students — that of *citrus fruit*. This concept may be introduced simply by stating that citrus fruits are oranges, lemons, limes, grapefruit, tangerines, and others.

It is assumed that percepts of oranges, lemons and other examples have previously been formed. Differences between them can easily be perceived. But in what respect or respects are they alike? Why are they called citrus fruits? One common property is that they all contain relatively large amounts of citric acid. But what is citric acid? It is defined chemically as $C_6H_7O_3$. But this definition is nonsense to students who have not studied chemistry. The point is that until the concept *citric acid* has been clearly formed the words "citric acid" mean only a kind of an acid that is found in one class of fruit. This example illustrates the point that the most distinguishing feature is not easily perceptible unless one's taste has been educated to the level of being able to identify a citrus fruit by tasting it. This being the case, the concept remains in a state of partial formation. From a practical standpoint this is no great disadvantage. The class of citrus fruits is relatively small. The concept can be acceptably formed by naming its members. Any fruit that is not on this list is known not to be of the citrus variety.

When the instances, or cases, are so numerous that they cannot all be named and classified into exhaustive lists, the learning task becomes one of being able (a) to define verbally the distinguishing features of a class; (b) to give examples of it, and (c) to recognize examples that do not belong to it. Most children think they know what a hotel is and can name a few examples. But do they know what it is about such a building that distinguishes it from other buildings of similar appearance? The answer is, of course, the kind of uses made of it. But similar uses are also made of homes and apartment buildings. The verbal formulation of what it is that distinguishes hotels from all other classes of buildings, by giving examples that fulfill and do not fulfill these specifications, is the major task of conceptual learning. This learning consists of bringing the response of giving correct examples under the control of the name or a verbal definition.

Very little is known about the relations of visual and auditory stimuli in concept formation. The stimulus materials used in laboratory experiments are mostly visual. Stimuli that activate any sensory reception are classified and labeled. The labels are always verbal. The members of the categories are for the most part percepts. Concepts are constructed from percepts. If the task is to give an example of a concept, the stimulus is the name or the definition, and the response is verbal. But if the task is to name the class to which an object belongs, the stimuli may be either the object, a picture of it, or its name.

Olson (21) compared the effectiveness of pictures, letters and numbers for the attainment of concepts by high school sophomores. The stimuli were presented on cards by adding one at a time. Each time one was added the subjects were required to identify and record the common element. If the correct element was identified on the appearance of the second stimulus the score was 10 points. It decreased as more stimuli were required to identify the common factor.

Two sets of pictures were used. One set was pictures of parts of a reciprocating machine, the other was pictures of levers. The letters were in groups of five with three in alphabetical order; and the numbers were in multiples of three.

For one group of subjects the order of presentation was from obvious to subtle (i.e., easy to hard); for another group the order was random; and for a third group it was from hardest to easiest. The results show that the order of presentation was much more important for the picture problems than for either the letter or number problems. This could be due to the fact that the number problems were intrinsically easier than the picture problems. For the picture problems of reciprocating action the mean score of the "easy to hard" group was 7.8, for the "random" group 3.3, and for the "hard to easy" group 2.3.

It is difficult to evaluate the results of this experiment without seeing the dissertation on which the article reporting it was based. The author reports that the selection of "obvious" and "subtle" examples of the pictorial concepts was based on rating by an independent sample of high school students, while instances of the letter and number concepts were selected by the experimenter.

3. The role of words and pictures in the acquisitions of responses of prehending and comprehending.

Here, the learning task is that of *grasping* a new idea, understanding an explanation, or comprehending the full meaning of a presentation. The notion of *getting something* from reading a book, hearing a lecture, or seeing a film runs throughout educational literature. Students often complain about a presentation being *over their heads*, or failure to *get anything* new from it. To seize, grasp or latch onto is to *prehend*; to grasp all there is to be grasped is to *comprehend*.

What, now, does one do to prehend and to comprehend? What kinds of responses are required, and how are they learned? Let us begin with the physical act of grasping and see if we can build up to higher mental processes. A monkey prehends the limb of a tree by wrapping its tail around it; and an infant prehends a pellet with its thumb and fore-finger; adults pick up and manipulate objects with their fingers or by the use of instruments. But with what bodily organ do they "pick up" ideas? The obvious answer is with their brains.

There are no doubt lines of connection between physical and mental prehension. There is a great deal of evidence, derived both from child psychology and the history of education, which clearly indicates lines of connection between object manipulation in early childhood and later manipulations of their surrogates. These lines of development are difficult to trace. There is involved, no doubt, a hierarchy of acquired abilities, beginning with the unlearned abilities of infants to manipulate objects. The line of development might stem from proprioceptive and autonomic stimuli produced by physical acts of prehending.

When a physical object is grasped, it may be reported as feeling hard or soft, large or small, round or oval or square, rough or smooth, pleasant or painful. Such verbal reports stem from feedbacks into the central nervous system of tactile, proprioceptive, and autonomic stimuli. These feedbacks provide several items of information—such as, the object is something that is round, hard, and smooth. It is the combina-tion and integration of these items of information that constitute an "idea" of the object. The idea is comprehended when all relevant in-formation is in and integrated.

The question now arises as to how one can grasp an idea of some-thing without the benefit of first-hand information obtained from physical grasping and manipulation. The obvious answer is, it is done by grasp-ing the meanings of the symbols and pictures that represent or stand for the idea. But what kinds of covert responses to surrogates correspond to the physical ones of grasping and manipulating? A good guess is that they are faint replicas of the physical responses. Replicas are muscular tensions, and other implicit responses, which produce autonomic and proprioceptive stimuli similar to those produced by physical manipula-tion. These covert replicas may be elicited by visual and verbal stimuli which by past experiences have become conditioned to them. By primary stimulus generalization, pictures of objects will elicit the same implicit muscular responses as seeing an actual object when it is out of reach. By the process of higher order conditioning, names of objects, verbal descriptions, and diagrams can gain control over the implicit responses of grasping. Thus, the implicit muscular responses and neural reactions could be the instruments by which ideas and explanations are grasped and understood.

A connection between responses required for the "mental" grasping of ideas and those involved in the acquisition of firsthand knowledge by manipulating and observing the physical environment is an instance of a more general proposition. The proposition is that all vicarious learning—i.e., by being told or shown, stems from, and is based on, responses by which knowledge is acquired by firsthand experiences. These primary experiences are observations and manipulations. A great amount of knowledge about the environment is acquired by looking, listening, touching, tasting, sniffing and noting changes as they are sensed. The sensing of environmental stimuli is basic to perceptual learning which, in turn, is basic to learning by observations, which is further basic to all observational sciences, such as astronomy.

This is not all. Humans can learn by observing the surrogates, or representatives, of the environment. An object, place, or event can be represented by a picture, or described in words. Such surrogates acquire meaning by the process of perceptual learning. It is only after such meanings have been acquired that it is possible to learn by observing surrogates. The more firsthand knowledge a child has acquired about various features of his environment, the easier it is for him to acquire new knowledge from A-V presentations, provided he has also learned the relation between visual and verbal representatives and the feature of the environment for which they stand.

Valuable firsthand information is also gained by manipulating objects in the environment and noting what happens. This is illustrated by operant conditioning, and other forms of learning by experience. Experience is defined by John Dewey as "doing and undergoing"—acting on the environment and taking the consequences. This may be mere doing for its own sake, as illustrated by the play of children. It may be the kind of doings that are characteristic of all experimental science.

When objects, places, events and relations are represented by symbols, either linguistic or mathematical, such symbols can be manipulated independently of the objects or concepts that they represent. Some symbols denote objects and relations, others connote features abstracted from the environmental objects, events and relationships. This makes it possible to acquire a great deal of new knowledge without undergoing firsthand experiences.

This view of the learning process puts us in a better position to assess the relative merits of words and pictures in understanding explanations and in comprehending abstract relations and concepts. Most of the responses here involved are, as previously indicated, the covert ones of prehending and comprehending. The question is, what are the relative merits of words and pictures in motivating, cueing and reinforcing these responses?

The properties of words and pictures are discussed elsewhere and need not be repeated here. The problem is how to utilize them for the achievement of different tasks. The rules are different depending on the functions that words and pictures are intended to serve.

The construction of visuals that will aid students in prehending and comprehending principles and abstract ideas presents problems of finding visual representations with which students are familiar. Visual representations are more likely to elicit correct responses than verbal descriptions. Bar graphs are useful for visualizing relations between quantities of statistical data provided the student understands that the higher the bar the greater the amount. Visualization of principles and abstract relations that do not elicit the desired responses may elicit wrong responses, or leave the student in a state of confusion. For example, May and Lumsdaine (19) found that an animated diagram of the movements of salt and water molecules through a semipermeable membrane failed to elicit the prehension of the point that the key to the explanation is the relative size of molecules in relation to the pores in the membrane. A general rule might be that the effectiveness of a visualization of an explanation, or of an abstract principle, depends mainly on the extent to which it contains a pattern of stimuli that will evoke the desired response.

A recent study by Vandermeer and Thorne (24), on the use of filmstrips for teaching the relations between *The Sun and Its Planets,* illustrates the problem of finding an optimum combination of words and pictures for teaching astronomical facts and principles. The visuals were mainly photographs or drawings of the sun and the orbits of its planets. The verbals were printed captions. The subjects were students in grades 5 to 12. Knowledge of the contents of the filmstrip was tested with a large number of multiple choice items.

This filmstrip went through three revisions. Each was based on the test items that were incorrect on the preceding version. The effectiveness of each revision was tested by assigning groups at random to the originals or to the first revision and to the second revision. Items correct on the revised version were compared with those incorrect on the original. Also mean total scores were compared.

The revisions of the graphic and pictorial elements that seemed to improve learning rather consistently were (a) increasing the "iconicity" of a frame showing how the waxing moon would actually look from the earth rather than from other positions; (b) the multiplication of similar cues without increasing the content to be learned; (c) the additions of cue identifiers such as directional arrows. Other revisions which improved on some but not all parts, and which were better in some, but not all grade levels, were labels of objects, and grouping objects in ways to facilitate an estimate of their numbers. Plane views instead of perspective, and boundary lines around significant cues were also improvements.

Verbal captions were improved by underlining or capitalizing key words. The uses of repetition and redundancy for unfamiliar audio-visual materials tended to facilitate learning.

This study illustrates the difficulty of finding combinations of verbal and nonverbal stimuli that will gain control over all criterion response for all students. Another interesting point is that the greater the "iconicity," or realism of a visual, the greater is the probability that it will elicit a correct response. This is attributed to previous learning. Gropper (10) reports an experiment in which a ball and ring were used to illustrate the principle that matter expands when heated. A cold metal ball is inserted in a ring and then heated. When heated the demonstrator could not pull it out of the ring. This visual demonstration of a principle was probably worth a good many words.

The relative merits of visuals and verbals for giving examples of abstract ideas and principles have also been investigated. In some instances a general principle may be understood from a simple statement. In the case of Gropper's experiment, the simple statement that "all metals will expand when heated" may be sufficient provided the concepts of "metals," "expand" and "heat" have been previously formed. A more general principle that "all forms of matter expand when heated" may require examples showing how metals, wood, water and gases obey this law. At this point visual demonstrations of examples may aid in comprehending the full meaning of this principle. As Gropper points out, it is not always possible to see what is happening when matter expands, but it is possible to see the effects, as in the ball and ring experiment. If the purpose is to go further and explain why matter expands when heated, visualization by animation showing the increases in speed of molecular action may be employed.

There are still other ways in which examples of abstract principles can be visualized. One is, as Gropper suggests, by analogy. Electromotive forces are analogous to hydraulic systems. The activities of electrons, protons, and other "trons" in various kinds of atoms may be represented by mock-ups.

SUMMARY: ACQUISITION RESPONSES.

Acquisition responses are controlled by the learning task. Different kinds of tasks may require different kinds of responses. There may be, however, one or more types of learning that are basic to all meaningful learning.

1. Associative Responses

All verbal learning, both meaningful and rote, requires the formation of new associations between stimuli and responses. The stimuli may be verbal or nonverbal, but the responses usually are verbal. Learning is faster and better retained when the stimuli and response terms are meaningful rather than when they are meaningless or nearly so, as in the case of memorizing nonsense syllables. Learning lists of names, verses of poetry, the vocabulary of a foreign language, the facts of addition and subtraction in arithmetic, facts of science, geography and other school subjects, are examples of meaningful verbal associative learning. Learning is meaningful when new associations are formed between terms, the meanings of which have previously been learned. If these meanings have not been learned previously, then associative learning becomes a matter of rote memorizing of meaningless words.[3] The result is "empty verbalization" which is frowned upon by educators.

2. The Acquisition of New Concepts

The learning tasks required by many A-V presentations go beyond the formation of new associations between terms and demand that fuller and more comprehensive meanings and implications of the materials be learned. This is called "concept" learning. This type of learning involves much more than merely memorizing dictionary definitions of terms such as "velocity," "rigidity" and "beauty." In psychological language a concept is defined as "any response, verbal or motor, that is under the discriminative control of a broad class of environmental objects or events" (Verplank, [25]). Terms such as "honest," "beautiful," "clever" are responses to discriminable properties of things and actions.

The process involved in concept formation occupies a prominent place in modern experimental psychology. The literature is very extensive.

3. The Understanding of Explanations

In many A-V presentations a major part of the learning task is grasping a new idea, understanding an explanation, or comprehending the full meaning of a principle. This is sometimes called "substance" learning in contrast to factual learning and concept learning. While the responses of grasping, understanding and comprehending the full meaning of a presentation involve the utilization of previously acquired associations and concepts, they also require a higher order of covert responding. This higher level is designated by Gagné(8) as "principles" learning. Beyond is a still higher level of problem solving.

3 There is evidence that nonsense syllables and meaningless nonverbal materials are learned by endowing them with meanings which mediate connections between stimulus and response terms; see Osgood (22), also Bugelski (3).

REFERENCES

1. Asher, J. J. *Sensory interrelationships in the automated teaching of foreign languages.* Psychol. Dept. San Jose State College, San Jose, Calif., *USOE Title VII,* Proj. No. 578, 1961.
2. Bern, H. A. *Learning and Physiological Responses to Various Word-Picture Combinations.* Unpublished Ph.D. dissertation, Bloomington, Indiana University, 1958.
3. Bugelski, B. R. "Presentation time, total time, and mediation in paired-associate learning," *J. Exp. Psychol.* 63:409–12 (1962).
4. Cofer, C. N. (ed.). *Verbal Learning and Verbal Behavior.* (New York: McGraw-Hill, 1961) p. 241.
5. Davidson, R. E. "Mediation and ability in paired-associate learning," *J. Educ. Psychol., 1964,* 55:352–56.
6. Dollard, John and Miller, Neal E. *Personality and Psychotherapy* (New York: McGraw-Hill, 1950).
7. Gagné, R. M. "The acquisition of knowledge." *Psychol. Rev.,* 69:355–65 (1962).
8. Gagné, R. M. *The Conditions of Learning,* (New York: Holt, Rinehart and Winston, Inc., 1965) pp. 308.
9. Goss, A. E. "Acquisition and use of conceptual schemes." In Cofer, C. N. (ed.), *Verbal Learning and Verbal Behavior.* (New York: McGraw-Hill, 1961) pp. 42–68.
10. Gropper, G. L. *A behavioral analysis of the role of visuals in instructions.* Studies in Televised Instruction. Metropolitan Pittsburgh Television Stations and the American Institute for Research, NDEA, Title VII, Project No. 637, 1963.
11. Hartman, F. R. "Single and multiple channel communication," *AV Commun. Rev.* 9:235–62 (1963).
12. Homme, L. E. and Glaser, R. "Problems in programming verbal sequences." In Lumsdaine and Glaser (eds.) *Teaching Machines and Programmed Learning.* (Washington, D.C.: Nat. Educ. Assn., 1960).
13. Kale, S. V. and Grosslight, J. H. *Exploratory studies in the use of pictures and sound for teaching foreign language vocabulary.* Pennsylvania State Univ. Instruc. Res. Program. U.S. Naval Training Devices Center, ONR. Tech. Rept. No. SDC 269-7-53, Port Washington, N.Y., 1955.
14. Kendler, H. H. "The concept of the concept." In Melton, A. W. (ed.), *Categories of Human Learning.* (New York: Academic Press, 1964) pp. 212–33.
15. Kopstein, F. F. and Roshal, S. M. "Learning foreign vocabulary from pictures versus words." Abstracted in *The American Psychologist,* 9:407–08 (1954).
16. Lumsdaine, A. A. "Cue and response functions of pictures and words." In May, M. A. and Lumsdaine, A. A. *Learning from Films.* (New Haven: Yale Univ. Press., 1958) pp. 123–149.
17. Lumsdaine, A. A. "Previous instruction on the topic of the film." In May, M. A. and Lumsdaine, A. A. *Learning From Films,* (New Haven: Yale Univ. Press, 1958) pp. 115–22.
18. May, M. A. "Patterns of words and pictures." In May, M. A. and Lumsdaine, A. A. *Learning from Films.* (New Haven: Yale Univ. Press, 1958) pp. 150–67.
19. May, M. A. "Verbal responses to demonstrational films." In May, M. A., and Lumsdaine, A. A. *Learning from Films.* (New Haven: Yale Univ. Press, 1958) pp. 168–80.
20. Melton, A. W. (ed.). *Categories of Human Learning.* (New York: Academic Press, and London, 1964) p. 356.
21. Olson, L. A. "Concept attainment of high school sophomores." *J. Educ. Psychol.* 54:213–16 (1963).
22. Osgood, C. E. "The nature and measurement of meaning." *Psychol. Bull.,* 49:197–237 (1952).
23. Sheffield, F. D. "Theoretical considerations in the learning of complex sequential tasks from demonstration and practice." In Lumsdaine, A. A. (ed.), *Student Response in Programmed Instruction,* (Washington, D.C.: Nat. Acad. Sci., Natl. Res. Council, 1961).

24. Vandermeer, A. W., and Thorne, H. E. *An Investigation of the Improvement of Educational Filmstrips and a Derivation of Principles Relating to the Effectiveness of these Media.* (The Pennsylvania State Univ. College of Education, University Park, Penna., 1964).
25. Verplank, W. S. "A glossary of some terms used in the objective science of behavior." *Psychol. Rev. Suppl. 64,* No. 6, Part 2 (1957).

Chapter 3

How can the media be used to develop and modify the attitudes of students?

What educational goals can be identified and met through attitude modification?

What determining factors affect the intensity, direction and durability of attitude change?

Are multi-media message combinations effective in systematically inducing behavior change?

DEVELOPMENT AND MODIFICATION OF ATTITUDES THROUGH EDUCATIONAL MEDIA

JOHN L. HAYMAN, JR., Executive Director of
Research and Evaluation, School District of Philadelphia

MARVIN DAWSON, JR., Coordinator,
Learning Resources Center, Auburn University

One possible use of media in education is the development and modification of attitudes. Whether or not they should be used for this purpose, however, depends on such things as the legitimacy of attitude modification as an educational objective, the extent to which attitude modification tasks can be made explicit and manageable in the educational setting, and the relative efficiency of media in accomplishing specific attitude modification tasks. In this chapter, we shall be concerned with these and other matters related to the development and modification of attitudes through educational media.

SALIENT CHARACTERISTICS OF ATTITUDE CHANGE

Some Generalizations.

What is an attitude? In the scientific sense, "attitude refers to a predisposition to behave in a particular fashion toward a given object or

40

class of objects." It is a predisposition which is learned and enduring, and it has "a directive effect upon feeling and action related to the object" (16, p. 50). In this vein, Schramm has said, "By attitudes we mean inferred states of readiness to react in an evaluative way, in support of or against a given stimulus situation" (49, p. 209).

Is this readiness to react in an evaluative way subject to manipulation, that is, can attitudes be changed? Very generally the answer is yes; attitudes can be changed. As Schramm commented more than ten years ago, there is no longer any doubt of this (49, p. 20).

Very few other broad generalizations can be made about attitude development and modification, for, as we shall see presently, the matter is very complex. Among these few generalizations are certain ones the reader should keep in mind as he proceeds through this chapter.

Modifying attitudes, for example, is a long-term affair. The one-shot program is likely to fail. One reason is that regression very often follows termination of an attitude modification program, particularly where the target attitudes are deep-seated (37, p. 290; 1, p. 480). Attitudes tend to slip back to their original position, and continued efforts to modify them are therefore necessary. Furthermore, recent evidence has shown that the effects of several related messages tend to summate (20), so continually adding information through a long-range program will result in the greatest attitude change.

Attitude modification programs will seldom be completely successful, because of the regression effects noted above and because many attitudes are highly resistant to change. As Klapper has noted, "attitude changes consist more often of modifications than of conversions" (37, p. 292). We should not be overly discouraged, therefore, at the failure to achieve complete success.

The same attitude modification program will have different effects on different people. Research has shown that these effects differ according to such things as current level of knowledge, types of past experience, level of ability, goals, and prior attitudes (11, p. 139; 49, p. 16). As Broudy has noted, "Each pupil is the bearer of a unique pattern of abilities, achievements, and possibilities" (8, p. 140), and to some extent, each will react in his own unique way to an attitude modification program. Thus, the need to think about individualization is just as pressing in attitude modification as it is in other parts of the instructional program (33).

Attitudes differ in their susceptibility to change, and different approaches are needed according to situational factors. Change is easier, for example, when *intensity* rather than *direction* is at stake. Someone can be made more or less favorable or unfavorable than he already is with relative ease; changing him from one side of an issue to the other is more difficult. One factor determining susceptibility to change is degree of internalization, and attitudes which have been internalized as part of the mores and folkways of the society are highly resistant to change (56, p. 347).

Attitudes normally become more inflexible and difficult to change as age increases (22). Modification programs, therefore, should begin as early as possible, even as early as kindergarten and first grade, for social attitudes and the like.

Finally, a great deal remains to be learned about changing attitudes (32). Considerable research is now in progress in this area, and the present scarcity of knowledge in several important aspects of it makes it incumbent on us as educators to keep abreast of findings.

Reference was made above to the fact that attitudes differ in their susceptibility to change. This susceptibility determines to a large extent the appropriate modification approach, and it is therefore important to understand so far as possible how susceptibility can be assessed. Unfortunately, there is no set formula for doing this, and value judgments are always involved. It is generally helpful, however, to consider two factors, intensity and direction, in relation to the attitudes in question.

Krathwohl, Bloom, and Masia have classified attitudes by levels according to degree of certitude. At the "acceptance" level, at one end of the scale, certainty is lowest, and there is more of a readiness to re-evaluate one's position than at other levels. At the "commitment" level, on the other end, certainty is highest, the attitude is likely to have been internalized, and there is the least readiness to re-evaluate (40, pp. 140–153).

The resistance of an attitude to change depends in part on its position on this certitude or intensity dimension. The further toward the commitment end the attitude is, the more deep-seated and difficult it is to change. Prior attitude status, therefore, determines to some extent the difficulty of the attitude modification task.

A second determining factor is the extent of change which is desired. Attitudes have direction as well as intensity; they are favorable or unfavorable. The certitude dimension can be thought of, therefore, as passing through a zero or neutral point with favorableness on one side and unfavorableness on the other. The further the attitude is to be moved along this dimension, the more difficult the task. This is subject, of course, to the qualification that movement at the extremes, or positions of greater certitude, is more difficult than movement near the middle or neutral point.

The difficulty of the attitude modification task determines the approach, which can be more or less passive or active. For the least difficult tasks, a passive approach to change is appropriate. As the task becomes more difficult, however, the appropriate approach becomes relatively less passive and more active. By passive, of course, we necessarily mean the subject is the recipient of information, and by active we mean he is engaged in some kind of overt behavior.

Media *per se* are involved with imparting information; therefore, the subjects are passive according to the above terminology. Media, therefore, can sometimes handle the complete attitude modification task alone, but most often they cannot. Even if they cannot succeed alone, however, they can be highly effective in combination with activities involving overt behavior. Let us consider some aspects of attitude modification through the use of media, that is, through the information approach.

The Information Approach.

Several writers have observed that the first essential in any communication act is to gain and then hold the attention of the intended receiver (49, p. 13; 29, p. 290; 11, p. 137). Once the person attends to the message, it is then necessary that he understand it. And, finally, he must accept it if the intended effect is to be achieved (11, p. 137).

In any information approach, therefore, special attention must be given to the matter of reaching the audience. In the schools, the information approach will be handled almost entirely through formal courses, and the audience will be the pupils. Their attention must be gained and held; the material presented to them must be understandable; and it must be presented in such a way that they accept it.

After the message reaches its intended audience, however, its efficacy still depends on a number of factors. Following Cohen, we will discuss these in terms of characteristics of the message, of the person sending it, and of the person for whom it is intended (11).

Accordingly, let us look first at the characteristics of the communication or message. As we have said, few attitude modification programs in the schools will be of the one-shot variety. The communication we are referring to, therefore, is likely in reality to be a long series of individual communication events (such as single lessons or parts of lessons), and the functional relationships we state must be thought of in terms both of individual events and of sequences of events. Possible techniques used with the communication include fear arousal, the drawing of conclusions, one- and two-sided approaches, and primacy and recency effects.

Communications which arouse fear are often used in programs such as health education and driver education where some physical harm might result from undesirable practices. Gruesome accident scenes are shown, for example, to illustrate why it is best to drive safely, and badly decayed teeth (with a reminder of the pain which restoring them will bring) are illustrated to promote good dental practice. The idea here is that a high state of fear or emotional tension is aroused and the message is then accepted and acted upon because it offers a way to escape the danger and therefore reduce the tension.

Since tension is to be reduced by following the communicator's recommendations, it is important that he state these recommendations immediately after arousing the tension and that he make them explicit (14, 29, 34). Furthermore, there is a limit to the degree of tension arousal which will facilitate attitude change. Inducing a very high level of tension has been found to weaken the appeal (22, 35), apparently because a subject will tend to eliminate an overly-horrible threat by discounting it through some psychological defense reaction rather than by doing something positive. In using this approach, therefore, a moderate rather than maximum arousal of fear should be employed.

The second matter is the stating of conclusions. In a communication designed to modify attitudes, is it better to state explicitly the point the communication is intended to convey, or is it better to let the audience draw its own conclusions? This is an important consideration in designing courses of the nature we are discussing. How often does one tell students what the course is designed to do? Are students banged over the head with it constantly, or are they, perhaps, never made aware of the explicit purpose at all? The early research on this matter suggested that conclusions should be stated in the course of each communication event (28, 29). Later results have shown that the issue is not so simple, for at least two additional factors need to be considered. The first is the complexity of the communication; the greater the degree of complexity, the greater the need for stating conclusions (41). Second is the intelligence level of the audience, and here an inverse relationship exists. The less the intelligence level of the audience, the greater the need for stating conclusions (55).

An especially important consideration in some areas such as government and political science is whether to present only information which supports the advocated position or whether to present information both for and against. Should a one-sided or a two-sided approach be used? The answer depends on whether the subject is likely to be faced with a counterargument at some later date and whether he is already familiar with some of the facts supporting the other side. More immediate change in attitude will occur if a one-sided presentation is given, but, if the subject is ever to face a counterargument, then a two-sided approach is essential (29). A one-sided approach is more effective when the audience is not familiar with facts supporting the other side, but, when some of these facts are known, then the two-sided approach is more effective (54). Apparently the integrity of the communicator is made suspect when a one-sided approach is attempted under the latter conditions.

Aside from these practical considerations in deciding between one-sided and two-sided approaches, however, there is a moral issue. We claim to value truth for its own sake in our society, and as Allport has said, "If we are going after the truth we must go after the whole of it—not merely after the part that is congenial" (1, p. 270). The two-sided approach seems desirable in most instances.

This brings up the matter of primacy and recency. If both sides of an issue are to be presented, which should be first? Does greater attitude change in the advocated direction occur if the favorable argument is given first, or does more occur if it is given last? Until recently, it was generally believed that the argument presented first had the advantage, but later research shows that this is not necessarily true, particularly where a series of communication events is involved (2). Whether the law of primacy holds depends on a number of factors, though the effects of many of them are not clearly understood at present. Among the factors are public commitment, warning against premature conclusions, and ability to hold attention.

If, after one side of an argument is presented, a person makes a public commitment to the point of view advocated, then the primacy effect is very strong; immediate change is unlikely no matter what kind of opposition argument is presented. The strength of this effect diminishes with time, however, so regression is likely as time increases since the person's public commitment (58).

Apparently, private committal makes a difference also, for the primacy effect can be weakened by avoiding early decisions (30). In education we often attempt this by advising that a person should get all the evidence before forming conclusions.

Primacy sometimes is simply a matter of attention. Subjects, for reasons of boredom, fatigue, etc., may attend better to material which is presented first (3, 53). Thus, it is important to insure that later communications are as well attended as early ones.

Let us now turn our attention to characteristics of the person who originates the communication. This will be the classroom teacher most of the time in the educational setting. In general, it has been found that the higher the credibility of the source, the greater will be the effectiveness of the communication in changing attitudes (12; 29, pp. 269–277; 36). Apparently the communicator can be 'credible' in a number of ways. He may be seen as impartial and trustworthy. He may be considered an expert in the area under consideration, or he may have great prestige. He may be perceived as intending only to inform his audience and not to manipulate them in any way. He may be similar to the receiver in some way, or he may simply be personally liked or disliked. Whatever the source of his credibility, however, it assists him in modifying the attitudes of the audience.

Again, the mechanisms by which the effect occurs are not fully understood. In some cases, credibility apparently relates to attention; the subject will not attend to messages from sources he does not consider credible. There are other considerations, however. Research has shown that equal amounts of information can be gained from different messages, but those messages attributed to the most credible sources still have the greatest effect on attitudes (29, p. 270).

Present knowledge allows certain other important generalizations in this area. The greater the change in attitudes advocated, the greater the change which will occur—provided the person advocating the change has high credibility. With a low credibility source, however, the greater the change advocated, the less it will occur, apparently because the subject builds up resistance to the message (4, 5, 6). He resents the attempt at manipulation by someone not highly regarded.

A second generalization concerns social pressure. A person's behavior is regulated to a considerable degree by expectations of approval or disapproval within his social climate, and he is usually alert to cues bearing on this point (50). Certain communicators gain their credibility by being perceived in some way as representatives of the social climate, and responding to their messages is seen as having to do with rewards and punishments. In this situation, the communication stands a good chance of effecting change in the advocated direction (51).

A third generalization relates to the desire not to be manipulated. We have mentioned already that intention to manipulate seems to relate in some way to source credibility. In something of a paradox, attitudes can sometimes be manipulated more easily when the subject thinks there is no intent to manipulate him (57, 18). This depends, however, on how much the subject personally likes the one trying to change him; the more he likes the communicator, the less he resents the attempt at manipulation (43). Thus, different components of credibility interact.

The problem of credibility is usually not as critical in the schools as it is in other communication situations. As Hovland, Janis, and Kelley have observed:

> Typically the classroom audience has initial expectations that the communicator's conclusions will be the "correct answers." Hence, the acceptance can usually be taken for granted and the primary problems are those of maintaining attention and insuring comprehension (29, p. 290).

What of the person for whom the communication is intended, that is, the one whose attitudes are to be modified? Research has shown that each person reacts differently to a message, according to his own unique goals, understandings, experiences, prior attitudes, and the like. Generally, one can say that a message is more likely to be effective if it is congruent with existing personality patterns or if it is in harmony with the norms of valued reference groups (49, p. 209; 17).

Thus, it is better in most cases to begin with where a person is and work changes gradually. Entering here is the phenomenon of selective perception. Klapper notes that:

> . . . by and large people perceive only what they wish to perceive, that they read or listen to only such material as espouses or can be misinterpreted to espouse their existing views, and in general use controversial material to reinforce the opinions they already possess (37, p. 303).

The extent to which existing patterns and needs affect the likelihood of a message succeeding depends on the degree to which the subject is already committed on the issue in question as well as the direction of his current stand. If the subject is deeply committed, he is less susceptible to change than if he is "on the fence" (1, p. 480).

Susceptibility to change depends also on a set of personality factors which might be referred to as self-dependence or self-sufficiency (15, 21, 27). The person who is more self-sufficient is more difficult to change.

Those who tend to be rigid in respect for and obedience to authority, for example, are more likely to be changed through persuasive communication, provided the source is highly credible.

Those who are other-directed, that is, who depend on relationships with other people, are more susceptible to change than those who tend to be inner-directed.

Somewhat akin to inner-directedness is the ability to abide social isolation. Those who are affected less by social isolation are likely to be affected less by communications designed to change attitudes.

A person's reference groups, and the extent of his dependence on them, affect his changeability. Every person has reference groups, and every person seeks approval from members of these groups to some extent. Attitudes, therefore, tend to change according to perceived group standards, though vulnerability to the threat of social disapproval from a group depends on the value placed on membership in that particular group (11, p. 41). A message should be designed, if possible, so that its agreement with the norms of one or more reference groups is emphasized.

This concludes the discussion of attitude change through informational approaches. It should be obvious to the reader that the pertinent effects are complex and that it is therefore risky to draw broad generalizations. Planning of a course or series of courses in which a major purpose is to develop or modify attitudes is a difficult task which requires understanding and care. It can be done, however. Research has shown that some fairly deep-seated attitudes can be modified through essentially verbal means in a planned course (26).

Behavior Approach.

As we have said, attitudes vary in their susceptibility to change through information alone. Those higher on the certitude scale, that is, which are more deep-seated, are likely to require some type of overt behavioral experience. This is not to say that anything other than knowledge is causing the change in attitude. The issue rather is how the knowledge is acquired; it is a matter of whether the person gains information about the field through the passive approach or acquaintance with the field through the active approach (1, p. 480).

We shall dwell but briefly on active or behavioral-based approaches, for media are almost totally concerned with supplying information—with providing knowledge about an issue rather than acquaintance with it through some kind of firsthand experience. As we have said, however, many programs will be most effective when information and overt behavior are combined in some way. For this reason, a few remarks about changes through behavior seem appropriate.

In the behavioral approach, the subject is by some means caused to behave in desired ways, and attitude change results. This is a reversal, of course, in the direction of causation implied in the development to this point. When we say that certain attitudes predispose a person to behave in certain ways, we imply that the attitudes come first and to some degree cause the behavior.

Actually, the relationship between attitudes and behavior is two-way, that is, the causation can occur in either direction. This means that when a person behaves in a particular fashion, he will emerge with attitudes and values which are in harmony with his behavior and will be predisposed to behave the same way in the future (47). As Raab and Lipset put it, "evidence indicates that specific attitudes shape themselves to behavior" (45, p. 41).

Left to his own devices, a person will, of course, behave according to existing attitudes and his behavior will simply reinforce these attitudes as they are. For attitudes to be changed, the subject must be induced to behave in ways discrepant to his existing predispositions.

By what means does this mechanism operate? The explanation is usually in terms of dissonance theory, that is, in terms of a person's mental discomfort in behaving in a way inconsistent with the way he thinks (or, perhaps, feels) he should behave (19). If he is somehow induced to continue the discrepant behavior, the only way he can reduce the inconsistency (and thus reduce the discomfort) is to change his way of thinking or feeling.

Two pertinent qualifying conditions are the amount of effort the person puts into the activity he initially is disposed against and the extent to which he perceives he is being forced to engage in discrepant behavior. The greater the effort the person puts into the activity, the more attitude change; and the less the perceived force, the more attitude change (11, pp. 93–97). The determining factor in each case is the extent to which the person can rationalize to himself what he is doing.

It has been found that only attitudes related to the specific type of behavior in question are likely to be changed (7, 15). Thus, going to school with people of a different racial group than one's own will change one's attitude toward going to school with them but not toward any other kind of activity. Living contiguously with those of other groups will cause one to develop favorable attitudes toward the others as neighbors, but these are the only attitudes which will be affected. The moral is that if the purpose is to develop more favorable attitudes generally, and this is likely to be the goal in education, then many different kinds of behavior are necessary. The behavior must be general if the attitudes to be changed are general.

Social attitudes, which are highly resistant to change and with which the schools are prominently concerned (46, 52), deserve special mention here. Evidence indicates that, to the extent possible, the behavioral approach should be followed in developing and modifying attitudes about people of different racial and cultural backgrounds. Many misconceptions can and should be corrected through carefully prepared information series, but numerous equal-status contacts are also essential in developing attitudes as free as possible from bias and prejudice (52).

ATTITUDE MODIFICATION AS AN INSTRUCTIONAL OBJECTIVE

Qualifications.

Is the modification of attitudes a legitimate objective of the schools? The answer, of course, depends on which attitudes are in question. The schools are concerned with some and not with others (15, 42).

Before we consider which are the province of the schools, we need, for purposes of clarification, to discuss the relationship between attitudes and values and the meaning of the word "modify" in this context.

Writers in the educational literature generally do not discriminate between attitudes and values; they tend to use the terms synonymously (40, p. 140; 46). An attitude is a readiness to behave according to some value, of course, so the practice of using the terms synonymously is not without foundation. The difficulty is that values, as opposed to attitudes, have no necessary behavioral correlate. Whether "value" or "attitude" is used in the discussion which follows, some behavior will always be implied.

As to "modify," we will mean more than just changing something which already exists. In reality, the educational system must both modify many of the attitudes and values which the child brings to the system with him, and it must develop attitudes and values where none exist. Therefore, when we speak of attitude modification as a function of the schools, we are implying both change and development.

What are the attitudes and values which the educational system is responsible for changing or developing?

Attitudes to be Modified.

Considerable difficulty is inevitably experienced in attempting to answer this question. In spite of the fact we have said we will limit our discussion to value-determined predispositions to behavior, in the broader view all education appears to meet this criterion. As Haan has said with regard to school experiences, "Values are inherent in all action. All experience involves ethical qualities" (25, p. 13). And Childs, after a penetrating examination of the problem, concludes: "In fine, education is a value-conditioned activity. The school seeks to cultivate selected values in the young by means of both the subject matters and the methods that it employs in its programs" (10, p. 100).

A helpful approach in delimiting the discussion is to consider how the society as a whole handles the education of youth in the matter of value systems. Broudy has performed this kind of analysis, and his work illustrates that many of the basic values, while reinforced in the schools, are the primary responsibility of some other element of society.

For example, he discusses milieu education, which is "more or less automatically a by-product of ordinary living" and which provides for conformity to society's folkways and mores (8, p. 6). Folkways and mores are, of course, an essential part of an individual's value system. They are internalized, that is, are accepted and used by a person as his own criteria, and they provide the framework within which all other values and attitudes fit. The important point here is that developing this essential set of values is not a primary responsibility of the schools.

The schools are engaged in formal education and have the primary task of teaching and training. They are necessarily concerned with the kinds of learning which can be controlled within their area of operation (8). Thus the schools can be concerned only with those attitudes (and related values) which are within their power to modify or develop. A significant problem here is determining which attitudes the schools have the power to control in some way.

Defining and Delimiting the Task.

The problem of determining what the schools *can* do in modifying attitudes as well as of determining how modification is to be accomplished is best approached through breaking broad modification goals into more immediate subgoals. Some way of classifying different parts of the overall task is needed to do this, and one useful classification scheme is illustrated in the following paragraphs.

To understand this scheme, consider first the role of the schools within the society. As we have indicated already, the schools have a unique role which compliments but which, in theory at least, does not conflict with the roles played by other societal institutions. Haan describes the role of the schools as follows:

> The role of the school in a free society is that of a supplementary institution, continuing, correcting, and expanding the socialization processes which began in the family. A school should pay attention to what it is in the individual's personality development, in the growth of democratic skills and attitudes, and in the community institutions that are necessary to maintain an open society (25, p. 7).

The kinds of things Haan mentions are functional to the ongoing of the larger society, and in the broad sense society has developed and maintained the schools so that this function will be performed. This is the schools' *raison d'etre*. They exist because they have a job to do and not because of their intrinsic worth. In making this point, Childs has gone so far as to say that, "the curriculum of a school is an index to the values of the particular human group that founds the school" (10, p. 96).

If one takes a closer look, however, he sees that Childs has overstated the case a bit. While the broad function of the schools with regard to supporting the larger society cannot be debated, the observer discovers that many values and attitudes developed by the schools are not altogether directly supportive of society.

Ask any public school teacher what values he would like his pupils to exhibit, and first he is likely to mention things related to his immediate task. He wants his pupils to value education and to be motivated toward high academic achievement. He wants them to conform to the rules of behavior established within his school and classroom and to avoid becoming disciplinary problems. He is, of course, mentioning the attitudes his pupils must display before he can successfully play his role, that is, before he can accomplish the larger task set by society. As Jaffa has said, "How a child behaves is a concern of all teachers" (33).

The schools, therefore, are engaged in developing two kinds of attitudes, and these attitudes can be separated according to the institution for whose purposes they are immediately functional. One set of attitudes and values is functional to the larger society, and these can be referred to as *societal* in nature. A second set of attitudes and values is functional to the school system, and can be referred to as *educative*.

A second division can be made according to the method by which the attitudes are developed or modified, that is, according to the approach employed. The schools achieve most of their goals through the formal curriculum, that is, through the set of formal courses offered to students. Many goals, however, particularly in the area with which we are dealing, cannot be achieved through formal courses. In regard to one such goal, Haan comments as follows:

> [The school] should be a laboratory for individuals to learn the methods and values of an open society with democratic ideals. The classroom, the playground, the school as a whole lend themselves for this purpose. Both formal, student government for example, and informal means are used to help children learn the personal character that enables them to live in and contribute to a democracy (25, p. 17).

Broudy speaks of another such goal:

> General education . . . has a great deal to offer to the values of personal relationships, but more through the effects of the total curriculum on self-determination, self-realization, and self-integration rather than through any specific course or courses (8, p. 177).

In other words, many goals in the attitudinal and value area are accomplished through the total curriculum, i.e., through combinations of many school activities, rather than through specific courses. Specific courses usually involve a communicative process in which the pupil receives information and is passive to a large extent. As we have seen, attitudes differ in their susceptibility to change through an approach which is essentially informational. The schools can achieve their goals with regard to the less difficult attitude modification tasks through formal courses. For the more difficult tasks, however, a formal course will not suffice, and other activities within the school setting must be designed to bring about the desired change.

This distinction provides another way of classifying those attitudes which are the legitimate concern of the schools. If they are susceptible to change through an informational approach, we can design a formal course which operates on them directly and immediately. If they are not so susceptible, we must design other activities which result in pertinent behaviors and to which the change in attitudes is concomitant. Any attitude, therefore, can be described according to the curricular approach through which it is modified. Either the modification is an *immediate* or a *concomitant* result of the approach followed.

Combining the two ways of classifying attitudes, we arrive at the following four categories:

1. Societal–immediate
2. Societal–concomitant
3. Educative–immediate
4. Educative–concomitant.

These categories are inclusive in that every attitude will fit into at least one of them, but they are not mutually exclusive because some attitudes may fit more than one. The scheme is meaningful to our discussion because, in attempting to classify an attitude according to it, a person is forced to break the overall attitude modification task into specific, manageable goals which are meaningful in terms of a media approach.

As an example of how this happens, consider the educational goal, 'respect for humanity,' which is one of 41 listed by the NEA's Educational Policy Commission (44, pp. 50–108). Respect for humanity is certainly an attitude, or more accurately a complex of attitudes, which is functional to the democratic society. It is also functional to the ongoing work of the educational system since classes operate more smoothly and the climate for learning is better when mutual respect exists among students and between students and teachers. Respect for other persons can be developed through providing direct information; a person can be taught the dangers of overgeneralizing and using stereotypes, for example, and he can be taught that behavioral variations result largely from environmental differences. Respect is even more firmly established through working together in activities such as student government, that is, through the equal-status contacts previously mentioned.

How can respect for humanity be handled according to our classification scheme so that we are aided in choosing media? To illustrate, let us first break the general concept into some components according to function.

Societal
    Judgment of people according to individual merits
    Support of programs to insure equal legal rights
    Courteous behavior toward all people
    Support of programs to insure equal vocational opportunities

Educative
    Courteous behavior toward teachers
    Courteous behavior toward other students
    Willingness to help others overcome school-based problems
    Fair treatment of others in athletics and other school activities

To complete the classification, we must subdivide these attitudes according to the means by which they can be modified. An arrangement like the following might result:

Societal–immediate

Knowledge of the history of different racial and cultural groups

Knowledge of ideals and goals underlying United States culture

Knowledge of democracy and other political systems

Knowledge of inequities among racial and cultural groups which exist and have existed in the United States

Societal–concomitant

Experience of visiting courts and seeing the legal system operate

Experience of traveling through the local area and viewing housing patterns

Experience of talking with people of different racial and cultural groups about job opportunities, educational opportunities, and the like

Educative–immediate

Knowledge of rules and regulations regarding conduct in the school

Knowledge of racial and cultural patterns within the school student body

Knowledge of democratic values as they apply in the school setting

Educative–concomitant

Experience of participating in student government

Experience of participating in athletics

Experience of working with others to solve academic problems.

This example is not meant to be comprehensive, nor are we prepared to argue whether or not we have thought of the best ways to approach respect for humanity. The point is, however, that classifying in this way forced a breakdown to subgoals that have direct meaning in terms of media. The subgoals in the "immediate" categories can be attained through a media or informational approach.

EDUCATIONAL MEDIA AND ATTITUDE CHANGE

Definition of Media.

How does one move from specific subgoals to a determination of the way media can be used in the task? This depends first on how the term media is defined.

We have already indicated that media are concerned with exchanging information, but this kind of loose, vague definition is not sufficient. A more precise definition is needed. It is very difficult, however, to derive a precise definition of educational media.

An abundance of current educational publications is concerned with such problems as administering *media,* multi-*media* and cross-*media* approaches in education, the effects of various *media* upon learning, *media* and educational innovation, etc. Yet, the meaning of media, and especially educational media, is unclear.

The vast majority of communications specialists define media in terms of various storage and retrieval devices. Klapper (37), for example, lists print, radio, screen and face-to-face discourse. A more inclusive list by Riley (48) includes television, radio, films, slides, laboratory demonstrations, recording instruments, "talking" workbooks, and learning machines. In a slightly different vein, Brown and Norberg (9) list print, lithography, audiovisual and electronic devices as various kinds of media.

Knowlton (39) has suggested that machine-oriented definitions such as those listed above would indicate excessive concern for gadgets. A more fruitful approach, he contends, would involve preoccupation with the nature of the message (i.e., pictorial or verbal), the intent of the communicator, and the response elicited by the communication. With regard to film, for example, he concludes:

> Film has been an often used variable in audiovisual research. But this variable either has no meaning or too many meanings, depending upon how one looks at it. To speak of the values of film independently of the messages contained is to speak of the lighting techniques used, the grain of the film, the quality of the sound, and so on. This would be like classifying books according to the number of pages, the size of the type used, etc. While this last is useful for some purposes, it is not generally the thing most useful for the usual purposes of the educator interested in teaching and learning (38).

Gropper (23), writing in a stimulus-response context, is clearly concerned with the nature of both verbal and nonverbal stimuli insofar as it assists students to acquire, retain, and transfer responses. In this sense he is definitely message rather than machine oriented in his approach to a definition of media.

A concept of media which may serve as a compromise to the different approaches discussed above is suggested in the following quotations from John Dewey.

> 'Medium' signifies first of all an intermediary. The import of the word 'means' is the same. They are the middle, the intervening, things through which something now remote is brought to pass. Yet not all means are media. There are two kinds of means. One kind is taken up into the consequences produced and remains immanent in them . . . Even bricks and mortar become a part of the house they are employed to build; they are not mere means to its erection (13, p. 197).
>
> A medium as distinct from raw material is always a mode of language and thus of expression and communication. Pigments, marble and bronze, sounds, are not media of themselves. They enter into the formation of a

medium only when they interact with the mind and skill of an individual (13, p. 287).

Dewey's definition of media was aimed at clarifying its usage in art. However, it can be generalized to the educational field. For example, when a filmstrip is produced by photographing an illustrated children's storybook, there is no reason to speak of this in terms of two media. The media involved are the same whether displayed on a paper page or a lenticular screen. In this context, the 35mm film, the filmstrip projector, and the bound paper pages can be conveniently defined as storage and retrieval devices, not media. In the case of a projected map versus a printed map, the situation is exactly the same. The media include certain colors, textures, lines and symbols put together according to rules developed by geographers. Again the projector, film, and paper serve as presentational and storage vehicles; i.e., they can *not* be distinguished from each other in terms of their roles in *mediating* the information being communicated. The map might just as easily have been printed in a book without loss of information.

From this discussion, one can conclude that:

(1) Media is *not* everything "seen, heard, read, talked about," etc.

(2) Media can *not* be defined on the basis of mechanical considerations, television, motion pictures, radio, etc.

(3) Media can *not* be understood by analyzing verbal and nonverbal stimuli and the responses elicited by them.

(4) Media can be defined only in terms of a particular gestalt formed by the coalescence of various media 'elements' which could, but do not necessarily, include cameras, projectors, words, sounds, bricks and mortar, but which do form a *particular mode* of language and consequently of communication.

It is important to think of attitude modification goals in relation to the totality of effects produced by particular configurations of media elements. Only through this approach is success in achieving such goals likely to be achieved.

It is also important that the difficulties faced be fully recognized. We have said previously that much remains to be learned about attitude modification, and the same can be said for media. Attitude formation and modification is psychological behavior in its most complex form, and it has been described in this paper as the product of a well-balanced, relatively stable, and highly organized complex of factors such as age, direction and intensity of prior attitudes and values, reference groups, etc. Each factor may differ in the degree of importance it plays in determining a particular attitude, and each may differ in the way it interacts with a configuration of media elements. Thus the matter is extremely complex and therefore difficult to handle. As we noted previously, complete success is not likely to be achieved.

Need for Specific Goals.

We have shown that a breakdown of broad goals into more specific ones is helpful in approaching the attitude modification task. Even more specificity than we have produced with the classification scheme is needed, however, to secure the highest probability of success. After the subgoals are stated, the process needs to be extended further.

This need for great specificity became widely recognized in recent months. New approaches to defining and achieving educational goals have been made a matter of concern as a result of experimentation with programed instruction and the development of systems approaches to education. Within this frame of reference, the educator is forced to limit the purposes of instruction to clearly definable (in operational terms) and precisely measurable goals. The questions asked by the educational technologist are:

(1) What is the student supposed to know or be able to do after taking the course that he did not know or could not do before?

(2) What can the student do to demonstrate his acquisition of the desired behavior?

(3) What combinations of devices, instructional materials, and direct experiences will result in the acquisition of desired behavior in the shortest possible time with the longest lasting effect?

Limitations of Media.

This paper has described four categories of attitude classification: societal-immediate, societal-concomitant, educative-immediate, and educative-concomitant. Media use will be most often limited to the "immediate" categories since the "concomitant" categories involve actual participation in, rather than knowledge about, the world. Limiting one's thoughts to the "immediate" situations, the following specific observations may be made concerning the use of media in attitude formation and modification:

(1) There are no clear-cut formulas to be applied willy-nilly in using media. The educator will be forced to assess the difficulty of the job in some fashion, that is, certain value judgments are necessary.

(2) Any single medium (or media element) might be sufficient to do any job, but it would seem that as the difficulty of the task increases so does the need for utilizing a variety of media.

(3) The world of attitudes belongs in the realm of nonverbal, subconscious behavior, so the media which can reach these levels will be

desirable. Consequently, the media which have the potential of presenting both visual and auditory symbols (such as sound-motion pictures and television) would seem to be the most efficient. The ability to combine nonverbal stimulus materials such as music, sound effects, concrete pictorial representations with the verbal, either written or spoken, makes television and motion pictures clearly superior in attitude formation and modification.

(4) Since most formal education operates on the induced attitude model (students are required to exhibit predetermined kinds of behavior and are rewarded for complicity), the student will rationalize many attitudes to fit this behavior. Once a particular behavior pattern and its corresponding attitude have become operational, media can play an important role in concept generalization—that is in generalizing the attitude to broader areas.

CONCLUSION

The information presented in this chapter leaves little doubt that the development and changing of attitudes is a major concern of educators and that educational media can aid significantly in the accomplishment of most attitude modification tasks.

There is no cut-and-dried formula for determining the exact role media should play in specific instances, however. Attitude modification is a very complex matter, and the means through which it can best be accomplished depend on a variety of factors. These are related to the attitudes to be modified, the people who compose the target group, and the context within which the modification task is to be accomplished.

The total task usually depends on both passive or information-gain activities and active or overt-behavior activities. The relative proportion of each type of activity varies considerably from task to task, however, and can only be determined in specific instances through careful division of the overall goal into immediate and specific subgoals. Where passive activities are appropriate, that is, where subgoals can be accomplished through information gain, media play the decisive role, for they are concerned with information exchange.

The many complexities of attitude modification assure difficulties in designing educational programs in this area. These difficulties are not insurmountable, however, and are no greater than those encountered in many instructional programs. As long as the educator approaches attitude modification carefully and realistically and stays alert to findings from the expanding research in the area, he can achieve significant success in meeting his responsibilities.

REFERENCES

1. Allport, Gordon W. *The Nature of Prejudice.* (Cambridge: Addison-Wesley Publishing Company, Inc., 1954).
2. Anderson, N. H. and A. A. Barrios. "Primacy effects in personality impression formation." *The Journal of Abnormal and Social Psychology.* 63:346–50 (1961).
3. Anderson, N. H. "Primacy effects in personality impression formation using a generalized order effect paradigm." *The Journal of Personality and Social Psychology.* 2:1–9 (1965).
4. Aronson, Elliot, Judith A. Turner, and J. M. Carlsmith. "Communicator credibility and communication discrepancy as determinants of opinion change." *The Journal of Abnormal and Social Psychology.* 67:31–36 (1963).
5. Bergin, A. E. "The effect of dissonant persuasive communications upon changes in a self-referring attitude." *Journal of Personality.* 30:423–38 (1962).
6. Berkowitz, Leonard and Richard E. Goranson. "Motivational and judgmental determinants of social perception." *The Journal of Abnormal and Social Psychology.* 69:296–302 (1964).
7. Brodie, Thomas A. "Attitude toward school and academic achievement." *The Personnel and Guidance Journal.* 43:375–78 (1964).
8. Broudy, Harry S. *Building a Philosophy of Education.* 2d. ed, (Englewood Cliffs, N. J.: Prentice-Hall, Inc., 1961). Copyright © 1961 by Prentice-Hall, Inc.
9. Brown, James W. and Kenneth D. Norberg. *Administering Educational Media.* (New York: McGraw-Hill, Inc., 1965).
10. Childs, John L. *Education and Morals.* (New York: Appleton-Century-Crofts, 1950).
11. Cohen, Arthur R. *Attitude Change and Social Influence.* (New York: Basic Books, Inc., 1964).
12. Dabbs, James M., Jr. "Self-esteem, communicator characteristics, and attitude change." *The Journal of Abnormal and Social Psychology.* 69:173–81 (1964).
13. Dewey, John. *Art As Experience.* (New York: Capricorn Books, 1958). Copyright © 1958 by Putnam's & Coward-McCann.
14. DeWolfe, Alan S. and Catherine N. Governale. "Fear and attitude change." *The Journal of Abnormal and Social Psychology.* 69:119–23 (1964).
15. Edwards, Ralph. "The development and modification of the elusive attitude." *Educational Forum.* 28:355–58 (1964).
16. English, Horace B. and Ava Champney English. *A Comprehensive Dictionary of Psychological and Psychoanalytical Terms.* (New York: Longmans, Green and Co., 1958).
17. Feather, N. T. "'Acceptance and rejection of arguments in relation to attitude strength, critical ability, and intolerance of inconsistency." *The Journal of Abnormal and Social Psychology.* 69:127–36 (1964).
18. Festinger, Leon and Nathan Maccoby. "On resistance to persuasive communications." *The Journal of Abnormal and Social Psychology.* 68:359–66 (1964).
19. Festinger, Leon. *A Theory of Cognitive Dissonance.* (Evanston, Ill.: Row, Peterson, and Co., 1957).
20. Fishbein, Martin and Ronda Hunter. "Summation versus balance in attitude organization and change." *The Journal of Abnormal and Social Psychology.* 69:505–10 (1964).
21. Goldstein, J. W. "Intellectual rigidity and social attitudes." *The Journal of Abnormal and Social Psychology.* 48:345–53 (1953).
22. Goldstein, M. J. "The relationship between coping and avoiding behavior and response to fear-arousing propaganda." *The Journal of Abnormal and Social Psychology.* 58:247–52 (1959).
23. Gropper, George L. "Why *is* a picture worth a thousand words?" *Audio-Visual Communication Review.* 11:75–95 (1963).
24. Guest, Lester M. "A longitudinal study of attitude development and some correlates." *Child Development.* 35:779–84 (1964).

25. Haan, Aubrey, *Education for the Open Society.* (Boston: Allyn and Bacon, Inc., 1962).
26. Hoover, Kenneth H. "An instructional approach to the development of an emergent value orientation." *The Journal of Teacher Education.* 14:402–405 (1963).
27. Hovland, Carl I. and I. L. Janis (eds.). *Personality and Persuasibility.* (New Haven, Conn.: Yale University Press, 1959).
28. Hovland, C. I. and Wallace Mandell. "An experimental comparison of conclusion-drawing by the communicator and by the audience." *The Journal of Abnormal and Social Psychology.* 47:581–88 (1952).
29. Hovland, C. I., Irving L. Janis, and Harold H. Kelley. *Communication and Persuasion.* (New Haven, Conn.: Yale University Press, 1953).
30. Hovland, C. I. (ed.). *The Order of Presentation in Persuasion.* (New Haven, Conn.: Yale University Press, 1957).
31. Hyman, Herbert H. and Paul B. Sheatsley. "Some reasons why information campaigns fail." In Eleanor E. Maccoby, Theodore N. Newcomb, and Eugene L. Hartley, (eds.), *Readings in Social Psychology.* (New York: Henry Holt and Company, 1958).
32. Jackson, Philip W. and Nina Strattner. "Meaningful learning and retention: noncognitive variables." *The Review of Educational Research.* 34:513–29 (1964).
33. Jaffa, N. Neubert. "The disadvantaged child." *The Instructor.* 74:39 (1964).
34. Janis, I. L. and Seymour Feshbach. "Effects of fear-arousing communications." *The Journal of Abnormal and Social Psychology.* 48:78–92 (1953).
35. Janis, I. L. and R. F. Terwilliger. "An experimental study of psychological resistances of fear-arousing communications." *The Journal of Abnormal and Social Psychology.* 65:403–10 (1962).
36. Kelman, H. C. and C. I. Hovland. " 'Reinstatement' of the communicator in delayed measurement of opinion change." *The Journal of Abnormal and Social Psychology.* 48:327–35 (1953).
37. Klapper, Joseph T. "The comparative effects of the various media." In Wilbur Schramm, (ed.), *The Process and Effects of Mass Communication.* (Urbana, Illinois: University of Illinois Press, 1955).
38. Knowlton, James Q. "A conceptual scheme for the audiovisual field." *Bulletin of the School of Education.* Indiana University. 40:3 (1964).
39. Knowlton, James Q. "The need for a conceptual rationale for the audiovisual field." In Henry A. Bern, (ed.) *New Directions in Audio-Visual Communications. Bulletin of the School of Education.* Indiana University. 36:44–61 (1960).
40. Krathwohl, David R., Benjamin S. Bloom, and Bertram B. Masia. *Taxonomy of Educational Objectives, Handbook II: Affective Domain.* (New York: David McKay Company, Inc., 1956).
41. Krech, David, R. S. Crutchfield, and E. L. Ballachey. *Individual in Society.* (New York: McGraw-Hill Book Company, 1962).
42. Mead, A. R. "Attitudes and education." *Education.* 84:427–32 (1964).
43. Mills, Judson and Elliot Aronson. "Opinion change as a function of the communicator's attractiveness and desire to influence." *The Journal of Personality and Social Psychology.* 1:173–77 (1965).
44. NEA Educational Policies Commission. *Purposes of Education in American Democracy.* (Washington, D. C.: National Education Association, 1938).
45. Raab, Earl and Seymour Martin Lipset. "The prejudiced society." In Earl Raab, (ed.), *American Race Relations Today.* (Garden City, N. Y.: Doubleday and Company, Inc., 1962).
46. Reeves, Katherine. "Attitude control." *Grade Teacher.* 81:8+ (1964).
47. Reiter, Harry. "Effect of orientation through small-group discussion on modification of certain attitudes." *Journal of Educational Research.* 58:65–68 (1964).
48. Riley, John W., Jr. and Matilda White Riley. "Sociological perspectives on the use of new educational media." In *New Teaching Aids for the American Classroom.* (Washington, D. C.: U. S. Office of Education, 1962).

49. Schramm, Wilbur. *The Process and Effects of Mass Communication.* (Urbana, Illinois: The University of Illinois Press, 1955).
50. Scott, W. A. "Attitude change through reward of verbal behavior." *The Journal of Abnormal and Social Psychology.* 55:72–75 (1957).
51. Singer, R. D. "Verbal conditioning and generalization of pro-democratic responses." *The Journal of Abnormal and Social Psychology.* 63:43–46 (1961).
52. Stein, David G., Jane A. Hardyck, and M. Brewster Smith. "Race and belief: an open and shut case." *The Journal of Personality and Social Psychology.* 1:281–89 (1965).
53. Steward, R. H. "Effect of continuous responding on the order effect in personality impression formation." *The Journal of Personality and Social Psychology.* 1:161–65 (1965).
54. Thistlethwaite, D. L. and Joseph Kamenetsky. "Attitude change through refutation and elaboration of audience counterarguments." *The Journal of Abnormal and Social Psychology.* 51:3–12 (1955).
55. Thistlethwaite, D. L., Henry de Hann, and Joseph Kamenetsky. "The effects of 'directive' and 'nondirective' communication procedures on attitudes." *The Journal of Abnormal and Social Psychology.* 51:107–13 (1955).
56. Trager, Helen G. and Marian Radke Yarrow. *They Learn What They Live.* (New York: Harper and Brothers, 1952).
57. Walster, Elaine and Leon Festinger. "The effectiveness of 'overheard' persuasive communications." *The Journal of Abnormal and Social Psychology.* 65:395–402 (1962).
58. Watt, Norman F. "Public commitment, delay after commitment, and change in verbalized expectancies." *The Journal of Personality.* 33:284–99 (1965).

Chapter 4

Can media be used for information transmission leading to creative thought and action?

Can analysis of message content, student receptivity and the creative process be functionally compared to a basic communication model?

Can general applications of information theory be used in producing media specifically related to creativity?

What questions remain to be answered in the use of stimulus materials to develop divergent thinking in learners?

CREATIVITY:
THEORETICAL AND PRACTICAL
CONSIDERATIONS FOR MEDIA*

FRANK E. WILLIAMS, Director, Creativity Project
Macalester College

The techniques of teaching by various media devices are not new. Means of communicating information through audio and/or visual media have been part of an educational and technological revolution during the past quarter of a century. Instructional media devices present a wide range of methods for storing information and provide a reliable means for retrieving it quickly and efficiently. Such devices involve two primary storage forms which include the electronic storage of audio information and the storage of images on film or other plastics. Retrieval of information which has been stored on tape and plastics appeals to the combined visual and aural senses of the learner and can be used as adjuncts to the important role of the teacher in school classrooms. Any reasonable recognition of differences in student abilities and learning skills would admit to the necessity of presenting students

*This chapter is reprinted by permission of the author and publisher from *Instructional Media and Creativity*, © John Wiley and Sons, Inc., N. Y., 1966.

with as wide a range of avenues and sensory inputs as possible when acquiring information which could lead to the fullest development of their creative talents while they are growing in knowledge. It may take combinations of books, tapes, films, machines, and the teacher to meet this challenge.

It is now known through measurement research on high-level abilities and talents as well as laboratory research on learning and concept formation that a rather large number of intellectual processes of the human mind can be identified and developed. Taylor[1] writes that students must have the experience of using and developing a great number of these learning and thinking processes during times when they are simultaneously acquiring a variety of information through subject-matter content in a total educational program. Without depreciating the important role that the teacher must continue to play in the total educational program, by the very nature of the growth in knowledge during the past decade along with the recognition that many intellectual and nonintellectual dimensions of the mind need to be developed, we can not neglect the manifold storage and retrieval possibilities that are available through instructional media devices. The students' task in the learning-thinking process must include acquiring information through memorization by traditional classroom methods along with developing the other intellectual processes of critical thinking, productive and creative thinking, planning, decision-making, and communicating. Other nonintellectual categories such as intuition, sensitivity, emotion and feeling, insight, involvement, and withholding judgment are likewise important when experiencing, practicing, and developing the mind's full range of potentialities. The unique and important role for teachers becomes that of how to bring this all about by the use of their own knowledge and techniques with the aid of a potential repertoire of perceptual inputs that various instructional media can provide.

Assuming one of the tasks of education is the development of those intellectual and nonintellectual processes leading to creation, it seems feasible that one should consider the basic research that has been conducted on the nature and nurture of creativity. The work done in this field over the past decade has shed considerable light upon the traits and characteristics of the creative person as well as the conditions under which the creative process might be developed. One of the purposes of this chapter is to define and discuss "creativity" and its relationship to information theory. Two conceptual models as aids in using or designing instructional media for evoking creative behaviors are then developed. Following this is a list of [tenable ideas for use by media

1 *Instructional Media and Creativity, op. cit.,* Chapter 2.

producers or teachers.] In conclusion, a list of research areas and questions, . . . as leads and needs for future study, is presented.

INSTRUCTIONAL MEDIA AS INFORMATION-TRANSMITTING DEVICES

By definition, media includes all the aids for transmitting information and learning via the senses, such as printed materials including books and programmed devices of instruction; the graphic arts including transparent slides, pictures, charts, filmstrips, and video tapes; audio materials including tapes, recorders, radio, and language laboratory equipment; and combination audiovisual materials including the sound motion picture and television. Media devices are visual and/or audio stimuli designed as external inputs to a receiver and can be classified in the following manner:

Visual Stimuli Inputs
Pictorial
Print
Audio Stimuli Inputs
Verbal
Non-Verbal

Information is defined from the psychological point of view as bits or items which the organism discriminates and which serve as communicative functions.

Instructional-media devices, as a means for transmitting information, have generally taken opposite trends for their design and use in school situations. One apparent trend has been for use in mass instructional situations. Such devices include educational television, radio broadcast, or video tape; mass motion picture or film strip series covering a specific subject; fragment film clips demonstrating a single principle, skill, or function; and vugraph or overhead transparencies. Another trend has been in developing individual instructional devices for reading, listening, reviewing, and programmed learning. These include textbooks, workbooks, tape recorders, and teaching machines, as well as language laboratory equipment. The latter category now includes libraries of electronic aids for individual instruction or student review of information previously presented in mass learning situations. Both of these trends in the development of instructional media materials have specific implications pertinent to the nurturing of creativity in the student.

It must be pointed out that all of these devices have been programmed to transmit information. Most of the studies on their effectiveness relate to the absorption and recall of presented factual information through the use of audiovisual stimuli, in contrast to situations not utilizing such stimuli. Methods of evaluating the amount of learning via instructional media make an implicit assumption that such a successful teaching device is one in which students who have participated are expected to differ from what they were before this experience, as revealed by an appropriate instrument measuring the amount of factual information they have acquired. An instructional-media device is considered an optimum aid to teaching so that a one-to-one ratio is more nearly approached between the amount of information presented to the student by the device and that amount which he can recall on a test. There can be no doubt that instructional-media devices can be of tremendous help in supplying a vast amount of information to the student, but unless the device is designed or used to allow something to be done by the student with this information, other than to merely receive it and recall it when conditions demand, its potential as far as developing creative behavior is seriously limited. It may be one thing to deal with ways to effectively transmit items of information for recall; it may still be another thing to impart and deal with an array of stimulus inputs which are necessary for creative thought and creative action.

Creativity related to information transmission

There are two kinds of talent consisting of different mental abilities which involve either acquiring information produced by and transmitted to someone else, or utilizing someone else's transmitted information to generate and produce one's own new ideas, pose different problems, or produce new knowledge. It is the development of these latter abilities which pertains to creativity. An abundance of rich sensory and perceptual input is not enough unless something is done with it beyond learning to recall. Creativity starts with a multitude of sensory and perceptual inputs, and the person desiring to create within any subject needs an abundance of input information about the subject. Conditions which facilitate creativity first depend on a storehouse of information within the person who is attempting to be creative. The amount of stored information of the potentially creative person seems to set the limit on such behavior. But sheer accumulation of information is not enough. It is how the person goes beyond learning to recall information, what he does with information, that makes him creative. MacKinnon[2] makes the point . . . that the more items of information the person has, the more likely it is, on purely statistical grounds, that he will be creative.

The process of creating is in large measure associating or putting together in new and original combinations the elements of information

[2] *Op. cit.*, Chapter 7.

which one has previously acquired. Thus, we must consider an originality or inventive factor as well as several kinds of flexibility factors that play a role in creative thought and action. Likewise, the more combinations one can form, the more likely it will be that some of them will be creative. Along with originality and flexibility are various fluency factors such as flow of ideas, flow of associations, and flow of expressions which also are important. The combining of items of information and the forming of new associations are outcomes of breadth and depth of knowledge, and the ability for their production depends on the establishment of associations between items of received information. Instructional media devices can quickly and effectively increase the student's items of information, which in turn can contribute significantly to the nurturing of creative potential, provided they are designed or used in the right way for this purpose.

Increasing the richness of stimulus input into a student's repertoire of knowledge and allowing him opportunities to work with such inputs seem to be the crux for teaching creativity through the means of instructional media. So it is that creativity may be defined as relating previously unrelated information, combining bits or pieces of information in new forms, fusing of past knowledge with the present flow of new information to produce original insights or unusual responses, or the conversion of accustomed knowledge to the unaccustomed idea, product, or act. However, research indicates that mere saturation of an individual with input information may have to be integrated with instructions or cued directions to be creative, opportunities for creating, or training in the utilization of mental processes other than assimilation, storage, and recall. The processes of exploring new associations from an array of input information are necessary prerequisites to making discoveries, and such opportunities must be granted students in order to develop their abilities for productive-creative thinking. Instructional-media devices as rich sensory inputs may only set the stage for the student to go on from where the device leaves off, providing it is arranged or manipulated for the student toward this purpose.

The problem becomes that of how this can be done either by the media device itself or by the teacher creatively using the device, or both. An interaction between the teacher and the device is necessary when attempts are made to structure or reorganize the presentation of input information for the student so as to produce student outputs to include all of the fluencies, flexibilities, elaborations, and original interpretations of knowledge that comprise the creative process. The teacher can then become a catalyzer in producing a need to create. The instructional-media device is used as a vehicle for a rich source of input which may then set the stage for the creative act to follow.

A MODEL FOR THE USE OF EXISTING MEDIA
OR FOR DESIGNING NEW INSTRUCTIONAL
MEDIA TO DEVELOP CREATIVITY

A proposed three-dimensional model for viewing the arrangement or manipulation of information transmitted via audio and/or visual stimuli for the purpose of evoking creative behaviors is presented in Figure 1.

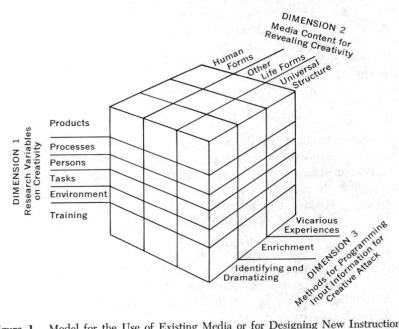

Figure 1. Model for the Use of Existing Media or for Designing New Instructional Media to Develop Creativity.

Each dimension of the model shall be discussed separately as follows: *The first dimension* takes into account the complexity of research on creativity which has been focused primarily upon six variables. These are:

1. the product created;
2. the process of creating;
3. the personality of the creator;
4. the tasks chosen for attacking or assessing creativity;
5. the environment or favorable climate in which creation occurs; and
6. the training techniques for developing or releasing all of the intellectual and nonintellectual abilities that manifest creativity.

These six variables may give clues from creativity research studies by which information can be arranged as sensory inputs via instructional media devices for developing creative behaviors. Thus, audio- and/or visual-input information may be devoted primarily to

1. appraisal of the products that require some criterion for measuring the degree of creativity shown by an individual;
2. exploration of the thinking and problem-solving processes involved;
3. investigation of the psychological and physiological traits or characteristics of creative persons;
4. examination of the kinds of tasks or problems selected and undertaken for creative attack or measurement;
5. study of the social climate and environmental variables that both aid or hinder creativity; and
6. the recognition of certain operational techniques and skills which have shown the most promise in developing or releasing creativity in learning situations.

It should be pointed out that these are not independent variables and that interaction between the six variables will most likely take place. The existence of such interactions should be capitalized upon for the design of an instructional device. For example, a film may portray the particular traits of a highly creative individual as they relate to the type of task upon which the individual works, the climate under which he produces, or the kind of thinking which he performs. All such interactions do exist and are important.

A *second dimension* involves the content which instructional media need to reveal when designed or used for developing creative abilities. This dimension deals with what needs to be presented. Mooney[3] has discussed the creative act in three forms which become relevant for designing media content.

The first form of content is that of revealing human forms of man creating in the way his body works, his mind functions, or how his society develops. This might involve content on the lives of highly creative people or the output of highly creative societies or groups of people in the processes of creation.

A second type of content for designing media devices is that of revealing other life forms such as plants and animals. This could reveal the birth and growth of species or events relating to creation in nature.

A third form of content deals with how the universe works. Here, instructional media could be designed around laboratory experiments, models, charts, or schematics revealing the physical or chemical operations of universal phenomena. A film, for example, might depict some physical principle in order to help students understand the underlying

---

[3] *Op. cit.*, Chapter 10.

structure of a phenomenon. This form of content could be used to portray the universal structure of knowledge. Thus, the content of instructional media could be designed upon the way man, society, other living forms and universal systems work in the processes of creation.

A *third dimension* of the model has to do with methods for presenting input information as an aid in the creative teaching process. This dimension deals with three methods of programming information for creative attack. Instructional media can be designed to present material to the student that would otherwise not be available to him in his ordinary classroom experience.

One method may be through presenting rich sensory inputs by which the student is given vicarious knowledge and experience consisting of a multitude of events supplemental to the curriculum.

Another method may be inputs designed and used merely for enrichment. These could be presented as extracurricular materials to embellish the life experience of the student. The greatest task here may be to program media for those not mentally or socially gifted; to deal with enrichment for the mentally- or culturally-deprived children who have to depend upon a rich source of materials from outside their life experience which might lead them to create.

A third method has to do with presenting materials as dramatizing events with which the student can closely identify in the act of creation. Examples of such materials might be the presentation of a historical event that is true in the spirit of creation, the nature film that dramatizes the struggle of a species in its habitat, the exemplification of an experiment or invention showing the dramatics of innovation, or exposure to greatness in many walks of life by documentaries about eminent people. Such identification and dramatizing devices might sketch out the history of what man has done to create, or people in the processes of creation. For example, a film pictorial presentation of Chaucer's *Canterbury Tales* may spark a student's interest and lead him to a genuine exploration of English literature that the printed book alone might not have stimulated. The student of history may be able to catch the spirit of the moment by hearing through magnetic tape the verbal creations of Winston Churchill or Franklin Roosevelt that neither teacher nor book can present.

In summary, there may exist instructional media devices which present materials to aid the teacher in extending the students' range of experience within the curriculum, in enriching areas which might never be opened up without such inputs, and in dramatizing the significance of events whereby the student can identify more closely with such events through their true realism. Thus, it seems conceivable that instructional media for developing classroom creativity can be used or designed around these three dimensions which consist of currently researched variables on creativity, by content composed of creative forms, through several methods or presentation. How one teaches creativity with the aid of such devices depends upon the skill and wisdom that both goes into the design of the device as well as the teacher's wise use of that device. Design and use become two programmed directions which will now be further considered.

CONCEPTUAL MODEL BASED UPON AN INFORMATION TRANSMISSION SYSTEM FOR THE DESIGN OR USE OF INSTRUCTIONAL MEDIA TO DEVELOP CREATIVITY

As a result of a study of information theory related to the audiovisual transmission of sensory inputs, an attempt has been made to develop a conceptual model concerning the design of new media or the teacher's use of existing media for evoking creativity. The block diagram of the fundamental elements involved in developing creative outputs by visual and/or oral inputs is shown in Figure 2. Although admittedly much

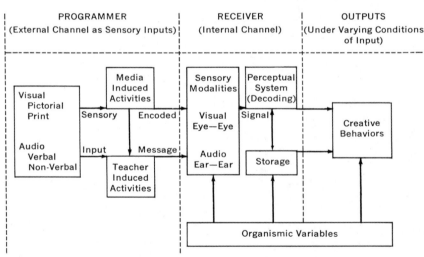

Figure 2. Information Transmission System for Evoking Creativity Through the Design or Use of Instructional Media.

more complex than transmitting a simple bit of information, the conceptual model could, because of its very nature, be considered synonymous to an information transmission system. It is a linear block model with external sensory inputs of visual and/or audio stimuli using the classification system of the Society of Motion Picture and Television Engineers as:

> Visual Stimuli Inputs
> Pictorial
> Print
> Audio Stimuli Inputs
> Verbal
> Non-Verbal

The programmer section on the left consists of these inputs as either a single input presentation in the case of an oral message transmitted by an audio tape or multi-inputs presented simultaneously such as a sound motion picture. At this time it should be pointed out that the programmer section is an external channel which means the transmitting medium is exterior to the body. By an internal channel, such as the receiver section next on the right, it is meant that the transmitting organs are within the body. By definition, any medium that will function to transmit energy from one point to another will serve as a channel. In the case of external channels such as sight or sounds, the most common medium is air. The different sensory modalities of eye or ear and their nerves are internal channels.

Transmitted messages are selected from the programmer's alphabet defined as any discrete sign-set such as letters, words, pictorial representation, music, or sounds as discrete concepts. The same alphabet must exist at both the programmer and receiver sections of the system. If the programmer were to use a different alphabet from that of the receiver, little or no information would be transmitted for each would supposedly be communicating in different languages.

The programmer scans its alphabet and from certain discrete signs constructs a chain of signs to form a message either as single inputs, for example, words in print, or combinations of inputs presented simultaneously, such as pictures accompanied by a narration.

The selection of words and/or pictures to form the message is the process of encoding at the programmer end and decoding at the receiver end. The model is shown to branch into either of two directions at the time of the encoding process. One programming direction involves producer design characteristics, and that block is labeled "Media-induced Activities." The other direction consists of ways in which a teacher elicits her own encoded message by audio and/or visual inputs, and that block is labeled "Teacher-induced Activities." It should be pointed out that there is a vertical arrow indicating a downward direction between these two blocks which takes care of the situation in which a media-encoded message by the producer is modified for use by additional teacher-induced activities. An upward direction is impossible since the teacher has no control over the encoded message that is designed by the producer.

Media-induced activities for creative outputs consist of design characteristics within the selected message encoded by the producer. Hence, it is important that if producers intend to develop media devices requiring creative outputs, they should indeed arrange or manipulate the encoded message in accordance with what is known about creativity and how it can be developed. Such a message is selected *a priori* and, in terms of the information theorist, is composed of a set of alternatives with which the programmer is concerned, known as his alphabet. In order to get the information transmitted with the desired outputs, the alphabet must be the same at both the programmer and receiver ends of the system. Already one of the greatest difficulties in designing instructional materials is obvious. It is imperative that the programmer have a specific knowledge of the audience for which the instructional device is intended in order to determine if his message is comprised from the same alphabet as that of the receiver.

For purposes of illustration, let us follow an information transmission through both branched directions of indiced activities beginning at the sensory input end.

Our first source of inputs will be from an educational film producer who has designed a sound motion picture for developing creative behavior. His alphabet, selected for the particular grade-level audience he wishes to communicate with, will consist of words, concepts, and pictorial perceptions. For simplicity, let us assume that the receiver, a student, has an understanding of the words and pictures used by the producer; and that the meaning of both the words of the narration, the pictures of the video portion, and their underlying concepts is common to the producer and the student. Thus, we have now satisfied the condition that the programmer and the receiver have the same alphabet from which to select signs.

The producer wishes to have the student create an original solution to a problem. Thus, he selects the factor of originality out of the paradigm of divergent thinking as one of the desired outputs for creative behavior. He chooses problem-solving as one way for developing original thinking and designs his device accordingly.

Then, suppose he has the knowledge from research evidence concerning a very simple but effective training technique for eliciting creative responses by posing questions with the instructions that original answers are desired. The producer designs an open-ended film known to be useful for developing the creative potential of viewers. Video and audio inputs are arranged to pose a problem with events leading up to a solution but not showing the solution. Furthermore, by the producer knowing that the technique of using questions with instructions to be original produces creative outputs, a media-induced activity could very well be that of inserting print questions at the crucial point in the film where the audience is asked what they would do to solve the problem and instructed to generate their own original solutions. Instructions should likewise be given to the teacher to turn the machine off at this point in order to allow students to create their own solution before being shown the solution as given in the film. This is an example of a media-induced activity for developing creativity which could be used without modification by any teacher.

Our second source of inputs might be teacher-induced activities which imply how a classroom teacher uses a multitude of stimuli, such as books, charts, video tapes, filmstrips, or sound motion pictures, out of which students may develop their own creations. For simplicity, let us cite the same technique discussed above for using a sound motion picture to aid in developing an original solution to a problem. Let us assume that the teacher also has the knowledge that questions and instructions to be original are effective training techniques for developing creativity, and she is able to select a film that poses a real problem. Then, by simply stopping the film at the crucial place, she could verbally ask questions and give her own instructions for students to be original in thinking up their own solution before turning the film back on to show the solution as given. This is an example of a simple teacher-induced activity as a modification of an existing audiovisual device, but used differently for creative attack.

It is important, however, to note that in both types of activities a knowledge by both the producer and the teacher of the creative process and how it can be developed is imperative. Hence, an understanding of the first model discussed in this chapter is important.

The media-induced and/or teacher-induced message is transformed into light rays (visual) and/or sound waves (audio) and transmitted via a medium to a receiver. In the usual sound film the medium is air, and is known as an external channel, meaning that the transmitting medium is exterior to the receiver. It is then taken in by the internal sensory modalities of the receiver.

While the message is being transmitted by the organs and nerves under the skin, the possibility exists that it becomes filtered or mixed with noise. Or the possibility also exists that the message can become mixed with noise in the external channel. This is probably more often the case than in the internal channel. Irrelevant information sent on the source channel would consist of sounds and images not programmed into the stimulus array but arising in the environment. Such disturbances which do not represent any part of the encoded message are usually considered noise and, having no bearing on the message, lead to an irreversible loss of information being transmitted. This loss in the information rate from the source of the message is called "entropy." Communication engineers have considered the possibility of a noiseless communication, or one in which no loss occurs. If a noiseless system were possible, then redundancy would serve other purposes than compensating for information loss due to noise. If this is not so, then redundancy in the transmitted message may be necessary in order to counteract for the results of noise with its consequent information loss. Redundancy, or an excess of various stimuli, between simultaneously presented inputs in the sound motion picture is not uncommon. For example, an explanation is given in the audio narration which refers to the visual picture. One is supposed to strengthen the other. It is not known, however, whether redundant cues should be presented simultaneously or whether they should be sequentially spaced so that the receiver need only to attend one at a time in order to decrease a loss resulting from interference.

As the message is carried further into the receiver's perceptual system, other transformations of the visual and aural waves occur in the brain which are known as "decoding." In the case of a human system, it is not possible to measure the reception of the message by its intended meaning other than through the measurement of the subject's behavior or output. Here again are many problems with regard to measuring outputs which are dependent upon the organism's character; hence, the underlying block of organismic variables. The decoding of transmitted information and a valid measurement by different types of actions or changes in behavior is indeed one area of extreme complexity.

Evidence indicates that the type and amount of decoding, with its subsequent output or change in behavior, is a function of how the inputs were arranged in its original transmission. It may be the way the message was transmitted which determines its value. A certain kind of message and arrangement of inputs may produce one type of output, but not necessarily other outputs. In other words, a message designed to produce originality may just only do that, but may not also be expected to produce fluency, flexibility, or elaborativeness. Likewise, if a motor-skill performance as an output is desired, it is likely that another type of message under differing arrangements of inputs is necessary other than those used for eliciting original associations. An implication may be that a message with certain manipulations of inputs may only produce one kind of output, and no others. A film designed to produce creative behavior may not also be expected to produce recall or develop a motor skill and vice versa. This is an area in which little research has been conducted.

TENABLE IDEAS FOR USE BY MEDIA PRODUCERS OR TEACHERS

Now that a general model of information theory and two of its applications have been discussed, it is in order to list some tenable ideas and research areas brought out during the conference.[4] These have been gleaned at random from the conference transcriptions, having no order in their importance, and credit for them should be given to all conferees. It is hoped they will serve as ideas upon which instructional-media producers as well as teachers will be able to innovate. Since instructional media are innovations, this section is intended to open up questions of what and where innovations are needed.

1. Program instructional media by taking into account the intellectual level of the intended audience. Develop media for those not performing well in verbal abilities, i.e., those not of highest measured IQ.

2. Design or use instructional media for stressing a multiplicity of approaches to solve problems.

3. Design instructional media taking into account individual differences, i.e., sex, intelligence, grade level, reading comprehension, creativeness, amount and type of deprivation.

4. Use instructional media to develop independence-of-thought activities.

5. Design media for teacher instruction and teacher preparation showing various means for rewarding and encouraging autonomy in the classroom.

6. Use instructional media for presenting modes of search and inquiry.

7. Design media depicting creative individuals making a work of art out of their own lives.

8. Design or use instructional media for the purpose of shifting from adjustment to development, i.e., show how failures or mistakes pay off, constructive discontent, anxieties and conflicts overcome, improvements made, things that bother people, and how these can be changed.

9. Media-producers and teachers must understand the various kinds or types of creativity in order to know which kind they are developing by what medium. Different ways of using or designing instructional media may be necessary for developing various kinds of creative behaviors.

10. Design instructional media around the utilization of principles of

4 Sixth Utah Creativity Research Conference, held at La Jolla, Calif., August 1964, supported by USOE, contract OE 516001.

creative thinking and problem-solving, i.e., analogies, similes, paradoxes, metaphors, attribute-listing, deferring judgment, check-listing, etc.

11. Design media which point out the two main value systems of creative people, such as aesthetic values, including elegance of product as well as theoretical values of functionality and practicality.

12. Use instructional media for the sole purpose of leading students to self-generated activities, independent thinking, goal-setting, and posing their own problems.

13. Design media around the mystery of things, i.e., birth, the universe, hypnotism, intuition, insight, etc.

14. Develop media for presenting biographies of creatively eminent people.

15. Develop media devices dealing with generalized problem-solving skills, i.e., preparation, incubation, illumination, ideation, verifications, etc.

16. Design different kinds of instructional-media devices to be used for teacher instruction, then for student instruction.

17. Develop teacher in-service training films around the themes of creative teaching (what it is) versus teaching for creativity (how to do it).

18. Use the technique of delayed feedback instead of immediate feedback when designing instructional-media devices for evoking creative behaviors.

19. Produce instructional media depicting the home environment of creative children or child-rearing practices for developing creativity based upon research evidence to be used for parent-teacher groups.

20. Locate a group of very creative teachers and find out what and how they teach. Produce an instructional-media device based upon their methods and procedures for teacher in-service training programs.

21. Produce two companion instructional-media devices (films), one to be used for showing the classroom teacher how to produce a need to create, followed by a second one for students containing rich sensory inputs for releasing their creative abilities. Both should be used together in a school.

22. Design instructional media as guided-planned experiences around scientific discoveries.

23. Develop new teaching materials or convert old materials to the productive-divergent thinking paradigm.

24. Develop instructional media for elementary school children around the techniques and methodology of research.

25. Design media which purposely present knowledge having incomplete gaps, i.e., knowns as well as unknowns of a field.

26. Produce instructional media which present rigidities in thinking or

functional fixation in the design of things, with questions posed of why they haven't been changed as well as how they could be changed.

27. Design or use media for teaching children how to live with change—how to change the environment rather than adjust to the environment.

28. Produce instructional media based upon the present contemporary goals of society: learning how to learn, learning how to change, learning how to create, learning how to adapt rather than adjust.

29. Design short film clips around a series of events depicting endurances, persistence, and perseveration with resulting incubation and verification—the insight!

30. Design media showing man in the process of creation and how he reaches into the unknowns and the unconscious.

31. Sketch out the history of what man has done to create through the use and design of various instructional media.

32. Design media around paradoxes of a field or subject.

33. Design media showing people in the process of toying with new information or ideas, i.e., how to care for and nurture infant ideas.

34. Produce media (training film) for experienced teachers which would help them to see what their *new* role is in teaching for creativity. Produce a similar film for student-teachers to help them to see their role as creative teachers.

35. Design media for teachers' viewing based upon research evidence depicting when and how teachers can reinforce creative behaviors in classroom situations. Design media for the same use but showing teachers' failure to reinforce creative behavior with their resulting consequences.

36. Produce media (filmstrips) to show samples of various tests for creativity.

37. Produce media (filmstrips) for experimenting with instructions to think creatively and drill procedures for such behavior.

38. Design media to provide more feedback for self-evaluation at different stages of the creative process.

39. Design instructional media solely for the purpose of transmitting rich sensory inputs by animation, color, sounds, noise, and all combinations of inputs to be used for releasing creativity through self-expression. (How do you feel by this color, sound, etc.)

40. Design media for showing how items of knowledge can be combined and new associations formed to produce the real creative idea, product, or solution. Use the theme "nothing new under the sun" and show the importance of associating and combining items of past knowledge to create something new.

41. Design instructional media which only pose problem situations or ask questions with rich inputs to clarify the problem situation and ade-

quately define it. Go no further, but leave it open for post-viewing problem-solving activities.

42. Design a series of short companion films each to portray three kinds of creativity. One could show sequences dealing with groups of people and interaction processes dealing with social creativity. Another could be an autobiographical sketch of a person dealing with his own relationship to himself, demonstrating personal creativity. The third could be the development of a highly original idea which was translated into the development of a novel product, demonstrating productive creativity.

43. Show the conclusion of a film and have students guess what the beginning was. Choose a film that poses a problem and solves it, but only show the solution and have students define the problem—or vice versa.

44. Design a trunk film for classroom use which defines a problem with very rich and embellished inputs about the problem situation. Have this accompanied by a number of shorter satellite films or film-strips, each showing a different solution to the problem. The latter could be used for individual viewing and verification only after each student has had the opportunity to create his own solution.

45. Produce films or filmstrips around leisure-time activities of inventors or patent-holders.

46. Produce a teacher-training film on how classroom teachers can use instructional media to set problems for different students and in encouraging students to set problems for themselves as suggested by the material seen in the media device.

47. Produce instructional media for portraying the early life anxieties, conflicts, and uncertainties of highly creative people with an emphasis upon how such problems were overcome or contributed to their creating. Such media materials could be used for counseling and guidance and mental health courses.

48. Design instructional media that will actually engage students to do and perform those things which they will be doing in creative-productive thinking situations; choose those requiring active drill and practice in the creative process rather than passive listening and watching.

49. Reproduce the symbolic and imaginative short film "The Hunter and the Forest" in *color* (Brittanica Films, Arne Sucksdorff photographer).

50. Design more of the spliced-in questions type of films such as produced by Churchill Films, Inc., Los Angeles, California.

51. Produce instructional media for teacher in-service training showing teachers interacting with students in the classroom when an unexpected, unusual response occurs. Show failure of teacher to capitalize on such a spontaneous situation with resulting closure, and then show how the

flexible and ingenious teacher learns not to be surprised and uses such responses to advantage.

52. Develop media for teacher-training showing teachers not capitalizing on classroom events or experiences that would foster creativity—how *not* to do it, or when one thing is not permitted to lead to another.

53. Develop a multitude of creative problem-solving types of visual aids, i.e., vugraph transparencies, mock-up boards, programmed learning devices.

54. Design media to show failures such as why inventions and discoveries did not work.

55. Design instructional media around perplexing social problems with no solution.

56. Develop tapes with narration consisting only of ideas and instructions for listeners not to prejudge but to use as springboards to generate more ideas on their own.

57. Use or produce instructional media showing the development of ideas instead of products.

58. Develop media around intuitive, exploratory borders of knowledge (hunches) without confining or testing hypotheses.

59. Develop media depicting how great ideas or innovative people get into trouble.

60. Design media with a negative viewpoint showing most effective ways to stifle or hinder creativity.

61. Develop subtle, single-channel media such as pictures without narration, or audiotapes of drama and comedy (like the old silent movie), where the message is enjoyed through the audience's own imagination.

62. Design or use media for the sole purpose of teasing out ideas and which permit creative behaviors or responses to emerge by the student himself, such as asking the question "What does this (color sound, image, etc.) make you feel like?"

63. Design or use media depicting a solution to a problem, and then require students to think up different problems which this solution created.

64. Develop instructional media around a case-study approach to a problem and then pose the question: "What would you do?"

65. Design a media device to show the highly developed learning skills children have by the time they enter school and how teachers should build onto these.

66. Develop media for strengthening attitudes that a student should have toward prior information that he possesses. Show the importance of using prior information to create.

67. Develop media showing idiosyncracies of creative people living in

the creative process way of life rather than in the conventional, traditional way.

68. A conceivable goal of education is learning how to change and adapt to change. Develop instructional media depicting change and adaptation in nature and parallel this phenomenon to human things.

69. Develop a sound motion picture or filmstrip designed around some of the most promising exercises requiring creative attack merely for the principle of warm-up for teachers' use before going into a lesson, i.e., brick uses, similes, brainstorming, nine-dot problem, match problems, etc.

70. Develop instructional media giving information about the creative process which could be used by teachers solely to motivate and orient students before taking up a new subject of study.

71. Design media (film) around respect and reward for unusual questions and ideas, with ways that teachers can encourage and give opportunities for such behavior.

72. Develop or use media for providing enlightenment concerning the nature and psychology of creative thinking skills.

73. Design a medium for comparing or contrasting creative thinking in the areas of science with the aesthetic areas of music, writing, and the visual arts. The first area might be shown as problem-solving; the second as problems of expression in artistic form.

74. Develop an animated film or filmstrip for viewing the human being as a processor of information, linking the creative process to information theory . . ., i.e., committing and coding information to storage, and retrieval of information in some new form or connection other than that in which it was learned and stored.

75. Develop media (film) depicting unresolved social issues of our contemporary time which require creative solutions.

76. Develop media for emphasizing the kinds of extended efforts which individuals need for invention, discovery, and creating.

77. Design media (film or series of films) which would present or extend the students range of emotional responses through effective damatizations.

78. Develop instructional media expressly for the purpose of identifying needs of people, and communicate these needs with considerable impact by effective use of an array of media.

79. Develop instructional media around dramatic problem situations in history by which students could not only easily identify with historical personalities but also be personally committed to their problems. Such media should not include the actual course of action taken in history, but instead require students to use their own ingenuity in devising possible courses of action by their own analysis of the situation.

80. Use and develop media which pose questions neither the teacher

nor the student can answer on authority, yet to which there obviously must be some definitive answers.

81. Develop a media device for motivating students toward an exercise in using their imagination for sketching out the kinds of things a particular field or area of knowledge might be comprised of a decade, a half century, or a century from now.

82. Develop media around the objective of people and events adjusting man's environment as contrasted to those who adjust to the environment.

83. Design programmed materials purposely for the development of the creative behaviors of transformation and evaluation, i.e., imaginative interrelation with knowledge and decision-making functions.

84. Develop programmed materials which cause students to search for all possible definitions of a problem.

85. Design a media device for teacher training showing how a wide repertoire of teaching styles performed by the teacher in the teaching act with varied opportunities for students to learn in different ways in a self-contained classroom will enhance the students' ability to learn.

86. Design media (film) comparing illustrative examples of people looking at information imaginatively by using it to see where it might take them, rather than judging information to see what is wrong with it or where it has taken them.

87. Stop a film or programmed learning device at some crucial point and have the students themselves create and design continuing inputs or information in order to bring it to a completion.

88. As a class project, make a home-made film (eight millimeter) around the life of some local person who is known to be highly creative.

89. Develop a silent film or filmstrip in pantomime of the process of some creative accomplishment with blank sequences where viewers are given the opportunity to guess what is occuring.

90. Have students choose for themselves ways in which they want to use information presented after a film or TV program, and allow them various opportunities to work with this information in committees, independently, or in groups.

91. Develop a three-part sound motion picture around some simple event or physical phenomenon which would lead students to ask questions about the event, guess things leading up to the event (causes), and guess things that might happen after the event (consequences).

92. Design a media device which identifies a problem and requires students to form their own hypotheses of how it might be solved.

93. Develop an animated biographical story of an animal or insect showing how it has solved problems of existence, innovation, and survival. Use this as analogous to man's solving such problems.

94. Show a film or filmstrip based upon some scientific principle and have students think of all the analogous uses the principle has.

95. Design a two-part film or videotape which would discuss and present examples contrasting critical reading, listening, and viewing with creative reading, listening, and viewing. Use this as an introduction to a unit on critical versus creative thinking.

96. Have film producers invite a team of creative curriculum supervisors and classroom teachers in for planning sessions when designing a new instructional-media device.

97. Develop self-instructional programs based upon the concept of originality in which likely or usual responses would be scored incorrect or penalized and unlikely responses accepted and rewarded.

98. Develop instructional media around the concept of mystery, such as presenting the principles of science so that students would be required to do detective work on the mysteries of nature.

99. Design film sequences showing a beginning and an outcome of an event, and ask students to create the intervening steps of the event.

100. Show an event or sequence of events on film, asking students to list all of the questions which occur to them as they view the film. Then have students suggest ways in which they can find out the answers to the questions listed. Finally, have them test their suggested ways by answering the questions posed.

101. Develop career-type media (films or filmstrips) of creative people in the work world, showing the kinds of things that contribute to creative success on the job. Show what creative workers do and how they behave. Use these as models of creative-work areas with which high school students can identify for career guidance.

102. Develop tape recordings or eight millimeter filmclips of the creative process taking place in a classroom situation. Have students analyze the tape or film to reinforce their learning and realization of how the creative process developed and unfolded.

103. Develop and use a checklist when previewing and evaluating an instructional aid based upon Torrance's twenty principles of creative thinking.

104. Develop instructional media for parents so that child-rearing practices for creativity can be stimulated in the home at a very early age.

105. Design media (film) depicting the principle of incubation, showing how it has worked in many instances. Follow this up with any information-type film, giving verbal directions that the film will be discussed at some later date after students have had the opportunity to incubate.

106. Develop a series of "What-I-would-have-done" type films or filmstrips based upon problems in particular fields. Use problems which

present difficult situations but which give no solution so that students do not become "set." Develop such films for teachers around controversial classroom situations and use as lead activities for teachers inservice training, discussion groups, or parent-teachers meetings.

107. Design instructional media that would take children to the forefront of scientific endeavors to give them the feeling of participation and stimulation in processes of innovation and adventure.

108. Use discarded film footage from commercial producers that would present raw information without answers available from which children could then hypothesize and draw their own conclusions.

109. Use instructional media to present the mysteries of scientific phenomena.

110. Design a trunk film to present an overview of a subject which poses questions for mass viewing with shorter satellite films that define, clarify, or answer questions for individual use.

111. Design media (trunk films) around the noncontroversial issues of a subject with shorter satellite films which present several controversial issues arising out of the subject from which teachers can then select those safe to use within their own community or setting.

112. Develop instructional media which stimulate categorization behavior and allow opportunities solely for classifying information.

LIST OF RESEARCH AREAS

The following questions [have been identified as areas] where future research is needed.

1. It is not known how best to program inputs—film-mediated, teacher-mediated, or combinations of both to develop creative behaviors.

2. It is not known if single-channel inputs via some teacher-mediated activities are more efficient for evoking creative behaviors than multichannel inputs.

3. It is not known if the same programmer strategy (inputs) will evoke more than one class of creative behavior as an output. For example, an arrangement of inputs to evoke fluency may not be the same as that to evoke elaboration, transformation, or evaluative behaviors.

4. Are single-channel inputs better for allowing the viewer to roam in his own imagination than multichannel inputs which too specifically compartmentalize the situation, leaving the viewer no alternatives within which to move?

5. Research is needed on the type and extent of prefilm instructions when film is used for developing creativity.

6. It is known that creative people prefer relatively complex visual stimuli. What is the relationship between preference for complex stim-

uli and ability to create after exposure to such stimuli via instructional media?

7. Is it necessary for the medium designer (programmer) to have a specific knowledge of the intended audience for which the instructional device is to be used (IQ-age-sex-developmental level) and if so how much and what kind of knowledge?

8. If instructional media posed different questioning techniques other than Who is? What is? How much is? When? and Where?—which all require convergent abilities, and instead asked questions requiring divergent abilities such as How to? How come? What if? and What other ways?—would they more likely develop creative responses?

9. Can instructional media be used or designed to point out similarities as well as differences in presented information for developing creative behavior?

10. Since creative people are more perceptive, are they more prone to become overloaded with multisensory inputs causing them to become anxious, frustrated, and confused, thereby hindering their creative potential?

11. Is the master creative teacher on television as effective an object of the student's identification as the same teacher in the classroom or, is the master teacher on television teaching creatively as effective as the regular classroom teacher who is creative?

12. What are the optimum ways of presenting information via instructional-media devices for highly gifted children (intelligent and creative) as compared to less gifted children or as compared to culturally- and socially-deprived children?

13. Are instructional-media materials presented in a simple, straightforward manner better able to develop creativity than those which are highly embellished with various attention-getting and arousal techniques?

14. Can creativity be better developed by instructional-media devices that present unsolved problems about a subject before or after presenting a solved problem in the subject? Laboratory research on timing and task-induced set is needed.

15. Can imagination and originality as creative factors be better developed by single-channel inputs, multichannel inputs, or combinations of channels to accommodate channel-switching in the human mind (listening, reading versus listening and seeing simultaneously versus all combinations)?

16. What is the optimum range for speed of presentation of various sensory inputs via audiovisual media for developing creative behaviors?

17. What type of inputs and follow-up techniques are most effective to stimulate creativity after a film or TV program broadcast in order for students to pick up where the instructional device left off?

18. Research is needed on the effects of directions before, during, or after using instructional media for fostering creative behaviors, i.e., cues, instructions, examples, practice, etc.

19. What types of feedback, knowledge of results, and reinforcement are most conducive for developing creativity by the use of instructional media?

20. Research is needed on the most effective agent for giving feedback, knowledge of results, or reinforcement, i.e., the teacher, the device, fellow students, etc.

21. Is there a basic structure of existing instructional media that "programs" or inhibits creativity?

22. What type and kinds of autoinstructional materials facilitate creative thinking?

23. Can modifications in the use or design of mass media programs covering specified subject-matter content (physics films series, etc.) be made to permit their use for developing creative thinking?

24. How can a well-designed instructional-media device with some built-in creativity developmental techniques be used for teacher in-service training to produce an effect on the classroom behavior of teachers?

25. Will a saturation of relevant inputs presented via multichannels simultaneously followed by instructions for the viewer to strive for new creative combinations out of this saturation produce creative behaviors?

26. How can instructional media be designed or used to permit the viewer to toy and play with information as it is presented so as to react to it creatively?

27. How can media be designed or used to permit an open system which encourages multiple approaches and divergent thinking about information being transmitted?

28. How can instructional media be used to encourage broadly diffused, instead of narrowly focused, attention to transmitted information so as to develop imaginative, original thinking?

29. Would the use of electronic-media devices interfere with or blot out any creativity effects that the teacher herself has been able to develop?

30. Experiments are needed with new ways for making books more effective for evoking creative behaviors, i.e., ways to involve the reader, ways to encourage the reader to question what is read rather than accept the information, etc.

31. Research support is needed for designing various samples covering the same information in school textbooks and experimenting with their individual effectiveness for deliberately developing creativity along with presenting subject-matter content.

32. Research is needed for ways of confronting the learner with sit-

uations via different instructional media by which creative behaviors are actually practiced rather than covertly or passively experienced.

33. How can teaching materials (instructional media) be constructed so that they may both orient the student to a clearly defined goal as well as energize the student to work toward this goal on his own initiative toward a self-generated solution?

34. Assuming teachers, not media, produce creative learning experiences, the question to be answered is if teachers can be sensitized via instructional media to teach creatively; and if so, with what kind of media?

35. How can information be provided via various instructional media so that students may probe the nature of problem areas and as a consequence of such trial activity, obtain feedback for further self-initiated problem-solving activity?

36. Does student interaction with instructional-media materials produce learning skills relevant to established academic school curricula?

37. How can pictorial style and use of words in the narration of programmed materials give a feeling of an open-ended interpretation rather than finality to a problem?

38. Using the book as a medium, how can the teacher interact with the student in developing the mental processes of making new associations, transformations, and implications from the presented information?

[In closing,] since little is yet known about the effects of various instructional media on creativity, a multiplicity of opportunities and a universe of challenges lie ahead for those venturesome enough to devote some of themselves to this exciting young field.

Part Two

MEDIA AND
EDUCATIONAL LEVEL

Chapter 5

How is the use of media in the schools interrelated with the use of mass media in our dynamic, changing society?

What are some of the characteristic interactions between teacher and learner that require consideration when selecting and using stimulus materials (e.g., audio materials, visual materials)?

What teacher techniques and procedures have proved effective, over the years, in integrating instructional materials into the on-going instructional process?

In the last two decades, what media research reports provided the prime basis for the rapid introduction of media into the public schools?

MEDIA AND
PUBLIC SCHOOL COMMUNICATIONS

TED C. COBUN, Head, Audiovisual Program, and Professor
College of Education, East Tennessee State University *

INTRODUCTION

Webster's Seventh New Collegiate Dictionary defines a medium as a substance through which a force acts, or an effect is transmitted. In education the force is communication, the substance is any of the means that we select to carry the message, and the effect is change in behavior. Educators seek to communicate through selected stimuli that which will generate changes in the behavior of the learner in relation to facts, information, ideas, concepts, skills, and attitudes. Therefore, communication media are relevant to the process of instruction and to learning.

Teachers need to have the ability to select appropriate forms of

*At the time this paper was solicited Dr. Cobun was Director of the Audiovisual Media Program at Niles Township High School District, Skokie, Illinois, a highly active and innovative public school program with extraordinary volume and variety of locally produced instructional materials—Ed.

media that are in existence, the skill and ability to create useful forms of media when they do not exist, and skill in the use of the media in various teaching and learning situations. In general, such media will be effective when they are designed and used to generate overt student behavior. Such overt behavior is required to provide feedback, and to allow measurement of the quantity and quality of the learning that resulted from the application of the media. Measurement provides information that is essential for carrying on the process of teaching and learning, and for improving it.

RATIONALE

Currently, the characteristic that most typifies our life is change. Our society is unlike that of the past. It can be predicted with confidence that the future will be unlike the present. The hope to control the quality of onrushing change lies in education, for through education the culture is transmitted to learners. We need to communicate to learners that which will assure the development of what we envision to be most desirable and enriching. The messages must be structured so that learners comprehend them, accept them, and act upon them. To the extent that our communication is effective, we can shape the nature of future society.

Together with our population, our economy, our society, and our technology, our fund of information is expanding explosively. In 1952, John Macpartland wrote in *Harper's* magazine that we are accumulating information as rapidly as a constantly expanding sphere accumulates new surface area. According to the estimations of Macpartland, every three months we are doubling the information of mankind since the beginning of recorded history. And, there is no reason to believe that the accumulation or the acceleration will stop at this point! It is therefore no longer practicable to 'cover' subject matter. The most effective kind of learning that offers continued benefits is the development of skill in the techniques of learning. The learner must find satisfaction and success in learning. He will then be more likely to develop attitudes, and further skills, that will lead him to continue learning for the rest of his life—as he must.

Research shows that the structure of a message should be directed by the nature and needs of the individual learners. The skillful structuring of a message requires that there are clear and specific curricular objectives which are stated in behavioral terms. To achieve these objectives the subject matter must be designed so that learners develop new meaning through the progressive rearrangement of old meanings.

Learners come to today's schools already conditioned to the impact of media. The mass media have continuous influence on all of us. More or less constantly, we are confronted by one kind of message or another. One can be sure, the messages in the mass media are the results of most carefully considered planning and do affect learning. One cannot be sure, however, in what direction the messages are biased other than to support the purposes of the source. To cope effectively with the immensity of the problems of our developing society, educators need to make the most skillful use of communication techniques as they manipulate the teaching and learning process, taking advantage of the preconditioning of learners' sensory channels.

EXPOSURE

Students attend school for a comparatively short period of their lives. If the life of man can be said to be about 70 years in length, the school-life of the average student is about one-fifth of this time. Too few learners have even this much opportunity to learn, and many of the people of the world have none of this opportunity. At the same time, writers, commentators, advertisers, politicians, and a host of others compete for our attentions and our behavior in the form of our purchases, our contributions, our loyalties, our commitments, our influences, and even for our minds. The skilled know-how of professional educators can be shared with learners through the effective use of media. Their use of media should be stronger and more effusive than the random media that gain students' attention after school hours.

In the second report of *A Cooperative Study for the Better Use of Teacher Competencies,* made a decade ago at Central Michigan College, a serious lag was found between the potential of modern communication techniques, materials, processes, equipment, and their adaptation to the purposes of our schools. This report included a comprehensive time study which showed that a significantly large number of teachers in the survey devoted less than forty minutes per day to lesson preparation! These preparations were found to be, in general, a repetition of the materials found in the textbooks. In support of the lesson preparations, nonprinted materials were used infrequently.

Again it is clear that professional educators should make more effective use of the media if they are to compete with other influences impinging on the students' minds.

THE UNIQUE LEARNER

The unique learner is possessed of worth and holds dignity. His capabilities and his needs are peculiar to himself. In all ways, he is an original, an exclusive. He is a learning device in his own right. He learns with most efficiency the things in which he sees (or can develop) meaning, and learns them on his own terms and at his own tempo.

At infancy, the learner begins to learn when he notices his environment and reacts to it. He adds to his fund of learning with every experience that provides a stimulus strong enough to get a response. The learner learns, to some degree, through every conscious act. In future acts, he is most likely to repeat responses which have been satisfying to him. He will continue such responses until he learns new ones which are more satisfying.

The learner tends to avoid situations which generate responses he feels to be unsatisfying or punishing. He will attend the stronger stimuli in his environment, and he will be bored by stimuli which he classifies as weak. The unique learner avoids not only dull stimuli and punishing responses, but the experience patterns which generate them, as well. It could be that this factor lies at the heart of our problem of school drop-outs.

Many patterns of school organization have been attempted as solutions to the problems of teaching and learning. More will be attempted in the future. Yet, no scheme of organization can take the place of good teaching! Ultimately, the teacher confronts the learner; the confrontation might be direct and immediate, or remote and delayed. The confrontation might be with massed classes, ordinary classes, small groups, or individuals. No matter what the conditions of confrontation are like, the learner remains unique, peculiar, and exclusive. Teachers must act with wisdom and skill to see that learning proceeds productively and coherently.

DIRECTING THE PROCESS

Skillful direction of the teaching and learning process requires that teachers recognize and understand the nature of behavioral patterns. If the learning (school) environment is to generate consistently positive and constructive learner behavior, it must provide stronger, more controlled stimuli than competing environments. The unconsidered stimulus in the learning environment often diverts attention from the true objective. An avant garde coiffure, a necktie askew, poor posture, harsh speaking and the like can create static and interfere with the intended stimulus. Relevant stimuli gain strength as they are directed toward precise single purposes—which are clear and uncluttered by distracting elements.

RELEVANCE

When we identify stimuli as artificial we are likely to form responses that are artificial, and forget these responses quickly. We tend to forget responses when we have little opportunity to put them to satisfying use. Stimuli and associated behavior are classified by learners as artificial when they are apparently related to the purposes of the teacher without relation to the purposes of the learner. When the learner must behave in certain ways because someone says that he must, the conditions of artificiality are fertile.

An essay, written by a ten-year-old girl some years ago, demonstrated considerable insight into one of the greater obstacles to teaching and learning. She wrote, "Education is what is in the book, and teacher is the only one who knows it!" The result is often labeled by learners as busy-work. The danger is that many learners will come to regard most of their learning experiences as busy-work.

The obvious choice is between generating academic successes or academic casualties. When learners know what the objectives of the learning experience are they can respond more relevantly. They need to understand the objectives clearly and precisely. They need to know what the stimuli are going to be like. They need to know what kind of behavior is expected in response to the stimuli. They need to know the acceptable limits, if any, of variability of response.

The process of coping with the developing mind of the learner is in no way casual, and, in fact, planning, production, presentation, evaluation, and re-planning require great amounts of expensive time. Indeed, the great delicacy of the task of precise teaching was highlighted by William James, the great teacher-philosopher, who said, "If it doesn't make any difference, what difference does it make?" In keeping with the philosophical admonishment, "On the clock of humanity, it is now five minutes to twelve!" professional educators cannot tolerate academic casualties. The price is eventual societal decimation, potential subjugation, and the loss of our cherished way of life.

GOALS: CONTACT

The media can do little more than carry the message to the learner. If he can, and if he will, the learner receives the message. Message reception is achieved by way of the obvious receiver inputs: taste, touch, smell, hearing and sight. For learning, some of the inputs are more effective than others.

We learn about 1 per cent through taste and another 1½ per cent through the sense of touch. The sense of smell provides about 3½ per cent, and hearing provides about 11 per cent of what we learn. An overwhelming 83 per cent of our learning is through visual experiences.

However, it is important that knowledge, once acquired, can also be retained. (For purposes here, retention is thought of not in terms of duration but rather of ready availability at the time the knowledge is needed for use.) We retain only 20 per cent of the 11 per cent we hear, for a net profit of 2.2 per cent of that which we were originally exposed to. By comparison, we retain 30 per cent of the 83 per cent we see, for a net profit of 24.9 per cent. The losses seem to be great. However, when visual and aural stimuli are combined in the same learning experience, the retention levels are also combined. Since about 50 per cent of what we learn through such combined senses will be retained, there is a net profit of 47 per cent of the original experience. This squares with other research findings that two or more sensory inputs can be more effective than a single input, if properly used.

It has been said that an effective way to learn about something is to teach it. There is evidence that learners retain about 70 per cent of what they say as they talk. And, when we know enough about something to demonstrate it as we talk about it, 90 per cent is retained. This would seem to support the case for learner involvement in the process of teaching and learning.

GOALS: ENVIRONMENT

To optimize results, stimuli should be presented to the student in a suitable environment. At the same time, as many ambient distractions as possible should be eliminated. Learners should be able to see clearly each significant detail, and they should be able to hear distinctly each relevant sound.

Light should be as bright as needed, yet without harshness or glare. It should be controllable by means of dimmer switches located at, or conveniently near the teaching position. The focus of attention is, normally, at the brightest spot in the room. A system of spotlights and floodlights should be available and controllable from the teaching position. They could be used to direct attention to the teacher, to the blackboard, to charts, displays, realia and the like. It is conjectural whether windows should be included in the learning environment or not. In general, the answer seems to be in the objectives of the school program and whether the environment outside the windows is supportive of those objectives.

When windows are a part of the learning environment, light control becomes an important consideration. An effective, low maintenance means of room darkening is as important as being able to illuminate desirable areas.

Acoustics must be considered if sound is to be heard clearly and without distortion. The basic structure of the room is one consideration. Acoustical tile on the ceiling and the walls can do much to control unwanted rebound of sounds, as can carpeting on the floors. (Experience indicates that carpeting also tends to decrease maintenance costs.) In large rooms, where sound must carry for some distances, sound amplification systems may be required, and the controls for such equipment should also be located at the teacher's position, or conveniently near it.

GOALS: STRUCTURE OF COMMUNICATION

Objectives

Clear and specific objectives offer the soundest basis for selecting appropriate materials, pertinent content, and methods that are predictably effective. When objectives are clear to the learners, they can better determine when their responses are appropriate.

Content Selection

Whoever transmits the message must say, show or do something which causes the learner to respond. This something to be said or done is the subject matter content. It must be carefully selected, direct and to the point, and relevant to the characteristics and needs of the learner.

Audience Analysis

Effective communication requires knowledge of audience characteristics. This analysis includes such factors as learners' reading level, comprehension, word fluency, ability in spatial relationships, memory span, knowledge of vocabulary and nonverbal symbols, mores, socio-economic background, previous educational experience, and pertinent physiological characteristics.

Structure, Meaning, Rate, Effect

Messages should proceed from the simple to the complex, and from the concrete to the abstract. Further, the message should be developed at a rate which gives the learner time for contemplation, comprehension, and rearrangement of old meanings into new ones. The accurate observation and interpretation of feedback from learners is a skill that requires a most sensitive perception in teachers.

FAMILIARITY WITH HARDWARE

Services need to be provided within the schools to enable teachers to do a sophisticated and successful job of teaching. Often, administrators are unaware of the services that need to be provided. On the other hand, teachers are often unaware of the services, the media, and the hardware that are available to them through programs of instructional support. In addition, technology is developing at an explosive rate and much of the media and hardware has been developed since teachers have had their last training in colleges and universities. In-service education is obviously required. For those teachers who develop skills in their use, the newer devices and techniques (such as multi-media presentations) permit a versatility of approach in the presentation of subject matter.

FAMILIARITY WITH GRAPHICS

Teachers need to be aware of the various graphic techniques that can produce instructional materials with dispatch and quality. It is important for teachers to know that it is possible, and not difficult, to mount useful captions and pictures on cardstock or cloth. They should also know that drawings or prints which have been made with a carbon-laden pencil or ink can be converted into transparencies in a matter of seconds. It is resourceful to know that color can be added to black and white transparencies within minutes and can enhance, emphasize, and add relevance to specific visuals.

Depending only on the length of time it takes them to dry, certain photocopy processes can produce various sizes of transparencies in less than one hour. Using natural scenes, other photographs, or prepared art work, it is a simple process to produce slides photographically and have them in sequence in a tray, ready for use within 36 to 48 hours. Relatively complex pictures can be manipulated, enlarged, or diminished by relatively untrained assistants by means of projection tracing. Labels, symbols or details can be added or deleted. Using files of pictures collected from old newspapers and magazines, or from clip-art sources, excellent paste-up work and mimeographic stencils can be produced rapidly and simply. Masters for liquid process duplication can be similarly produced.

FAMILIARITY WITH UTILIZATION

The effectiveness of any medium of communication is largely a result of how it is used. A general plan of utilization can be applied to most media, and, for the purposes of this discussion, the motion picture will be taken as the example.

The pattern of use described takes into account many of the significant findings of research. It is intended to (a) derive the most predictable learning from valuable material with (b) the greatest enjoyment by the learner (c) in the least amount of time and (d) with the greatest guarantee of retention.

Administration—5 minutes.—At the opening of most classes, teachers need time to do the administrative portion of the class routine. They take the roll, make announcements, collect homework, pass out graded homework, and generally get the class settled for instruction.

Orientation—10 minutes.—Learners need to know what they are about to see, what they are expected to do about it, and how it relates to the class objectives. They need to know what the highlights of the motion picture or other medium will be. They should be aware of any discrepancies or biases that will come to their attention. They need to know what details require their attention and they need to know what, if anything, to ignore. To develop the best understanding of the medium, learners need to develop meaning for terms and symbols that are part of the presentation.

Research shows that a significant increment of learning is gained when students are informed that they will be tested on the content of the medium after it is displayed to them. It takes about ten minutes to make an orientation, depending on the background of the learners and the nature of the message.

First showing—11 minutes.—Research shows that students learn significantly more from two showings of a motion picture than from a single showing. Also, retention is improved. It takes about 11 minutes to show 400 feet (one reel) of 16mm motion pictures, unless only selected portions are used.

Second showing—14 minutes.—To rethread the motion picture and show it the second time takes about 14 minutes. About three minutes of the time is available for question-answering, discussion, or re-orientation between showings.

Test, Question-answering, and Discussion—10 minutes.—After the second showing, the promised test should be given. It does not need to be lengthy or involved, but it should be related to the objectives of the lesson and the highlights of the message.

Following the test, a period of question-answering and/or discussion can be conducted. Assuming the teacher has previewed the motion picture and is thoroughly familiar with the details of its content, she should have a list of questions and discussion points on hand to guide the activities of this session. Learners might ask questions as well as answer them. Panels might lead discussions. (There is also valuable opportunity for student involvement during the preview phase of the motion picture, as well as some opportunity for independent learning.)

Closing—5 minutes.—The remaining five minutes of the class are used for making assignments, summarizing, and closing the class.

The total process takes about 55 minutes. Obviously, when the school organization demands it, modification must be made in the length of the various sessions. Media oriented segments of instruction can be shortened by omitting introductions and/or conclusions, or by use of only the relevant segments. Showings can be divided into segments usable over two or more class periods and, by such means, content can be made more pertinent. These are matters which require skilled judgment by the professional teacher.

MASTERFUL PRESENTATION

As a part of his report, *Images of the Future*, J. Lloyd Trump said that a democracy demands of its education both quality and quantity. In a foreword of the booklet, *New Teaching Aids for the American Classroom*, Wilbur Schramm held that our schools are challenged to achieve unprecedented qualities and quantities.

Both authors declared the need to teach even greater numbers of slow and average learners while providing, at the same time, more and special opportunities for the brighter learners. The massive challenge is to raise the general quality of the educational product higher than it has been ever before in all of history.

The illustrated booklet, *Design for ETV*, points out that presently there are, and will be in the future, more learners than we can educate effectively by current techniques of administration and teaching. The pressure of sheer numbers promises to grow. Unless there is a creative wisdom in the technique and application of media, the situation in the future will become even more acute.

In *New Teaching Aids for the American Classroom*, there is the pointed comment that in a comparatively few years we must come to understand, learn to use skillfully, and evaluate objectively the worth of these new devices in their various forms. We must learn as much about them in a few years as we have learned about textbooks in hundreds of years.

It seems imperative that we instill in neophyte teachers the techniques of message design and masterful presentation, for the benefit of increasing numbers of learners. Former president Henry Hill, of George Peabody College for Teachers, wrote in *The Atlantic* magazine that there are both amateur and professional teachers. The chief difference, he said, is that professional teachers are in teaching for life, or for an extended period. He might have added that the professional teacher should be well-equipped with a thorough mastery of his subject matter area and a philosophical framework, as well as a thorough mastery of the tools of teaching and skill in the design of tailored messages to fit the tools. The teacher should be prepared to make the best use of any medium which is most appropriate for conveying the subject matter to the mind of the learner in the most effective manner.

Both *Images of the Future*, and *New Teaching Aids for the American*

Classroom emphasize the necessity of future handling of massed classes (100, 200, or more learners). There are benefits to be obtained through teaching large numbers of learners by means of masterful presentations. A point of economy exists in reducing the numbers of presentations required for even greater numbers of learners. Also when small teams of teachers serve large numbers of learners, other teachers are released for small group discussions, seminars, individual student attention, supervised independent learning, and special projects. The teachers themselves achieve added time for planning and producing further masterful presentations.

GOALS: PRODUCT

Recently, a prominent educator asked, "What is it that you can teach me that I cannot live as well without knowing?" He implied that the goal of education is not a stock of memorized information. The goal for each individual is that he live differently. Living differently means living better, more productively, more contributively. To do this, learners must acquire sound value structures, constructive attitudes, versatile skills, and the ability to learn supporting information effectively and independently. Most learners need to learn how to learn. Through considerable success and numerous satisfying experiences, learners can develop an insatiable taste for learning.

Teachers need to have an expert knowledge of how learners learn. They need a 'bag of tactics and a sack of strategy' to enable them to meet the learner on his own terms. They need, also, a knowledge of the characteristics of the learner's environment and how it can be dealt with creatively. Teachers should then create learning situations which offer a fair guarantee of success. We must act on the certain knowledge that individual differences are real and vital aspects of the conditions of learning.

Whatever else is said, learners must do their own learning. There is an old Chinese proverb that says, "The teacher opens the door. One must walk through the door himself!" The responsibility of teachers is to create opportunities through which learning is likely to take place efficiently and with enthusiasm.

BIBLIOGRAPHY

Adams, H. F. "The effect of climax and anti-climax order of presentation on memory." *Journal of Applied Psychology*, 4:330–38 (1920).

Ash, P. "The relative effectiveness of massed versus spaced film presentation." *Technical Report SDC 269-7-3*, (State College, Pennsylvania: Pennsylvania State College, Intructional Film Research Program, 1949).

Beck, L. S., Van Horn, C., and Gerbner, G. "A study of audience 'involvement' or 'interest' in a training film." University of Southern California, unpublished, March, 1954.

Brenner, H. R., Walter, J. S., and Kurtz, A. K. "The effects of inserted questions and statements on film learning." *Progress Report No. 10,* (State College, Pennsylvania: Pennsylvania State College, Instructional Film Research Program, 1949).

Edwards, Allen L. *Experimental Design in Psychological Research.* (New York; Rinehart and Company, Inc., 1951). "Effects of selected 'set' inducing instructions upon learning from multiple film showings." Boston University, 1954.

Faison, E. W. J., Rose N., and Podell, J. E. "A technique for measuring observable audience reactions to training films." *Technical Note,* (USAF Training Aids Research Laboratory, Chanute AFB, Illinois, 1955).

Gage, N. L., (ed.), *Handbook of Research on Teaching,* American Educational Research Association, (Chicago: Rand McNally and Co., 1963).

Hoban, Charles F., Jr., and Van Ormer, E. B. *Instructional Film Research 1918-1950 (Rapid Mass Learning)* Technical Report No. SDC 269-7-19, NAVEXOS P-977 Special Devices Center, Port Washington, L.I., New York, 1951.

Hovland, Carl I. "A 'communication analysis' of concept learning." *Psychological Review,* 59: 461–72 (1952).

Hunter, Dr. Ian J. L. *Memory, Facts and Fallacies* (a Pelican Book) reports on recall following a verbal discussion of a familiar subject.

Jaspen, N. "Especially designed motion pictures: I. Assembly of the 40mm breechblock." *Progress Report No. 9,* (State College, Pennsylvania; Pennsylvania State College, Instructional Film Research Program, 1948).

Kanner, J. H. and McClure, A. H. "Varied versus identical repetition in filmed instructions on micrometer reading." *Technical Note,* Chanute AFB, Illinois: TARL, August 9, 1954.

Kanner, J. H. and Sulzer, R. L. "Overt and covert rehearsal of 5-% versus 100% of the material in filmed learning," Chanute AFB, Illinois: TARL, AFPTRC, January 8, 1955.

Kendler, H. H., Kendler, T. S., and Cook, J. O. "Implications of learning theory for the design of audio-visual aids." *Human Resources Research Laboratory Memo Report No. 12-A,* November 1951.

Kendler, T. S., Cook, J. O., and Kendler, H. H. "An investigation of the interacting effects of repetition and audience participation on learning from films." Paper presented at American Psychological Association, Cleveland, Ohio, September 1953.

Lathrop, C. W., Jr. "Contributions of film instructions to learning from instructional films." *Progress Report No. 13,* (State College, Pennsylvania: Pennsylvania State College, Instructional Film Research Program, 1949).

Lindquist, E. (ed.), *Educational Measurement,* (Washington, D.C.: American Council on Education, 1951) p. 23.

Long, A. L., "The influence of color on acquisition and retention as evidenced by the use of sound films." Unpublished doctoral thesis, University of Colorado, 1946.

May, Mark A. "The psychology of learning from demonstration films." *Journal of Educational Psychology,* 37: 1–12 (1946).

May, Mark A., and Lumsdaine, A. A. *Learning From Films.* (New Haven: Yale University Press, 1958).

McClusky, S. D., and McClusky, H. Y. "Comparison of motion pictures, slides, stereographs and demonstration as a means of teaching how to make a reed mat and a pasteboard box." In F. N. Freeman, (ed.). *Visual Education,* (Chicago: University of Chicago Press, 1924), pp. 310–34.

McGuire, W. J. "Factors influencing the effectiveness of demonstrational film for teaching a motor skill: II. Slow motion, added narration and distributed showings." Unpublished, 1953.

McGuire, W. J. "Length of film as a factor influencing training effectiveness." Unpublished, 1953b.

McGuire, W. J. "The relative efficacy of overt and covert trainee participation with different speeds of instruction." Unpublished, 1954.

McGuire, W. J. "Serial position and proximity to reward as factors influencing teaching effectiveness of a training film." Unpublished, 1953c.

McGuire, W. J. "Slow motion, added narration and distributed showings as factors influencing teaching effectiveness of a training film." Unpublished, 1953d.

McLean, W. P. "A comparison of the effectiveness of colored and uncolored pictures." Unpublished thesis, University of Chicago, 1930.

Mercer, J. "The relationship of optical effect and film literacy to learning from instructional films." *Human Engineering Report SDC 269-7-34.* (State College, Pennsylvania: Pennsylvania State College, Instructional Film Research Program, 1952).

Michael, D. N. "Some factors influencing the effects of audience participation on learning from a factual film." *Memo Report 13 A* (revised), Human Resources Research Laboratory, 1951.

Michael, D. N., and Maccoby, Nathan. "A further study in the use of 'audience participation' procedures in film instruction." *Staff Research Memorandum,* Chanute AFB, Illinois: AFBTRC, Project 504-028-0003, March 25, 1954.

Miller, George A., and Selfridge, J. "Verbal context and the recall of meaningful material." *American Journal of Psychology,* 63: 176–85 (1950).

Miller, J., and Levine, S. "A study of the effects of different types of review and of 'structuring' subtitles on the amount learned from a training film" *Memo Report No. 17,* Human Resources Research Laboratory, 1952.

Miller, J., and Levine, S., and Sternberger, J. "The effects of different kinds of review and of subtitling on learning from a training film (a replicative study)." Unpublished, 1952.

Neu, D. M. "The effect of attention-gaining devices on film-mediated learning." *Progress Report No. 14-15-16.,* (State College, Pennsylvania: Pennsylvania State College, Instructional Film Research Program, 1950).

Roshal, S. M. "Effects of learner representation in film-mediated perceptual-motor learning." *Technical Report SDC 269-7-5,* (State College Pennsylvania: Pennsylvania State College, Instructional Film Research Program, 1949).

Sulzer, R. L. and Lumsdaine, A. A. "The value of using multiple examples in training film instruction." Memo Report No. 25., Human Resources Research Laboratory, 1952.

Vandermeer, A. W. "Relative effectiveness of color and black and white in instructional films." *Progress Report No. 9.,* (State College, Pennsylvania: Pennsylvania State College, Instructional Film Research Program, 1948).

Vandermeer, A. W. "Relatively effectiveness of exclusive film instruction, films plus study guides and typical instructional methods." *Progress Report No. 10.,* (State College, Pennsylvania: Pennsylvania State College, Instructional Film Research Program, 1949).

Vandermeer, A. W. "Relative effectiveness of instruction by: films exclusively, films plus study guides, and standard lecture methods." *Technical Report SDC 269-7-13.,* (State College, Pennsylvania: Pennsylvania State College, Instructional Film Research Program, 1950).

Weiss, W. "Effect on learning and performance of controlled environmental stimulation." *Staff Research Memorandum,* Chanute AFB, Illinois: Training Aids Research Laboratory, 1954.

Wendt, Paul R. *Audio-Visual Instruction.* #14 in a series of pamphlets on "What research says to the teacher," (Washington, D. C.: Department of Classroom Teachers, American Educational Research Association of the National Education Association, 1957).

Wulff, J. J. "The teaching effectiveness of a film mechanical assembly demonstration with supplementary nomenclature training." Yale University, unpublished, 1954.

Wulff, J. J., Sheffield, F. D., and Draeling, D. G. " 'Familiarization' procedures used as adjuncts to assembly task training with a demonstration film." *Staff Research Memorandum*, Chanute AFB, Illinois: Training Aids Research Laboratory, 1954.

Yale Motion Picture Research Project. "Do 'motivation' and 'participation' questions increase learning?" *Educational Screen*, 26: 256–59, 274–83 (1947).

Chapter 6

How well have the colleges and universities succeeded in fulfilling their traditional leadership role through adoption of innovative teaching practices?

What unique relationships exist between teacher, learner and the media in the college or university setting?

What are the prerequisites for support of media service centers if a systems approach to instructional development is to be successfully undertaken?

What trends appear to be developing in the role of the professional educator and in the use of technology?

HIGHER EDUCATION
AND MEDIA INNOVATION

ROBERT A. WEISGERBER, Senior Research Scientist
American Institutes for Research, Palo Alto

It is widely accepted that the responsibility for leadership in educational process and curriculum development is the special province of higher education. The curious aspect of this designated role is that leadership has been traditionally defined as scholarship resulting from educational research, and its concomitant writing, public speaking, and consulting, yet the outcomes of such activity, in general, have not been adequately translated into demonstrated excellence in educational process in the college classroom itself.

Nevertheless, in recent years there has been a re-evaluation of the educational process among the professorial ranks, and a marked trend exists toward establishing a balance between research and teaching excellence. This has been paralleled by an acceleration in professorial attention to the use of modern technology and new media. There is every indication that traditionally conservative lectures in higher education are now giving way to more flexible and creative formats for instructor-student communication. W. J. McKeachie (1), writing in the

Handbook of Research on Teaching, has pointed out the wide range of variables that affect learning success in the lecture format in college and university teaching. It would appear that much has long been intuitive about this type of teacher-student relationship, and that teaching procedures should be varied from this traditional method toward techniques more likely to generate motivation and involvement, especially where the learner is expected to master concepts or problem-solving skills.

Recently national attention has been focused upon the new image of the professor as a teacher through such popular communications channels as *Life* magazine and network television programs. Promotions committees and faculty organizations have upgraded excellence in teaching methods in their list of criteria when selecting outstanding faculty members. Boards of trustees, as in the California State Colleges, are establishing cash awards for teaching excellence. It is clear that the next move is up to the college faculty themselves as they are challenged to become fully resourceful as educators.

It is the purpose of this chapter to review particular aspects of college instructional patterns and the new relationship of technology and media to college programs. In particular, note will be made of various forms of excellence now being applied at various institutions—examples of outstanding innovation in educational process that will eventually make it possible to live up to the responsibility of leadership long assigned the colleges and universities. It is *not* the intent of this chapter to recite any listing of specific media and their particular applications, chiefly because this writer believes there are no practical limits for media applications in the college curriculum, except the limits imposed by the user's imagination.

James Cass (2), writing in *Innovation in Education,* has succinctly summarized the challenge.

> Technology will spark the most dramatic changes in elementary and secondary classrooms in the next decade. Educational television, language laboratories, teaching machines, films, and the whole range of other mechanical and electronic means of communication will become increasingly important. Not long ago the potential of these devices for improving classroom learning was largely theoretical, but today they have proved themselves in many experiments. What remains is to rub the gloss of novelty off these innovations and find how they can best contribute to learning day by day.
>
> The changes that face American higher education in the ten years ahead are less well known and understood, but are no less revolutionary. The same underlying factors will affect the nation's colleges and universities . . .[1]

[1] Reprinted with permission from Matthew B. Miles, *Innovation in Education,* (New York: Teachers College Press, 1964). © 1964 by Teachers College, Columbia University.

Achieving excellence in classroom practice has long been an objective of all concerned with higher education. More specifically, we have particularly sought to accentuate those skills which are singularly human: factors involving human relationships, personality, value judgments, critical thinking, and creativity (3). Since teacher education involves not only college faculty but also future faculty at all grade levels it has been doubly important to upgrade classroom practice by innovation and experimentation, and to pay special attention to technology (4). That change and innovation are now vastly accelerated in the colleges over what they used to be is made clear by Alvin Eurich (5) who suggests that there has been greater progress in the colleges in the last 10 years than in the previous 100 years.

INSTRUCTOR AND STUDENT INFORMATION TRANSMISSION AND ASSIMILATION

Colleges and universities have a curricular structure which directly influences the teaching-learning relationship existing between students and faculty members and also among faculty themselves. Students, by virtue of the diversity of course content they are required to take, are exposed to a wide variety of professorial teaching styles. As graduates they are products of a milieu of instructional situations, and this collegiate experiential repertoire shapes their own actions in post-graduate years. This collage or variety of experiences not only fosters individuality in each graduate but also in undergraduates, for they show considerable diversity in their *approach* to learning.

Instructors, on the other hand, tend to gravitate into mutual interest clusters, based on teaching assignments. There is little doubt that most institutions have very real problems in horizontal communication between departments, and especially those departments whose faculty have little in common in the content they teach. One unfortunate outcome is the relative lack of information exchange between professors regarding classroom communication processes. It is easy to empathize with the common student practice of having coffee while making comparisons of professors' teaching abilities. In the faculty lounge a similar process of analyzing colleagues' classroom procedures is less seldom undertaken, partially because of ethical considerations. The implication, inescapably, is that the students who discuss and make judgments on the worth of various teachers' methodologies profit from the analytic process but little similar benefit accrues among professional ranks.

Notwithstanding the above, there are notable differences where media are introduced. Professors appearing on television, for example, invite colleagues' comments by their very appearance in a public setting.

Similarly, the professors who are innovators and who place heavy emphasis on the functional integration of media in their teaching bring attention to the classroom activity, largely through the atmosphere of change thus generated. The attention paid by colleagues to positive gains accomplished through media innovation is probably the greatest single factor responsible for the increasing number of faculty who turn their attention to technology as a fruitful new avenue for improving college instruction. Nothing breeds success like success, as the saying goes, and this has clearly been the experience of professors who establish sound objectives, engage in careful planning, and have effective implementation of multi-sensory media techniques.

The college environment is potentially the most fertile ground of all educational levels for the adoption of new patterns of responsibility in the teaching/learning quotient. Student maturity and the typical diversity of student learning objectives are important ingredients which encourage a climate of self-motivation, self-direction, and self-evaluation, and make possible extensive individualized study programs using appropriate media. Similarly, there is a branching and specializing in content that characterizes student progress from freshman to senior level, not to mention the graduate level. This raises the possibility of large group instruction at the freshman level, reaching students by the hundreds, and smaller class sizes at each succeeding level, with senior classes that are very small indeed. The full gamut of media capabilities is challenged in such a variety of situations. Yet technology has developed in diverse ways as well, and for each situation appropriate media *can* be identified. As one example, progress has been noted at the University of Miami in using multi-media with varying class sizes (6). In one research report social science and humanities seminars were found to benefit from specially designed media packages (7).

STUDENT INVOLVEMENT

The pattern of instruction at the college level depends to a great degree upon student participation. This participation is readily recognized in science laboratories, music rehearsal rooms, art studios, gymnasiums, and in practice-teaching classrooms. Less apparent but no less significant is active student involvement in the entire range of courses, from freshman English composition to senior courses in audiovisual methods of instruction. The significance of this high degree of student participation can be appreciated when the process of classroom communication is analyzed and compared to theoretical models showing closed-loop feedback. These young adults enjoy a role that is more than passive, or even reactive; they have much that is original to contribute and do not hesitate to do so. Communication *is* a two-way exchange in the college environment. A colleague of the writer's recently said, facetiously but with some truth, that the "current crop of college students will learn no matter whether the instructor shows films, lectures while standing on his head, recites in Chinese, or even forbids the students to learn." The implications of such a statement are enormous, for if learner readiness is so self-evident, then a new look at professorial roles is imperative in order to provide alternative avenues for learning.

The media are apparent as alternative avenues for learning, but it is essential that their use is not divergent with the two-way communication principle just described. Leslie J. Briggs (8) has pointed out the typical open-loop nature of one-way communication such as film, TV, etc. and cautioned that with *all media* provision must be made, as it is in programed instruction, for student involvement and for some confirmation or correction to the student with respect to the progress he is making.

Traditional lists of the so-called audiovisual teaching methods frequently include the technique of bringing in a guest expert or authority to speak or demonstrate to the student group. In a larger sense this technique occurs continuously on the college campus, for nearly every campus is international in the composition of its faculty and student body. The world figuratively comes through the door of the college or university, and this cosmopolitan gathering often results in a mutual exchange of ideas that transcends the campus, the immediate community, or even the state. Inevitably programs develop on the campuses which extend beyond the requirements for local service. Often the programs, such as the Indiana University Audio-Visual Center's A.I.D. contract with Nigeria, are communications oriented and lead to considerable instructional material preparation for use both on campus and in the foreign country. Through the enlargement of experience, brought into the classroom by foreign students who represent different cultures and value systems, a dimension is added to college teaching that is at the same time intangible and indispensable. In a sense it is like having live media always available in infinite variety.

The media, then, are used in many ways by both instructors and students. *They serve as agendas for discussion, as expositions of points of view, as instruments of analysis, as expressions of esthetic value, as transmitters of information, as demonstrators of skills, and as many other uses as the educational participants generate.* There is no question that the cross-fertilization of ideas is greatly fostered by those creative students and professors who are versatile in their use of media as vehicles for educational interaction.

THE MEDIA CENTER ROLE

The media center is pivotal in the spread of information which leads to the adoption of innovative teaching techniques. There is logic in this, since the media center is, sooner or later, a useful resource for virtually every faculty member, and, once contact has been established, its commitment to support and service encourages further contact.

The professional communications specialist in the media center cannot be a content authority in the many diverse courses in the college curriculum, and hence is not a source of criticism for professors who seek help. Instead, discourse between professor and communications specialist has usually taken an initial form and direction preferred by the instructor, later extended into new dimensions through the initiative of the media specialist. The initial request for service may involve no more than a rented film, but it is likely that even this brief contact will lead naturally to other, more complex services. There is virtually no limit to how far this type of team relationship can go. In the last several years the full-scale participation of the media specialist in the shaping of instruction has been best realized in the systems approach, described more fully later in this chapter.

Of course, the capacity of the media center to provide complex services must be established if such team relationships are to be meaningful. Toward that end, Boyd Mitchell (9) has developed criteria showing the factors deemed essential for the effective operations of college media centers as they now exist. Specifications for future media centers will differ markedly.

THE RENOVATION OF TEACHING PATTERNS

To date there have been *three general conditions* which characterize the universities or colleges that have moved ahead prominently in the renovation of teaching patterns and the assignment of a prominent role to technology. *The first condition is that top level administration must exercise active rather than passive leadership in innovation.* Charles Hoban (10) has pointed out a critical factor in the adoption of media in classroom practice. He observes:

> No matter which of the new educational media is introduced, the situation into which it is introduced is transformed by the introduction. Acceptance of *management of learning* as a central problem of organized and institutional education would, at least, permit the admission of a wider range of alternative procedures, techniques, and methods in teaching — without threatening or substantially altering the critical functions of education, teaching, or learning. (Italics this writer's)

No better example comes to mind than the milestone passed in 1960, when the president of Michigan State University, John Hannah (11), listed seven proposals for progress in a report to the board of trustees. From an outsider's viewpoint it is remarkable to note how the university has progressed toward fulfillment of these specific guidelines.

1. It is proposed that the student be encouraged to assume progressively more responsibility for his own learning, and that this encouragement be offered by giving earlier skills and by far more comprehensive advising by faculty in time released from repetitive and nonproductive tasks.

2. It is proposed that we facilitate independent learning by defining educational objectives more concretely and specifically and organizing courses and curricula to serve the purposes of the student.

3. It is proposed to redefine the responsibilities of faculty members with due reference to rank and to most productive use of their time.

4. It is proposed to put to use discoveries already made concerning the learning process itself, and to stimulate further research through the establishment of a Learning Resources Center to include and encourage the use of closed-circuit television, film, teaching machines, programed studies, and other aids.

5. It is proposed to improve the environment for learning by making greater academic use of the residence halls, and of the time students spend in them, thus eliminating as best we can physical inconvenience as an impediment to learning, and capitalizing upon our great advantage as a residence university.

6. It is proposed to give consideration to designing a model for the University combining the advantages of comprehensiveness with the conveniences and identification of smaller groups.

7. It is proposed that forward planning and budgeting be carried out by the several colleges and departments in a manner to give effect to these proposals, and that the Board of Trustees and officers allocate the financial resources of the University so as to support and encourage those colleges and departments actively engaging in the process of redesigning their programs in keeping with the over-all development framework.

Perceptive leadership has been increasingly demonstrated at well established institutions, and also new institutions. In numerous instances the momentum for change has centered around central administrative planning.

The second condition which has promoted change at the college level is the need for economical quality. That is, institutions have been pressed into a re-evaluation of their *efficiency* of instruction as a means of protecting the *quality* of instruction in the face of rising costs from every quarter. A number of institutions have concluded that this is a function of continued self appraisal.

> The University of Southern California recognizes the need for an ongoing program of self-evaluation, and, in consequence, an Office of Institutional Research is being created. The purposes of this office include exploration of the use of team teaching, teaching machines, computers, television, language laboratories, and every available audio-visual device in order to maintain the best possible learning environment. New methodologies and techniques are being adopted where appropriate (12).

Sometimes this recognition of need, followed by insightful exploration of possible solutions, has taken place at school or department levels. A notable example of this is the well-known (and inspirational) innovation in teaching/learning in the biology department at Purdue University. Here the faculty, led by S. N. Postlethwaite (13), have gone through a major transition in methods. They have turned away from lecture methods, unfavorable teacher-student ratios and consequent depersonalized and steadily weakening teacher-student relationships, to a thoroughly new media-based mode of instruction. The new format is clearly learner oriented and observation reveals an awareness of this fact by the students. As Postlethwaite describes it:

> Emphasis on student learning rather than on the mechanisms of teaching is the basis of the integrated experience approach. It involves the teacher identifying as clearly as possible those responses, attitudes, concepts, ideas and manipulatory skills to be achieved by the student and then designing a multi-faceted, multi-sensory approach which will enable the student to direct his own activity to attain these objectives. The program of learning is organized in such a way that students can proceed at their own pace, filling in gaps in their background information and omitting the portions of the program which they have covered at some previous time. It makes use of every educational device available and attempts to align the exposure to these learning experiences in a sequence which will be most effective and efficient. The kind, number and nature of the devices involved will be dependent on the nature of the subject under consideration.

Students have evidenced both greater achievement and greater appreciation of the faculty, as signified by their selection of Professor Postlethwaite as the campus' outstanding teacher.

Professional educational associations are also encouraging full integration of media in their respective curricular fields, even where such patterns were not traditionally evident (14). Undoubtedly this will help to make media 'academically respectable' among college faculty. Teacher education associations are equally aware of the impact of instructional technology as evidenced by the purposes of the Teacher Education and Media Project, jointly undertaken by the American Association of Colleges for Teacher Education and the Associated Organizations for Teacher Education (15).

The third general condition which has been prominent in the introduction of new methodology is the increasing number of media personnel who are qualified to attract research monies, and who choose to perform their research in an applied setting in the college or university. Unfortunately, there are fewer such individuals than one would expect, and even less who relate their findings to a variety of disciplines, thereby stimulating adoption throughout the campus.

One interesting interdisciplinary research effort is the work of the Coordinated Science Laboratory at the University of Illinois. There, the PLATO Project, under the direction of Donald Bitzer (16), has centered on exploration of practical variables in computer-based instruction to varying numbers of individual students, and has found application in engineering, nursing, education and psychology as well as other disciplines and other grade levels. Perhaps the most exciting potential application for such a project is in the area of continuing adult education. Through the power and speed of computers a direct interface with large numbers of remote student locations may become practical, allowing individual study from the home. When fully operational, this type of action research on learning methodology could have broad impact on the curriculum.

Other media research has equally exciting possibilities for higher education. A thorough review of the broad topic of media research, its findings and applications, is contained in A. A. Lumsdaine's chapter in the *Handbook of Research on Teaching* (17).

CURRICULUM REVISION BY THE SYSTEMS APPROACH

To say that the curriculum is constantly undergoing revision is to state the obvious, but to state that *the revision process can be optimized* toward specified goals and, at the same time, course content can be made both effective and efficient is to make some important inferences about the procedures employed. One such effective procedure is *the analysis and design of instructional systems.* James Brown and Kenneth Norberg (18) have briefly and lucidly presented basic relationships between the systems approach and the educational media. They consider it a technique for planning that begins with a comprehensive analysis of objectives and functions, then follows by relating optimum configurations of human and technical resources to achieve performance goals. Brown (19) also has outlined eight generalized steps to be incorporated in any systems procedure.

Extensive work has been started in developing and adapting systems procedures at the college level. Leading in this effort are the projects at Michigan State University, University of Syracuse, Oral Roberts University, University of Colorado, University of Miami, Stephens College, Grand Valley State College, Florida Atlantic University, New York Institute of Technology, University of Wisconsin, Delta College, Oklahoma Christian College, St. Louis Jr. College District and selected other institutions (20) (21). Oakland Community College, working with Litton Industries, has applied systems procedures, from the establishment of behaviorally stated terminal objectives to the implementation of audio-tutorial media, as a means of achieving a total multi-track academic and technical program for individual students possessing unique prerequisite skills (22). Other instances of college-industry collaboration in systems procedures are noticeably evident and it will be interesting to see whether industries, such as the aircraft/airline industry, fully adopt systems procedures before higher education does (23) (24).

The systems approach to instructional design appears to be the single most productive development promising an optimal combination of curriculum, technology, and personnel that is *actually* an educational whole greater than the sum of the parts (25). The advent of systems procedures will very likely require a new definition of roles, including those of the traditional audiovisual specialist (into instructional communications engineer) and the lecturer (into learning content strategist). As optimum working procedures for analyzing educational problems are developed, many of the assumptions of staffing, funding, and facility design, which have been held for years by administrators and boards of trustees, will be severely challenged. The funds allocated to faculty salaries, permanent and inflexible buildings, and considerable amounts of standard equipment for traditional lecture rooms may be reassigned into more innovative strategies and practices.

RESPONSIBILITIES OF THE COLLEGE INSTRUCTIONAL TEAM

Clearly, with so much at stake in so many divergent activities, the college and university professorial cadre relies increasingly on media techniques as a way of optimizing the instructional and service programs. Though leadership in adoption of media techniques can originate from faculty, administrative, or media personnel, it takes a team effort on the part of all of them to truly implement successful and significant curriculum transition.

The well qualified team member from the teaching faculty is a person who

(1) is well versed in the subject matter and well informed on new developments in methodology in his content area,

(2) is flexible and dynamic in his approach to the teaching of his specialty,

(3) is concerned about learning, as well as teaching, and is responsive to student needs and capabilities,

(4) recognizes the value of feedback concerning his instructional techniques and welcomes full involvement by a communications specialist in designing effective instructional strategies.

The well qualified team member from the media center is a person who

(1) has extensive education and experience in the broad field of communications,

(2) is cognizant of the psychological, physiological and behavioral aspects of the teaching/learning phenomenon and incorporates this awareness into his functional role in the team,

(3) has technical competence in the design and creation of instructional materials as well as their effective utilization, based on perception/cognition research,

(4) is able to elicit a clear set of teaching objectives from the teaching faculty member, relate these to learning objectives on the part of the students, and correlate these aims with practical, innovative strategies.

The well qualified administrative team member is a person who

(1) recognizes the need for continuously changing and evolving teaching/learning methodologies,

(2) allows for flexibility in funding and in use of facilities to encourage creative approaches,

(3) makes adequate provision for higher costs during the research and developmental stages of innovation in a similar manner to the special allowances made in R. & D. programs by business and industry (education *is* a big business!),

(4) evaluates the productivity of the instructional team not only on a quantitative basis but also on a qualitative basis.

FUNDING FOR MAXIMUM UTILIZATION

In higher education there is an extremely wide variety in methods and amount of funding both at the institution level and at the media center level. The implications of funding are so serious as to warrant special consideration, even though this chapter is less concerned with administration than instruction.

Irrespective of the talents of media professionals and their willingness to 'go the extra mile,' there are budgetary imperatives for any appreciable upgrading of the role of media as components of instruction.

The first budgetary requirement is for flexibility, with ample allowance for (a) variability in hardware costs; (b) the need for purchasing series and sets of materials; (c) hiring more professional media personnel as the volume of usage grows (by way of comparison, the institution always expects to add more faculty when student enrollment goes up); and (d) the production of local materials for campus needs at a quality level sufficient to warrant their reproduction if useful to other institutions.

The second requirement is for adequacy in funding, with a built-in minimum of support. In this latter respect, it is essential to avoid the trap of a support formula tied to the size of student population. Unless regular revision is provided for in such formulas, it is virtually inevitable that growth in staff will lag behind growth in work load with the result that the support 'floor' soon becomes a support 'ceiling.' As a guide that would be entirely defensible in a technological society which is now two thirds of the way through the twentieth century, the budgeting for media services should begin to approach a par with budgeting for library services.

A third requirement is for consistency between federal, state or private sources of funds. In general, the state provides a more stable source but private sources provide the greater flexibility and the greatest chance to capitalize on innovative opportunity which could not be foreseen. While federal funds have helped to achieve adequacy they are so fluctuating in supply as to prevent their being depended on in long-range budgetary planning.

There exists a continuum in the degree and nature of funds available, ranging from heavily endowed or heavily research funded universities to struggling institutions nearly wholly dependent on student fees. Strangely enough, media programs and teaching with modern technology are not consistently identified with the richer schools, since some of these are steeped in academic tradition (the lecture method). It is the contention of this writer that advocates of the media have been at the back door of higher education seeking flexible, adequate and consistent funding for years, a circumstance which is due for reversal with the advent of instructional systems design procedures.

MEETING LOCAL NEEDS

Campus media services are available to faculty either on a free basis (media center controls its own funds) or on a charge-back basis (college departments pay for services from their own funds). In general, the former arrangement has encouraged greater media utilization by the individual faculty and leads to increased instructional experimentation. Where free services are available to the instructor one might expect that the rush to the media center would be overwhelming. But, since the funds provided to the center are finite and fixed for each year, the temptation to innovate is tempered by the realization that dollar resources are not inexhaustible.

There is a prevalent contention, not universally held, that faculty users are themselves the most sensitive determiners of their own needs in instructional communications. This implies a need for great freedom of choice open to the professor in the selection of particular materials appropriate for each teaching point and it also implies that those materials would, in fact, be made available on request. Realistically, however, instructors are generally rationed in the degree of media choices and support services available. Real options, such as local production of 16mm films, are not always open to them. Occasionally, however, we are able to find rather free-wheeling media development programs where professorial involvement toward developing comprehensive teaching materials represents a large segment of the faculty. Some 50 per cent of the faculty in the St. Louis Jr. College District, for example, are engaged in materials development projects on (paid) 'extended time' during summers.

Even where funds are lacking for local development of specialized media, the typical campus has its share of faculty who so strongly feel the need for heavy media use in their instruction that they are willing to seek external sources of supplementary funds to make production possible. An examination of the booklet entitled *Science Course Improvements Projects,* published by the National Science Foundation (26), quickly illustrates the point. This publication lists numerous faculty from colleges and universities throughout the country who have committed themselves to extended programs of curriculum development or research and are engaged in extensive media creation as their form of scholarly contribution to their chosen subject field. Because of the flexible scheduling of class loads and special arrangements by which professorial time can be bought on a reimbursed basis, it is possible for faculty to engage in these types of activities on either a full- or part-time basis. It is repeatedly demonstrated that agencies and foundations lend considerable financial support to programs which develop new teaching materials and innovative methods.

Similar to the externally funded professorial salary is the externally funded audiovisual service. Some media centers, particularly those with outstanding reputations, such as the one at Indiana University, have attained their large organizational structure through various self-supporting means. The center at Indiana, for example, derives the majority of its funds through the sale of its own film productions, television kinescopes and self-initiated projects which attract outside monies. These monies then are placed in a revolving fund which provides staff, materials, and equipment for new projects and productions, which renew the cycle. With the capacities introduced by this fiscal flexibility, and with the additional support directly obtained from the state of Indiana, the center is able to offer applied experiences in a remarkable range of undergraduate and graduate educational communications courses (leading to the doctorate) which would be unlikely if the center were dependent solely on legislative appropriations.

MEDIA SERVICES AVAILABLE TO INSTRUCTORS

In considering the use of media by college instructors it may be helpful to consider representative kinds of services that are typically available in varying degrees from campus to campus.

On-Campus Services

1. Consultation: Communications media personnel are frequently involved in the planning and presentation of summer institutes (NDEA, etc.), and of large (200 plus) classes, because of the heavy use of media in these instructional situations. They also serve on committees working toward the design of new instructional facilities; and in numerous ways it has become apparent that curriculum planning, in its broad sense, requires a heavy involvement of the media or communications specialist. The role he plays in these various contexts is essentially that of a catalyst, for he introduces innovations in teaching practice yet always maintains a staff (rather than line) relationship to the teaching faculty.

2. Production: The production of graphic, photographic and electronic images has become commonplace in college and university media centers. However, the range of quality and type of materials produced *on campus* for local needs is striking. In the more traditional production units within audiovisual centers, there is considerable faculty demand for lettered charts and posters and for 2 x 2 slides copied from existing source materials. In more versatile production units, there is a rapidly increasing volume of faculty requests for graphic representation in the form of overhead projectuals and for 8mm cinematography in the form of films on single concepts. In sophisticated and innovative production centers, artwork and photography are being integrated in complex ways in closed-circuit television, in 16mm film production, and in multi-media systems presentations.

3. Utilization: It is probable that the criterion that most determines faculty use of instructional materials is their ease of access to those materials. Ideally, instructors and students in the seminar room, auditorium, laboratory, study carrel and dormitory, should all have fingertip retrieval of the whole range of college owned materials. Dial access systems are extant now, with both audio and video retrieval possible. Institutions like Ohio State University (27), with 267 student stations, nine campus locations, and over 35,000 users per week, are pioneering in this direction. (This writer is convinced that at a future date such dialing will not be directed to either owned materials or campus located materials but rather to huge regional information retrieval banks.) In planning any new campus this kind of instructional capability is an obvious desideratum. There have been developed some generalized criteria by which cost analysis of such equipment can be estimated at the time of planning (28).

In a long established campus, full implementation of dial access to remote media may not be possible without prohibitive remodeling, resulting in a need for maximum dispersion of equipment and materials to locations convenient to the users. This latter ideal is tempered by several factors. First, there are certain kinds of materials, notably many film titles, which are of interdisciplinary value and need to be available on a shared basis. This requires some form of centralized scheduling and circulation. Second, there are practical factors of security, maintenance, and cataloging which lend themselves to centralized but not to decentralized equipment and material collections.

Some institutions have begun to bridge the gap between total electronic distribution systems and the 'bicycling' of equipment and materials to and fro across campus. Where closed-circuit television has been installed, and a film chain is available, it can be used to send films to remote locations. Where television is not available, or when inappropriate (as in the case of subject matter where color is essential, but the campus transmitter is only black and white), other methods have been devised.

One approach has been the use of rear projection installations. In auditoriums and other large rooms audiovisual equipment is installed behind the front wall, and the screen transmits, rather than reflects, the projected light. Southern Connecticut State College, Rochester Institute of Technology, Illinois Teachers College-Chicago North, Foothills College and numerous other institutions have adopted this large group technique. Architects have been developing reliable engineering data on the optimum design of such facilities. In undertaking new construction, colleges are now able to avail themselves of architects who specialize in media and who are in a position to avoid the 'little' mistakes that later affect utilization (29). In average size classrooms the "communications wall" has been suggested with some justification. In this design the equipment is contained within a free standing wall with rear projection screens on the front surface. In both types of rear projection facilities, it should be noted, the problems of storage and security for decentralized equipment have been overcome by the limited access nature of the rear projection room. The advantage to the college professor's classroom flexibility is obvious when compared to the alternatives of (a) chance equipment availability; (b) difficulty in obtaining adequate room darkening; and (c) disruption of class continuity to provide for projection equipment temporarily brought into the room.

Instructors have the benefit of a new dimension of flexibility in their classrooms when vidicon cameras and video tape recorders are utilized. These devices have rapidly earned a major function in education in their ability to provide instant playback of group or individual performance, and to permit enlargement or selective focus for control over material being presented. Teacher training has especially benefited.

The advent of individualized learning (as opposed to group instruction) poses new problems since the escalation of cost becomes a major factor if the individual learning station is *multi-media* designed. This problem has not been resolved, but is the subject of much discussion by manufacturers. It is likely that various *modular* audiovisual instructional systems will be marketed in the near future as a direct result of this changed curricular requirement (30).

The utilization of programed learning materials for independent study has been attempted to some degree at most institutions of higher education. Much of this has been research oriented (31) leading to clearer understandings of learning theory (32). Still, there have only been isolated instances where adoption in the college and university setting has been either as permanent or widespread in the curriculum as it has at Oakland Community College. It is likely, however, that the major contribution of programed instruction to college instruction will be not the programs per se, but rather the concomitant attention to stated, measurable objectives, the structuring of learning experiences, and the tailoring of progress to learner's needs and pace; all of which are likely to result in more scientifically prepared instructional materials (33) and ultimately into what might be termed 'instructional engineering' (34).

The next decade will see truly radical changes in the optimum methods for utilization of instructional materials. New technological advances will continue to be a prime factor in encouraging those in higher education to innovate more freely in utilization patterns.

4. **Evaluation:** Probably the least adequately developed service function in media centers within higher education is that of evaluation. As used here the term implies two factors, first, the selective rating of ma-

terials for their potential worth in meeting the professor's *specific teaching objectives* as a precondition to purchase and second, the measurement of *effects on learning* brought on by the use of those materials.

Regarding the first factor, many institutions provide reference catalogs and source books which suggest the national whereabouts of teaching materials, and many also engage in some form of written evaluation to be filled out by the faculty member who obtains materials for preview. At first this appears adequate, but when one examines (a) the extreme variety and complexity of content that characterizes the college curriculum and (b) the minority of nationally marketed materials which are available at the *college* level, one is immediately conscious of the inadequacy. Relying on standard references simply does not suffice for providing specific materials relevant to the college teacher's specialized subject matter.

A more useful approach is the provision of client-tailored searches by evaluation specialists resulting in selective listings with evaluative comments on each item included. This type of media center service should be complementary to the provision of basic reference catalogs and source books already mentioned, for the latter can be arranged (color coded) so that faculty can use them without the presence of professional media personnel. There is no doubt that the time-consuming nature of such client-tailored searches by media personnel is the main deterrent preventing institutions from full implementation throughout the curriculum. However, most institutions of higher education today utilize computers, and ultimately it will be through this technological avenue that complete specialized listings will become routine. It is likely that the 1970s will see a national system allowing automatic print-out of specialized media lists, available on demand from central information storage centers through the local campus computer service center. Further, this will be available according to concept and in a form which includes qualitative evaluations of the materials by other college professors. A long step toward such a national information retrieval system is the U. S. Office of Education Project ERIC (with a Media Information Center at Stanford University), intended to expedite the handling of research findings.

Once appropriate materials have been identified and obtained for review, there remains the task of applying objective criteria to ascertain whether purchase or repeated rental is the more preferable alternative. Points to be considered include: (a) frequency of use; (b) difficulty of guaranteeing rental availability; (c) transiency of content; (d) similarity to other items in the existing collection; (e) special purchase opportunities and price adjustments, and (f) evaluation of effectiveness toward attainment of instructional objectives.

With regard to the effects on learning brought about by the use of media, much remains to be done. Clearly language laboratory tape decks have been useful to provide knowledge of student progress. There has also been exploratory use of the Edex Teaching System as an evaluation tool to provide the student with cumulative scores and the instructor with a means for simple item analysis (35) (36). Videotape and 8mm films have both been successfully employed as direct documentations of student skill attainment with the intent of critical self-evaluation leading to new educational design and improved performance (37). However, the computer represents the medium most adaptable to objective evaluation of all phases of learning, whether conceptual, motor or affective in nature (38) (39). The full impact of cybernetics and communication theory, in its mathematical form, is yet to be determined (40).

Off-Campus Services

1. **Consultant programs:** As indicated in the opening paragraph of this chapter, colleges and universities are looked to for leadership in the field of education. For this reason the faculty are consistently called on to act as consultants in the community, the state, and the nation in industrial, military, and educational undertakings. Consistently, this writer has observed that faculty appearances before lay, business, government, or educational groups have been most enhanced and most successful in impact when the presentation goes beyond the verbal approach. Since this is the case it is obligatory that the consulting faculty expert be alert to current developments in his field *and* competent in his mastery of communications techniques in order to transmit his specialized information more effectively. Not infrequently effective presentation techniques have a secondary result in increased use of new media within the consulting organization. This has been clearly evidenced in the various auxiliary educational programs (Project HEADSTART, etc.) which have been federally organized and are now being coordinated by academic professionals.

2. **International Programs:** Higher education's involvement in overseas activities has expanded drastically since World War II. In global perspective two factors are prominent which tend to encourage still greater participation. The first is the changes occurring and recurring in transportation and communication. The second is in the rapid emergence of new nations into a technological world.

Relevant to the first factor, economy jet flights and special student rates on other transport systems encourage the development of student-exchange programs. Numerous opportunities for foreign study are available and their number increases constantly. A unique aspect of such exchange programs is the need for surmounting language deficiencies quickly in order to allow the visiting student to be 'competitive' with other college students. Here media, particularly tape-recorded lessons, have been extremely effective. Similarly, language laboratories are being used by professors who are learning new languages prior to overseas assignment.

Not only is transportation flexibility encouraging personal relocation for study, but with the advent of communications satellites there appears a very real possibility for a world 'classroom,' where simultaneous involvement via television can be accomplished, offering considerable flexibility and convenience to the attendees. Significant here is the fact that the *only* means for achieving such simultaneous international education is through new media techniques.

Regarding the second factor, the emergence of new nations in a technological world, there has been considerable assistance in transitional phases through the involvement of larger colleges and universities. Frequently, they establish contract teams to work with young governments which are seeking to bypass the centuries of struggle that are usually implicit during agrarian-to-industrial transformation. Almost without exception, the professorial teams on contract have found that media are a key to the acceleration of skill training, attitude modification, and concept mastery that are so essential for the native populations of those countries. Frequently, these teams have included media specialists and, largely through the support of the Agency for International Development (AID) in Washington, media have become integral parts of training programs developed for these emerging nations.

3. **Marketed Products:** Some, though still a minority, of the larger colleges and universities, such as Indiana University, University of Southern California, State University of Iowa, and The University of California, create and distribute media products. In many instances the particular item produced, (be it a film, tape, or other medium) is originally created to fill a specific need at that campus, but which can similarly benefit other schools or agencies. In such cases, arrangements are made to market the item, and this provides revenue often used for internships and assistantships for students. The process is, at the same time, strengthening community and national resources by providing additional avenues of media production and distribution.

4. **Regional and National Centers:** Certain institutions, such as East Texas State College, have achieved a high level of integration with their community through establishment of regional media cooperatives. The principle on which these centers operate is simply one of pooled purchasing power and shared resources. It is a particularly effective technique where materials collections in large urban centers do not already exist. Where the scope of stored materials is narrowed to a single class

of item, then a national center is more appropriately established. In this latter approach the University of Colorado has become the national repository for audio tapes, Indiana University for National Educational Television kinescopes, and the University of Massachusetts did pioneer work as the coordinating center for overhead projectuals.

The newest trend in the establishment of regional and national centers is in the area of curriculum development. Long-range projects, especially those funded by the federal government and major nonprofit foundations, are now supporting research and development centers where the newest ideas and curriculum research can be translated beyond the syllabus stage and into actual demonstration practice. Without exception, at all such national centers, media are considered as an essential component of modern educational methodology.

IN SUMMARY

Evidence is accumulating that the methodological lag in college and university teaching is undergoing rapid change. It now appears that higher education will soon regain a true leadership role and will serve as the testing and proving ground for innovative teaching/learning practices. This will be accomplished partly by the external factors of (a) government financial support, (b) community, national and international involvements and (c) sheer pressure from the publics served. But it will also be accomplished partly from within, by (a) new assignment of roles within the professional ranks, (b) increasing sophistication in the use of technology and media and (c) experimentation in the systems approach to curriculum development and instructional design (41) (42).

Truly, there is an air of revolution on the campus, and while students are demonstrating a marked change in their attitude toward learning, there is another, quieter revolution—the change away from formalized lectures toward dynamic, media-integrated instructional systems. It is a sign of leadership regained.

REFERENCES

1. McKeachie, W. J., "Research on teaching at the college and university level," *Handbook of Research on Teaching.* Chicago: Rand McNally, 1963, p. 1218.
2. Cass, James, "Changes in American education in the next decade: some predictions," reprinted with permission from Matthew B. Miles, *Innovation in Education.* New York: Teachers College Press, 1964. © 1964 by Teachers College, Columbia University.
3. Pullias, Earl V., and Lockhart, Aileen, *Toward Excellence in College Teaching.* Dubuque, Iowa: Wm. C. Brown Co., 1963, p. 133.
4. Zacharias, Jerrold R., *et al., Innovation and Experiment in Education.* Panel on Educational Research and Development, President's Science Advisory Committee, March 1964, p. 79.
5. Eurich, Alvin C., "A twenty-first-century look at higher education," *Revolution in Teaching.* Bantam Books, 1964, reprinted from *Atlantic Monthly.*

6. Tharp, Charles Doren, *Learning and Instructional Resources Center.* Coral Gables, Fla.: Univ. of Miami, 1964, p. 21.

7. Diamond, Robert M., *The Use of Multi-Media Instructional Materials Within the Seminar.* Report 5, Office for the Study of Instruction, Univ. of Miami, July 1964, p. 11.

8. Briggs, Leslie J., "The teacher and programed instruction," *Audiovisual Instruction,* N.E.A., May 1964.

9. Mitchell, Boyd, "Evaluative criteria for college instructional materials centers," *Audiovisual Instruction,* N.E.A., September 1965.

10. Hoban, Charles F., "From theory to policy decision," *AV Communication Review,* Summer 1965.

11. Hannah, John A., *Report of the President 1960–61,* Michigan State Univ., Publication 56, No. 6, November 1961.

12. *Report of the President: University on the Move.* Univ. of Southern California, October 1964, p. 59.

13. Postlethwaite, S. N., Novak, J., and Murray, H., *An Integrated Experience Approach to Learning: with Emphasis on Independent Study.* Minneapolis, Minn.: Burgess Publishing Co., 1964, p. 114.

14. Swanson, Edwin A. (ed.), *New Media in Teaching the Business Subjects.* National Business Education Association, N.E.A., 1965, p. 206.

15. "Current and future use of new media in teacher education", *Audiovisual Instruction,* N.E.A., June–July 1965.

16. Bitzer, Donald L., Lyman, Elisabeth R., and Easley, John A., Jr., "The uses of PLATO, a computer controlled teaching system", *Audiovisual Instruction,* January 1966.

17. Lumsdaine, A. A., "Instruments and Media of Instruction", in *Handbook of Research on Teaching.* Chicago: Rand McNally, 1963, p. 583.

18. Brown, James W., and Norberg, Kenneth, *Administering Educational Media.* New York: McGraw-Hill, 1965, p. 355.

19. Brown, James W., "The 'systems' solution to college problems," *Educational Screen and Audio Visual Guide,* May 1966.

20. Brown, James W., and Thornton, James W., Jr., *New Media in Higher Education,* N.E.A., 1963, p. 182.

21. *The Sound of Learning at Oklahoma Christian College,* tape and workbook. Oklahoma City: Oklahoma Christian College, 1966.

22. Canfield, Albert A. *et al.,* *A Learner-Centered Instructional Systems Approach,* preprint of speech. National Society for Programmed Instruction Convention, April 1966.

23. Corrigan, Robert E., Kaufman, Roger A., *Why Systems Engineering,* Palo Alto, Calif.: Fearon Publishers, 1965, p. 71.

24. Kaufman, R. A., and Nunnelly, C. L., *Instructional System Approach to Training: Design and Implementation Model.* Douglas Aircraft, Report #LB 32497, September 1965.

25. "The Systems Approach," (complete issue) *Audiovisual Instruction,* May 1965.

26. National Science Foundation, *Science Course Improvement Projects,* National Science Foundation, July 1964, p. 77.

27. "Tapes Let Students Dial a Lesson," *College and University Business,* Vol. 40, No. 5, May 1966.

28. Stewart, Donald K., *The Cost Analysis of Dial-Access Information Retrieval Systems for Education.* Mimeographed, Univ. of Wisconsin, 1966.

29. Justin, J. Karl, *Lecture Hall and Learning Design: A Survey of Variables, Parameters, Criteria and Interrelationships for Audio-Visual Presentation Systems and Audience Reception,* preprint of speech (98–14). Society of Motion Picture and Television Engineers Convention, November 1965.

30. Trow, William H., *A Modular Audiovisual Instructional System,* preprint

of speech (98–87). Society of Motion Picture and Television Engineers Convention, November 1965.

31. Schramm, Wilbur, *The Research of Programed Instruction.* Dept. of H.E.W., Office of Education, OE-34034, 1964, p. 114.

32. Glaser, Robert (ed.), *Teaching Machines and Programed Learning II: Data and Directions.* Dept. of Audio Visual Instruction, N.E.A., 1965, p. 831.

33. Fleming, Malcolm L., *Influence of Three Teaching Machine Factors — Feedback to Programer, Participation by Learner, and Feedback to Learner — on the Production and Utilization of Science Films.* N.D.E.A., Title VII, Project 800, U.S.O.E., July 1963, p. 93.

34. Kersh, Bert Y., "Emergence of the Science of Instructional Engineering," *Programed Instruction,* Vol. IV, No. 8, May 1965.

35. Stack, Edward M., *The Language Laboratory and Modern Language Teaching,* Oxford Univ. Press, 1966.

36. Weisgerber, Robert A., "Instructional Experimentation and Methods Research Using Systems," *AVEAC Research Bulletin,* Audio Visual Ed. Assoc. of Calif., Vol. V, No. 1, 1965–66.

37. Smith, Karl U., and Smith, Margaret F., *Cybernetic Principles of Learning and Educational Design.* Holt, Rinehart and Winston, 1966, p. 529.

38. Loughary, John W., *Man-Machine Systems in Education,* Harper and Row, Publishers, 1966, p. 242.

39. Lyman, Elisabeth R., "A Descriptive List of PLATO Lesson Programs," *CSL Report R-186,* Coordinated Science Laboratory, Univ. of Illinois, 1965.

40. Pierce, J. R., *Symbols, Signals and Noise; The Nature and Process of Communication.* New York: Harper and Brothers, 1961, p. 305.

41. Briggs, Leslie J., Campeau, Peggie L., Gagné, Robert M., and May, Mark A., *Instructional Media: A Procedure for the Design of Multi-Media Instruction, A Critical Review of Research, and Suggestions for Future Research,* Center for Research and Evaluation in Applications of Technology in Education (CREATE), American Institutes for Research, Palo Alto, 1967, 176 pp.

42. Weisgerber, Robert A., "The Compleat Communicator," *Improving College and University Instruction,* Oregon State Univ. Press, Spring, 1967.

Chapter 7

What is the background and the underlying function of adult education?

Have adult education programs taken advantage of innovative instructional practices?

How can the various media make unique contributions and be used to special advantage for the instruction of adults?

What are the promising future developments which may make the education of adults increasingly convenient and meaningful?

ADULT CONTINUING EDUCATION
AND EDUCATIONAL MEDIA

LEE W. COCHRAN, Director, Audiovisual Center
University of Iowa

Adult education, in one form or another, has been in existence since the dawn of history. Mankind always has been willing to tell or show others how to do something. The information provided might have been conjecture, but it was provided willingly, because the act of instruction enhanced the ego of the informant. In Europe, for centuries, apprenticeship training flourished, with a young person binding himself in contract to an experienced person to learn a chosen trade. Some apprenticeships took many years before the individual was released from his contract to set up his own business or practice his chosen trade. There is little question that some of the basic visual teaching devices were used in this early apprentice training, including such things as models, charts, drawings and demonstrations.

Adult continuing education, as we know it today, was started about 1885 and developed rather rapidly just before the turn of the century. It has been estimated by persons involved in the early development of university extension work, that by 1890 there were over two hundred organizations carrying on some form of extension teaching in nearly every state of the union. In 1891 in Philadelphia, colleges and universities involved in extension instruction organized a national conference to discuss common problems. It is noted that not all of the so-called extension instructional programs were offered by colleges and universities, but also by institutes, learned societies, and others. Prior to college and university extension teaching programs, such organizations as the Lowell Institute in Boston, Cooper Union in New York and the Peabody Conservatory of Baltimore, conducted what might be termed adult education classes. Other early developments contributing to adult education were the lyceum bureaus, Chautauquas, literary societies, scientific groups, and various correspondence study schools.

Adult continuing education at present is decidedly non-captive. The motivation of the individual, whether it be to improve his economic situation, learn a new trade, or just to improve his background of knowledge about certain things, is the deciding factor. With the vast expansion in knowledge in the past twenty years, many adults are experiencing the truism: "learning is a continuing process from the cradle to the grave." The adult student is not controlled by a specific course of study and does not have to meet formal school requirements. He is seeking knowledge to improve his status in society, or to improve his job, or to satisfy his creative curiosity. Needs of the adult student are varied and are often subconscious needs rather than those that the individual can clearly define.

The objectives of instruction must meet these needs and interests of the adult. The courses must be concise, direct, and provide orderly, specific information that can be recognized by the individual student as pertinent to his objectives. In contrast to formal types of education where programs are planned to create a background leading to subsequent development of a topic, adult education courses invariably must be adjusted to the immediate interests, needs, and background understanding of the adult.

For clarity, adult education types of instruction are separated into the following:

Adult classes—credit: to provide opportunity for individuals to pursue a degree program (high school, undergraduate, or graduate).

Adult classes—non-credit: for persons seeking knowledge or to improve skills in a trade.

Short courses—non-credit: improving knowledge within a profession or trade.

In-plant instruction—non-credit: upgrading of employees, or retraining for new jobs in the industry.

Correspondence study—credit: to provide opportunity to continue a degree or certificate program.

Correspondence study—non-credit: opportunity to acquire knowledge in desired subjects.

Correspondence study—non-credit: offering training in a specific job, i.e., electronics, radio repair, television repair, etc.—often terminating with a certificate of completion.

On-the-Job Training—non-credit: can be either an apprentice type training in a specific job, or part class combined with experience on-the-job.

Job Corps Training—non-credit: created in the mid 1960s to train young adults, or school dropouts from poverty stricken areas in simple homemaking, customs, proper dress, and background of job procurement and in some instances, basic on-the-job training in different services.

Retraining—non-credit: retraining persons from jobs that have been eliminated by automation to do other types of work.

One of the major problems in group instruction of adults is the broad spectrum of individual interests. The reason for taking a given course may vary with each student. Thus the instruction must be quite flexible to meet individual needs. Most adult students, because of economic factors, must secure the desired information in the shortest possible time. They are willing to attend long periods of instruction that would be impossible in formal public school or college, but adults must at all times see the results they are obtaining.

With few exceptions, the credit continuing education courses are sponsored by the extension divisions of the larger colleges and universities. The National University Extension Association is an organization of approximately one hundred colleges and universities who offer a wide variety of opportunities to adults seeking knowledge. This organization, established in 1915, stated, "This then is the purpose of University Extension—to carry light and opportunity to every human being in all parts of the nation; this is the only adequate ideal of service for the University" Within the National University Extension Association there are now many different departments offering services to adults:

Audiovisual Communication—provides libraries of educational films and related instructional materials to educational groups and public and private schools. Also many institutions operate radio and television stations to extend learning to a larger and ever-growing audience.

Community Development—cooperates with individual communities in planning and developing needed changes to meet the rapid growth in many towns and cities.

Correspondence Study—offers a large variety of both credit and non-credit courses for individual instruction.

Conferences and Institutes—develops conferences, institutes, workshops, etc. This program serves both professional and service personnel by providing the latest information on changes in professions and developments in our ever-changing society.

Evening Colleges and Class Extension—offers credit and non-credit courses from colleges and universities to groups of persons interested in furthering their education. (Some states have established extension centers in larger cities, thus making university instruction available many miles from the campus.)

Arts and Humanities—provides guidance and assistance to cultural groups such as music, art, dramatic art and related groups in their own community.

WHAT SORT OF INSTRUCTION LENDS ITSELF TO ADULT CONTINUING EDUCATION?

Instruction for the adult must be direct, meaningful, and have a specific relationship to reality. Most adults do not want theory, but desire a practical, straightforward approach. Many adult centers are well equipped with laboratories, shops, language laboratories, and related instructional facilities. In most instances, adult instruction must be accelerated, making it imperative to use every type of media and related equipment. All media, including texts, workbooks, charts, maps, graphs, models, slides, filmstrips, transparencies with overlays, films, magnetic tapes, closed-circuit television, and broadcast television are adaptable to adult instruction.

Many of the more sophisticated adult training programs are systems of instruction. A systems approach implies use of varied media, such as a motion picture, 2″ x 2″ slides, and magnetic tape programed to carry the instructional message. This combination of media and method may be implemented by use of automated equipment to operate several projectors, each presenting a specialized segment of the lesson. In one such device, magnetic tape provides sound, gives verbal instructions to the students and with inaudible signals starts and stops a motion picture projector, a filmstrip projector and a slide projector. The instructional message is presented in pictures in motion on one screen and/or in still pictures on a second and third screen. To test learning and continuously involve the students, questions are projected to a screen. Time is allowed for each student to answer by pressing a selector button on the responder box at his station. Multiple choice or true-false questions are used. Before continuing to present more information, the system projects the correct answer on a screen thus avoiding erroneous assumptions which hinder a student's understanding the developing lesson.

Some industrial training programs have reduced training time as much as 50 per cent by using this systems approach in instruction. In industry, where time is money, large organizations have extensive training programs and find it financially advantageous to invest in a system of instruction due to the saving in training time. To develop a system of instruction is time consuming and therefore expensive. The investment in initiating such a program is paid off in increased efficiency in learning—a shorter term of instruction and greater retention of facts. If a large percentage of the students miss a given question, it is the fault of the system and must be corrected so the students can progress, with the right impression or answer, to the next phase of the instructional program.

Programed instruction, often in costly so-called teaching machines, was developed and used by the early 1960s. As the programs developed, it was found in many instances that the machine was unnecessary and the programed instruction could be printed in special types of books or manuals which questioned students as they progressed through the program and provided them immediately with correct answers. Industry once again was the leader in developing programed instruction for adults, with some companies spending large sums of money to develop programs. They realize a return on the investment of the money through a shorter in-training or retraining time.

Programed instruction is important in the adult education field because one individual can study a program by himself, whenever convenient, and proceed at the pace he desires. The program is a private tutor. This individual study can be pursued at home by using programed workbooks. In the near future, learning resource centers will house a type of study area called a carrel. This is a semi-enclosed booth containing projectors or viewers and audio playbacks for individual use in studying films, filmstrips, slides, tapes and records. Some of these carrels will have rear projection screens and ear phones. The student will dial his choice of study materials and pictures with sound will be transmitted to the screen in his booth from a central projection studio.

One of the problems of both systems of instruction and programed learning is finding educators with the ability of developing such materials. This development of step-by-step learning is different than most authors of texts or producers of projected media had ever experienced. It was necessary to establish courses in many colleges and universities to train people to write such programed texts and to develop systems of instruction. In addition, The Center for Programed Instruction of the Institute of Educational Technology, Columbia University, was organized to assist in providing information and research findings on methods of writing and planning such programs.

The specific type of instruction often depends on the age of the individuals receiving instruction. Young, vigorous people, who, for one reason or another, need to continue their education, will face the challenge with confidence. On the other hand, some middle-aged persons may underestimate their ability to learn or relearn and hesitate to start an educational or training program. Yet, many institutions find retired senior citizens enrolling in correspondence courses. Retirement has provided the time to study certain subjects denied them when they were active in business or industry.

ANALYSIS OF DIFFERENT MEDIA IN ADULT EDUCATION

Let us look at different types of media and some of their applications to adult education. The motion picture has been used in adult education for many years. One of the early producers of educational motion picture films was the U.S. Department of Agriculture. This government department started film production during World War I, and continues to produce films on a wide variety of agricultural subjects, including reports on new developments and research in many of the agricultural colleges. The films produced in the field of agriculture, over the past fifty years, provide an outstanding history of the developments resulting in increased yields in most crops.

The educational training film was used extensively during World War II to train a vast army of industrial workers to produce the machines of war. In 1940, a special service was established in the U.S. Office of Education to produce motion pictures and filmstrips to retrain people to work in the war industries. No doubt, one of the largest adult training programs ever attempted was in the Armed Services during World War II. All branches of the Armed Services used a wide variety of audiovisual materials, such as motion pictures, slides, models, mockups, charts, maps, electric circuit boards, and the larger overhead transparency projector. This projector was developed during the war to teach navigation, and refined after the war to its present state of development. Originally the overhead projector used a 7" x 7" transparency, which later was standardized in the 10" x 10" size presently in use.

Some of the educators loaned to the various services to direct the important training aid programs for the war effort were: Floyde Brooker, Industrial War Training Films; Charles Hoban, Jr., U.S. Army; Francis Noel, U.S. Navy; Walter Bell, U.S. Marine Corps. Hundreds of other audiovisual specialists from education also joined this program for the Armed Services and developed a vast program in audiovisual materials that made a major contribution toward training and morale building of our fighting men all over the world. These training programs authenticated the value of visual teaching materials to learning. It might be added that proper motivation was inherent in the situation. At the same time, the fact that successful training from the "training aids" was a matter of life and death placed an awesome responsibility on the originators and directors of these programs. Education owes a considerable debt to these innovators of the 1940s.

College and university film libraries, through the extension divisions, also made a major contribution to adult education over the past fifty years. Some of the early film libraries distributed 35mm films before the development of the 16mm film. Films were widely used by county agricultural agents and by many other groups seeking information. Many industrial groups or companies also contributed to the early development of the motion picture for instructional purposes. Such companies as General Electric produced many films in the general area of cotton and wool processing and food preparation to show the contribution of electricity to manufacturing.

The present day use of the motion picture in industrial organizations might better be measured by the fact that there are over 400 film companies who are engaged in the production of films for industry. Some of these are public relations films, others are specific training films, and still others are employer-employee relations films used to keep the entire labor force aware of company policy and new developments. Some large corporations produce films to report to stockholders since they can show new plants in operation or new products being developed.

The educational motion picture has gone through many metamorphic changes during its existence. One of the early size films, used extensively on the East Coast, and in parts of Canada, was the 28mm film. In most instances the projector was hand cranked, with light from an electric bulb operating from a battery or an electric circuit. During World War I, the educational film changed to the 35mm film so popular in theatres all over the world. In 1925 the 16mm silent film was perfected, giving great impetus to the use of films in all levels of education. About ten years later, sound was made available for 16mm film. Acceptable color film was released about the same time. To its ability of providing pictures in motion and color, sound was added, thus expanding the "learning senses" of the educational film. The educational film producers were satisfied they had arrived at a film size that was acceptable to all educational, industrial, and religious interests, only to see the 8mm film start to emerge and force itself into education about twenty-five years later, around 1960. The 8mm film, for the first time, is bringing about a change in production methods of educational film. Instead of the production of a film to fit a certain size reel, came the short single concept film to fit a single idea. This new film varies from two to four minutes in length, often silent. Sometimes sound is added in the form of a magnetic strip on the 8mm film. A controversy over the exact format of the film, delayed the development of a satisfactory optical sound track on 8mm films until 1965.

It is not anticipated that the 8mm film will replace the 16mm in education as was the case when the 16mm film and related equipment were perfected in 1925, and over a short period of time completely replaced the use of 35mm film in classrooms. It is thought that the 8mm and 16mm are complementary: the smaller film being used for small groups and individual instruction, and the 16mm film continuing to be used for larger groups. There can be little question that the 8mm width film has arrived in education and probably will make a much greater impact than all of the other size films combined.

Slides, one of the early forms of visualization, have been in use since before the start of the twentieth century. They were first available in the so-called U.S. standard size lantern slide, $3\frac{1}{4}$" x 4", later to be somewhat replaced by the 2" x 2" slide. Around 1935, with the development of color film, the larger glass $3\frac{1}{4}$" x 4" slides were practically eliminated. At present, adult education teachers have a wide variety of color slides to augment their instructional programs, often supplemented with magnetic tape for the audio part of the presentation. Slides are used extensively in conference, institute, and workshop types of meetings, to supplement the lecture. Many persons using the 2" x 2" slides prefer them to the light weight and smaller filmstrip, simply because they can alter the presentation by changing the organization of the slides.

The filmstrip, a short sequence of 20–100 pictures on 35mm film, was developed about 1925. The introduction of color about 1935 helped the filmstrip make a major contribution to all forms of education. The filmstrip was the answer to many adult educators' prayers, allowing them to carry a very light weight projector and a large number of filmstrips for use in varied instructional programs. The low cost filmstrip made available, for the first time, a widely accepted form of visualizing instruction. It was accepted immediately by industry and most levels of education. It allowed for the development of step-by-step visualization in such fields as automotive repair, methods of assembly, and maintenance of large equipment. Many manufacturers would start the production of a series of filmstrips on the repair and maintenance of new equipment prior to its being released for sale, thus insuring against faulty, expensive mistakes by the repairman. Several large commercial audiovisual companies were built on the financial backing they received for the preparation of filmstrip kits for the automotive industry.

Industrial training groups were also the first to recognize the great value in the sound filmstrip as an important phase of supplementing instruction. The first sound filmstrips were made available with the audio on a large transcription disc recording. Following World War II, with the development of the magnetic recorder, equipment for the audio on sound filmstrips was also made available on magnetic tape. Both record disc and magnetic tape for sound filmstrips are still in wide use. In some instances, the audio can be purchased on either record or tape, depending on the type of equipment available for reproducing the sound.

The 10" x 10" transparency projector, although the last of the projection types to be developed, has, no doubt, made the greatest strides in acceptance by all forms of education. It can be used in step-by-step development of an idea or a process. It permits the manipulation of objects on the stage of the projector and the use of overlays. For several years following the development of the overhead projector, it was not broadly accepted. With the development of complete sets of transparencies in many instructional fields, it provided the ready made instructional package so many teachers were seeking. The overhead transparency projector is quite versatile and can be used in many training situations where other forms of projection would be ineffective. Its light source provides adequate illumination for projection in a normal room light, making its use possible in the shop, in industrial training areas, and in many rooms where light control has not been provided. The simplicity of producing projectuals for the overhead projector makes it quite popular with the instructional staff, since they now can produce their own visuals, with a minimum of production equipment and time. Diazo foils used for producing one kind of transparency also allow for use of color as an emphasis or as a method to differentiate between objects in the presentation. For comparison of methods and other developmental lessons, the overhead projector provides an ideal teaching tool. Although the equipment is rather bulky to move, some of the later portable types of overhead projectors can be moved easily to wherever the instruction takes place.

One of the old forms of visualization, the feltboard, has been used in many types of adult education, but with the more sophisticated presentations in this medium being developed in industrial training. Prior to recent developments, the feltboard was one of the few ways step-by-step development could be shown or developmental phases changed as the lesson progressed. It was quite adaptable to showing such things as organizational charts, and other presentations where the instructor wished to show development, explaining each step, as he continued with the feltboard visualization.

Another manipulative type board is the "Hook 'n Loop" that came into use in the early 1960s. Its purpose is much the same as the feltboard in step-by-step development of an idea or a process. Its unique contribution is that it will hold heavy 3-dimensional objects, yet permit them to be moved as desired. It is of special use to persons who wish to plan a presentation using things as small parts to be assembled into a larger unit, or the tools needed in certain industrial jobs can be displayed and introduced one-by-one. The nylon cloth with the 'loop' is stretched over a board or metal background. The 'hook' cloth, also nylon, comes in strips of different widths, and can be cut and glued to the instruments or items to be used in the presentation. This type of presentation has wide application in varied educational presentations, but is of special benefit when used to hold heavy objects.

Audio devices are also widely used in adult continuing education. The record player has been found of great value in such subjects as language instruction, where the student can hear a foreign language in a repetitive situation. They have also made a contribution to many forms of art, such as music, literature, the dance, and for other types of recreational programs.

The magnetic tape recorder has, in a large part, replaced the record player because of its versatility in providing the playback feature of the record player, and in addition, a recording capability. This record-play-back feature provides a much wider range of utilization in such subjects as speech, language, foreign language, business education, and many other fields. The ability of the recorder to erase the tape for re-use makes it an economical instructional tool.

Many states have, through a college or university, or the State Department of Public Instruction, installed tapes-for-teaching libraries. Such libraries collect master tapes from such sources as the National Tape Repository, University of Colorado and the National Association of Educational Broadcasters, and provides a service of rerecording the tapes for all levels of education in their respective states or area. Such libraries have high speed tape duplicating equipment that can turn out many duplicate tapes in a short time, with a maximum of quality. Magnetic tapes in many subject areas are available in adult education. Some college and university correspondence study departments and correspondence study schools offering training in industrial subjects, often use taped programs as part of the course. Some schools have purchased small, inexpensive magnetic tape playbacks and distribute them to the correspondent student, along with the taped programs. Rerecording tape services are quite inexpensive, allowing an institution or individual instructor to build a large collection of tapes for use in his instruction, with a minimum investment.

The recent development of tape cartridges that can be easily inserted into a small magnetic tape recorder, will greatly expand the use of recorded lessons. Many students at the college or adult education level, have purchased tape recorders to use in classes, conferences, institutes or workshops to capture the total lecture or discussion on tape, for replay and study at a later time.

Radio, in its early stages of development, was thought to be the panacea for adult education programs. It could carry instruction to a vast audience, and expand the classroom to an entire region, state, or to the nation. In retrospect, radio had the horsepower, but seemed to be using the wrong kind of gas. The 'low power gas' was in the programing, often by educators with outstanding teaching records, but who had little knowledge of what an adult radio audience would accept. Programs were built by the best experts of the day, but when the audience was surveyed, few were listening. It should be said that educational radio did make its contribution to cultural programs in music and dramatic presentations but few of the so-called classrooms-of-the-air made an educational contribution to other than the well educated. It did not reach the market of the vast number of persons who needed the educational information, because of the lack of knowledge in programing for the 'average United States Citizen.'

Before leaving radio, it must be said that the overall impact of this medium has been outstanding, but not necessarily in the educational program. Radio changed the way of living of millions of Americans from 1920 to the advent of television, and many of the entertainment programs expanded the general cultural knowledge of a large percentage of the people. Some of the so-called commercial radio programs were well financed, making it possible to obtain the best talent available, and the cultural wealth contained in such programs over the years cannot be measured in terms of our present social advancement. Educational radio is not dead; it needs imagination and a new look at its programing to enable it to compete with other broadcast media.

Educational television, at its inception in 1953, was welcomed as the great educator. It not only had the sound of radio, but visual presentation as well. As many broadcast specialists working in radio said, "we will not make the same mistakes that were made in educational radio; we now know how to program this new medium, television." But once again, several years were wasted in finding out how to write for television and how to produce the programs, and often educational television had to do a complete job of training many of its staff, prior to going on the air. Educational television lost much of its potential adult audience through the release of poor programs in the early developmental stages, and never regained them when the programs were improved.

In the fifteen years since the first educational television station opened in Houston, Texas, great strides have been made in this medium. Colleges and universities have established many educational programs for the television writer, director, cameramen, sound technicians, and the electronics technician who will maintain and repair the equipment.

Many of the people who worked in the developmental stages of educational television thought that it could serve all levels of education: elementary, secondary, college and adult. Within a very short period of experimentation, it was found that one broadcast circuit would be limited in its service, if it focused its attention on only one level of education, and in most instances, the elementary and secondary education programs won out, leaving little time for the educational television station to devote to college or adult education. Some fine programs have been produced for the adult learner, but they are a very small percentage of the total effort being put into educational television.

Educational television's contribution to adult education will probably continue to be small, due to the high cost of maintenance and programming. Adult education may continue to eke out a few evening hours in the educational television schedule, but its general impact on society will probably be small. A National Educational TV Network would no doubt be of great value, but at present it is only in the experimental stage.

A major problem in the use of educational television, with the average person seeking adult continuing education, is that when he returns to his home in the evening, after a hard day's work, he seems to find the entertainment channels of much greater interest. It is hard for advanced mathematics or other academic courses to compete with Bob Hope, or many of the other high cost commercial color television programs.

While educational broadcast television has, as indicated, made little contribution to the adult learner, closed-circuit television has a great potential. Closed-circuit TV can adapt itself to almost any in-plant training program, and is also of great value in many adult programs operated by colleges and universities. It can provide a means of extending a class presentation to large groups, and give each student a very intimate view of what is being demonstrated. A company can produce materials at its home plant for its entire training operation, and by recording the programs on video tape, they can distribute the programs to every branch plant in the country, thus providing a uniformity of training, taught by the best of their instructional staff. Closed-circuit television can also be used in industry for on-the-job training. By installing small television screens at each training station, one supervisor, or a video tape recorder, can send step-by-step assembly instructions to a large group of persons in training, thus making them productive while learning the job.

Due to the high cost of adequate closed-circuit equipment, industry will no doubt take the leadership in its use, but other adult education agencies will probably make use of this valuable tool to disseminate instructional programs to larger and larger groups. The television projector permits larger sizes of groups in training or retraining programs. Industry is finding it cannot depend on other educational organizations to retrain their workers for new jobs brought about by automation. Closed-circuit television offers industry a tool that can greatly expand their training programs, and at the same time cut the cost by reducing the need for a large staff devoting full time to instruction.

The wide use of kinescopes in the early developmental stages of television and now the low cost video recorder can provide the means of greatly expanding the use of television programs. They can be used for one class, put on the shelf until needed again, or until such time as revision is needed, then the video tape can be demagnetized and used over again. The kinescope, although used very little at the present time for direct recording from television programs, does provide a means of rerecording from video tape, so programs can be used on any 16mm sound motion picture projector.

Who Selects the Media?

Educational media, like texts, workbooks and references, must be selected and integrated by the instructor, as a part of his course objectives. Media have been added to many courses as an afterthought, and often duplicate the information provided in printed form, thus losing its potential impact on the learner.

All materials for the adult course must be carefully previewed by the instructor. Whether the educational materials are to be used by the instructor in the group instruction process, or by individual students in learning carrels, the instructor must know the content. Since titles of films, filmstrips, slide sets, tapes, and other visual materials are often misleading, the instructor cannot depend on the catalog description in making his selection. Previewing is of special importance in planning courses for adults, who are quite critical of materials produced for children, even if they were educational dropouts at a young age and received a minimum of formal schooling.

Where team teaching is being carried on by several instructors, it is of great importance that the entire team know the complete content of all media being used, in order to evaluate its specific contribution to the course. Team teaching will continue to gain impetus in adult education because of the breakdown of a process into many specialties, making it mandatory that many different specialists contribute to an overall training program. No longer can the training director carry on a complete program. In mass industrial production today most persons need know only one small phase of the total process, but each must be well trained in his specialty.

AFTER FORMAL EDUCATION IS TERMINATED WHAT OTHER CHANNELS OF LEARNING ARE AVAILABLE?

It has been said that more knowledge has been acquired about our universe and the people in it during the last ten years than was known prior to that time. New discoveries are taking place at such a rapid rate that most people find it impossible to keep abreast of the new developments. As an example, as late as 1953, articles and editorials were being written about the impractical thinking of scientists who thought they could put man into orbit and travel to the moon. Some authors even went to the extent of saying that the scientists had no hope of accomplishment, but these were the dreams of technological men. It is interesting to note that five years later Russia put a man into orbit in outer space, causing somewhat of an educational revolution in the science instruction in the United States.

The unknown of today is the known fact of tomorrow, and to exist each man must realize that his education is never completed. The formal education in elementary, secondary schools and colleges provides only the background on which to build, to explore, to experiment and to continue to search for the unknown. The more education an individual has, the more he realizes there is no terminal point in education, only a terminal point in formal classroom instruction. The same fact is true for the person who is trained for work in a factory, or at a trade. A training director stated, in 1965, that the person coming into the labor market as of that year would probably be retrained three times or more during his productive lifetime. This is the real challenge to groups providing adult continuing education. They must be ready to meet this never ending need for the search of knowledge.

Man continues to learn every day of his life, unless he isolates himself from the world around him. He meets new people, observes phenomena all around him, reads newspapers, magazines and books, listens to radio and watches television. It is agreed there are some nonreaders, but the percentage is small, and they are not the lifestream of our society.

The Adult Learner is a unique individual
- Possessing a wide variety of
  interests
  abilities
  beliefs
  prejudices
- Emerging from a diversity of
  social
  economic
  religious
  educational
  vocational backgrounds.

Some adults are constantly striving for more knowledge; others think they have reached their pinnacle of life's objectives, and are willing to accept the status quo. A major problem is how to encourage a continuing learning attitude in those individuals who have accepted the existing level of information. Education is one of the few ways we can answer our social problems of unemployment and poverty of those who are not acceptable in industry.

Within the last twenty years, great strides have been made in mass communication. Over 90 per cent of the homes in the United States have television. This medium might be said to be the informer of the masses, reaching into homes of the very lowest income groups. A family may not have a bathtub, but it will often have a television set, making available to most people news and information, cultural programs, and exploration. Now with communication satellites, they can view events from all over the world. Such programs can be used immediately, or video taped and used at a later time, when the information may be of greater value to the understanding of an entire subject.

Another communication device coming into use for mass instruction is the tele-lecture and the electro-writer. The tele-lecture is a telephone amplifying system for two-way communication between a lecturer and a class. The students can ask questions of the speaker and receive the answers over the system. Persons lecturing over a tele-lecture system often send slides or transparencies in advance which can be used in the classroom and reference made by the speaker who may be a thousand miles or more away. The electro-writer system also sent over regular telephone lines, makes it possible for a person to write with a stylus on the surface of the electronic equipment and the image is transmitted over the telephone lines for hundreds or thousands of miles. At the receiving end the message is projected by a device much like an overhead projector onto a screen, making it possible to teach large groups a great distance from the source of the information. One of the early experiments with the electro-writer was in Iowa, where the State College of Iowa taught a course in modern mathematics to a group approximately 300 miles away from the campus in the northwest part of the state. With receivers in several different towns, the instruction was received by five hundred teachers and over two thousand parents who wanted background information in modern math. The electro-writer is an inexpensive method of transmitting pictures of written materials, figures, such as used in teaching modern mathematics, and related information.

The public school is also a source of many informal adult courses, as well as credit and noncredit courses. A survey by U.S. Office of Education in 1959 indicated that approximately 5000 public schools were involved in teaching adults in such subjects as Americanization and citizenship, literacy education, high school academic education (for dropouts), personal development and group relationships, family relationships, homemaking and consumer education, business education and trade courses.

TO WHAT EXTENT DOES THE EMPLOYER ASSIST
IN FURTHERING TRAINING AND/OR RETRAINING?

There is no denying the fact that education is big business, and getting larger every year. A statement recently made by an assistant commissioner, U.S. Department of State, indicated "One-third of the population in the United States is involved in some kind of educational endeavor."

There has been a great reversal in the attitude of some industrial organizations in the last few years regarding the training of their employees. The old idea that an individual had to be trained before he could accept a job is disappearing, and in its place in some industries comes a fresh new look at the entire responsibility for training and retraining of industrial workers. Many national and state organizations have started studies in manpower requirements which attempt to numerically set goals and types of occupational training apparently necessary for the national growth. Industry and business have found that to have adequate manpower, they must be a part of this huge task of education and training. There seems to be a strong trend by both industry and government to study human resource development and also how to best utilize the developed manpower.

In recent years the government has become one of the major educational systems in this country. When you add the Armed Forces training program to other training programs in varied departments and commissions, it shows a huge educational program in our government. All over the country the United States Office of Education has, in the past few years, given vocational and adult programs a great impetus, through funds appropriated for such purposes by the Congress. It is now realized that eight out of ten students now in high school will probably not continue in college, thus a vast program of vocational education must be planned. This accelerated program is also endeavoring to eliminate the training for jobs that no longer exist, and replace it with training programs for existing or emerging positions in industry.

In 1965, a number of research projects were started through funds allocated by the Division of Adult and Vocational Research, U.S. Office of Education, to try to find answers to many existing problems in vocational education. The research program is also trying to find what part educational media plays in the vocational training program. Another project is trying to find if teacher behavior can be modified through research dissemination, etc. Still other studies are being made on how to train teachers to recognize potential talent in students as well as recognizing the possible dropout. Recent studies have shown that the potential dropout can be recognized at about the seventh grade, but many problems regarding how to prevent the student from leaving school at an early age still exist.

There continues to be a major problem in getting all industries to accept training and retraining as a part of their responsibility. In 1965, the Division of Adult and Vocational Research estimated that only one out of five industries had adequate training programs, but that progress was being made to improve this low percentage.

Efforts are also being made toward finding the answers on how to help the 6 per cent to 8 per cent of the so-called hard core of the deprived. Most of these people cannot accept employment because of inexperience in most phases of life, including such things as how to catch a bus, how to secure the services of a doctor, and in many instances do not know how to deal with problems in their own environment. These people first need basic education for social literacy, before they can be trained for a job whether it be in services or in industry. They feel defeated and isolated.

There is a movement at the present time to encourage organizations, schools, producers of media, etc., to develop instructional materials for use with the social illiterate. The materials must be of a nature to be usable by the average citizen, not necessarily the experienced teacher, since many of the programs developed will be in a community educational project, with many citizens contributing their time and talents. Although the great need at present is for training people from grades 0 to 5, the educational media must be for adults, since illiterate adults will immediately reject anything made for children.

It needs to be pointed out that it is not only the illiterate who must be trained and retrained. Many of the high school graduates are not prepared to enter the labor market, because their educational program was pointed toward continuing into college. If their education is terminated at the twelfth grade, the high school students often have little knowledge that will help them get a job and hold it. The vastly expanding program of area vocational schools, in many parts of the country, will be of great help to the student who will not pursue a college program. As mentioned previously, the person receiving training for a specific job today may have to be retrained several times during his lifetime, or before he reaches retirement.

In summary, it is being recognized that the problem of adult continuing education in this country is a major problem, if our society is to flourish and grow in stature. The federal government, through its many training and retraining programs, is facing the problem. Many states already have fine programs for adult continuing education, and yet others seem not to recognize the need for immediate action. Many communities already have taken steps to assist in this ever-growing problem. Industry and business, in many instances, are aware of the need for taking a hard look at the problem and their responsibility in developing training and retraining programs.

There is little question that the United States was slow to recognize this great need for educating all people. Currently, a major governmental effort is developing a variety of programs, such as the Job Corps, vocational education, and others, that should benefit citizens all over this country. One such program, the Higher Education Act of 1965, and especially Title I of this Act, gives considerable assistance in financing "Community Service and Continuing Education Programs." The planning now taking place in the various states indicates some exciting new programs will be developed that should have powerful effect on upgrading the entire Continuing Adult Education Program.

Part Three

PROGRAM PERSPECTIVES
AND MEDIA CONSIDERATIONS

Chapter 8

What are 'arts' programs and how have they evolved in the schools?

What complexities have been attendant in the introduction of media into the arts curricula?

What relationships between teaching objectives and specific media seem most feasible for adoption in arts instruction?

What new kinds of media experimentation seem especially promising for development by educators in the arts?

INSTRUCTIONAL PROCESS AND MEDIA INTEGRATION IN THE CREATIVE ARTS

WARREN I. RASMUSSEN, Associate Professor of Music
San Francisco State College

WHAT ARE THE CREATIVE ARTS?

The term creative arts is a relatively new one in education. As yet, it has attained neither established usage nor precise definition. Unlike the term liberal arts, it has no foundation in *trivium* or *quadrivium* to lend it historical prestige and academic distinction. Further, it is a coined term which is composed of two words, neither of which has ever been adequately defined. The essence of creativity remains a mystery, and the standard dictionary definition of art runs the gamut from a skill to a trick or wile.

Though it is difficult to find a concise definition of creative arts, there is general agreement as to the type of subject areas to which the term applies. Broadly interpreted, the creative arts include study and performance in any of the fine, applied, or decorative arts. The very existence of the term creative arts testifies to an attempt to end, at least for educational purposes, the dichotomy which has existed between the fine arts on the one hand, and the applied or technological ones on the other. To admit that a real distinction still does, in fact, exist between the esoteric purpose and value of an article of functional use as opposed to a painting or a symphony is not to say that the subject areas cannot be considered together—particularly in their educational setting.

Subject areas deserving consideration in any discussion of the arts would include such specifics as art, design, architecture, industrial arts, music, theater, dance, visual arts, writing, and crafts. The mere listing suggests the impossibility of doing justice to all within the confines of a single chapter. Music, art, and industrial arts have been selected for primary consideration here because they are most commonly found in the public school curriculum. The term arts, as used in the remainder of the chapter, should be understood to refer generally to these three areas. The other arts, no less important, but certainly less common as public school curricular subjects, will be considered peripherally.

ARTS IN THE CURRICULUM.

Ever since their gradual inclusion in the public school curriculum at the end of the nineteenth century, the exact position and prestige of the arts has been unclear. Mid-nineteenth century experimentation with arts instruction in the schools was based on its utilitarian rather than its aesthetic values. Music instruction grew out of Lowell Mason's desire to have the children of Boston better prepared to sightsing their Sunday School songs. Art, in the form of drawing, gained acceptance on the basis of its importance for later technical training in an increasingly industrialized society. It was also considered a good way to use up bits of time during the school day which, it was felt, might otherwise be completely wasted.[1] Industrial arts entered the curriculum as manual training, and was designed to provide vocational training for the many students who did not go to college. The term manual arts was not adopted until the early years of the present century. It, and the even later term industrial arts, indicated an attempt to stress the creative and imaginative aspects of a curriculum designed for general students rather than one devoted exclusively to vocational goals.[2]

In keeping with the educational philosophies of the times, and also because of its novelty as an untried curriculum, arts instruction began with extremely formalistic methodology. Copybook accuracy in the sight-singing of a melody or the reproduction of a drawing seemed to be the major goals of instruction. John Dewey, one of the early influential

[1] Logan, Frederick M. *Growth of Art in American Schools*. New York: Harper Brothers, 1955, pp. 21–22.

[2] Roberts, Roy W. *Vocational and Practical Arts Education*. 2nd ed. New York: Harper and Row, 1965, pp. 75, 77.

philosophers in creative arts education, felt that the arts had more to offer children than dry formalism and copybook routine. His interest in the arts permeated his work at Chicago University and later at Columbia Teachers College.[3] In *Art as Experience*,[4] which appeared in 1934, Dewey called for a curriculum in the arts which was both experience-centered and child-centered. The impact of his thinking gave impetus to a movement in arts education which put greater stress on imagination, creativity, and aesthetic values.

Dewey characterized art as "a quality of doing and what is done."[5] This definition provides one of the common threads running throughout the fabric of arts instruction. Though specific subject matter, methodology, and goals may vary, all the creative arts have in common some skill or technique to be learned, and a product which is the result of its application. The painter learns the techniques of brush and perspective and paints a picture. The musician discovers methods of organizing and manipulating sounds and composes or performs. The industrial arts student manipulates tools and materials to create objects of function and beauty.

A somewhat more elusive bond uniting the creative arts is their common concern with attitude building as an essential part of the learning and creating process. While no subject area desires a negative attitude on the part of its students, the creative arts are perhaps more concerned than other areas with the necessity for building positive attitudes, not only as an adjunct to effective learning, but as an integral part of that learning.

There is a third way in which creative arts instruction is not only consistent within itself, but is also significantly different from many other curricular areas. This is in the desire to stimulate what has been termed divergent rather than convergent thinking.[6] The emphasis on divergent thinking is perhaps the essence of, or at least the prerequisite for, creativity itself. The instructor who is concerned with teaching the parts of speech or the binomial theorem is rightly stressing convergent thinking. Arts instructors are sometimes concerned with the same type of thinking, as, for example, when the music teacher asks that students know the year of Beethoven's death. On the other hand, to paint a picture or to play a melody is not a matter of finding *the* correct way. It is, rather, one of finding *a* way which is creative and expressive. This aspect of arts instruction has consistently caused problems in group instruction since the methodology involved lends itself most naturally to develop-

[3] Logan, *op. cit.* p. 112.
[4] Dewey, John. *Art as Experience.* New York: Minton, Balch and Company, 1934.
[5] *Ibid.* p. 214.
[6] Lowenfeld, Viktor and Brittain, W. Lambert. *Creative and Mental Growth.* 4th ed. New York: The Macmillan Company, 1947, p. 10.

ment of convergent rather than divergent thinking. The same type of problem presents itself in utilizing media. If imitative response and convergent thinking are not the desired result of instruction, media designed for such goals may be inappropriate.

The validity of creative arts instruction as a part of the school curriculum seems, today, beyond dispute. The exact nature of that curriculum, especially in the arts, is not so clear. Instructional process and media integration in any area are closely bound up with an articulated curricular structure. It is in precisely this area that the creative arts need further examination.

CURRICULAR GOALS IN THE CREATIVE ARTS.

To attempt to write about even three of the creative arts as one area, unified in goals and techniques, is to run the danger of oversimplification. An even greater difficulty in explaining the goals of arts instruction may lie in communicating a concept of the essential nature of the arts. The late "Fats" Waller, on being asked what jazz was, replied, "If you don't know by now, don't mess with it!"[7] While this anecdote is usually told for its humor, it illustrates a problem which has increasingly plagued the cause of instruction in the arts. Instead of finding better means of communicating the goals of arts instruction to the public, teachers in the creative arts sometimes retreat to a defensive position. They seem to imply that these goals should not have to be explained to anyone who is sensitive to artistic values.

Such an ivory-towered attitude on the part of arts educators is increasingly inappropriate for present-day curricular conditions. The arts today are crowded in a school curriculum which seems to be outgrowing the space-time possibilities of the school day. Music and art in particular are feeling the effects of an emphasis, possibly an over-emphasis, upon college preparatory subjects—especially languages, science, and mathematics. This curricular pressure, and the increasing necessity for each subject area to substantiate its right to student time, is having a profound effect upon the arts in several ways. Perhaps the most obvious is in what might be called an agonizing reappraisal of the curricular structure of the arts.

Though histories of instruction in the arts indicate that there has been development and improvement in curriculum and methodology, the arts remain poorly organized by comparison with such curricular areas as science and mathematics.[8] The lack of curricular development and, more particularly, the organizational problems of the arts have been

---

7 Stearns, Marshall W. *The Story of Jazz.* New York: Mentor, 1958, p. 11.

8 Monroe, Thomas and Reed, Herbert. *The Creative Arts in American Education.* Cambridge, Massachusetts: Harvard University Press, 1960, p. 5.

increasingly recognized by professional educators and groups within individual arts areas. The "Yale Seminar Report,"[9] devoted to music education, has called for development of a sequential, articulated curriculum in music. A recent research monograph devoted to art instruction has made the same recommendation for that subject.[10] K. E. Dawson, writing on industrial arts, has commented upon the dormant nature of instruction at levels which have not had adequate and far-seeing curriculum development,[11] and John Feirer has suggested the need for a national curriculum for industrial arts.[12]

ARTS IN THE ELEMENTARY SCHOOL.

The self-contained classroom concept of elementary education has undoubtedly contributed to the lack of definition of goals in the creative arts. In the elementary classroom, one teacher is expected to provide instruction in all areas of the curriculum. For the creative arts, this implies that not only verbal information, but also guidance in skills, techniques, and understanding must be provided by teachers who have varying degrees of arts competence. The degree to which the self-contained classroom has been satisfactory in highly verbal areas has been open to some question. In the area of the creative arts, there has never been any real doubt that the average elementary teacher is likely not equipped to provide adequate instruction in all three of the subjects commonly taught.

The frustration of the professional arts educator with the elementary situation may be illustrated by the case of music, which has, in the past, attempted to provide some definite curricular goals for the elementary grades. A study reported that what was actually being accomplished musically in elementary schools fell so far short of the announced goals that music educators needed to become more realistic about what could and would be accomplished in the self-contained classroom.[13]

The philosophy of the child-centered curriculum, which developed during the early years of the present century, rightly emphasized an arts curriculum which encouraged creativity and self-expression. The severe lack of professionally trained arts personnel for the general elementary student has, however, tended to create a situation where this creativity and self-expression are attempted on the basis of a minimal

9 "Music in our schools," prepared by Claude V. Palisca. U. S. Department of Health, Education and Welfare. Bulletin 1964–28.
10 Stoops, Jack. "Music and art in the public schools," Research Monograph 1963–M3, NEA, reported in Art Education, XVI:9 (December, 1963), pp. 15–21.
11 Dawson, Kenneth E. "K–6 industrial arts," Art Education, XVI:1 (January, 1963), p. 24.
12 Feirer, John L. "More on a national curriculum for industrial arts," Industrial Arts and Vocational Education, 52:8 (October, 1963), p. 15
13 Encyclopedia of Educational Research. Chester W. Harris, ed., 3rd ed. New York: The Macmillan Company, 1960, p. 910.

understanding of technique and skill. The feeling is growing among arts educators that these early years of instruction are too important, and the potential accomplishments too significant, to force elementary teachers who feel unprepared in one or more of the arts areas to provide instruction which satisfies neither themselves nor the goals of arts instruction.

While individual teachers throughout the years have done some exemplary work in elementary arts instruction, no one suggests that this type of work is to be found consistently. With the almost uniform tendency to build all arts instruction around the social studies program in the elementary schools, it has seemed impossible to build an articulated, solid arts curriculum.

Districts which provide special consultant help in the arts are aware of the problems of personnel and curriculum, but these stopgap measures are effective only to the extent that the specialists are superior teachers whose visits are regular and frequent. This has not been a common pattern, and with the growing exigencies of finance it seems to be becoming even less common. Even where such help is provided, however, arts programs tend to be a highly individualistic reflection of the specialist or classroom teacher, rather than an effective implementation of some standard curricular goals arrived at by philosophers and teachers in the specialized areas.[14]

To summarize, elementary instruction in the arts is most often carried on by the classroom teacher, and geared to implement and enrich the social studies program. It emphasizes self-expression through the various art forms with a minimal amount of technique imparted or required. There is a growing belief among arts educators that the true aims of creativity and self-expression can be more adequately met by increasing emphasis upon basic understanding and technique. They also feel that this new emphasis can be established only by better curricular planning and increased utilization of trained arts personnel.

ARTS IN THE JUNIOR HIGH SCHOOL.

It is at the junior high school level that most students contact, on a regular classroom basis, personnel who are professionally trained in the arts. Both because of student maturation and the availability of professional instruction, the arts at this level begin to place more emphasis on expression through skill and understanding. At the same time, however, experiences in the arts remain largely exploratory. This is true because the philosophy of the total junior high curriculum, outside the traditional academic subjects, is one of exploration. It is also the result

14 Mills, Fred V. "Modern approaches to the understanding of art," *Arts and Activities*, 58:4 (December, 1965), p. 28.

of necessity, for the students in a seventh grade art or music class come with widely divergent backgrounds and understanding in arts areas. Music provides performance groups for those interested in singing or playing instruments, as well as general music experience for the non-performer. Art and industrial arts offerings vary according to the size and financial structure of the school. The basic art course and the general shop provide the usual minimal offerings.

ARTS IN SECONDARY AND HIGHER EDUCATION.

At the high school and college level, the arts must usually be chosen as a major or as elective subjects. High school curricula in the arts tend to include offerings for those who intend to continue in the arts and those who are interested in them only as a part of general education. Curricular goals are accordingly performance or appreciation oriented. With the exception of larger and more progressive districts, high school offerings in the arts have tended to remain the traditional ones. Music includes instrumental and vocal performance groups and sometimes academic classes in the history, theory, and appreciation of music. Art classes may be diversified and include such special areas as ceramics, sculpture, and general appreciation. As evidenced by the recent introduction of pre-technical interdisciplinary instructional patterns, industrial arts appears to be breaking away from the traditional orientation of wood, metal, and drafting shops.[15]

The colleges have a threefold function in the arts. First, they continue, or sometimes begin, the general education or appreciation approach for the benefit of the general student who wishes merely to know something about the arts. Secondly, they provide basic offerings which will bring the potential professional to a level at which he can begin arts instruction of collegiate calibre. Thirdly, they provide professional preparation for those who will make the arts their vocation.

THE CURRICULUM OF THE ARTS.

There is today no standard curriculum, or even curricular pattern, in any area of arts instruction which begins with the elementary grades and continues through higher education. The varied quality and quantity of instruction which is available in the arts throughout the public school years is undoubtedly one reason for the lack of development of such standard curricula. Another important factor, however, may be the apparent reluctance evidenced by many teachers in the arts to engage

---

[15] Feirer, John L. "Are we building the right kind of shops?" *Industrial Arts and Vocational Education*, 52:3 (March, 1963), p. 31.

in careful research related to goals and methodology, not to mention the special aspects of learning psychology in the arts.[16] It is true that there is an increasing amount of descriptive research being reported, but solid, basic research is still lacking.[17]

This research problem may be traced, in part, to an honest belief that the essential qualities of the arts, and therefore of arts instruction, defy analysis and measurement. It may also, however, be based on an overly romantic notion of what arts instruction should be, especially for those who are involved with rudimentary phases of instruction in the various art forms. It must also be admitted that the teacher giving full time and energy to daily instruction seldom has additional hours to give to long-term research projects for improving instruction.

Regardless of the cause, there is little doubt that the lack of clear curricular goals, methodology, and means of evaluation in the arts not only impedes effective education but also makes it more difficult to justify the importance of the arts in the curriculum. Increasingly, arts educators are seeking for better definition and articulation of instruction. This search is also, in some measure, a reflection of the increasing impact of new thinking in instructional process and the developments of instructional technology. These developments have stimulated arts educators in their search for more specific data on precisely what should be taught and when that teaching is best done. Technology has obvious potential for improving the quality of instruction, and offers some partial solutions to the problems posed by inadequate professional staffing for instruction in the arts. It is also possible that recent developments in educational hardware will make it possible to carry out useful research in arts instruction which has heretofore been impossible.

TRADITIONAL MEDIA IN THE ARTS.

Teachers of music, art, and industrial arts are probably in the forefront of those who admit that the arts have not, as yet, found ways of taking full advantage of available instructional media. It is, therefore, of interest to recall that the arts could hardly have entered the curriculum at all without media utilization. Music instruction began by using sol-fa ladders, player pianos and the victrola. Art and industrial arts made use of pictures, models, and lantern slides. From that time on, however, the arts seem to have adopted readily only those instructional aids which improved upon techniques already in use. Music has come to use the stereophonic phonograph and the tape recorder. Art and industrial arts are making use of improved projectors and more complex models, but

---

16 *Encyclopedia of Educational Research*, op. cit., p. 77.
17 Eisner, Elliot W. "A role for research in the education of the teacher of art," *Art Education*, 15:9 (December, 1962), p. 8.

they are doing essentially the same things with them that they did with the first lantern slides and models. All areas have made some use of motion pictures and film strips. Nevertheless, it seems fair to suggest that even these traditional media are not used as widely or effectively as they might be.

Some of the reasons for this lack of utilization are fairly clear, though not always, perhaps, completely valid or defensible.

(1) Many teachers in the arts tend to have what they, at least, regard as a pro-personal, antimechanical approach to instruction. The music teacher used the victrola with considerable reluctance at first as only a poor substitute for attendance at a real concert. The art teacher would usually prefer a trip to a museum to showing the same pictures by means of a projector. It may be that, from the very beginning of arts instruction, teaching aids were viewed by arts teachers as nothing more than poor substitutes, to be used only when the real thing was not available. And even when they were used, they were often regarded as interposing something mechanical and undesirable between the student and the art form.

(2) Some teachers feel not only an innate bias against what they term mechanical, but also a frustrating inability to cope with the manipulation of equipment. The music teacher is often accused of a lack of sympathy for those who do not comprehend the mysteries of the tonic sol-fa system. The mechanically adept should have some understanding for the music teacher who finds the phonograph recalcitrant, or the art instructor whose knowledge of the slide projector does not extend to easy replacement of a burned-out lamp.

(3) It is sometimes difficult for arts teachers to know just when a given instructional aid will be wanted. The curricular haziness which has been alluded to — and haziness is not used in an entirely pejorative sense — makes it difficult to plan an art or music course as one might be able to structure lessons in English or mathematics.

Compounding this problem, the teacher who wishes to make use of media must too often go to some relatively distant central location to search for materials and place a request for them. The availability of given materials is not always certain, and their prompt arrival at the desired time seems too often a matter of some question.

(4) The quality of instructional aids for the arts has too often been poor. The scratchy phonograph record, cracked or blurred slides, and the vintage film are still too common in the schools. The importance of attitude building as an essential part of the educational process in the arts requires that instructional aids be of the highest quality. It is possible that poor reproductions of pictures and music may do more harm than good in the formation of positive attitudes.

(5) Another factor which has undoubtedly had considerable influence upon the use of instructional media in arts curricula is the fact that any product-oriented process is, by definition, intimately connected with a primary medium—that which comprises the art form itself. Music deals with instruments and tones. Art explores an ever increasing variety of media such as paints, clay, woods, materials, and metals. The industrial arts deal with tools and materials. It may be that attempting to separate media into two categories—teaching media and product media—is, in effect, splitting hairs. Yet, it seems possible that the arts instructor who is already concerned with the medium of the art form is less sympathetic than he might be to media which are only 'about' the art.

CURRENT MEDIA UTILIZATION.

Despite the problems which have been suggested, media have, of course, found considerable use in arts instruction, and that use is inevitably increasing. It is not yet possible, however, to provide anything approaching a complete résumé of instructional and media experimentation in the arts. First, such experimentation appears to be slow in coming. The reluctance of arts educators to engage in research has been cited. Secondly, there is no doubt that much experimentation which has taken place has not yet been reported in professional journals.

It is unfortunate that, as yet, there exists no single authoritative source for media in the arts curriculum.[18] The *Educational Media Index*, though admittedly incomplete, provides what is probably the most extensive listing of available media for a wide variety of subject areas, including the arts. Media specialists interested in assisting the arts educator should be aware of some of the following types of sources for media in the creative arts. The list is intended to be suggestive rather than complete or comprehensive.

(1) Advertisments and articles in the several professional journals. Among them would be the following:

> *Music Educators Journal*
> *Journal of Research in Music Education*
> *Art Education*
> *Research in Art Education*
> *Arts and Activities*
> *School Arts*
> *Industrial Arts and Vocational Education*

(2) Sources for general media:

> Sources of Information on Educational Media. OE 34024. Washington: US Department of Health, Education and Welfare, 1963.

---

[18] Lanier, Vincent, "Instructional media: Sources of media," *Arts and Activities*, 58:2 (October, 1965), p. 35.

Educational Media Index. New York: McGraw-Hill, 1964.
Index to 16mm Educational Films. McGraw-Hill, 1967.
Indiana University Film and Educational Television Guide. Bloomington, Indiana 47401.
Society for Visual Education. 1345 Diversey Parkway, Chicago, Illinois 60614.
"Appendix: Source Lists," in Kinder, James S. *Using Audio-Visual Materials in Education.* New York: American Book Company, pp. 188–195.

(3) Specialized catalogues and source lists for creative arts areas:
Film Guide for Music Educators. Donald J. Shetler, ed. Washington: Music Educators National Conference, 1961.
Barnard, D. P., "Sources of Audio-Visual Materials for Industrial Education," *Industrial Arts and Vocational Education.* 54:52 (September, 1965).
Burdette, Walter E. "Instructional Aids in Industrial Education." Arizona State University.
Films on Art. Compiled by Alfred W. Humphreys. Washington: National Art Education Association.

(4) Commercial sources: Many industries and corporations have an educational division which provides, free of charge or at nominal cost, teaching aids related to their products. The Ford Motor Company, which offers filmstrip and workbook combinations for auto mechanics, and the Conn Instrument Company, offering a wide variety of teaching aids in music, are only two examples of such sources. Such major art gallerys as the National Gallery of Art in Washington, D.C., also have extension divisions which provide such aids as flat pictures, slides, and filmstrips.

The utilization of newer media in creative arts instruction is limited only by the suitability of given media for a particular task, and the ingenuity of teachers and media specialists in devising new techniques for utilization. The problem of suitability was stressed by William Allen in a recent national conference on media in the arts. In emphasizing the importance of selecting appropriate media, he charted the effectiveness of various media approaches to the many curricular objectives of the arts.[19] (See Table I.)

The absence of standard national curricula in the creative arts has made it impossible for commercial media sources to develop anything approaching a media curriculum which could parallel it. Accordingly, individually devised and prepared media remain a necessity by virtue of both cost factors and sheer availability. A recent government publica-

[19] Allen, William H. "Instructional media research and the art educator," *Transcript of Selected Portions of the Symposium on the Uses of Newer Media in Art Education Project.* Washington: National Education Association, 1965, p. 24.

Table I. Instructional Media Stimulus Relationships to Learning Objectives.

Learning Objectives / Instructional Media Type	Learning Factual Information	Learning Visual Identifications	Learning Principles, Concepts and Rules	Learning Procedures	Performing Skilled Perceptual Motor Acts	Developing Desirable Attitudes, Opinions & Motivations
Still Pictures	Medium	HIGH	Medium	Medium	low	low
Motion Pictures	Medium	HIGH	HIGH	HIGH	Medium	Medium
Television	Medium	Medium	HIGH	Medium	low	Medium
3-D Objects	low	HIGH	low	low	low	low
Audio Recordings	Medium	low	low	Medium	low	Medium
Programed Instruction	Medium	Medium	Medium	HIGH	low	Medium
Demonstration	low	Medium	low	HIGH	Medium	Medium
Printed Textbooks	Medium	low	Medium	Medium	low	Medium
Oral Presentation	Medium	low	Medium	Medium	low	Medium

tion has reported on the extensive development of teaching aids by one school district.[20]

Allen has recommended five steps toward effective application of any instructional medium to teaching in the arts.

(1) State the exact behavior to be expected of the learner.

(2) Identify the type of learning objective being met by the instruction.

(3) Write down the particular "instructional" event that will occur.

(4) Determine availability of the instructional media.

(5) Arrange for preparation of unavailable instructional media.[21]

The steps may seem unduly detailed and, indeed, may not always be followed completely. Nevertheless, the subjective nature of arts and arts in-

[20] "Improving the learning environment," U. S. Department of Health, Education and Welfare, Circular 718, OE 34031. 1963.

[21] Allen, William H., *op. cit.*, p. 20.

struction would appear to make it desirable to have as objective an approach as possible in planning for good teaching.

REPORTS ON MEDIA UTILIZATION.

Though catalogues and advertisements indicate that there is an increasing supply of commercially prepared media for arts instruction, the potential for media utilization cannot be fully realized without extensive research and experimentation by arts teachers in the classroom. Reports of such experimentation are sketchy and incomplete. Some observations may, however, be made on recent projects involving media utilization.

Overhead projector.

The overhead projector is finding significantly increased use throughout the area of the arts. One reason for this, in addition to the obvious advantages of relative classroom illumination and teacher-student eye contact, is the increasing availability of commercially prepared transparencies, and the potential of effective schoolmade transparencies using such processes as Thermofax. Prepared transparencies are available in the areas of music reading, art, and industrial arts.[22] Teachers have reported utilization of overhead projection techniques in such specific lessons as drafting instruction,[23] creative drawing directly on the acetate sheets,[24] and teaching general music classes to play the recorder.[25] It appears almost axiomatic that any teacher demonstration done at the chalkboard can be more effectively done with the overhead projector. Use of such materials as overlays, carbon-film sheets, and colored transparencies offers possibilities for variety and interest in arts classes.

Programed learning.

Of all the newer instructional media, programed learning techniques and materials have had perhaps the least experimentation in the field of arts instruction. *Programs '63* listed three programs in music notation and fundamentals, but none in the general area of art or industrial arts.[26] A more recent publication lists eight programs in various aspects of music instruction which are commercially available.[27] Reports have been made

[22] "Shop Talk," *Arts and Activities*, 57:1 (February, 1965), p. 48.
[23] Warner, M. E. "Teaching drafting with transparencies," *Industrial Arts and Vocational Education*, 53:4 (April, 1964), p. 29.
[24] Metzke, Fred W., Jr. "Project inspiration big as life," *Arts and Activities*, 58:2 (October, 1965), p. 36.
[25] Debski, Merrill. "A new 'musical' instrument: The overhead projector," *Music Educators Journal*, 52:3 (January, 1966), p. 122.
[26] "Programs '63. "A guide to programed instructional materials," Lincoln F. Hanson, ed. U.S. Department of Health, Education and Welfare. OE 34015–63, 1964, No. 3.
[27] Dallin, Leon, "A survey of programed music teaching materials," *Music Educators Journal*, 52:4 (February–March, 1966), p. 198.

on experimentation with programed materials in teaching manipulative skills,[28, 29] the preparation of programed units for industrial subjects,[30] and a systems approach to instruction in music listening.[31]

At this time, most of the arts literature on programing remains in the areas of theory and philosophy. The potential of such instruction in music,[32] visual arts,[33] and industrial arts[34] has been explored, but practical applications are still not numerous.

Educational television.

A 1965 report indicated that there were 102 educational television stations in operation across the country.[35] And this figure does not include the many public school and college closed-circuit stations. It is obvious that educational television is well out of its infancy but still lacks adequate money and personnel to do its job most effectively. Experimentation has been reported in the closed-circuit television teaching of industrial arts classes,[36,37] art classes,[38] general music classes,[39] and such specialized music areas as the teaching of violin and cello.[40]

Recorded television lesson series are available in elementary and secondary music and art as well as college level fine arts.[41] The National Center for School and College TV offers, for example, four courses on music—two elementary, one secondary and one in-service.[42]

The expense involved in educational television has encouraged the formation of state and even regional educational television areas. Such a regional plan is exemplified by the Great Plains Regional Instructional Library, with headquarters at the University of Nebraska. A recent item

[28] Hofer, Armand G. "Teaching manipulative operations with programed materials," *Industrial Arts and Vocational Education*, 53:8 (October, 1964), p. 49.

[29] Shemick, John M. "Teaching a skill by machine," *Industrial Arts and Vocational Education*, 54:8 (October, 1965), p. 30.

[30] Drozdoff, Gene. "A plea for teacher–prepared programed units for industrial subjects," *Industrial Arts and Vocational Education*, 53:8 (October, 1964), p. 43.

[31] Rasmussen, Warren I. and Weisgerber, Robert A., "Eighty ears a teacher," *Music Educators Journal*, 52:2 (November–December, 1965), p. 79.

[32] Goldiamond, Israel, and Pliskoff, Stanley, "Music education and the rationale underlying programed instruction," *Music Educators Journal*, 51:4 (February–March, 1965), p. 43.

[33] Quirke, Lillian M., "There is a place for programmed instruction in the teaching of the visual arts," *School Arts*, 63:7 (March, 1964), p. 31.

[34] Feirer, John, "Programed learning in our instructional tool kit," *Industrial Arts and Vocational Education*, 53:8 (October, 1964), p. 25.

[35] "Educational TV, the next ten years," U.S. Department of Health, Education and Welfare, O. E. 34036, 1965, p. xii.

[36] Barnard, David P. "Audio visuals," *Industrial Arts and Vocational Education*, 52:1 (January, 1963), p. 10.

[37] Gilbert, H. G., "Television in industrial arts education," *Journal of Industrial Arts Education*, 24 (March, 1965), p. 37.

[38] Baumgarner, A., "TV in art education," *Art Education*, 18 (February, 1965), p. 15.

[39] Hasen, Carl F. *Report on an Experiment in Teaching Elementary School Music by Television in the Washington Public Schools*. Washington, D.C. Board of Education, 1952.

[40] Justice, E. "TV plays a major role in new teaching techniques for violin and cello," *School Music*, 36 (October, 1964), p. 38.

[41] "Educational TV: The next ten years," p. 271.

[42] "Telecourse catalogue: 1966" National Center for School and College Television. Bloomington, Indiana.

from their catalogue is a thirty-lesson art course designed for use with second grade classes.[43]

Educational radio.

Interest in educational radio appears, with the possible exception of music, to have declined somewhat since the advent of educational television. Especially when combined with instructional workbooks or slides, however, radio still has a considerable contribution to make to arts instruction. The Cleveland Public Schools combine radio broadcasts in art instruction with prepared slides which are distributed to classrooms to be used in conjunction with the radio presentation.[44] The Standard School Broadcasts, sponsored by the Standard Oil Company of California, remain one of the musical staples for elementary classroom music appreciation.[45]

Sight and sound.

The expense of more sophisticated educational hardware and the lack of professionally prepared programs for instruction in many areas has encouraged the 'home' preparation as well as the commercial availability of various types of sound and sight combinations for instruction. Art history can be effectively presented and illustrated with a combination of slides and prepared tapes.[46] The Jam Handy Organization, 2821 East Grand Boulevard, Detroit, and Bowmar Records, 10515 Burbank Boulevard, North Hollywood, are among distributors who offer extensive sight and sound combinations for music and art instruction in the elementary schools. Tape-workbook courses in theater, music, and art have been developed at the college level.[47]

One of the newest hardware developments in the sight-sound area is the Westinghouse Phonovid. This device projects still pictures and audio on a built-in television screen from a disc similar to a phonograph record. Applications to all areas of instruction in the creative arts should be numerous once it or something like it becomes commercially available.

Use of sight and sound as separate media is also continuing. Experimentation has been reported in the preparation of slides for art and industrial arts,[48] and an interesting use of double-image slide projection

---

[43] Great Plains Regional Instruction Library. University of Nebraska. Lincoln, Neb.

[44] Day, Ronald N., "Radio makes art a public affairs program," *Arts and Activities* 58:5 (January, 1966), p. 16.

[45] Standard Oil Company of California, Public Relations Department, San Francisco, Calif.

[46] Florian, Virginia L., and Novotny, Dorothy F., "Enrich art history with sight and sound," *Arts and Activities*, 58:1 (September, 1965), p. 38.

[47] "The sound of learning at Oklahoma Christian College," Tape and workbook, Oklahoma Christian College, Oklahoma City.

[48] Abrams, F. Russel, Jr., "Techniques for preparing slide film lessons for industrial arts," *Industrial Arts and Vocational Education*, 53:9 (November, 1964), p. 26.

for art appreciation.[49] The tape recorder is being utilized for prepared lessons in music listening as well as individual study and self-evaluation in music and industrial arts.[50]

Films.

The use of motion pictures is not, of course, an example of new media utilization, though the enormously increased number of appreciation and instructional process films available in the arts is making traditional use more effective. The 8mm film loop is providing an interesting example of new applications and techniques with older media. The film loop appears to offer considerable potential for teaching manipulative operations and visual comprehension in music,[51] art, and crafts.

LOOKING AHEAD.

This brief survey of reported current practice reveals that, as yet, no more than a beginning has been made in realizing the potential for media utilization in the creative arts. It appears that some of the factors which have militated against wider usage of media have also had a deterrent effect on experimentation with creative ways of using media in the arts. There is a gap to be bridged between the media specialist and the creative arts educator. Perhaps the best hope of achieving better communication will be in the media specialist's encouragement and active support of creative arts personnel who have a feel for media development.

It is difficult to single out particular instructional media which provide areas for fruitful research and development in the creative arts since, as has been indicated, there is room for improvement and experimentation in all. Some developments in technique and technology may, however, be briefly considered as pointing the way for media utilization in the years to come.

(1) Programed instruction. The development of systems packages in which audio, visual, and evaluative techniques are combined appears to offer great potential in the arts area. Such packages can be designed for group or individual instruction. They may well provide part of the answer to the problem of insufficient arts personnel in the elementary grades, and make possible an enriched curriculum for talented students at all grade levels. Further, the development of such packages, and the research which goes into that development, will tell arts educators more than they have ever before known about what constitutes effective teaching and learning in their own subject area.

[49] Tierney, Lennox, "Double image slide projection technique," *Art Education*, 15:8 (November, 1962), p. 17.

[50] Zacco, M. L., "How to individualize instruction with a tape recorder," *Industrial Arts and Vocational Education*, 52:2 (February, 1963), p. 19.

[51] Koskey, B. Eugene, "New visual techniques for music," *Music Educators Journal*, 51:4 (February–March, 1965), p. 51.

(2) Educational television. The personnel problem is an acute one in educational television. Students who are accustomed to watching "slick" commercial programs, or the professional and artistic performance of a Leonard Bernstein, can not be expected to react favorably to the classroom teacher or arts specialist as an amateur television personality. The problem can, to some extent, be solved by adequate coaching and directing, but a real search needs to be made for arts specialists who are not only good classroom teachers, but have the ability to project their teaching personality via the television receiver.

(3) The tachistoscope. While this device is not considered an example of new media, it apparently has found little use in the arts. It seems possible that any area which makes important use of visual acuity and rapid perception, e.g. music sight-reading, perception of artistic structure and basic design, should find considerable value in experimental use of the tachistoscope. Its values would appear to lie in research, diagnosis and instruction.

(4) Video tape. The video tape offers great possibilities in all areas of the performing arts. Theater, dance, and music students will be able to perform before the television camera and get an immediate playback during which they, together with other students and teachers, can evaluate the performance.

(5) Multiple-track tape recording. Though tape recording is not new, the development of multiple track recording allows music students, for example, to record a solo performance along with a pre-recorded accompaniment, or even a duplication of the solo part. This technique should have value in teaching not only fundamental aspects of music, but also the more subjective areas of style and interpretation.

(6) Computer aided instruction. The potential of computer aided instruction and automated classrooms in the creative arts has had little investigation. Indeed, the cost factors involved have allowed for little but administrative and research experimentation in data retrieval. Nevertheless, the possibilities for instruction through branching programs, and the potential for actual attitude changing[52] make the field of computer instruction well worth the future attention of the creative arts educator.

(7) The arts center. Though pleasant, tastefully decorated and appointed arts centers are not yet found in most schools, they should be. Sheldon Wiltse has reported on the development of a unified arts area in an ungraded school,[53] but such developments are still rare. An essential feature of the arts center will be extensive provision for media: overhead, opaque, slide and motion picture projectors; stereophonic high-

---

[52] Bushnell, Donald D. "The role of the computer in future instructional systems," AV Communication Review, II:2, (March–April, 1963), p. 65.
[53] Wiltse, Sheldon R., Jr., "Developing a unified arts area in an ungraded middle school," Industrial Arts and Vocational Education, 54:3 (March, 1965), p. 44.

fidelity phonographs; multi-track tape recorders; television and radio receivers; a video tape machine; and a systems device to provide for group and individual programed instruction. Such centers will be in use throughout the school day, and provide superior facilities for evening adult instruction. The time in which an appreciation and understanding of the arts is to be developed in a formal classroom with a minimum of superior audiovisual support is passing. Schools of the future will have not only the hardware to do the job, but readily available teaching programs, 8mm film loops, video-taped courses of instruction, slide and tape sets, and the usual file of prints, phonorecords and tape recordings to serve all areas of the creative arts.

At least two promising approaches to media utilization in the arts need to be explored. First, large school districts need to provide released time for competent, interested arts personnel to work with the media specialist in developing appropriate materials. The media specialist, often not trained in any of the arts areas, can, alone, do little more than suggest sources of hardware and software and help with utilization. The arts instructor with a full teaching load has little time to engage in extensive and long-range media development.

Second, masters and doctoral candidates in the arts need to be both allowed and encouraged to do basic research on curricular and media goals, materials, and methodology. A concept of valid graduate research as primarily historical or statistical does not meet today's educational needs. The best thinking of arts educators is essential for solving the problems of reaching students through an articulated curriculum in the arts supported by creative media utilization. It is apparent that a functional integration of media and the arts is both possible and on the increase. Where joint efforts by art educator and media specialist are applied to a given curriculum, such as music,[54] helpful guidelines can result.

The future for media utilization in the arts is a rich and promising one. Instructional improvements and an infinitely greater understanding of the nature of teaching and learning in the arts will be important results of the trend toward "going media."

[54] Sur, William Raymond, and Schuller, Charles F., *Music Education for Teen-Agers,* Harper and Row Publishers, 1966, p. 603.

Chapter 9

What is the essence of science education and how can
resources and organizational patterns be effectively utilized
in support of it?

What are the essential requirements for further improvement
of science instruction?

What innovative methodologies could be employed to build a
logical scientific approach to instruction in a given situation?

In the case of an actual institution, what method of attack is
used in developing and operating a technology-based curriculum?

SCIENCE EDUCATION
AND INSTRUCTIONAL SYSTEMS

ALEXANDER SCHURE, President
New York Institute of Technology

Education in the United States has come far in the last half century. The nation has many fine schools, serves a substantial portion of the formal school age population well and derives benefits from strong and widespread support, both public and private, for education. The massive new attacks proposed to solve educational problems begin from a position of some strength. Yet, the very needs, challenges, aspirations and benefits of changing modern society have led to deficiencies in the educational programs. Acceptance of the broad social objectives of education for all, and the reemphasized recognition of the potentials of education as a means of achieving a truly eminent society, have lead to a concentration of effort to improve all of education in general, and special segments, such as science education, in particular.

The next decades are propitious for a new forward surge, with many component elements at hand to make giant strides possible. One of the more important forces is the present national, state and local support and concern for educational improvement. Other apparent trends include a national recognition and emphasis upon long term continuous educational

163

development, from early years forward and projecting over the span of a lifetime, the emergence of techniques for dealing with the educational problems of the underprivileged, a concern for realizing the maximum potentialities of each individual in the society, interest in the development and structuring of new curriculum patterns, and efforts directed at the improvement of existing courses of study. Add to these directions the availability of an information processing, retrieval and communication technology ever increasing in sophistication, the broadening diverse role of the media in attaining instructional objectives, and the development of systems engineering and management techniques applicable to fundamental educational problems. In total, the compound impetus yields a favorable prognosis for the realization of bold educational advances in new directions within the forseeable future.

As of this date, however, most approaches to educational problems have touched only segments of the total educational structure, with various piecemeal solutions proposed as answers for given aspects of educational needs. Valid critiques are usually applicable to these partialized approaches. Thus, educational innovations are often planned or implemented for such relatively short periods that follow-through, restructure, retrial, and long-term evaluations become inadequate or neglected. Oftentimes, in a fragmentary approach, educational products are not tied meaningfully to implementation as, for example, a major national curriculum restructuring taking place without accompanying teacher reeducation. Then, again, proposed designs may fail as the outcome of inadequate communication between the elements of the applicable power structures, among and between the educational agencies, the universities, the colleges, research laboratories, the schools, the state education departments, the administrative organizations, the teacher agencies, all engaged sincerely but usually with virtually separate efforts to improve the education of the individuals concerned. There is all too frequently a failure to bring together those available but characteristically uncoordinated resources which, once organized, would permit a more concentrated attack upon educational deficiencies.

It becomes apparent, as a result, that we must consider education in its totality as an operating system, one in which science education is a subsystem. We may define such a system as a heterogeneous assemblage of equipments, personnel, and procedures operating within the constraints imposed by its environment to satisfy the mission for which it was designed.

The elements which then govern judicious integration of resources and organization into the instructional process are those which are deemed most desirable for the solution for the wide range of problems identified at the level of actual pupils, in actual classrooms, and in actual programs.

The thrust must always be a total one. It must touch upon the real needs of the pupils, under the true role and purpose of the institution itself and with the proper emphasis on the information, guidance, and motivation provided by the teachers and their equipment to effect accomplishment of desired learning goals. It is here the problem exists and, upon its recognition, where results will be effected.

The merits of individualizing instruction are now largely accepted. Professionals and the public are in general accord that it is desirable to structure educational arrangements within which learning experiences are geared to the pupil's needs, individual capabilities, learning rates and interests. Education within such setting takes on the responsibility for achievement by each individual of all he is capable of learning and being, not only with respect to academic pursuits, but personal development as well. Response by the educational system is required to the continuously growing sensitivity of multivariate differences that distinguish one individual from every other individual and to the satisfaction of particularized needs. What evolves, as logical consequences, are the needs to structure operational facilities capable of implementing the conduct of training and education which simultaneously present a variety of curriculums, each with nonidentical content, at varying rates, to heterogeneous populations of students.

Each innovative methodology which seeks to alleviate an inadequacy in the educational process is subject to those fundamental integrations which are the basics of a total educational process. Succinctly, interrelational elements within a complete educational structure must result from assessments of the overall environment in which the learner functions, the resources, information storage and dissemination capacities available within the environment, the objectives of the educational system evolved by environment, learner, or institution, and the dynamics of interaction between the individual and the system. These interactions govern the shaping of the logistic and economic patterns which will characterize any particular formal institution. The resultants are reflected in the variety of structured or unstructured cognitive, social and emotional tasks imposed by a specific institution upon its pupils as essentials to be mastered in their education, and, the adaptive and coping patterns characterizing the students populating that institution.

Generalizations are drawn from these tasks to form patterns relating the building of pupil skills, the development of conceptual thinking, modification of pupil attitudes and the stimulation of creativity in student thought and action to the organizational, curriculum and economic configurations of the institution. Particular tasks, such as delineating the specific natures of science-instructional objectives, require further elaboration of the generalized objectives. Thus, the science-instructional objectives for the building of skills may include application of basic mathematical and other abstract skills to the solving of problems of the real universe, application of basic language and oral skills for the expression of scientific content and concepts, development of manipulatory and technical skills in the performance of experiments, development of increased sensory perceptions (observation, selected hearing, etc.) for data-acquisitions and scientific tests, and coordination of simple skills into more complex organization and relationships.

Not all objectives are capable, as yet, of scientific analyses. It is in the appreciation of the interplay of structure and function, much more so than in the storage of rote content, that attitude formation takes place. This modification of attitude as a function of exposure time to enthusiastic science teaching is as natural as it is a rewarding outcome. Related, elusive and of enormous consequence to society is the quality of creativeness. It has resisted quantitative analysis, and its very criteria are nebulous. Opinion of peers is, perhaps, the present most dominant evaluative mechanism, but its subjective bias is hardly a satisfactory determination point for a constructive teaching program. Emerson's words "Emulate, then be original" should not be lightly dismissed. Creativity may not be a virtue that can easily be taught, but certainly the example set by a creative resource be it teacher, or film, or instructional science kit, can stimulate the student to try something new. The questioning attitude and desire to experiment are the heritage of human nature. They must not be dulled by the formal constraints of unresourceful education. Curiosity killed far fewer cats than man did.

Many efforts are now ongoing which concentrate on the improvement of science education, all contributing to a better understanding of the educational problems involved in the learning process as they affect a wide range of student maturity. The necessity of achieving a meaningful, relevant science education has become important to a broader spectrum of population as science continues, at a most rapid rate, to become an integral part of more of the activities of our culture. The consequent results for development of better methods of teaching science are applicable to populations which possess a wide variety of talents, perceptive attitudes and motivations. Concurrently, the means must be provided to allow teachers with less than ideal skills and training to service adequately the increasing numbers of students requiring science education.

Within the frame of the prime objectives for the teaching of science are the more conventionally expressed secondary objectives. The list, which includes the establishing of relationships of man to his environment, the influence of science on government, on society, on health, and wealth, the lessons of the birds and the bees, not to mention the history of how it all took place, goes on ad infinitum. From these voluminous possibilities it becomes somewhat subjective to define precisely the totality of fundamental objectives. For the teacher of a given student group, however, this is required before the application of methodology and resources.

A number of requirements which will contribute to the improvement of science instruction have been identified. Among the more important are:

1. identification of the means by which the educational system can best cope with the pressures and changes of modern society upon it
2. utilization and integration of innovations stemming from system analysis into the instructional and educational process
3. attention to the development of clear, cogent, more accurate presentations
4. well organized team efforts by leading scientists, working with outstanding media and other specialists, applied to the development of educational materials and apparatus
5. the development of a variety of approaches and resources to a particular subject
6. integration of traditional disciplines
7. increased understanding by science faculties of the psychological and behavioral aspects of the learning process, with consequent reduction of the gap between scholars concerned with the learning process and the practitioners of teaching
8. development of a cadre interested and competent in both science education and educational research
9. sponsoring of a broadly based increase in professional competence and interest in science teaching
10. increased attention to training and retraining of science teachers, under appropriate conditions and forums
11. assessment of the educational environment's influence upon the student
12. requirements for better understanding, correlation and utilization of student capacities, behavioral patterns and personality factors as they relate to the educational process
13. the need to optimize learning environments
14. integrating and involving media, management, computer, simulation processes, game theory and other pertinent sophisticated techniques as applicable to the educational process
15. development of refined testing and selection methodologies to insure better use of testing as an educational tool for diagnosis and guidance.

The efforts to accomplish meaningful improvements in science education of necessity focus on concrete problems and activities. Resources may include the human, conventional texts, programed texts, machine presented programs, films, video tape, audio tape, ETV, dial remote resources, computer systems and teams of teachers, among others. They always depend upon the software researched and developed by competent authoritative sources and upon validation of material for effectiveness in the system. A science curriculum is generally formulated by a committee which seeks to define content and resources of a program compatible with its objectives.

The effectiveness of a curriculum is not easily identified. Courses in a curriculum as well as items in a course must relate to the methods of teaching for learning to be effective. The combination of teaching resources (whether human or other), curriculum, and learner forms a closed system that cannot be assessed if we ignore any of its elements. Yet, too often, curriculum analysis treats only of the content or method of the curriculum without reference to the other components and without the quality control and feedback which will insure improvement. In some cases where safeguards have been built into the system the delay time of the analysis precludes effective remedial action. Further complicating the problem is the continuous updating and upgrading necessitated by the advent of an exponentially changing scientific and technological era. Finally, the recent awareness of the need for educationally escalating heterogeneous populations places heavy demands on curriculum development, which must now treat a complex set of requirements at a time when solutions to simpler cases are still unsatisfactory. Scientific analysis of curriculum development and implementation of successful innovations are still in the primitive stage despite the crucial role that curriculum plays in the education of our population. Innovations in the development of curriculum which treat the total dimensions of the problem may point the way to the alleviation of this nationwide problem. It is ironical that a scientific approach to the teaching of science has not become more common. Conventional education is failing in its responsibility because of the demands engendered upon the educational system by an ever increasing student body, by a heterogeneous student population, and by the need for constant updating and upgrading of scientific materials. To date, the curriculum development in science does not differ from that in many other disciplines, except for the constant revisions necessary as the result of modern scientific advancement.

Curriculum development as well as any other entity in the total educational process requires very precise stipulation and definition, capable of being assessed, of content and method. It requires the integration of those materials and methods which prove to be successful into ongoing educational activity. The curriculum, dependent as it is upon methodology, must be sensitive to the diverse media required. It must be sensitive to the fact that there are not enough instructors and certainly not enough eminent instructors for the population demands. It must also be sensitive to the fact that most materials have not been developed with the heterogeneous student population in mind. It must be equally sensitive to the rapid changes which are taking place.

The introduction of innovative methodologies is complicated by resistance from insufficiently oriented faculty members and insufficiently oriented students. Therefore, a multipronged attack upon the entire curriculum problem is essential. No one factor can be ignored.

It is necessary that the educational practicioner maintain an awareness of the needs of relating curriculum development to the changing set of constraints, constituent members, materials, relationships, dimensions and influences that constitute an educational system. Viewed within such a systems framework, it becomes possible to hypothecate a logical procedure whereby a science (or other) curriculum may be analyzed, utilized, and then improved in efforts to attain a maximum efficiency in the teaching-learning situation. It has been suggested previously that most formal learning patterns are outgrowths of dynamic socio-political economic systems which employ extensive arrays and mixtures of resources, approaches and techniques to meet their objectives. A systems characterization study would identify the responses made by any particular system, including a curriculum 'system', resulting from demands upon it for changes in the quality or quantity of its product. It would identify the kinds of instrumentalities and the character of the decision points, as well as the operational elements that govern changes in the mixture of resources, or the execution of approaches, to facilitate realization of objectives.

Let us hypothecate a science department which desires to restructure itself for more effective performance of the curriculums relating to its educational tasks. It may desire, by such curriculum reorganization, to better prior performance of its services, enlarge, reorganize, or expand areas dealing with its substantive curriculums, raise its objectives, or perhaps, accomplish all of the above goals simultaneously. The requisite changes may be massive. Of necessity, the minimum commitments for success include resolutions of questions of the priority, timing and sequence of efforts which will allow effective and orderly change within the department. Yet, as with any educational system, the science department requires (a) information, derived from inputs both outside of and within the institution that relate to its objectives, methods, and curriculum purposes; (b) its procedures, that set of designs and practices by which this institution functions; (c) the decision structure through which its decision making managers, administrators, interested individuals, and its public present, review and select relevant options; and (d) awareness of its available resources, including the people, buildings, technological facilities, materials, and (obviously to be ranked in the priority lists) monies. To realize its aspirations in terms of curriculums, it may have to integrate the factors described above with available new instructional methods, with new intelligence or information dissemination capabilities, and with new administrative patterns. It must consider the new forms of school architecture and the use of data-processing systems to accommodate more flexible divisions of labor among students and instructional staff. In essence, the members of the department would be concerned with the descriptive aspects of their situation (this is the way it functions now) and the prescriptive natures of what and how is to come (this is the manner in which the system must change to be responsive to meaningful innovations).

With such understanding, a hypothetical pilot model system of the department could be structured which would include curriculum relevences. It would identify the critical elements affecting the department and serve as a unifying framework for subsequent research on the real system. The objectives of the department would be clearly specified in the model and as a result of the experimental program the entire departmental educational operation could be evaluated and then modified to maximize the extents to which its objectives are met. For maximum efficiency in assessing the idealized model, the department should bring together a highly competent supplementary staff (to complement its cadre), one which would include access to a variety of subject matter specialists, media experts and behavioral scientists. Working together as teams, the capacities would exist to produce well integrated curriculums designed to fulfill both the departmental objectives and the outputs predicted for the model.

If prior practices are any indication, preliminary pilot efforts with the model would yield a very wide gap between the idealized model version and actual school practices. The more common of the reasons for 'noise' in the early models are found in the problems of stipulating curriculum objectives precisely; in the integration of separate courses and disciplines into an entire curriculum spectrum which is then reviewed and analyzed as a totality; and the difficulty of evolving evaluative measures against which the desired outcomes may be assessed with a high degree of confidence. As soon as the stipulation of objectives become precise, when the spectrum of sequences comprising the total desired curriculum are derived, and, when satisfactory evaluative measures are structured, the model becomes operational. It now serves to provide guidelines about which the departmental organization can synthesize a meaningful and concentrated attack upon its deficiencies. Through the organizational structures suggested by the model, the department (or school) should be able to demonstrate the successful methods and directions of truly modern approaches. Concurrently, in all likelihood it will experience the failures that are the inevitable result of early experimentation.

Trial, error, failure and reorganizations for success are the basic fundamental ingredients of the truly experimental laboratory. This same process can be applied with great effectiveness to curriculum development, acknowledging that early approaches for any beginning technology tend to be primitive. An evolving technology, though, soon moves from evaluations based upon its earliest products. Successive innovations designed to overcome the limitations of first efforts yield new and valued tools. New systems must be made to work—they are rarely satisfactory at the first attempt. Mere structuring of an idealized hypothetical experimental system alone is far from arrival at the successful operation of a complex school department. A pure research approach alone will not be successful in a rapid implementation of an experimental model system because it does not result in a sufficient development of instructional resources and mixes sufficient for the total task. The assessment of well-designed and well-constructed educational products, along with the terms of their utilization within an actual operational system, is extremely important towards a broad-based innovated pattern within any specified school or department. Mere insertions of a few innovations are not adequate.

The value of traditional experimental methods common to educational research programs is acknowledged, but, to be effective, they must be introduced and integrated into the total educational structure. Then, the total operation must be assessed and redesigned by repetitive, empirical procedures. To a considerable extent, such a cut-and-try iterative approach must replace narrower a priori hypothesis-testing experiments. What is suggested is a series of successive experimental revisions, each with progressively improved features being developed until the desired levels of performance and the behavioral objectives sought are actually achieved.

Logic and trends of present developments, which continuously return us to the earlier conclusion of the totality of the educational structure, indicate good reasons for much of the present concern with systems, systems analysis and systems operations. The efforts to make available to the learner better, more efficient resources, instructional patterns, methodologies, curriculums and teacher techniques are increasingly viewed as improvements which are effective only within a total educational program. Educators at all levels of the educational stratum are realizing they must deal with learning system approaches that combine learner, teacher, faculties, materials and technological innovations, under controlled conditions, so as to achieve optimum learning conditions. There must be a *systems* integration of all the available resources components, with the unique potentialities of each element, teacher, machine, materials, and techniques orchestrated to produce a totality more effective *as a whole* than any one resource used alone.

The choices made for particular situations in any projected man-machine-materials organization must take into account the realistic causes of educational operational problems. When consideration is given to the overall inputs and outputs of the total systems environment, we are dealing with a system concept. The analysis of the complex inter-actions of the interrelated components that comprise the entire functional system can be understood best when they are treated as a whole system through a systems approach. Acknowledging that the components within the system may themselves be optimized, the greatest improvement re-sults when the system is examined from that total perspective which permits the interrelationship of its parts to be understood. The analysis itself and the detailed procedures which result from the analysis of the system give rise to the terminology "systems analysis."

There are both important principles and actions involved in the sug-gestions made here. The introduction into the educational system of small unrelated components, an innovation in one place and another innovation in a different area, without fitting these pieces into a total unified process, may create as many problems as it solves. Intruding some new part into a dynamic school organizational structure may merely replace older problems and have minimal effects. In fact, it may be the reasons for 'static' and 'noise' in the system since the new components may make many kinds of adjustments necessary, add to existing work loads, and cause resentment among faculty members. Unless there is an analysis and a picture of the whole educational structure before the introduction of the innovation, the resulting disruptions may, in all too many cases, merely interfere with the introduction of very promising innovations.

Many current innovations stem from a systems analysis approach to education. Systems engineering analysis offers a scientific method to the educator for the organization, statement, and derivation of alternatives in the solutions possible to the many complex problems of education. Its techniques require precise stipulation of objectives, resources, alternatives, and criteria. Proposed modes or methods of organization may then be derived and structured. The selected mode permits the allocation of various choices to be applied to a particular problem. It may also infer new techniques, equipment and facilities better suited to a specific objective.

Systems engineering analysis offers a relatively new orientation with which to approach the many complex problems of education. Its main objectives are to permit maximum utilization of faculty skills, improve the learning rate of students, permit each student to realize his capacities at his individual optimum pace, control the content and quality of curriculums, and create greater efficiency in teaching methods. A systems approach may use a combination of media for mass instruction (such as television) along with media for individual instruction (such as programed learning). It requires the integrated application of teaching teams, related technical personnel, machines, and programed or sequenced materials. Since the aim is greater productivity without sacrificing standards of quality, a systems approach involves the use of labor-saving devices such as teaching machines, constituting one factor within a system, and means for rapid data acquisition and analysis. The system should be self-improving, based on constant feedback information at all stages. The systems are totalities, however, and pieces (sub-systems, such as science education, or media usage) must be viewed as support elements in a systematic attack of total planning for a self-improving system. Use of systems analysis and a systems approach differ from heuristic, trial-and-error accidental success methods by which all too many innovations are introduced. Systems analysis utilizes controlled restructure and feedback to give support to an overall plan.

Within any total system, particular media may be considered aids in the communicative process, or in the broader sense, communication sub-systems. There are a broad range of learning media available, of varying sophistications, which can be used—singly or in combinations—to increase the efficiency and effectiveness of education. The devices, along with their ancillary materials and methods, have become an integral part of the fabric of education. Media relate strongly to the attainment of the objectives of the analysis-synthesis-restructure of content and function previously described, whether for curriculum reorganization or for conventional educational practices. Intelligent use permits approaches to the improvements in quality, efficiency and individualizations sought as mainstreams of contemporary educational aspirations.

Media increase the opportunities for learning, and their importance to effective application of system-analysis is fundamental. Basically, in addition to presenting information in a variety of ways so as to meet particular learning objectives, selection among the media makes possible creations of learning situations that otherwise could not be accomplished (such as the televising of current events or computer assisted instruction) to groups varying in size from individuals to national audiences. Under proper conditions, with proper facilities, media may introduce economies, accelerate learning and release teacher time. In the teaching of science, as an example, some media permit students to work under situations without teacher guidance or supervision; others (sometimes the same ones) allow for individualization of curriculums by presenting either identical information, or variations of the same information, to different students at different times. Under other or identical circumstances, the newer media may extend the motivation to learning by bringing the dynamics associated with the best teachers, be it via the presentation medium of television, film, videotape, discs, or other, to more students.

The growth of media has extended the combinations and reorganizations of the educational innovations now permeating our schools. A random listing of such innovations marks the ways in which present day patterns are formulated and evaluated to improve teaching content. Any partialized list would touch upon: (a) *design of curriculums* (regional curriculum development projects, curriculum study groups, nongrading continuous progress methods, independent learning, computer sequenced curriculum analysis, multiple track curriculums); (b) *the improvement of administration* (computer-based scheduling, data processing, registration tracking and evaluation techniques, systems designs, automated test-scoring processing); (c) *organization of staff* (teacher aids, multi-discipline teacher teams, team teaching); (d) *the grouping of students* (multi-age, multi-class groupings, individual study, differential pacing, frequent varied regroupings, large groups, be they in multiple spaces or in single lecture spaces or taught via radio, wire or television); and (e) *the organization of time* (co-op work plans, extended school periods, modular class periods, student organized class periods, trimester, quarter, full school-year plans). As the above lists are extended, a compatible corollary statement can be drawn listing the expanded resources and media which make the innovations possible. Specifically, such an itemization would include systems approaches to use of media; local, regional and national organizations for broadcasting, collection and production of instructional aids, audio tape recording, language laboratories, student response systems, computer assisted instruction, commercial and non-commercial television (open-circuit, airborne, closed-circuit, discs, video-tape, and 2500 megacycle systems), telephone and telelecture communications systems and projectors, slides, overhead, opaque, 16mm, 8mm and micro-projectors; to all of which must be added the entire catalog of information, storage, and retrieval devices and materials.

It remains for the decision maker, whether learner, teacher, administrator, or team to select from the resources by determining (a) what it is hoped will be done, (b) if the way in which it will be done is the best way for all concerned, and that (c) there is an attempt to be sure, by assessment, that the mix actually chosen eventually represents the best selection among the available means. The choice of methods and ways to reach desired objectives are set, in the final analysis, by the system logistics (the way information is to be presented to the learner) and the economics of the system (those factors governing the wherewithals by which resources may be made available). The decision maker must continually ask the vital pertinent questions relative to the system, whether the questions involve the formulation of only a single unit of material, or encompass a sequence of courses comprising an entire curriculum.

The greater precision of systematized approaches inevitably results in an awareness of the constraints and limitations that affect the promises inherent in media usages. Despite considerable impact and growth (studies of the potentialities of media have resulted in substantial production of tangible, significant educational products and byproducts), learning media are not being used extensively in American education. At this date, less than one per cent of our total educational budget is being spent for learning media and instructional aids.

Faculty attitudes, ranging from indifference and anxieties to misunderstandings and outright hostility are a limiting cause restricting wide usage. Considered together with administrative complexities, possible leadership inadequacies, budget implications and the needs of special design considerations for facilities, the problems which restrict implementation of the uses of media in contemporary education become clearer. The need, then, to give considerable attention to planning for successful introduction of media innovations is apparent. Education of a faculty to the potentials of man-machine-systems is a prerequisite to education of students using machines. Since teaching and supporting staffs play a key role in the use of media, strong, consistent educational leadership must be available. It is up to such administrators to lead the faculty and staff into the development of the skills, programs, and above all, states of mind which allow the use of media to become effective in an operant situation. Workshops, development of in-service programs, and joint administrative-staff planning at early points in the decision process all help. With provisions of proper production and dissemination facilities, manned by technical and support staff, faculty anxieties tend to be alleviated and cooperation greatly increased.

A description of the systems and computer-oriented developmental programs for educational escalation at the New York Institute of Technology might well serve as a specific example of the formation, development and conduct of research programs which are systems based.[1]

The programs resulted from the establishment of a systems and computer-oriented Research and Development Center for educational escalation at the New York Institute of Technology. The operating philosophy of the Center is based upon the conviction that educational escalation is

[1] System is defined as a heterogeneous assemblage of equipments, personnel and procedures operating within the constraints imposed by its environments to satisfy the missions for which it was designed. The systems study includes the complete communication patterns inherent in an entire operant school system that is the New York Institute of Technology. Acknowledgement to Dr. Bertram Spector, Vice President of Research, N.Y.I.T., for use of the ULTRA diagram and supporting materials is herewith gratefully made.

always possible. This philosophy permits a major assault upon the wide gamut of scientific, occupational, vocational, and technical training needs. Further, it is emphasized that one of the primary considerations of the effort is the generation and implementation of mechanisms by which innovations that emerge from the activities of the Center can be incorporated into educational institutions.

The systems and computer-oriented Research and Development Center for educational escalation at N.Y.I.T. is founded on the assumption that through the systems approach to education a model functional educational system will evolve. This educational system will have the capabilities of mass implementation, yet it will match the inventory and potential of each individual in a heterogeneous population to his subsequent career environment. The door will never be closed to educational escalation. Methodologies and resources must be provided to develop human talent in an optimal way, and with a high probability of attainment. A prime objective is to extend the range of college opportunity to students, who, under conventional educational practices, would be deprived of this educational possibility. In addition, the Center must be responsive to those who can not enter formal institutions of learning. Therefore, the talents, facilities, methodologies, and technological support must be provided to serve the following functions:

a. To educate and train both within and without the constraints of a formal institution.

b. To make manifest the problems associated with the introduction of these techniques.

c. To serve as the vehicle for the solution of these problems.

d. To permit the generalization of the obtained results to curricula not under investigation, and in situations and with populations different from those for which the Center was designed.

e. To relieve geographical restrictions by utilizing modern communication means for the exercise and the dissemination of educational methodologies and resources.

A major concern of the program is to structure educational systems which are compatible with and may be linked to regional and national systems and computer centers. A corollary objective of the Center is to do the research and development necessary to provide the tools for:

a. The acquisition of data for the efficient application of design effort for operational educational application.

b. The determination of the relative efficiency of alternative functional design recommendations at each level of system organization.

c. The determination of the comparative efficiency of alternative means for system implementation.

d. The provision of validating evidence for design recommendations.

The requirement for research and development derives from the fact that in a complex, interacting system of the type under discussion, it is frequently unfeasible to predict the consequences of modification of one part of the system to its over-all output. In some cases, indeed, it may be difficult to describe the output. Further, being mindful of the necessity for parsimony of effort, a comprehensive initial phase is required for validating design recommendations prior to commitment to expensive, but perhaps inapplicable equipment whose existence might coerce its use.

Given the requirement for the tool, the problem then becomes one of providing the basis for specifying its characteristics and the means for its use.

The following method of attack on the problem is being proposed:

a. Description of the missions of the system, derivation of criteria of systems effectiveness, and the measures of effectiveness which relate to these criteria.

b. Description of the operational, technological, social, and economic environments within which the simulated system must function.

c. Functional analysis, including the operational description of the functions which the system (and its simulation) must perform, and the information processing, and the control required to satisfy each of these.

Much of the ongoing continuing research and development at the Center is basic to the overall concept of Project ULTRA (*UnLimited TRaining for All*) illustrated in Figure 1. Project ULTRA represents the blueprint for the systems philosophy at the New York Institute of Technology.

The present programs underway concentrate on selected promising phases of Project ULTRA. The design of even the preliminary programs involves sophisticated programming and computer techniques, and requires services of eminent educational advisors, systems management personnel, computer programmers, data processors, admissions and guidance counselors, coordinators, and curriculum development teams. The associated materials and resources which provide the software and hardware, the facilities to house them, and the communications links for the dissemination of information are also vital to the successful implementation of the program.

The preliminary programs are being adapted to the following:

a. An off-campus program currently underway for paratechnical personnel.

b. On-campus programs serving heterogeneous populations.

One offshoot of the research is Project X (see Figure 1). The result of this has been the development of a self-organizing, computer-based

Figure 1.

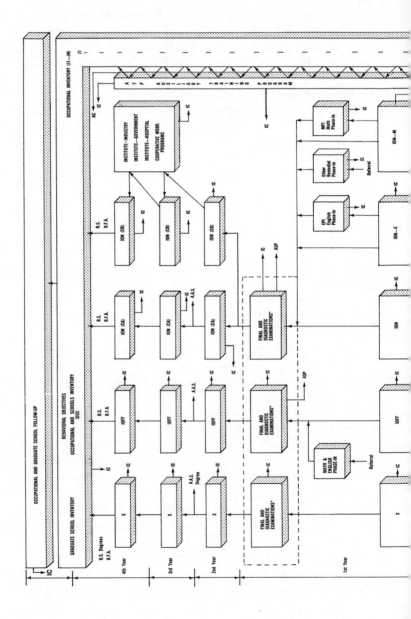

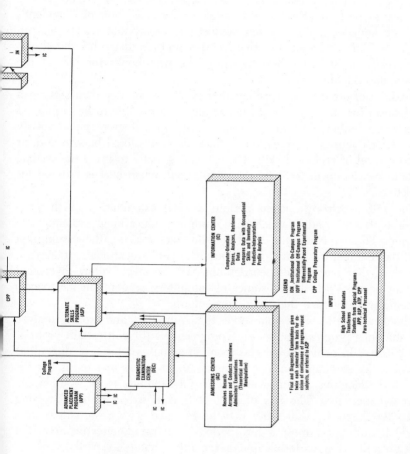

ULTRA
A Schematic Outline
of the Overall Concept

educational system by which a computer makes diagnostic examinations of a student's level of knowledge, offers him the learning materials he requires, checks his progress, and helps him to achieve successful completion of the objectives specified for a particular course.

The individual diagnosis permits a student or participant to enter a learning situation at that point most closely related to his needs and capacity to perform. Having discovered the precise point of a student's level of knowledge in a given subject, the computer selects his appropriate learning resources—the lectures and seminars he should attend, the best texts for him to study, the best books for him at the library, and the films for him to see.

In this self-organizing learning method, the computer then sets up a mechanism for checking the learner's progress according to his stipulated objective, whether it be to complete credits for a degree course, satisfy a need for continuing education, update his professional background, or reach a level of technical skill. The student is ready to leave the system, without restriction to artificial time limitations, when he has satisfied his objectives.

The self-organizing system permits critical examination of the 'unalterable truths' under which many present educational systems now operate. These include the fixed student-teacher ratio, the assumption that the number of years determines student educational attainment, and the belief that present curriculum patterns meet widely diversified student needs. With the assistance of computers, students in the schools to come will organize their own curriculums.

The computer in the system serves to acquire data and rapidly analyze the student's progress and rate of progress, his difficulties and patterns of difficulty. In conventional classroom situations, patterns of difficulties exhibited by students may not be apparent for weeks or months. By the time the difficulties are uncovered, it may be too late to effect adequate remedial measures. The loss of student time is irrecoverable. Utilizing computer diagnosis, difficulties may be revealed within the course of a single period or at most a few periods, and rapid, effective remedial measures may be undertaken. On the other hand, as patterns of accomplishment are revealed, accelerated measures for advancement may be instituted.

The self-organizing computer-based system is the kind of system that tailors an educational program to meet a specific individual need. There are normally two kinds of goals common in educational organization. One arrangement is the typically formal curriculum that exists in our conventional institutions. Thus, for example, when a young man in high school or in college elects a specifically oriented program, one which includes a course in mathematics, he will, at the conclusion of a finite time, take a series of objective examinations. The results, coupled with other evaluations made by the teacher in the classroom, are used to determine his competency in that subject. In both high school and college this kind of formal authoritarian structure is amplified to include a number of required courses leading to either a diploma, a degree, or to some professional objective. There is another type of educational organization where this structure and responsibility is either less evident or completely absent. In the wide gamut of continuing education, whether the impetus be social or concerned with the upgrading of a technical or a professional skill, the objectives are less formal. Such goals, if stated at all, are usually less precise than in the formal educational system, and most often are evolved by the learner in the system. Thus, a practicing physician who wishes to stay abreast of the field may say, "I must have certain knowledge relating to a new kind of drug." He has now formulated his objective and proceeds to organize his own method, entering the educational system to do a number of things to satisfy the need he has expressed. For example, singly or in combinations, he may attend a seminar being given by a professional group, or use the resources of the best available libraries, or ask his colleagues about the persons or groups having the most knowledge relative to his problem, visiting these people in order to get the specific information he desires. The moment he has satisfied his defined objective he says, "I may now leave the educational system for the moment, having completed this particular task."

Education is not really a series of separate little compartments of knowledge. Over the last decade this belief has been shaken, steadily and progressively, throughout school and college organizations previously founded upon recurring quarter, semester, or annual intervals. The concepts of advanced collegiate placement, non-graded classes, dual-progress schools, and multitrack programs are evidences of an increasing orientation towards nonroutinized pupil time organization.

It is only when full range is given to the flexibility of schedule inherent in a fully adaptive and differentially paced teaching mode that the capability of the mode to react to various pupil differences, or to situational exigencies, becomes primarily related to one single factor—time. This is the truly revolutionary quality of an adaptive teaching mode, replacing the rigidity—native to outworn patterns of scheduled, routinized learning—by a flexible, learner-time based system.

The hypothesis put forth in organizing the computer-based system is that it is perfectly possible to design a system, aided by the computer, where, with great precision, the satisfaction of defined objectives can be met. Here the computer can guide not only the student, but in addition all those concerned with the student, including, among others, the teacher, the professional guidance counselor and the psychologist. The system declares precisely and exactly what it is that the student is accomplishing, and the learning experiences that he should undertake to complete the particular educational task he has in mind. A typical experimental operation of such a system, and its application at the New York Institute of Technology is related to courses now being given in college physics. The description will give the reader an understanding of how the system works in practice.

The teams responsible for evolving the software, or programs, structure their materials in accordance with specific goals defined by responsible faculty members in the physics department. These objectives are normally specified as heuristic in nature. In effect, they tell the learner embarking on a freshman course in the theory of physics that he is expected to be able to solve a number of mathematical and conceptual problems relating to physics, and that once he has demonstrated his capacity to do so, he has completed the course for formal credit. The student's progress through the course is purely individual, completion ranging from one week to sixteen weeks. (In practice, the most rapid progress for a student without prior background is six weeks.) A series of diagnostic examinations is organized to test the knowledge of each student who enters the system. He takes this series of examinations on special apparatus which automatically translates the information in a form that may be fed into the computer (an IBM 1620). The computer makes a series of analyses including the structuring of a pupil profile pattern, and integrates these tests with prior indices of performance, such as IQ, reading level, and mathematics capacity of the student. It then projects, in terms of such measures, the areas in physics in which the student has achieved competence, the segments in which further learning is required because of demonstrated deficiencies, and the specific institutional resources available to the student to help meet the objectives for that unit.

As an example, if the student were concerned with learning something as simple as the fundamental units relating to measurements, the computer would produce a routine record outlining all of the resource material available to the student to supplement the demonstrated areas of deficiency relating to the use of such measurement units. This record would include additional study programs, references to textual material in the library, available films or video tape recordings, pertinent seminars or lecture classes offered by professors in the department, the times these are available, all as they relate to his learning objective, along with final diagnostic post tests to verify the student's progress. A student, in accordance with his attitudes, capacities and desires, chooses from among these resources and organizes his own schedule of learning. The computer may indicate suggestions derived from the attitudes of the student, but the responsibility for organizing his educational program remains with the learner. He may choose from among the available resources those which are sufficient to bring him to the next point stipulated in the objectives defined for the course. Note that he may select any resources he chooses, including the human resources available in the faculty, to the extent he desires, as available within the institution. Whenever he meets the 'terminal' objectives put forth for the particular course, he has completed that course. He then 'leaves' the learning system, in the sense of having no further needs relating to this course.

The mechanism for meaningful independent study thus allows a more complete utilization of the human resources of both the student and his educational institution. Experimental work to date has indicated a major reduction in the time necessary to complete typical courses in degree curriculums. Such a computer-oriented program may make possible individual education on a mass basis, within or outside other formal educational institutions.

Related to the ULTRA projects are the efforts necessary to produce meaningful systems of media and curriculum reorganization. A description of these innovations follows.

INNOVATIONS IN CURRICULUM DEVELOPMENT

An intensive curriculum research and development program has been initiated at the New York Institute of Technology designed to insure the following:

1. That a detailed list of items for each course in a curriculum be formulated, and that the objectives for teaching each of the items be coded for later evaluative purposes.

2. That there be smooth transitions between successive courses within a departmental curriculum.

3. That courses taken in one department be closely linked with those taken in other departments, so that needless repetition of material be avoided; that each item of material be sufficiently covered; that prerequisites be supplied in time; and that newly acquired tools be put into use as quickly as possible.

4. That the materials for the courses be available; that the student know exactly how he should use the material; and that he be able to proceed at the rate best suited to his learning abilities.

5. That means be provided to continually evaluate the student's progress so that he can be advised of appropriate problem sessions, discussion groups, lectures and other services, and facilities of value to him.

6. That the student be able to observe his own progress; that he learn of his mistakes quickly and be referred to remedial material; and

that he be stimulated to proceed at a rate which will ensure both effective learning and good use of time.

7. That the courses of instructions be continually assessed for quality and effectiveness.

These objectives are certainly not new, nor are they mentioned here merely to illustrate an awareness of some of the age-old problems in education. Nevertheless, they have not generally been met in total for homogeneous populations, and not even approached for heterogeneous student populations.

Curricula Analyses

To insure smooth transitions between courses, and close cooperation between departments, it is necessary to define precisely each course content. To this end, detailed curricula analyses are being carried out in many courses, using the work done in analyzing the first two years of the Electrical Technology curriculum in N.Y.I.T. as a guide. Eventually these analyses will be carried out in all disciplines. Currently, projects are underway in the areas of electrical technology, mathematics, applied physics, science survey, English curricula, and social sciences.

The curricula analyses serve the following functions:

1. For immediate use they facilitate analyses of
   a. the precise items,
   b. the reasons for teaching each item,
   c. the order in which items are taught,
   d. deficiencies in particular areas,
   e. the relation, in time, of each item to prerequisite items,
   f. the level of each item,
   g. the alternate methodologies of teaching each item,
   h. applicable references and diagnostic examinations for each item.

   They also serve as
   i. guides for students and faculty to primary and secondary sources so that they may obtain alternate approaches towards particular items and groups of items,
   j. guides for teachers in assigning outside reading or extra projects,
   k. means for directing each student to self-instruction at his optimal pace (differential-pacing).

2. For long term use, they serve as aids in
   a. updating and upgrading the curricula in inter-related departments,
   b. scheduling prerequisites more accurately,
   c. making fuller and prompter use of technology and knowledge acquired in other curricula.

Although closely related to prerequisites, this is not an identical concept. Prerequisites are necessities, whereas, the depth and breadth of additional knowledge enriches the student and may act as a motivating influence.

Table 1. List of Abbreviations and Code Designations.

A. *Method of Presentation*
   01 CP   Class Presentation
   02 PT   Programed Text
   03 MP   Machine Presented Program
   04 FL   Film
   05 LK   Lecture
   06 VT   Video Tape
   07 AT   Audio Tape
   08 CN   Course Notes
   09 NT   Normal Text
   10 ST   Self-study (self-taught)
   11 LM   Laboratory Manual
   12 WK   Theory and/or Problem Workbook
   13 BT   Abridged Textbook
   (99 such designations may be permitted)

B. *Academic Level*
   00   High School
   01   1st Semester College
   12   12th Semester College
   (09–12 are graduate level)

C. *Information Categories**
   AT   Analytical   pencil and paper operation
        Technique
   BG   Background, general
        information
   CP   Concept   a mental construct—an idea not based upon
                            sensory perceptions alone
   DF   Definition   statement or meaning of a term
   ED   Engineering   circuit or physical object designed and/or built
        Device
   ET   Experimental   operation in lab or shop
        Technique
   FA   Fact   experimentally verified theory
   FD   Factual data   units, constants, constraints and properties of
                            materials as needed to effect a design of an
                            instrument or an engineering device
   IN   Instrument   a device used primarily for making an observation
                            or a measurement
   LW   Law   a statement summarizing a body of experiences
                            or a logical deduction from basic principles
   PE   Percept   phenomenon we become acquainted with through
                            the senses
   PR   Principle   plays the role of axiom or postulate and cannot
                            be derived
   SI   Special   item presented in class as an illustration of a topic
        Illustration   already discussed
   TH   Theory
   PF   Proof   rigorous mathematical or logical proof

*Based on the following work:
Trent, Horace M. and Eva Mae Trent, *The Engineering Science Program at Dartmouth College; contents of the core curriculum*, page 13; 1963

Figure 2. Diagnostic Questions.

ET5011

ET00010 If Hg. changes from a gas weighing 32 grams, to a solid, how many grams
will Hg. weigh when it is in its solid phase?

1.
    1) 45 gms.

    2) 64 gms.

    3) 32 gms.

    4) 48 gms.

ET00020 The core or nucleus of an atom consists of _____, which
have _____ and _____ charges respectively.

2.
    1) Protrons and neutrons; positive; zero.

    2) Positron and a neutron; positive; zero.

    3) Proton and an electron; positive; negative.

    4) Protron and a positron; positive; positive.

ET00030 In the Millikan experiment, the oil drop presumably obtained its negative
charge via:

3.
    1) The electric field.

    2) Induction.

    3) Friction.

    4) Heating.

ET00040 A substance that cannot be broken down into simpler substances is
called a (an):

4.
    1) Molecule.

    2) Element.

    3) Compound.

ET00050 The material least likely to make a good permanent magnet is:

5.
    1) Steel.

    2) Nickel.

    3) Cobalt.

    4) Soft iron.

Student Evaluation Through Testing

For continual student evaluation it is important that frequent diagnostic examinations be given. This becomes feasible only through the use of computer-oriented methodologies so that the burden on a staff is not excessive. The N.Y.I.T. diagnostic procedures have the following characteristics:

1. Diagnostic examinations are of the multiple-choice type, and are given at least once a week.
2. The examinations are graded by computers.
3. The student receives the results of the examination shortly after he has completed it.
4. The student is given a complete set of referrals, following a correlative analysis of his answers.
5. On the basis of his examination, which is for diagnostic purposes only, and therefore not reported for grades, he is referred to problem sessions and/or lectures and other resources which are geared to his level of understanding of the material, as evidenced by his examination scores.

In generating the examination procedures and their implementation, it was felt that for a 15 section curriculum, broken down into approximately 200 items or topics (this number will be increased at a later date), an average of 4 questions should be generated per topic. Three exami-

Figure 3. Diagnostic Answers.

ET5011

ET00010 If Hg. changes from a gas weighing 32 grams, to a solid, how many grams will Hg. weigh when it is in its solid phase?

1. 3) 32 gms.

ET00020 The core or nucleus of an atom consists of _____, which have _____ and _____ charges respectively.

2. 1) Protrons, and neutrons; positive; zero

ET00030 In the Millikan experiment, the oil drop presumably obtained its negative charge via:

3. 3) Friction

ET00040 A substance that cannot be broken down into simpler substances is called an:

4. 2) Element

ET00050 The material least likely to make a good permanent magnet is:

5. 4) Soft Iron

nations, consisting of 10 questions each, will be generated for each of the 15 sections. Hence, from approximately 800 questions, 450 would be assembled into examination papers for use during the term. The remaining 350 questions will be available for special examinations when requested by students or advised by the instructor.

Since questions may be used in alternate or even consecutive semesters, the need for minimizing student collaboration is evident. This need is at least partially filled by

    a. scrambling the order of multiple choices for a given test question on consecutive usages;

    b. varying the order in which the questions appear on examination papers; and

    c. generating additional questions with time.

More important, however, is an orientation for students which will emphasize that these examinations are for the student's benefit and that by compromising on examinations they are doing themselves a disservice. The attitude must be impressed upon the student that if he is conscientious, and progresses at the rate which best suits his ability, then he will gain a better understanding of the material and consequently his achievement will be recognized.

Curricula Updating and Upgrading

The responsibility of curricula updating and upgrading falls entirely on the faculty, but the task is greatly facilitated because of curricula analyses by specially trained teams. The analysis clearly identifies new material introduced into the curricula, both horizontally (between departments) and vertically (within a department). With the cooperation of interdisciplinary teams consisting of delegates from various disciplines, adequate prerequisites can be provided, and the information gained via this new approach may be used effectively in subsequent courses. This implies the necessity for a flexible and energetic staff. N.Y.I.T. is taking vigorous steps in this direction.

Detailed Information

With this brief outline of general considerations, a detailed description of the information in an analysis is presented as follows:

    1. Topic Number

    2. Topic Title

    3. Information Category (see table of abbreviations)

    4. Time spent in Class Presentation (to be supplied later by the instructor)

    5. As many Source References as desired — called out by reference number (10 references were used for ET 5011, 9 for ET 5030)

    6. For each source the following information is provided

        a. page numbers on which the treatment begins (up to 4 allowed)

        b. method of presentation (see table of abbreviations)

        c. estimate of the academic level (see table of abbreviations)

    d.   extent of treatment — an intuitive judgment, graded 1 to 5

    e.   a statement of prerequisites (maximum of 4) called out by topic number, and referring only to courses not directly in the same sequence as the present course, since an understanding of that material is assumed.

A sample of this type of analysis is shown in Figure 4.

Figure 4.

DETAILED REFERRALS: STATIC ELECTRICITY

ET00010 States of Matter   G LW PR

ET00010 0140 0001, 0003 # 02 00 1 #   A. Topic Number

ET00010 0155 0009 # 09 00 1 #   B. Source Reference and Number

ET00010 0375 0017 # 03 01 1 # #   C. Page(s) on which treatment begins

             V V V

A   B   C   D E F   D. Method of Presentation

                           E. Academic Level

ET00020 Atomic Structure   TH   F. Extent of Treatment

ET00020 0140 0006 # 02 00 2 #   G. Information Category

ET00020 0150 0005 # 09 01 1 #   H. Prerequisites (if any)

ET00020 0151 0004 # 09 01 1 #

ET00020 0155 0010 # 09 00 2 #

ET00020 0125 0201 # 02 01 1 #

ET00020 0100 0449 # 09 01 1 #

ET00020 0095 0278 # 09 01 1 #

ET00020 0375 0033 # 03 01 2 # #

ET00030 Millikan Oil Drop Experiment; charges on electron ET AT

ET00030 0155 0012 # 09 01 1 #

ET00030 0100 0487 # 09 01 1 # #

ET00040 Elements, Compounds, Mixtures   LW

ET00040 0140 0004 # 02 00 2 #

ET00040 0155 0009 # 09 00 1 # #

etc . . . .

Note: Prerequisite behaviors have been evaluated prior to student entrance. Since this is an introductory course there are no prerequisites shown for the items analyzed herein.

This is actually the second step in the development. The first step is a less detailed version of the same, giving only the topic number, the title of the topic and, for each source referenced, the pages on which the material is covered. This format is especially useful for instructors who wish to scan the course topics, get an idea of the topics treated and the extent of treatment. An example of this format is shown in Figure 5.

Students and faculty will have access to this condensed listing. Binders containing these analyses for all the courses will be kept in convenient locations. The material will be periodically updated.

Figure 5. Condensed Referrals. Course: ET5011 Subject: STATIC ELECTRICITY

| TOPIC | | SOURCE REFERENCE NUMBERS AND PAGES | | | | | | | | | |
NUMBER	TITLE	140	150	151	155	125	100	95	160	375	105
ET00010	States of Matter	3-4 7			9				1-4	17-32	
ET00020	Atomic Structure	6-8	5-8	4-7	10-12	2-1	449	278		33-50	
ET00030	Millikan Oil Drop Experiment (charge on electron)				12		487		36-40		
ET00040	Elements, Compounds, mixtures	4-6			9						
ET00050	Law of Electric Charges	8-10	207 21	241	6	1-1	449-50	277	4-7	51-77	
ET00060	Constitution of charges and charging	11-14			5	3-1, 4-1	452-4 509	294 297		188-99	
ET00070	Atoms & Ions	15-17		7-8	12-13					70-8	
ET00080	Coulomb's Law Force Between Charged Bodies	17-21	209	241-44	7	5-1	456	280	12-13 18	51-77 215-36	136
ET00090	Distribution of Charges	26-29		243		8-1, 11-1	486	282-283	34-36		
ET00100	Detection Devices Electroscope	24-25			8	5-1 3-1	453 457	279	7-11	200-28	
ET00110	Energy & Energy Levels	7									

The detailed referral information shown in Figure 2 will be placed on punched IBM cards. All the cards relevant to the course in which the student is being tested will be fed into the computer at the time his examination is graded. At the end of the examination, the computer will print out the detailed referral information relevant to the questions he answered incorrectly.

It may be seen that with this type of referral and curriculum analysis information available, faculty members have precise information of what is being taught in their own and other disciplines. This is desirable since it represents an effective communication link between faculty members in different disciplines. One result is that a mathematics curriculum team can note where they might best introduce a given topic into the curricula for application to solve a problem in physics or electronics. A second result is that the progression of the student will be logical, since both sequence and difficulty of material can be rigidly established. Other consequences have been considered previously and reflection will undoubtedly suggest more.

Examinations

Brief mention was previously made of examinations. The method of conducting these examinations and their usefulness will now be discussed.

Considerable flexibility in the examination procedure will be available via three provisions, to wit:

1. Part of an examination may be taken. This is advantageous in variable paced programs since a student may wish to take an examination on a certain body of material, but is not ready for an examination which covers additional material as well. Hence, the instructor can specify which questions the student should answer. (An alternative, time permitting, would be to make up a new examination from the bank of questions available.)
2. Optional omissions may be permitted. This gives the student a choice of questions. Numerous possibilities for the use of the statistics suggest themselves. For example, if a test were given to a large group, a knowledge of the questions students omitted could be quite revealing. It could mean that the question was too difficult or that insufficient emphasis had been placed on that material by a teacher, etc. Covariant analysis might establish probable factors in a carefully designed experiment.
3. Variable weighting will be permitted. Among various reasons for this flexibility, it may be noted that different disciplines choose to emphasize different aspects of a particular item or topic. It is feasible, using variable weighting, to give the same examination to students of different majors, and to emphasize the point of view of the desired major.

Referrals

It was mentioned earlier that it is desirable for the student to receive the results of diagnostic examinations as soon as possible. This will indeed be the case in a computer-oriented methodology, and he will receive a considerable amount of additional information, namely:

1. For each student
   a. student identification number,
   b. number correct, wrong, omitted, omitted through option, and score,
   c. those questions answered incorrectly,
   d. the topic numbers of the referrals corresponding to the questions omitted or incorrect (see 3, below).
2. For the class; overall examination analysis containing
   a. question number,
   b. the number of students who selected each of the multiple choices,
   c. identification of the correct choice,
   d. the number of students who omitted a question,
   e. the number of students who omitted a question by option,
   f. the percentage of students who answered the questions correctly,
   g. the grade distribution—the number and percentile of the class who achieved less than a given score,
   h. the number of students who took the examination,
   i. the mean, sum of scores, and the sum of scores squared.
3. The curriculum analysis information corresponding to the topic numbers to which any of the students were referred.
4. In addition, selected data for the students' class-analysis will be put on permanent record for the purpose of long term analysis.

Summary

The methodology described in the preceding material is quite encompassing, yet sufficiently flexible to permit periodic revision, inclusion of new methods, etc. Considerable effort will be made to evaluate the effectiveness of these methods, since it will establish a model for an integrated systematic approach to curriculum development.

The devoted dedication that almost all teachers bring to their task is not enough to satisfy the problems which exist today. In the many sectors of human endeavor, the field of education is among the last to which technology has made any truly substantial contribution. There now exists, therefore, in terms of present efforts to modernize the educational structure, an urgency to provide appropriate and adequate technological measures, sufficient to support the resources and dedication offered by the human teacher. Without the application of educational technology, it is difficult to see how the teachers of today, small in number in proportion to our enormous student population, will be able to lead each student to explore, to learn, to evaluate and to master the prodigious quantities of evolving knowledge.

The systems approach to technology, particularly as it relates to educational technology, is not just a collection of hardware—it is much more. It is a social activity involving people, ideas, methods, machines, communications and various interacting systems. But always, it comes back to people. Utilization by people is always the prime objective. The effect of interjecting technology into education is to come up with an efficient and rational division of labor between men and machines, subject always to the rational control of the human being. Once we have done this, we have an opportunity to expand the benefits that human personalities bring to the process of education, and through technology to relieve much of the rote work normally associated with the educational process. In no way would we be restricting human values. The responsibility for the design and operation of the system proposed heretofore relates to both the professionals who practice in the educational world, and to their students, the scientists and humanists of tomorrow.

Chapter 10

Is there a need and a direction for change in existing teaching practices relating to the social sciences and humanities?

What essential points of agreement exist regarding the areas of instruction, the objectives of these areas, and the organization of the curriculum?

How do area studies and technology interrelate toward systemized instruction?

How can media and methods be used innovatively in such a manner as to encourage students' development of values, critical thinking, and intercultural understanding?

SOCIAL STUDIES
AND HUMANITIES*

WILLIAM CLARK TROW, Professor Emeritus
School of Education, University of Michigan

While instruction in the natural sciences, mathematics, and languages has been moving ahead with the generous public support and the assistance of scholarly and technological innovations, the social sciences and humanities have been becalmed in the backwaters of general apathy. True, researchers have been active in carrying on their experimental studies (1), but most of these involve relatively minor educational readjustments. Although the value of science and mathematics and of their applications in the present technological age is not questioned, and improvements in language instruction are long overdue, no one can reasonably question the values inherent in the content of the social sciences and humanities. Dealing as they do with the relations of people to each other and to the impersonal — often seemingly hostile — world, they are or should be of concern to everyone, in contrast to the relatively few

*This chapter is a revision and enlargement of an article which appeared in *Social Education*, Vol. 29, March 1965, pp. 142–6, under the title "An Area Study Social Studies Curriculum," and is included here with the permission of the National Council for the Social Studies.

who will employ the mathematical technologies and foreign language skills.

No more auspicious time than the present could be found for a thoroughgoing analysis of the situation, since change is in the air, and new content and new methods and media of instruction are available to make even drastic changes possible. While improvements can be made within the framework of the present course structure, if they are attempted, the familiar baffling situations will present the same old quandaries. Many of these may be avoided if a new structure is employed, particularly if it will leave continuing opportunities for changes in details that further research may suggest. In fact, what is good can be used in the new structure, but the way lies open for its more effective use.

It is the intent of this chapter, after a brief analysis of the present state of affairs, to propose a new curricular structure, that of area or regional study, which will include the general content of the social studies but focus on a limited number of significant cultural epochs, and in so doing follow a pattern of the humanities and include the arts. Before elaborating the possibilities, let us first examine the present structure.

Present Status

One of the difficulties in drawing up a curriculum in the social studies and humanities is the matter of definition. With 'the best that has been thought and said' sitting on one side of the fence, with the empiricism derived from the social sciences on the other, and with history claimed by both, definition is not easy, and any kind of consolidation is seemingly impossible.

So far as the humanities (2) are concerned, there seem to be three main divisions: 1. history, chiefly of the ideas of Western man and of significant cultural epochs; 2. values to be found in great books, particularly those in the democratic tradition, and those in which there is a comparison of cultures; and 3. the arts—their understanding and appreciation. Usually included are history, philosophy, religion, and literature, while some scholars accept and some reject music and the visual arts—painting, sculpture, architecture, and the dance.

Now, however, we have for the first time something that can be called an official definition. The Commission on the Humanities, co-sponsored by three learned societies published a report (3), aimed to enlist federal support for an independent agency to be known as the National Humanities Foundation. In the report, the humanities were defined as "the study of languages, literature, history, and philosophy; the history, criticism, and theory of art and music; and the history and comparison of religion and law." The claim was made that "throughout man's conscious past [the humanities] have played an essential role in forming, preserving, and transforming the social, moral, and esthetic values of every man in every age." But they are more than the mere "study of," for the report states that "The humanities may be regarded as a body of knowledge and insight, as modes of expression, as a program of education, and as an underlying attitude toward life."

These categories are elaborated as follows:

> The body of knowledge is usually taken to include the study of history, literature, the arts, religion, and philosophy. The fine and performing arts are modes of expressing thoughts and feelings visually, verbally, and aurally. The method of education is one based on the liberal tradition we inherit from classical antiquity. The attitude toward life centers on concern for the human individual, for his emotional development, for his moral, religious, and esthetic ideas, and for his goals—including in particular his growth as a rational being and a responsible member of the community.

The above statement concerning the arts goes considerably beyond "the theory of art and music," of the original definition. And Barnaby C. Keeney, president of Brown University and chairman of the commission, in an address entitled, "A Proposed National Foundation for the Humanities" (4), went still farther: "We place the creative and performing arts within the scope of the Foundation on the grounds that they are the very substance of the humanities, and embrace a major part of the imaginative and creative activities of mankind."

Some mildly negative voices have been heard, like that of Arthur E. Wright of Yale, writing for the Association for Asian Studies, who averred that

> the humanities have two strikes against them, since in spite of their glamorous tradition, their practitioners often have the reputation of being pedants and antiquarians indulging their curiosity and as a rule conducting research that is 'scattershot' in nature unrelatable to any known problem or theme.

And one might inquire how the humanities, with their objective of transmitting the cultural heritage and enriching the lives of everyone, can be made to fit into grades K to 12. It is generally assumed that such an array of content cannot be made into any one course of study; but as we shall see, this is a false assumption, although as one surveys the academic landscape, he is likely to be somewhat cynical as he notes the military and political history, the samplings of literature, the music played by the school band, the banishment of religion, and the neglect of the arts. The liberal tradition of classical antiquity seems to have fallen by the wayside, and more concern for the human individual is to be found in the guidance services than in the curriculum.

While there are a number of official statements as to what the social studies are, in order not to prolong this statement unduly we can perhaps simplify the definition by stating that they present more or less systematized knowledge derived from the social sciences and adapted to the instruction of young people in schools. They therefore include data in varying amounts from anthropology, history (where they overlap the humanities), geography, psychology, sociology, economics, and political science. Other subjects are sometimes added, such as personal adjustment, guidance, driver education, safety and health, conservation, alcohol and narcotics education, economic geography, and current events.

The social studies, unlike the humanities, do not suffer from neglect so much as from misuse. Students criticize the subject as dull, monotonous and useless, with too many names and dates to remember. Scholars have criticized the textbooks as encyclopedic, superficial, sometimes lacking in precision, sometimes erroneous, with unfortunate omissions, partial explanations, failure to generalize, often lacking in objectivity, and revealing undue bias and ethnocentrism. There is too much esoteric information for the grade level intended, and concept loads are too heavy. Collateral readings are limited, and much of the fugitive literature is not adapted to the age of the pupils. In comparison with other subjects, little advantage is taken of audiovisual materials and programed instruction. Group discussions are random and desultory, a sharing of ignorance, and teachers are inadequately prepared.

The seven subjects listed for the social studies together with the eight for the humanities (counting art and language each as one subject) constitute the content here under consideration. It is physically impossible to insert all fifteen subjects in the curriculum as separate courses. Or if they were listed, no one student could elect and so profit from more than a few of them. They must in some way be combined. Selections of content must somehow be made in the light of accepted educational objectives and means employed to make the instruction of at least minimum value to the students.

Objectives. The objectives usually listed are entirely commendable, but there is considerable disparity between them and actual instruction. Studies reveal that there is real concern for the development of skills and attitudes. The skills range from map reading to critical thinking and problem solving, and the attitudes frequently mentioned are toward life, toward democracy, and toward one's fellow man, usually expressed as intercultural understanding.

A number of strategies and models have been designed to provide training in critical and constructive thinking in connection with social studies content. Some emphasize the determination of causal factors, while others stress deductive reasoning, the dangers of dogmatic beliefs, logical concepts and operations, the method of discovery, and thought quality. It is impossible to say which of the various approaches is most productive, but there is no doubt that some such approach is far better than none at all—desultory discussions and merely asking students what they think. It may be that convergent thinking on the part of the experts will gradually produce a superior model for general use.

Effective ways to develop desirable attitudes have been less fully explored. School elections, mock national elections, cooperative community enterprises, and other projects have more or less successfully supplemented the regular instruction. But the current framework is a bit too shaky to support additional units and special projects. Both effective thinking and attitude development are phases of transfer which must necessarily stem from rather effective learning procedures that call for a greater degree of student involvement than is usually fostered by current procedures, but which seems more likely if a thoroughgoing area-study pattern is followed.

Curriculum. As a rule the humanities are difficult to locate in the curriculum even when history, languages, and the arts are taught. It may be that the comparison of ideas and the search for meanings and motives, to say nothing of creativity in the arts, are beyond all but a few students of elementary and secondary school age. So the fine objectives tend to be forgotten in the pursuit of facts.

The social studies are distributed by grade, as a rule, with many variations but for high schools they are about what was recommended in the 1916 Report of the Committee on Social Studies, of the Commission on Reorganization of Secondary Education:

    I.   Home and school life

    II.   Participants in community life

    III. The community concept, U.S. and elsewhere; satisfying needs

    IV. History and geography, settlements, culture groups

    V. American history (first round), biography, periods

    VI. World regions and countries—geography, history; some economics and sociology

    VII. History and geography of local and other regions; European backgrounds

  VIII. American history (second round)

    IX. Civics, government, U.S. constitution, citizenship problems, vocations, boy-girl relationships

    X. World history

    XI. American history (third round)

    XII. Problems: democracy, government, world geography, international affairs, economics, sociology, psychology, etc.

The list reveals different principles of organization—the spiral form with repetition of content but supposedly at higher levels of complexity; the principle of adaptation to youth tasks and needs; and the principle of discovery of social facts and problems. Historical continuity necessarily conflicts with otherwise desirable course sequences, and geographical grouping of blocs, e.g., the Arab World or the Far East, is likely to overlook important differences within a bloc.

Concurrently, the most intriguing problem at the elementary level is deciding the age at which different kinds of content can be introduced. It is argued that since the interests of the children in the first three grades are wide, they should not be deprived of a knowledge of geographical and other events of current interest, especially if it can grow out of field trips and other explorations. It has been urged that more content should be provided earlier since outside the immediate environment, children showed a broad interest in geography and government and 'knew the meaning of' terms used. Similarly a unit on economics showed that children could obtain an 'understanding' of economic concepts. Such knowledge and understanding, limited as it is, can be obtained, however, only through careful, systematic instruction. The tendency to push more advanced work into the earlier years is by no means generally approved. Learning is likely to be rote instead of meaningful. In the second grade, lack of precision in answers was found; children were unable to keep two factors in mind at once, they had difficulty in responding to the key word in a question and had little grasp of time and place concepts. In the first grade they were unable to read available social studies materials, and 15-minute periods and oversimplification were found necessary.

There is no need to try to crowd children into a level of maturity they will gradually reach anyway. It would seem wiser to allow the growth processes to have their salutary effect. One investigator discovered that the higher the grade the more effective was the understanding of necessary concepts, and he was probably not greatly surprised. But readiness is, of course, not the sole criterion: even if sixth graders can be brought to think reflectively about current events, it does not necessarily follow that increased time should therefore be given to current events. On the other hand, as this is being written, the photographic exploration of Mars would presumably provide an excellent opportunity for those who are studying arid lands, whether in the American Southwest, Africa or Arabia, to inquire into the conditions necessary to support life and learn of the irrigation canals, ancient and modern, the viaducts and dams and other means of reclaiming the desert and bringing water to farms and urban populations.

Methods and Media. It is desirable to distinguish, as is often not done, between methods and media. A method is a form or pattern of continuing instruction, while a medium is the means whereby the method is made to operate. For example, the lecture is a method, but there is a variety of media which may be employed—the direct human voice, overhead and opaque projection, sound film, television, tape recording, and the printed page. In addition there are certain supplementary devices which the lecturer may employ, e.g., notes, manuscript, and teleprompter.

Various media, particularly the audiovisual and programed materials, can be employed in connection with different methods, but unfortunately social studies teachers have not made as much use of them as they might, though a number of methods have been employed, including the lecture-demonstration, the recitation, teacher-pupil planning, field trips, individual study, role playing, outside readings and oral report, so-called research papers, surveys, class and community projects, simulation and games, and dramatization including songs and folk dances. In general, however, there has not been as much diversity in instructional method as is possible or desirable.

A few special projects might be mentioned. The Cardozo Peace Corps Project in Urban Education (5) took a leaf from the Peace Corps training to acquaint teachers with the life of city youth and provide a relevant history course. Innovations included poetry and fiction and even myths from Babylon and the Book of Genesis to illustrate cultural diffusion. The Lexington Project (6) was initially limited to twenty-four college-bound high school seniors meeting frequently for a semester to discuss the "crucial problems of man," the various efforts at finding solutions, the implied values, cultures with conflicting values, and the possibility of their resolution. The Yorker Club Project (7) is of long standing and furnished the precedent for a number of similar clubs in other states. The New York State Historical Association organized so-called Yorker Clubs in junior high schools throughout the state. The members do research and write reports on local historical events, many of which are published in the monthly journal. The CUE system (8) is an experiment in the humanities which attempts to integrate the arts into the on-going New York State curriculum at the ninth-grade level. CUE stands for Culture, Understanding, and Enrichment. Lesson plans and audiovisual materials including films, pictures, and posters were packaged and provided for thirteen schools of different types, traveling exhibits were supplied, field trips to museums and galleries encouraged, and performing artists rode the circuit.

Area Study and the New Technology

As may be inferred from what has been said above, the present flexible pattern of instruction in social studies and the humanities in many schools provides opportunities for good teaching and good educational content. But the patchwork curriculum itself offers the temptation to fall back on routine methods and rote learning with little challenge to introduce new content and new instructional methods and media. By way of contrast, an area-study approach tends to suggest desirable innovations and to put a premium on the construction of designs (9) involving a partnership of teacher and technology in systems of instruction that give promise of something far more valuable than is possible under present conditions.

Region or area study came into being in a serious way during World War II when it became necessary to prepare civil affairs officers to follow the troops into occupied territory and reconstruct the civilian services. Since that time, departments of area study have been organized in a number of universities, usually coupled with a study of the local language or languages. The need for such study has been frequently affirmed in connection with the training of technical assistants and others to be dispatched to do business abroad, particularly in some of the less highly-developed countries. The facts and principles of the social and other sciences, instead of being taught separately or not at all, are brought to bear on a particular area or region and their interaction studied as it affects the lives of those living in the area.

The newer technology refers not only to the media of instruction—audiovisual materials including television and programed instruction—but also to modifications in class size, team teaching, and the questioning of such traditional items as the Carnegie unit, the self-contained classroom, and the grading, marking, and promotion systems. These latter have come to be questioned and modifications urged primarily because of the emphasis which programed instruction necessarily places on statements of course objectives (10). Traditional procedures tend to nullify the efforts to reach educational goals.

Visual media can make much more vivid the nature of the life and times in various parts of the world at different periods of history, and auditory media can improve instruction particularly in languages and music. Programing reduces the amount of teacher contact time needed for instruction and provides a peculiarly efficient kind of independent study that permits the student to move ahead at his own rate. Television and team teaching can enlarge class size almost indefinitely, and listening can be carried on individually or in small or large groups. Discussion generally calls for small groups unless an audience situation is desired. Let us first see how the new synthesis might look as a consequence of a shift to the area-study approach.

In developing a curricular structure for any subject the primary task is to do justice to the organized discipline from which it is derived and at the same time to maximize its application or transfer values. For the social studies and humanities the task is difficult since they draw on a number of disciplines, and the content must be applicable in the complex pattern of social living.

The Social Sciences and Experience

What seems to be needed is a plan which deals with experience in life situations and draws on the appropriate social sciences to provide the needed understanding. History reveals a country's past and geography its surface features, so to speak, which is all right as far as it goes, and provides an excellent start. The other social sciences, however, contribute general principles and select the facts culled from various sources that tend to illustrate, support, or negate them. But the interplay of various social factors in some locale where people live is likely to be neglected. Yet this is exactly what young people, future citizens of their country and of the world need to know.

Like the civil affairs officer or the technical assistant, the citizen of today meets situations in which phenomena studied separately in the social sciences are inextricably intermingled. There are political, economic, and social factors as well as others complicating the problem of Viet Nam, civil rights, or the local bond issue. As long as social studies is taught like courses in separate social sciences, any unity will be difficult to find and effective transfer doubtful. But if one looks for ways to acquaint the learner with the nature of the world in order to help him become a reasonably happy, competent, and thoughtful participant in its on-going activities, the problem takes on a different shape, and needed improvements suggest themselves. No perfect solution emerges but area study offers valuable possibilities.

Only in school does a child see his world as made up of a number of different subjects. Outside, he sees his friends and others going about their various activities interested in different undertakings. It is a complex world, and as he grows older he becomes aware of greater complexities that he as a person or as a citizen has to deal with in one way or another. So in meeting his problems he is likely to be baffled, to be thrown back on childish or on primitive beliefs and to employ irrational methods to justify his thoughts and actions.

One chief function of the social studies and humanities is to help this individual and his confreres to understand this world better and so be able to deal with its problems more intelligently than he otherwise could. It is here postulated that the student can advantageously be a participant not only in his own culture but vicariously in others including those that have contributed to it, or that clash with it in one way or another. He can see the problems of different peoples, why the problems exist, the solutions that have been tried, and, if not successful, why no satisfactory solution was found.

Principles of Area Study

The brief overall plan for an area-study curriculum presented below embodies a number of principles and procedures:

1. Coverage includes the usual objectives, content, and methods of the social studies curriculum and its variations. In this sense it is not new and should not be. United States history, world history, and world affairs, the spiral development of concepts, and the like are taken care of, but the organization permits and even encourages more satisfactory coverage and progression and carries with it other advantages.

2. The organization requires that successive stations or observation posts be chosen—each some locale that is at the center of things during a significant period or cultural epoch; for example, Athens in the age of Pericles. Thus history and geography are meaningfully related. The life and times of each period are explored. All that is known about it, whether from the social sciences or other sources, is drawn upon to make the period become alive. Particularly in the earlier years, the students should have the empathic feeling of climbing out of a time machine, and of living in the midst of and even participating in ongoing events.

3. For more complete coverage, the flashback and the 'flashahead' present the past and the future of the period in order to pick up earlier events, trace causes and look into consequences. This is a variation of the history-backwards principle.

4. There is a meaningful continuity or progression in moving from one of these areas and epochs to another through elementary and high school so that later work can build on what has gone before. Cross relationships are pointed out to give a realization of the contemporaneity of events separated in space, as well as of similarities of events separated in time.

5. Progression is in part from the familiar to the unfamiliar, with many related strands that tend to prepare the student for what is to come, as for example a study of the home regions includes the origins of the settlers, although the countries they come from are not studied until later.

6. Progression is also from the simpler to the more complex. The less highly-developed cultures, or those in connection with which higher-level abstractions may not be necessary, are studied earlier. Concepts can be presented first in simple contexts and later on with increasing complexity and depth.

7. Certain social science phenomena in one period are noted later

in different contexts (e.g., arid land, autocracy), and thus the students' concepts are enlarged and clarified, and the advantages of the spiral organization accrue with a repetition of principles but not of content. The nature of the abstractions is better understood, and the features of unity in diversity are recognized.

Contributions of each of the social sciences and of the humanities to each area studied presumably would develop such concepts as are suggested below to aid in understanding the life of the people in different places and times. It should be emphasized, however, that although events as classified in the different subjects will be included, they should not be presented in any formal order. The list below is not an outline for the treatment of a region but a source of material. The organization would instead be around people and places, events and activities.

In general, an area or cultural epoch would be introduced by orientation films or video tapes showing the region as it now is. Filmed lecture demonstrations of artifacts and reconstructions of historical sites would be supplemented by readings and by appropriate literature of the period, paintings, samples of musical and dramatic recordings, and other art products. Maps would be studied and constructed showing physical features, political divisions, highways and waterways, products, and so on, and chronology would be clarified graphically. While programmed instruction is widely adaptable, it seems most readily fitted to teaching facts and concepts. After such a grounding, students would be ready for discussions of some of the political, economic, or social problems of the times based on some systematic procedure that would develop skill in the thought processes.

Anthropology. (How do they live?) Anthropology deals with people, their beliefs, traditions, customs, religion, recreation, archeological artifacts. The whole curriculum might be called anthropology in the sense that it is the study of man in different cultures. Certainly the point of view should be maintained. Pictures and lecture-demonstrations will be particularly helpful here. Students can identify with different peoples, as it has been found they do not do in social studies courses, taking advantage of simulation techniques, and in some cases authentic games, folk dances, and other activities. In discussion, differing customs and value systems and the universality of sanctions however varied, together with culture concept itself and others, like that of social anchorage, will lay the foundation for the development of international understanding.

History. (What have they done?) The sequence of events, cause and effect; factors affecting stability and change. History is recognized as providing the time line for the underlying structure which symbolizes the contemporaneity and succession of events, and so students will construct parallel time lines relating different periods. History is also recognized as the temporal matrix within which all things have occurred, and so, if events are to attain visibility and concepts clarified, slides and films will be quite as helpful as for anthropological data. Military history, however, should not be allowed to submerge other events; and the natural suspense motivation of the story, to find out what happened next, should be exploited more fully than is customary.

Geography. (Where do they live?) Earth surface structure, ecological factors; land masses, waterways; flora, fauna, agriculture and conservation; divisions: natural (altitude, soil, climate), and political (states, countries). Geography provides the maps which symbolize the spatial relationships and influences. So students will learn to make, read, and interpret maps of the different regions studied. Geography is the spatial matrix wherein all things have occurred, and so yields easily to visual presentation which is often needed to supplement the verbal methods, including programed instruction. But visuals can only be looked at, and in spite of occasional dramatic features, can be forgotten unless appropriate techniques such as anticipation, tabulation, and review are employed.

Psychology. (What is their nature?) High school courses in psychology generally feature how-to-study procedures or difficulties in individual and social adjustment. The first of these should be acquired as the course proceeds; the second is not particularly germane. But a number of psychological factors are of interest including growth, development, attitudes, knowledge, and skills. Efforts to discover national or racial psychological characteristics and traits have not been very successful; hence the important emphasis here may be the negative one—that of avoiding unsubstantiated generalizations characterizing peoples, say, as cruel, religious, ignorant, fun-loving, warlike, and so on.

Sociology. (How do they live together?) In the usual social studies curriculum, emphasis on crime and delinquency, over-population, racial conflict, poverty, and breakdowns in family life has suggested that the sociology strand would be more fitly characterized as social pathology. While information on these matters may be appropriate, positive factors could well be accented: tribal and other groupings, social class; leadership, communications, and institutions.

Economics. (How do they make a living?) Unfairly tagged as the dismal science, economics has a doubtful place in the school program despite the widespread interest in money. Memorizing exports and imports doesn't help much. Perhaps an approach through picturing occupations, markets (black and other), pricing, exchange, and the like would be effective, leading to transportation, wealth, and the influence of science and technology.

Political Science. (How are they governed?) Formerly referred to as political economy and usually called civics in high schools, political science is perhaps one of the worst taught of the social studies when it should be one of the best. The study of the different regions would include such topics as sources of power, governmental forms, political parties; lawmaking, interpretation, enforcement, concepts of justice; power groups (external, internal); war and peace. As in sociology, and economics, methods would include reading and discussion with considerable use of games, role-playing, and simulated activities. The knowledge gradually built up from the study of different countries presumably would provide a basis for a rather thorough understanding of the meaning of political democracy.

Health, Education, and Welfare. (How do they take care of themselves?) All the social sciences and others contribute to the professions of medicine, education, and social work, and their status in a culture is a remarkably sure criterion of its level of development. Because of their importance in the affairs of a region they call for special consideration. Their neglect in the ancient world and in the under-developed countries contrasts sharply with the support that has evolved in recent years, and acquaintance with the agencies and institutions concerned should contribute to good citizenship and the understanding of social democracy.

Art. (How do they express themselves esthetically?) This topic would include the literature, art, and music of the Report of the Commission on the Humanities, and also crafts, ceramics, sculpture, architecture and the dance, as they are found in the areas studied. The attention given them would naturally not take the place of specialized courses in music, literature, and the visual arts. However, students who did not take the specialized courses would be well informed artistically and would have an excellent background and motivation for any potential esthetic interest. Slides, preferably colored and not administered in large doses, would be highly important for the visual arts, as would recordings for poetry and music of the times. Selections for the literature characteristic of the period, but adapted to the developmental level of the students, should be available as well as current documents and fictionalized biographies and other stories.

Philosophy, as such, is rarely studied in the schools, but some might well be included under political, social, or economic theory, particularly in relation to autocratic and democratic forms of govenment. Law, to the extent desired, is included under political science. The religions of different peoples, with citations from their literatures are included appropriately in the anthropology and history columns and would be taught but not advocated—instruction without indoctrination.

This organization leaves languages in a separate category, even though they are a proper phase of area study, since there would be no effort to teach the languages of all the world areas studied, though something might be done with English words derived from some of them. For the one or two languages chosen by any one student, it would seem that instruction should be continued long enough to result in effective use, however that might be defined. This goal is now approachable with the tapes and booths of the language or sound laboratory. The correct use of the mother tongue would properly be emphasized in English, itself a composite subject, and would include, as it does now, various forms of literature, although it might be well to differentiate more clearly than is customary between selections that should be viewed artistically and humanistically. It would be expected, however, that imaginative as well as expository writing would find a place in the individual and group projects of the area program.

The emphasis given to the data from these different sources will of course vary with the different region studied. As has been pointed out, they are to be considered not as an outline, but rather a checklist. There are no sections devoted to interpersonal behavior for discussing the sins of omission and commission on the part of pupils, as is occasionally done in social studies courses. It would seem advisable to keep the content objective, and to handle behavior problems separately and directly, or through the regular pupil personnel services of the school.

AREA-STUDY OUTLINE

The outline of a possible area-study curriculum which follows should serve as a kind of architect's preliminary sketch. There is a danger in presenting it, for some may disapprove of certain aspects and immediately vote it down. However, there are advantages in seeing what it might look like when it is constructed. And one might ask himself whether he would have preferred such a curriculum to the social studies he took when he was in school—or any with which he is now familiar.

In the outline are events at home and abroad that should be common knowledge, or relate to matters of current interest or concern. The locale and periods (in italics) are often designated by place names. Although less space is given them in the outline than to the suggested 'before and after' continuities, their coverage would be more complete. No brief is held for the specific places, periods, and events listed; others may be better for a variety of reasons. The (a) and (b) divide the year's work into convenient terms or semesters. The Roman numerals refer to the larger units for the grades in the present school organization. They begin with grade III since there is so much uncertainty about what social studies should be for the first years, and according to recent studies there is some question as to whether younger children have reached the level of development required for readiness to handle cause-and-effect and other relationships.

THE AMERICAN HOMELAND

III. The School

(a) **The Present Site:** Room, building, yard. Floor plans of rooms, corridors, playground. (The beginning of graphic symbolic representations —the map.) Landscape design. Projects: Care and improvement; tree planting, school garden, etc.

(b) **The Local School:** Elementary, secondary. Personnel, curriculum; financial support, administration, government. Democracy, decision-making. Project: room government.

IV. The Community

Neighborhood, village, parish, township, county, city, state.

(a) **The Local Community:** Street plan, homes of pupils, public buildings, parks, etc. Old houses, interviews with old-timers, letters, documents, museums, landmarks. (Dateline to begin development of time concept.) *The State Capital:* County and state maps, auto maps, roads, waterways, land masses, climate, weather. Early settlement, agricultural and industrial development; historical figures, events, markers. Population centers. Government services, spot maps—health, crime, soil fertility, etc., causes and cures.

(b) **The Home Region:** Same for wider area, regions to be marked off on maps of the United States (see regions, V, below). One or two historical periods are selected for each, and area concepts related thereto. The back and ahead to be treated more lightly, but to reveal chronological continuity. The remaining four areas are to be studied during the fifth year, two semesters each. (Although Alaska and Hawaii appear later, in the outline, those living in these states may wish to add their state history to the Pacific coast region.)

V. Regions of Continental U.S.A.

Here, as elsewhere, first a general view of the area today.

(1) **North Atlantic Region.** *Boston or New York: the Colonial period.* Back to exploration and settlement. Ahead to Declaration of Indepen-

dence, Revolution. *Philadelphia:* The constitutional convention, political democracy, industrialization.

(2) The South. *A Plantation: antebellum South.* Back to early settlement, colonial period—Williamsburg, slave trade—New Orleans, agrarian feudalism. *Richmond:* War between the States, reconstruction. Ahead to T.V.A., one-party system, etc.

(3) The Midwest. *Northwest Territory: Detroit.* Fur trade, French and Indians. *St. Louis:* From plains to fences. Back to the covered wagon, migrations and settlements, Indians and U.S. troops. *Chicago,* industrialization, scientific farming.

(4) The Uplands. *Louisiana Purchase. A ranch:* the moving frontier. Cowboys, Indians, Spanish, Mexicans, Mormons, etc. *Denver:* mining wealth, ghost towns, natural resources, deserts, national parks.

(5) The Pacific Coast. *San Francisco: Gold rush.* Back to Indians, Spanish missions. Purchase. Forests, fisheries. Ahead to statehood, migrations, industries, etc.

VI. The Americas

Natives and immigrants.

(a) **Alaska:** *Gold rush.* Eskimos; back to purchase, immigration. Ahead to development, statehood. *Canada and U.S.:Field trip*—nomadic, pastoral, and agricultural Indian tribes (e.g., Iroquois, Sioux, Navajo). *A settlement.* Settlers and whence they came. Pacts, wars, treaties, Indian reservations. Ahead to *United States.*

(b) **Latin America:** *Antigua.* Back to Mayas, Aztecs, Incas, *et al.* Conquest, immigration, settlement—Spanish Portuguese; Negro, East Indian. *Mexico City.* Back to rebellion, feudalism, nationalism, and revolution in various countries. Ahead to the Monroe Doctrine, Panama, U.S. Border. Ahead to Cuba, Organization of American States.

THE WESTERN HERITAGE

VII. The Mediterranean World

Greek and Roman

(a) **Athens:** *The age of Pericles.* Back to Crete, Homer, first Olympiad, Phoenicians, Solon, Thermopylae, etc. Ahead to Alexander, Hellenistic Age.

(b) **Rome:** *The age of Augustus.* Back to the 12 Tables, Carthage ('coexistence'), Caesar (Gaul, England, Egypt). *Jerusalem*—Back to Abraham, Moses, David, Christ, St. Peter, St. Paul. Ahead to the Papistry, Hadrian, decline and fall, invaders.

VIII. The Mediterranean World

Christian and Moslem

(a) **Rome:** *The Western Empire,* Charlemagne, the Holy Roman Empire. Back to kingdoms, monasteries. Ahead to national developments (English, Scandinavians, Germans, etc.) Languages, universities. *Constantinople: The Eastern Empire.* Constantine, Turks, crusades.

(b) **Mecca:** *The Mohammedan World.* Arabia, India-Pakistan. Babylon: Mesopotamia. Back to Hammurabi, ancient Babylon; Persia, Darius; Jerusalem. *North Africa: Moslem Alexandria.* Back to ancient Egypt, Nile, pyramids, papyrus, etc., (Helenes, Romans). Carthage, Cordova. Ahead to Spanish influence in Latin America, Southern California. Imperialism, nationalism.

IX. Europe

Renaissance, Reformation, exploration, nationalism.

(a) **Florence:** *The age of the Renaissance man.* The Renaissance moves north: Rome, Florence, Venice, Milan. Ahead to Munich, Vienna, Berlin. *Paris: The Napoleonic age.* Back to Middle Ages, English wars, the monarchy, the age of Enlightenment, revolution. Ahead to the twentieth century.

(b) **London:** *The Elizabethan age.* Back to the conquest, Magna Charta, etc. Ahead to the Reformation—early protests, the Inquisition, monasteries, Luther, Calvin, Henry VIII, Cromwell. Migrations to the U.S. *London:* The British Empire. *The Victorian age.* Back to the Spanish Armada. Commerce, wealth, Napoleon, Egypt, India. Ahead to the twentieth century.

WORLD RELATIONSHIPS

X. The Eurasian Heritage

(a) **India:** *Delhi: British rule.* Back to Buddha, Alexander, Asoka, Akbar and the Moguls. Ahead to *Gandhi, New Delhi,* Independence, Pakistan. *China: Peking; nineteenth century.* Back to Confucius, significant dynasties including Manchu, relationships with Europe, U.S., Open Door, Boxer Rebellion. Ahead to republic, Communists. *Japan: Tokyo, with the Army of Occupation.* Back to Jimmu Tenno, feudal nobility, samurai, Shoguns (treaties, ports), Mikado. Wars with China, Korea, Russia. Co-prosperity sphere. War with U.S.: new constitution. Ahead to postwar recovery. *South-East Asia: Bangkok.* Indonesia, Malay peninsula. French, English, Dutch, Japanese, Independence, Communist encroachment. *Philippines: Manila*—U.S. Territory. Back to occupation by Spain, Aguinaldo. Independence. *Australia and New Zealand.* Migration, colonials, development, commonwealth. *Oceania.* Ahead to development. *Hawaii: Honolulu: U.S. missions.* Back to origins—settlers. Ahead to development, statehood.

(b) **The Communist World:** *Moscow: the Bolshevik revolution.* Back to Mongols, Genghis Khan, the Czars, "Mother Russia," wars with Poland, Turkey, Sweden, Japan. Conquests to East and South. Hegel, Marx, Lenin, Trotsky, the Party. Forward to Stalin, communization. World War II, expansion. Relations with U.S. ('co-existence'), the 'free world,' China.

XI. U.S. and World Neighbors

(a) **London. c. 1900:** Science, industrialization, nationalism, balance of power, imperialism. Back to Germany—Bismarck; England—India, South Africa, Boer War. apartheid. U.S.: *New York, c. 1900.* Back to Civil War, industrialization. Spain. Democracy, financial development. The Renaissance in U.S. (Greek revival) vs. the Frontier.

(b) **The Twentieth Century:** *Washington: World War I.* League of Nations; Depression, Fascism, National Socialism, Communism. Technology. *World War II.* United Nations. Marshall Plan. Reconstruction, NATO. Japan, Korea. British Commonwealth. *North and Central Africa,* imperialism, nationalism. Problems: conservative vs. progressive, regionalism, space exploration, science vs. humanities, population explosion, scarcity and abundance, new underdeveloped nations, desegregation, etc.

XII. Systematic courses in social sciences and/or participation in socio-civic projects, or concentrated study of selected national and world problems.

As has no doubt been noted, the elementary grades deal primarily with the Americas, beginning at home and gradually moving out to establish an awareness of the rest of the world through an exploration of the national origins of their peoples. The junior high school concentrates on the Western heritage, the senior high school on wider world relationships.

METHODS AND MEDIA

Much depends on the methods and media used for the success of the area-study approach, but it provides opportunities for an interesting variety of procedures, many of them familiar to social studies teachers.

Probably first in importance are actual field trips to the sites studied, but these are necessarily limited, as are excursions to museums and galleries. Artifacts and restorations of whatever sort give a sense of reality. Sometimes class members will have visited the places studied and brought back articles of various kinds including rocks, dishes, costume dolls, jewelry, and the like.

Of greatest general value, probably, are the wide range of visuals to give reality to imaginary visits to distant times and places and clarify the concepts of objects and activities: historical films, travel films, video tapes, slides, prints and different kinds of maps. Travel folders and encyclopedias can be studied. Television, of course, has the advantage of being able to include a wider audience—all sections of a class, and even students in outlying schools can participate.

A fictional family of the period might in some cases be assembled, with members of which the students can identify or fraternize, discuss their problems and study the history that *they* will study for the flashback. Both original and secondary sources will be consulted, models of various kinds planned and built, various kinds of role playing, informal dramatization, and even more complicated simulation techniques employed. Anachronistic newspapers can be edited with such headlines as SOPHICLES' OEDIPUS SMASH HIT, or CRISTOBAL COLON RETURNS—FROM WHERE? and solutions of problems of the period can be proposed and compared with what was actually done.

As work progresses toward and into the senior high school, the efforts to give reality to past events will continue, but methods employed will be adapted to the growing maturity of the students. It is probable that the habits of thinking derived from the earlier experiences will continue, and problems can be discussed in the abstract but with the continuing realization that they were and are problems of people.

There is, of course, a danger of employing poor methods with a good medium; for example, of showing too many buildings, statues, pictures, working scenes, and so on. Ideally, each should be presented only for a well-defined purpose. An explanatory sound track lessens the teacher's load. Recordings of music can be used directly or through the medium of the sound laboratory, illustrating different periods and places, and occasional literary masterpieces may be presented more effectively in this way than in any other.

But instruction is not all looking and listening, and should not be, although much can be taught in this way. There will necessarily be a great deal of factual material to be learned and concepts from the different social sciences to be clarified. Factual materials, the contributions of great men, key dates and places, and important concepts lend themselves to the use of programed and other self-instructional materials and can effectually assume much of the burden of content, the framework of facts and their relationships that necessarily constitute such a large part of school learning, and do it more efficiently than is possible in the classroom with large numbers of pupils of widely differing abilities. The area context, it can be predicted, will result in greater ease of learning and with a higher level of interest and retention.

Audiovisual materials and programed lessons will do much to overcome one of the chief criticisms of social studies teaching—the usual large amount of aimless, uninformed, and profitless discussion. It is possible that three kinds of specialists are needed: one for telling (lecture-demonstration), one for programing, and another for leading discussions. But even with a not so skillful discussion leader, questions growing out of the facts observed and studied are attacked at a more mature level than is otherwise the case. Children and young people thus informed who argue, for example about why such and such action was taken, and in the light of the consequences what might have been a better course to follow, will gradually gain the experience that will enable them to meet their own current problems more intelligently. At least this seems not too much to hope for.

And lastly, the matter of projects. Ideally, every student would be engaged in an individual or group project, following his line of special interest. The projects might involve constructs of one sort or another—models, ceramics, art work, illustrated posters, maps or diagrams and the like, or they might be the preparation of papers on one aspect or another of the area being studied. In any case it would be expected that the instructional materials center, or its equivalent, would be consulted, and that it would be equipped in personnel and supplies to furnish the needed support for such efforts.

Advantages of Area Study

The first four advantages listed below are methodological; the others relate primarily to content. Many of the advantages of an area-studies curriculum are to be found in the usual social studies-humanities instruction, but it is believed that under the area-study program they could be more abundantly realized.

1. It adapts easily to the level of development of the students without making unjustifiable demands upon them, as does the history of the world, in one year. Simpler cultures, or those which necessitate less detail, are studied earlier, but the treatment of any area may be adapted to the level at which it is believed it should be taught.

2. It provides systematically for diversification, less repetition, and more reality than the usual social studies curriculum. Whitehead's "inert ideas" are more easily avoided since all are taught in relation to life as it is being lived.

3. It is sufficiently flexible to permit whatever variations in emphasis and method may be considered desirable at different times and in different schools. Other materials can be substituted in different units, and even whole units can be switched.

4. It furnishes a basis for subsequent high school or college courses in one or more of the separate social sciences by providing an understanding of the context from which they are drawn.

5. It transmits the cultural heritage, which along with the development of values is an important aim of education, and does it in a way that makes it meaningful and applicable to current happenings and problems.

6. It includes commonly neglected regions of the world. Many studies have shown that the countries of Asia, and now of Africa, have been inadequately treated in the textbooks, preference being given to the Western heritage. Now that one of these countries has become a leading world power, there should be an end to this neglect; and area-studies provides a form within which the needed supplementation can be provided.

7. It introduces the basic concepts of the different social sciences in different forms and in different social structures or cultures as the curriculum advances. This is valuable not only for further study, but also for practical application.

8. It provides the content for experience in problem-solving and critical thinking in the area of human interaction. The errors of the past come up for review, the ignorance, prejudice, and short-sightedness, as do also the wisdom, foresight, and courage and the sources of knowledge on which wiser judgments might be based. Students can learn to recognize dogmatism, tolerate necessary ambiguities, and make intelligent choices. This is at least part of what is desired by those who want the schools to train young people to think.

9. It provides the content for intercultural understanding, for which the various current shortcuts are helpful but inadequate.

10. It provides a basis for developing value judgments in the area of both public and private morality. It is time for values to be examined in the school life of young people, and for them to learn that cultural relativism does not imply an absence of all sanctions. And further, the story of the world in which young people must learn to live and make their choices should be presented with scientific objectivity, but it need not be an expurgated edition. They can learn to make more right choices. They can be brought in on the side of good government and humanitarian effort. They can learn the responsibilities of the average citizen, and of those above average. And they can be brought to see some of the many things that need to be done and have a hand in doing them.

REFERENCES

1. Gross, Richard E. and Badger, William V., "Social studies," in Chester W. Harris (ed.), *Encyclopedia of Educational Research*, (New York: The Macmil-

lan Co., 1960), pp. 1296–1319; and Harrison, Sylvia E., and Solomon, Robert J., "Review of research in the teaching of social studies: 1960–1963," *Social Education*, XXVIII (May 1964), 277–92, and *idem.*, "1964," XXIX (May 1965), 281–90, 298.

2. Dressel, Paul L., and Lorimer, Margaret F., "Humanities," in Chester W. Harris, *op. cit.*, p. 576.

3. *Report of the Commission on the Humanities*, of the American Council of Learned Societies, the Council of Graduate Schools in the United States, and the United Chapters of Phi Beta Kappa. New York: American Council of Learned Societies, 1964.

4. *The Key Reporter*. Washington, D.C.: United Chapters of Phi Beta Kappa, Autumn 1964.

5. Cuban, Larry, "The Cardozo Peace Corps Project: Experiment in urban education," *Social Education*, XXVIII (December 1964), 446–49, 456.

6. Lyons, Richard G., "Philosophy and anthropology in the study of mankind," *Social Education*, XXVIII (November 1964), 405–6.

7. *The Yorker*, The Directors Report. Cooperstown, N.Y.: State Historical Association, 1964, XXI (May–June 1964) 1–16.

8. *The CUE Report: An Experiment in the Humanities Using Newer Media.* Albany: the Univ. of the State of New York, State Educational Dept., Division of Educational Communications, 1965, p. 14.

9. See Trow, William Clark, *Teacher and Technology — New Designs for Learning*. New York: Appleton, Century, Crofts, 1963, chap. V.

10. See Bloom, Benjamin S. (ed.), *Taxonomy of Educational Objectives: Cognitive Domain*, (New York: Longmans Green and Co., 1956); Krathwohl, David R., *et al.*, *Taxonomy of Educational Objectives: Affective Domain*, (New York: David McKay Co., Inc., 1956); and Mager, Robert F. *Preparing Objectives for Programmed Instruction*, (San Francisco: Fearon Publishers, 1962).

Chapter 11

How has business education evolved in order to stay current and meaningful for the student during the rapid changes in business and industry?

How has the availability of technology influenced the teaching of 'traditional' business courses?

What differences in skills and abilities will be required of business education graduates in the future?

What can be done to make business education dynamic and more "businesslike" through the use of media?

INSTRUCTIONAL MEDIA AND EDUCATIONAL PREPARATION FOR BUSINESS AND INDUSTRY

ALVIN C. BECKETT, Professor of Business and Education
San Jose State College

INTRODUCTION

Trade—the backbone of profitable business and industry! Paperwork—the cartilage that serves as the link between the buyer and seller, employer and employee, owners and union or government, educator and educated, and anyone else who desires to get involved. What were some of the forces that led to the superabundant demands of business and industry as we know it today?

Certainly the documented movements of the crusaders that began in the year 1096 did much to establish the multi-pronged avenues of trade between the insular domains of Europe and the East. The discovery of a large volume of products, coupled with extensive markets for those products, provided an unusual impetus for an increase in business transactions. The combination of growth, complexity, and the question of profit preceded the need for Fra Luca Pacioli's book, *Summa de Arith-*

metica, Geometria, Proportioni et Proportionalita, in 1494—one of the earliest guides for the proper recording of such transactions. This, together with Johann Gutenberg's movable type, and the art of paper-making acquired from the Chinese by the Germans, made the basic tools possible for business and industry to promote itself. Through a system of apprenticeship, the competence to maintain the records of industry was transmitted from master to novice.

Unfortunately, the number of trained clerks was found to be insufficient as the tempo of increased colonization throughout the world trebled the need for records. The Colonial period in this country (1635-1789) yielded the first private classes of instruction in bookkeeping, arithmetic, and handwriting for vocational purposes (1). From this modest beginning in business education, some of the private academies joined the movement to include similar courses and at the same time develop a more unified and systematical preparation of clerks. A few city public schools added business courses in the early 1800s and declared the same objectives—the training of clerks.

Private business colleges came into existence as the result of increased demands for trained clerical workers required by burgeoning industries. The period when this occurred, the mid-1800s and the Industrial Revolution, reflected little change in the courses of study until stenography was added to the program in 1863. The invention of the typewriter in 1873 mechanized writing and served as a complement for the shortened form of calligraphy. Private business colleges were, and continue to be, a form of private enterprise organized to supply business education in exchange for profit on capital invested in the operation of the school.

The character of formal business education offered in private business schools did not assume any appreciable change in major emphasis until 1881 when Joseph Wharton endowed the University of Pennsylvania with sufficient funds to establish a "School of Commerce and Finance" (2). This underwritten private venture, followed by similar assistance from the American Bankers Association for the University of Chicago in 1889, gave impetus to a change in ideology. The broader aspects of training for responsible positions of authority in business and industry were stressed, and the merits of college degrees in business awarded by accredited institutions were cited as evidence of the value of a broad college education.

When did the public high school begin to evidence a show of strength? At the turn of the century, public secondary-school enrollments totalled approximately one-half million students. Sixty-five years later, enrollments in public high schools had grown to 15,321,000 (3). A relatively stable average of 10 per cent of those persons who have pursued a public secondary-school education have elected courses offered in the business education program throughout the entire time (4).

Where else may a student seek an education to prepare for positions in business and industry? Post-secondary education, evident in the terminal and transfer programs of the private and public junior colleges, offers such a possibility. Designed for the thirteenth and fourteenth years and viewed either as an extension of the high school, or the first two years of college, the products of these programs accept permanent employment immediately, or pursue added studies for greater depth.

Who is to say where the job of preparation for business and industry can be done best? Ultimate judges of the product, the employers, are certainly entitled to voice their opinions. Generally, the level on which preparation is received in order to train for jobs in business and industry is of little concern to the employers. The persons who do the hiring are prepared to budget the amounts of money they consider apropos for the work done, and in turn they expect persons equipped with the threshold skills and knowledges that are useful in business and the community.

MAJOR AREAS OF CONCENTRATION

Formal education designed to prepare students for jobs in business and industry may begin at almost any stage of maturation. Business subjects may be taught on many different educational levels, but there is a time when particular knowledges and skills have more meaningful purpose for individuals who recognize such needs. Properly introduced, at a time when those who are counseled to enroll in business courses realize why they are there, learning becomes more meaningful.

Four major areas of concentration ordinarily exist within the business education curriculum. These are broadly identified as secretarial, bookkeeping/accounting, distributive education, and general/clerical. National secondary level enrollments for business subjects in these areas of concentration most recently announced were (4):

Typewriting I	1,301,663
II	273,992
Shorthand I	490,641
II	113,249
Secretarial Practice	48,414
Bookkeeping I	571,713
II	54,106
Business Arithmetic	230,109
General Business	356,051
Business Law	103,807

Distributive Education	45,317
General Clerical Practice	231,640
Consumer Education	57,843
Business English	50,954
Business Organization	24,862
Economic Geography	19,047
	3,973,408

The treatment of these business subjects in the presentation that follows is intended to coincide with the order of importance of the subject and the area of concentration with which it is most closely identified.

Typewriting

Legibility and the Typewriter. The art of handwriting, which formerly was one of the keystones in business education programs, has become a lost art. The distinct flourishes and characteristic embellishments that typified the trained penman have virtually disappeared. This decline began in 1873 when the first mechanizations of the art of handwriting were embodied in the output of Christopher L. Shole's crude typewriter (5). Today, the serifs and curlicues are quickly made from a selection limited only by the machine and supplementary equipment at hand.

The Changeable Type kits for the SCM Electra 120, in combination with many type faces and styles, enlarge the potential selections available on the ordinary fixed keyboard. The innumerable printing elements available as optional equipment for the IBM Selectric make this typewriter a handmaiden for today's printer's devil. Hundreds of different type fonts for the VariTyper—one of the first machines to offer a variation in type styles at the fingertips—provide unlimited choices for the mechanically-minded printer-typist. Typit keys are designed, without restriction, for use with typewriters that lack any key imaginable (6). The complete mechanization of writing tasks that were formerly taught and practiced for many decades has improved the results of these manual rituals. Small wonder that time formerly spent in the business program to control handwriting has been relegated to the mastery of the typewriter keyboard.

How early in life can a child be taught the rudiments of typewriting? Gifted children have been introduced to electric typewriters as early as the age of two years seven months by Omar Khayyam Moore (7). These children were taught to recognize the letters of the alphabet by location on the keyboard, strike the proper letters when characters were projected onto a screen, arrange letters into words, and eventually construct simple sentences. With the aid of tape recorders, these children repeated the sounds of the letters as they typed them, read their own typed material, took dictation on the typewriter from other recorded voices, and dictated their own short stories. Within 68 weeks, children in the experimental group were able to read at the fourth-grade level, type autonomously, print, and take third-grade material in dictation. These children were given this instruction on the operation of the typewriter in order to teach them orthographic symbols which would permit them to translate written symbols to spoken ones, and spoken symbols to written ones.

Refinements of procedures employed in subsequent experiments with kindergarten pupils have utilized special purpose computers to replace human instructors and thus set up an automated responsive environment (8). Here, the typewriter keyboard was synchronized with a voice recording. Each time a key was pressed, a voice repeated the letter or number struck; within three or four sessions, most of the children became familiar with the keyboard. In the next phase, the recorded voice said a letter and the child pressed the appropriate key as the letter appeared on a screen at the top of the machine with a pointer over the appropriate letter. Here, the major purpose was to recognize groups of letters and words to improve reading ability rather than seek proficiency on the typewriter as the major purpose.

What is the best way to implement the elementary school typewriting course? Experiments conducted by Nathan Krevolin to assess the contributions of typewriting mastery to the language arts areas—reading, vocabulary, spelling, capitalization, punctuation and usage—resulted in the publication of a new text for elementary school typewriting instruction (9). Encouraged by a typewriter manufacturer and offered to a fifth-grade class, twenty-minute lessons were given for a total of seventy periods throughout one semester. The twenty-minute lessons were recorded and played; this permitted the instructor to stress fundamentals, praise achievement, assist those who had difficulties, and free himself from the more formal approaches to instruction. Clearly evident was the genuine interest exhibited by elementary children who were under no pressure to qualify for grades. They accepted the use of records and music as additional inducements to relax while learning, and were determined to apply their newly acquired skills to their personal needs rather than vocational demands. The greatest weakness noted was the lack of typewriter stations accessible to those who had learned to type; once their term of instruction ended, it became an individual problem to find another typewriter elsewhere for further application of the skills acquired.

Why do most students learn to type in junior and senior high schools? A review of the national secondary level enrollments for business subjects immediately discloses that typewriting was first, with 1,301,663.

The closest competitor was bookkeeping, with 571,713. Estimates of the number of students who took typewriting courses in grades lower than these claimed no more than 1,000 enrollees throughout the entire nation.

Contemplate the elementary school course requirements—English, sciences, social studies, mathematics, physical education, music or art or homemaking, foreign languages (California)—and the usual length of the class day; one of the major reasons for the omission of typewriting is evident! Add to this the costs of equipping a room—30 to 40 manual typewriters could cost $5–8,000, or the same number of electric typewriters (preferred) could cost as much as $16,000—plus the peripheral equipment that should be in the room. Then provide a properly trained typewriting teacher. Multiply cost factors by the number of elementary schools in the district and the magnitude of the problem is enough to deter any cost-conscious administrator who is being pressured constantly to supply quality educational programs with emphasis upon subject-matter oriented classes. It is easier to sidestep a problem than to compound those that already exist.

If students are to make use of this newly gained knowledge, then such knowledge should be acquired as near as possible to the time of use. As an illustration of this theory put to the test, note the competences stressed for those who take the course for personal use: announcements, memoranda, short reports, personal notes, postal cards, letters, minutes of meetings, long reports, manuscripts, tables, personal correspondence, and common legal documents (10). Secondary school, with its emphasis upon club activities and social gatherings, together with the demands for more written work in any number of courses taken by college-bound students, is immediately a logical choice. For those students who envision employment immediately after graduation—to earn a living, or help meet the costs of a college education—the additional letter styles, report forms, business papers, work on duplication equipment, and stress upon increased production requirements qualify vocational enrollees for such a purpose. Graduation from high school merely signifies an opportunity to put this knowledge to the supreme test.

Should typewriting instruction be offered beyond the high school level? This question, often issued as a challenge when such courses are offered on the college level, can be countered through restatement of the question by substituting such courses as general biology, elementary German, freshman English, United States history, or economic geography. If courses such as these have not been taken at a prior time, and if the knowledge and skills to be gained from these courses are a necessary part of the educational pattern, then why not in college?

College level courses in typewriting proceed at a much faster pace than those offered on secondary or elementary levels; one semester of the former is equivalent to two terms of the latter. The vocabulary employed throughout the text is intended to be more relevant to that which is used in business, and the syllable intensity averages 3.4, and higher. The amount of motivation deemed necessary for success on the secondary level becomes decidedly less on the college level; student maturity and an awareness of the purposes for taking the course encourage such an attitude on the part of the teacher.

What can be done to facilitate the learning process in typewriting? Innumerable multi-sensory materials and devices have been available for classroom use for a number of years. What appears to be brand new to many of today's advocates were in many instances discoveries of an earlier period.

Filmstrips and films have long been used to introduce new keys to those learning to type, and were available from Coronet Films before World War II. How-to-do-it slides, prepared for more deliberate observation of selected techniques, were the output of cameras that utilized slower film, lacked color, and relied upon either the skill or luck of the amateur with a practical idea; the addition of Polaroid Swingers or Kodak Instamatic flash-cubes together with super-sensitive color film has given the output a more professional appearance. The cumbersome combination of weight and bulk of the old-fashioned opaque projector, together with extreme heat from bulbs with high wattage, deterred many teachers who preferred the slow deterioration of bulletin board displays to that of the 'infernal magnifier.' The experiment of Fred Winger (11), in which he used the tachistoscope to accelerate typing skills, was followed by the commercial output of the Educational Developmental Laboratories' Skill Builder and Controlled Reader filmstrips (12). Reports of experiments with such visual media technology should lead to wholesale adoptions, for the old cliché that "one picture is worth a thousand words" has been substantiated again and again in a number of trials.

Audio media are more plentiful than ever. The original equipment that relayed instructions via records, belts, cylinders, wire, and tape has been improved to an extreme that defies the imagination. Soundproof chambers and cumbersome recording paraphernalia belong to a bygone era; the transistorized tape recorder makes it possible for thoughts to be modified a few moments before instruction begins. Students on all educational levels today accept recordings and playbacks as a way of life.

How can this, and much newer equipment, be utilized to best advantage by the forward-thinking teacher of typewriting?

A combination of the previously mentioned multi-sensory materials can be blended in the following manner. Taped instructions for warm-up drills and introductory reading, followed by mood music, while typewriting takes place, free the teacher for administrative detail tasks and development of the traits sought in each student. Controlled reader exercises can be used to vary the drills and increase the reading response speed. The overhead projector can be a tool to hasten the presentation of illustrations that are designed to give the students a visual image of the end product. This can also be varied with examples of techniques or finished copy captured on film with today's ultramodern photographic apparatus and shown on slides or filmstrips. Lessons that put into practice these extensions of an individual's ingenuity do diminish the number of lectures delivered from force of habit, and heighten the possibility of achievement through artful stimulation.

Many schools have been constructed in the last decade and are now wired for television. Receivers are mounted in many classrooms, or are sufficiently mobile to make them available. The study completed in 1955 by William Pasewark (13) set forth the feasibility of teaching touch typewriting via this medium. His recommendations led to the publication of *Teaching Plans for the Gregg TV Typing Course* and a companion course guide in 1958 (14). The invention and constant improvement of video tape since then have resulted in the marketing of video tape recorders for the home, and quite logically for the classroom. Why not capture the unbounded enthusiasm of the most effective typewriting teachers on video tape for an entire series of lessons, to be transmitted at whatever times classes are scheduled to meet, and closely monitored by teachers in charge? These video tapes could be duplicated for all other schools in the system—the entire country, for that matter.

Typewriting may also be self-taught in the classroom. Such programed instruction lesson materials as those developed by International Educational Services, Inc. (15) for typewriting do instruct students in the operating techniques, correspondence, rough drafts, manuscripts, centering, tabulation, and speed tests. The same procedures could be used for formal classroom instruction and thus make learning an individual matter of concern.

The use of FM radio to teach typewriting to dropouts and retrainees, through a program called *Mind* sponsored by the National Association of Manufacturers, couples the use of tapes and the broadcasting medium to teach the students in their own homes. Students with little or no previous typewriting instruction currently employed by business to perform other tasks are loaned typewriters, transistor sets, and headphones throughout the period of instruction. The FM station operates several channels and the student selects the band with the program which approximates her own speed while she learns or improves her typewriting ability at night at home (16).

Enoch J. Haga maintains that "automated typing instruction is on the way" (17). Inasmuch as keyboard instruction and directions for exercises and problems already exist on tapes, it is a simple matter to correlate these tapes with automatically projected slides, filmstrips, motion pictures or multimedia demonstrations. Now add individual learning stations, each equipped with a keyboard, viewing screen, earphones and various other controls and data communications links. Put the teacher behind a console to individually control each student's learning experiences by electronically sequencing him into desirable instructional patterns. Follow this with testing and measurement tied to the same system. All of these operations, punched on the tape by the typewriter, can then be compared with computer-stored models for evaluation and criticism. Follow this plan and automated typing instruction can become a reality.

Why is the ability to type proficiently so important to business and industry? Evidence of a shortage of trained clerical personnel is offered again and again in newspaper reports, research and statistics published by various State Department of Employment bureaus, and magazine articles. When firms such as Western Electric "now hire(s) people with 'substandard typing skills' and give(s) them a typing course" (18); Edith Green, ranking member of the House Committee on Labor and Education, calls attention to one million high school dropouts who need vocational training (19); and published monthly reports of the "Characteristics of Retraining Applicants" cite the fact that the major number of retrainees enroll in clerical (and sales) classes (20), the need for such instruction while students are still in school is emphasized. The demands for trained typists will be even greater as calls for communications between automated pieces of equipment become more pronounced.

The copy which followed the headline "Mail letters over the phone!" (21) to introduce the new Xerox Magnafax Telecopier described the simple procedure of sending a letter any distance from one Telecopier to another Telecopier over ordinary telephone equipment. A successive advertisement (22) reproduced the letter that was transmitted via the Telecopier, but the letter that was transmitted was *originally typed*. The equipment is ingenious, but the typist is not replaced.

IBM's joint experiments with Pennsylvania State University (23) link students with computers by telephone lines to pursue courses in cost accounting, engineering economics, mathematics for elementary school teachers, and special education courses. Instruction begins when the computer causes a question to be typed on the student's typewriter. The student must then *type the response* to the computer for evaluation. Learning takes place with the aid of the typewriter. The May 1966 AT&T Bell Telephone System advertisement in *Forbes* pointed out that colleges and high schools are currently using teletypewriters for computer-assisted instruction, and the trend continues to grow.

The keyboard printer with paper tape transmitter (24) operates like a typewriter. As the typist strikes the keys to print a message, coded signals activate a distant machine to print the identical message. The added advantage of the paper tape is that it may be used again and again for later transmission—but a typist has to prepunch the paper tape.

Visual Display Terminals (24) provide visual presentation of information stored within a computer system. Questions or information typed on the keyboard of the terminal are relayed to the computer by telephone lines and in this instance the responses to the inquiries are transmitted in return to a Teleregister, or television-type screen mounted in full view behind the typewriter. A typist must inaugurate the request to the computer.

Advertisements for Teletype equipment reinforce the demand for trained typists when they advise businessmen-readers that "This typist has just transmitted sales order information directly to other Teletype sets in the production, shipping, and accounting departments—all at the same time. . ." (25). Data communications depend upon trained typists.

Businesses, such as title insurance firms, utilize clerk-typists to prepare information tapes on such machines as the Dura Mach 10—basically an electric typewriter with automatic tape punch attachments. The output eliminates the need for lower echelon file clerks and routine research clerks; once again, however, the key person is the clerk-typist.

When businesses are prepared to pay $10,000 for the new IBM Magnetic Tape Selectric, then the demand for accurate typists may be compromised. If this machine is used and typing mistakes are made, the typist simply backspaces, retypes, and keeps on going while the machine automatically corrects the magnetic tape during these steps. Furthermore, the magnetic tape may be replayed and further edited. What happens to the magnetic tape when the job is finished? The magnetic tape becomes the key for as many repeat performances of the copy as the production manager envisions. The typist is still the key person!

Spellright typewriter ribbons (26) can save time and work for the typist too. Errors are chemically treated with the top half of the ribbon (similar to the process of eradication) and the bottom half does the regular job. Ko-Rec-Type kits (27) do the same work as Spellright typewriter ribbons when applied to the errors manually.

Laser erasers (28) may become standard equipment on electric typewriters of the future. The beam from lasers will erase typing errors without leaving a trace of the ink.

Automation will have a profound affect upon the work of the typist. Electric typewriters will replace manual machines in order to provide input tapes for electronic machines. Automatic typewriters will perform repetitious production jobs. However, the typist will still have to be trained in the basic skills of typewriter operation.

As school budgets are prepared in anticipation of the replacement of existing pieces of equipment, those that call for new electric typewriters should look ahead now. The Smith-Corona 250 KPT (29) is an electric typewriter with a keypunch keyboard that couples the usual automatic features of electric typewriters with full-size special numeric and alphabetic keypunch keyboards. Its optical scanning type is compatible with type used on data processing equipment. Purchase of this equipment can bridge the gap between the classroom and actual business practice without necessitating the addition of expensive data processing equipment.

Undoubtedly, such rare items as the music typewriter which has 42 keys and 79 symbols (30), and the Chinese typewriter with its 1500 characters (31) will not warrant automation applications. The market is a highly limited one and the demand is not sufficient enough to warrant excessive costs embodied in training and purchase of equipment. Understandably, there will never be an oversupply of trained typists for the operation of such machines.

The typewriter skills demanded for entry jobs must be taught in the classroom if future clerk-typists, human links with computers, or other possessors of these skills plan to qualify for their goals.

What about tomorrow? There is a good possibility that future typists may be taught by speech teachers. Results of experiments, reported by RCA in 1962 (32), yielded a typewriter that printed in English or even translated into another language when commanded to do so from a selected vocabulary of 100 words. At that time, the threat that such sentences as "the spirit is willing but the flesh is weak" might be incorrectly translated as "the whiskey is strong but the meat is poor" were quite real. Those original experiments have continued and the claims of RCA now are that the response is correct 90 to 99 per cent of the time (33). Voice control of telephone dialing, adding machines, computers, and typewriters can now be accomplished laboriously. RCA claims that 28 of the 40 phonemes, or basic sounds, are within the dominion of their equipment. Progress evidenced in the capabilities of the present generation of computers can lead to just one conclusion: typewriters, controlled by voice, must be recognized as a future threat to the preponderant attention given to the major course of instruction offered in business education—typewriting.

Shorthand

Should it be forgotten? Throughout the past century, countless systems of abbreviations for shorthand—cryptic and lettered—have vied for top favor with would-be secretaries and stenographers. Such names as Gregg, Thomas, Forkner, Isaac Pitman, and Ben Pitman have been linked with instruction in shorthand, Notehand, Alpha-Hand, Briefhand, and many other names given to the shortened system of handwriting. Stenotype, a system that depends upon the operation of a machine to take notes, has occupied a position apart from the manual methods. During the same period of time, machine dictation and transcription have steadily encroached upon the position of dominance shorthand systems have held, and enrollments in shorthand courses continue to diminish. Will the need for persons highly trained in the art of shorthand die out completely? Never—as long as the members of the fair sex continue to beguile the employer and his customers into the recognition that the individual touch lends a lot of polish to the raw materials.

What makes an executive secretary's qualifications more attractive than a typist and a machine transcription operator from a pool? Training and the degree to which independence of action is permitted in the fulfillment of duties are hallmarks in such identification. Although thoughts can be transferred to dictation machines of many types, the privilege of immediate edit coupled with helpful opinions when wanted make the machine less desirous than the human counterpart. Add to this attraction the many other tasks performed throughout each working day by an efficient secretary, and the continued demand for persons with shorthand skills defies prediction for obsolescence.

What can be done to facilitate the learning process in shorthand? One thing is common to the development of the ability to take dictation with any degree of speed: plenty of practice. This practice usually takes the form of reading the abbreviated outlines or letters, copying many combinations of outlines or letters, taking the dictation of this theory again and again, and transcribing the work that has been dictated. What can be done to free the teacher and the students from the monotony of the humdrum routine of study/practice/read/write/transcribe and repeat?

A number of companies (e.g., Gregg, Dictation Disc, Electronic Futures, Inc.) have marketed complete sets of records or tapes that repeat orally all the principles contained in the textbook lessons. Record players or tape recorders make it possible for the teacher to counsel students individually while the practice dictation is given. The dictator's voice is foreign to the students' ears—a good bridge for the move to a job some day. This equipment provides a way, too, for the absentee student to receive the previous day's instruction while the class advances, or else borrow this instruction for additional practice at home.

The complete electronic classroom, with its individual listening stations and its battery of tape recorders for the transmission of different applications of practice simultaneously, is the logical expansion of facilities for the teacher who needs centralized variation of dictation speeds for students with different abilities, or help for absentees who missed previous instruction and drill work needed after their return to class. Some classroom equipment, such as that manufactured by the Electronic Futures, Inc., a learning system, needs no installation because it is wireless, broadcasts from transmitter to listening channels within the classroom, accommodates multi-track magnetic tapes for 5½ hours of material, and makes it possible for the teacher to use the transmitter or student receiver for microphone input (34).

The emphasis placed on the ability to take dictation in shorthand should be supplemented with similar stress on the proficiency needed to transcribe notes. In beginning shorthand, oral transcription—reading aloud in a group, or individually—can be stimulated through the use of tachistoscope and controlled reader filmstrips. Introductory materials, correlated with the textbook, may be projected line by line (tachistoscope) for response. As the work of the course progresses and the need for increased transcription speeds becomes a part of each day's goals, the projection of outlines at varying speeds (controlled reader) facilitates such goals. Educational Developmental Laboratories (35) has marketed filmstrips for shorthand courses, as well as typewriting and business machines filmstrips, for projection in pacing machines.

Programed units for self-study, such as the Alpha-Hand programed course (36), can shorten the learning process. The combination of a programed workbook-textbook with dictation records returns the responsibility to the individual. The recognition of the merits of this method for the self-instruction of adults is evident in the wide range of business courses—including shorthand—developed by Educational Methods, Inc., and used in pilot programs sponsored by the American Bankers Association (37). The National Cash Register approach to programed instruction in shorthand (and other courses) differs in that instructions are given by tape recorder, with pauses for response and reinforcements of the responses; here, the trainee couples visual with audio instruction (38). **What can be predicted for the secretary and stenographer of tomorrow?** The ultimate goal for students who seek vocational careers with the aid of their shorthand skills should be recognition as a Certified Professional Secretary. The title is awarded to those secretaries who have presented evidence of a combination of secretarial experience and education, and who have passed a certifying examination, developed and administered by the National Secretaries Association. The two-day examination includes tests in six fields: secretarial skills, secretarial procedures, secretarial accounting, business law, business administration, personal adjustment and human relations (39).

"The secretary of the year 2000 won't have to take dictation or type." This is the prediction of Richard L. Sheppard, one of the vice presidents for the 3M Company (40). "Her boss probably will do all of his dictating into a microphone connected to a computer which takes down his words, then transcribes them and types them onto a letter." Until that time arrives, those students who must prepare for this and the next generation of office procedures face the prospect of learning how to typewrite and also present evidence of stenographic skills in order to successfully compete against today's applicants.

Bookkeeping/Accounting

What are debits and credits? The basic rules formalized by Fra Pacioli in his treatise of 1494 have been enlarged considerably since that time in order to apply to more complicated transactions. However, the mandate that the total debits (the left side) must equal the total credits (the right side) after balances of all accounts are ascertained has not been modified one whit. The principle of balance is basic to the work of all bookkeepers (those who record transactions and determine whether accounts are in balance) and the understanding of all accountants (those who verify the work of the bookkeepers and then make further interpretations).

As is the case of other skills that must be thoroughly learned in order to be properly applied, the ability to manage sets of books for selected business firms necessitates adequate practice. Once the explanations, demonstrations, and questions related to principles to be mastered have been covered, then the students must solve series of problems, verify their solutions, review, and be subjected to examinations in order to prove their mastery of techniques.

How can instruction and application of theory be provided effectively? Traditional visuals, such as charts, enlarged forms, portable cardboard headings for columns ruled on blackboards, and posters have been an adjunct to the well-schooled bookkeeping/accounting instructor's classes since time immemorial. Commercially prepared films and filmstrips, such as those sold or rented by the Society for Visual Education or by the Text-Film Division of the McGraw-Hill Book Company quickly illustrate some of the major accounting principles (41). Intended for use with overhead projectors are such items as the kit of visual aid materials that includes complete sets of projectuals for demonstration problems, solutions for text problems, series of overlays for working papers, and accounting forms (42).

Programed instruction for bookkeeping/accounting by such firms as the International Educational Services, or the Addison-Wesley Publishing Company (43), are intended for students who wish to proceed at their own speed. Similarly, the programs sponsored by the American Bankers Association and other business groups are intended for those who are employed and who wish to upgrade their qualifications.

Is the demise of the bookkeeper/accountant inevitable? A good portion of the work currently performed by the bookkeeper is repetitious. Thousands upon thousands of credit transactions are recorded daily in such retail businesses as Macy's and Lord & Taylor. Billings mailed by these and the thousands of firms like them at the conclusion of predetermined periods summarize these transactions, seek payments, and then demand additional hours of posting. Such work is the subject of data processing equipment appetites. Any job that can be reduced into a myriad of simple steps for the subjugated "mind" of a machine will be eliminated in businesses of reasonable size within the next decade. Films and filmstrips produced by the major manufacturers of data processing equipment are intended to promote the sales of this equipment; however, it is just as advisable to instruct those who will be required to bridge the gap between these data and the balance of the business records—bookkeepers and accountants alike.

The proof of what lies ahead is evident in the Federal Reserve System predictions for drastic changes in the payments system of the United States (44). In the payments system envisaged, the average citizen will pay his monthly bills to the doctor, utility company, department stores, and elsewhere not by mailing checks to each of them but by instructing (with a combination Data-Phone/Card Dialer) the bank holding his deposit account to transfer specified amounts from his account to the accounts of designated payees. Furthermore, the money in the citizen's account will have been placed there on payday by his employer through an interaccount process rather than by individually deposited payroll check. Demonstrations of this equipment in Bell System films are a revelation of tomorrow's business practice.

What remains for bookkeepers/accountants to do? Machines depend upon myriads of repeated procedures; these are limited to subsidiary records. Entries in the general ledger will continue to come from highly individualized journal transactions that result from singular appraisals, and the bookkeeper/accountant will still have to record these odd financial facts. Basic training for this work must be offered in classes of some type, and those classes will produce qualified personnel through a continued blend of teaching methods that couples the statements of the textbook with the many media that illustrate actual practice.

Business Arithmetic

How can students profit from another term, or year, of arithmetic? Those students who take a course in business arithmetic possess a wide range in their quantitative aptitudes and skills. Most of these students ordinarily are average or below average in their mastery of basic skills and are weak in problem solving ability. A well-designed course should improve their skills in fundamental operations, and prepare them to be able to handle quantitative problems they may expect to encounter in business areas such as savings, payrolls, taxes, insurance, installment sales, investments, various types of discounts, measurement applications, graphs, and the like. The dual problem of providing remedial instruction while encouraging those with aptitude to proceed at a much faster rate can be solved through the introduction of supplementary media to serve as an extension of the teacher.

One of the best ways to provide self-instruction for those who should be allowed to forge ahead at their own speeds is through the use of programed texts in business mathematics such as the four-volume series prepared by Harry Huffman (45). The intent is similar in the materials prepared for the American Bankers Association, the National Cash Register sales training programs, and Educational Methods, Inc.

Extensive practice intended for the increase of speed and accuracy in mental and written calculations of fundamental operations can be offered with the aid of controlled reader training courses available from Educational Developmental Laboratories (46). Although designed for use in machines classes, the expected outcomes may be the same whether the operations are performed manually or mechanically.

Arithmetical figures enter into conversations in the business world in a number of ways. Consequently, training in the recognition and working with aural direction can be used to advantage in business arithmetic. A series of tape recorded exercises in which the material progresses into more difficult problems and requires students to mentally arrive at answers, record various type of problems and then solve them, and listen carefully for variations on directions provide another approach for the subject. At the same time, tape recorded work can be used to promptly settle arriving students into the daily class routine, take examinations without written materials being provided, or review the work they have learned.

General Business

To explore, or to better understand American business? Fifty years ago, this course was intended to introduce ninth graders to business programs they might pursue on the high school level in order to meet initial job entry requirements upon graduation from high school. Emphasis was placed upon a study of various business occupations, terms used in business, spelling, business arithmetic, and simple job entry skills. Known by a variety of names—junior business training, general business, basic business, introduction to business—the course offered today is most frequently offered on an elective basis and recommended as essential general education for all American youth. The emphasis has been switched from exploration for job entry purposes to that of the development of a better appreciation of the American free enterprise system. Beginning with the position of that of consumer, continuing into the mechanics of production of goods and services, and concluding with an analysis of exchange and sharing of the resulting benefits, the course is broader in purpose. How are these concepts reinforced?

Films and filmstrips available through such firms as Modern Talking Picture Service or Business Education Films, or the many members of the National Association of Manufacturers, provide an endless source of audio and visual examples of the topics considered. Delta Pi Epsilon, the national graduate business education honorary society, has produced several volumes of annotated film evaluations for business education (47) in order to simplify selection.

Copying machines make it easier to update and make more localized the planning of itineraries (travel unit), the costs of communication (via mail or telephone), the charges assessed for credit, or similar units of study. The products of copying machines may be prepared for use with duplicators for quantity distribution, or in transparency form to project for discussion purposes.

Self-contained units of instruction simplify preparations for classroom lessons. Such a resource unit, "The How and Why of Banking," prepared by Michael Bronner and underwritten by the California Bankers Association in 1963, is complete with fourteen large wall charts, four filmstrips, student workbooks, final examinations, and a Teacher's Guide for the presentation—all packaged in a mobile leatherette covered box, half the size of a grandfather's clock, and supplied gratis to every high school and junior college in California. The California Real Estate Association underwrote a similar project that produced manuals for students, guides for teachers, examinations, and charts. Doubtless, the only reason additional projects have not been made available for every other chapter covered in general business is simply that proposals for such units have not been formulated and presented for the approval of some other generous sponsor.

Business Law

Why is this course offered in the business program? The legal aspects of the business activities performed daily necessitate an understanding of basic principles whether this be for self-protection or an awareness of someone else's rights. Instruction from a technical or vocational approach is decidedly inadvisable; most teachers of this subject are not lawyers, and students do not appreciate bodies of highly technical facts. Familiarity with the operation of different court systems, the ordinary civil circumstances that are an outgrowth of contractual relations, the many involvements with various forms of negotiable instruments, and orderly dictation of post-death actions through instructions contained in wills are fundamental to personal interpretation of responsibilities and rights. Here, in the business law classroom, the opportunity to employ the case approach method in order to bring business practice into the experiences of students is greater than it might be in other business classes. Dynamic presentations create deeper respect for the points of law that are advanced.

What should be done to make business law instruction more dynamic? Illustrations of simple contract forms, different negotiable instruments used in the course of trade, partnership agreements, standard clause wills, and legal papers related to other topics covered in the textbook are divorced from the everyday world of students. Textbook illustrations cannot be localized for areas of the country that they serve; furthermore, publication dates are forever behind the times. It is a very simple matter to supplement the materials supplied by the author with much more interesting clippings of a local and current nature. Examples of such possibilities might be guidelines for the recognition of unacceptable negotiable instruments provided in the Teller's Manual supplied to employees of local banks; occasionally published "Last Will and Testament" declarations of well-known people (in recent years those of Henry Ford, Bernard Baruch, and John F. Kennedy, or madman Charles Lounsbury of the State of Illinois); agreements between labor unions and local employers; rules for Medicare (which definitely are not in the textbook), or forms used for various purposes in the petitioning of local courts for redress. Transferred to transparencies and then projected for class consideration and discussion, business law becomes a much more meaningful experience.

The adaptability of television for this particular course makes it one of the most suitable means for introducing reruns that have meaningful purpose. Reruns of original television programs such as "Perry Mason," "The Defenders," or "Divorce Court" taped at home (with home television tape recorders such as the ones manufactured and sold by Sony, Fairchild, or Ampex) can review materials on the court system with professional actors as teachers. Closed-circuit television equipment, or television sets that are part of the home television tape recording system, coupled with additional monitors can repeat the program for everyone within viewing distance of the sets. With the addition of a television projector, such as the Tele-Beam (48), maximum teaching value may be achieved from this medium. Transistorized equipment facilitates the start of the class and the program without a moment's hesitation.

The advent of telephone circuits now linked with Electrowriters and television equipment has resulted in so-called telelectures, blackboard-by-wire lessons, and Picturephone interviews. Depending upon the extent to which the teacher wishes to have his guest speaker illustrate his thoughts, any one of the three aforementioned media could be used to transport the outsider psychically to the waiting class. Busy persons of national stature can speak and be interviewed on matters related to scheduled class discussions for the cost of telephone connections.

Truly articulated business course instruction in schools that have equipment designed to record, classify, sort, and retrieve data can be achieved in the following manner. Data related to possible clauses and types of contracts can be selected and edited by the business law class; business machines or typewriting classes can prepare the input for data processing equipment; secretarial practice classes can retrieve the data in accordance with job instructions and then prepare this information for whatever the assignment is to be. When this stage of instruction is reached, then the vocational uses for business instruction will become truly meaningful.

Distributive Education

Just what is distributive education? Distributive education is more than a retail training program. Properly taught, distributive education is applied to the total marketing system. It is an interweaving of advertising, display, marketing research, marketing, sales promotion, and other marketing functions that come under the blanket that covers production to consumption. A program that utilizes single subject approaches toward the coverage of all facets of distributive education misses the market; it fails to integrate these experiences. Properly brought together, Hampton (49) suggests that distributive education embrace the following:

> (1) *Basic and social skills* — the 3 R's and abilities in human relations, grooming, attitudes, and the like. (2) *Technology of products and services* — i.e., the specialized knowledge that is needed in a particular job such as color, line, design, and construction needed by the clothing salesman. (3) *Marketing know-how* — consisting of the basic knowledge of distribution, principles of sales, consumer behavior, marketing computational skills, and similar content. (4) *Programs for specialized areas of distribution* — like restaurant management, real estate, or specialty selling.

How do we do the job? Human relations, grooming, attitudes, and other individual abilities to be nurtured in those who subscribe to the program need emphasis daily; they should not be embodied in units to be covered today and then put aside in favor of the next scheduled topic. Films, filmstrips, guest speakers, demonstrations, and slides preview the ideas and purposes; then it becomes a matter of posters, transparencies to serve as case reviews for the opening minutes of class periods, and the personal examples set by the teachers who guide the destinies of the program. Good habits are an outgrowth of constant reminders and practice.

The need for practice in marketing computational skills and the 3 Rs compares to the suggestions made elsewhere in this chapter for the improvement of mathematics and similar areas of weakness. The regular supplementation of class work through lecture and discussion by that of tape-recorded problems, spelling exercises, and similar hear-and-do assignments reinforces the knowledges sought as outcomes here. Projection of problems, reading exercises, and the like on controlled reader or tachistoscope machines become variations of the same techniques.

Closed-circuit television hook-ups make it possible to bring any stage of marketing from the actual scene of operation to the contemplative atmosphere of the classroom. Speakerphones coupled with the television connections, with separate transmitters and loudspeakers, provide the means for the students to question the experts who are on the marketing scene. The many hours consumed along with the outlays of monies to move classes to these locations can be saved while the periphery of visits can be extended well beyond the natural boundaries imposed by accessibility. Video tapes of this and other solo visits can then become the beginning of a pool of materials for future years of instruction as well as a depositary for all schools in a district to utilize.

Pupil interest can be intensified if the courses that are pursued in the distributive education area ultimately lead to work experience in retail establishments. The combination of theory with actual practice represents the transitional step from the classroom to the eventual job. It is extremely important that harmonious relationships be created between school administrators, work experience coordinators, students and employers. An excellent film, produced at Indiana University, titled *Vocational Distributive Education—The Program and the Plan,* could serve as the vehicle to initiate a work experience program.

In Summary

When does the school meet the clerical and secretarial needs of business or industry? The businessman presumably hires employees for office positions who can think and who also possess skills in typewriting, spelling, other written communication abilities, and other job skills he cites in his job specifications. The elimination of many of the routine clerical jobs through increased automation has resulted in a more selective process which envisions employees who are ready to keep pace with the demands of tomorrow. Unfortunately, most schools are still equipped with the discarded and outmoded equipment of yesterday. How can teachers inform their students and train them to meet the challenges of tomorrow?

Certainly one of the best ways to keep students abreast of new developments in office and secretarial equipment is to take them to business shows such as those sponsored by the American Management Association in the large cities of the nation. If this is not possible, then regular reading of company house organs such as *Think, DuPont Magazine, Oilways,* and *Steelways* (subscriptions are at no cost to the recipient), business publications such as *Business Week, Forbes, U. S. News & World Reports,* and *Fortune,* and such business newspapers as *The Wall Street Journal, Barron's,* and the Fairchild Publications (e.g., *Women's Wear Daily*) will create an awareness of what is new. House organs will in turn provide leads to company films, brochures, and other instructional materials obtainable upon request to be shared with others. Equipment demonstrations are readily available when company representatives are convinced that students who are to see and try this equipment are but a term or less away from employment in places of business where they will participate in decisions to purchase. Lastly, new media must be imaginatively integrated into *all* facets of business education.

The classroom that is intended to simulate an office must look like an office, be equipped like an office, and be run like an office. The measure of the products of such an office, when applied by a businessman, is simply: "Can they do the jobs for which they are going to be paid?" When there is an obvious affirmative response, and when the response receives the maximum amount of nationwide publicity, then and only then will business programs in education be considered businesslike.

BIBLIOGRAPHY

1. Knepper, Edwin C. *History of Business Education in the United States.* Ann Arbor: Edwards Bros., Inc. 1941, 221 pp.
2. Strong, Earl P. *The Organization, Administration, and Supervision of Business Education.* New York: The Gregg Publishing Co., 1944, 358 pp.
3. "The magnitude of the American educational establishment — Fall 1965," *Saturday Review,* XLVIII (September 11, 1965), p. 68.
4. Tonne, Herbert A. "Signs of the times," *The Delta Pi Epsilon Journal,* 4:3 (May 1962).
5. *A Brief History of the Typewriter.* New York: Remington Rand, 1958, 11 pp.
6. *Typit Symbols.* Alexandria, Va.: Mechanical Enterprises, Inc., 8 pp.
7. Moore, Omar Khayyam. *Orthographic Symbols and the Preschool Child — A New Approach.* Draft copy later published in the Proceedings of the Third Minnesota Conference on Gifted Children held October, 1960, University of Minnesota. 17 pp.
8. *San Jose* (California) *Mercury-News,* May 28, 1961.
9. Lloyd, Alan C. "So much in so little time," *Business Teacher,* 43:5 (May-June 1966).
10. Wanous, S. J. *Personal and Professional Typing.* 2d ed., South-Western Publishing Company, 1962, 190 pp.
11. Winger, Fred E. "The determination of the significance of tachistoscopic training in word perception as applied to beginning typing instruction." Unpublished Ed.D. thesis. University of Oregon, Eugene, 1951.
12. *Typing-Skill Development.* Huntington, New York: Educational Developmental Laboratories, 4 pp.

13. Pasewark, William R. "The effectiveness of television as a medium of learning typewriting." Unpublished Ph.D. thesis. New York University, 1955.

14. Lloyd, Alan C. *Teaching Plans for the Gregg TV Typing Course.* New York: Gregg Publishing Division, McGraw-Hill Book Co., Inc., 1958, 26 pp.

15. *How Do You Get Ahead in Business?* Scranton, Pennsylvania: International Educational Services, Inc., 6 pp.

16. *The Register* (Huntington Beach, California), April 3, 1966.

17. Haga, Enoch J. "Get ready for automated typing instruction," *The Journal of Business Education,* XLI: 250–51 (March 1966).

18. *Wall Street Journal* (Pacific Coast Edition), May 3, 1966.

19. *Wall Street Journal* (Pacific Coast Edition), April 12, 1966.

20. *Research and Statistics.* (Published Bi-Weekly) Department of Employment, State of California.

21. *Wall Street Journal* (Pacific Coast Edition), May 3, 1966.

22. *Wall Street Journal* (Pacific Coast Edition), May 5, 1966.

23. *Wall Street Journal* (Pacific Coast Edition), September 29, 1966.

24. Gentle, Edgar C. Jr. *Data Communications in Business.* Instructor's Edition. New York: American Telephone and Telegraph Company, 1965, p. 69, 131.

25. *Business Week,* April 9, 1966.

26. *The World's First Spellright.* Washington, D.C.: Spellright Corporation, 3 pp.

27. *Ko-Rec.* Brooklyn: Eaton Allen Corporation, 2 pp.

28. "Laser eraser chases mistakes." *Telephone News* (June 1965). (PT&T)

29. "Key Punch Typewriter." (New Business Equipment section) *Business Education World,* 46:56 (May 1966).

30. *San Jose* (California) *Mercury-News,* December 15, 1960.

31. *The Record* (Penns Grove, New Jersey), November 19, 1964.

32. *The New York Times,* July 8, 1962.

33. *Wall Street Journal* (Pacific Coast Edition), March 30, 1966.

34. *Listen and Learn with the EFI Audio Secretary.* Lafayette, Indiana: Electronic Futures, Inc., 4 pp.

35. Ruegg, Robert J. "Skill Building Through Reading Instruments," *Business Education Forum,* 14:17–20 (January 1960).

36. *Alpha-Hand Programed Course.* Scranton (Pennsylvania): International Educational Services, Inc., 62 pp.

37. Jones, Lloyd D. "Bank reports on programed instruction," *Banking,* 57:52–54 (August 1965).

38. "New technique used to teach computer programming . . ." *NCR Electronic Data Processing News Report,* September 1963. 4 pp. (The National Cash Register Company, Dayton 9, Ohio.)

39. "What's all this about CPS?" *Today's Secretary,* 68:34, 78–79 (May 1966).

40. *San Jose* (California) *Mercury-News,* November 3, 1965.

41. Musselman, Vernon A., and Johnston, Russell A. "New media for teaching bookkeeping and accounting," *New Media in Teaching the Business Subjects,* p. 102, National Business Education Yearbook, No. 3. Washington, D. C.: National Business Education Association, 1965.

42. *Business and Economics Textbooks and Supplies.* Cincinnati: South-Western Publishing Company, 1966, p. 7.

43. Anthony, Robert N. *Essentials of Accounting.* (Programed by Matthew L. Israel) Reading, Massachusetts: Addison-Wesley Publishing Company, Inc., 1964, 126 pp.

44. "The Giro, the computer, and checkless banking," *Monthly Review,* Federal Reserve Bank of Richmond (April 1966), pp. 2–5.

45. Huffman, Harry G. *Programmed Business Mathematics: Concepts, Skills, and Applications,* (in four parts, or books) New York: Gregg Division, McGraw-Hill Book Company, 1962.

46. Ruegg, Robert. *Ten Key Training Program.* Huntington, New York: Educational Developmental Laboratories, 50 pp.

47. Delta Pi Epsilon. *Film Evaluation for Business Education.* (Volumes I & II) Stillwater: Oklahoma State University Press, 1960.
48. Zeitler, Richard J. "Projection TV in the Schools," *View,* 9:10, 18–19 (February 1966).
49. Hampton, Robert E. "Distributive Education Strengthens its Offerings to Meet Change," *Business Education Meets the Challenges of Change,* p. 286, National Business Education Yearbook, No. 4, Washington, D. C.: National Business Education Association, (NEA) 1966.

Chapter 12

What instructional innovations might facilitate the specialized attention that is needed by exceptional children?

What are some of the factors that should be considered in the use of programed learning and automated instruction as strategies for individualizing educational experience?

Can the tutorial-interaction between student and machine program have spin-off import, for example, could it suggest the use of other mentally retarded students as tutors?

How is an auto-instruction program developed and utilized for special education applications?

PRINCIPLES
FOR PROGRAMING LEARNING MATERIALS
FOR MENTALLY RETARDED CHILDREN

LAWRENCE M. STOLUROW, Director, Computer Aided Instruction, Harvard University

An important but unsolved problem in education is the method of teaching that should be used in order to maximize the rate at which mentally retarded children learn. This is obviously a complex problem which has to be dealt with in terms of its separate facets. One facet about which we know little is the organization, or programing, of teaching materials to promote rapid learning, retention, and transfer. Another facet concerns the important unsolved problems of stimulus control, or guidance, not only to promote learning, but also to aid retention and transfer. Still another basic set of problems relates to the development of concepts and methods for tailoring instructional procedures to individual differences in aptitude and ability.

INDIVIDUALIZED INSTRUCTION

The present research* is only an initial effort to delineate and examine the basic problems of individualizing instruction. It was undertaken to determine the usefulness of a set of hypotheses extracted from laboratory research on learning. These hypotheses were chosen because they appeared to be useful in the development of programed learning materials. While there have been many promising efforts to develop psychological theories of learning, there has been relatively little effort to develop the technology of learning which would permit the translation of these theories into educational practices. Programed learning and automated instruction are a promising potential contribution to the technology of learning which in its more comprehensive and highly developed form is educational engineering. The development of conditions of learning to fit a design based upon an individual's needs would be particularly useful to special education in view of the highly individualized requirements of these students.

The Research Potential of Programed Instruction

If the individualization of education is a goal of educational technology, then several basic kinds of information are needed so that decisions can be made about the selective use of teaching strategies to accomplish specified educational objectives. In order to generate this type of information, it is necessary to identify relevant variables over which sufficient control can be exercised to permit the establishment of reliable relationships with learning outcomes. In educational research, control over factors that otherwise would confound the effects of an instructional method, such as variations among teachers, has been an obstacle to the identification of significant variables relating to instructional effectiveness. Individualized instruction requires a level of precision in the control of variables that has not been possible by conventional means. Furthermore, potentially useful data, such as the individual responses of students, have not been available for use in evaluating the "fine grain" of instructional procedures.

While the potential importance of programed instruction for advancing the individual student has been pointed out by many, the potential research contribution of this approach to basic problems in the development of a theory of teaching has not been given equivalent attention and recognition even though, in fact, it is a prior condition. Whether or not programed instruction becomes a widely used school method is really less critical at this time than whether or not it takes hold in educational

*This chapter is extracted by permission of the author from USOE, Cooperative Research Program No. 661, S.A.E. 8370, completed while the author was at the Institute for Research on Exceptional Children, University of Illinois, 1963.

laboratories and is used to its fullest extent for the development of new knowledge about the psychology of teaching and learning. The principles that are revealed by the use of programed self-instruction are not just "machine principles"; if they work and accomplish desired objectives they are principles of teaching in the most general and desirable sense. If a machine can accommodate a program written to conform to a learning principle, then it is likely that a teacher can be taught to do the same thing, if that is desired. The more basic problem to be solved is that of developing information and theories about methods for most effectively teaching a given subject matter to a learner who has particular abilities, interests, and personality characteristics.

Programed self-instruction requires that particular conditions and variables be made explicit. Consequently, once they are formulated sufficiently to be used, they are under adequate control and are stabilized enough to be used with as many groups of students as are desired to determine their effectiveness. For theoretical purposes, different conditions can be used and reused to teach groups in ways that vary systematically from one another. Replicability has a further advantage in that specific defects are revealed in a program. This means that possible ways of eliminating them can be more efficiently discovered. Thus, the good parts of the program can be retained and the weak ones eliminated. The cumulative effect of a consistent effort to develop a set of instructional materials can be expected to be one of demonstrable improvements in student achievement. New educational practices can be discovered and evaluated through an understanding of the basic instructional processes.

PROGRAMED INSTRUCTION FOR THE MENTALLY RETARDED: A REVIEW[1]

Research on programed instruction (PI) for the mentally retarded was reviewed prior to the initiation of this project (Stolurow 1960, 1961). An article and a monograph reviewed both the few PI studies using mentally retarded children and the related issues that were of current interest. Silberman's excellent chapter in the April 1962 *Review of Educational Research* included several subsequent reports. The earlier studies, based primarily on language programs, indicated that programed instruction was indeed feasible for, and applicable to, educable mentally handicapped (EMH) children and slow learners. Without normative behavioral data based upon alternative methods of instruction, it is not possible to make quantitative comparisons with other methods of instruc-

[1] Based upon Stolurow (1963).

tion. However, the relative efficiency of PI and of other methods is typically less important as an issue in the education of the retarded than in the education of children of average or superior intellectual status. Those who are institutionalized, for example, often have minimal educational opportunities. Hence, any use of effective methods would be helpful.

This chapter attempts to represent the kinds of proposals, plans, and findings that are being developed in this country. It reviews the types of studies, the plans, and findings of the investigators, however tentative and sketchy they may be.

Table 1 lists the 14 projects about which some information has been available. Blanks represent gaps in this writer's information. These 14 projects dealt variously with language (reading, spelling, language arts), arithmetic, intelligence and step size, inductive reasoning, and total program for educable mentally handicapped.

Table 1. Studies of Programed Instruction with Mentally Retarded Students.†

Principal Investigator	Institution	Supporting Agency	Topic
D. Ellson	Indiana Univer.	USPHS	R
M. Woolman	Inst. of Educ. Res.	NIH	R
L. Malpass	Univer. So. Florida	USOE Coop. Res. Br.	RS
J. Price	Partlow Sch., Alabama	USOE Title VII	A
J. Kleiser	Devereaux Foundation	NIH	A
F. Payne	McFarland Jr. High Washington, D. C.		RSA
J. Birnbrauer	Univer. of Wash., Seattle		TP
L. Stolurow	Univer. of Ill.	USOE Coop. Res. Br.	LA
L. Blackman	Johnstone Trng. Center	USOE Title VII	IR
G. Cartwright	Univer. of Ill.	USOE	A
D. Merachnik	Berkeley Hts., N. J.		A
C. Shay	Univer. of Calif., L.A.		I & S
Naumann & Woods	Cent. Wash. St. Coll.		S
J. Holland	Fernald St. School		IR

Key:
   Topics: R—reading, S—spelling, A—arithmetic, TP—total program, LA—language arts, I & S—intelligence and step size, IR—inductive reasoning.

   †A summary of the proposed work on many of these projects is available from the Science Information Exchange, Smithsonian Institution, Washington 25, D. C.

Language Studies

In view of the language problems that EMH children have, it is not surprising that PI reading has been a popular topic for research. In spite of decades of research on reading, its nature is not well understood.

Hopefully, programed instruction will contribute to our understanding of the learning processes in reading. To date, PI studies have dealt with specific aspects of the total process rather than with all aspects at once. This is typical, since PI research is highly specific. It therefore remains for future work to extend these interesting and promising beginnings to other facets of reading. If the total reading process is considered in terms of some of its major stages, then teaching a sight vocabulary is seen as only one stage with two distinguishable aspects: (a) reading aloud and (b) reading silently. Different investigators have worked with each of these aspects.

Picture program in teaching sight vocabulary. Ellson and others, who have been working on a project titled "Machine Teaching of Reading to Retarded Children," have developed a "workable teaching machine program," which has been found to be effective for producing rapid increases in the learning of a reading vocabulary. Their work, summarized in a mimeographed report, indicated that the automation of oral reading poses a technical problem difficult to accomplish. In their own words, the problem is essentially that "machines do not listen well —they cannot distinguish (and thus differentially reinforce) correct and incorrect oral responses with the proficiency required for teaching purposes." Consequently, Ellson and others have used a human listener to simulate a machine. In fact, the listener serves some other related functions; however, since most of his behavior is determined by the program, he can be called a "programed tutor."

In one study, in which 38 retardate residents of Fort Wayne State School participated and in which both experimental and control groups took part, 82 words were selected from *A Reading Vocabulary for the Primary Grades* prepared by Gates (1935). Each word was paired with a picture, which the children were to name correctly. The statistically significant mean gain was 11.8 words in favor of the experimental group. At the end of one month, there was a 43 percent loss in performance.

To determine the generalization of the programed instruction, a 150-word vocabulary test was developed by selecting every tenth word from the Gates list and by arranging each in order of difficulty, with words employed in the program excluded. The test was administered before and immediately after a five-trial learning session. The experimental group gained, on the average, 7.1 words ($p < .05$); the control group, 2.8 words ($p < .20$).

The program was branched in teaching each word—*intra*-item programing—but the words themselves were not placed in sequence according to any programing rule—*inter*-item programing. The intra-item arrangement is a sequential decision procedure: In Step 1, a word is shown, and, if the oral response is correct, the subject is reinforced by a flashing light, and the next word is shown through use of the same procedure. However, if the response is incorrect, Step 2 follows. Step 2 involves showing the word with a picture (prompt). If the oral response is correct, Step 3 follows. However, if the oral response is incorrect, the tutor names the picture correctly, the learner names the picture, and then the learner proceeds to Step 3. In Step 3, the picture is removed (vanished), leaving the word visible by itself. If the oral response is correct, the subject is reinforced and the next word is shown, as in Step 1. If the response is incorrect, the tutor names the word correctly (prompt), the learner does the same, and the next word is then shown (Step 1).

Use of retarded tutors. A second experiment was an informal test of the feasibility of using retarded children as tutors of others. Two retarded children, in approximately two hours, were taught without difficulty to administer the picture program used in the above experiment. The tutors, who had IQ's of 71 and 58, were 14 and 17 years of age, respectively. One taught another child seven words; the other taught four other retarded children a mean of 28 words. The average learning rate was "23 words per hour." Certainly the method is potentially valuable, particularly for institutional use.

Sentence program using verbal prompts. A "sentence program," developed and tested with three groups for eight sessions, used consecutive sentences in a story for primary readers. Like the picture program, a correction procedure or "part method" was used that provided a branch program in a sequential set of five decisions. In Step 1, the sentence is shown. If it is read correctly, the tutor reinforces the subject, who then proceeds to the next sentence. If the sentence is incorrectly read (error in reading any word), the tutor goes to Step 2. In this step, the tutor reads the sentence, then shows each word in the sentence in a random order A by pointing to each one. If the word is read correctly, the tutor reinforces the subject, and the learner goes to Step 3. If any word is read incorrectly, the tutor reads it to the subject, who first repeats it and then proceeds to the next sentence and follows the Step 1 procedure. If incorrect (error in any word), the learner proceeds to Step 4 in which the sentence is shown. The tutor reads the sentence and, leaving the sentence visible, names words of that sentence one at a time in a random order B (different from Step 2); the learner points as the tutor reads. If all words are pointed to correctly, the learner proceeds to Step 5. If any word is not indicated correctly, the tutor points correctly, and then the learner points. After the last word, the tutor has the learner proceed to Step 5, in which the sentence is shown. If it is orally read correctly, the tutor reinforces the learner, has him proceed to the next sentence, and initiates the Step 1 procedure. If an error in any word occurs, the tutor reads the word orally, and the learner repeats it. After the last word, the tutor proceeds to the next sentence and uses Step 1.

The program was used in eight one-half hour sessions, two per week for four weeks, followed one month later with a retention test. Three groups, each consisting of four children, were taught with this program: (a) normal first graders; (b) slow first grade readers; and (c) retardates (like those in the first experiment). Normals gained, on the average, 30.5 words; slow learners, 20.0; and retarded children, 19.5 words. Mean rates were five words per hour for retarded and slow children; 7.5 for normals. Retention was nearly 90 percent for all groups after one month.

Comparison of classroom and programed learning techniques. Four groups of 16 retarded children were used: (a) *program*—taught individually with sentence programs; (b) *class*—taught same material by usual classroom procedures with groups of eight children; (c) *alternation*—taught in alternate sessions of program and classroom procedures; and (d) *control*—no training between tests. Pretests and posttests of reading vocabulary and of comprehension (meaning of sentences) were given to all groups. The mean vocabulary gains were 32.9, 18.1, 37.6, and 6.6, respectively. Differences in mean gain between control and program groups, between control and alternation groups, and between class and alternation groups were significant. No significant comprehension gains were obtained.

The procedures of alternation and program also were compared after an additional six sessions that yielded a total of four sessions per week for three weeks. Results from the posttest given after the 12th session showed that all groups gained significantly more than the control sample. Furthermore, the gain in comprehension was significant for the alternation group only. At the time of the final comprehension test, the subjects in the control group read correctly 25 percent of the words; the program and class groups averaged 33 percent; and the alternation group, approximately 50 percent.

Present plans call for revision of the programing procedure to restrict practice to words not read correctly rather than to all words in sentences in which an error occurs.

Word learning.

In Wechkin's (1962) study, the relative efficiency of four conditions, made up of combinations of auditory and visual modes of presentation, were studied. He used 32 delinquent institutionalized girls. Their minimum IQ was 90, and their ages ranged between 14 and 17 years. An auditory cue stimulus, coupled with visual response alternatives, did produce significantly faster learning ($p < .001$), and subsequently better retention, than did auditory response alternatives to visual cue stimuli.

Results were interpreted to support the differential fading of the cue stimulus trace. Thus, the findings suggested that program for the retarded should *not* remove the cue stimulus before the learner makes a response, especially during early trials.

Research has been conducted at the Edward R. Johnstone Training and Research Center in Bordentown, New Jersey, (Blackman and Smith, 1964) relating to the course that instruction should follow in the very beginning of reading, in that attention has been directed toward four "basic skills:" (a) sight word recognition, (b) sight word meaning, (c) phonics, and (d) comprehension. Over 300 programs in word recognition, sentence recognition phonics, and story comprehension were developed. Machines were developed according to specifications for use at Bordentown in two experimental rooms of 10 children each. During the remainder of the 1962–63 school year, an evaluation of the effectiveness of the programs was made in terms of learning as well as retention. Basic data relating to learning and retention also were collected while the classroom demonstration study was taking place. For example, learning and skill in transfer of printed letter-sound associations, as well as the effectiveness of a minimum versus a maximum change in programing training materials were studied and evaluated.

Spelling. Naumann and Woods (1962) have made a preliminary report of an automated basic spelling program for EMH children. Three boys and three girls in a special education program (whose chronological age varied between 10 years, 1 month, and 16 years, 2 months, and whose *Wechsler Intelligence Scale for Children* IQ's ranged between 59 and 74) were taught 62 words from representative spelling lists with 15 Skinner-type program units, which varied in length from 25 to 34 frames. Teaching machines were used. All children were given selected parts, including spelling, of the *Gates Reading Diagnostic Tests* before starting and after completing the program.

All children showed some gains on the spelling tests. Observations indicated (a) the child should always write the whole word, not just the missing part; (b) it was preferable to write programed instruction units in story form; (c) children responded favorably to programed instruction; (d) machines had "play appeal"; and (e) basic training in phonics should be emphasized in pupil's readiness experiences.

Arithmetic Studies

Working with 36 retarded children at Partlow State School for Mental Deficients, Price (1962) compared one group whose answers were constructed with another group taking the same program under multiple-choice conditions. He also included a conventionally instructed control group. The samples were equated for chronological age, mental age,

IQ, and arithmetic achievement level. The linear program constructed for the study contained 3,635 problem frames including counting (59 frames), addition (1,107 frames), subtraction (629 frames), arithmetic sign discrimination (100 frames), and mixed addition and subtraction (1,740 frames). The material was presented through use of a machine. Two tests, in which children responded orally to problems presented to them both visually and orally, were designed to measure progress. Each test consisted of 43 addition and 24 subtraction problems.

Both programed instruction and conventional teaching produced significant improvements. The multiple-choice method resulted in significant improvement in subtraction; however, no significant improvement was observed either for the group that constructed its answers or for the group that received conventional teaching. Addition appears to be teachable to EMH children with either type of PI materials. The two groups receiving programed instruction spent only 86 class periods on the material, whereas the conventionally taught group spent 130 class periods.

Research on programed instruction with arithmetic materials not only has indicated that the method is feasible but also has suggested that it might be more efficient than many of the alternative methods of instructing EMH children. Studies of methods of programing and of the relationships between type of programing method and various aptitudes appear to be among the most promising possibilities for future research. Repetition in programed instruction seems to facilitate learning and to augment retention. The academic use of programed instruction might well consider allowing time for repetition of task material whenever possible. Although there seems to be a general effort to secure retention data as well as learning scores, too few attempts have been made to determine transfer effects. Relatively few studies are being designed to test hypotheses concerning the learning process or to increase the knowledge of professional personnel concerning the special needs of selected subgroups within various segments of the general ability range with divergent thinking abilities.

Intelligence and Step Size

Shay (1961) studied the relationship between level of intelligence and three different sizes of step for a fourth grade unit in the teaching of Roman numerals. Ninety fourth graders in four Los Angeles elementary schools were used. In terms of IQ scores, one-third of the children were at or above 110; one-third, between 93 and 109; and another third, at or below 92.

The results supported Skinner's position to the effect that one program can serve different ability levels. At all three levels of ability as size of step decreased there was an accompanying increase both in posttest score and in time required to complete the program.

Inductive Reasoning

Holland (1962) reported briefly on studies which are potentially promising. Through use of a specially constructed device, visual displays are presented to the subjects as sequences of forms. The child is asked to press a button at the bottom window to indicate which form is to be added to the series on the right extreme. By various grouping plans, different logical operations can be displayed (without the use of language) simply by manipulating color and form of the objects in the sets.

Automated Curriculum

Birnbrauer (1962) has described an entirely "programed" classroom for the EMH. The "programed learning classroom" was established to develop effective and efficient teaching procedures and programed materials to cover the current curriculum for EMH. The curriculum includes "reading, writing, arithmetic, communication, and a number of practical subjects and skills." Each learner attends class for 1.5 hours daily. Usually the students work at a machine, customarily at their own rate. Some commercial programs are being used with a multiple-choice format, since the children cannot write.

Programs and procedures are constantly being revised. Experience suggests that an entirely programed classroom for retardates is feasible.

INDIVIDUALIZED USE OF AUTHOR I: A CLINICAL APPLICATION OF A COMPUTER-PREPARED PROGRAM[2]

AUTHOR I, written in SPS (a computer language), uses the console typewriter of the IBM 1620 to out-put the learning material which it generates. As in-put it uses three types: (1) sentence forms; (2) lists of words designated as objects, attributes, verbs and modifiers; and (3) sentence codes. The program interprets the sentence codes, selects a sentence form and inserts words as the variable elements into the sentence forms. It can, if called for, perform some grammatical corrections and vanishing operations which could be any rule for eliminating portions of the variable elements of the sentence (e. g., the last letter of a word, then the second to last letter, etc.). There are two optional modes of use: (a) printed or punched out-put or (8) simulation of an on-line teaching system. The former is used to prepare materials for off-line applications which are in the format of a linear program with blanks to be

2 The data were collected by Peggy S. Mooney, educational programer and therapist. [Tables have been renumbered.]

filled in by a student and so located on the page that they can be inserted in the typewriter for a different mode of presentation to the student. The latter is accomplished by having the student sit at the console typewriter and observe the out-put as it is prepared. The typewriter is programed to stop at points where the student is to respond. Once a student responds, the system interprets the response, displays the result of a comparison with an expected standard and prints out a message indicating correctness or incorrectness of the student's response and then goes on to display the next frame of material.

One use of the AUTHOR I computer program is to generate learning materials organized on a specified basis and presented to the student in programed learning format typical of the constructed response type.

The off-line application of the program is particularly desirable when the out-put can be a stencil for mimeographing materials to present to students, all of whom require the same materials. A still more interesting application occurs when the out-put of the typewriter is generated uniquely for an individual student. One case of this exists when the general logic of instruction, or the instructional strategy, is to be the same for all students who differ, however, in their particular needs for practice. For example, students may need spelling practice but may differ in the kinds of errors they make. They would, perhaps, be differentially benefited by the presentation of different sets of words. Similarly, the students with reading disabilities may show particular patterns of disability (e.g., encoding), suggesting that each of them could benefit by the same instructional strategy but the materials best used for each of them may differ. One child who has a motor encoding deficiency may need second-grade material and another with the same deficiency may need fifth-grade material.

Problem

The present study was an attempt to individualize the use of AUTHOR I for the purpose of meeting the unique requirements of a child who had sufficiently severe learning disabilities to have been passed from teacher to speech therapist to psychologist. For this particular application of AUTHOR I the words were specified to meet the particular requirements of the child and a general code was written for the sentence forms to generate a unique set of materials for his disability. The Illinois Test of Psycholinguistic Abilities (ITPA) revealed that the child had a severe encoding deficit. Consequently, the codes for sentence forms and vanishing were prepared for this problem. His test results are summarized in Table 2; they indicate that he was at least average in his general intellectual ability. He was unable, however, to express language either motorically or vocally. He was also unable to make multiple asso-

Table 2. Ability Measures on the Child who Received Programed Instructional Materials Generated by AUTHOR I.

Pre-Training

Wechsler Intelligence Scale for Children (vocabulary test omitted)	CA 9–11	California Mental Maturity (10–63) IQ	99
Verbal	IQ 118	Non-Language IQ	116
Performance	IQ 114	Language IQ	82
Full Scale	IQ 117	*Post-Training*	
Ravens Progressive Matrices I	CA 9–11	Ravens Progressive Matrices I	CA 10–10
IQ Equivalent	113	IQ Equivalent	119
Goodenough Draw-A-Man (12–63) (motor encoding task)	CA 9–11		
	IQ 73		
	MA 7–3		
Peabody Picture Vocabulary Test	CA 9–11		
	IQ 128		
	MA 9–4		
California Achievement Test (elementary) (9–63)	CA 9–8	California Achievement Test (elementary) (9–64)	CA 10–8
Reading Vocabulary	2.0	Reading Vocabulary	2.3
Reading Comprehension	3.4	Reading Comprehension	3.5
Arithmetic Fundamentals	3.2	Arithmetic Fundamentals	4.5
Arithmetic Reasoning	3.0	Arithmetic Reasoning	5.0
Language Mechanics	3.4	Language Mechanics	3.7
Informal speech test	No errors	Informal speech test	No errors

ciations to simple words even when given an example. He was able, for instance, to use a single characteristic describing "apple" as in the phrase . . . A red apple . . . but was unable to expand this idea of apple, giving alternative characteristics such as would be the case in the phrase . . . A round, red apple. He had no flexibility of responses, and alternative responses to a single problem were not possible. He could memorize a 14-line poem and recite it from memory. His comprehension and storage of material, if assessed by requiring only a "Yes" or "No" answer, was superior.

The child, in addition, did not have a conception of hierarchical associations or of the existence of categories. Everything appeared to be a separate entity to him; relationships between phenomena were not linked although facts were stored. His problems appeared to be one of associative organization for storage, or of retrieval and expression.

The educational therapist felt that this child needed a small-step program with carefully-controlled vocabulary and sequencing. Our feeling was that he also needed very carefully controlled practice in expressive behavior under precise stimulus control and with an obvious associative pattern or structure. This was a set of requirements for remediation which suggested the potential value of AUTHOR I. This student appeared to be one who could be helped by programed instruction in reading. An approach very different from classroom instruction was desirable because of prolonged resistance and defeat in that environment. Integration of the motor and vocal areas was defined with the educational objective of teaching the concept of roundness. A sample of the programed sentences used with the boy are presented in Figs 1 and 2.

A STONE CAN BE A ROUND THING.
ROUND
AN APPLE CAN BE A ROUN* THING.
ROUND
A BASEBALL CAN BE A ROU** THING.
ROUND
SOME GRAPES ARE RO*** THINGS.
ROUND
A BUTTON OFTEN IS A R**** THING.
ROUND
A BEET CAN BE A ***** THING.
ROUND

Figure 1. Sentences used early in the program.

SOME ROUND, PURPLE THINGS ARE GRAP**.
GRAPES
A ROUND, LONG THING OFTEN IS A CHA**.
CHALK
A ROU**, PURP** THING OFTEN IS A GRAPE.
ROUND PURPLE
SOME ROU**, LO** THINGS ARE CHALKS.
ROUND LONG
SOME ROU**, FL** THINGS ARE BUTTONS.
ROUND FLAT

Figure 2. Sentences used late in the program.

Figure 1 shows sentences used early in the program. Figure 2 shows sentences to which the child was required to respond with multiple attributes. Each figure represents the number of sentences used in one session.

The six sentence forms used to generate his materials were:

---

a. A(n) O can be a A thing.*
b. Some O(s) are A things.
c. A(n) O is a A thing.
d. Some A things are O(s).
e. A(n) A thing often is a(n) O .
f. A(n) A thing can be a(n) O .

---

*Note: O= object word and A=attribute word;
   (n) indicates the change from a to an;
   (s) indicates the plural form.

The mode of presentation of these sentences was to have the child place the page in a standard typewriter. He then turned the platen until the sentence came into view. After reading the sentence, he typed the response word(s) above the dashed lines. Once he had made his constructed response, he rolled the platen forward into view and compared his answer with the correct one. A portable tape recorder was used simultaneously to involve the vocal encoding channel. The child read each sentence, each word he typed, and the sentence with the word filled in, and then listened to himself (see Fig. 3 for the step-by-step flow chart of remediation procedure and Table 3 for the orderly progress of the program's schema).

Table 3. Step-by-Step Schema of the Vocal-Motor Encoding Program.

Step	# of attributes[a]	order[b]	word vanished[c]	vanishing pattern[d]
I	1	O-A	A	1–5
II	1	A-O	A	1–5
III	1	O-A	O	2, 5
IV	1	A-O	O	2, 5
V	2	O-A	A	4, 5
VI	2	A-O	A	4, 5

[a] Number of attribute words appearing in each sentence.
[b] Order in which the object and attribute are presented.
[c] Word in which the vanishing takes place.
[d] The step-size of vanishing: 1-5 means that one letter at a time is vanished; 2, 4 means that first 2 and then 4 letters are vanished at a time; similarly for 4, 5.

Results

The results obtained with this use of AUTHOR I were encouraging. The child enjoyed the sessions with the therapist and looked forward to

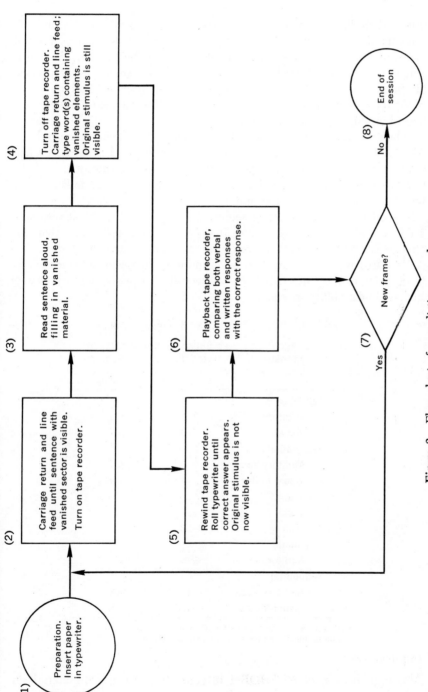

Figure 3. Flow chart of remediation procedure.

this part of his lesson. He became adept at typing the words and the time involved decreased, indicating that his ability to express himself (encoding) had increased. When the sessions began, this boy was almost unable to express himself. In the school classroom, he had raised his hand voluntarily but, when called upon to respond, had remained silent for as long as the teacher would wait. He was also unable to express himself adequately in writing.

When he returned to school in the fall, after having received the AUTHOR I generated materials during the spring and summer, he had a new reading teacher. She reported that he answered questions verbally using one or two-word sentences. In committee work he talked freely with classmates and often supplied ideas.

The change in the encoding scores (shown in the ITPA test results in Table 4 and Fig. 4) is dramatic. It cannot, of course, be said that this change is totally a result of exposure to the programed materials. The AUTHOR I materials, however, were undoubtedly beneficial since everything prior to their use had been unsuccessful in producing any change in the child's ability to encode.

Table 4. Illinois Test of Psycholinguistic Ability.

Language Age Prior to and Subsequent to the Use of Programed Instructional Materials With One Subject

Subtest	Pretest Age*	Posttest Age*
Decoding		
Auditory	7–6	**AN
Visual	8–9	**AN
Association		
Auditory Vocal	9–0	9–0**AN
Visual Motor	7–2	**AN
Encoding		
Vocal	2–7	6–0
Motor	3–10	7–4
Automatic		
Auditory Vocal	9–6	**AN
Sequential		
Auditory Vocal	7–10	**AN
Visual Motor	7–10	**AN

*Pretest C. A. was 9–11, Posttest C. A. was 10–10
**Indicates that he achieved the maximum score.

Implications

Although this use of AUTHOR I to generate instructional materials involved only one child, the results were encouraging. Further uses of

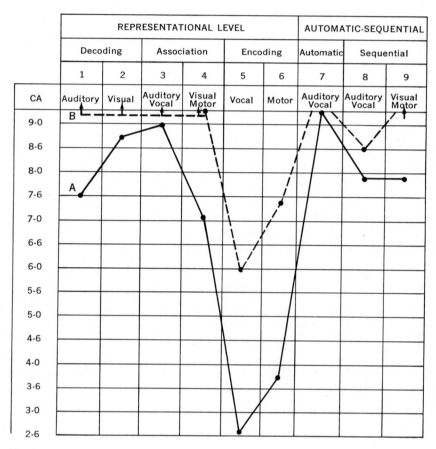

Key:
A Pre-Remediation, CA 9–11.
B Post-Remediation, CA 10–10.

Figure 4. ITPA profile for Tommy, a reading disability case treated with a program generated by AUTHOR I, SOCRATES.

AUTHOR I for supplying materials for individual instruction are possible.

The use of an on-line typewriter or a cathode ray tube display with a keyboard under computer control would be a desirable way to present materials generated by such a computer program. Under such a condition the computer could adapt the educational program to the student's responses. Progression of the frames from minimal change to maximal change, for example, would be handled individually in reference to a particular child's needs. If he made more errors than expected for instance, the rate of change could be slowed down. If he made fewer errors than anticipated, the change could be speeded up. The use of a digital computer for teaching in this manner could achieve a relatively high degree of adaptivity to a student's specific needs.

SUMMARY

In summary, programed instruction for retardates is clearly feasible. Programed instruction needs to be used to determine the special educational requirements of the retarded. It may be more efficient than the alternatives presently available, particularly in institutions. Work is needed on the factors that make it most effective for learning and transfer. The studies conducted thus far reveal a developing rapprochement between the psychology of learning and educational practice. Hopefully, programed instruction will continue to be a catalyst in effecting applications of the psychology of learning to teaching activities.

REFERENCES

Angell, D. and Lumsdaine, A. A. *Prompted Plus Unprompted Trials versus Prompted Trials Alone in Paired-Associate Learning.* (Pittsburgh: American Institute For Research, AIR-314-60-1R-129, Air Force Office of Scientific Research, Rep. No. AFOSR-TN-60-808, October, 1960.)

Birnbrauer, J. S. *The Rainier School Programmed Learning Classroom.* (Seattle: University of Washington, 1962.) (ditto)

Blackman, L. S. and Smith, M. P. *The Development and Evaluation of a Curriculum for Educable Mental Retardates Utilizing Self-Instructional Devices or Teaching Machines.* (Boonton, N.J.: E. R. Johnstone Training and Research Center, 1964.)

Bloomfield, L. and Barnhart, C. L. *Let's Read.* (Detroit: Wayne State Univer. Press., 1961.)

Carr, H. A. Teaching and Learning. *Journal of Genetic Psychology,* 1930, 37, 182–218.

Cartwright, G. P. Two types of programed instruction for mentally retarded adolescents. (Unpublished masters thesis, University of Illinois, 1962.)

Cook, J. O. Supplementary report. Processes underlying learning a single paired-associate item. *Journal of Experimental Psychology,* 1958, 56, 455.

Cook, J. O. and Kendler, T. S. A theoretical model to explain some paired-associate learning data. In G. Finch and F. Cameron (eds.) *Symposium on Air Force Human Engineering Personnel and Training Research,* (Washington, D.C.: National Academy of Science, National Research Council, 1956,) 90–98.

Cook, J. O. and Spitzer, M. E. Supplementary report. Prompting versus confirmation in paired-associate learning. *Journal of Experimental Psychology,* 1960, 59, 275–276.

Detambel, M. H. and Stolurow, L. M. Stimulus sequence and concept learning. *Journal of Experimental Psychology,* 1956, 51 (1), 32–40.

Dubois, P. H. The design of correlational studies in training. In R. Glaser (ed.) *Training Research and Education.* (Pittsburgh: Univer. of Pittsburgh Press, 1962,) 63–86.

Ellson, D. G. Programmed learning of elementary reading. In *Selected Convention Papers.* (Washington, D. C.: Council for Exceptional Children, National Education Association, 1962.)

Fleishman, E. A. and Fruchter, B. Factor structure and predictability of successive stages of learning Morse Code. *Journal of Applied Psychology,* 1960, 44, 97–101.

Gates, A. I. *A Reading Vocabulary for the Primary Grades.* (New York: Columbia Univer., 1935.)

Holland, J. G. New directions in teaching-machine research. In J. E. Coulson (ed.), *Programmed Learning and Computer-Based Instruction.* (New York: Wiley and Sons, 1962,) 46–57.

Irion, A. L. and Briggs, L. J. *Learning Task and Mode of Operation Variables in Use of Subject Matter Trainer.* (Lackland Air Force Base, Tex.: Air Force Personnel and Training Research Center, Tech. Rep. AFPTRC-TR-57-8, October, 1957.)

Kirk, S. A. and Hegge, T. G. *Teaching Reading to Slow-Learning Children.* (Boston: Houghton-Mifflin, 1940.)

Kirk, S. A. and McCarthy, J. J. The Illinois test of psycholinguistic abilities — an approach to differential diagnosis. *American Journal of Mental Deficiency,* 1961, 66(3), 399–412.

Kopstein, F. F. and Roshal, S. Learning foreign vocabulary from pictures versus words. *American Psychologist,* 1954, 9, 407. (abstract)

Lindquist, E. F. *Design and Analysis of Experiments in Psychology and Education.* (Boston: Houghton-Mifflin, 1953.)

Mattson, D. E. The effects of sharing and overlapping in a paired-associate learning task. Unpublished masters thesis, Univer. of Illinois, 1961.

Morton, R. L. *et al. Making Sure of Arithmetic. Grade 5.* (Morristown, N. J.: Silver-Burdett, 1958.)

Naumann, T. F. and Woods, W. G. *The Development of an Automated Basic Spelling Program for Educable Handicapped Children.* (Ellensburg, Wash.: Central Wash. State College, 1962.)

Osgood, C. E. *Method and Theory in Experimental Psychology.* (New York: Oxford, 1953.)

Postman, L., Jenkins, W. G., and Postman, Dorothy L. An experimental comparison of active recall and recognition. *American Journal of Psychology* 1948, 61, 511–519.

Premack, D. Toward empirical behavior laws. I. Positive reinforcement. *Psychological Review,* 1959, 66, 219–233.

Price, J. E. *A Comparison of Automated Teaching Programs with Conventional Methods as Applied to Teaching Mentally Retarded Children.* (Washington, D. C.: U. S. Office of Education, NDEA Title VII, Project No. 670, 1962.)

Shay, C. B. Relationship of intelligence to step size on a teaching machine program. *Journal of Educational Psychology,* 1961, 52, 98–103.

Sidowski, J. B., Kopstein, F. F., and Shillestad, Isabel J. Prompting and confirmation variable in verbal learning. *Psychological Reports,* 1961, 8, 401–406.

Silberman, H. T. Self-teaching devices and programmed materials. *Review of Educational Research,* 1962, 32 (2), 179–193.

Smith, Leone M. Programed learning in elementary school. An experimental study of relationships between mental abilities and performance. *Dissertation abstracts,* 1963, 23, 4231, No. 63-3337.

Stolurow, L. M. Utilization of class-descriptive cues in the learning of technical information — studies in task engineering. In G. Finch and F. Cameron (eds.) *Symposium on Air Force Human Engineering, Personnel, and Training Research.* (Washington, D. C.: National Academy of Sciences, National Research Council, 1956, Publication No. 455,) 248–266.

Stolurow, L. M. *Teaching by Machine.* (Washington, D. C.: U. S. Office of Education, Cooperative Research Monograph No. 6 [OE-34010], 1961.)

Stolurow, L. M. *Psychology of Learning and Instruction. Proceedings of the National Electronics Conference.* (Chicago: National Electronics Conference, 1962,) 428–446.

Stolurow, L. M. Programed instruction for the mentally retarded. *Review of Educational Research.* 1963, 33 (1), 126–136.

Stolurow, L. M. *A Taxonomy of Learning Task Characteristics.* (Wright Patterson Air Force Base, Ohio: AF 33(616)-5965, Tech. Doc. Rep. No. AMR-TDR-64-2, January, 1964.)

Stolurow, L. M. *Some Educational Problems and Prospects of a Systems Approach to Instruction.* (Urbana, Ill.: Univer. of Illinois, Training Research Laboratory, NONR 3985(34), Tech. Rep. No. 2, 1964.)

Stolurow, L. M. and Bergum, B. Learning diagnostic information-effects of direction of association and of prose vs. paired-associate presentation. In G. Finch and F. Cameron (eds.), *Air Force Human Engineering, Personnel, and Training Research.* (Washington, D. C.: National Academy of Science, National Research Council, 1958, Publication No. 516,) 69–84.

Stolurow, L. M., Hodgson, T. F., and Silva, J. Transfer and retroaction effects of association reversal and familiarization training in trouble shooting. *Psychological Monographs,* 1956, 70, No. 12 (Whole No. 419).

Stolurow, L. M. Jacobs, P. I., and Blomme, R. W. *Tables of Estimated Letter and Letter Combination (Bigram and Trigram) Frequencies in Printed English.* (Urbana, Ill.: Univer. of Illinois, Training Research Laboratory, Memo. Rep. No. 13, 1960.)

Stolurow, L. M. and Smith, Leone M. *The Effectiveness of Two Different Sequences of Programed Elementary mathematics.* (Urbana, Ill.: Univer. of Illinois, Training Research Laboratory, U. S. Office of Education Project No. 711151.01, Tech. Rep. No. 1, September, 1963.)

Thorndike, E. L. and Lorge, I. *The Teacher's Word Book of 30,000 Words.* (New York: Columbia Univer., 1944.)

Thurstone, Thelma G. *Primary Mental Abilities Test.* (Chicago: Science Research Associates, Inc., 1953.)

Underwood, B. J. and Richardson, J. Some verbal materials for the study of concept formation. *Psychological Bulletin,* 1956, 53, 84–96.

Wechkin, S. Word learning in an automated teaching situation as a function of display condition. *Journal of Educational Psychology,* 1962, 53(4), 165–169.

Woodworth, R. S. *Experimental Psychology.* (New York: Henry Holt, 1938.)

Wulff, J. J. and Stolurow, L. M. The role of class-descriptive cues in paired-associate learning. *Journal of Experimental Psychology,* 1957, 53(3), 199–206.

Chapter 13

*What is the scope of challenge involved in providing
adequate educational opportunity for the economically
and culturally deprived?*

*In view of the odds operating against the student
with a disadvantaged background, what adjustments
need to be made in the curriculum?*

*How can media be used to promote effective
conditions of learning for the deprived?*

*What resources are available through which educators can
begin organizing meaningful instructional programs?*

MEDIA IN PROGRAMS
FOR THE ECONOMICALLY
AND CULTURALLY DEPRIVED

GORDON C. BLANK, President
Western Piedmont Community College
Morganton, North Carolina

THE BRAVE NEW WORLD OF EDUCATIONAL CHALLENGE

American education has come of age. It is no longer a sterile desert
of professionalism, nor is it the stepchild of our society. Increasingly,
education is looked upon as a major means by which we as a society
can not only survive but flourish. It is a paradox that, on the brink
of a new golden age of mankind, we are struggling for the sheer survival of civilization itself. The renaissance of American education in
recent years is every bit as significant an event as when Galileo imposed
system and design upon the Elizabethan world. The vibrant urgency of
our times has opened new horizons and challenges and has precipitated
massive efforts to enable us to meet the critical demands that our times
present. One need only read newspaper headlines or listen to news

telecasts to realize that education can no longer afford the luxury of archaic goals and obsolete methods. The education of yesteryear cannot cope with the endless problems of today and tomorrow. We as a nation have come to recognize that space-age problems cannot be solved by horse-and-buggy tactics. The modern educator must face not only a brave new world of educational problems but also the past inadequacies of our educational system. The point of no return has long since been reached, and the challenges are clearly before us.

Recognition of the challenges of our times and the inadequacy of the past are, however, not enough. The implications of a true educational renaissance are so staggering as to demand a major restructuring of basic concepts of the educational process.

Heretofore, the educational *zeitgeist* has tended to view education as based on what might be termed a funnel model, in which the world of knowledge is somehow imparted by injection through the funnel of the teacher into the awaiting mind of the student. With the advent of more psychologically-oriented learning models, the emphasis has tended to shift to the learner himself in recognition that knowledge is not an entity unto itself that acts upon an indifferent organism. Since the post-World-War-II impact of technology and media on educational thinking, a growing awareness of and sophistication with theories of communication has tended to embrace models of education that emphasize the role of process in the interactions among content, students, teachers, media, and all the components of a total system.

Clearly, the challenge before us is not only one of knowledge, nor just one of people, but also one of communication processes. As there are old assumptions about the nature of knowledge, old assumptions about the nature of people and how they learn, so it is that there are old assumptions and models upon which concepts of communications are based.

Part of the legacy of the past failures of our society and our educational system involves a major segment of our population who live in a world that exists on our very doorstep but is unknown to most of us. It is a world containing the human debris of the richest and most technologically advanced society in history. It is the world of the deprived— a gray and bleak world in which the spirit is twisted and the soul maimed; a world of the educationally crippled. It is a world about which we do not like to think, for it is an admission of failure. Yet it is a world we must attempt to understand. Our well-being as a nation demands that education, in concert with other societal institutions, cross that world's moat of apathy and neglect and enter its walls to minister to its ills. It is, however, a hostile world, and its walls are formidable. The Greek legend of Augeas, king of Elis, has implications for what we as educators must do. Augeas left his stables neglected for thirty years. It took the strength of Hercules to remedy the problem. Education must have this herculean strength and will to deal with the world of the deprived.

Granted that we as educators have the will and strength to attack the Augean stables of the deprived, we must first address ourselves to the question of what we mean by the deprived. Who are the deprived? Where do they exist? What are they like? Only then can we begin to ask ourselves what can be done about their educational needs insofar as curricula, methods, and media are concerned.

THE WORLD OF THE DEPRIVED

Our educational system takes great pride in the democratic philosophy on which it is based. Yet the educational world of the deprived is the very antithesis of democracy. It is a world apart from and alienated against the rest of our democratic society. Indeed, the only thing democratic about deprivation is that it knows no bounds of race, creed, or national origin. The deprived are from various racial and ethnic origins. They live in remote rural areas as well as in major urban centers. They are of varying ages and religious backgrounds. In short, the only pervasive characteristic of the deprived is that they exemplify the old saying "To them that hath not is taken away." They are impoverished economically, socially, culturally, educationally, physically and psychologically. They form a subculture of deprivation that exists outside the mainstream of American life. They live in a harsh and cold world that is characterized by a web of crippling disabilities, alienating them from the bright, clean, colorful world of middle-class America. It is often said that the people in America's subculture of deprivation are better off than the teeming millions who have a subhuman level of existence in non-industrialized emerging nations. This is paltry justification for the ironic situation in which millions of deprived people exist in the richest nation on earth.

Michael Harrington, in his work on poverty in the United States, appropriately entitled his book, *The Other America.*[1] He referred to the conditions which trapped, according to his estimate, 40 to 50 million Americans who are defeated and deprived, whose existence is masked by the familiar America we know of as an affluent society. Harrington wrote of the disadvantaged as the victims of our society who think, feel, and act differently from the Americans of suburbs and Madison Avenue. He described a world of pessimism, hopelessness, and despair. He de-

[1] Michael Harrington, *The Other America: Poverty in the United States* (New York: The Macmillan Company, 1963).

picted the life of the deprived in the United States as one in which life was looked upon as a fate involving an endless cycle from which there was little hope of deliverance. Harrington viewed the impoverished and disadvantaged as being internal aliens in our country, who, while possessing some of the characteristics of the major society of which they were a part, were sufficiently separated from the middle-class norms of our country to constitute a "subculture of poverty."

It is obviously not an easy task to define accurately the disadvantaged, for there are many complex factors involved. One factor of crucial importance is that of income. In 1962, the Conference on Economic Progress estimated that more than 38 million Americans lived under conditions of poverty in the United States, while another 39 million lived under conditions above poverty but short of minimum requirements for a modestly comfortable standard of living.[2] Thus, from one index, two-fifths of a nation were not sharing in the economic blessings of the majority of our population.

Numerous other agencies have attempted to define the disadvantaged in economic terms. In 1964, the Committee on Education and Labor of the House of Representatives reported that of the 47 million families in the United States in 1962, some 9.3 million families, containing more than 30 million persons, had total family incomes below $3,000.[3] The Committee indicated that there is no clear and unvarying standard of what constitutes a minimal level of living, but that it is obviously difficult for a family with four or more children to subsist on less than $3,000. The committee further reported that whereas the annual per-capita income in 1962 of men, women, and children in the United States as a whole was $1,900, there were 35 million Americans whose annual per-capita income was only $590. The committee further reported that the heads of over 60 per cent of all poor families had less than a grade-school education. The geographic distribution was such that 54 per cent lived in cities, 16 per cent lived on farms, and 30 per cent were rural, nonfarm residents.

The topography of poverty reveals many statistics, and many authorities disagree on the various economic categories that should be used in classifying the impoverished and the disadvantaged. Regardless of the statistics, the fact remains that millions of men, women, and children in the United States live in a world lacking in material comforts, human dignity, and fulfillment. Poverty is a way of life that forms a subculture in which irresponsibility, immorality, disease, indifference, crime, ignorance and human misery flourish. It is not only a personal, local, or state

[2] *Poverty and Deprivation in the United States: The Plight of Two-Fifths of a Nation* (Washington: Conference on Economic Progress, April, 1962).

[3] *Poverty in the United States,* Committee on Education and Labor, House of Representatives, 88th Cong., 2d sess. (Washington: U.S. Gov't Printing Office, April, 1964).

problem; it is a national disgrace that these millions of American families live in a society of abundance but do not share in it. Recognizing the severity of the problem of the disadvantaged is the first step in launching the war on poverty. One of the most shocking yet enlightening experiences that a middle-class American educator can engage in is to walk in the world of the "Other America"—to participate firsthand in seeing, smelling, and tasting the world of the deprived.

It is every teacher's responsibility both as a citizen and as an educator to make every effort to understand the plight of the deprived. It is only out of understanding that proper diagnosis can be made, curative measures be formulated, and appropriate action taken.

THE SPIRAL OF DEPRIVATION

The taproots of the economically and culturally deprived are enmeshed in a complex of factors. Deprivation may be thought of as an inverted spiral in which a multitude of factors continually interact with one another, further aggravating other problems involved. The deprivation spiral, once it begins, tends to worsen as it feeds upon itself in a self-generating fashion. The deprived are submerged in unemployment, lack of education and employable skills, poor housing, poor food, poor physical and emotional health, low aspiration, and alienation from society. Each factor has a multiplying effect on all the others. As a result, we have, in this country, spawned generations of the same families on relief whose offspring tumble deeper into the maelstrom of misery and hopelessness. The children of poverty become the parents of poverty. The adjectives used to describe these children are many; among them disadvantaged, deprived, underprivileged, and impoverished. Regardless of the terms used, the syndrome is typically the same. The children of the poor, many of whom are from minority groups, bear scars that affect the rest of their lives and their children's lives. And so on the spiral continues to bleed them and their progeny. Human dignity is difficult to maintain for 35 million Americans who have less than 70 cents a day for food and less than $1.40 a day for all other needs. Poverty is a deep and very personal wound.

THE NEW INDUSTRIAL REVOLUTION

A myth about the deprived has long permeated our society. The myth, in effect, holds that the deprived are inherently inferior to the rest of society and are reaping the bitter fruits of their own laziness. The American Dream of social and economic mobility from rags to riches took place in the Horatio Alger era, when waves of immigrants entered this country as unskilled laborers filling the great demand for the industrial revolution of days gone by. The following statement exemplifies the nature of the difficulty of economic and social mobility among the deprived in the new industrial revolution we face today.[4]

> We are now in a new industrial revolution. The changes of locations and sources of power, the changes in the characteristics of machines, the processes of automation, the demands for new and highly technical skills, the changes in rural-urban populations, and many related developments bewilder the imagination. The effects of the new industrial revolution on the character of labor demands are dramatic. The labor market for the unskilled is shrinking rapidly; there is a decrease in "blue collar" jobs, a decrease in demands in the traditional "trades." On the other hand, there is increasing demand for the technically trained and those who have had the advantage of a college education.

The changing complexity of our labor market is further pointed up by Edgar May, in his book, *The Wasted Americans.*[5] May says:

> In agriculture, farm workers employment dropped from 9.5 million in 1940 to 5.2 million in 1962, pushing a massive contingent of unskilled men into the urban labor force. In manufacturing, the Bureau of Labor Statistics reports peak employment of almost 18 million workers was reached in 1943 and has never been equalled since. There were fewer workers in manufacturing in 1959 than in 1953. While white-collar employment increased between 1948 and 1961, blue-collar employment fell. Union leaders say that from 1956 to 1962, a total of 1.5 million production jobs in factories was lost.

Among the hardest hit by unemployment are the youth of the deprived. About two-thirds of all workers who never completed high school are employed in unskilled or semi-skilled jobs. They are often the last to be hired and the first to be fired when technological displacement occurs as a result of automation or relocation of industry. Unemployment among young people is often two to three times as high as it is in the total labor force. There is a dreary future for the uneducated and unskilled youth of the deprived.

EDUCATION OF THE DEPRIVED

In the light of modern economic and societal requirements, it is imperative that the educational levels of the deprived be raised. Youth who are the misfits of our educational system have limited potential for coping with an increasingly technological economy. The damage done

---

[4] Quoted by permission of Donald C. Agnew, Director of the Education Improvement Project, Atlanta, Ga.

[5] Edgar May, *The Wasted Americans* (New York: Harper and Row, Publishers, Inc., 1964), p. 65.

to these people is more than crippling economic harm, however. The economically and educationally deprived youth is often a psychological dropout as well as a potential school dropout. He faces a hostile society and often becomes alienated against it. His spirit is warped and diminished; he roams a lonely world in which few opportunities and gratifications exist. He often exhibits low levels of aspiration, marginal feelings of social responsibility, hostility, disregard for established order, insensitivity to civilizing values, gross irresponsibility, and apathy. Overt manifestations of these factors are often reflected in statistics dealing with rates of delinquency, promiscuity, illegitimacy, alcoholism, narcotics addiction, crimes of violence, and mental illness.

The behavioral patterns of the deprived are not inherent. They are the result of the dismal cesspool of rural and urban slum life. The homes of the disadvantaged, if indeed they may be called homes, provide a paucity of stimulation for learning, and there is little to encourage the inculcation of socially desirable values. The preschool years at home do not give the children the background to properly participate in the school environment. The children frequently lack verbal skills and have difficulty in learning to read and write. Their speech typifies the patterns of those with whom they associate in the slum home and neighborhood. They often lack the visual discrimination necessary for reading books and learning from audiovisual materials. They generally cannot concentrate on learning and are prone to develop poor study skills. The slum hostility toward constituted authority often transfers to the school environment, and slum youth tend to look upon the school staff with negative attitudes, suspicion, and resentment. Above all, the conditions of life in the disadvantaged home are alien to the accepted value patterns that are necessary for success in our society. Deprived children enter school with two strikes against them.

If poverty and its resultant deprivation struck at random, its percentage among various racial and ethnic groups would be expected to be similar. Obviously, discrimination against particular groups increases the likelihood of an increased percentage of poverty and deprivation. Although 80 per cent of the nation's poor families are white, nearly one out of every two nonwhites live under poverty conditions. The American Negro has borne the brunt of deprivation in our society. In the book, *Slums and Suburbs*, Dr. Conant describes the educational plight of Negro youth in urban areas:[6]

> I can now take up the educational problems in the Negro slums of certain of our largest cities. I wish that I could do more than take them up. What I should like to do is to create in the reader's mind a feeling of anxiety

6 James B. Conant, *Slums and Suburbs* (New York: McGraw-Hill, 1961), pp. 18–19, with permission of Conant Studies, Educational Testing Service, Princeton.

and concern. For without being an alarmist, I must say that when one considers the total situation that has been developing in the Negro city slums since World War II, one has reason to worry about the future. The building up of a mass of unemployed and frustrated Negro youth in congested areas of a city is a social phenomenon that may be compared to a piling up of inflammable material in an empty building in a city block. Potentialities for trouble — indeed possibilities of disaster — are surely there. Let me describe a slum that might be in any one of several of the large cities I have visited. The inhabitants are all Negroes and with few exceptions have entered the city from a state in the deep South anytime within the last month to the last three years. Often the composition of a school grade in such an area will alter so rapidly that a teacher will find at the end of a school year that she is teaching but few pupils who started with her in the fall. I recall the principal of one school stating that a teacher absent more than one week will have difficulty recognizing her class when she returns. This comes about because mothers move with their offspring from one rented room to another from month to month and in so doing often go from one elementary school district to another. I am told that resident tenements look more like transient hotels. I write "mothers" advisedly, since in one neighborhood, by no means the worst I have seen, a questionnaire sent out by the school authorities indicated that about a third of the pupils came from family units (one hesitates to use the word "home") which had no father, stepfather, or male guardian. This particular section was by no means homogeneous, of course. For while many moved about from room to room, a quarter of the parents reported that they owned their homes. Only 10 percent of the parents had graduated from high school and only 33 percent had completed the elementary school. Contrast the situation in which a third of the parents have completed elementary school with that in a high-income suburb where as many as 90 percent of the parents have bachelor's degrees, if not graduate degrees from a university.

When Dr. Conant visited urban-area slum schools, he found teachers and administrators struggling against appalling odds. The flight of middle-class Americans from decaying urban centers to residential suburban areas has become an established phenomenon. Into the vacuum of the urban core come the destitute, resulting in what Dr. Conant called "social dynamite." The slum school is faced with an increasingly compacted concentration of educational cripples. The upsurge in race riots in recent years can never be justified in a land of law and order, but it can be understood in the light of the causative conditions.

The Negroes are not alone in being destined for deprivation, however. Other minorities—migrant workers, Indians, Americans of Mexican and Puerto Rican origin, and others share the twin burdens of discrimination and deprivation.

Mounting anxiety among knowledgeable educators about the plight of the deprived has resulted in the evolvement of compensatory programs to remedy their educational handicaps. Opponents are quick to indicate that such programs 'bend over backwards' and discriminate against the nondeprived. This narrow point of view does not allow for the humanistic and democratic educational philosophy of enabling individuals to achieve the maximum of their capabilities, nor does it recognize the incalculable price that we as a nation pay for maintaining a large segment of our population in the grip of educational handicaps. Opponents will frequently point to the results of culture-laden intelligence tests and standardized achievement tests to reinforce their feelings about the inherent ignorance and lack of capability among discriminated-against minorities and other deprived youth. This frame of reference neglects a growing body of research indicating that the results of such tests are environmentally influenced. The educational handicaps of such youth stem for the most part from the chronic impoverishment of an environment that victimizes youth and provides slim educational nourishment.

Education is not a panacea for the plight of deprived youth; but it is a major factor in reversing the spiral of deprivation. The leadership that educators must exert was well stated by Harold Taylor, when he wrote:[7]

> The educator must go to the root of the matter, and he must deal with the whole child. The root is in the social and economic conditions in which the child exists. The educator must deal bluntly with those who support the residential segregation of the colored people and the poor. He must fight those who wish to profit in real estate at the expense of the children. He must think of education as a total process, in which the conditions of society deeply affect the child's mind, the level of his achievement, and the range of his possibilities. The curriculum, the classroom, the guidance office are instruments for dealing with one part of the child's life. But they do not and cannot function in a social vacuum.
>
> Nor is it permissible any longer to say that the social environment of the child is not the problem of the educator, that it belongs to city planners, social workers, economists, housing experts, or society. It belongs to everyone, but most of all to the educator. The educator is not a personnel manager, an administrator, an organization man, although his work involves organizing, managing, and administering. He is a social and intellectual leader, and he begins to exercise his leadership when he recognizes the conditions of his society and brings to bear upon them the force of a humanitarian philosophy.

Although deprived youth as a group tend to share some similar characteristics stemming from their environment, it is important to think of them as individual human beings who range widely in abilities, attitudes, interests, and needs. Some have overcome their backgrounds and risen

[7] Harold Taylor, "The Whole Child: A Fresh Look," *Saturday Review,* Education Supplement, XLIV (December 16, 1961), 42–43.

to great heights in our society; most have not and will not unless the conditions causing deprivation are remedied. The function of education is to enable each and every youth to realize his maximum potential in our society.

The history of education gives insight into ways and means by which other nations have handled the deprived. Historically, nondemocratic societies have determined the education of their youth on the basis of social class and have thus tended to fix the station in life a particular class could attain. American democracy provided a stark contrast to the rigidity of older European and Asian socio-economic systems. American education evolved as a key that could unlock the door of opportunity, enabling youth to reach for the stars. When older societies provided education for the poor, their purpose was only to enable poor youth to better perform the menial tasks that were necessary to maintain and support the aristocracy so as to further safeguard the *status quo*. American public education is a unique outgrowth of democratic philosophy which is aimed at all the youth of our land. Has American education missed its mark by too great a margin in recent years? Do we need to reconceive and revitalize our concept of mass public education? What can we do to provide proper educational opportunities for all our youth?

CURRICULUM FOR THE DEPRIVED

In Riessman's *The Culturally Deprived Child,*[8] the applicability of existing curriculums for the other world of deprived youth is aptly summarized in Watson's introduction when he stated:

> The American public school is a curious hybrid: it is managed by a school board drawn largely from upper-class circles; it is taught by teachers who come largely from middle-class backgrounds; and it is attended mainly by children from working-class homes. These three groups do not talk the same language. They differ in their manners, power, and hierarchies of values. In the current flurry of concern over the "gifted," most well-to-do families are pleased to think of their own children as being given well-deserved special consideration. Teachers are gratified because "higher standards" are in vogue. Yet the great reservoir of undiscovered and undeveloped intellectual talent in America is not in upper-class or middle-class neighborhoods. While the proportion of high I. Q.'s may be lower in underprivileged areas — this is a slippery question, as Professor Riessman demonstrates — the actual numbers of intellectually very bright children in poor homes are far in excess of those to be found in the relatively few homes of business and professional leaders.

[8] Frank Riessman, *The Culturally Deprived Child* (New York: Harper and Row, Publishers, Inc., 1962), p. x.

What is needed now is some fresh approach to the discovery and cultivation of the talents that undoubtedly exist among millions of children from unpromising backgrounds. The usual tests won't identify these able pupils; the usual curriculum won't challenge them; the usual teachers won't inspire them. While additional research would be helpful, the more urgent needs seems to be for creative teaching on the basis of a different set of assumptions. It won't do to parade excuses, or to blame the individual, or the neighborhood. These pupils may not score high on verbal tests, but they are clever about many other things. They may be "uncooperative" in carrying out traditional assignments, but they often show extraordinary loyalty to their families or their gangs. Their parents may not volunteer for P. T. A. committees, but it would be wrong to assume that these parents are not concerned about what their children are able to achieve. Even their preference for television and movie shows over storybooks may arise from authentic awareness that print is actually a devious and impoverished medium in comparison with the presence of speaking, acting persons.

It is a sad commentary on our educational system to realize that we have generally failed to provide a proper education for the deprived. In many slum communities, less than 5 per cent of the youth go to college. In many of these same communities, the average IQ measures below 85 and continues to drop as the children get older. The fact that education is but a reflection of our society at large, and in many cases is one of the few social institutions feverishly trying to remedy the problem, is little consolation for the children who mark time in an educational wasteland. The insularity and educational provincialism of the slum environment school at best works with the symptoms and sometimes does not even do an effective job of that. Our society owes a great debt to the harried teachers in slum schools for their efforts in struggling with insurmountable odds. These teachers and their administrators simply do not have the resources to cope with the special needs and requirements of the deprived. The problem is more than just a matter of additional funds, although this is sorely needed. Among other things, it involves a reconstruction of curriculum for the deprived. The curriculum for middle-class youth cannot be effective when it is merely shifted to the other side of the tracks.

THE DEPRIVED CHILD

A starting point for curriculum is the child himself. These are some of the special characteristics that tend to typify the deprived child in the slum school:

1. Social and economic misfortune have tended to give him low educational aspiration and ambition. He does not care about schooling.

He and his parents have a long history of being defeated at every turn, so he may feel that learning is not worth the effort.

2. He may be antagonistic toward his teachers. Teachers represent an authority figure, and he has been taught by his slum environment to be suspicious and resentful of all authority.

3. He may be emotionally frustrated and readily discouraged. The oppressive conditions of slum life do not lead to an emotionally stable nor confident outlook.

4. He may not have the physical stamina that proper learning requires. His diet is likely to be low in protein or at least imbalanced through lack of money or parental indifference and neglect.

5. He probably does not possess middle-class value systems of conventional rewards for school achievement. In some slum schools, the mark of success is to 'buck' the system and fail as soon and as often as possible.

6. His orientation to language tends to be less symbolic and more particularized than middle-class youth. He cannot cope well with abstractions or categorical representations that are beyond his experience. His speech patterns reflect the selective retardation that his environment has provided.

7. He tends to have poor perceptual discrimination skills. His visual and auditory discrimination suffers from lack of stimulation and practice in the home. He is usually not told stories by his parents, not read to at home, not given stimulating reading or viewing materials by his parents. His home undoubtedly lacks the wealth of toys, objects, pictures, recordings, and other materials that early enable middle-class youth to develop referent categories so important for language and reading development.

8. He has difficulty in concentrating on learning. His attention span is probably limited. It is difficult for him to attend to what he perceives as meaningless and abstract.

9. He cannot readily identify with educational experiences as presented by conventional school books, films, and other materials. These materials are beyond his limited background of experience and alien to his way of life.

10. He may be callous towards his teachers and peers. He may have difficulty in accommodating to essentially middle-class social conditions of learning. He has likely not experienced much love and affection. He may be subconsciously crying out in the wilderness, "Don't teach me—love me. No one else has!"

Such is a hypothetical profile of the deprived child. What role can media play in reorienting curriculum to his special needs?

ROLE OF MEDIA

There are no simple answers to the complex problems involved with educating the deprived. Thoughtful educators everywhere recognize that major sustained efforts must be made to effectively and efficiently cope with the education of the deprived. There have been many mistakes made and there will likely continue to be mistakes made, with time, effort, and money expended in the process. But we as educators must attend to the problems of the deprived in order to restructure our educational methods. Means and instrumentalities must be found that will facilitate the learning of the deprived to enable them to catch up with the rest of our society. Neither the transfer of traditional ways of teaching nor the transfer of conventional materials will enable the deprived to gain the education that we must provide. The problems of educating the deprived are too vast and too complex to be solved by resorting to the dead hands of obsolescence and inefficiency. Clearly, the need exists for new and better instructional practices. The fruits of education's long-awaited technological revolution may provide a solution to the problems of the deprived. It is a paradox that the very same technology that is a partial determinant of the plight of the deprived may enable education to reap benefits that can contribute to breaking the spiral of deprivation.

Focal to any consideration of education are the media by which people learn. The successful accomplishment of education involves the delicate structuring of conditions of learning, and media can play a major role in this endeavor. Properly conceived, the employment of media resources, although they are no guarantees for promoting effective learning, can significantly influence learning behavior. A growing body of research clearly indicates that, used properly, media can provide effective conditions of learning. The term media, as it is here used, refers to all stored information (in the generic sense, instructional content), regardless of the form of storage of the associated display mechanism. As such, the term media encompasses books, pamphlets, encyclopedias, magazines, newspapers, documents, programed and other self-instructional resources, motion pictures (8mm, 16mm, kinescopes), telephonic means (tele-lecture), television, radio, recordings, (audio, disc, and video), flat pictures, filmstrips, slides, transparencies, drawings, microformat materials, maps, charts, globes, graphs, cartoons, models, diagrams, and posters. This listing is meant to be neither comprehensive nor exhaustive. Its sole function is to convey an impression of the wide range of diversification of materials and equipment for communicating knowledge. Other chapters in this book deal specifically with media systems in greater detail. Suffice it to say that the potential for using media with the deprived has not been fully tapped. Imaginative, creative use of the rich fund of media resources could be of great value to the teaching of the deprived. The key factors, however, are the skills of the teachers involved and the total restructuring of the educational environment.

Fundamentally, the basic rationale for the employment of media resources with deprived youth is no different from that used with advantaged youth. Educational media are instrumentalities designed to enable students to learn effectively. Differences lie in the appropriateness of the media for the kinds of learners for whom they are designed and in the degree of inventiveness with which they are used. All too often, the media utilized with the deprived reflect the middle-class world that is foreign to the deprived. They reflect levels of abstraction beyond the comprehension of the slum child. They are geared to the motivations and psychological frames of reference of suburban America. There is no one-to-one relationship between learning and exposure to media. The media do not act on sponge-like minds which soak up knowledge. Each student differentially perceives media content within the boundaries of his own world of experience and understanding. In short, when media are used with the deprived, they must be designed for the deprived. This does not mean that all we need do is water down media content in order to have it understood by slum youth, for this outlook envisions the deprived child as a diluted version of his middle-class counterpart. But it does mean that the deprived child has a unique set of goals, symbol repertoire, language abilities, perceptual patterns, and background experiences that must be taken into account by the designers and users of media resources. Materials produced must be aimed specifically at the deprived. Such materials must be designed for the low motivations, impoverished backgrounds, and abilities characteristic of the deprived. In effect, standard materials, which invariably are based on middle-class norms, expectations, symbolism, and experiences, speak a foreign language to the slum child. This was forcibly brought to the attention of the writer when, a few years ago, he showed a film, which typically was enthusiastically but seriously received by middle-class students, to a group of slum children. The catcalls and laughter practically drowned out the sound track. The communication breakdown that occurred during the showing was directly attributed to the inappropriateness of the film to the students.

This is not to say that the teacher of the deprived cannot use the wealth of standard materials available. But it does place on the teacher a heavy burden of responsibility for the judicious selection and adaptation of existing materials. In some cases there is sufficient overlap of background experiences among both slum and nonslum children so as to allow for use of standard materials; but the wise teacher of the deprived must always keep in mind the 'other world' of the slums.

The nonverbal nature of many media of an audiovisual nature can often be used to advantage with the deprived because they can provide pegs on which the deprived can hang meanings and build toward subsequent development of more verbally oriented experiences. It should be kept in mind, however, that the deprived may exhibit illiteracy in a visual sense to the same extent that they may exhibit illiteracy in a verbal sense. Impoverishment of background is likely to exist on both a verbal and nonverbal level. Audiovisual materials do not by their nature reach low nor are they primarily intended for the intellectually unsophisticated. Indeed, some of the best audiovisual materials are used at medical schools and with other highly select and sophisticated learners.

The point is that whatever materials and media are employed must be appropriate to the learners. The same 'learning to learn' phenomenon that applies to verbal symbols also applies to nonverbal symbols. The unique capabilities of all media resources must be utilized to full advantage with the deprived. By proper use of the vast storehouse of media resources, disadvantaged youth may be able to leapfrog their deficiencies and attain equal educational footing with other students. Such does not occur by sheer use of media. It can only occur by skillful manipulation of all the elements of the learning environment by competent professionals who are well versed in curriculum, methods, media, content, and the special requirements of deprived youth. Imaginative media programs for the deprived can only come from the combined efforts of knowledgeable teachers, administrators, curriculum and media specialists, psychologists, and experts in the education of the deprived who are supported in their efforts by local, state, and federal officials and who have the full cooperation of parents and taxpayers.

Skillful teachers have long been aware of the diagnostic and therapeutic effects of various media. Intense involvement with films and other media may well be used to advantage with deprived youth, who frequently exhibit the torments and stresses of an oppressive environment. Use of media may provide for recognition, identification, insight, or catharsis, enabling deprived youth to better cope with their tensions and anxieties. This process of interaction between viewers and media might be termed mediatherapy. Mediatherapy might occur as a viewer vicariously experiences a situation portrayed in a film, telecast, or other medium. By identifying his real or imagined problem with that shown, he is able to gain insight into his difficulty, secure personality gratification, or undergo an anxiety-relieving catharsis.

Involvement with media may be of a preventative nature by providing deprived youth with a rich backlog of experiences that they would otherwise not readily obtain, thus enabling them to cope with future problems that might arise. In this manner, they may stockpile solutions to potential problems, conflicts, and difficulties. The creative uses of media for such purposes of diagnosis and therapy offer the educator a wealth of opportunity for fruitful research and development.

PROGRAMS OF SIGNIFICANCE

The upsurge of interest in the plight of the disadvantaged in this country has resulted in a multitude of special programs. It is beyond the scope of this chapter to deal with these in detail, or even to attempt to provide a comprehensive listing of them. The sole purpose here is merely to convey an impression of the scope of the activities that are currently in progress, some local, others statewide, still others national. Some programs are supported by foundation, philanthropic, private, or charity funds. Others are tax supported. Since deprivation involves the totality of the deprived environment, education is but a part of many programs. Some programs are successful, others are unsuccessful, and the success or failure of others remains to be seen. About the only thing that may be said concerning the multitude of various programs is that there is a great proliferation and diversity of them and, most important, that they are all significant in the sense that this nation has at last launched a frontal assault on human degradation in its aspirations to become a truly great society. So long as poverty and deprivation exist, the vision of our founding fathers is unrealized.

SOME EXAMPLES OF PROGRAMS FOR DEPRIVED INVOLVING MEDIA SUPPORT

The unique capability of the medium of television for bridging space offers great promise in reaching deprived children. Recognizing that preschool learnings are fundamental to success in later school years, a number of school districts, in cooperation with television stations, have telecast programs involving curriculum-linked preschool experiences to homes as well as to specially located public receiver locations where many deprived children can view them. Most commercial children's television programs provide valuable background experiences, of course, but it is especially significant that curriculum-linked programs of an instructional nature are being telecast. A characteristic of these instructional telecasts is that they are produced in cooperation with kindergarten and primary-level curriculum committees in an effort to provide a coordinated continuity from preschool to school years. Among the urban areas making use of such programs are Albuquerque, Memphis, Miami, and Denver. Many such programs are designed specifically for children from deprived homes; others are applicable for all children.

An example of the use of media enabling youth to leapfrog their impoverished environment is that provided by the Prince Edward Free School Association in Virginia. Integration difficulties resulted in the shutdown of the public schools in the county. Faced with a desperate situation, a group of foresighted educators, with the assistance of various funding organizations, established a school system in Farmville, Virginia, in an effort to provide educational opportunities for deprived children who had been without school for four years. It was early recognized that traditional educational practices were inadequate to cope with a severe educational situation. In addition to the establishment of nongraded programs, team teaching and extended contact time, the system placed heavy emphasis on media-oriented methods of instruction. Wilbert Edgerton, the audiovisual director, reported significant improvement of instruction at all levels through the use of media. Once students were able to master fundamental competencies, they were able to then engage in more advanced learnings. The following are noteworthy aspects of the media program:[9]

1. Use of the Language Master, a device containing a magnetic sound track on a card enabling students to see written words and pictures. This device was especially useful in teaching reading, writing, and speech.

2. A centralized program of materials and equipment, headed by a professionally trained director, which provided a diversity of materials, equipment, and services.

3. Involvement with educational television courses transmitted from Richmond, Virginia.

4. Inservice training in the use of educational media, involving both teachers and students.

5. Use of community resources. Students were frequently taken on field trips to broaden their horizons. Many students who never had the opportunity to travel outside their county visited major urban areas and attended museums, historical sites, industries, and symphonies.

6. Showing of educational and recreational films. These materials were used in conjunction with a summer-school program and were also available during the regular school year to the community at large.

It was evident from the results of the program that media played a significant role in serving the deprived youth of Prince Edward County.

In Omaha, deprived youth were able to overcome some of their handicaps of limited vocabulary and attention span by means of directed listening experiences provided by guides and worksheets used in conjunction with specially prepared tape recordings. Students from deprived

9 Wilbert D. Edgerton, "Prince Edward County: AV Helps Virginia's Deprived," *Audiovisual Instruction,* (January, 1965), 18–23.

homes who exhibit a potential for creative work have been involved with the production of tape-narrated color-slide sets. Participation in this and other materials-production programs has tended to evoke great satisfaction and increased understanding on the part of the students as well as to reduce disciplinary problems.

Cook County, Illinois, has been experimenting with electronic distribution for teaching reading and social adjustment to high-school dropouts. Each student used a carrel equipped with a small TV monitor, a headphone set, and a microphone. Lesson content originated from film and slide chains, tachistoscopes, and controlled readers, and was transmitted electronically. Teachers and students could also privately communicate through microphones and headphones. The carrel setting tended to provide fewer distractions than a conventional classroom. The typical short attention span of dropouts seemed to improve as students progressed at a pace determined individually by ability. In addition, the carrel-based learning tended to lessen the impact of social pressure and embarrassment that poor readers often experience from their peers in a regular classroom. An interesting finding of this pilot project was that students who progressed most in reading skills exhibited improved behavior patterns.

The children of migratory workers pose special problems insofar as education is concerned. The mobility of their families is such that their educational development is often severely limited. The use of various media has successfully been employed in many programs with migrant children. In Cedartown, New Jersey, a special educational program used a variety of media carefully integrated with units of study designed to compensate for the barren educational backgrounds of the migrants. One such unit of study involved films, demonstration, and actual equipment to teach the use of the telephone. Most of the children had never used a telephone before. It was found that the combined use of a variety of media significantly aided the educational development of the deprived children of migratory workers in overcoming their cultural disorientation and communications difficulties.

The San Diego schools, long known for their imaginative use of media in education, have evolved programs for deprived children that capitalize on the unique capabilities of media. A series of relatively inexpensive filmstrips dealing with community resources was prepared. Each filmstrip contained a teachers guide and many were provided with taped narration. The filmstrips were produced in order to provide broad community experiences to children whose neighborhood experiences tended to be isolated and insular at a time when funds for field trips had been eliminated. Another media project of interest is that of amplified telephone technique—telelecture—in order to bring resource people into classrooms by telephonic means. The technique permits an entire class to listen to and discuss matters with resource people who otherwise could not directly come into the class. Sometimes the phone calls are made on a prearranged basis. Other times they are spontaneous, arising from class consideration of various topics. Tape recorders with earphone attachments enabling small groups to listen to taped material without distracting other class members have also been used to advantage with San Diego's disadvantaged school children. This listening-post technique is especially useful in providing opportunities for deprived children to overcome their linguistic difficulties stemming from their impoverished home and neighborhood experiences.

New York state has a number of pilot and demonstration projects of significance to the educationally disadvantaged in which varied media resources are used. Among these are Project ABLE, Project STEP, Project REENTRY, and Talent Search Project. Project ABLE is a demonstration project of cultural enrichment and compensatory educational practice in which funds are allocated for upgrading programs. Participating school districts use funds for hiring additional personnel, purchasing instructional materials and equipment, hiring consultants, and increasing administrative and clerical support. Project STEP is designed to assist potential dropouts to remain in school or to better prepare them for employment if they leave school, through careful guidance, counseling, and supervised work experience. Project REENTRY is aimed at encouraging dropouts to return to school and to help them remain and succeed in school through intensive guidance efforts. Talent Search Project has been designed to encourage and develop the potential and to enrich the educational horizons of deprived students who seem to academically perform at a lower level than their ability suggests.

The North Carolina Advancement School in Winston-Salem was established to provide special programs for underachievers. The media program utilizes modern technological advances in media and has an extensive program in media research and development. Of particular interest is the instructional systems-design approach to the problems of students, many of whom come from disadvantaged environments. As is characteristic of well-conceived media programs, competent professional leadership coupled with carefully planned faculty and student involvement in media activities is a keynote of the program.

Another project to improve educational opportunities for inner-city deprived children is the Detroit Great Cities School Improvement Project. Considerable emphasis in this project is placed on the use of media programs and activities. This project employs the community school as its focal point of operation and makes extensive use of a wide range of media resources, ranging from televised reading-improvement programs and reading pacers to specially prepared preprimers in which the characters have been racially integrated.

The "black-power" inspired riots in Detroit and other major urban ghetto areas represent what amounts to civil insurrection from the lunatic fringe of deprived slum dwellers. Rap Brown and Stokely Carmichael are much more appealing to slum youth than Dick and Jane. Imaginative media programs can help to meet the educational needs of the deprived; but the immensity of the problem requires an equally immense effort. A BB gun is grossly ineffectual against a wounded charging rhinoceros.

A confluence of pressing educational needs has precipitated the rapid emergence of an ever-growing movement in higher education—the community college. Called democracy's colleges, these comprehensive new institutions are closely geared to local educational needs and offer a broad spectrum of minimal-cost educational opportunities. Among the many programs typically offered are those designed for youth and adults from deprived environments. Speaking of the unique role that judicious use of media can play in such programs, Herbert Stallworth, a leader in establishing media-oriented community colleges, recently stated: [10]

> Teaching work and learning work have been neglected—for whatever reasons—in the exciting movement in our time to deliberately study and engineer all kinds of human effort. Education, as a human enterprise, is, and should be, just as much subject to the intelligent application of technology as any other human enterprise. Perhaps we shall see the bonds of custom broken more adventurously and helpfully in community colleges. The comprehensive community college, because it has many different missions and must serve the widest spectrum of student backgrounds and interests will, I predict, find itself in the vanguard of the movement to improve teaching-learning processes through a judicious use of media.
>
> Having already broken through the "tradition curtain" in the area of educational purpose, the community college movement can reasonably be expected to overcome custom-based impediments in the area of educational practice.

The Educational Improvement Project embraces two programs for the improvement of educational opportunities in schools primarily for Negroes. One program was initiated by the Southern Association of Colleges and Schools. The other program was proposed by the College Entrance Examination Board. Both programs bring to bear stimulating resources and techniques for learning on the problem of bridging the culture gap that deprives many of adequate educational achievement.

Project Opportunity, conceived by a group of colleges and universities working with the Southern Office of the College Entrance Examination

---

10 Quoted by permission of Herbert F. Stallworth, President, College of the Mainland, LaMarque, Texas.

Board and the Southern Association of Colleges and Schools, is a plan to prepare culturally isolated yet talented students for admission to higher education. The program is directed toward the disadvantaged student in the belief that his success will affect community attitudes toward equal educational opportunity. Potentially talented students will be identified in the junior-high years, and their progress will be followed and supported in an effort to qualify them for college through stipends, materials, special educational programs, and counseling and guidance. The use of media is expected to appreciably add to the instructional quality of the progress of the youth involved.

A NATIONAL EFFORT

The immensity of economic and cultural deprivation, with its consequent educational effects, has become a problem of national scope. A veritable flood of federal programs has been unleashed and will likely continue to flourish in a massive effort to increase the life-chances of the deprived. These programs reflect a growing awareness of the tragic waste of human resources because of the circumstances of birth and environmental conditions. The Community Action Program, The Job Corps, Project Head Start, VISTA, The Neighborhood Youth Corps, The College Work-Study Program, Adult Basic Education, The Aid to Migrants Program, and many other programs pay credence to the humanitarian and democratic nature of our goals as a nation. The schools, along with other societal agencies, will share a major burden of responsibility in the national effort to remove the cancerous malignancy of deprivation. The perplexing yet provocative challenge confronts us. The deprived student does not exist as an abstract category. He is flesh and blood. And we are equally human in our efforts to help him and our nation. Artfully contrived programs of rich media resources may help. But there is no royal road to success.

BIBLIOGRAPHY

Books, Pamphlets & Reports
Allen, Charles M. *Combating the Dropout Problem*. Chicago: Science Research Associates, 1956.
Baltimore City Public Schools: An Early School Admissions Project Related to In-School Learning Activities and Experiences for Culturally Deprived Children. Baltimore: Baltimore Public Schools, 1962.
Bienstock, Herbert, compiler. *Factbook on the School Dropout in the World of Work*. New York: Bureau of Labor Statistics, U. S. Dept. of Labor, 1963.
Bloom, Benjamin S., *et al. Compensatory Education for Cultural Deprivation*. New York: Holt, Rinehart, and Winston, 1965.
Burchill, G. *Work Study Program for Alienated Youth: A Casebook*. Chicago: Science Research Associates, 1961.
Carricker, William R. *Role of the School in Prevention of Juvenile Delinquency*. Washington, U. S. Gov't Printing Office, 1963.

Chansky, Norman M. *Some Psychological Characteristics of School Dropouts: Findings Based on Research Related to Operation Second Chance.* Raleigh: North Carolina State University at Raleigh, Department of Education and Psychology, April, 1964.

Chapple, Dorothy S. *The School Dropout: An American Calamity.* New York: Birk & Co., 1963.

Clark, Kenneth B. *Prejudice and Your Child.* 2d ed. Boston: Beacon Press, 1955.

Clearing House on Urban Teacher Education Report. No. 1. New York: The City University of New York, April, 1965.

Coleman, James S. *Social Climates in High Schools.* Washington: U. S. Gov't Printing Office, 1961.

Conant, James B. *Slums & Suburbs.* New York. McGraw-Hill Book Company, 1961.

Cutts, Warren G. *Reading Unreadiness in the Underprivileged.* Washington: U. S. Gov't Printing Office, 1963. Reprinted from *N.E.A. Journal,* (April, 1963), 23–24.

Davis, Allison. *Social Class Influence Upon Learning.* Cambridge: Harvard University Press, 1948.

Educational Policies Commission. *Education and the Disadvantaged American.* Washington: National Education Association, 1962.

Educational Research Service. *School Programs for the Disadvantaged.* Circular No. 1. Washington: National Education Association, January, 1965.

Evans, Luther H., and Arnstein, George E. *Automation and the Challenge to Education.* Washington: National Education Association, 1962.

Finley, Otis E., Jr. *Meeting the Challenge of the Dropout: New Horizons in Education in the Sixties.* New York: National Urban League, 1963.

Fusco, Gene C. *School-Home Partnership in Depressed Urban Neighborhoods.* Washington: U. S. Gov't Printing Office, 1964.

Hannah, Arlene, and Riessman, Frank. *Teachers of the Poor.* New York: Mobilization for Youth, May, 1964.

Harrington, Michael. *The Other America.* New York: Macmillan, 1962.

Jewett, Arno, *et al. Improving English Skills of Different Youth.* Washington: U. S. Gov't Printing Office, 1964.

May, Edgar, *The Wasted Americans.* New York: Harper & Row, 1962.

Miller, Leonard M. *The Dropout: Schools Search for Clues to His Problems.* Washington: U. S. Gov't Printing Office, 1963. Reprinted from *School Life,* XLV (May, 1963), 5–7, 30–33.

Miller, Leonard M. *References on Dropouts: Related to the Identification, Causes, Prevention, and Counseling of Dropouts at the Elementary, Secondary and Higher Education Levels.* Washington: U. S. Dept. of Health, Education and Welfare, Office of Education, October, 1962.

Miller, S. M., and Saleem, Betty L. *The Neglected Dropout: The Returnee.* Syracuse, N. Y.: Youth Development Center, Syracuse University, 1963.

Myrdal, Gunnar. *An American Dilemma: The Negro Problem.* New York: Harper & Row, 1944.

Neisser, Edith G. *School Failures and Dropouts.* New York: Public Affairs Committee, July, 1963.

New England Council for Economic Research. *Report on School Dropout Problem.* Boston: The New England Council for Economic Research, 1964.

Passow, A. H. *Education in Depressed Areas.* New York: Bureau of Publications, Teachers College, Columbia University, 1963.

Plenty, Ruth C. *Reading Ability in High School Dropouts.* New York: Teachers College, Columbia University, 1956.

President's Committee on Youth Employment. *The Challenge of Jobless Youth.* Washington: U. S. Gov't Printing Office, 1963.

Programs for the Educationally Disadvantaged. Bulletin No. 17. Washington: U. S. Dept. of Health, Education, and Welfare, 1963.

Project TRUE: A Final Report, 1962-1964. New York: Hunter College, 1964.
Riessman, Frank. *The Culturally Deprived Child.* New York: Harper & Row, 1962.
Sanford, Terry. *Operation Second Chance: Special Youth Contract.* Raleigh: Governor's Office, 1963.
Schreiber, Daniel. *Guidance and the School Dropout.* Washington: National Education Association, Project: School Dropouts, 1964.
The 1963 Dropout Campaign: Summary and Analysis of the President's Special Summer Program to Combat School Dropout. Washington: U. S. Gov't Printing Office, 1964.
The Impact of Urbanization on Education. Washington: U. S. Gov't Printing Office, 1962.
Weary, Bettina. *School Dropout: Selected and Annotated References.* Washington: U. S. Dept. of Health, Education, and Welfare, Office of Education, April, 1962.

Periodicals
Association for Supervision and Curriculum Development. "Disaffected Children and Youth," *Education Leadership,* XX (February, 1963).
Ausubel, D. P. "Teaching Strategy for Culturally Deprived Pupils: Cognitive and Motivational Considerations," *School Review,* LXXI (Winter, 1963) 454–63.
Barko, Naomi. "Dropouts to Nowhere," *Reporter,* XXVI (March 29, 1962), 34–36.
Bellenger, M. E. "Guidance for the Disaffected," *Educational Leadership,* XX (February, 1963), 297–99.
Bloom S. "Improving the Education of Culturally Deprived Children Applying Learning Theory to Classroom Instruction," *Chicago School Journal,* XLV (December, 1963) 126–31.
Brunner, Catherine, "Project Help: A Program for Early School Admissions," *Maryland Teacher,* XXL (November, 1963) 8–10.
Clift, Virgil A. "Factors Relating to the Education of Culturally Deprived Negro Youth," *Education Theory,* XIV (April, 1964), 76–82.
Coles, R. "Racial Identity in School Children," *Saturday Review,* XLVI (October 19,. 1963), 56–57.
Conant, J. B. "Social Dynamite in Our Large Cities," *Vital Speeches,* XXVII (July 1, 1961), 554–60.
Cutts, W. G. "Special Language Problems of the Culturally Deprived," *Clearing House,* XXXVII (October, 1962), 80–83.
Davis, Donald A. "An Experimental Study of Potential Dropouts," *Personnel and Guidance Journal,* XL (May, 1962), 799–802.
Della-Dora, Delmo. "The Culturally Disadvantaged: Educational Implications of Certain Socio-Cultural Phenomena," *Exceptional Children,* XXVIII (May, 1962), 467–71.
Dentler, Robert A. "Dropouts, Automation, and the Cities," *Teachers College Record,* LXV (March, 1964), 475–83.
Fisher, John J. "Who is the Lower-Class Child?" *Journal of Educational Sociology,* XXIV (March, 1961), 309–11.
Fishman, Joshua, et al. "Guidelines for Testing Minority Group Children," *Journal of Social Issues,* XX (April, 1954), 127–45.
Gellman, William, and Gendell, H. "Motivating the Unmotivated Youth," *American Child,* XLIV (May, 1962), 16–20.
Goff, S. M. "Some Educational Implications of the Influence of Rejection on Aspiration Levels of Minority Group Children," *Journal of Experimental Education,* XXIII (1954), 179–83.
Gordon, Edmund W. "A Question of Culture," *American Child,* XLV (March, 1963), 11–14.
Gottlieb, David. "Goal Aspirations and Goal Fulfillments: Differences Between Deprived and Affluent American Adolescents," *American Journal of Orthopsychiatry,* XXXIV (1964), 934–41.

Greene, J. E. "Comparison of the School Morale of White and Negro Students in a Large Southeastern School System," *Journal of Negro Education,* XXXI (Spring, 1960), 132–38.

Greene, J. E. "Discipline and Morale Among White and Negro High School Students," *Journal of Teacher Education,* XII (December, 1961), 437–47.

Harrison, E. C. "Working at Improving the Motivational and Achievement Levels of the Deprived," *Journal of Negro Education,* XXXII (Summer, 1963), 301–7.

Haubrich, V. "Culturally Different; New Context for Teacher Education," *Journal of Teacher Education,* XIV (June, 1963), 163–67.

High, P. B. "Educating the Superior Student in the Deprived Area," *American Teacher Magazine,* XLVIII (December, 1963), 5.

Jencks, C. "Slums and Schools," *New Republic,* CXLVII (September 10, 1962), 19–22; (September 17, 1962), 13–16.

Karraker, C. H. "Education for Our Rural Slums," *School and Society,* XCI (October 5, 1963), 276–77.

Kelley, Carl C. "The Dropout — Our Greatest Challenge," *Educational Leadership,* XX (February, 1963), 294–96, 318.

Kirman, Joseph, "Teacher Survival in Difficult Schools," *High Points,* XLV (April, 1964), 69–70.

Krugman, M. "Culturally Deprived Child in School," *N. E. A. Journal,* L (April, 1964), 23–24.

Larson, R. "Method of Identifying Culturally Deprived Children," *Exceptional Children,* XXX (November, 1963), 130–34.

Liddle, Gordon P. "Psychological Factors Involved in Dropping Out of School," *High School Journal,* XLV (April, 1962), 276–80.

Lipton, A. "Cultural Deprivation," *Journal of Educational Sociology,* XXXVI (September, 1962), 17–19.

McDonald, Keith H. "The Relationship of Socio-Economic Status to an Objective Measure of Motivation," *Personnel and Guidance Journal,* XLII (June, 1964), 997–1002.

McQueen, R. "Intelligence and Educational Achievement of a Matched Sample of White and Negro Students," *School and Society,* LXXXVIII (September 24, 1960), 327–29.

Maleska, Eugene. "Stirrings in the Big Cities: New York," *N.E.A. Journal,* LI (May, 1962), 20–23.

Mitchell, C. "Culturally Deprived: A Matter of Concern," *Childhood Education,* XXXVIII (May, 1962), 412–20.

O'Gara, J. "Doctor Conant's Social Dynamite," *Commonweal,* LXXV (November, 1961), 166.

Porter, John W. "The Heart of the Dropout Problem: Early Identification," *Michigan Education Journal,* XL (January, 1963), 362–65, 397.

Rehage, K. J. "Culturally Deprived Child," *Elementary School Journal,* LXIII (January, 1963), 186.

Riessman, Frank. "Culturally Deprived Child: A New View," *School Life,* XLV (April, 1963), 186.

Riessman, Frank. "Teaching the Culturally Deprived," *N.E.A. Journal,* LII (April, 1963), 20–22.

Ritchie, Robert R. "The High School Dropout — An Educational Dilemma," *Bulletin of the National Association of Secondary-School Principals,* LXVI (November, 1962), 45–47.

Schreiber, Daniel. "The School Dropout — Fugitive from Failure," *Bulletin of the National Association of Secondary-School Principals,* XLVI (May, 1962), 233–41.

Schreiber, Daniel, *et al.* "School Dropouts," *N.E.A. Journal,* LI (May, 1962), 51–58.

Sembler, I. T. "Comparative and Developmental Study of the Learning Abilities of Negro and White Children Under Four Conditions," *Journal of Educational Psychology,* LIV (February, 1963), 38–44.

Singleton, R. "Some Problems in Minority Group Education in the Los Angeles Public Schools," *Journal of Negro Education,* XXXII (Spring, 1963), 137–45.

Sloane, Frank. "Stirrings in the Big Cities: Miami," *N.E.A. Journal,* LI (January, 1963), 14–16.

Sorensen, Mourits A. "Low Ability Drop-Outs Versus Low Ability Graduates," *Personnel and Guidance,* XXXIX (October, 1960), 144–45.

Utter, L. W. "Helping Our Culturally Impoverished Children," *N.E.A. Journal,* LII (November, 1963), 28–30.

Velie, Lester, "No Room at the Bottom," *Reader's Digest,* LXXXIV (April, 1964), 169–73, 176–80.

Vogel, Anita. "How to Check Drop-Outs: Six Case Histories," *School Management,* V (November, 1961) 73–84.

Walton, George. "Uncle Sam's Rejects," *Saturday Evening Post,* CCXXXV (December 8, 1962), 10–13.

Ware, K. "English Programs for the Culturally Different: Significant Aspects of the Saint Louis Program," *Elementary English,* XL (October, 1963), 611–14.

Weiner, M. "Another Look at the Culturally Deprived and Their Levels of Aspiration," *Journal of Educational Sociology,* XXXVI (March, 1963), 319.

Whipple, G. "Multicultural Primers for Today's Children," *Education Digest,* XXIX (February, 1964), 26–29.

Wolf, L. "Sociological Perspective on the Education of Culturally Deprived Children," *School Review,* LXX (Winter, 1962), 373–87.

Wolman, M. "Cultural Factors and Creativity," *Journal of Secondary Education,* XXXVII (December, 1962), 454–60.

Motion Picture Films & Kinescopes

Ask Me, Don't Tell Me. 30 min., b&w. CON, 1961.[11]
The Baltimore Plan, 21 min., b&w. AFL-CIO, 1953.
Big City — 1980. 54 min., b&w. CAROUF, 1960.
Building Better Cities. 28 min., color. COFC-US, 1961.
Cast the First Stone. 42 min., b&w. ADL, 1960.
The Challenge of Change: The Case for Counseling. 28 min., color. NET, 1962.
The Challenging City. 16 min., color, CF, 1962.
Children Without. 29 min., b&w. NEA, 1964.
Christmas in Appalachia. 29 min., b&w. CF, n.d.
City in Trouble. 20 min., color. FF, n.d.
Colorado Cares. 20 min., color. CSDH, 1958.
Day after Day. 30 min., b&w. CON, n.d.
Depressed Area. 14 min., b&w. AFL-CIO, 1962.
The Devil is a Sissy — Court Sequence. b&w. TFC, 1946.
The Dropout. 10 min., b&w. DAVP, 1962.
The Dropout. 29 min., b&w. IFB, 1961.
Farewell Oak Street. 20 min., b&w. AFL-CIO, 1953.
The Forest of the Night. 30 min., b&w. NAAJSSA, 1956.
Gang Boy. 27 min., color. DAVP, n.d.
Green Thumb in the City. 30 min., b&w. NAAJSSA, n.d.
Hard Brought UP. 40 min., b&w. IFB, 1955.
Harvest of Shame. 54 min., b&w. MGHT, n.d.
High School — Your Challenge. 13½ min., b&w. CORF, n.d.
Home is a Long Road. 54 min., b&w. WISU, n.d.
The Hurrying King. 24 min., color. USAC, 1962.
I Never Went Back. 16 min., color. CCA, 1964.
If These Were Your Children. 50 min., b&w. MLI, n.d.

---

[11] Abbreviation in capital letters refers to producers or distributor. See listing for full name and address.

Lewis Mumford On the City, Part 5 — The City as Man's Home. 28 min., b&w. STE, n.d.
A Morning for Jimmy. 28 min., color. ADL, 1961.
Mike. 11 min., b&w. USC, 1962.
Mike Makes His Mark. 29 min., color. NEA, 1962.
Neighborhood Story. 30 min., b&w. SU, 1956.
Old Man Stone. 30 min., b&w. NAAJSSA, 1956.
Our Race Problem, Parts 1 and 2. 29 min., b&w. NET, 1958.
Population Patterns in the United States. 11 min., b&w., CORF, 1961.
Problem of Pupil Adjustment: The Drop-Out. 20 min., b&w. MGHT, 1951.
Problem of Pupil Adjustment: The Stay-In. 19 min., b&w. MGHT, 1951.
The Quiet One. 70 min., b&w. CON, 1956.
The Revolution in Human Expectations. 29 min., b&w. UU-AVC, 1958.
Stay in School and Graduate. 15 min., color. USNRS, 1957.
Step by Step. 20 min., b&w. IFB, 1954.
Superfluous People. 28 min., b&w. AFL-CIO, 1962.
This is Tomorrow. 10 min., b&w. AFL-CIO, n.d.
To Promote the General Welfare. 13 min., b&w. AFL-CIO, 1954.
The Urban League Story, 25 min., color. HURTE, 1956.
When I'm Old Enough — Goodbye! 28 min., b&w. AFL-CIO, 1962.
Why Johnny Can't Get a Job. 29 min., b&w. TGP.
You Can Go a Long Way. 21 min., b&w. EBF, 1961.

Tapes & Records

It's A Changing World. 46 min., 1-track 7½ ipw. COLU, n.d.[12]
The City — A Place to Live. 30 min., 7" 1-track tape. COLU, n.d.
The Local Police and Prevention of Juvenile Delinquency, Parts 1, 2. 7" 1-track 7½ ips. 60 min., COLU, n.d.
Migration and Urbanization. 30 min., 7" tape 1-track 7½ ips.
The Precocious. 15 min., 5d, 1-track 7½ ips. COLU, n.d.
These Great Americans. 13 fifteen-minute programs, 16" record, 33⅓ rpm. ADL, n.d.

Filmstrips & Soundstrips

Continuing Your Education. 24 min., (2 records, 2 filmstrips), color. HP, 1964.[13]
Dropping Out: Road to Nowhere. 26 min., color. GA, 1964.
High School Diploma. (2 records, 2 filmstrips) 24 min., color. HP, 1964.
Men and Machines: Our Expanding Economy. 55 frames, silent. NYT, 1963.
Stay in School. b&w. VEC, n.d.
The Story of Our Town. b&w. ADL, n.d.
A Time for Decision. 24 min., (2 records, 2 filmstrips), color. HP, 1964.
Trade . . . The Future. 1 33LP, 1 7½ ips, 1 FS, 1 Manual. Convair, 1959.
What Good Is School. 32 frames, color. SVE, 1961.

Listing of Producers or Distributors of Audiovisual Reference Materials

ADL	Anti-Defamation League of B'nai B'rith 515 Madison Ave. New York, N. Y.
AFL-CIO	AFL-CIO Department of Education 815 16th St., N. W. Washington, D. C.

[12] Abbreviation in capital letters refers to producer or distributor. See listing for full name and address.

[13] Abbreviation in capital letters refers to producer or distributor. See listing for full name and address.

BYU	Brigham Young University Division of Communications Services Salt Lake City, Utah
CAROUF	Carousel Film, Inc. 1501 Broadway New York, N. Y.
CCA	Charles Cahill & Associates 5746 Sunset Blvd. Hollywood, Calif.
CF	Churchill Films 6671 Sunset Blvd. Los Angeles, Calif.
COFC-US	Chamber of Commerce Audio-Visual Department 1615 H. St., N. W. Washington, D. C.
COLU	University of Colorado National Tape Repository Boulder, Colorado
CON	Contemporary Films 267 W. 25th St. New York, N. Y.
CONVAIR	Convair Division of General Dynamics Corporation Educational Services 3302 Pacific Hwy. San Diego, Calif.
CORF	Coronet Films 65 E. South Water St. Chicago, Ill.
CSDH	Colorado State Department of Health 4216 E. 11th St. Denver, Colorado
DAVP	Sid Davis Productions 1418 N. Highland Ave. Hollywood, Calif.
EBF	Encyclopaedia Britannica Films 1150 Wilmette Ave. Wilmette, Ill.
FF	Stuart Finley Films 6996 Mansfield Road Falls Church, Virginia
GA	Guidance Associates PO Box 5 Pleasantville, N. Y.
HP	Horizon Productions 301 W. 73rd St. Kansas City, Mo.
HURTE	Leroy E. Hurte Productions 4477 W. Adams Blvd. Los Angeles, Calif.
IFB	International Film Bureau 332 S. Michigan Ave. Chicago, Ill.
IUAVC	Indiana University Audio-Visual Center Bloomington, Indiana

MGHT	Metropolitan Life Insurance Co. 600 Stockton St. San Francisco, Calif.
NAAJSSA	National Academy of Adult Jewish Studies of the Synagogue of America 1109 5th Ave. New York, N. Y.
NEA	National Education Association 1201 16th St., N. W. Washington, D. C.
NET	National Educational Television Film Service Audio-Visual Center Indiana University Bloomington, Indiana
NYT	The New York Times Office of Educational Television 229 W. 43rd St. New York, N. Y.
PUAVC	Purdue University Audio-Visual Center Lafayette, Indiana
STE	Sterling Educational Films 6 E. 39th St. New York, N. Y.
SU	Syracuse University Educational Film Library Syracuse, N. Y.
SVE	Society for Visual Education 1345 Diversey Parkway Chicago, Ill.
TFC	Teaching Film Custodians, Inc. 25 W. 43rd St. New York, N. Y.
TGP	Theodore Granik Productions 1627 K. St. Washington, D. C.
USAC	U. S. Continental Army Command Fort Monroe, Va.
USC	University of Southern California Department of Cinema University Park Los Angeles, Calif.
USNRS	U. S. Navy Recruiting Service
VEC	Visual Education Consultants 2066 Helena St. Madison, Wisc.
WISCU	University of Wisconsin Bureau of Audio-Visual Instruction Madison, Wisc.
WSU	Wayne State University Audio-Visual Utilization Center Detroit, Michigan

Part Four

THE DEVELOPING
TECHNOLOGY
OF MEDIA SYSTEMS

Chapter 14

---

*What is educational technology and how does it relate to
education as an institution and education as a process?*

*How has educational technology developed through the years,
and how has this development been reflected
in the 'hardware' of the media field?*

*What have been the significant implications of technology
on curricular reform, organizational patterns,
and the psychology of learning?*

*What is likely to happen in the future to provide for
optimal information storage and retrieval, communication
methodology, and cybernetics in education?*

THE EMERGING
TECHNOLOGY OF EDUCATION*

JAMES D. FINN, Director
Instructional Technology and Media Project
University of Southern California

INTRODUCTION AND DEFINITION

Education in the United States can be viewed as an institution—social,
political, economic. It can also be viewed as a process whereby humans
learn and are taught. Subject matter content or skills are also sometimes
loose referents to the word "education," in the sense of such phrases as
scientific education, physical education, or education of teachers. Finally,
there is always a definition which represents a description of the effect
of personal experience, as in the classic *Education of Henry Adams,* or
in such a phrase as "that experience taught me a lesson in (or gave me
an education in) human relations."

*This chapter is reprinted by permission of the author from *Educational Implications of Tech-
nological Change,* the report of the National Commission on Technology, Automation and Economic
Progress, 1966.

These separate but somewhat overlapping concepts (and they are by no means exhaustive) suggest that care need be taken when addressing the problem of the relationships of technology to education. It would appear that the Commission should be interested in the bearings that technology has on education as an institution, a process, and its content.

There is also some disagreement within the educational profession as to what is meant by the expression educational technology (or instructional technology). A group of experimental psychologists would like to confine the term to an empirical approach to the process of teaching and learning.[1] That is, they refer to the work in experimental psychology as a developing "science of learning," and applications of this science—for example, applying the principles of operant conditioning to teaching through programed instruction—as the "technology of instruction."

While these psychologists admit that there is, by no means, a one-to-one relationship between their version of the science of learning and the technology of instruction, they view this relationship as the ultimate goal. There are some real weaknesses to this point of view and it will not be the one from which this paper is written.[2] However, since this relationship does exist to some extent, it will be considered within a broader context of educational technology.

Educational or instructional technology is sometimes too narrowly thought of as confined to hardware. Thus, for example, closed-circuit television or language laboratories represent to many educators the sum total of instructional technology—making it very easy to discuss or dismiss. Actually, much more is involved in the concept. If the point of view is taken that the institution of education in the United States is now the subject of and is moving into the general scientific-technological revolution, then hardware, materials, systems of organization, and new roles for teachers and administrators are all a part of educational technology. Within this broad umbrella, there are subtechnologies; for example, psychological testing, the development of new hardware such as the cartridge-loading 8 mm. film viewers, and the creation of whole systems of materials such as those designed for the Physical Science Study Committee by Professor Jerrold Zacharias to teach high school physics.

Further, when education is viewed as an institution, technology of a sophisticated type can (and is, to a small extent beginning to) play a part in the management and operation of the entire enterprise. For ex-

---

[1] See, for example, A. A. Lumsdaine, "Educational Technology, Programmed Instruction, and Instructional Services," in *Theories of Learning and Instruction*, 63d Yearbook of the National Society for the Study of Education, part I (Chicago, Ill.: The National Society for the Study of Education, 1964); and James D. Finn, "Instructional Technology," *The Bulletin of the National Association of Secondary School Principals*, vol. XLVII, No. 283 (May, 1963), pp. 99–103.

[2] Among other problems associated with this point of view is that the "science of learning" must be a particular psychological position; e.g., Skinner or Bruner. More important is the fact that psychology is not the only science of learning. Social and economic factors introduce other variables.

ample, data processing machinery and techniques are being used for scheduling, pupil accounting, etc.; modular construction of school buildings is being tried; information storage and retrieval processes are being considered as applicable to age-old library problems.

There are, in addition, economic and other aspects to this general concept of educational technology. These will, in this paper, be interwoven as the discussion criss-crosses between education as an institution and as a process. The general emphasis, however, will be on the subtechnologies most closely related to instruction, as it is felt that this is the current interest of the Commission. These include hardware, materials, systems, organization, and psychological applications.

SOURCES OF PRESENT CONCERN

Since World War II the national concern with education has been increasing, a concern that took a quantum jump with the unveiling of the first sputnik. Since that time, the national effort to improve the educational system has redoubled several times. However, from the point of view of instructional technology, all concerns cannot be said to originate in the space race. The efforts of the Ford Foundation in the development and promotion of educational television, for example, antedated Sputnik I by several years.

The concerns for education represent a sort of catalog of problems and issues relating to instructional technology. These can be briefly listed:

1. The population explosion with all it implies in terms of more students and fewer teachers and the necessity for new educational arrangements.[3]
2. The information explosion, which presents great problems in curriculum construction (what to teach) and requires greater efforts in increasing the efficiency of teaching and learning (more learning in less time).[4]
3. The general rising throughout the world, including the United States, of the depressed sectors of mankind. Education is seen as the main weapon in the war on poverty, for example, and the requirements of such an educational war include new methods and techniques to reach these people—here and overseas.
4. The urge to raise the quality of life for all, which, in turn, requires raising the quality of education even though the institution is

[3] A recent report from the TEMPO Division of General Electric in Santa Barbara, Calif., projects the total U.S. population under 20 years of age in the year 2000 at 143 million.

[4] A paper on the explosion of knowledge will soon be released by the Instructional Technology and Media Project at the University of Southern California. In the meantime, a good general reference on a portion of the knowledge explosion may be found in Derek J. de Solla Price, "*Little Science, Big Science,*" New York: Columbia University Press, 1963.

pressed on all sides by population, knowledge, and various kinds of special demands. This situation also sets a requirement, although in a different way, for a more efficient educational process.

5. Research and development on all aspects of education have generated more knowledge about the process and the institution as part of the general knowledge explosion. From this situation rises a drive to introduce all kinds of innovations—most of them relating to instructional technology—into the educational system. Practice in education has, until the last few years, lagged about 50 years behind research and theory. Today the process of educational innovation itself is under study in an effort to speed up the rate of change.

6. The need for education and reeducation and for training and retraining of manpower to meet individual personal needs and national needs increases as society becomes more automated and technologically sophisticated. If, as is often said these days, an individual may have to learn several jobs in a lifetime, the same problems of educational efficiency involving possible uses of instructional technology arise—both on a formal and an informal basis.

7. The ill-defined drive toward a new value system, symbolized by the student revolts at Berkeley and elsewhere and by very personal concerns on the part of a segment of the intellectual community, suggests, among other things, dissatisfaction with the abstract, status-oriented, large-scale organization of the college and university characteristic of a technological culture. Since a return to the colonial college is impossible, solutions to these problems, too, must be found in technology, although the student spokesment would not understand this. The effort to find technological answers, however, is a function of a technological society as noted by such students of technology as Ellul.[5]

8. There is a cluster of economic pressures pushing for more technology in education. Several foundations, particularly the Ford Foundation, have poured money into the system for developments in this area. The drive to diversify on the part of the aerospace and defense industries (possible sources of educational hardware, materials, and services) as part of the general move into the public sector is another, little understood, aspect of this problem.

No claim is made that the catalog above is complete or that the application of technology to the educational system or to instruction will

[5] Ellul, Jacques, *The Technological Society,* translated by John Wilkinson, New York: Alfred A. Knopf, 1964.

solve all the problems listed. It is true, however, that a component of educational technology will have to be present in any attempt at a broad solution. It would, perhaps, be well to examine some of the dimensions of instructional technology as it has developed in order better to understand its possibilities.

A SHORT HISTORICAL BACKGROUND

For the problem at hand, it is crucial to understand the history of the development of instructional technology for the last 50 years. However, the interested scholar may chase this development back much further than the overworked Greeks, if he desires. The great Sumerologist Samuel Noah Kramer puts the invention of writing on clay tablets at Sumer at about 5,000 years ago and then notes that "the Sumerian school was the direct outgrowth of the invention and development of the cuneiform system of writing."[6] To some extent, the development of devices and techniques of communication—the development of a technology of instruction—has affected education ever since.

Skipping over thousands of years, the history of 19th century American education is replete with effective technological developments—including the development of textbooks (to which there was some objection), the blackboard, and even improvements in pens and ink.[7] However, from the point of view of the Commission, the crucial period has been roughly from the turn of the century.

The last 60 or 70 years have been marked by social historians as the period of the so-called "communications revolution"—steam driven rotary presses, photography, motion pictures, radio, etc., with accompanying developments in psychology, mass communication techniques, school organization and finance, etc. The following discussion will break down some of these developments to aid in obtaining perspective.

Conventional Audiovisual Devices and Materials

The best date to mark the beginning of the modern trend of using audiovisual devices and materials in education is about 1920. Before that time, the glass slide, the phonograph record, and to a very limited extent, the 35 mm. motion picture had been in some use. After 1920 developments speeded up, partly due to the use of films during World War I. By 1926, 16 mm. safety film and equipment for education were available, and a start had been made by the Eastman Kodak Co. in producing educational films; radio had reached its commercial stage and a beginning had been made with educational radio; other devices and materials were

6 Kramer, Samuel Noah, *History Begins at Sumer*, Garden City, N.Y.: Doubleday and Co., 1959.
7 Anderson, Charnel, "Technology in American Education, 1650–1900." New Media for Instruction Series, No. 1, Washington, D.C.: U.S. Office of Education, 1962.

either developed or improved. Another big change—perhaps the big change—came in the middle thirties with the development of the 16 mm. sound motion picture, the workhorse of the audiovisual movement.

Accompanying these hardware and material developments had been parallel developments in the study of learning from audiovisual materials, beginning with the first studies made right after World War I by K. S. Lashley and John B. Watson, the great experimental psychologists of their day. This connection between some very able research psychologists, students of mass media, etc., and the audiovisual field has continued to the present and has resulted in a respectable literature, much of which is unknown to general educationists, other psychologists, and to many vocal subject matter experts outside the field of education. It is also safe to say that while these developments did occur—partly through the generosity of the Carnegie and Rockefeller Foundations—the application to American educational practice was very limited. There were, for example, only slightly over 600 sound motion picture projectors in the schools of this country in 1936.[8]

By the time the United States entered World War II, an instructor could have had an adequate instrumentation at his disposal. It included still and motion projectors of several varieties, recording devices and players, various forms of printing, chart production, etc., and sound and communication equipment. In addition, a fair amount of material to use with this equipment (educational film, for example) was available, and quite a lot of know-how derived from research and practice was at hand. In fact, however, very few American school teachers had even seen much of this technology, let alone having it available. (In some of the larger cities, of course, it was available, but not too extensively.)

The wide—almost saturated—use of audiovisual materials in the military and industrial training programs during World War II has been well told in several places.[9] This was the first successful mass application of the technology of instruction to the training of large groups of men and women.

Following the war, a renewed interest arose in the American public schools in the use of audiovisual materials. Some States, such as California, made a great effort and supplied funds in quantity for this development. Across the United States, however, the reaction was spotty, and the additional know-how derived from the war effort had little effect in many places.

---

8 Finn, James D., Donald G. Perrin, and Lee E. Campion, "Studies in the Growth of Instructional Technology, I: Audiovisual Instrumentation for Instruction in the Public Schools, 1930–60 – A Basis for Take-Off.,, Occasional Paper No. 6, Technological Development Project of the National Education Association, Washington, D.C.: Department of Audiovisual Instruction, National Education Association, 1962.

9 Miles, John R. and Charles R. Spain, *Audiovisual Aids in the Armed Services*, Washington, D.C.: American Council on Education, 1947.

In the meantime, hardware developments added to the impetus and the confusion. The development of wire and then magnetic tape recording, the long-playing record, improvements in the optics of projection equipment, and the adoption of the overhead transparency projector which had been developed during the war all contributed. Producers rushed in to turn out motion pictures, recordings, filmstrips, slide sets. Research—some of it financed by the armed services—in the problems of learning from these materials was carried on. However, as we approached the middle of the decade of 1950–59, educational interest in what has come to be called conventional audiovisual materials tailed off somewhat. Present developments date from that time and will be discussed below.

Psychological, Sociological, and Educational Developments

Even a brief account of the history subsumed under the title above could fill one or more volumes. The intention here will be merely to outline some of these related developments. The work of Thorndike at Teachers College, Columbia, early in this century set the stage for the development of a scientific psychology of education. Thorndike even anticipated teaching machines and programed learning.[10] S. L. Pressey of Ohio State University, as is well known, discovered certain principles of machine instruction while attempting to produce a test scoring machine in the twenties.

In the early days of modern educational psychology, there was a tight connection between laboratory experimental psychology and educational practice. Gradually this connection eroded. The experimental psychologists shut themselves in their laboratories. Some educational psychologists turned their attention to psychological, achievement, and other forms of testing and developed a formidable subtechnology that has been the object of some recent crticism.[11] Others turned to the field of guidance. The effect on practice, however, was highly variable. By 1955, this trend toward separation of experimental psychology and practice reversed somewhat and added a forceful element to the developing educational technology. This, too, will be discussed below under the present state of the art.

In the meantime, other research workers, principally in the field of social psychology (and, to some extent, related fields), had turned their attention to the mass media of communication. The work of Paul Lazarsfeld both before and after World War II is an example. This, together

---

10 Finn, James D., and Donald G. Perrin, "Teaching Machines and Programed Learning, 1962: A Survey of the Industry," Occasional Paper No. 3, Technological Development Project of the National Education Association, Washington, D.C.: National Education Association, 1962.

11 See, for example, Banesh Hoffmann, The Tyranny of Testing, Riverside, N.J.: Crowell-Collier Press, 1962.

with the work of communication and perception theorists and industrial psychologists interested in group dynamics, had certain fallout value for educational practice. An educational technology began to develop in the group field which had quite a vogue until the middle fifties. The work of the mass communication specialists and perception psychologists has had some effect on the theory back of the educational use of audiovisual materials.

With respect to the process of education itself—learning and teaching taking place in an institutional setting—theorists in the twenties had great hope of developing something called "educational engineering." The great leader of this movement was W. W. Charters of Ohio State University.[12] Charters' ideas were attacked and pretty well demolished during the thirties by both the social reform and the child-centered philosophers of education. From the middle fifties onward, the Charters' concepts were revived, although in a new form, and were seldom attributed to him.[13] Interestingly enough, Charters also had a great interest in audiovisual communication and founded the Institute for Education by Radio and Television at Ohio State in the thirties.

Industrial and Governmental Developments

Industrial developments relating to a technology of education can be briefly discussed with reference to (1) the design, development, and marketing of hardware and environments, (2) the production and distribution of materials of instruction, and (3) intraindustry use of instructional technology.

Generally speaking, hardware, at least until very recently, has not been designed for use in schools. A manufacturer would produce, for example, a motion picture projector designed for the industrial, home, or military market. Small changes might be made for the school market, but the design and reliability needs of educators went unheeded. There was many a tragic joke about the 110-pound school teacher who had to carry a 45-pound projector up three flights of stairs. The whole question of the design of instructional equipment is discussed in a paper of the Technological Development Project of the NEA.[14] Badly designed equipment and equipment mismatched to educational needs were among the causes for the failure of schools to rush to adopt innovations during the postwar period.

School buildings provide spaces for learning—learning environments.

---

[12] One of the writers has on loan from Ohio State University a manuscript for a book being written by Charters when he died. The title is "Educational Engineering"; the date approximately 1952.

[13] An exception is Silvern who has related Charters' ideas to the present situation and credited him for his contributions. See, for example, Leonard Silvern, *Systems Engineering in the Educational Environment,* Hawthorne, Calif.: Northrop Corp., 1963.

[14] Leverenz, Humboldt W. and Malcolm G. Townsley, "The Design of Instructional Equipment: Two Views," Occasional Paper No. 8. Technological Development Project of the National Education Association, Washington, D.C.: National Education Association, 1962.

As such, they are part of the technology that should aid in learning and obviously should be matched with other technologies that have the same end. Since before World War II, this had not been true. Recently, some signs of change are evident.

School architects have done a pretty good job in providing space for certain special educational functions—gymnasiums, auditoriums, shops, etc. They have, over the last 30 years, immensely improved the aesthetic quality of the school environment—color, light, etc. They have made the environment more healthful with such things as better lighting and ventilation. They have done almost nothing to help the general instructional process by providing for modern instructional technology. Until recently, the concentration on using natural lighting through acres of glass windows has prevented full use of projection equipment, and many schools today still do not have adequate light control, acoustic treatment, or wiring. Beginning about 1955, this situation, too, has changed for the better.

Problems of the design of instructional equipment over the last 50 years and, to a certain extent, problems of the design of buildings are inextricably related to the economics of education. The manufacturer could not invest the necessary capital to create special educational equipment because his chances of recovery in a reasonable time were almost nil. The manufacturer, therefore, adapted existing commercial equipment and made very few changes in the fundamental models marketed for educational use once they were set. One manufacturer used the same stampings for the body of a projector for about 20 years, ignoring both the needs of the teacher and the technological developments that had occurred during that time.

The economic problems involved in providing an educational technology during this period (1920–55) were complex. The educational establishment had no precedent and no great inclination for investing in a machine technology at all. The local and State system of finance left little money in educational coffers for investment in technological capital. The local nature of the educational market (Robert Hayes, with insight, once called the educational market "clumped," as opposed to homogenous or monolithic) together with local bidding procedures prevented large scale selling. The distribution organizations of the manufacturers were primitive, ranging from one-man camera and music stores to a few large audiovisual dealers with service departments.

The materials side of the developing educational technology over the same period also suffered from a lack of market on the part of the schools and a lack of capital, vigor, and imagination on the part of the producers. The first three large scale efforts to produce educational films were subsidized for many years by industry—partly in the hope of eventually developing a profitable market and partly for what have to be philanthropic reasons. Eastman Kodak subsidized Eastman Teaching Films in the twenties; Western Electric subsidized ERPI Classroom Films (now Encyclopaedia Britannica Films) beginning in the thirties and running for about 20 years; David Smart began producing Coronet Films on his own estate, using the profits of *Esquire*.

The textbook market, while no doubt profitable over the same period of time, never realized its potential. School systems sometimes kept the same textbooks in use for periods as long as 25 years—with all that implies in terms of outdated learning. It is only very recently that the development of libraries for elementary schools has taken hold, and many junior high school and high school libraries still are pretty bad.

In 1948, the textbook industry had a study made by a consulting firm to see if the industry should expand generally into the audiovisual field. The conclusion was that it should not.[15] McGraw-Hill, a firm that had already made a beginning in this direction, ignored the recommendations and now occupies a commanding position as an overall producer of all kinds of teaching materials. In general, the publishing industry is still not facing up to the general technological developments that are occurring.[16]

As more of the newer media—long playing records, tapes, etc.—came in, the same marketing procedures applied. The supply a school had of new and older materials could only be said to be fortuitous; it often depended upon who called on the superintendent. Maps had to be obtained by mail order or from a salesman who worked a large territory out of his house; the supply of textbooks depended upon the vagaries of State law—in Kansas students had to buy them, but in California they were supplied free (and this had certain political implications in selling); the demand for films, slides, filmstrips, etc., was conditioned upon equipment available and the extent of library service; this was a classic chicken-egg situation and is, incidentally, one faced with the introduction of any new media or technology of instruction (teaching machines —programs, language laboratories—practice tapes).

Beginning with the National Defense Education Act in 1958, the general marketing picture changed radically and with it improvements in the overall technological capital of the educational system. Figures available to 1960, however, indicate that the technological capital of the American education system is still in a primitive state; Finn has suggested that the Rostow concept of five stages of technological growth of a primitive society can be applied to the educational system and that

15 *A Report to Educators on Teaching Films Survey*, conducted by Harcourt and Brace and other publishers, 1948.
16 Redding, M. Frank, with additional material by Roger H. Smith, "Revolution in the Textbook Publishing Industry," Occasional Paper No. 9, Technological Development Project of the National Education Association, Washington, D.C.: National Education Association, 1963.

the American educational system may be about ready for technological "takeoff."[17]

Some time and space have been spent on this very sketchy account of the development of some aspects of educational technology in American education in this century because many educated laymen (and for that matter, educators and subject matter experts now attending to the educational problem) are not aware of these developments. Many seem to assume that the concept of educational technology sprang full blown from the forehead of B. F. Skinner about 1954, or began when the Ford Foundation blessed instructional television with money the same year. To some degree, judgments as to what will and should happen with educational technology have to be conditioned on its history—even if every decision made up to this point in time has to be reversed.

These developments, set arbitrarily from 1955, have led us to the present time. All the evidence suggests that the middle of the fifties marked a shift, a quantum jump, in technological development for American education. This shift brings us to the present state of the art, and it will be described in the following section.

PRESENT STATE OF THE ART AND A VIEW OF THE FUTURE

As was indicated above, the year 1955 has been arbitrarily set as the beginning of modern developments in instructional technology that have given rise to such expressions as "the technological revolution in education." This period was examined in some detail in 1960 by Finn.[18] A brief overview of developments in the 10-year period after 1955 should provide a reasonable description of the state of the art.

Hardware

More or less all technological developments during this time—machines, materials, techniques, organization patterns, etc.—may be conveniently classified into two large categories: (1) A technology of mass or large group instruction, and (2) a technology of individual instruction. Developments in instructional hardware fall neatly into these categories.

Television is the instrument par excellence of mass instruction, even if the receiver is watching alone. The promoters of educational television in the beginning viewed television as an instrument designed to help solve the teacher shortage by providing quality instruction with fewer teachers. Television may be either broadcast, closed-circuit, or broadcast on the 2500 mg. band (very short-range broadcasting).

There are now about 100 educational television stations in the United States. The tendency in recent years is for these stations to transmit

17 Finn, Perrin, and Campion, *op. cit.*
18 Finn, James D., "Technology and the Instructional Process," *Audio-Visual Communications Review,* winter 1960.

more cultural programs and more programs of a general educational nature for both adults and preschool children. School broadcasting (instructional television) still occupies some time on these channels. For reception, there were about 50,000 television receivers in the schools in 1962.[19]

Closed-circuit television and the adoption of the 2500 mg. band provide a more direct means for using television in school instruction. The adoption of closed-circuit television has not been spectacular. As of 1963, there were approximately 600 such installations of all kinds in schools and colleges in the United States.[20]

Related to television development has been the development of the video tape recorder. In the beginning, the price was prohibitive for educational channels, but the Ford Foundation eventually supplied the Nation's educational television stations with professional video tape recorders. In the last 5 years, efforts, including competition from the Japanese, have tended to reduce the size, complexity, and price of this equipment. There are still problems of broadcast compatibility (the smaller, less expensive units produce tapes that cannot be broadcast over standard broadcast equipment without some difficulty; they can, however, be used on closed-circuit systems). Video tape recording, of course, permits the freezing, storage, and free scheduling of television instruction.

The other large development has been the language laboratory, a sophisticated combination of sound equipment centering on the tape recorder, now often called the learning laboratory. The language laboratory is a device making it possible to drill many students in speaking and listening at the same time but as individuals. Further, since there are oral (and aural) aspects to other subject and skill areas (spoken literature and stenographic dictation, for example), the possibilities of expanding the use of such a facility are being explored in many places. There are about 10,000 units in the United States, making this development the most spectacular from the point of view of adoption and expenditure of funds.[21] These laboratories range all the way from small portable units that can be set on a table or wheeled around on a cart to very large and complex installations.[22]

[19] Finn, Perrin, and Campion, *op. cit.*

[20] Campion, Lee E. and Clarice Y. Kelley, "Studies in the Growth of Instructional Technology, II: A Directory of Closed-Circuit Television Installations in American Education With a Pattern of Growth," Occasional Paper No. 10, Technological Development Project of the National Education Association, Washington, D.C.: Department of Audiovisual Instruction, National Education Association, 1963. This figure is now somewhat low due to expenditures in the last 3 years provided under the National Defense Education Act.

[21] Finn, Perrin, and Campion, *op. cit.*

[22] About 2 years ago the American Association of School Administrators launched an attack on the language laboratory, using some research done at the Institute of Administrative Research of Teachers College. The Association is opposed to categorical Federal aid to education, from which funds (NDEA) were, for the most part, used to provide these laboratories to the schools. The NDEA was up for renewal at the time.

A third technological approach to large group instruction is called multimedia, or multimedia-multiscreen. Here the hardware innovations are in the form of control equipment which can operate several different types of projectors, projecting on two or more screens, singly or together. Projection may be from the rear, as in the case of the Multi-Media Laboratory of the University of Wisconsin, or from the front, as in the case of a system developed at the University of Southern California. This technique permits the projection of slides, motion pictures, and overhead transparencies as well as the playing of tapes and recordings, very often with teachers or lecturers playing an integral part in the presentation.

There have been small improvements in other forms of mass instructional technology as the conventional audiovisual devices have undergone some development, as, for example, the semiautomatic threading 16 mm. motion picture projector and the semiautomatic or automatic slide projector. In some ways, principally due to improvements in the equipment which made it much easier to use and to a superb approach to marketing by one large company, the Minnesota Mining and Manufacturing Co., the overhead transparency projector has now become a great contender for the educational technological innovation of the decade, after languishing since its development from the bowling alley projector by the Navy in 1941. Coupled with the tremendous increase in the equipment has been a tremendous increase in eggs or chickens, as the case may be. Transparency materials of all kinds, some prepared transparencies, some materials making it easy for teachers to prepare, and some sort of in-between arrangements, like cake mix, have become available. By far the most widely used process recently has been the heat transfer, office copy machine since transparent materials have been developed to use with it.

Principally due to publicity, the technology of individual instruction is thought by many to center on the teaching machine. This is not the case. When B. F. Skinner published his famous article in *Science* in 1958,[23] a great interest developed in teaching machines and programed learning. This interest not only engaged psychologists, but also segments of industry from small inventors to large firms. From late 1959 to 1962, a rash of companies went into the teaching machine business (see Finn and Perrin).[24] Most of the small ones have disappeared, and most of the large ones have dropped the projects.

This situation had several causes. The educational community was hardly ready for such a startling innovation; the whole business suffered from the same old chicken-egg situation. There were not enough pro-

23 Skinner, B. F., "Teaching Machines," *Science*, vol. 128 (Oct. 24, 1958), pp. 969–977.
24 Finn and Perrin, *op. cit.*

grams for the machines; the machines were not standardized so that one program could fit another; most machines were poorly designed; most programs violated all principles of programing. Research showed no difference between machine and book-type programs. Programed instruction survived in the form of books, notebooks, and other ways of using printed material without machines and is, at present, the captive of publishers who are not particularly interested in a machine approach.

The teaching machine, however, is not dead. Some experimentation continues across the country. In a few places, third and fourth generation machines have been produced. The basic problem in the early days was that teaching machines attempted to present verbal information only. This was all that most programers knew how to prepare. The capability of a machine, however, is in the direction, on the one hand, of a complex stimulus—picture, sound, color, as well as words—and, on the other, of a complex response mechanism relating the student's response instantaneously to the task at hand. This leads to audiovisual stimulus machines and computer control—items that will be discussed in the next section.

In addition to teaching machines per se, a range of devices is in use or development that constitute a solid technology of individual instruction. Using phonograph records and, later, magnetic tape, some teachers began experimenting with "listening corners" in the elementary school shortly after World War II. Headphones on gang jacks were developed so that several children could listen at once without disturbing the class. Later, illustrative materials in the form of filmstrips and slides and various kinds of workbooks and directions were added. A sort of home grown individual instructional technology was developed in a few places.

Following on the heels of this, several manufacturers brought out well-designed listening and viewing devices for filmstrips, tapes, sound filmstrips, etc. (Various types of reading pacers fall into this category.) The materials producers have not kept up with this development too well, although they have produced some materials. A lot of work remains to be done to produce the proper kind of material for individual as opposed to group use.

However, the most significant development on the individual instructional technology front has been the growth of 8mm. film. About 1960, sound was added successfully to 8 mm. film; this event triggered a large number of developments in 8 mm., many of them, interestingly enough, in the silent field. Although 8 mm. may be projected for fairly large groups and, with the new format just announced, will probably generate a projected image about as good as 16 mm. was 10 to 15 years ago, it is in the field of individual instruction that 8 mm. seems to be destined to make its mark.

The small, inexpensive technicolor cartridge-loading projector for individual viewing is already finding much use and has started a new materials movement known as "the single concept film." The single concept film is a 2- or 3-minute film on a self-winding cartridge that may be inserted in the projector and be ready to project. It covers a single idea, for example, nuclear fission. The Air Force recently ordered a quantity of these projectors with stop-frame devices which make it possible to program the films and use the projector somewhat as a teaching machine. Viewing devices for 8 mm. sound film are also coming on the market. What this will do to television is still not clear, especially since there are other developments in the video tape recording field that bear on the problem of individual viewing and listening.

Materials—Systems

In the last 5 years, a great deal has been heard about the "systems approach" in education. This interest has increased recently; there are projects at Syracuse University, Michigan State University, and the University of Southern California that are working on certain aspects of the problem. The systems concept in education is related both to materials and to hardware as well as to certain psychological and philosophical concepts.

Technically, if you consider such expressions as the educational system, the school system, and the State system of higher education, then an instructional system is a subsystem. It is this subsystem that is generally the object of the systems approach in education.

One way to understand the developing instructional system is to approach it through the materials of instruction. In this sense, the idea is not too new; for example, with the introduction of graded readers accompanied by workbooks, etc., in the twenties, a sort of system of teaching reading was introduced into the schools. However, the decade we are examining has seen a speeding up of trends toward systematic organization of the materials of instruction. This trend was identified by the Technological Development Project of the NEA as "from kits to systems."

There are now available all sorts of kits for teachers to use which consist of a variety of materials organized around a topic, such as a country (Japan), a process (wheat-bread), or a concept (energy). These kits often include paperback books, filmstrips, realia, phonograph records or tapes, etc. The kit is accompanied by a manual which suggests how the resources may be deployed.

Another systematic approach to instruction began several years ago with the production of a whole series of film lessons (162 half-hour films) in the field of physics. This was followed by other film series in other areas. These were not simply "aids." They were systematic presentations of content accompanied by suggestions for other activities and related, to some degree, to texts or other materials.

The concept of the Physical Science Study Committee project under the direction of Professor Zacharias developed an even more systematic approach. Here, beginning with a thorough textbook revision, laboratory exercises, an apparatus, a whole film series, and some other materials were prepared. This development was accompanied by tryouts in the schools and a program in the summer for training physics teachers to use the materials. While not developed exactly according to accepted principles of systems design, it could be said that the Zacharias group developed a system for teaching physics.

The foreign language field has recently contributed some very systematic approaches to instruction. There is one system for teaching elementary French which consists of books, workbooks, tapes, records, and films. These materials can be supplied in a case with the necessary hardware. The films supplied, while in color, come in both 8 and 16 mm., and can be used on television.

Throughout the materials field, organized and semisystematic collections of instructional materials continue to make their appearance. Eight millimeter single concept films are being marketed in sets and are related to textual materials; even the textbook industry is publishing sets of books, workbooks, tests, and materials from which overhead transparencies can be copied. Some of the newer work, as, for example, by the AIBS (biology) group is even more systematic. Materials now being tested by this group lead the teacher almost step by step through the teaching process.[25]

It is, I believe, safe to say that this move toward organization and system in the instructional materials field is one of the most solid trends of the technological revolution in education. Its implication for the role of the teacher of the future, is, of course, tremendous.

The systems approach to instruction also has a hardware aspect. Up to the present time this has shown up principally in an attempt to bridge the gap between the technology of mass instruction and the technology of individual instruction. In a sense the language laboratory has always done this, as the individual student in the laboratory deals with what is, in effect, a mass communication system.

---

[25] See, for example, Biological Sciences Curriculum Study, *High School Biology, Special Materials: Teacher's Manual (Revised Edition)*, Boulder, Colo.: Biological Sciences Curriculum Study at the University of Colorado, 1964.

However, there are several devices new being used that bridge this gap more directly. These devices provide for mass stimulus (television, projection, or multimedia presentation) but allow each individual student to react to what he sees by pressing a button, turning a dial, or otherwise informing the system as to his response. These devices go under the general name of classroom communicators. One such device is now being used in several of the Job Corps camps. The data derived from the students' response can be processed in several ways; for example, providing the teacher with an immediate readout of how well the students are performing. The materials for such a system have to be very carefully programed and are, of course, highly systematic. This requirement is the biggest problem in connection with the use of this equipment.[26]

There are several other ways to consider the systems approach to instruction. For example, the small group interested in computer applications to education seems to take the position that the only systems approach to education is through the computer. This will probably be the ultimate systems approach.[27]

Organizational Concepts

As was indicated by the introductory material, organization is a major aspect of technology. As might be expected, organization concepts better fitted to present educational needs are being suggested and applied. We are considering here only organization for instruction—not other proposals having to do with the governing and financing of the educational system as a whole.

In essence, there are two such organizational patterns on the current scene which have many common aspects. The first, usually associated with the name of John Goodlad, reorganizes the elementary (and junior high) school into an ungraded pattern, permitting the individual student to progress much more easily at his own rate. The system of grade classes, imported from Germany in the 19th century, is unrealistic in the sense of human variability. It was, in its day, a technological solution to a chaotic problem. Whether the ungraded elementary school is the answer for 1965 yet remains to be seen. The requirements in terms of materials, individualized instruction, and the like are frightening.

The second new system of organization is applied to the secondary school and is usually referred to as the Trump Plan after its originator, Lloyd Trump. Trump has attempted to break up the "egg crate," 30-student-to-a-classroom situation in the high school and provide for large group instruction (40 percent), small seminar instruction (20 percent),

26 The best such program the writer has seen is one developed for the retraining of bus drivers by Western Greyhound using films and slides on a system known as the EDEX.

27 See the paper prepared for the Commission by Donald Bushnell for a complete discussion of this aspect of educational technology.

and individualized instruction (40 percent). This concept is formally referred to as the Staff Utilization Plan. Inherent in this system is the idea of team teaching where teams of teachers, sometimes under a master teacher, manage these several responsibilities. Various aspects of this plan have been tried out all over the United States, and the idea seems to be moving into practice. It should be emphasized that the Trump Plan is also postulated on a much wider use of instructional instrumentation than now exists, particularly for large group and individualized instruction. (Many existing team teaching experiments do not have this component.)

Curriculum Reform

Another aspect of the technological revolution in education is curriculum reform. Reference was made above to the Physical Science Study Committee. The PSSC set the pattern for curriculum reform, backed by money from private foundations and the National Science Foundation. Since that time, following the PSSC pattern to some extent, groups in biology, chemistry, mathematics, and many other fields have been organized. As of 2 years ago, the NEA identified 37 such projects. Almost all of these have an orientation to instructional technology in some or all of its aspects—television, programed instruction, films. In other words, the approach to the radical revision of the educational process is through the materials and devices of instruction.

The Current Situation in Educational Psychology

If the approach to change in education is viewed, at least in some quarters, through the materials and devices of instruction, it follows that the psychological orientation of these devices and materials within the teaching-learning process is of crucial importance. This is the area of applied educational psychology, or, as was indicated in a previous section, what some theorists, such as Lumsdaine and Glaser, consider to be the technology of instruction.

The current situation, however, within educational psychology is, to say the least, mixed. Very few theorists or practitioners would be willing to say that one given point of view has achieved all of the answers. In the general practice of school-keeping today, an eclectic point of view as to theory coupled with a large portion of experience-passed-on-down constitutes the operational base.

Within the general literature of learning theory and related matters, there have been many attempts to distinguish, describe, even to reconcile various theories of learning. Hilgard, for example, in a classic work treats nine theories of learning.[28] Such considerations are important to

[28] Hilgard, E. R., *Theories of Learning* (2d ed.), New York: Appleton-Century-Crofts, 1956.

the scientist exploring this area, but it is highly likely that most practitioners today—teachers, materials producers, etc.—could not make the sometimes subtle distinctions between these points of view, and certainly could not consciously apply these distinctions to real life problems of teaching and learning.

The uninitiated person reading only a portion of the literature might get the impression that the matters of teaching and learning were pretty well settled by the psychologists. This is not the case. However, since the educational process is ongoing and since children and adults come to school daily, some kind of commitment to a point of view is often made, particularly at the growing edge of educational technology. The following brief description of the situation must be read with this fact in mind and also remembering that most practice does not have a coherent theoretical base.

The most dominant point of view within the area of instructional technology today is that of Prof. Jerome Bruner of Harvard. Professor Bruner's point of view has been adopted by the Zacharias group which began the national movement of curriculum revision through the materials and devices of instruction with the physics course of the Physical Science Study Committee. This group has extended its activities to such areas as elementary school science,[29] and its point of view and methodology are, it is believed, dominant throughout almost all national efforts at curriculum revision, even including music and the fine arts.

At the great risk of oversimplification, Bruner and his colleagues, because they have carefully and brilliantly studied what is known as cognitive structure (an individual's organization, stability, and clarity of knowledge in a particular subject matter field at a given time), have emphasized two general concepts: (1) Knowledge in a given field has a structure that can be taught and on which all individual facts and events can be hung; and (2) such a structure is best learned by the method of "discovery" or "inquiry," which in turn will help the learner be more creative and able to learn all his life. Bruner's ideas have received great acceptance among scientists, mathematicians, and, interestingly enough, from many old-line progressive educators. A popular source for Bruner's ideas is his little book *The Process of Education.*[30] His concern with other aspects of learning may be found in another small volume, *On Knowing.*[31]

Again, recognizing the difficulties of oversimplification in a brief treatment such as this, B. F. Skinner, also of Harvard, can be thought of as holding a point of view almost directly opposite to that of Bruner.

29 See, for example, *A Review of Current Programs,* Educational Services, Inc., Watertown, Mass., 1965.
30 Bruner, Jerome, *The Process of Education,* Cambridge, Mass.: Harvard University Press, 1960.
31 Bruner, Jerome, *On Knowing,* Cambridge, Mass.: Harvard University Press, 1962.

Skinner has recently criticized the Bruner position in a popular article[32] and in a technical essay.[33] Skinner, recognized as the father of teaching machines and programed instruction in the modern sense, has a theory of teaching and learning known as operant conditioning in which the individual learner's behavior is "shaped" by positive reinforcements administered under certain contingencies and following certain schedules. Theoretically, programed instruction of the so-called linear type is designed to do this. In practice, very few programers write programs according to pure Skinnerian principles. Skinner has had an enormous influence on the thinking of psychologists, and it is safe to say that most psychologists today are behaviorists who would be willing to accept a great deal, if not all, of Skinner's point of view. The fact remains, however, that his influence on educational practice, particularly on educational technology as it is being applied, is small compared with that of Bruner.

A third point of view, for the moment somewhat outmoded, may be described as antitechnological and existential. It is stubbornly held, however, by a portion of the educational community, notably those most concerned with child development and the person, and some of those concerned with creativity. These latter often accept much of the Bruner position in addition. In some ways this position combines a little of the old Gestalt concepts with the so-called assumptive view of perception and a great deal of emphasis upon self, self-actualization and self-perception. These concepts, combined with certain others derived from psychotherapy are often referred to today as "existential" psychology.

As was mentioned, there are, of course, other theories of teaching and learning; the so-called neobehaviorists, for example, adhere to a range of closely overlapping points of view. We are speaking here primarily of the views of practitioners (considered broadly) concerned with developing educational technology. In this connection, several newer positions which appear to have promise for or are related to instructional technology should be mentioned. Studies in neurophysiology have resulted in a theory of thought in behavior dealing with the electrochemical functions of the central nervous system; memory has been studied with reference to changes in nervous structure, etc. Such a viewpoint is appealing to some theorists in instructional technology, probably because of its science-technology relationship. One of the leaders in this field is D. O. Hebb.[34]

[32] Skinner, B. F., "Why Teachers Fail," *Saturday Review*, Oct. 16, 1965, p. 80.

[33] Skinner, B. F., "Reflections on a Decade of Teaching Machines," in *Teaching Machines and Programed Learning, II: Data and Directions*, Washington, D.C.: Department of Audiovisual Instruction, National Education Association, 1965, pp. 5–20.

[34] Hebb, D. O., *The Organization of Behavior*, New York: John Wiley and Sons, 1949.

Closely related to the interest in neuropsychology and even more closely related to developments in technology in general is what is often referred to as the cybernetic model of behavior and learning. Essentially, this viewpoint undertakes to explain thought and behavior in terms of models derived from the studies of computers. An excellent statement of this position may be found in Miller, Galanter, and Pribham.[35] In many ways, this theory can be considered an information theory of learning and is related to an even more elaborate concept, J. P. Guilford's structure of intellect.[36] David Ausubel has recently published a theory relating only to what he calls "reception learning," or the processes of learning meaningful verbal materials, arguing that this type of teaching is what is principally done in school.[37] All of this work suggests that it will influence technological applications in education within the next decade. If this is true, some changes in current trends will occur.

Finally, it should be noted that both dominant and emerging theoretical positions in the literature (which have been applied in small areas of technological practice in some instances) merely emphasize the fact that the educational practitioner cannot turn to a science of learning for his answers. This has resulted in a technological or empirical approach to solving practical problems of teaching and learning. This point of view in espoused by Ofiesh and is contained in part II.* The empiricists hold that materials, devices, and processes must be validated in advance in terms of well stated objectives of instruction on the students on which they are to be used. In other words, materials, processes, and devices are produced on a best-guess basis, are tried out, are refined or changed as necessary, and are tested again. The process is repeated until a system that works is derived. Such a concept can be considered as a sheer technological or engineering approach and is so referred to by those who advocate it.

If present efforts at research, development, and theory construction continue to expand; if, for example, the national research and development centers and the regional educational laboratories take root and grow, it can be expected that a much greater alignment of theory and practice of teaching and learning will come about within the next two decades. While it is unlikely that the answer will be achieved in this first new thrust, the move toward the classic relation of science to technology in the field of education will be speeded up.

35 Miller, G. A., E. Galanter, and Karl Pribham, *Plans and the Structure of Behavior,* New York: Holt, Rinehart and Winston, 1960.
36 Guilford, J. P., and P. R. Merrifield, "The Structure of Intellect Model: Its Use and Implications," Los Angeles: University of Southern California Psychological Laboratory (Report #24), 1960.
37 Ausubel, David, *The Psychology of Meaningful Verbal Learning,* New York: Grune and Stratton, 1963.
*Reference is made to Part II of the original document from which this paper was reprinted.

Research and Development

The history of research and development in the field of instructional technology is a long story in itself.[38] Contributing to the quantum jump of 1958 in this field was the passage of title VII of the National Defense Education Act. Title VII provided both for research in the new media field and for dissemination of information about new media to the educational community. Although the amounts of money available have been small (too small), the effect has been large. Psychologists and other educational research workers have turned their attention to educational media, and fundamental questions concerning effectiveness and use of the technology of instruction have been investigated.

The Cooperative Research Group in the U.S. Office of Education has also funded some studies in the field of instructional technology, and some research has been backed by other Government agencies concerned with manpower retraining, etc. Compared to the need, this research effort is still too small and the dissemination of the results of this research leaves much to be desired.

The new Elementary and Secondary Education Act of 1965 contains a provision for $45 million for what are known as regional educational laboratories. These laboratories (actually, they will probably be more like groups of cooperating institutions and school districts) are supposed to do research and then apply the results of this research to practice. The task force, which worked preparing the background for the bill, had in mind something like Professor Zacharias' Educational Services Inc., a nonprofit corporation which produces the materials for PSSC and other curriculum projects. However, it is likely that the organization of the laboratories will be much broader. There is no doubt, however, that there will be a large component of activity relating to instructional technology in these laboratories.

While many important research questions need to be settled, the great problem is the dissemination of the results of this work and the application of these findings to practice. To take just one example, there is very little evidence that the research findings on programed instruction have actually been applied in the construction of many programs that are available; further, the use of programed instruction in the schools remains at a minimum level—the movement has not affected practice a great deal.

The great foundations of this country have contributed both to the research effort surrounding instructional technology in this decade and to the development work associated with it. Actually, foundation sup-

---

[38] The Instructional Technology and Media Project at the University of Southern California will soon release a paper covering the history of research and development in instructional technology.

port has principally been for development and, as such, it has been more of an economic than an intellectual force. Because of this, it will be treated in the next section.

The Infusion of Capital

If technological capability—machines, materials, etc.—is viewed as capital, the educational system of this country is still poverty ridden. Using hardware as a measure of this capability, Finn, Perrin, and Campion found it to be relatively low.[39]

This low capital level is why, during this crucial decade of 1955–64, foundation support has in many cases been decisive and has turned the path of American education into new, technological directions. The role of the Ford Foundation in this picture cannot be underestimated. Especially in the field of television, the support from the Ford Foundation was decisive. This included help for weak educational television stations, the establishment of the National Educational Television Network Service, support for a national effort in instructional television, the institution of the airborne television program in the midwest (MPATI), etc. Millions of dollars helped build technological capability and, of course included other activities besides television; for example, the founding and support of the Educational Facilities Laboratories which are designed to improve educational construction of all kinds.

Other foundations, notably Carnegie, also contributed to this buildup. However, other than television, viewing the needs of the country as a whole, all the foundation money put together could only be described as seed corn. It remained for the U.S. Congress to provide funds for a much larger capital infusion into the American educational system.

From the point of view of educational technology, title III of the National Defense Education Act made all the difference. In its original form, it provided money on a matching basis for States to furnish local school systems with funds to purchase materials and equipment for teaching science, mathematics, and modern foreign languages. This provision has since been expanded to cover other areas of the curriculum. Under the older restrictions, approximately 60 to 70 percent of the funds went into science equipment and the balance into audiovisual materials and equipment. These percentages are no doubt changing and, during the last year, the amount of money expended under the provisions of this title was about $90 million.

Almost all of the acts relating to manpower (manpower redevelopment and training, vocational education, etc.) are designed to provide money for research and for teaching equipment and materials. No esti-

[39] Finn, Perrin, and Campion, *op. cit.*

mates were available to the writer as to the exact amount of such funds, but they are considerable and will contribute to the overall increase in technological capital for the educational system.

Acts of the Congress relating to manpower were climaxed with the passage of the Economic Opportunity Act of 1964—the so-called War on Poverty. In the act, provision is made for centers for the basic education and vocational training of jobless youths. In the organization and development of these centers, the assumption has been made that a great deal of use must be made of instructional technology because the system of instruction, it is believed, must be considerably different from that used in schools from which these young people dropped out in the first place. Because the main Job Corps training centers are being operated by private industry in many instances, every effort is being made to apply the best that is known in the instructional program of these camps. Money is available. Camp Parks, for example, installed about $90,000 worth of television equipment. This development will have far-reaching effects, but they have yet to be assessed.

The latest act of Congress affecting instructional technology is the Elementary and Secondary Education Act of 1965. Mention has already been made of the laboratory provision. One title of the act provides for the strengthening of library services, and this will add to the technological capital available to schools, as library services will include materials other than books. Another section provides for supplementary educational centers. These are conceived very broadly and will contain everything from guidance and remedial services to resident musicians. These centers will obviously have a media component and may end up as, among other things, regional centers for more sophisticated technological services. Plans for these programs are just being laid.

There are other governmental influences in the field of instructional technology; for example, the wide use of many of these techniques in the training programs of the Armed Services. Further research in the field of instructional technology is being conducted by HumRRO for the Army and by other defense agencies.

The picture adds up to the fact that an increase in the technological capital of the educational system of the United States can be expected in the next few years as a result of Government programs. The extent of the increase, its general acceptability, and its effect remain to be seen. At present, from the point of view of the existing, let alone the future, technology, the American educational system is undercapitalized.

The Response of Industry—Diversification and Reorganization

Accepting the fact that the American educational system remains primitive from the point of view of technological development, it is no different from other parts of the public sector, such as the field of social work. This concept, of course, can be traced to Galbraith who suggested in the *Affluent Society* that investment must move into the public sector and that we should treat such institutions as education with at least as much generosity as we do Las Vegas or the Strategic Air Command.

In addition, the economics of the defense and space programs cannot forever remain at the same levels. These programs have created great scientific-based industries with tremendous technical and manpower capabilities. Reduction in space and defense programs could cause social problems of no mean magnitude. It is no accident, therefore, that the Galbraithian concept of beefing up the public sector of the economy should be linked to the potentials of the aerospace, defense, and science-related industries.

With some anticipation in the earlier manpower acts, this policy became reality when the Economic Opportunity Act of 1964 provided for the participation of industry in the Job Corps and other programs. This put the science-related industries into the education business and, in the perspective of the general scientific-technological revolution, was inevitable anyway. Further, many of these industries or industrial groups had made previous passes at private educational developments (teaching machines, computer scheduling services to schools, etc.) and already had created some special educational capability.

The various acts discussed above provide a considerable amount of money and are an enticement for the science-based industries to enter the educational field. Since most of them have a quick-reacting capability, it was to be expected that the last few months have been occupied with tooling up, preparing proposals, reorganizing in the direction of what can only be called "educational diversification," and otherwise preparing to move into this new enterprise.

Several of the large Job Corps camps, as was indicated above, are being operated by these industries, sometimes in combination with a university. However, the most interesting signs are those related to mergers, acquisitions, joint venture agreements, and the like. Raytheon has purchased EDEX, a classroom communicator manufacturer, and Dage Television. Xerox has created a research laboratory in the basic behavioral sciences and has acquired Basic Systems (a programing group) and American Educational Publishers; Westinghouse has acquired the entire programing capability of Teaching Machines Inc.; Litton Industries and Hughes Aircraft have both built up inhouse capabilities in these fields and, particularly in the case of an acquisition-oriented company like Litton, acquisitions of various kinds may be expected. This is a partial and very incomplete list, but it is illustrative.

These industrial groups are aggressive and have access to highly educated manpower both inhouse and on a consulting basis. The effect of these developments is not yet clear, but some of them ought to be pretty obvious. There is not too much manpower available in the instructional technology field, and hence, there will be competition for manpower.[40] The very existence of technology-based instructional programs in Job Corps camps, etc., will put pressures on the schools. School board members may not be so reluctant to vote funds for instructional technology once the industrial factor becomes evident, and they may even put pressure on school administrators.

Since this is just the beginning of this phenomenon—essentially a phase of the scientific-technological revolution—much more can be expected to come out of it.

TRENDS—A FORECAST

The preceding section covers the current situation with emphasis upon the decade 1955–64, a crucial period for the development of educational technology. The changes occurring during this period were so striking (and some of them, such as the language laboratory, so unpredictable) that forecasting in this field appears extremely risky. Further, it cannot be overemphasized that developments involving any appreciable degree of novelty are still very slow to affect educational practice. In effect, events occur at two levels: An analogy might be to consider the interest in research and development now occuring in educational technology as the upper level of ocean currents which can be seen and measured, and actual practice in the majority of educational institutions and systems as the deep, slow swelling, cold currents that move in their own time and are difficult to detect.

Nevertheless, there are probabilities and trends in the situation, and prediction is possible, although its accuracy cannot be stated even with the precision of probability statements now used in weather forecasting. What follows in this section is such a prediction; it is the sole responsibility of the principal author. For reasons which should become clear, this forecast is divided into two parts—a short-range forecast and a long-range forecast.

The Next 5 to 10 Years

An analysis of the situation suggests that the next 5 to 10 years will be a period of consolidation and spread into educational practice of the technological developments of the last decade. The educational system has, in effect, been threatened with novelty; in the coming decade the novelty will be absorbed to the point where it will be no longer novel.

[40] One of the writers had one doctoral candidate in the spring of 1965, who received four job offers in 1 week. Two were from universities and two were from industries. He took an industrial job.

There will be some new developments; these, however, will tend to be in the political-social-economic sphere and not, as many of the current thinkers in educational technology suppose, in materials, hardware, and psychological breakthroughs. Breakthroughs and novel developments are always possible these days, but the current trends continue to suggest that their time is, perhaps, a decade or more away.

Based on the generalization that consolidation of gains will characterize the next decade, the following forecast is made from current trends:

1. Innovation—Change. It has become the official policy of the U.S. Office of Education to encourage educational innovation; further, the concept of innovation is "in" with the entire educational community at State, regional, and local levels. Three forecasts can be made in this area:

a. The principal site of education innovation will change from the lower levels of the school system to higher education. Colleges and universities will be forced to innovate, principally due to the flood of students, but with other factors acting as an influence as well. Universities, while sources of innovation for the whole culture, have been loath to make drastic changes in their own procedures, particularly their teaching procedures. The innovations which will be forced on the higher educational system during the next decade will, therefore, cause a great deal of strain.

b. With respect to the system as a whole—particularly the public school system—educational innovation will become institutionalized, centering upon the U.S. Office of Education and secondarily, the several State departments of education. Existing legislation and plans and the influence of a new educational establishment will all combine to push this now visible trend into actuality.

The principal instruments for this institutionalization are likely to be the regional laboratories now being set up by the U.S. Office of Education together with regional educational centers to be set up under title III of the Elementary and Secondary Education Act of 1965. The regional centers do not have to have this function, but at this writing, it looks as though part B of this section of the law, which does provide for exemplary (i.e., demonstration centers designed to spread innovative ideas) projects, will receive precedence over regional educational services. However, even if these instruments are not used for one reason or another, others will be found, and the innovative process will be institutionalized.

c. With the institutionalization of educational innovation, two things will happen. First, the innovations themselves as they are picked up by units of the system (schools, school districts, colleges) will become simplified and vulgarized, sometimes beyond recognition, and will lose a great deal of their power. This is principally due to the fact that the system as a whole is not sophisticated enough to absorb many of the new processes and procedures with all of their subtleties and qualifications. Secondly and more important, as the process of innovation is institutionalized, innovation will gradually become little more than change. This is based on the assumption that the "invention of the method of invention" as applied to educational innovation—and that is the avowed purpose of this institutionalization—will not necessarily work with the same force that it has with industrial technology. It is likely that the true innovators will begin to drop out of such an institutionalized system, and the remaining bureaucracy will not be capable of far-reaching innovation.[41]

2. The Development of the New Educational Establishment. American education has always seemed to have more common procedures, goals, and even buildings and teaching materials than are warranted by existence of 50 autonomous and presumably different State school systems. There are many reasons for this, but among those often cited is the existence of an educational establishment. In the past, it has been stated that this establishment has consisted of the national educational professional associations, the teachers colleges and schools of education in universities, and the State departments of education. After 1950, this establishment came under heavy fire, and beginning about 1955, a new educational establishment began to emerge.

The significance of this new educational establishment for this paper is that it has a scientific-technological base. Essentially, it consists of four or five of the leading higher institutions in the United States, several foundations, a component of the new scientist-politicians that have emerged in the last 20 years and some able individuals both within and without Government. Its relation to the older establishment is almost nil.

The next decade will see the complete domination of educational thinking in this country by this new establishment as it develops and consolidates. Nothing in this statement should be construed as suggesting that there is anything conspiratorial about this emergence. It is doubtful, for example, whether individuals now belonging to the new establishment even know it as such. Rather, the emergence of such a group of intellectual leaders for education was almost foreordained by the development of our advanced technological society. Henceforth, the new establishment will orient American education more in the direction of science and technology as associated with its own processes and will absorb only that part of the older establishment which will fit this overall scientific-technological pattern.[42]

[41] This is why the principal author has some doubt as to Ofiesh's proposal in part II. The proposal is for another form of institutionalization. For an interesting discussion of the difficulties of change in an educational bureaucracy, see the article by H. Thomas James, "Problems in Administration and Finance When National Goals Become Primary," *Phi Delta Kappan*, December 1965, pp. 184–187.

[42] In this connection it is fascinating to note that recent news stories report that the new Russian educational program was prepared by a commission composed of members from the Academy of Sciences and from the Academy of Pedagogical Sciences.

3. **The Systemization of the Materials of Instruction.** The already well-developed trend toward more systematic organization of instructional materials will reach fruition in application in schools and colleges within the next few years. Systems of teaching the structure of subject matters and certain skills such as reading will be applied on an increasing scale. These systems will make use of all of the available instructional technology[43] and will absolutely control the curriculum in the areas (such as physics) where they are applied. To some degree, competing systems will be created, and schools and colleges will be asked to choose among systems; however, since these systems are expensive and take years to develop, the choices will be limited. Further, there will be problems of obsolescence and logistics associated with them for which the schools and colleges are ill prepared.

The materials within these systems (films, programed learning sequences, videotapes, books, etc.) will increasingly be tailored directly to learning tasks and will represent much more of a rifle approach than the historic shotgun approach of the standard textbook or educational film. As such, their overall effect should be much more efficient. Further, research now going on in several places should have begun to supply some answers to the general question as to which medium is the most effective for a given purpose. If these answers do develop, the emerging instructional systems will also reflect this knowledge. Increasingly large amounts of money will be spent on developing these systems.

4. **Developments in Hardware.** Hardware, particularly in sophisticated systems, such as military weapons systems, can change or develop rapidly. On the other hand, in the consumer field, such as refrigerators and automobiles, the changes tend to be slower and are often more apparent than real. In the field of instructional technology, both possibilities are present.

a. *Optical-photographic versus electronic systems.* Because of the long leadtime that optical-photographic (conventional audiovisual) systems (projectors, film, etc.) have had on electronic systems (television, videotape, etc.) existing instructional hardware is heavily weighted toward the optical-photographic for pictorial (and audio) storage and transmission. Further, photographic information is still superior to electronic by a factor of, perhaps, 100 to 1. There are other influences as well, such as accessibility.

The next few years will see a continuing invasion of this field by electronic transmission. Improvements will be made in the information capabilities of electronic systems; the transmission of color will become cheaper and easier; accessibility will be improved through cheaper

---

[43] It is believed that forecasts which claim all instructional systems will be computer controlled in the near future are wrong by at least 20 years.

videotape-type storage; and videotape recorders and players will become smaller, less expensive, and easier to operate with reliability. By the end of the decade, a new balance will have been achieved between these two (partially) competing systems. Neither will disappear, but electronic storage and transmission or combinations of electronic and optical-photographic systems will claim a much greater share of existing hardware designed for pictorial storage and transmission than is the case now.

b. *Television, videotape, etc.* As indicated above, videotape players and recorders will become smaller, cheaper, and more reliable. Whether the current methods of recording on magnetic tape will still be in use might be in question, as there are several other ways to use electronic impulses to record information on some medium; thermoplastic recording is an example. The precise means is unimportant from the educational point of view. What this does mean is that images and sound will be available in inexpensive, easy-to-use form.

In addition, it is to be expected that television will expand in its educational aspects during the same period of time. This expansion will principally be in the closed-circuit and 2,500 mg. areas and not in broadcast television for schools and colleges. The expansion will occur first in higher education, and it can be fairly confidently predicted that interinstitutional cooperation in the use of television, such as has been experimented with in Oregon, will be extended as the pressures on higher education increase. A professor in one institution teaching a class in another, or several others, will not be at all unique except in small enrollment, prestige institutions. Even in such cases, lectures from Nobel Prize winners and the like will probably be delivered by television.

Along with these developments in television and, for a while at least, overshadowing them, will be an enormous increase in the use of telephone lines to transmit certain kinds of educational materials. The last few years have seen some growth in the so-called "tele-lecture" technique where the lecturer at one location can speak to a group via amplified telephone at some other location. Recently, as at the Harvard Business School and in connection with various medical education projects, conference-type seminars between groups have been held using the telephone system. A new invention makes it possible for a teacher to draw while lecturing over the telephone and have the image projected by a special overhead projector at the receiving end; slides and other materials distributed in advance have also been successfully used with tele-lectures. Since this procedure is relatively inexpensive and very useful, it may be expected to grow spectacularly during the decade.

c. *Other hardware developments.* While improvements and changes may be expected in all audiovisual equipment, it is likely that the major advances will occur in the field of self-instructional devices. There are, at present, several prototypes under development of multimedia machines (still and motion picture and sound) designed as individual instruction devices. While the history of this type of teaching machine has not been too spectacular up to this point, it seems reasonable to predict that the next decade will find several types of these in use. This, of course, will set a new requirement for programing and production of materials.

The 8 mm. film, particularly with the new format (40 percent more information per frame), will constitute the most important development in the audiovisual field in the next few years. Following Professor Forsdale of Teachers College, it is believed that 8 mm. will be used primarily for individual instruction, although with the new format classroom projectors for groups of up to 50 in size may be expected to become quite common. As 8 mm. comes in, a technological lag problem will become apparent with the huge investment the educational system has in 16 mm. film and projectors. One way around this problem will be to develop individual instruction devices for use with 8 mm. film, particularly devices that permit student response. Considerable resistance to this development may be expected.

Multimedia-multiscreen techniques for large groups will continue to expand during the next 10 years. Lecture halls and briefing rooms will be built with such hardware requirements in mind. Automatic projection equipment will be redesigned in order to operate in gangs for this purpose, and control equipment will be developed on a miniaturized, high reliability form.

d. *Computers and the interface problem.* Since a separate paper has been prepared on computer applications to education, computers for computer-based instruction will not be discussed here. However, it may be important to point out or reemphasize that there are certain needed hardware developments related to computer-based instruction which will probably occur during the decade under consideration. These developments are referred to as the interface between the computer and the student and have been the subject of a recent study by Glaser, Ramage and Lipson.[44] In the next 10 years various ingenious interface devices will be developed so that students may receive stimulation in various forms from a computer (pictures, words, numbers, sounds, graphs), may manipulate the subject matter so presented with instruments such as light pens, and may be informed on other portions of the interface device as to progress, what to do next, etc. Until such interface devices

[44] Glaser, Robert, William W. Ramage, and Joseph I. Lipson, *The Interface Between Student and Subject Matter.* Pittsburgh: Learning Research and Development Center, University of Pittsburgh, 1964.

are developed, computer-based instruction will never achieve its full potential.[45]

Essentially, at least a portion of what should go into such an interface device is the result of developments which, in the computer field, go under the general name of information display. Although the existing literature seems to suggest it, there is nothing in the educational picture which would require all such display techniques to be confined to devices requiring student response and controlling student behavior in detail. It is reasonable, in fact, to predict that information display techniques which are essentially electronic or electronic-optical in character will also be used in connection with television, other wave-propogated transmission and telephone to convey teaching materials from one point to another without elaborate response and measuring devices. As yet, with the exception of a few experiments, the techniques of information display in use with sophisticated systems, such as space and space support systems, have not been tried with education problems.[46] The next decade will see many developments in this area, including simulation.

5. Information Storage and Retrieval. An area which may develop as spectacularly in the next 10 years as the language laboratory and associated teaching techniques did in the 1955–64 decade is the area of information storage and retrieval. As such, in its educational applications, it could represent an exception to the general orientation of this section.

The problem of the information explosion is well known; the fact that much information today never reaches the book stage in time but remains in the form of documents, articles, etc., has given rise to a whole new profession known as "documentalists"; experts in information storage and retrieval are calling themselves "information scientists"; and there are signs within the old-line professional library field of a deep schism between conventional librarians and information scientists and documentalists.

Obviously, new technological information storage and retrieval techniques can be (and are now, to a certain extent) applied to the problems of a conventional library. However, except for large university libraries, it does not seem likely that these techniques will make much of an inroad into school and college libraries during the next decade.

What is likely to happen is that sort of an end run will occur, and the new technology of information storage and retrieval will reach the educational system in some strength outside of the main library stream. There are several reasons for this. Again, the position of the U.S. Office of

[45] There are, of course, other requirements for the ideal computer-teacher. See, for example, the abstract of the Case and Roe study in the *Audiovisual Communication Review*, vol. 13, No. 4 (winter 1965), p. 453.

[46] One example of such an experiment is that undertaken by Licklider. See Licklider, J. C. R., "Preliminary Experiments in Computer-Aided Teaching," in J. E. Coulson (ed.), *Programmed Learning and Computer-based Instruction*, New York: Wiley, 1962, pp. 217–239.

Education may be crucial; however, it is the considered opinion of the writer that even if that office were not a factor, this phenomenon would occur.

The U.S. Office of Education, however, will play a large role in this development providing present plans for its proposed Educational Research Information Center (ERIC) are implemented with sufficient funds and personnel. Operating from a center in Washington, D.C., and from, perhaps, up to 200 satellites or clearinghouses located in higher institutions and research centers of various types, microfiche (small sheets of microfilm) chips containing research documents will be supplied educational users ordering from a system of indices, bibliographies, and abstracts also provided by ERIC. This system is now underway on a small scale.

The availability of this information will create a demand for microfilm readers of various types and for equipment to reproduce hard copy from microfilm. Such readers are all—with some modification—potential teaching machines; further, the ability to reproduce hard copy presents the possibility of expanding such services to instructional materials too current to be available in any other form. Such a procedure has been experimented with in San Diego County, Calif., for some years with great success, where local industries and scientific institutions have been supplying schools with current scientific materials produced in this way.

If this development proceeds as suggested—and the probabilities are high—a full-fledged educational information storage and retrieval system may grow up outside existing channels. Further, because the hardware and services are adaptable, it is possible that a new generation of teaching machines will come into being based on the microfiche reader, thus short-circuiting a whole series of obstacles. The presence of hard copy-producing equipment might speed up the use and adaptation of newer curriculum materials, both in programed and in more conventional forms. Such a development would tend to restore a certain amount of curriculum independence to local school districts, providing staff and facilities were made available to take advantage of it. This latter development is highly unlikely. What is more likely is, as the State departments become stronger, curriculum materials will be supplied by the State departments in this easier-to-use form and curricular autonomy will be lost, not gained, at the school and district level.

6. Standardization. One of the strongest trends in the next decade will be a general move toward standardization, a move inevitable in any highly technical society. With respect to equipment and materials, several forces are at work that, potentially, could force standardization. The first of these is the so-called "State plan" by which many of the Federal educational programs dispense money to the States. In its most simplified form, the State submits a plan for a program, for example, dispensing funds under title III of the National Defense Education Act. Once this plan has been approved, the State, in effect, sits in control of the disbursement of the funds to its local and regional units. All the State has to do is to require standards for equipment in its plan and standardization becomes a reality. With the so-called "Compact of States" within the immediate future, providing for efficient communication between the States on educational matters, standardization could soon become national.

A second force, which has been discussed for many years but has never been released, is possible if the major cities of the United States were to combine in order to write common specifications for equipment and materials. Such cities represent a large share of the market and now contribute to the chaos in educational equipment standards by requiring annoying and, most often, useless differences in specifications. This raises the price per unit on such items as projectors, complicates bidding procedures, and localizes purchases. Economic considerations may force the end of this practice and a move to joint bidding or even centralized purchasing. Such a possibility is only a possibility and it is more likely that the provincial practices of the educational bureaucracies of such mammoth systems as New York and Los Angeles will remain at the level of their archaic city building codes. Of the two forces, the State force, even including centralized purchasing (a procedure opposed vigorously by the audiovisual industry), will probably prevail, and equipment and, to a certain extent, materials standardization will occur during the decade under discussion.[47]

At a broader level, greater standardization will be forced on the present quasi-autonomous school system than now exists through such factors as the increasing influence of Federal educational programs, even if no direct control is sought or applied; the inevitable cooperation of States and regions in educational matters; the introduction of whole systems of instruction; the possibility of a national assessment program; the reduction in the number of educational materials suppliers; the reduction in the total number of school districts in the United States; the general increase of communication; the prevalence of large-scale industrial thinking as it moves into the public sector; and the move toward computer data control.

7. The National Assessment (Testing) Program. Earlier in this paper it was mentioned that testing had been developed over the past several decades into a formidable subtechnology within the broader field of

---

[47] Materials standards are equally, if not more, chaotic than equipment standards. One of the earliest problems with teaching machines, for example, was that there were no standards for programs —either mechanical or educational. An abortive effort of a group of professional organizations to set up standards produced nothing.

educational technology. The influence (some call it tyranny) of the New York Regents Examinations upon the curriculum of the schools in New York State has been commented upon for many years. Recently, this type of influence has extended throughout the Nation with the examinations of the College Entrance Examination Board, the National Merit Scholarship Examinations, the Graduate Record Examination, etc. Attention here is devoted to examinations that affect the curriculum of the schools and not to other forms of testing, such as psychological and attitude.

The next decade will see the institution of some form of national educational assessment program. The word "assessment" is used advisedly because the sponsors of the idea (essentially the new educational establishment) are proposing to combine standard achievements testing techniques with sampling techniques similar to those used in public opinion polls to assess "how well the schools are doing." Such a program would not be achievement testing in the accepted sense. A good discussion of the pros and cons of this issue may be found in a recent *Phi Delta Kappan*.[48]

Once such an assessment program is underway, it will become another powerful force for standardization. The technical capability (test construction, sampling techniques, computerized statistics) already exists. Current moves underway to make this capability operational by taking the necessary political, social, and economic steps will no doubt be successful. The claims already being made that such a program will not force a certain amount of standardization are rejected by the writer. That is not the issue anyway. The questions that remain to be answered are what kind of standardization and whether or not the standardization so created will be good or bad.

8. Trends in Administration. Many trends in the field of school and college administration could be singled out for projection. For example, at the brick-and-mortar level, school buildings will continue to improve and be made more compatible with the existing and developing instructional technology. Of all possible predictions in the field of administration, four are selected for comment.

The first . . . will only be mentioned briefly. Data processing equipment and computers will become common tools for the school administrator in handling many routine problems; better decisions will be possible because of the immediate availability of better data. Centralized data-gathering centers will appear, probably as regional centers within the several States. Later, and inevitably, these will be joined into some kind of a national network.

48 Hand, Harold C., "National Assessment Viewed as the Camel's Nose," *Phi Delta Kappan*, XLVII, No. 1 (September 1965), pp. 8–12; Tyler, Ralph W., "Assessing the Progress of Education," *Phi Delta Kappan*, XLVII, No. 1 (September 1965), pp. 13–16; and "The Assessment Debate at the White House Conference," *Phi Delta Kappan*, XLVII, No. 1 (September 1965), pp. 17–18.

Secondly, the most important function to be developed during the next decade will be a logistics of instruction. Everything within the new instructional technology—systems, complex use of materials, sophisticated equipment, new patterns of organization and buildings—requires formidable logistical support. The whole system will break down without it. Such support involves planning based on precise objectives and data, materials flow, equipment maintenance and replacement, backup manpower to the teacher, etc. Such thinking at present is almost completely foreign to school administrators at all levels except in a primitive form that provides sufficient pencils and sweeping compound for the year. Logistical thinking has rarely been applied to instruction; first, therefore, a theory of instructional logistics will have to be created. The pressures of the developing instructional technology will force it into being within the decade.

The third projection is somewhat broader than the first two but is related to them. Essentially, it is that organization patterns will move into larger and larger units for administrative purposes and that control will become more and more a part of what is sometimes called a corporate structure. In other words, the educational bureaucracy will enlarge, with an effort to make the parts (teachers, subadministrators, etc.) interchangeable.

The precise pattern of the enlarging units may take several forms during the decade ahead. The main point is that there will be an increase in size which, of course, will in turn increase the distance between the top levels and the point of contact with students. All State systems of education will tend to become real systems instead of the semisystems now existing. The regional laboratories, the Compact of States, and other such developments mentioned above, when combined with State plans, school district consolidation, and urban growth are all forces operating in this situation. It is hard to see anything but a diminution of local control of schools in the next 10 years. This diminution will tend to accelerate toward the end of the decade.

Finally, it is probable that one or more new private school systems, national in scope, will be started during this same period. These systems will be developed by the new industries moving into the educational field and will feature highly standardized, relatively fully automated, high-quality education designed essentially for upper and upper middle-class clientele. Such a system or systems will be accompanied by, but probably not related to, similar systems of private vocational training centers. This movement, too, will be gaining impetus by the end of the decade.

The school administrator required by these and many will quite clearly be a skilled professional manager, not the Latin scholar or part-time chemist-administrator, as desirable as such characteristics seem to many people; and he will not be so much the community-oriented, faithful service club member so highly valued in some school administration circles today. Subject matter scholars, through the technique of curriculum development projects, have learned to short-circuit school boards and administrators in matters of curriculum content. Increasingly, as methodology becomes more precise within educational technology, the same effect will be achieved by psychologists and educational engineers; thus, the issue of the ideal subject matter expert or liberal arts generalist qua school administrator will become completely dead, remaining to be mourned in the columns of literary magazines. The concept of the successful community-oriented administrator will also die, although a little more slowly, and the mourning will be heard at the annual steak fry.

9. **The Research, Development, Dissemination and Adoption Syndrome and the Resistance to Innovation.** As the process of research, development, dissemination, and adoption begins to operate with force (see part II), the traditional resistance of the educational system to change will crumble at an increasing rate during the next 10 years. Some enthusiasts for educational technology of any variety have consistently underestimated the power of the resistance of the system in the past; in the future, however the timespan between idea and practice will increasingly be shortened. The current timespan between the development of a new process and its adoption by a substantial majority of units of the system has been estimated at about 35 years. During the next 10 years this timespan will be reduced to about one-quarter of that length, or from 8 to 10 years.

10. **General Developments in Educational Psychology and Methodology.** Barring unexpected breakthroughs in understanding the physics and chemistry of the central nervous system which are, of course, possible, the situation in educational psychology as described above will not change much during the decade. Cognitive structure, inquiry, structure of knowledge, creativity, and student response manipulation will still be key concepts both for pure and applied research and for the development and testing of instrumentation and materials. Increasingly, a dialogue may be expected to develop between the cognitive structure-inquiry school and the operant conditioning school; a hard core of each will hold firm, but borders will become increasingly friendly. Experiments attempting to turn one system into another, as, for example, that recently reported by Schrag and Holland,[49] will increase.

In the meantime, newer viewpoints, particularly those associated with cybernetic principles and information theory, will begin to gain momen-

---

49 Schrag, Philip G. and James G. Holland, "Programing Motion Pictures: The Conversion of a PSSC Film into a Program," *Audiovisual Communication Review*, vol. 13, No. 4 (winter 1965), pp. 418–422.

tum. A recent book by Smith and Smith may be a bellwether.[50] Research patterns using these developing theories will begin to intrigue younger psychologists. The decade will end with some newer points of view having enough adherents to threaten what will then be "old hat" psychology.

Because the psychological situation will remain unsettled, the educational engineers will build bridges of learning on an empirical basis. The decade will see a great commitment to the empirical approach in the production of instructional materials and hardware. Materials and processes will be tested increasingly on suitable populations and will be revised until they work. The engineers, of course, will use whatever can be used from the studies of the pure psychologists; further, more research will be based on realistic student populations rather than small laboratory situations from which it is difficult to generalize.

The combination of the empirical approach and increased pure and applied research throughout the whole field of education and educational psychology represents one force that will turn a current form of thinking completely around so that it will point in the opposite direction.

The second force in operation relates to the national commitment to education as *the* uplifting force in our national life. For example, developing learning programs for such things as Operation Headstart and the Job Corps training centers are very difficult technical problems; they require, for their solution, large doses of educational technology considered broadly—methods, processes, machines, organization, skilled specialist manpower. Pious claims to the contrary, a knowledge of subject matter alone will be of little or no help in dealing with a 16-year-old illiterate from the Kentucky hills.

These two forces will combine into a pressure that will result in the rediscovery of educational methodology. From about 1950 to 1960 it was extremely fashionable to decry educational methodology as useless, as a fake medicine sold by charlatans, as something certainly not needed in the process of instruction. Those that grudgingly conceded that methodology did exist equated it with "tricks of the trade"—something that could be picked up overnight on an apprentice basis.

An illustrative example relates to the problems which led to the creation of Operation Headstart, a huge national operation designed to provide missing background for young, deprived children so that they might be ready to learn in school. It is now ironically forgotten that many critical books and articles appearing from 1950 to 1960 claimed that there was no such thing as "readiness" for learning and that professional educators, in maintaining that there was, were perpetrating a

[50] Smith, Karl U. and Margaret Foltz Smith *Cybernetic Principles of Learning and Educational Design*, New York: Holt, Rinehart and Winston, 1966.

fraud on the American public. These books were read by the upper level economic group and the articles appeared in the "best" magazines. This general downgrading of methodological concepts, which resulted in its own mythology, is being attacked by events and will result in a complete destruction of this posture. Further, since control of subject matter is now secure through the technology of instructional systems, the entire dialogue between method and subject matter will be wiped out.

11. The Buildup of the New Educational Industry. As was indicated earlier in this memorandum, one trend of the last decade was the emergence of the science-based industries into the educational scene. The result of this in the next decade will be a pattern of power struggle, mergers, acquisitions, and new combinations, such as joint ventures between such industries, universities, and nonprofit corporations of the "think-tank" variety.

It is hard to see how the old-line publishing firms and audiovisual producers and suppliers can retain their current organization, appearance, and way of doing business. The next 10 years will see enormous changes in the educational business, which will generally be in the direction of larger, more diversified enterprises that will absorb many of the smaller companies and will force others out of business. The time of the lone salesman working out of his house for the small company and calling on a friendly territory will run out in this decade.

The existence of this larger educational industry will gradually force a change in bidding and purchasing procedures, and, hence, will influence the formation of the logistics of instruction. Such an industry will also permit more communication between the training segment (military, industrial, etc.) and the pure educational segment (schools, colleges, etc.) because materials and equipment will be supplied to both. If the pattern continues in the direction it seems to be going at the present time, these industrial giants will, through contracts, also be operating educational enterprises. The current operation of some of the Job Corps training centers by industrial groups and nonprofit corporations will be followed by the development of a general contracting capability under which such companies will provide instructional materials and services, build buildings, process data, catalog books and even hire or provide teachers and administrators for schools and colleges. Some of them may well develop their own school systems.

Chapter 15

---

*How did the concept of integrated instructional materials
'packages' evolve from the earlier orientation of the textbook
as the basic instructional material?*

*What are the implications of packaged instructional programs
for flexibility in selecting appropriate teaching strategies?*

*What variety exists in the various commercial approaches
to packaging of instructional kits?*

*Is it probable that the trend will be toward uniform packages
or will diversity tend to continue?*

PACKAGED PROGRAMS

PHILIP LEWIS, President
Instructional Dynamics Incorporated
Chicago, Illinois*

EVOLUTION OF A CONCEPT

It was just a short time ago that the concept of instructional materials
for the classroom generally assumed the basic textbook to be the main-
stay for the teacher and for the learner. It was also an accepted idea
that a teacher's edition was essential to successfully implement the
unique or special approaches built into the texts by the authors and
subject matter authorities involved. A further outgrowth of this development was the addition of coordinated workbooks to provide skill development exercises and application opportunities for the students.
Another attempt to assist in the instructional process was the provision
of unit and chapter tests to enable the teacher to more validly assess the
progress of her charges.

During this same period publishers and producers got together to provide lists of so-called correlated films, filmstrips and recordings that
keyed-in with texts. These products were independently produced and

*At the time this chapter was developed, Dr. Lewis was Director of Research, Development
and Special Projects, Chicago Board of Education.

had only coincidental elements in common with each other as well as with the texts. It was evident that such identified relationships served only enrichment purposes for use when and if time permitted.

The development of the field of programed learning brought with it a new and important reassessment of theories of learning and also put into focus the need for more specifically identifying educational objectives in planning for the use of instructional materials, teaching techniques and learning resources.

As a result of this new emphasis educational publishers began to provide filmstrips as an integral part of their textbook-workbook-test package. Initially, these visuals often only reproduced illustrations from the text. As experience was gained, however, the filmstrips became more effective as they were specifically designed to achieve certain learning objectives not as easily obtained through the printed material alone.

As this development continued, the idea of instructional kits and packages took root and incorporated not only filmstrips but motion pictures, disc and tape recordings, manipulative devices and even realia to assist in the teaching-learning process. Within this framework the visuals, manipulatives and other items changed their customary roles. They were no longer to be considered as instructional aids or enrichment resources, but rather essential and integral parts of a total plan. Each and every part of the instructional 'package' performs an important function and cannot be eliminated from use without in some way impairing the thoroughness of the plan.

Subsequent recognition of the benefits of multimedia approaches brought with it the requirement for associated equipment in terms of projectors, audio reproducing devices, language and learning laboratories and other such facilities. The mere fact that many instructional items involving several media are put together in a single package does not necessarily result in a truly integrated instructional unit.

In order to qualify in this connection, the prescribed use of a coordinated instructional package should result in the mastery on the part of the learner of the information or skills or in the attitude shaping originally established as specific educational and instructional goals. An analysis of such materials indicate at least three major approaches in their organization and implementation:

1. The formulation of materials used by the teacher in conjunction with her students.
2. The organization of materials so that they are self-directed, self-administering, so that the student may learn on his own. This latter approach need not necessarily be a true programed learning situation although in some cases it may incorporate programing in lesser or greater degree depending on the design involved.

3. In some instances a combination of the two approaches just described have been used successfully. At certain times the teacher participates to promote interaction and at other times the students are self-directed and independent in their learning activities.

IMPLICATIONS FOR CURRICULUM DEVELOPMENT

There are important and pervasive implications in the advent of "packaged materials" for the field of curriculum development. It is currently conventional practice in formulating a course of study or a resource guide to proceed essentially, through the following major steps:
1. The establishment of general educational objectives.
2. The identification of specific learning goals.
3. The listing of appropriate classroom and other activities necessary to assist the learner to achieve the goals and objectives established.
4. The selection and listing of materials, devices, equipment and working facilities useful in presenting or working with the concepts involved.

It may be helpful in pinpointing the need for modified curriculum-making procedures to discuss briefly the relationships that exist in the teaching-learning situation. Actually, the teacher, the learner and the medium of communication are the three basic concerns in this process. If a change is made in the role, function or emphasis of any of the three factors listed, then the role of the two remaining elements is directly affected. For example, a teacher who on occasion lectures to her students takes on the role of a person dispensing information. The resultant role of the learner is a passive one—a mere receptor of what is being presented. If the teacher, however, should employ the chalkboard to use graphics to visualize certain concepts being presented, then her role is significantly changed and the learners receive stimuli through visual as well as auditory means.

Even more dramatic is the realignment of roles when the teacher employs overhead projection transparencies, a filmstrip or a motion picture as part of her lesson presentation. In such instances her role is no longer that of a lecturer but rather that of a resource person with the visual medium taking on signal importance in the relationship. When a discussion ensues the learner becomes active in the process and the teacher's role becomes that of moderator, guide and stimulator. While all of the examples just presented may seem quite obvious, they do highlight the need in the curriculum development process to consider *the teacher, the learner* and *the medium* simultaneously as planning is done, rather than sequentially, as is now the case. In this way the activities, the devices, the program, etc., become important and integral parts of the plan, each of which is not mutually exclusive.

CHANNELS OF COMMUNICATION FOR TEACHING AND LEARNING

There are three main channels of communication in the teaching-learning process. These are:

1. The teacher working directly with the student or students.
2. The teacher employing media in working with the students.
3. The students working directly and/or individually with media that have been structured for such activity.

This listing is not intended to indicate one channel of communication as being more important than the others. The approach to be employed at a particular time, to fulfill a particular objective, must be selected as being the most effective for the specific purpose. If this premise is acceptable then all three channels of communication are available for use in designing configurations most appropriate in the overall picture. The introduction of packaged programs fit in with the two latter communications approaches.

TECHNOLOGICAL DEVELOPMENTS AFFECT THE PACKAGE

In order to indicate some of the scope and potential of the packaged concept, it may be well to list briefly some of the elements that lend themselves to such arrangements:

Filmstrip Projectors and Viewers

This development has been used traditionally for small as well as large group instruction. More recently, however, the production of compact, table-top viewers has encouraged the use of such visuals on an individualized basis. Some manufacturers now supply machines that will use half and quarter frame images in addition to conventional full frames to permit the presentation of information, the introduction of challenges in the form of questions to be answered or problems to be solved, and finally the provision of reinforcement in terms of indicating the proper responses. Further developments include the synchronization of such projectors with prerecorded audio sources on phonograph discs or magnetic tapes as well as built-in tachistoscopic facilities.

The Language Master

A relatively recently marketed audio and visual combination device, the Bell and Howell Language Master, (Figure 1) employs cards of

Figure 1. Language Master.

various sizes for its operation. Each card has a strip of magnetic tape adhered to it about ¼" from the bottom edge. The basic equipment unit permits students to place the cards, one-by-one in a grooved track or channel. At a certain point the card is pulled through the machine by a motor arrangement and the word, phrase or sentence recorded on the master track of the tape is reproduced audibly through a built-in loudspeaker or headphone attachment.

The cards may either be purchased commercially or prepared locally, Card sequences can be used with sight-impaired children where large type faces are imprinted on prepared materials. Similarly, blind children can utilize the equipment when braille characters are embossed on the cards. Preschool youngsters may work with cards having color patches imprinted or tactile swatches adhered to the card to learn basic concepts of colors, of rough and smooth textures and as readiness for reading. Other applications include card sets for vocabulary development, speech correction and speech therapy approaches, foreign language instruction and other possibilities limited only by the imagination and creativity of the user.

The learners, after hearing the 'models' recorded on the teacher track while at the same time viewing the graphics, are able to record their own version on the student track for review and comparison purposes. Language Master units are also employed as decks in learning carrels or booths and are even interconnected in language or learning laboratory formats.

Tape Recorders

Despite the fact that magnetic tape recording has been on the educational scene since World War II, it was only in recent years that many of the exciting developments and applications have occurred with this device. There are now single-track, dual-track and quarter-track machines with accompanying features that allow these devices to be programed as self-instructional units.

The incorporation of solid-state techniques with the resultant miniaturization of equipment opens up new horizons in terms of instructional applications. The smaller machines can be taken home, used in carrels or employed for interviewing and other techniques. Experiments conducted recently with techniques variously known as 'compressed speech' or 'speed discourses' indicates that the human hearing mechanism capability far exceeds the vocal speaking rates. Short exposures to speeded up recorded materials indicate that learners can assimulate material at a far greater rate then is now conventionally employed. The ease with which recordings and other materials can be produced, programed and supplied provides resources never before available in the classroom or for the self-directed learner.

Repetitive Film Loops

It has been conventional procedure to produce 16mm educational motion picture films on 400, 800, 1,200 and 1,600 foot reels. Because of these relatively lengthy presentation limits, it is generally the practice to include a great deal of information in the footage, in addition to long introductions, credit frames and other information on trailers.

A new idea evolved recently in terms of the production of films of short duration (anywhere from 30 second to 4½ minutes) which deal with a single concept, one or two ideas or a step-by-step process in a brief but pertinent presentation. The Technicolor projector (Figure 2), a device weighing about 7 pounds and roughly the size of a loaf of bread, utilizes Magi-Cartridges (Figure 2C). These latter items are plastic cassettes in which the film is loaded and spliced end-to-end. It is possible to thread the projector by the simple insertion of the cartridge in a matter of a few seconds. As the film is projected, it continuously rewinds itself so that it is ready for another showing upon completion of the first exposure. Using this approach, it is possible for an individual learner or for a small group to view and to repeat a sequence as many times as may be necessary to develop skills or to effectively absorb the information.

Figure 2. (*A, B*) Technicolor "800" and "810" 8mm motion picture projectors with small screen rear projection unit. (*C*) Insertion of Magi-Cartridge into Technicolor "1000" 8mm projector.

A second model of this projector is equipped with a start button on the top of the machine. Part of the preparation of the film in explaining a step-by-step process would be to manually notch the film after each step before loading it into the cartridge. In use the motion sequences for the first step in the process is projected after which the machine automatically stops itself to enable the learner to actually perform the action indicated. Upon completion of this step the button is pressed by the learner and the machine projects the material relating to the second step after which it stops again. This procedure is repeated for each of the individual sequences built into the film. Many shop and laboratory applications lend themselves to this approach—learning to use a microscope, preparing a slide, developing skill in grinding an edge on a woodworking tool, acquiring technique in the proper operation of an analytical balance, etc.

A third model of this projector employs an extension cord with a remote control switch. Locally produced 8mm films of persons executing a tennis or golf swing, fingering a musical instrument, bandaging a wound, etc. may be loaded into the plastic cartridges. It is possible to view the motion sequences in a conventional manner, but by depressing one of the buttons, a single frame is projected as a still picture. Each successive pressure on this button advances the film one frame at a time. In this way, analysis of complicated procedures are easily achieved.

These projectors, at present, do not have accompanying sound track, and, therefore, all of the techniques of the silent film are involved. However, experience has shown that audio is not essential for many learning activities. Adapters, however, have been produced by other manufacturers which will synchronize sound with these cartridge films. The new Technicolor "1000" motion picture projector incorporates optical sound but utilizes cartridges that will accommodate up to 30 minutes of film footage. This product, however, is not intended to replace the "silent" models, but to provide a smaller, lighter, and automatic film machine.

Combining These Media.

The examples above represent a sampling of the many devices now available on the market. It is the purpose of these illustrations to indicate the unique capabilities of such innovations and in this way to justify consideration of including one or more of these approaches in a multimedia package.

An example of an interesting combination of media used for self-directed instruction is a botany laboratory in operation at Purdue University. Here the professor has organized the work thoroughly and systematically so that students may report for lab sessions without adherence to rigid schedules and may progress at their own rates. For example, if a student completes the required assignment in a single session, he is not required to report to the laboratory for the rest of the week except perhaps to take on extra assignments at a more challenging level.

In operation a student reporting to the laboratory will scan a card rack. If cards are in the rack he selects one which bears a number. This relates to a vacant work station. The student goes to this station, puts on the headphones located there and starts a tape recorder. The prerecorded material gives the background information and instructions for the experimental work to be done. The student turns to the display of plants or whatever might be on the schedule for that week and goes through the sequence of required activities, makes entries on worksheets and solves problems that accompany the assignment. In addition, he may view a slide sequence, a single concept film or some other resource designed to assist him in mastering the assignment. At the conclusion of his work, the tape recorder may be started again as a follow-up or as a check on the work done. When the student is satisfied with the results of his efforts, he then takes an examination on the unit. If he passes it satisfactorily, he is relieved of further laboratory attendance for that week. This arrangement gives the professor complete freedom to assist students individually in the laboratory to better serve their needs.

Multimedia Kits and Instructional Packages

The production of coordinated and integrated materials based on total instructional plans are relatively new in the field. Therefore, it is expected that the products will not necessarily fall into clearly identified patterns. Rather, they appear in many and diverse forms. Perhaps the best way to illustrate the wide range of designs being developed as part of this trend is to list a limited number of examples:

Science Research Associates Education Programs.

    a. Our Working World. An elementary school studies program designed to teach economics concepts to pupils in the first, second and third grades. This program incorporates records, a selection of specially authored books along with a comprehensive teacher's manual.

    b. Reading Laboratory. This boxed series approach was introduced in 1957 and to date has been used by nearly 7 million children throughout the country. The "lab" assortment is available for kindergarten through 12th grade and contains materials based on multilevel concepts of individualized instruction. In use these programs are practically self-administering and self-testing.

    c. Contemporary Composition. This program presents a modern approach to teaching the fundamentals of English composition. It consists of a series of 510 acetate transparencies for use with an overhead projector. An attachment facilitates the use of the transparencies and provides a writing surface which permits the instructor to superimpose additional markings on the projected images. The visuals are divided into 24 books to present the 12 major units in the course. Units in the total package include instructor guides, student manual, answer key and Flipatron.

Benefic Press Developments.

    a. Science Shelf. A supplemental science program intended to update and enhance basic science textbook series. The shelf consists of 6 copies of 6 different titles plus 6 filmstrips. Each filmstrip is related to the text and is accompanied by a teacher's guide.

    b. Uni-A-Kit Program. A series of 6 copies of 5 different titles for a total of 30 books. Included in a filmstrip for each text in the group as well as a teacher's guide.

    c. Animal Adventure Series Recordings. An assortment of six 10-inch 33⅓ rpm records which carry the stories contained in a series of 6 supplemental readers for grade 1. The author's voice on the records tells each of the stories as the child is directed to follow it in his book.

V-M Corporation Basic Language Courses. This company has available three packaged and functional basic language course kits dealing with French, Spanish (Figure 3), and English for Spanish-speaking persons. The components include books containing words, phrases and sentences which are illustrated by photographs on facing pages, programed magnetic tapes adapted to the Add-A-Track feature on the V-M Tape-O-Matic Tape Recorders (Figure 4) to allow learners to listen to native speakers and to record their own spoken versions for comparison, a glossary of words, and an instruction booklet outlining procedures to be followed. A number of unique features are incorporated in the design of the tape recordings and a bilingual approach is employed.

3M Tape–Filmstrip Discussion Course. This instructional kit includes a group leader discussion guide, teacher review manuals, filmstrips and audio tapes. All are packaged in a functional service box. The various parts of the course are color-coded to facilitate in coordinating their use. The educational objectives of the kit are focused on assisting the teacher of modern languages in dealing with the proper use of electronic laboratories and associated equipment and materials.

Learning Through Seeing Materials. This instructional resource contains a tachistoscopic device (an inexpensive arrangement to flash images on the screen for a fraction of a second). The unit adapts existing filmstrip projectors for the purpose (Figure 5). An assortment of special filmstrips are provided to assist in the development of learning skills. A teacher's manual to instruct in proper procedures is also supplied.

Educational Development Laboratories. EDL has evolved a number of approaches to assist in developing proper reading and related skills.

  a. Their reading carrel (Figure 6) is equipped with a 'skimmer,' a controlled reader, a hand held tachistoscope and all of the accessory printed materials to permit effective and individualized skill development. The line is quite comprehensive in terms of printed materials as well as other media.

  b. The newest EDL addition is known as the Aud-X (Figure 7). This unit combines the phonograph capability with filmstrips in a unique design. For example, electronic controls enable the student to hear a part of a sentence and when a new word is introduced, it will appear on the built-in screen as a visual stimulus. A number of interesting variations are included in this approach.

Stansi Scientific Company Kits. These science packets provide a convenient approach to supplying materials and equipment for use in science experiments. The requirements of science curricula are analyzed to identify items to be packaged (Figure 8). In this way the replacement of chemicals, wire and other consumable materials eliminates the need for detailed and arduous reordering of small quantities of inexpensive items. These kits are particularly adaptable to the use of mobile science labs.

Welch Scientific Company. The Rol-Lab (Figure 9) and Rol-Labette represent a trend that is supporting science instruction through demonstration and experimentation in classrooms that cannot ordinarily afford a full-blown laboratory. These mobile units provide a water supply by means of pumps and storage bottles, heating facilities using compressed gas units fitted with changeable tips for Bunsen applications and other purposes, batteries for DC current supply and duplex plug-in box for AC supply. In addition, the facility has storage space for apparatus, glassware and refuse. A complementary unit is a stationary wall cabinet containing plastic tubs. Each container provides individual storage of classified groups of materials, each dealing with an area in science such as 'living things,' heat transfer, or air pressure. The assortment is further augmented through the inclusion of an instruction book for the teacher which not only outlines the use of the facilities, but includes instructions and illustrations relating to basic experiments generally a part of every science curriculum.

Hickok Teaching Systems. Here in a single assortment are contained:

  a. All materials required for a beginning course for vocational and technical students in electricity-electronics. The storage cabinet

Figure 3. Spanish Language "Treasure Chest."
Figure 4. Tape-O-Matic Tape Recorder with Add-A-Track.
Figure 5. Filmstrip Projector with Tachistoscopic Device.

Figure 6. Learning Station.

Figure 7. Aud-X.

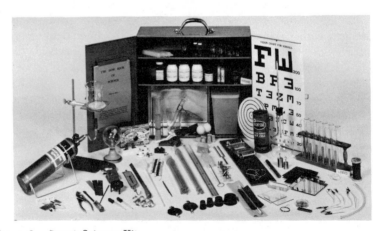

Figure 8. Stansi Science Kit.

Figure 9.   Rol-Lab.

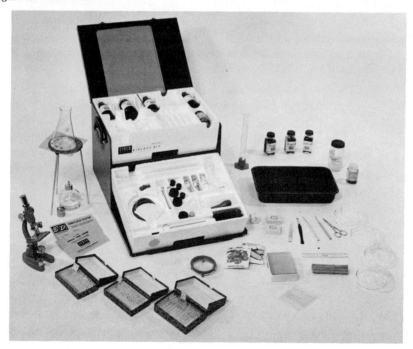

Figure 10.   Biology Kit.

accommodates trays of various electrical components as well as baseboards to accommodate modular assembly of single or multiple stage circuits. In addition, basic test equipment is also supplied. The manual included is employed throughout the course, and one such kit will serve two students simultaneously.

b. Hickock also offers a physics laboratory and an electronics-mechanics kit as well as a microwave technology assortment styled along the same lines as described.

Central Scientific Company. Produces kits in biology (Figure 10), microslide assortments, and general science materials for a variety of instructional levels. These assortments are complete in terms of equipment, materials and instructions.

IN CONCLUSION

It must be concluded from this analysis that the effectiveness of the design of instructional kits is a direct result of the degree of creativity, imagination and careful study expended to assist the classroom teacher in solving some of her instructional problems. It is unlikely that only a single pattern of use and format will suffice. Rather, a large number of varying approaches will be validated for use in different situations. Built-in flexibility of use may well determine the degree of acceptance of any package made available.

As time goes on the benefits of new research in learning, the increased effectiveness of applications of instructional technology and materials, and the updating and upgrading of curricula will join together to make learning not only profitable but economical of students' time.

Chapter 16

---

*How has the historical development of instructional film
contributed to our knowledge of specific
teaching-learning principles?*

*What can film accomplish in the instructional environment and
how does film relate to the responsibilities
of the classroom teacher?*

*How does the nature of the film medium enable it to accomplish
specific effects through manipulation of stimuli?*

*What specialized types of film exist and what future
developments in the use of film can be forseen?*

THE MOTION PICTURE:
COMMUNICATION CHANNEL FOR
INFORMATION, CONCEPTS, SKILLS, ATTITUDES

RICHARD A. SANDERSON, Director, Communications Center
University of Hawaii

THE MOTION PICTURE IN EDUCATION

Thomas Edison, credited as the American inventor of the motion picture, was perhaps one of the first to realize the potentials of his invention for education. It was ironical that he considered his invention
of more use to education than as a great potential for commercial
entertainment. It was for this reason that he failed to take out world
patents on his invention and was subsequently forced out of the motion
picture business by competitors who imported their adaptations of
his motion picture camera and projector into the United States and
developed a thriving entertainment business.

The birthdate of Edison's motion picture is set at 1894. The tremendous development of this new medium was reflected by the fact
that over 1,800 motion pictures were registered with the United States

Copyright Office between 1894 and 1904. These were short vignettes of action, events, and vaudeville, and although the trend towards entertainment was unmistakable, the content of some of these films indicated that a documentary or educational approach was evident to some extent (17).

The first fully organized effort in developing films specifically for education was represented by the Yale University "Chronicles of America Photoplays" series of 1922. These films, like all motion pictures at that time, were silent and were on 35mm film. Within ten years sound was added to 35mm film. The reduced 16mm noninflammable film was introduced in 1923 for educational purposes, capitalizing on the possibilities of utilizing less expensive and more easily operated equipment for classroom use. By 1930, sound was added to the 16mm classroom film (5).

The development of the educational motion picture had progressed by 1960 to the point where over 160 major film companies, universities, and educational organizations were producing or distributing films for educational purposes (15). With the stimulation of instructional media programs by National Defense Education Act matching fund grants and Elementary and Secondary Education Act projects, the production and distribution of educational films has been expanding even more rapidly since 1960.

The quantity of educational films available does not necessarily indicate the effectiveness of their contribution to learning. The content of a film, the treatment of its subject matter, and the effectiveness with which it makes use of the film medium for communicating are more important as factors in evaluating contributions to learning. Charles Hoban and Edward Van Ormer, in their review of instructional film research from 1918 to 1950, concluded that there were at least two other principles contributing to the influence of an instructional film: the psychological make-up of the *audience,* and the social and instructional characteristics of the *situation* (12). Transferring these principles to the classroom situation places as much or even more responsibility upon the teacher as it does upon the film producer for the effectiveness of instructional films in a learning situation.

Hoban and Van Ormer summarized their review of thirty-two years of film research by presenting ten basic principles or postulates of film influence. These ten principles can be related directly to the responsibilities of the classroom instructor in properly selecting a film, preparing the students for viewing it, and carrying on follow-up activities after the viewing. They are summarized and paraphrased with this application in mind (12).

1. A film will have greater impact when it is used to reinforce and

extend previous knowledge, attitudes, and motivations of students. Similarly, reinforcing experiences conducted before, during and after a film viewing will increase the learning resulting from the film. For the learner, viewing a film can constitute an experience just like any other learning experience. To become more effective and lasting, these experiences must be repeated as necessary or reinforced with similar experiences—in other words, film review and viewing of additional films may serve as reinforcement.

2. A film cannot be used effectively for broad, general objectives; it must be used with specific learning objectives in mind. However, over a period of time a series of film viewings and related activities may eventually lead to broader generalizations.

3. Film learning can be increased when the content of the film is directly related to the concepts to be learned. Extraneous and irrelevant material should be eliminated.

4. The ability of students to learn from films may vary in relation to their previous experiences with films, their previous experience with the subject, their attitude toward the subject, and with their academic ability. This places further emphasis upon adequately preparing a class for film viewings and suggests that small group or independent learning with certain films might be more effective than large group viewing.

5. The visual aspect of a film is (or should be) the primary source of learning. The film which can be used effectively as a learning device with the sound turned off may be more useful for repeated showings, review, and independent study. If the visualizations carry the greatest share of the film's content, verbalizations can be made by the teacher and by students, relating the descriptions more closely to their own needs and experiences.

6. Students will respond to a film in relation to how they may equate their own needs and experiences to the content and in relation to how significant it appears for their purposes. Providing students with some familiarity of the film content or film setting and relating the significance of the content to the students' needs will increase acceptance and receptivity during the film presentation.

7. Students will respond most efficiently to a motion picture film when they become involved in the presentation and view it subjectively. Involvement in the film may be directly related to the ability of students to identify with the characters portrayed, the situations presented, or the method in which problems or tasks presented by the film are resolved.

8. The rate of learning demanded by a film should not be too rapid for effective instruction. The teacher must relate the rate of de-

velopment to the ability or intellectual level of students and make necessary adaptations. A presentation which is found to be too rapid may be slowed by merely stopping the projection periodically for discussion or review. Portions of the film may be shown again by reversing the projector or reviewing parts of the film (or seeing the entire film a second time). A complex and rapid presentation by a film may indicate that student study guides or teacher-prepared outlines of the film content should be utilized before, during, or after the viewing.

9. The instructional effectiveness of films is increased when they are supported by established instructional techniques provided by the classroom teacher. The most common techniques to be employed are:

    a. Properly orienting the students to the film before viewing, and summarizing after viewing.
    b. Indicating that a test or check on the learning accomplished will be given after the film viewing.
    c. Repeating the important points through review or through a second viewing.
    d. Encouraging student participation either during or after the film showing and allowing the student to practice what he has learned.
    e. Revealing to the student how much knowledge he has gained from the film by evaluating student responses or performances during or after the viewing.

    (Additional support for film learning can be provided through the use of other audiovisual devices or techniques such as exhibits, demonstrations, still pictures, field trips, etc.)

10. The instructor's leadership qualities directly influence the efficiency by which his class learns from the film.

Films cannot serve as a complete substitute for the teacher, and particularly in exercising leadership. The greatest responsibility for the effective use of an instructional film is placed upon the teacher who selects, prepares, conducts the class viewing, and provides follow-up activities in using classroom films. The teacher who wishes to accomplish these tasks effectively must know the medium with which he is dealing.

THE SPECIAL CHARACTERISTICS OF FILM

In selecting and utilizing a motion picture the classroom teacher must first consider the suitability of subject content and appropriateness of the grade level approach. But beyond these considerations a broader analysis of the value of any film should be made before incorporating it into the classroom program. The method of classroom utilization may depend heavily upon the type of film involved—documentary, instructional film, entertainment film, 8mm single concept film, etc. However, the real value of any film as an effective instructional device may depend on the unique opportunities for learning which it contains.

Film and the Learning Environment

Most summaries of the motion picture as a classroom instructional tool reiterate the basic characteristics of film which make it an effective means of learning in the classroom. (1,3,4,9,23)

1. **Provides a common experience.**—The level and variety of experiences in any classroom group usually are widely diversified. Providing a common experience to all through motion picture film creates a plateau from which the teacher can progress, using the plateau as a frame of reference.

2. **Attracts and holds attention.**—Interest and even curiosity in the film has been developed by the instructor; the lights are dimmed and attention is virtually compelled to the bright image which appears at the focal point in front of the classroom; further attention is attracted to the sounds of the film, to the brilliancy of color, to multiple views of objects, to close-up views, and to the motion of both subjects and camera.

3. **Provides visuals in motion in combination with environmental sounds.** —An appropriate blend of moving images and sounds effects a realistic portrayal of life, yet the film can also be purely symbolic through animation and creative sound.

4. **Overcomes classroom barriers of time, distance, and space.**—A motion picture can break the time barrier in several ways. First it has the ability to view events of past history (in either an actual recording or a re-created episode) or of future time, through animation. The distance bridged may be from country to country, city to village, mountains to desert—all within a brief period of time and presented with extreme selectivity and guidance.

Many objects are too large to bring directly to the students. Through film these oversized materials may be examined in the classroom and often in a closer, more detailed way.

5. **Presents materials in a way accomplished by no other device.**—There are special characteristics of motion picture photography which enable the motion picture to bring unique experiences into the classroom—

a. Slow motion photography—slowing down rapid and complex movements for closer observation and analysis (such as the pumping of a heart or the movements of an athlete in action).

b. Time-lapse or *stop motion photography*—speeding up long and time-consuming processes and movements by photographing the movement sporadically over a long period of time (illustrated by the budding of a flower, germination of a seed).

c. Animation—creation of symbols and drawings in simulated motion by taking a series of single photographs of the artwork as the movement progresses.

d. Cine photomicrography—photography of specimens through the microscope for detailed study.

e. X-ray motion photography—making visible the interior structure and movements of animals, humans, and other objects capable of examination by X-ray.

COMMUNICATIVE ELEMENTS OF THE MOTION PICTURE

Beyond the visible elements of moving images and their accompanying sound, there are the many variable elements of a motion picture which can be manipulated or controlled during its planning and construction. Weisgerber identified four major phases in the making of a film: (1) *orientation*, which involves the identification of audience, purpose, and limitations; (2) *formulation*, covering the determination of filmic content and its treatment; (3) *execution*, or creating the final product from the plan; and (4) *evaluative testing* to determine if the goals and purposes have been met. In each of these four phases consideration must be given to properly utilizing the elements of a motion picture film for effective communication (22). The way in which these elements are used and the manner in which all of the elements are formed together to accomplish the final product will determine how effectively the film will transmit its message.

Selectivity and Condensation of the Filmic Content

What are the most important aspects of the subject to be covered? Which topics should be covered in detail; which should be touched upon lightly or excluded entirely? What is the best way of visualizing the subject? How can the selection of various angles of view, close-ups, long shots, or juxtaposition of these, best reveal what needs to be seen? Which sounds of the environment should be included; what verbal description should accompany the image? All of these questions and many more must be answered by the film producer and his staff before he can begin to put the effective elements of film to work in his production.

Planning.—The planning stage of the film should include a collection of authorities and resources relating closely to the subject. It is a team-teaching approach with the subject specialists determining content and approach, and the film production staff determining the best method of visualizing and placing the content into a filmic form. Their efforts may be examined by undertaking some type of pre-production testing through short film clips, still pictures, or storyboard sketches (16). This type of test might be performed on a sampling of the intended film audience, examining their interest, their comprehension, and the apparent effects upon developing understandings and retention of information.

An analysis and evaluation of a film for instructional purposes should be made with these 'behind the scenes' elements of selectivity in the planning and preparation stages taken into account. Does the film reflect a continuity of purpose, a condensation of all that is pertinent and relevant, an accuracy and reliability of subject approach, and a suitability to student levels and needs?

Photography.—Selectivity continues throughout the production of the film. The photographic images should reveal a choice of angles and composition of each picture which are not merely aesthetically pleasing, but also contribute to the subject and help tell the story. Long shots and medium shots permit a view of the subject in its environment, and close-ups are useful for detailed investigation. When photography of the actual item does not communicate all the facts and understandings, special processes such as slow motion, time lapse photography, and animation are available to the film maker.

Editing.—With the film script planned and the photography complete, the elements of selectivity in film production are still present in the editing processes and in the final recording of the sound track. The film editor controls the relationship of one image to another and controls the over-all tempo or rate of development of the film. His selectivity enters into the choice of the best image or of the best action or view of action; the length of time one image remains on the screen before being replaced with another is his determination; the juxtaposition of one image with another, showing relationships and contrasts, is under his control; special laboratory effects such as dissolves, fades, wipes, super-imposures are located in the film and indicated by the editor. The skill with which these choices are made may determine whether the images on the screen clarify or confuse—whether they communicate the meanings intended or cloud the issues with fleeting and meaningless images.

Sounding.—Selection and control of the sound images is as important an aspect for filmic communication as the selection of the visual images. The human ear is selective; we automatically exclude extraneous noises which do not pertain to the sounds created at the center of our interest or attention. Since microphones and sound recording apparatus are not selective the selection process must be performed by the film maker. This requires skill in mixing the various sound sources at the proper time and at the proper volume levels. The combination of sync-sound (screen dialogue viewed and simultaneously heard), musical background, narration, and miscellaneous environmental sounds and special sound effects is an involved process. The success of the film sound track depends greatly upon its relationship to the images projected simultaneously on the screen. This relationship is a close-knit one in which sound and picture support each other towards communicating the same theme, each contributing the most when it can accomplish the task more completely.

Utilization of Multiple Communication Channels

Within the basic elements of visual image and sound are several sub-elements which also contribute to the film's communicative powers.
View of image.—The choice of pictorial images and their arrangement have much to do with the progression and development of the subject matter. However, the angle of view, the proximity to the subject, and the relationship of one view to another can communicate in themselves. For example, the view from a low angle gives a subject added stature and power; a view from above the subject looking down will reduce stature and weaken the subject. John Grierson, the 'father' of the documentary film in England, felt this power of the camera along with the power of intimacy and of detail through close-ups, and the elements of changing angles, gave added dimension to the subject and creative power to its filmic description. He emphasized that still further powers for communicating were made possible on the film cutting bench (11). A sudden and extreme close-up of a subject or part of a subject from a longer view may serve to shock or surprise the viewer. A 'cut-away' from the center of attention to a separate but related action may serve to indicate a subtle relationship or sidelight with the main subject. These are filmic techniques which through their own power can communicate ideas, attitudes, or emotions.

Other filmic elements which tend to communicate (or confuse—depending upon their use) are the size of the image itself in relation to the screen, the use of color (or, in black and white film, shades of gray), the composition within the picture frame, and the movement of both the subject matter and the camera while the scene is being photographed.
Movement.—Since the portrayal of motion is one of the special characteristics of motion picture film, subject and camera movements become important elements for communicating effectively through film.

In addition to the normal movements of subjects being photographed, the camera can add movements of its own.

1. Panning and tilting movements of the camera permit an investigation of the subject or its environment much as the human eyes would in scanning the horizon or searching over an object.

2. Follow-action and trucking movements involve a movement of the camera along with a subject, keeping it in view as the human eyes would in watching a person walk down the street or in following any subject as it moves.

3. Dollying a camera 'in' and 'out' and using 'zoom' lenses are techniques for bringing the camera closer to or further away from the subject as it is being observed in action.

To these basic movements of the camera are being added all of the visible and pertinent movements of the subjects being photographed. The subject movement must be revealed as unbroken and continuous while being viewed from a variety of angles. This requires an overlapping of the action from shot to shot. For instance, the chemist preparing a solution in one view must be completing the same actions when the camera comes in for a closer view in the next shot. Continuity of movement is also important when the subject is moving from one definite location to another. Screen direction must remain constant from one side of the screen to another as the subject is seen from various angles while moving to the next location. Were the screen direction to change abruptly, the subject would appear to be returning to his original position.

These elements of motion must be carefully used, providing subject or camera movement only when it is called for or when necessary to adequately reveal the subject or action and to communicate the intended information.

Sound.—The auditory channels of communication within a motion picture have a dual role. One is that of supporting the visual symbols and providing additional meaning for the visuals; the other role is that of adding distinct meaning or information which is not possible solely through visual images. The motion picture is essentially a visual medium; sound is required as a background accompaniment or as a concurrent explanation or clarification of the visual images. A continual stream of indiscriminate narration, background music, and sound effects can be more detrimental to a motion picture than no sound at all. All too often the narration of a film will continue a point of information which is remotely connected to the visual images being shown. This may be an indication of three things: the film maker is attempting to cover more of the subject than is possible in the time limit imposed; the visualization of the subject is incomplete and narration is being used to overcome such inadequacies; or, in extreme cases, the subject would have been much better suited to some other medium not requiring visualization in motion.

Properly used, the sound track of the motion picture can provide at least five separate channels of auditory communication.

Dialogue or 'lip sync' provides a means of seeing and hearing the person on screen speak. The most obvious advantages of this use of sound would be in the film designed to teach a foreign language. In such instances facial expressions, movement of lips, etc., are prime communicating factors along with the sounds that are simultaneously produced. In places or situations calling for sync dialogue, narration is sometimes used as a crutch. It is much easier and less expensive in film production to shoot silent and then cover the dialogue with some type of 'voice over' narrative (meaning a voice recorded over or in place of what normally would have been dialogue). An evaluation of a film should include the consideration of whether the use of narration in place of the actual dialogue contributes to the overall effectiveness of the film.

In a nondramatic film, narration is most often the method used for carrying the verbal explanation of the content. This is not done necessarily as a production expediency, but because in this type of film the visualizations and not the image of the person guiding the audio portion of the film experience are the most important aspect of the film. The obscure narrator has the ability of preparing the viewer for visualizations to be seen next, pointing out details, calling attention to important factors, explaining related factors which may not be immediately visible, and providing continuity between ideas and visualizations by relating one concept or visual presentation to the next or by referring to previous visualizations.

Background sounds produce that additional factor of realism and can often be as strong as the visual cues; in some cases an auditory cue can recall experiences or impressions which will fill in and complete a rather sketchy visual cue of such an experience.

Music is one of the auditory communication channels of a motion picture which is most often overused or misused. Too often a continual and rather meaningless background of music is carried throughout a film. Music properly used serves as a signal and scene-setter for the introduction and conclusion of a film, as a device for a change in scene or topic, or as a means of providing an emotional or rhythmical background for special situations or scenes in a film.

Special effects in the film sound track cover a wide area of auditory cues which are limited only by the subject matter and by the creative imagination of the film maker in utilizing sound. They include providing sound for certain actions or movements in the film which demand a special sound to complete the image or impression, as well as providing additional meaning or emphasis through the use of creative sound. Such examples might best be found in animated portions of film where sound is created to accompany the actions and movements of creative images and symbols.

Audience (Learner) Acceptance

One of the basic characteristics of film as used in the learning environment is the attention which the moving image and its accompanying sound attract from the learner. This phenomena of the attractive force of a moving image is one of the elements of motion pictures which makes the medium such an effective communicative device.

Not only is the human eye attracted to movement of any type, to the play of light and dark, color and shade, but certain perceptive forces are at work in the viewing of a motion picture film. The strongest of these forces (or one of the most effective for learning) is involvement. The content of a motion picture is perceived by an individual in the same manner that most human experiences are perceived—in relation to past experience and associations. This perceptive process involves a continual structuring of the film's content in relation to the viewer's own experiences or knowledge related to the subject. He becomes personally involved in the film presentation through this attempt at relating events, ideas, or concepts to his own frames of reference or past experience (19).

In their summary of film research, Hoban and Van Ormer identified six factors which contributed to involvement of an audience in a film experience (12).

1. The theory that audience identification with the film content or subject resulted in increased learning through involvement was indicated but not strongly proved beyond the experimental stage.
2. Familiarity with the film setting or type of activity shown can heighten audience involvement leading to personal meanings.
3. A subjective approach (especially in the skill or training film) which shows the subject from the learner's point of view will heighten involvement.
4. The intensity of audience involvement and response can be heightened if some anticipation of situations is possible.
5. Involvement can be in the form of actual audience participation incorporated into the film after some initial learning has taken place.
6. Dramatic structuring of a film has proved to produce effective emotional involvement, but the development of this type of in-

volvement with expository type films has not been demonstrated.

This ability of motion picture film to involve the viewer is not a feature which can be built into every film; nor is it necessarily a strong characteristic of every film. It is a characteristic which the educator who uses films effectively can capitalize upon by proper utilization through preparation of the learner for the film learning situation.

FILM AS AN INSTRUCTIONAL MEDIUM

The motion picture film is capable of contributing significantly to four major areas or types of learning situations. As a communication channel in the learning process, film has the capacity of transmitting factual information, of presenting ideas and building concepts, of developing skills, and of influencing attitudes. For the purpose of investigating such capacities, these four major areas will be discussed separately; however, in actual use these types of learning situations are greatly intermingled.

Transmitting Factual Information

Our perception of the world around us is based upon our previous experiences in life (14). In a similar way, our *knowledge* of the world around us is based upon the factual information which we have assimilated. A command of the basic facts is essential for the learner who is to comprehend such information and put it into an intelligent framework for problem solving, creative thinking, or any other form of intelligent behavior. The imparting of factual information is a basic process of education and the motion picture is one of the instructional tools which has proved to be effective in this process.

Much of the research dealing with the effectiveness of films in the instructional situation have dealt with the ability of these films to impart factual information. In general, according to the results of these studies, factual information is significantly increased when the normal instructional methods are supported by an instructional film. The retention of factual information is significantly increased through the use of films. This increase in gaining and retaining factual information was found to be much greater when the film content dealt with specific items which related closely to the instructional goals. Hoban and Van Ormer, in their summary of research related to the ability of film to impart factual knowledge, concluded that film effectiveness depends on how well content relates to specific instructional objectives (12).

These conclusions on the ability of films to transmit factual information stress the values of supporting regular classroom instruction with appropriate motion picture films, but also place a heavy responsibility upon the film user. The supporting role of the film must be supplementary, not merely repetitious. The film and the on-going instruction in the classroom must be mutually reinforcing in order to obtain the greatest results in the transmission and retention of factual information. Perhaps the greatest responsibility of all for the classroom instructor is to insure that the content of the film is related to a specific instructional objective. This is not an inherent characteristic of the instructional film but is dependent upon the instructor and the ways in which the film is incorporated into the broader instructional plan.

Some characteristics of motion picture film for imparting factual information must be carefully considered for their negative associations or variables. Holaday and Stoddard, in their study of the effects of theatrical films on children and youth, discovered that general information presented incorrectly in motion picture films was often accepted as valid (2). This characteristic should warn the film user to carefully explain any inaccuracies which may appear in a motion picture because of an outdated, incomplete, or out-of-context presentation of factual information. A detailed and extensive study of the effectiveness of the "Why We Fight" film series produced for armed forces trainees during World War II revealed that the amount of factual information obtained from a film varies greatly with the age level, educational background, and intellectual capacity of the viewer (13). To insure the effectiveness of a motion picture film in transmitting factual information, the classroom instructor must correlate the factual content and its presentation in the film with the experiences and capacities of the students.

Presenting Ideas, Building Concepts

Factual knowledge is only one of the steps toward learning. Without an understanding, an application, and a utilization of factual learning the process is incomplete; factual learning remains passive and inert without comprehension and conceptualization. Learning from a motion picture, through even the most factual film presentation, is not (or should not be) a passive experience. The student is seated quietly in a semi-darkened room, may make no verbal response or have no visible interaction with the film, but this does not indicate complete passivity. With proper utilization a great deal of mental activity can be taking place during the film viewing—activity in realizing new relationships, comprehending new applications of learning to different situations, and relating new concepts to previous experiences. As Hoban and Van Ormer stated, research has not shown film learning to be passive, that is, instructional films do not impede the transfer of learning to somewhat different or new situations (12). In fact, their summary of several research studies indicated that the ability of films to develop concepts and contribute to comprehension and understanding of the subject was even greater than their ability to transmit factual information and skills.

One of the basic characteristics of the motion picture is both an advantage and disadvantage in relation to its ability to present conceptual learning experiences. The ability of a film to expand or condense time and to present related ideas or situations into a meaningful sequence of events creates an effective device for comprehension and conceptual learning. This destruction of the time sequence or of the cause and effect cycle may also lead to a distortion of time relationships. In his utilization of such motion picture sequences, the classroom instructor must re-establish the time-line for the student through proper introduction and follow-up explanations.

Demonstrating and Developing Skills

The industrial and armed forces training films developed and used during World War II revealed the effectiveness of motion pictures for training students in perceptual motor skills. The necessity of speeding up the training processes and making this training more effective led to the production and use of motion picture films designed to teach skills which required the coordination of body or hand movements, the manipulation of materials, or the performance of some task through physical movement. Research on the utilization of such films indicated that the medium played a significant part in more effective learning. Learners who viewed such films were able to develop skills more rapidly and the training time involved was shortened in many instances (12).

The subjective approach in teaching skills through motion pictures has been found to be more effective. This subjective approach reveals the actions as though the camera were performing the activity and the learner may closely relate the procedures to the movements he himself must make in performing the skill. In teaching the manipulation of materials (such as assembling and disassembling objects) a subjective view revealing the entire process has been shown to be more effective than showing completed steps of the process in a series of still images. The training film appears to be most effective when it deals with more complex skills requiring prolonged instruction and practice. Student participation in actual practice of the skills either during or immediately after viewing the training film is an essential part of effective learning from such films. It has been found that learning is improved by requiring students to perform certain 'mental' practice during the viewing of a training film. Such mental exercises can be stimulated by asking students to think of the motions, how his muscles feel as he performs the motions, and words and phrases which will later guide his performance (12).

Certain characteristics of the training film indicate that it is effective for small group study and independent learning. Research by Beck and Lumsdaine for the U.S. Army indicated that groups using training films seemed to develop a greater spirit of cooperation and performed better as a team than groups not using films. Those viewing the films required less on-the-job instruction, indicating there was more independent learning within these groups with less dependence on the instructor for help and guidance (12).

Stimulating Motivation; Modifying Attitudes and Opinions

Research on the capabilities of influencing motivation, attitudes, and opinions through the use of motion pictures has generally revealed that the film medium is as effective as other media for these purposes. Films tend to reinforce existing motivations and attitudes which are consistent with the existing social forces and the experiential background of the viewers.

Concrete evidence of the ability of films to stimulate motivation is more significant. One of the most significant examples of motivational forces arising from the use of motion picture films is in the stimulation of reading. In 1929 Knowlton and Tilton reported that students in classes utilizing the Yale "Chronicles of America Photoplays" (7th grade history) showed an increase of 40 per cent in voluntary reading over those students who did not view the films. This increase was in the percentage of pupils reading as well as in the amount read (12). A similar study of the reading habits of students who viewed sound films in their classes was reported by Wittich in 1946. This study revealed over 50 per cent more voluntary reading over classes not utilizing films (23). Another study by Wittich in 1952–53, designed to show the effect of sound films on the reading ability of children in the second grade, showed greater increases in the quality of reading—95 per cent improved in reading, 95 per cent revealed vocabulary improvement, and 70 per cent participated better in class discussions. Wittich concluded that the films produced the desire, interest, and readiness by pupils for more reading and for more comprehensible reading (23).

Instructional film research conducted in the area of attitudinal changes indicates that a motion picture film is more effective for influencing changes on a specific attitude rather than general attitudes (12). The ability of mass communication techniques to change attitudes becomes more effective as the recipient is prepared to accept the change and has received a suggestion to accept it. This suggestion is likely to be more acceptable if it meets existing needs and drives and is in harmony with group norms and loyalties. The suggestion for change through a communications media which is reinforced in a face-to-face communications situation and by related events is more likely to be accepted and carried out (19). All of these factors leading to the successful influence of attitudes and opinions by films indicate that the teacher must provide the suggestion and acceptance for change with classroom discussion and related activities.

SPECIAL TYPES OF FILMS FOR INSTRUCTIONAL PURPOSES

The characteristics and potentials of motion picture film for educational purposes as discussed up to this point pertain in general to all classifications of educational films. Most films utilized in the classroom are made specifically for such instructional purposes. These include the individual instructional films centered around specific subject matter and designed for specific age levels and the filmed courses composed of a series of films containing the major content and presentation of a complete course of instruction. There are other types of films which are not necessarily designed specifically for use in formal classroom situations. These should be considered by the classroom teacher as important resources for instruction. The *principles* of effective utilization remain the same—the *techniques* of utilization will vary according to the type of film, the purposes of the instructor, and the situation in which the film is used.

Skill or Training Films

The film designed specifically for the purpose of providing training in some task or skill, basically an instructional film, requires consideration as a special type of film.

Step-by-step operations can be shown in motion, repeating key actions or slowing down the motion such as in the slow-motion photography of the football player or pole vaulter. Ample opportunity for the student to practice what he has observed in the skill or training film must be built into the film or be incorporated into its utilization in the classroom. It may be that only repeated viewing of the operations supported by student exercises in the skill to be learned will accomplish the training task. The necessity for detailed analysis and study of the motor skills and motions viewed may require that the film be stopped frequently during projection, be viewed over again, or perhaps be held for still projection of single frames. Such needs may be accomplished through independent or small group viewing and study. These utilization techniques are closely related to the capabilities of the 8mm single concept film.

Entertainment Films

Among the thousands of theatrical films which have been produced in Hollywood and produced abroad by foreign film companies are many films which are suitable as supplementary learning resources in the classroom. Such resources may be useful because of the subjects with which they deal, because of the type of presentation or treatment represented by the film, or because they represent an adaptation of famous literary works.

Some of the problems involved with the use of entertainment or feature films in the classroom are related to their length (usually over an hour) and to their availability in 16mm film for classroom projection. Several companies specialize in distributing selected feature films for educational use on 16mm film; one company has developed a program of taking excerpts from feature films or cutting the film to a more suitable length for classroom use.[1]

In addition to the more obvious uses of feature films of literary works (in English for literature studies and in foreign languages for use in language programs), there are the historical treatments of past events and sociological treatments of contemporary problems. The use of any feature film, however, must justify the time and expense involved in obtaining and projecting the film. A lack of close relation to learning outcomes will result in little more than a pleasant break from classroom routines to see a film for entertainment purposes.

Documentary Films

The term documentary film is often confused with travelogue. The travelogue is one type of documentary film but is not necessarily representative of the broad category of films falling under the classification of documentaries. The most common definition of a documentary film is one which represents it as an *approach* to subjects of social significance; its theme is one of contemporary thought and activities dealing with society in its present state (18). John Grierson, leader of the documentary film movement in England, stated that the documentary purpose was an educational purpose and was developed as a movement to bring alive the world about us and to bridge the gap between the citizen and his community (11).

The documentary film, under such definitions, becomes an asset to the

---

[1] Teaching Film Custodians distributes abbreviated versions of feature films. Among other major companies distributing full-length feature films in 16mm are Brandon Films, Films Incorporated (affiliated with Encyclopaedia Britannica), and Contemporary Films. Many smaller distributing companies provide similar services, often specializing in certain types of feature films.

classroom for a study of all types of social situations and of other countries and other peoples. Although these definitions cover a broad area, the quantity and quality of resources are even broader. The instructor using documentary films for classroom use must select wisely from such sources as governmental agencies, outlets for television news documentaries, educational organizations, and business and industrial companies. In many instances propaganda is considered an element of the documentary. Consequently, the original purpose of the films must be taken into account and the content must be carefully evaluated and related to the learning objectives at hand.

Sponsored Films

Large business and industrial firms, as part of their public relations programs, sponsor the production of films generally with the purpose of informing the public about the company or its products. These films are then distributed free of charge.

Many of these sponsored films serve as excellent resources for classroom use. The blatant commercials once common are not as prevalent today. Companies have discovered that a straight-forward exposition of their company or product will find a more willing and less suspicious audience. In fact, many companies have produced public service films whose subject is not directly related to their products.

The instructor's prime responsibility in selecting and utilizing sponsored films is in making sure that the film content is related to the learning needs of the students and does not present a biased approach or persuasion to patronize one product or company. With such criteria in mind, sponsored films can bring into the classroom knowledge of the community and its business enterprises, insight into the function of large industrial firms and their products, and can create an awareness of the wide range and place of free enterprise in our economy.

Single Concept Films

In 1962 the first major innovation in the projection of educational films since the introduction of the 16mm sound film was introduced by the Technicolor Corporation in Great Britain. This innovation was a three to four minute silent presentation on 8mm film, completely enclosed in a small and relatively inexpensive automatic projector which required no threading and would show the film continuously in a well lighted room with rear projection screens. This innovation with 8mm silent film was termed the single concept film. The brief three or four minute viewing, covering a single idea, could be repeated as many times as was necessary for study and comprehension. Within three years over 1,800 single concept titles had been produced by major film companies and were being used in business, in industry, and in the classroom (10).

A few advantages of the single concept film are:

1. The presentations are completely teacher- or student-controlled. Since the films are silent, the verbal commentary is the responsibility of the user, permitting a great deal of flexibility in their use.
2. The simplicity of operation and the content of the single concept films make them ideally suited for small group instruction or independent learning.
3. With a minimum of skill and expense, teachers may produce their own single concept films by photographing the content on 8mm film, editing the processed film, and sending it to the Technicolor Corporation for insertion into the plastic cartridge.

The uses of the 8mm single concept film are limited only by the instructor's imagination and his ability to either obtain suitable concept films or produce his own. Some of the basic areas of utilization are:

1. Observation of demonstrations which visualize processes involving movement (such as the flow of blood through the heart, chemical reactions, movement of biological specimens).
2. Instruction in the development of particular skills (such as manipulating tools or equipment).
3. Visualization of situations or problems which require an active verbal response from the student.

An evaluation of any single concept film should be made with the realization that the essential contribution of this technique is that of visualizing motion, and that the information being presented must not be complex but should present a central idea—a single concept.

The use of 8mm film in education is not limited to the silent single concept film. Programs for incorporating this narrow gauge film into other areas of educational use are in process. However, these applications are more significant to the availability and methods of utilization of educational film than they are to the content of films. The development of 8mm sound films and 8mm sound cartridge projectors opens up new avenues for the application of all the uses described for the 16mm sound film in education and may serve as a direction for motion pictures in the classroom of the future.

FILM IN THE CLASSROOM OF THE FUTURE

To meet the problems of efficient learning in the midst of an information explosion as well as an enrollment explosion, educators are investigating and experimenting with media systems, multimedia packages, independent student-guided learning, computer controlled learning situations, media-oriented study carrels, and dial-access information retrieval systems. In all of these situations the motion picture plays an integral part in the expansion of learning facilities and the improvement of learning efficiency.

Independent Study and Small Group Instruction

The complex nature of 16mm projection equipment and the cost of films and equipment have been the greatest limitations toward the use of motion picture films as student-guided study materials for self-learning. The availability of machines and films, the necessity of training time for proper operation, and the possibilities of film damage have been some of the problems which have in the past made it rather impractical to incorporate motion picture films into a program of independent study. With the development of the 8mm single concept cartridge film, the 8mm sound cartridge film (capable of 30 minutes showing), and retrieval systems capable of channeling film projection into study carrels, these problems are being solved. As part of an automated or semi-automated program of instruction, they can provide key visualizations in motion which can be combined with audio tapes, slides and written instructions. By following directions and operating the proper switches in the study carrel students activate the projection and sound devices at the proper time.

Super 8mm and 8mm Sound

Although 8mm motion picture film has been in use since 1932, its application to educational uses had been limited by the small image, considered rather inferior for successful projection in a large classroom, and its usefulness was reduced by the lack of sound. However, film stock and photographic processes have improved to the point where 8mm can be compared to the quality of 16mm a short time ago (6). The development of magnetic (and later optical) sound tracks has eliminated the other deficiency of 8mm film.

Eastman Kodak further improved the 8mm image when it released a redesigned format called Super 8 in 1965. Using the same width of film stock, the picture area of the 8mm frame was enlarged 50 per cent by reducing the size of sprocket holes and the width of lines between picture frames. Although Super 8 introduced the problem of not being able to photograph or project such film on existing 8mm equipment, the improved quality of the image opened up wider fields for 8mm film in education. With sound and with an image suitable for larger classrooms, 8mm film has been introduced as the paperback of the educational film (8). The reasoning behind such statements relies not only on the availability of more simplified methods of projection (such as cartridges), but upon the possible savings in production costs and consequently the reduced cost of film prints. Through an interrelated chain of events—slightly reduced production costs, reduced projection costs for 8mm, a greater market for less expensive classroom films, a decentralization of film libraries into schools and classrooms, and the development of mass production techniques to fulfill increased demands for films—the cost of the classroom film could be dramatically reduced (7).

Media Packages

Research into the classroom use of motion picture film has shown repeatedly that when film is used in conjunction with other types of instructional materials and learning devices, the amount of learning and the retention of learning is greatly increased. Such advantages can be capitalized upon through the distribution of film as part of a 'media package' containing related materials in the form of filmstrips, models or specimens, audio recordings, flat pictures, slides, transparencies, etc. These materials would be designed to provide the content of a subject lesson where each particular instructional device could do the best job of instruction.

Through the use of media packages the teacher does not take a backseat and merely observe while the elements of the package do her work. The package serves as a resource, and the essential job of the classroom instructor in selection, preparation, and guidance of the learning experience is still of prime importance.

Automation and Information Retrieval

The motion picture film plays an important role in automated systems in providing instructional materials which require the additional communicative values of motion. Examples of the wide range of application are:

1. Use of 8mm cartridge sound motion pictures in conjunction with other study materials by students in individual study carrels.
2. Viewing one of several multiple screen projections through a glass window of a study carrel while carrying on related study activities independently with other instructional materials such as prerecorded tapes, study guides, programed materials.
3. Viewing films transmitted simultaneously to individual carrels through multiple television channels from central transmission facilities where cartridge films are 'called up' by number or scheduled at specific times for projection into the television system (including the use of color television).
4. Computer tie-in with viewing screens, TV and audio transmission

systems, and a student response system, in which basic information is provided through audio and visual materials. (As such systems become more and more automated and electronically controlled, the motion picture film in the photographic form in which we now know it may disappear in favor of electronic video tape storage and playback. However, the motion picture film will remain as an important intermediary step and resource for the production of electronic tapes.) The content of prime network television programing has been estimated to be from 70 to 80 per cent on—or originating from—motion picture film.

5. The transmission of audio and visual materials to remote locations via telephone lines. (This has been in use for audio materials and is possible for still pictures through the use of slow-scan television transmission over standard single-circuit telephone lines (20). The development of refined television transmission for phono-vision or video-phone systems where the person is seen and heard simultaneously will open up the possibilities of transmitting motion picture images to remote areas via telephone lines).

Highly automated systems of access to visual materials open up a wide range of possibilities for both classroom and individual student use of motion picture resources.

> The adaptability of the film medium to systems and to electronic transmission has increased the volume of the product, extended the scope of its screen, the nature of its audience, and the uses to which it may be put (21).

Although transmission techniques may be accomplished through electronic transmission, the *principles* of utilization and of original production will remain the same as those previously established for motion pictures as an effective medium for educational purposes.

SUMMARY

Motion picture films have been utilized in the classroom and have been the subject of research and experimentation for their contributions to learning for over 50 years. This research has shown that films contribute significantly to learning, improve the retention of that learning, and stimulate student motivation towards further learning. The classroom instructor plays an important part in effective learning through films by coordinating their use with other instructional materials and techniques and by providing the leadership necessary in planning and guiding the film learning experience.

A motion picture film can accomplish several tasks in the classroom which cannot be performed as easily or as effectively with any other type of instructional material. In addition to providing a reproduction of movement and accompanying sound, film has an inherent ability to attract and hold student attention and can serve as a basis for common experiences in the classroom. The historical past and the predictions of the future can be realistically re-created in the classroom through motion pictures. Some special characteristics of motion picture film which are unique to the medium and serve as unusual techniques for learning are slow motion and time lapse photography for slowing down or speeding up motion, X-ray and micrography to show minute or 'invisible' objects in motion, and animation to create graphic materials in motion.

In the production of a motion picture film designed for instructional situations many basic elements may be selected and manipulated to increase the communicative effectiveness of the film. In his initial planning with educational specialists, the film maker lays the groundwork for the purposes and methods through which he will select or create the correct visuals, sound, and movement to reach the final goal—the utilization of all communicative elements of motion picture film to reach, stimulate, and produce the desired effect upon the audience.

As an instructional medium, film is capable of performing effectively in the four major areas of transmitting factual information; presenting ideas and building conceptual understandings; demonstrating and developing manipulative or manual skills; and stimulating motivation towards learning or modifying attitudes and opinions. Films which are suitable for performing these functions are available from many sources and represent several different basic types of motion pictures. The most common resources are among the instructional films designed and produced specifically for classroom use in specified subject areas and for definite age groups or levels of ability. Filmed courses provide the complete instructional package in a series of films designed to provide most of the learning experiences for an entire course of instruction through the 'film studio teacher.' Skill or training films are similar to instructional films in their design for specific learning tasks, but offer resources for teaching manipulative skills. Among the vast number of entertainment films, documentary films, and commercially sponsored films are many excellent resources for the classroom. The silent 8mm single concept film in cartridge form for automatic projection offers a more recent film resource ideally suited for small group and independent learning.

As film resources expand and as the technology for utilizing films in the instructional situation develops, new and wider applications will be found for the advantages which motion pictures can provide as a communicating force for education. The single-concept film and other developments in 8mm film will produce a more flexible, less expensive, and more prolific utilization of motion pictures in the classroom. Rapid and continuing developments in the simplicity and efficiency of projection facilities will be coupled with the complex integration of the film medium into instructional systems utilizing media packages and a vast array of automated and programed instructional facilities. These facilities will serve as basic learning references for the student, permitting the teacher to spend her efforts more efficiently in channeling, guiding, and stimulating efficient learning which leads to the utilization of facts and concepts and the development of creative thought and critical thinking.

BIBLIOGRAPHY

1. Brown, James W., Lewis, Richard B. and Harcleroad, Fred F. *A-V Instruction: Materials and Methods.* 2d ed. New York: McGraw-Hill, 1964.
2. Charters, W. W. *Motion Pictures and Youth.* New York: Macmillan and Company, 1933.
3. Dale, Edgar. *Audio-Visual Methods in Teaching.* Rev. ed. New York: Dryden Press, Inc., 1954.
4. Erickson, Carlton, W. H., *Fundamentals of Teaching with Audio-visual Technology.* New York: Macmillan Co., 1965.
5. Finn, James D., Perrin, Donald G. and Campion, Lee E. *Studies in the Growth of Instructional Technology, 1: Audio-Visual Instrumentation for Instruction in the Public Schools.* Occasional Paper No. 6 of the Technological Development Project. Washington, D. C.: Department of Audiovisual Instruction, National Education Association, 1962.
6. Finn, James D., and Rosengren, Joan, "8mm sound film – a full-dress conference at TC," *Audiovisual Instruction,* 7:90–93, February, 1962.
7. Forsdale, Louis. "An educator looks at 8mm sound film," *Journal of the Society of Motion Picture and Television Engineers,* 70:593–595, August, 1961.
8. Forsdale, Louis, "8mm motion pictures in education: Incipient innovation," In Matthew B. Miles, (ed.). *Innovation in Education.* New York: Teachers College, Columbia University, 1964, pp. 203–229.
9. *Gateway to Learning.* Publication prepared by the Audio-Visual Commission on Public Information, New York (n.d.).
10. Happé, L. B. "The silent educational single-concept film," *Journal of the University Film Producers Association,* 17:3–7, 1965.
11. Hardy, Forsyth (ed.). *Grierson on Documentary.* New York: Harcourt, Brace and Company, 1947.
12. Hoban, Charles F., Jr., and Van Ormer, Edward B. *Instructional Film Research 1918–1950 (Rapid Mass Learning).* Technical Report No. SDC 269-7-19, NAVEXOS P-944 by the Instructional Film Research Program at the Pennsylvania State College. Port Washington, L. I., N. Y.: Special Devices Center, 1950.
13. Hovland, C. I., Lumsdaine, A. A., and Sheffield, F. D. *Experiments on Mass Communication.* Princeton, N. J.: Princeton Univ. Press, 1949.
14. Krech, David, and Crutchfield, Richard S., "Perceiving the world," Wilbur Schramm, (ed.), *The Process and Effects of Mass Communication.* Urbana, Illinois: Univ. of Illinois Press, 1955, pp. 116–137.
15. Lirones, Daniel S. (comp.). *Sales Service Policies of Educational Film Pro-*

ducers: A Handbook for the Film Buyer. New York: Educational Film Library Association, Inc., (n. d.).

16. Rose, Nicholas, and Van Horn, Charles. "Theory and application of pre-production testing," *Audio Visual Communication Review*, 4:21–30, Winter, 1956.

17. Sanderson, Richard A. "An historical study of the development of American motion picture content and techniques prior to 1904." Unpublished doctoral dissertation, Univ. of Southern California, Los Angeles, California, 1961.

18. Sanderson, Richard A. "An investigation into the elements of documentary film and their use in the production of the television film series, 'Dragnet'." Unpublished master's thesis, Univ. of Southern California, Los Angeles, California, 1958.

19. Schramm, Wilbur (ed.). *The Process and Effects of Mass Communication.* Urbana, Illinois; Univ. of Illinois Press, 1955.

20. Stewart, Don (ed.). "Dial-access information retrieval systems for education," *Articulated Instructional Media Program Newsletter*, Vol. 11, No. 3, Univ. of Wisconsin, September, 1965.

21. Wagner, Robert W. "The educational film in transition," *Audiovisual Instruction*, 9:174, March, 1964.

22. Weisgerber, Robert A. "The compleat communicator," *Improving College and University Teaching*, pp. 122–124, Spring, 1967.

23. Wittich, Walter Arno, and Schuller, Charles Francis. *Audio-Visual Materials: Their Nature and Use.* 3d ed. New York: Harper and Brothers, 1962.

---

Chapter 17

*In view of the momentum already generated toward adoption
of instructional television, what is the nature of the
deterrents yet to be surmounted?*

What are the advantages and limitations of instructional television?

*What are the essential differences between closed-circuit
and open-circuit, and between classroom and studio television?*

*In what instances is television best considered as a supplement to
teaching and when is it best considered as basic to teaching?*

INSTRUCTIONAL TELEVISION
IN PERSPECTIVE

ROBERT M. DIAMOND, Director,
Instructional Resources Center
State University College, Fredonia, N.Y.

Within the next decade, the television set will become a standard
fixture in most classrooms. The question is no longer *if* television will
be used, but *how*. What is the role of television in providing for our
students the most effective and efficient educational program possible?
The uses that teachers and administrations have found for the medium
are as varied as the problems that exist and often change from district
to district, school to school, and course to course. While the early concept of a school teaching an entire curriculum by television has generally
been abandoned, it can be expected that, in time, each student will
receive *some* of his instruction utilizing the medium in one form or
another. In this chapter an attempt will be made to put instructional
television into perspective and, in the process, highlight some of the
applications now found in the classroom.

TELEVISION IN THE CLASSROOM

Television is, after all, nothing more than a process of transmitting
sound and pictures. Its successes and failures have been those of the

administrators, teachers, production personnel, and technicians who utilized it rather than of the medium itself. When the application was planned with care, it usually proved effective. When preparation of lessons was rushed, when emphasis was placed on production aspects at the expense of instructional planning, and when the basic purpose was saving money rather than improving instruction, the project usually failed, quite often with much notoriety and fanfare. Thus, in effect, it is the insight of the educators, both teachers and administrators, who utilize television that will determine the role television will play and the ultimate effectiveness of the medium within our classrooms.

Television by its very nature is an effective teaching tool because it can bring a new dimension into the classroom. With television we find:

1. *Maximum use of resources:* Specialists and demonstrations normally unavailable to most classroom teachers now become available. Every teacher, in districts large and small, rich or poor, has the services of outstanding scientists, artists, musicians, politicians, teachers, etc. Television also provides for maximum use of local school district and community resources, and, when combined with some form of team teaching, may allow for more effective use of existing facilities.

2. *Economic feasibility:* Television production, when done well, is expensive. An average half-hour lesson may require over 100 man hours of preparation and the services of close to a dozen highly skilled individuals. Under the normal teaching procedure, the average teacher is limited in both time and resources. Television teachers are, or should be, given enough planning time and have the services of subject matter specialists, graphic artists, etc. to provide optimum instruction. While this type of support and planning would be too expensive for use within a single classroom, when a lesson is utilized in hundreds or even thousands of classrooms the cost per student becomes nominal.

3. *Wide applications in both subject and use:* Once television is available, educators are finding that it has not only a wide variety of applications in many subjects but administrative uses as well. Several of these—orientation programs, test administration, and in-service training—will be discussed later.

4. *Advantages of taping and editing:* With the use of the video tape recording technique, resources can be recorded when they are available for later utilization. The potential of immediate playback is ideal for evaluation and instruction in the fields of teaching, public speaking, and physical education. Editing of video tape is relatively simple and offers the educator the ability to form-fit the material to his specific needs. This process also permits a relatively

inexpensive recording and editing process when compared with standard filming techniques.

5. *Image magnification:* In its simplest form, television can serve as an image magnifier and transmitter. Uncomplicated equipment which is relatively inexpensive and easy to operate is now being utilized in many courses and, in time, may become a standard piece of equipment in laboratories where it will serve more as an additional piece of audiovisual equipment than as a tool unto itself.

6. *Utilization of all the other instructional media:* Of all the technological teaching tools now available, only television utilizes the others—films, slides, tapes, transparencies, etc. Thus, in effect, television is a technique through which many other instructional materials may achieve their own most effective utilization. School systems are finding that a single copy of a film can be seen in hundreds of classrooms, solving the problem of seasonal demands when during a single week every teacher requests the same film. This, of course, raises the problem of copyright, which is rapidly becoming an extremely complex and important consideration.

7. *Maximum availability:* Once a receiver is available, a simple turning of a switch will bring the lesson into the classroom. Lighting is rarely a problem and additional equipment is not required.

LIMITATIONS

In any discussion of television requiring a studio production there are limitations that must be considered. As mentioned previously, instructional television, properly produced, takes talent, time, and money. Often this expense can be distributed over a large number of students; in many instances, however, the number of students involved is extremely limited and thus it may be too expensive and administratively unsound for a district or university to operate its own production unit. In many instances it makes far more sense to provide the classroom teachers with maximum resources than to embark on an extensive television project (see Table 1).

A major problem has been the large number of school districts that have rushed into using television without studying possible alternatives, been negligent in providing necessary production support, or been negligent in providing television teachers with enough time to prepare superior presentations and study guides to be used by the classroom teacher. The administrative rush that took place several years ago to get on the television bandwagon actually has been a major handicap to the development of effective uses of the medium. If television is

Table 1.   Criteria for Studio Television.

Use if:

Presentation is outstanding, difficult to repeat, or otherwise un-available.

or

Reception is required in more than one room simultaneously with enough students involved to prove financially practical *but* only for that aspect of our teaching that *belongs* in the one-way trans-mission situation.

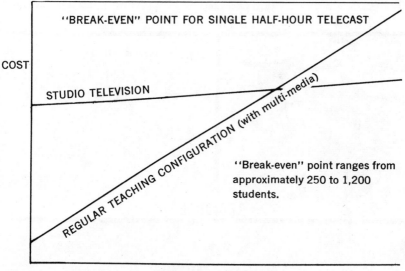

"BREAK-EVEN" POINT FOR SINGLE HALF-HOUR TELECAST

COST

STUDIO TELEVISION

REGULAR TEACHING CONFIGURATION (with multi-media)

"Break-even" point ranges from approximately 250 to 1,200 students.

NUMBER OF STUDENTS

used, it must be used properly. It reaches too many students and is too expensive to be used poorly.

APPLICATIONS

In any discussion of television, several terms should be clearly defined. The television picture can be transmitted into the classroom by either open- or closed-circuit or by a combination of the two. With *open-circuit television* the signal is sent out from a transmitter over a general area and may be received by any set tuned to that particular frequency. An open-circuit system may cover a local area, a larger region by use of an airplane or translator station, or several countries by use of a translator (see Illustration 1).

In *closed-circuit television*, the signal is transmitted from the cameras

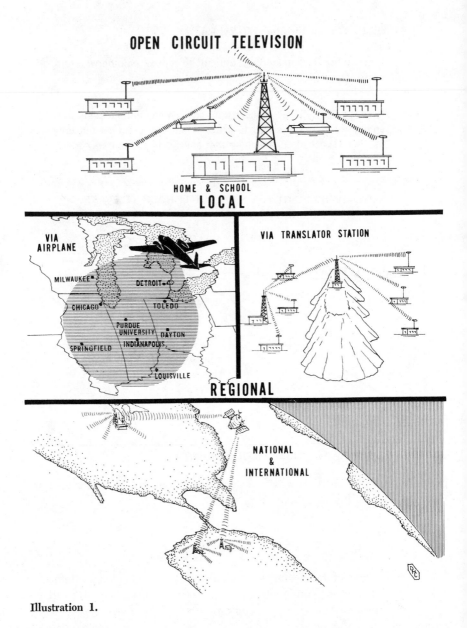

Illustration 1.

to the receivers by a cable system or by a microwave link. With a closed-circuit installation, the signal can only be seen on those receivers directly included in the system (see Illustration 2).

A *microwave link* is a technique where the audio and video signals are sent from transmitter to receiver in a directional line-of-sight beam.

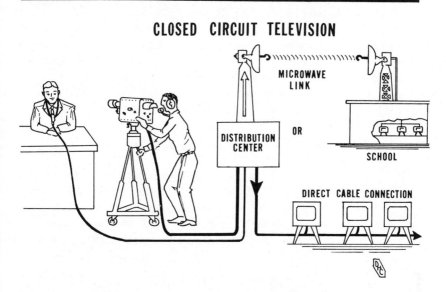

CLOSED CIRCUIT TELEVISION

Illustration 2.

The vast majority of educational television stations transmit via open-circuit television. Quite often, in a particular school where the signal being received is weak, a single large antenna will be constructed with the individual rooms then being connected directly to this antenna by cable.

Most independent school or district operations are of the closed-circuit variety with a recent growth in the open-circuit use of the specially licensed, low power 2500-megacycle band. Both these techniques can permit more than one signal to be transmitted at a time and are usually less expensive and far more flexible than the standard broadcasting station.

Recently independent stations have begun combining with regional and state educational television networks, both open- and closed-circuit. This type of linkage has provided each of the member stations with a far wider choice of programing than would otherwise be possible. As will be noted later, one of the best educational bargains now available to many schools is the use of regional educational stations where, for a few dollars per student per year, a wide variety of excellently produced programs are available.

As more and more series are produced for national distribution, it must be remembered that the wider the use of a lesson the less chance there is for form fitting it to the needs of a specific district. Extensive use of a television series requires agreement upon content and sequence. If individual teachers or districts do not agree upon content, level, or sequence, the use of television becomes questionable. It is not surprising, therefore, that maximum use of educational stations has been on the elementary level where there is more agreement upon objectives and greater freedom in scheduling. To provide maximum flexibility, many districts, when funds are available, are planning to combine the use of an educational station with some locally produced materials.

SINGLE-ROOM TELEVISION

Often overlooked in any discussion of instructional television is what may be called single-room television. In this approach, the simplest type of closed-circuit system, a television camera, operated by the instructor, is connected directly to one or more receivers within the same room (see Illustration 3). Unlike the standard studio camera

SINGLE-ROOM TELEVISION

CAMERA DIRECTLY CONNECTED TO ONE OR MORE RECEIVERS - NO AUDIO

Illustration 3.

which usually requires additional equipment for operation, the small, less-than-20-pounds camera is self-contained, with all the operating and transmitting equipment built into the camera housing.

To provide maximum flexibility, a zoom lens is often used. While more expensive than a combination of standard lenses, the zoom permits an instructor to go from long-shot to close-up with a minimum of effort. This approach brings to the classroom and lecture hall an exciting new teaching tool and, at the same time, is relatively inexpensive and extremely easy to operate. A complete installation including camera, lens, stand, and TV receivers usually costs less than $1,500. In most instances the entire package of equipment can be set up and taken down by one person in less than 10 minutes.

Single-room television has one basic advantage; it allows the image magnification advantages of television to be used within the student-teacher interaction situation. It has allowed new content to be included in courses and standard areas to be taught more effectively and efficiently. Of all the uses of television, this approach has also had the least amount of teacher resentment and resistance. Many administrators have found this approach an excellent way of introducing a faculty to television.

Science

In science the single-room television camera is being widely used in both laboratories and large lecture halls. Its ability to enlarge a three-dimensional object makes it a natural tool for many science demonstrations. While the number of receivers required may vary from two or three in a laboratory to six or eight in a large lecture hall, the operation remains basically the same.

In high schools, instructors have conducted a dissection with students working along, step-by-step. Result—less time required, more effective learning. For many laboratory periods the time needed to complete a unit has been reduced by 50 per cent or more by eliminating the need for repeated demonstrations. Of particular importance is the ability of the teacher to answer any question a student may ask by utilizing his own specimen which the student can clearly see on the television screen. Demonstrations once omitted because of the inability of students to see are, for the first time, being included.

At various colleges and universities, the unit is a permanent piece of equipment on the demonstration table and used not only with three-dimensional objects but as an overhead and an opaque projector.

In addition, the vidicon-tube of the camera can be focused on a microscope to serve as an excellent microprojector. In most cases, to provide maximum flexibility and effectiveness, the television unit is used in conjunction with overhead, slide, and motion picture projectors.

Business Education

In several experiments, teachers have found that typing and general office machine operation can be effectively taught by using the single-room television camera. Kelley (3) in a detailed description of a project in the teaching of typing reported:

> From the experiences this writer has had with the use of television in the typewriting classroom, he has come to the conclusion that three basic advantages exist over the traditional approach in teaching this skill. First,

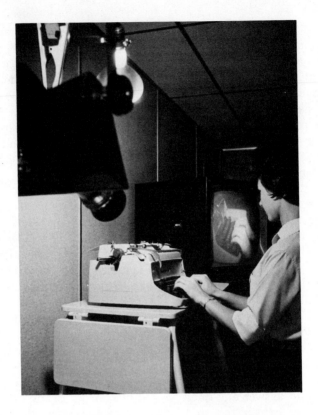

Figure 1.

valuable time is saved in the high school or college typewriting classroom. Second, thest techniques can make it possible for large numbers to be taught typewriting at the same time. The number of students in this type of class is limited only by the size of the room and the number of typewriters. Third, with the use of television it is possible for the instructor to become an improved teacher with students performing better, and, as mentioned above, this improvement can be reached under reduced instructor time.[1]

In this project the equipment was used in the teaching of speed development, letter placement, office forms, stroking, and in correcting poor techniques. By focusing the camera on the instructor's keyboard and having students imitate the stroking, the entire keyboard was mastered in 50 minutes.

The time required to cover letter placement, manuscript typing, and office forms was reduced by over 50 per cent, with a far greater

[1] From *A Guide to Instructional Television* by R. M. Diamond (editor). Copyright © 1964, McGraw-Hill Book Co. Used by permission of McGraw-Hill Book Co.

achievement in speed development. This same technique has been widely used in teaching computer and other basic machine operations.

Other Subjects

The single-room television camera is an excellent tool for demonstration in many other subjects, including drawing procedures, jewelry design, and finger movements on a string instrument within a music course. It has been used in shop instruction to demonstrate tool handling. One photography teacher had his students set up a picture with lighting, etc., in front of the camera, utilizing the receiver as a viewer. Once the student was pleased with his composition, the instructor and class could evaluate, discuss, and make immediate adjustments. In psychology and testing, the unit has been used to demonstrate specific tests and has proven particularly effective for those instruments where manipulation of objects or materials is involved.

Limitations

The self-contained television camera has certain limitations. If one of the standard models is purchased ($600–$800 of the total $1,500 expenditure), it will not have the quality of the normal studio camera. In some demonstrations, particularly those in anatomy, high quality resolution is often required, necessitating the purchase of a camera in the $1,200–$1,500 range. Also, when high quality resolution is required, the standard home TV receiver usually has to be replaced by a video monitor of a type found in a television control room. This receiver will cost approximately $500 compared to $150 (the school price for a standard 23″ receiver). In addition, the zoom lens of the inexpensive camera does not have the quality of a standard lens. In short, the $1,500 expenditure for the complete installation will usually be sufficient for most applications, but when extra high quality image reproduction is required, more expensive equipment will probably be needed. Some instructors have found that when an extremely small area is to be seen or when movement is necessary, a student assistant is required to help with focusing.

The basic unit has neither audio nor color and thus is limited in some demonstrations. In several areas of anatomy and chemistry, color is extremely important. To solve the problem of sound transmission, several schools have combined the single-room TV unit with a standard PA system, allowing students to see a dangerous experiment conducted at a safe distance in an adjoining room. In some instances, a demonstration is so complex that it must be carried out in a studio where maximum production is possible. However, for a simple magnifier of three-dimensional objects within a student-teacher interaction situation, the single-room television camera is ideal.

STUDIO TELEVISION

The major problem facing education today is logistics. More information must be taught to more students by relatively fewer teachers. The elementary teacher often finds she must teach entirely new content in math and science and in many cases new subjects—geography, one or even two foreign languages, etc. At the junior and senior high school level, content once taught in college now forms the basic part of many courses. Colleges and universities are finding that freshman class sections of several hundred are rapidly becoming the rule rather than the exception.

At the college level a shortage of skilled faculty is also becoming acute. It has been estimated that from 1965 to 1980 college enrollment will increase from 5.2 million to 10 million. (5) During this period the doctoral output of our graduate schools will double from approximately 14,500 to 29,000, but, of this number, less than half will go into teaching, and a majority of these, with the present emphasis on research, will not teach a full academic load. One study conducted by Harold Orlans of the Brookings Institution reported that from 1930 to 1960 the average teaching load of faculty lowered from approximately 16 to 12 hours. The teaching load in 'eminent' universities is even lower, 6 hours per week in the science areas and 8.3 in the humanities. Clark Kerr, former president of the University of California, has stated that he could use all the Ph.D.s coming out of the nation's colleges and universities for the next ten years. Results of a study by John Jamrich at Michigan State University indicated that, just to maintain their present ratios, the states of Illinois, Ohio, and Michigan would require nearly 70 per cent of all Ph.D.s going into teaching.

Television is a mass media and by its very nature is ideally suited to cope with this problem. Thus we find that the most dynamic uses of instructional television have been to:

1. Provide better utilization of existing resources.
2. Provide the assistance of subject matter specialists and outstanding demonstrations, making available new and improved resources.
3. Reduce duplicate effort on the part of teachers and increase the amount of time a teacher can spend with individuals or small groups of students.
4. Improve space utilization.

In reviewing the present applications of studio television within our educational program, we find that the uses tend to fall into several major categories.

Television as a Supplementary Teaching Aid. (*In this type of use the television lessons are scheduled once or twice a week on a regular basis to provide a basic resource for the classroom teacher.*) Supplementary programs might be classified as a resource to regular courses of instruction. Most of the series designed for the elementary classroom in the area of science are of this nature. While the bulk of the total teaching responsibility still lies with the classroom teacher, television is providing demonstrations and experiments that would otherwise be omitted or difficult to produce, as well as the services of subject matter specialists.

To facilitate effective utilization, many of these series have additional supplementary materials available. The "Patterns in Arithmetic" series produced by the University of Wisconsin includes two classroom presentations and one teacher orientation per week plus extensive teacher's guides and student's workbooks. Many of these series have been produced with the support of governmental agencies and private sponsors. As a result, students in every state of the union are receiving instruction by some of the most effective teacher-scholars that this country has to offer. In each case the television teacher is supported by a production staff and subject matter specialists not available to the classroom teacher.

A rather interesting use of television in social studies is the several "News Time" series for different grade levels produced by WMHT in Schenectady. Utilizing available network news clips provided by a local commercial station, three different news series, geared to specific grade levels and curriculums, are presented regularly in hundreds of classrooms.

Direct Teaching by Television. (*The basic instructional program is provided by television with the classroom teacher performing the vital introductory, drill, and follow-up functions.*) Series of this type are most common in those areas where we find many classroom teachers having little specialized training. For example, it has been estimated that the average elementary teacher is responsible for over 15 different subject areas. Television has been successful in filling this gap in such areas as foreign language, art, and music instruction. In South Carolina, a statewide closed-circuit operation has made available to the majority of high schools a high calibre college preparatory curriculum.

In 1962, the Anaheim District in California hoped to implement a major conversational Spanish program. Over 20 subject matter specialists were required, and yet, after an extensive recruiting campaign, only three qualified individuals were found. By the use of television it became possible to implement a program that has proven to be extremely effective on both the in-class and in-service levels with these three teachers, while, at the same time, actually providing the program at a cost well below the figure required if the standard format had been possible. In the same district, with television, a single music specialist was able to provide one hour of music instruction per week to over 8,200 students.

Total Teaching by Television. *(The primary instructional program is presented on television with little or no direct contact with the student.)* Series of this type are predominantly found in two areas: where teachers with the required skills are not available, and in the field of adult or continuing education. In many rural areas small schools have been unable to provide high quality courses for the more able student. By using television in conjunction with a wide range of related textbooks and programed materials, thousands of students in remote areas are, for the first time, receiving advanced courses in science and mathematics. The range of adult and continuing education programs now available is as broad as one could imagine. There are effective reading and writing programs for the illiterate, basic skill training for the dropout, and advanced courses for the professional. The South Carolina Television Network has provided series for physicians, nurses, pharmacists, dentists, lawyers, and insurance agents, to name just a few. In Chicago, students have been able to obtain a junior college degree via that city's extensive television college program. The use of associated study guides and programed sequences is proving to be a key supplement to series of this type and should, whenever possible, be built into such series.

Television as Enrichment. *(These programs use outstanding local or national resources which are televised on a flexible schedule.)* Programs interviewing foreign visitors, scientists, policemen, musicians, artists, politicians, businessmen, etc. are available on almost every station and in every closed-circuit project. During election campaigns, student interviews of politicians are commonplace. Using television, many school districts are, for the first time, making effective use of local resources. When possible, many of these presentations are taped and stored for use when they more closely fit the curriculum. Television is rapidly replacing radio in bringing news as it happens to the classroom.

Television as an Administrative Tool. *(Television has uses not related directly to the in-class instructional program.)* Often overlooked is the fact that once television is available it can have many administrative applications.

Orientation: At the beginning of the school year, Joe Hall, superintendent of the Dade County, Florida, Public Schools, speaks directly to 8,000 teachers over the local ITV station. Anaheim used the district's CCTV operation to improve staff communications. Each Wednesday at noon, news of the district activities, major events, and board of education activities were discussed during the special 'staff chats' program. Most districts utilizing open circuit have found the medium to be an excellent means for building community relations and for contacting parents. WTHS in Miami telecasts a weekly "This is Your School" program designed specifically for the public. Many schools and colleges use television as a major tool during the orientation period. One large junior-senior high school televised its library orientation from the library itself to all its English classes and completed the orientation program in less than two days; a month was required previously.

In Hagerstown, Maryland an effective series of guidance programs for seniors is offered. Representatives of the various colleges present an overview of their schools for the college bound student. As a result a single representative can reach hundreds of students simultaneously. It has been found that by this process students are able to identify, for application, those colleges that will most closely fit their needs, reducing substantially the number of students who apply to institutions that either do not meet their requirements or where they have little chance of acceptance. This series also presents scholarship information and other data of interest to the graduating class, plus other programs designed for students interested in various careers and technical training programs.

In-Service Education: Another important administrative application is using television for in-service education to orient new teachers to district policies and practices and to introduce new materials and techniques on a district-wide basis. With the constant change in faculty, the continuing developments in curriculum and the availability of new teaching tools and techniques, school districts are faced with a growing problem of in-service education. Both funds and consultants are limited. Many districts have found that even when the necessary financial support was available they were unable to conduct an effective and efficient program of in-service education simply because there were not enough experts available to direct the required number of workshops. Even when available consultants are rarely able to effectively reach more than a small percentage of the total teachers within a district.

The need for in-service education has been further increased by the dynamic and immediate changes possible in curriculum when television is used. Within a single year, the content of a mathematics or science program can change fundamentally within every classroom in the district. With the success of any academic program resting with the classroom teacher, the need for an effective and immediate in-service program is obvious.

For example, the State of California recently required the teaching of elementary school geography. In one populous county only 10 per cent of the teachers had ever had a geography course, and, of this number, the vast majority had their course over ten years before. The use of television was the only possible answer, not only for in-class instruction but for the training of teachers as well. San Jose State College, working closely with the local school districts, presented, at their request, an in-service series on this subject. This was but one of many in-service series developed in this manner. One of the series, teaching elementary school science, had a weekly audience of over 5,000 teachers viewing on their own time.

In-service education by television is also relatively inexpensive. A survey of the school districts in the San Jose area determined that the average cost of a consultant, per teacher contacted, was approximately $2.15. The cost of television, based on a viewing audience of 2,000 teachers, was less than 25 cents per half-hour lesson. To further expand the program, in-service telecasts were kinescoped for repeat use on regular 16mm projectors within the individual school. In this manner many districts have designed their faculty workshops around available kinescoped presentations.

Observation by Television: Another effective use of television within the in-service program is in classroom observation. For example, the Fontana Unified School District in California utilizes its closed-circuit equipment for a regular schedule of classroom observations. By this technique teachers can observe a classroom in operation, see close-up details, and discuss what is happening without disturbing the students. The equipment is small, relatively inexpensive, and controlled from outside the classroom. This approach has proved extremely effective for introducing new teaching techniques, observing excellent teachers in operation, and serving as a basis for in-service workshops sponsored by the district. One major study found that the amount of live observation in a teacher training program could be reduced by 50 per cent without detrimental effects, (4) when combined with a carefully prepared series of television observations.

Delta College (near Bay City, Michigan) has made excellent use of the observation technique in its extensive program for business and industry. To improve their communications techniques, managers are given a problem and required to present a sales pitch, give a talk, etc. Then, individually or in small groups, their taped presentations are viewed for evaluation and discussion. The ability to replay a video tape immediately has found substantial use in public speaking courses, teacher training, and physical education. The number of schools using this approach increased substantially with the recent decreases in the cost of video tape recorders.

Recent experimentation in "micro-teaching," the use of short taped sequences for self-evaluation, has opened up an entirely new and effective approach to certain aspects of teacher training.

Testing by Television: It has been estimated that the average student, by the time he graduates from high school, will have taken approximately 50 hours of standardized tests. Unfortunately, conditions for testing are usually far from ideal, with crowded rooms, noise, and nonstandardization of instructions generally prevailing. With television, one test officer is able to give instructions simultaneously to students located in many rooms. By utilizing an enlarged testing form, student errors in filling out the required information can be substantially reduced, at a saving of hundreds of man-hours required for hand scoring. In addition complete standardization is obtainable. At the University of Miami, the first time this approach was applied, student error in completing the required information—student ID, seat, and section number—was reduced by 80 per cent.

Medical and Dental Education: Television has become a standard tool in a majority of our medical and dental schools. Both instructors and students have found that observation of an operation by this technique provides maximum viewing combined with the opportunity to discuss the operation without disturbing those in the operating room. In many of these projects the cameras are controlled by those in the viewing room, utilizing remote controlled equipment. Several chains of hospitals are now connected together by a closed-circuit network to provide observation of the basic operating room and to permit clinical discussion, with doctors in several hospitals viewing X-rays or other data simultaneously. Thus a patient with his records in one hospital can immediately be treated in another.

A comprehensive plan for connecting all the state-operated mental, tubercular, and charity hospitals, state schools for the retarded, the central office, and the two medical schools in the state of Louisiana is now being put into operation. The long-range effects of this system are as broad as the ways in which it will be used. The rationale has been stated as follows:

> This system is designed to provide complete and continuing medical training for all professional and non-professional department personnel. ETV will make possible more efficient sharing of highly experienced instructors and costly medical equipment throughout the State. Permanent documentation of significant events as they happen will be made possible

through videotaping of televised programs. Through the ETV network, the Department of Hospitals will be able to program lectures and demonstrations concerning all phases of new medical techniques, provide intern and resident training, perform live psychiatric consultations, and conduct administrative conferences and other activities as they are required. (2)

Other Applications: One of the most exciting facets of television is the creative uses being made by teachers and school districts once it is available. To provide constructive use of the culturally deprived youngster's time between school dismissal and his parents' return from work, several community groups in Oklahoma City support a TV series designed specifically to raise the level of cultural appreciation of these students. Local high school students serve as group leaders. In the same community, two elementary teachers, faced with the problem of student motivation and preparation, developed a cartoon series "Exploring Our Universe" which appears in the local Sunday paper and is designed specifically to prepare students for the in-school television lesson that they will see later in the week.

Many districts are utilizing their studio and production areas as training facilities for a wide variety of technical training programs. Hundreds of students presently are being trained as technicians, cameramen, and graphic artists.

As television sets have become common in the home, more and more teachers are assigning viewing of specific late afternoon and early evening programs for homework. Assignments range from regular news reports to outstanding special features.

THE TEACHER, THE ADMINISTRATOR, AND THE STUDENT

The Classroom Teacher

The key to the successful use of television within any classroom rests with the classroom teacher. Since the inception of instructional television, an image of the master television teacher supported by a host of subsidiary classroom teachers has been developed. This image is not only questionable, but often damaging. More than one project has seen its star system develop into a source of internal friction and poor quality instruction. To be successful, television requires—or, to be more emphatic, demands—close cooperation between the television and classroom teachers.

That part of a lesson that can be covered by a one-way transmission can successfully be left to television. However, the guidance of the individual student, class discussion, evaluation, and the assignment of individual tasks can only be accomplished under the direction of an effective classroom teacher. It is his responsibility to mold the television presentation into the entire teaching configuration.

The Teacher's Guide: It is, therefore, imperative that this close working relationship be developed with care. The classroom teacher should be involved as much as possible in the early planning stages. The anticipated role of the television presentation should be clearly defined, and the classroom teacher must be given enough information to use the lesson with maximum effectiveness. Many of the study guides designed to serve this purpose are, unfortunately, virtually useless.

The guide must serve two basic purposes: it must help the teacher and administrator decide, first, *if* a particular series should be used and, second, *how* an individual program can be used to its best advantage.

To facilitate these decisions, certain information must be included:

1. day, time, and length of presentation
2. specific intended audience—grade level, ability level, stage of development
3. objectives of lesson (in behavioral terms)
4. content
5. how the program is designed to be used.

To further assist the classroom teacher in using the lesson, additional information must be provided. What does the television teacher assume that the student already knows (concepts, terminologies, etc.) and what activities are suggested for the student before, during, or after a particular presentation? (Several districts have found that student activity can be effectively built into a televised lesson with the television teacher pausing for several minutes while the classroom teacher directs an activity or leads a brief discussion and answer period.)

The main problems handicapping the development of more extensive guides are: first, when done well they are both extensive and expensive and, second, the television teacher rarely has been given the time and administrative support to do the job well.

The Administrator

The administrator has many responsibilities with television. It is his basic decision as to whether or not television is to be used and if so, how. As the key factor in implementing change, (1) he is responsible for how the classroom teacher is introduced to the medium and how television is introduced to his district, to students, to teachers, and to parents. The administration must plan carefully for faculty orientation as most teachers will not automatically use television properly. A positive climate must be developed *before* a project begins. Where the application has been successful, the administrator has done his job. Where the project has met resistance and hostility, the failure also rests with the administrator. If the project is district operated, he must provide his television teachers with adequate support staff and preparation time when possible; a sound evaluation procedure should also be developed. And of fundamental importance, the administrator must impart to his district a sound rationale for the use of television.

The Student

With television, the role of the student is not easy. He must concentrate and learn how to take effective notes; it is not, as so many have assumed, a rest period. Basically, the student must learn how to learn from television. Since many television instructors have found that they can effectively cover from two to three times the amount of material in the same amount of time, the student must not only be motivated to learn but be trained in those skills that are required. Many districts and colleges have found it advisable to spend time at the beginning of each academic year to orient the students to use television effectively.

TELEVISION, YES OR NO?

Should television be used? If so, in what form—single-room image magnification, independently operated studio, educational station, or in combination? One basic problem has been the tendency for these questions to be answered long before the facts on which a wise decision can be based are known.

1. Statement of Objectives

Step one in making any decision is determining, and stating, the behavioral objectives of a course, the units within the course and, if possible, the objective for individual lessons. Stating objectives serves two purposes, making possible both an effective evaluation of the program, and maximum teaching and learning efficiency and effectiveness. When objectives are clearly stated, a team of individuals can work independently or in small groups toward specific goals with a minimum of confusion and duplicated efforts.

2. Allocation of Objectives

Once the objectives are stated, it becomes possible to allocate specific objectives to each of the three basic teaching and learning configurations; independent study, student-teacher interaction, and large group (one-way transmission) instruction. This decision should be based on seven factors:

    A.   faculty availability

    B.   space availability

    C.   anticipated number of students

D. available instructional resources (including television)
E. budget
F. time available (for planning as well as teaching)
G. research findings.

When these factors are stated, a rationale for a configuration for a specific course to be taught in a particular district and in an individual school within that district can be determined. It can be expected that when this system approach is used properly a wide range of teaching and learning configurations will exist and rarely will the same course be identical in two different schools.

3. Criteria for Television

As highlighted throughout this book, television is but one of a series of instructional tools now available to the administrator and to the teacher. An attempt has been made in this chapter to present the broadest range of applications. In review, possible criteria for television might be as follows:

1. If within a small group or lecture hall, simple image magnification is required, use single-room television.
2. If a specific resource is required in more than one place at a time, use studio television.
3. If a single presentation must be seen in enough rooms to provide a sound financial base, use studio television.
4. If the total number of students involved is less than several hundred, provide the classroom teachers with maximum production and resource support instead of utilizing television.
5. If maximum resources are required and minimum funds are available, explore the use of a local educational station, average cost per student per year $2.00. (A list of programs available on just one station will be found in Table 2.)
6. If the answer is television but lessons are not available on an area educational station, explore a school- or district-owned station, making sure that enough funds and staff are available to insure quality.[2] Quite often the answer will be a combination of the two.
7. And under all circumstances, use studio television *only* for those aspects of a course that can be effectively taught in a one-way transmission (no student-teacher interaction).

---

[2] To plan and produce a single lesson well is expensive. A quality studio operation requires, in addition to the TV teacher, an extensive staff: producer-director, engineer (one or more), graphic artist(s), and cameramen. It has been estimated that 100 man-hours are required to produce a quality half-hour lesson. In the three districts reported by Bretz ("Closed-Circuit ITV Logistics — Comparing Hagerstown, Anaheim, and Santa Ana," *NAEB Journal,* July-August 1965), the annual ITV operating cost ranged from 1.25 to 4.8 per cent of the total school budget with television use on the elementary level averaging 10 per cent of the total school time.

Table 2.

SERIES AVAILABLE 1967-68
WMHT, Channel 17, Schenectady, New York

Elementary

Outdoor Surprises	K-1	American Historic	
Science Spy	2	Shrines	4-6
Eye on Science	3	Reading Newspapers	5-8
Science Today	4	Children of other Lands	4-6
Focus on Science	5	Parlons Francais	3-6
World of Change	6	French II	3-6
Working with Science	6	French III	3-6
Exploring our Language	4-6	Primary Math	K-2
Library Skills	4-6	Shapes in Space	3-4
Treasure in Books	4-6	Speaking of Numbers	5
Tell Me a Story	K-2	It's a Wonderful World	K-3
Phonics	K-2	Doorways to Art	4-6
Window on the World	K-2	Let's Make Music	K-2
Newstime	3-4	Understanding Music II	3-4
Assignment: The World	5-6	Understanding Music III	5-6
Dateline America	K-6	Meet the Arts	4-6
Americans All	4-6	Adventures in the Arts	K-6

Secondary

Variations on a Literary Theme	International Zone
American Literature	Cultures and Continents
Books that Live	Driver Education
Little Orchestra	Of the People
Curtain Call	Practical Politics

In-Service

Ages of Math	English: Fact and Fancy
Third R	Project Talent

THE FUTURE

It is anticipated that by 1970 over 90 per cent of our students will be in schools capable of receiving instructional television programs originating from one of the more than 170 stations that will then be incorporated in the National Educational Television Network. Additional hundreds of thousands will be in schools operating their own closed-circuit faculty. It can, therefore, be expected that within a few years most students will be receiving some part of their educational program by television. The use of television will range from the variety of presentations we now find available to short televised segments utilized within a system of computer-based individualized instruction. While the total use of television will increase substantially, the amount of television will rarely exceed one hour per day for an individual student.

Not only will the use of television increase substantially, but the quality of the individual lessons will markedly improve. There will be a decrease in the number of live programs being produced by the individual station, with major series being prepared and taped with the support of private and governmental funds. Local productions will be primarily of the type designed specifically to meet area or regional needs. It can be anticipated that television presentations may, in time, become one part of a computer-based learning sequence utilizing a wide range of instructional media.

The single-room television camera will become an integral part of the laboratory and lecture hall and will be handled in much the same way as any other audiovisual devices.

The use of small, compact, relatively inexpensive video tape recorders will increase substantially for replay of regular lessons and for evaluation, and the use of television for observation will become an integral part of teacher training, speech instruction, and physical education.

IN RETROSPECT

There can be little doubt that instructional television is here to stay. What remains to be known is its maximum role within a particular subject within a specific classroom. It is but one of a series of tools that are now available to assist the educator in improving the quality of instruction within our schools. The long range effectiveness of the medium rests on the insights and the attitudes of those using it, the quality of the lessons, and how it is molded into the entire learning sequence.

REFERENCES

1. Brickell, Henry M., *Organizing New York State for Educational Change*. Albany: University of the State of New York, State Educational Department, December 1961.
2. *Eductional Television Bulletin,* Southern Regional Education Board, May–June, 1965, from a mimeographed paper by R. B. Walden.
3. Kelley, Edward C., "Television and the teaching of typing." In Robert M. Diamond (ed.), *A Guide to Instructional Television*. New York: McGraw-Hill, 1964.
4. Rogers, William R., "Television utilization in the observation program for teacher education," San Jose State College, 1962.
5. *The Flight from Teaching,* Carnegie Foundation, 1964.

Chapter 18

How has the concept of remote resources evolved from
its language laboratories beginnings?

How does the use of remote resources benefit or facilitate the
teaching-learning process?

What are the operational characteristics of a dial-remote system
in actual use?

Is it likely that the dial-remote concept will incorporate other
multimedia, including computers, in the future?

DIAL-REMOTE RESOURCES

GEORGE POTTER
Vice President for Academic Affairs and Dean of Faculty
Grand Valley State College

Technology and education go forward hand in hand. New technological
processes give rise to the need for modifications in the educational
program. Educational developments encourage technological change
in business and industry. The new products of business and industry
facilitate changes in educational techniques. These relationships are
particularly evident when we examine the fields of electronics and
education, and will emerge continually in this discussion of the development and use of dial-access information retrieval systems in education
since the end of World War II.

There is no doubt that the educational subject area most directly
affected by the new electronic equipment available in the early postwar
period was that of language instruction. Wartime developments in
language teaching techniques had led to a new emphasis on the use
of native speakers in intensive language drill programs but when
more and more colleges sought to introduce this emphasis into their
programs they found it necessary to resort to recorded drill materials
in place of a direct use of native speakers on their campuses. Even
when such speakers were available, they could not easily be installed

as regular staff members of the institutions. Hence, faculty members interested in language teaching sought the assistance of the electronics industry and, for example, as early as 1947 Louisiana State University had established an installation that provided its students with access to disk recordings of foreign language drills.

Thus emerged the first electronic information retrieval tool to be employed in education, the language laboratory. This aid to education provides for the recording and storage of language exercises, which are then presented to students as audio programs for their observation and imitation. The language laboratory can take many forms, from a simple tape recorder in the back of a classroom, to an electronic marvel feeding dozens of programs to scores of students in remote classrooms or isolated individual study booths.

Despite the early postwar interest in the use of electronic aids in language teaching, difficulties in the supply and reliability of available equipment delayed the general development of language laboratory facilities. Problems associated with the local production of recordings for use on phonograph equipment led many schools and colleges to look instead to magnetic recorders as the basis of their systems, and it was eventually the improvement of the magnetic tape recorder that removed the final technical obstacle to a more general use of electronic equipment in language teaching.

By 1957 the use of language laboratory facilities had extended to 64 secondary schools and 240 colleges or universities across the country. The installations in use in these various locations varied greatly. In some cases the older disk equipment remained. Other schools made use of standard tape recorders. Some installations provided only listening stations at which students could listen in to recordings that were being played back from the control console. Still others provided each student station with a magnetic recorder on which the operator could copy a master tape distributed electronically from a teacher's console, and then add his own recording for comparison with the recorded model. Except where recordings were manually distributed to students for use in language study booths, the range of programs available to students at a particular time was generally limited to only very few possibilities, and the selection of these possibilities was usually at the discretion of the teacher seated at the control console. The concept of giving every student the opportunity of remote electronic access to a large library of programs was still only a wild dream. For most students a session in the language laboratory was an exercise in frustration, as he tried nobly to thread a tape onto a reel, and then sought to switch in to the control console, hopefully to catch up with the teacher's comments before she set the master tape in motion.

Eventually the kinds of equipment available for use in language laboratories became more and more suitable. Gradually the early full-track recorders were replaced by double-track, and eventually four-track machines, while the difficult-to-manage reel-to-reel equipment gave way to cartridge tape units that students could more easily manipulate. Progressively also the advantages of laboratory instruction in language courses were ever more generally acknowledged, and, as will emerge from the following list, it came to be recognized that at least some of these advantages would apply equally to instruction in other topics. Because of this, the long-term trend towards the general use of electronic recording, storage and play-back equipment in education gathered momentum.

The advantages to be achieved through the use of language laboratory and similar equipment include the following:

A. ADVANTAGES TO THE STUDENT

1. Students can work alone and at their own speed, providing that the equipment permits them individual access to the tape sources. The student who is quick to learn can move forward through his program without waiting for the class. The slow learning student can repeat programs in his own time as often as may be necessary.

2. The facilities provide students with individual access to excellent instructional materials, prepared under good studio conditions, and, if a foreign language is the topic, presented by a native speaker.

3. Students are able to evaluate their progress by comparing their audio or written responses with those on the tape or on accompanying study manuals.

4. Students are assured considerable audio and visual privacy in their study situations. Distractions are minimized.

5. The teacher is released from general class activities and permitted to spend more time with individual students in the laboratory, or in other ways.

B. ADVANTAGES TO THE TEACHER

1. The teacher no longer has to give direct supervision to repetitive study activities, but is relieved to spend more time in creative teaching situations.

2. Teaching staff can monitor students' programs and coach those found to be having difficulty with their assignments.

3. Teachers may themselves participate in the preparation of the

study materials, or, if they need specialized support, such materials may be prepared by experts in the area involved.

4. Teachers may improve their own teaching techniques, or expand their own knowledge, through cooperation with others involved in the preparation and presentation of the study materials.

C. ADVANTAGES TO THE INSTITUTION

1. All students can be assured access to first-class study materials, even in subject areas that are difficult to staff with subject area specialists.

2. Through the use of recorded tapes a wider range of courses, or increased number of class levels, can be handled without the necessity of adding to the teaching staff.

3. Students' schedules can be adapted without upsetting the entire curriculum. If materials are on tape, a student can begin a course at midterm and continue to proceed at his own pace without disrupting others.

4. Materials can be in use, with minimum supervision, for the full time the school buildings are unlocked.

It is evident that the extent to which any or all of these advantages can be achieved will be dependent on the quality of the programs made available, the number of programs available, the range of services available to the student and teacher, and on the extent to which these services can be individualized for use by particular students. Assuming that good quality program materials are available, then the utility of the system will be increased if a large quantity of different programs can be distributed to different students at the same time. Similarly the utility will be enhanced if students are able to respond to the tapes and to record their responses for comparison with the master tapes, in addition to fulfilling the basic function of listening to them. The teachers, moreover, will very likely be more effective if they are able to monitor the students' activities and to communicate with them if they wish to do so. Given all these additional features, however, the value of the system will still be dependent on the ease with which it can be used by individual students on a random access basis. If the system includes 30 stations, all of which are closed down when the staff leave their offices for the day, then the system will have only a limited value. If the 30 stations are regarded as available to all departments, and if they are all equipped for individual operation outside of regular classroom hours as well as during the teaching day, then they may very well prove to be of major value to the instructional program.

At this point, a word of caution is in order. Along with the advantages outlined above, there are some disadvantages to be considered. Not all language teachers agree that it is important for students to spend their time developing listening and speaking skills. Some teachers in other subject areas are unwilling to give students too many opportunities for individual consultations. Other teachers are inclined to place too much responsibility on their students' shoulders—to the extent that they might neglect necessary class or tutorial meetings that would augment the work students undertook during their own time. Some teachers would not have time to prepare excellent materials for use in the system. Other teachers would resent the suggestion that off-campus experts should be brought in to supplement their efforts. Particular students might be quite lost in a situation in which they were cut off from their classmates, alone in a study booth working with the disembodied voice of an expert speaking from some 'distant source.' In the presence of any or all of these negative conditions the value of the electronic system will quite clearly be reduced and it could, conceivably, become an encumbrance to the institution.

Returning to a more optimistic frame of reference, it is an accomplished fact that, encouraged by the success of language laboratory installations, educational pioneers in schools, colleges, and universities across the nation have moved along in their use of such installations to the point where they have added programs in a wide range of subjects, and have multiplied by many times the number of students who can be served by their facilities.

Gradually they have removed the direction of their installations from the language departments, and have placed them in locations at which they are accessible to all departments. In some cases this move has placed new responsibilities upon the library staff, and at the same time, has enhanced the function of the library as a source of instructional materials. Some colleges have extended their networks to dormitories as well as to classrooms. They have added video channels to augment the more traditional audio components. A new concept—that of the Learning Resources Center—has emerged.

Although it would probably be misleading to give credit to any particular school, college, or university as being the first to conceive of the establishment of a Learning Resources Center (Stephens College, Missouri; Oklahoma Christian College; Ohio State University; Florida Atlantic University; Nasson College, Springvale, Maine; Grand Valley State College in Michigan; and others all claiming the honors) credit must nonetheless be extended to the Educational Facilities Laboratories for the help which this organization has given to the concept. Many ideas now applied at these various institutions were conceived under the auspices of EFL, and their application in many locations is a direct consequence of a series of fine publications brought out by this organization.

CASE STUDY

When I turn, therefore, to my own institution, Grand Valley State College, to illustrate the part to be played by a Learning Resources Center in the life of the modern college student, it is not with the thought that we alone have been innovators in this field. It is simply that I know this system from top to bottom. I know it to be typical of installations elsewhere in the nation, and I am close enough to our operation to be able to point out its inadequacies without causing grave offense to its designers or operators.

Grand Valley State College is a new college, located near Grand Rapids, Michigan. We were founded in 1960, and admitted our first students in the fall of 1963.

One of the first decisions taken at Grand Valley was the decision that we should attempt to make special arrangements to give students individual attention in the development and completion of their study program. Hence, the decision to introduce an element of decentralization into the overall college plan—so that all students could be members of small academic complexes on campus, working directly with the faculty members located in these complexes. Hence, also, the interest in providing individual study carrels in each academic building—to give each student his individual study headquarters on campus.

These interests, along with considerations concerning the successful use of electronic equipment in college teaching situations, and with the impending shortage of college teachers, led to the notion that a decentralized campus should be generally provided with equipment of this kind, to supplement more traditional approaches to instruction. Thus, late in 1961, the college authorities approached the Educational Facilities Laboratories for support in securing the services of an independent consultant to advise us on kinds of equipment that we might need to help achieve these educational objectives. Our request was granted, and with the assistance of the consultant and other advisers we reached the following conclusions:

1. in a campus with decentralized facilities there could be real merit in establishing closed-circuit television links between each of the decentralized units;

2. in view of the impending shortage of teachers, there could be real merit in using equipment that could amplify or extend the output of our instructional staff—enabling them to teach additional stu-

dents without overloading themselves or diluting the instructional program;

3. since photographic slides, films, audio tapes, records, video tapes, teaching machines, computers, and remotely originated programs can provide enrichment to support many kinds of instructional activities, we should attempt to provide the funds necessary to make these sources available on the campus whenever our faculty members called for them, either as classroom aids, or to supplement students' individual study programs;

4. in keeping with our plans to give students individual attention, we should provide students with individual study booths or carrels. These carrels would become each student's personal headquarters on campus. They would be equipped to display audio and video materials distributed on the campus AV system;

5. given the availability of the electronic equipment and study carrel installation outlined above, some parts of the instructional program could be automated, at a probable saving in the time of the faculty members, and possibly, at a minimum cost per student.

Armed with these conclusions we pushed ahead in 1962 and 1963 with the development of the integrated audio-video system outlined in the illustration appearing on pages 398–99, and over the recent years we have gradually been bringing the system into operation.

Referring to the illustration, and recalling that our immediate interest in this chapter is with dial-access information retrieval systems, we should note, first of all, the units pictured at the top of the page. Each of these units, namely study carrels, lecture hall lecterns and classroom monitors, are equipped with telephone type dials through which students or instructors can activate the automatic switchgear to make selections from among the audio programs stored on playback machines located in the audio-video center. In the case of the study carrels, the selected audio programs are heard on headsets located in the carrels. In the lecture halls and classrooms, the audio is distributed to a local public address amplifier, allowing everyone in the rooms to listen to the program without difficulty. Given the specifications of our switching equipment, up to 120 audio programs can be made available at any time, and a similar number of listening positions can be served.

Other electronic features of the study carrels included in the initial installation are microphones, which allow students to communicate with the AV center, and permit them to elect a record mode when working with student record and playback machines; and jack plugs, connected to our video distribution system, which are designed for use with small television monitors that students can obtain from a nearby library circulation desk for their individual use in the carrels. Volume controls are installed for use with the microphones and the headsets, and desk lights are included to augment the general room lighting. Originally, all carrels were equipped with loudspeakers rather than headsets, but it was discovered in practice that these led to interference with students working in adjoining carrels.

Seated in a study carrel, the student thus has electronic access to 120 audio programs. By dialing a three digit number, the student operates relays located in the audio-video center. The relays set up impulses which set in motion the cartridge-type tape playback machine carrying the selected program, and they further identify the audio track (one of four) on which that program has been recorded. Once started, the tapes run through progressively until they are played out, at which time they go automatically in a rewind cycle and are available for re-use. Alternatively, they can be rejected by the student by action of the dial selector. Ninety-six of the programs are played back on machines that allow for a maximum program time of 30 minutes. Longer programs are available on the other tracks of recorded sound, up to a maximum of one hour per track. Twenty-four of the carrels at any time can also provide access to additional two-track tape recording machines that run in conjunction with any machine already playing back a selected program, rerecording this program, and, at the same time, recording students' responses carried from the microphones in their carrels. By operation of the dial selectors, students in these carrels can cause the tape recording machines to rewind and to play back the recordings they have made, along with the rerecording of the program tape. Thus they are able to compare their own recorded exercises with the voice that was carried on the program tape.

Another aspect of our audio system featured in the illustration is the teacher console, through the use of which the instructional staff can monitor students' use of the system, and which provides opportunities for communication between the teacher and his students.

Although our original plan called for video program materials to be switched in the same way as audio programs, so that we could offer remote electronic access to these materials, we have not yet been able to introduce this feature. Accordingly, the student in the carrel is limited to a selection of only eight video programs at any time. All eight program channels are scheduled directly from the AV center, and the students operate a dial selector on the television monitor to choose the program that they wish to view. Until video tape recorders come down in price to the level of audio tape machines, and until a more elaborate switchgear and distribution system is installed, this will be the limit to the number of video programs we can make available.

How Grand Valley State's ETV System Functions

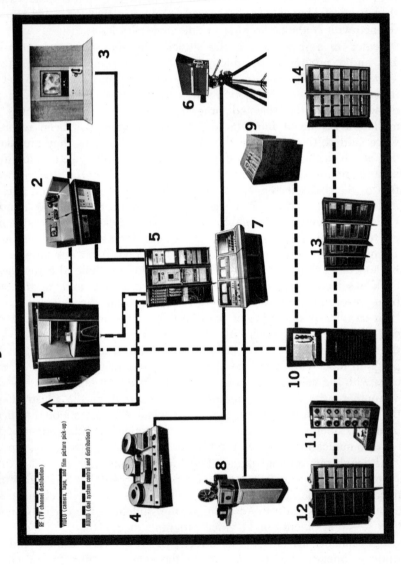

RF (TV channel distribution)

VIDEO (camera, tape, and film picture pick-up)

AUDIO (dial system control and distribution)

1. 118 CARRELS: Students can select any of 120 audio programs and 8 TV channels on the small TV sets.

2. AUDITORIUM AND LECTURE HALL LECTERN: Allows Instructor to select any of the 8 TV channels or 120 audio programs and display or broadcast them to the class. Has camera inputs, automatic record facilities, PA system, lighting control. Contains built-in monitor for instructor viewing of classroom programing.

3. CLASSROOM MONITORS: Through the telephone handset, instructor may dial the control room and ask for any tape he desires, or play any of the 120 audio programs to the classroom. He can also select any one of the 8 TV channels. He may request TV cameras be brought into the classroom for direct televising, for program video-taping from the classroom, or program distribution over the RF distribution system.

4. VIDEO TAPE MACHINES: Two helical scan machines record on two-inch Mylar tape, very similar to an audio tape. Tape may be erased and used for recording. Sound and picture are recorded on the same tape.

5. TV DISTRIBUTION PANEL: Provides 8 simultaneous TV channels, for either off-air or closed circuit distribution. Signal is fed by cable to each carrel, classroom and lecture hall. The equipment allows monitoring of anything distributed through the system, an interconnection of all sources.

6. TV CAMERAS: 3 Blonder-Tongue cameras equipped with zoomar lenses capable of focusing on anything from a very small object to a large scene with the turn of a handle. Have both RF (radio frequency) output, and high resolution video output. All transistorized, easily portable on light aluminum dolly, and reused in the class-rooms, lecture halls and TV studio.

7. STUDIO AND AUDIO CONTROL CONSOLE: Allows remote control of video tape recorder, film chain and allows making programs from any lecture hall, classroom or auditorium on campus, or from the studio. Audio and video controls allow switch-ing of one source to another to provide a finished production.

8. FILM CHAIN AND MULTIPLEXER: The Blonder-Tongue Film Chain combines into a single camera, a 16mm film projector, a 35mm slide projector and one other source, if desired, through a half silvered mirror-lens system.

9. TEACHER CONSOLE: Allows the instructor to listen to and correct students using audio record carrels, either all at once or separately. Also allows multiple testing and correcting.

10. CARREL INDICATOR & PATCH PANEL: Light indicates carrel in use whenever a student dials for any tape. If assistance needed, technician is alerted by flashing light and bell. He then answers student through headset on the panel. Difficulties in carrels can be located by patching on this panel. Also allows interchange of carrel record facilities.

11. RECORDER AND DUBBER: All program tapes are made on this unit through a duplicating tape machine. As many as four lectures can be recorded on each machine simultaneously.

12. 24 STUDENT RECORDERS: 2-track machines: on one track students record a copy of the program dialed in; on the other, they record the copy of the program dialed in, plus whatever the student says into the microphone. Controlled by dial, fast forward, stop, rewind, play.

13. DIAL (CROSSBAR) SWITCHING: Built like a modern telephone exchange, each bank will handle ten students and 120 programs. Three banks to each rack. 4 racks total. This gear switches in a dialed call to a selected program.

14. 96 "AT-READY" PROGRAM SOURCES: 4-track machines play back four tracks simultaneously. Any number of students can dial into any number of programs simultaneously. Machines will rewind as long as any student is dialed in and will stop when last student dials out. Each number under the machines represents a dial number.

Looking once again at the illustration, we should realize that four classrooms and three lecture halls are connected to the AV system and have access to all the sources which were available in the carrels, and that, in addition, it is possible to originate television programs from these locations. Representative illustrations of our video production and distribution equipment are included in the diagram. In addition to the closed-circuit programing opportunity, we can also receive and distribute four commercial television channels and the airborne educational television programs.

THE SYSTEM IN USE

The system just described is still in its infancy. The video program potential was only introduced at the beginning of 1965, and we have only more recently added the professional staff needed to operate this equipment effectively, so our comments about its use must be inconclusive. However, a few preliminary comments are in order.

A first comment relates to the expense and availability of the equipment required in any reasonably extensive dial-access system. The initial cost is considerable. In our case we have already invested more than $250,000, and we still have much to add to the installation. Such an amount need not be prohibitive when spread over the useful life of the equipment, which may be set at ten years, but the initial cost may dismay some administrators. Another difficulty will be the question of the supply and installation of the equipment desired. This is still a pioneering field. Equipment is still passing through the developmental stage and some delays in supply are almost inevitable. Few local companies are able to undertake the elaborate kinds of installations that are called for, so further delays may arise. We count ourselves fortunate in having specified reliable equipment, and in having the equipment installed by an enterprising local organization; but even so, the delays in completing the installation were frustrating.

A second kind of comment about our equipment relates to the carrels. These were developed to our own design and were custom built. They are not generally available, which is just as well, for they need modification. It is perhaps too costly to provide carrels that are completely sound protected, although we went to some expense in an attempt to secure such a feature. As I have indicated, the attempt failed, and we were obliged to replace the original loudspeakers with headsets to reduce the transference of sound between carrels. As time passes, there will continue to be new kinds of carrels made available by special manufacturers, and these will quite likely be acceptable from the standpoint of sound isolation providing that headsets are specified, or if the carrels are to be used in situations where noise transference does not present a problem.

Thirdly, there is a more detailed criticism of our equipment, a criticism which challenges the entire concept of remote dial-access systems. For the sake of economy we are using four-track playback machines. Hence, if one track is selected and started, the other three are in operation—to the dismay of any student now dialing into one of these programs. To be sure, he can listen in to the program, but it is sometimes frustrating to have to come in on the middle of the lesson and have to wait around for the first part to be repeated after the tape has completed its cycle. A related problem involves the extent to which the tapes can be rewound and played back through use of the dial selector. If one student is attempting to perform this manoeuver while other students are eager to carry on with the same program, then frutrations arise. One solution to both of these problems is no doubt to expand the scope of the switchgear installation, and to multiply the number of playback machines in the system, but this can be a costly procedure. New technology is being developed to circumvent this problem by making a high speed copy for each student to use when he is ready, and the cost of playback machines is coming down, so perhaps we can be optimistic regarding alleviation of this difficulty in the future.

Other factors relating to the use of a dial-access information retrieval system are the attitudes towards such a system held by students, by faculty members, and by the administration. At Grand Valley, where we are operating a tutorial program involving regular faculty meetings with students in groups of three or four, our students do not react negatively towards the use of electronic study aids. The fears of some observers that students would find this equipment impersonal or 'soul destroying' do not seem to be borne out by our experience to date. In fact, students enthusiastically recommend use of the equipment in an expanding range of courses. Whether or not they would be as enthusiastic about a program in which there were to be no personal contact with faculty members in tutorial or other meetings, and whether or not such a program would be successful, remains to be tested, although experience with various kinds of programed instructional courses encourages optimism on this latter point.

Faculty members traditionally have worked as independent agents in the classroom. Although programs were perhaps drawn up by curriculum committees, and textbooks selected by subcommittees, the teacher was left to his own approaches and methods when he closed the classroom door. Such independence is no longer his privilege. Once the doors are opened to instructional media of various kinds, the teacher becomes a member of a team. Generally speaking he will emerge as the captain of this team, and he will retain control of the direction in which the team is to move, but he will have to make some concessions to the other team members. He will have to publish his course plans well in advance, and relate them to materials already available within the learning center library. He must collaborate in developing a schedule for the preparation of any additional programs that are required, and collaborate with such artists, audio specialists, cameramen and program directors as are needed to produce these materials. Finally, he must submit his efforts for use and evaluation by his students, in the knowledge that he will have no immediate control over the use of these materials, nor any immediate opportunity to revise them. With all these considerations in mind, it is not surprising that many faculty members balk at the prospect of utilizing AV instructional techniques when the matter is first raised. Then, as they go through the agonizing process of developing their first taped, filmed, or programed course sequences, they are alarmed at the amount of time that must be spent on the preparation of first-class materials. Consequently the level of faculty interest in the use of instructional media is slow to rise, and it is only when faculty members are given clear explanations as to the long-term necessity of their use of these media, as a means of reducing future teaching loads or raising future salaries, that their interest begins to increase.

It is the administrative group in any school or college that is the most enthusiastic about the advantages that an effective use of instructional media can bring about. This group, comfortably removed from the day to day problems of the classroom, and free of the frustrations of working with primitive audio-video installations, are most immediately aware of the increasing demands that must be made on our educational institutions in the years ahead, and can see that good instructional techniques will provide solutions to many problems. If a school system wishes to provide foreign language programs, but can only obtain the service of a very few gifted language teachers, then use of audio-video materials will permit these teachers to work with lesser qualified colleagues in presenting a program in every school in the system. If a group of colleges wish to secure the services of outstanding faculty members, then this can be arranged via telephone and television links between their institutions. If a new teacher wishes to augment his teaching activities with first-class illustrations or cartoons, then specialists working in an AV center can be assigned to collaborate with him. It is up to members of the administrative group to call for development in the quality and versatility of instructional media produced by the electronics industry, so that an ever growing range of their application becomes acknowledged, and in order that our methods of using them may be improved. They must also bring this equipment to the attention of the teaching staff, and must work with teachers who welcome these resources in order to bring about their general acceptance.

LOOKING AHEAD

As the needs of our specific situations, coupled with the inventiveness of industry, lead toward a more general use of instructional media, then we can look forward to important developments in the use of dial-access information retrieval systems in our schools and colleges. Video sources of information will be incorporated in future systems as extensively as audio services have been used in existing systems. Networks of cables and radio communication links will connect local schools and colleges into wider systems of education. Materials stored in one remote location will be reproduced for students studying in another part of the state or country. New information, stored in local or remote computer sources, will be made available to a student who dials a switch or presses a button. Students will be able to interact with computers programed with their courses of study and the machines themselves will keep a record of the students' progress. Technically, it would even be possible to develop the facilities needed to support the distribution of materials via dial access retrieval systems to all students at their homes via their telephones, radios, and television receivers, but this may not be a near-term development.

Education is, of course, much more than the mere presentation of information and grading of student assignments. It is a human experience and it demands the interaction of students with each other, and with an interested group of teachers. From its very nature, this aspect of education will not be programed, but through skillful use of instructional media in the other aspects of the program teachers will be freed to devote their time to this humanistic activity.

BIBLIOGRAPHY

Johnston, Marjorie C., and Seerley, Catherine C. *Foreign Language Laboratories in Schools and Colleges.* U.S. Department of Health, Education and Welfare, Office of Education Bulletin, 1959, No. 3. Washington: United States Government Printing Office, 1959, 86 pages.

Hutchinson, Joseph C., *Modern Foreign Languages in High School: The Language Laboratory.* U.S. Department of Health, Education and Welfare, Office of Education Bulletin 1961, No. 23. Washington: United States Government Printing Office, 1961, 86 pages.

Stickler, Hugh, *Experimental Colleges: Their Role in American Higher Education.* Tallahassee: Florida State University, 1964.

Chapter 19

During the brief span of its general use, what factors have influenced the programed instruction movement?

What functions are similar and dissimilar between the human teacher and the teaching machine?

To what degree are current auto-instructional programs dependent on the psychology of behavior and stimulus control?

What distinctions should be made between experimental use and classroom use of programed materials?

REFLECTIONS ON
A DECADE OF TEACHING MACHINES*

B. F. SKINNER, Professor of Psychology
Harvard University

To the general public, and to many educators as well, the nature and scope of teaching machines are by no means clear. There is an extraordinary need for more and better teaching, and any enterprise which may help to meet it will not be left to develop normally. The demand for information about teaching machines has been excessive. Articles and books have been published and lectures given; symposia have been arranged, and conferences and workshops have been held and courses taught. Those who have had anything useful to say have said it far too often, and those who have had nothing to say have been no more reticent.

Education is big business. Teaching machines were soon heralded as a growth industry, and fantastic predictions of the sales of programed texts were circulated. Devices have been sold as teaching machines which were not well built or designed with any understanding of their function or the practical exigencies of their use. No author was ever more warmly received by a publisher than the author of a

*This chapter is reprinted by permission of the author and *Teachers College Record*, from the November, 1963 issue.

programed text. Many programs, to be used either with machines or in textbook form, have been marketed without adequate evaluation.

TEACHERS AND DEVICES

The "mechanizing of education" has been taken literally in the sense of doing by machine what was formerly done by people. Some of the so-called computer-based teaching machines are designed simply to duplicate the behavior of teachers. To automate education with mechanical teachers is like automating banking with mechanical tellers and bookkeepers. What is needed in both cases is an analysis of the functions to be observed, followed by the design of appropriate equipment. Nothing we now know about the learning process calls for very elaborate instrumentation.

Educational specialists have added to the confusion by trying to assimilate the principles upon which teaching machines are based to older theories of learning and teaching.

In the broadest sense, teaching machines are simply devices which make it possible to apply our technical knowledge of human behavior to the practical field of education (10). Teaching is the expediting of learning. Students learn without teaching, but the teacher arranges conditions under which they learn more rapidly and effectively. In recent years, the experimental analysis of behavior has revealed many new facts about relevant conditions. The growing effectiveness of an experimental analysis is still not widely recognized, even within the behavioral sciences themselves, but the implications of some of its achievements for education can no longer be ignored.

An important condition is the relation between behavior and its consequences; learning occurs when behavior is "reinforced." The power of reinforcement is not easily appreciated by those who have not had firsthand experience in its use or have not at least seen some sort of experimental demonstration. Extensive changes in behavior can be brought about by arranging so-called contingencies of reinforcement. Various kinds of contingencies are concealed in the teacher's discussions with his students, in the books he gives them to read, in the charts and other materials he shows them, and in the comments he makes on their answers. An experimental analysis clarifies these contingencies and suggests many improvements.

SHAPING BY PROGRAM

An important contribution has been the so-called "programing" of knowledge and skills—the construction of carefully arranged sequences of contingencies leading to the terminal performances which are the object of education. The teacher begins with whatever behavior the student brings to the instructional situation; by selective reinforcement, he changes that behavior so that a given terminal performance is more and more closely approximated. Even with lower organisms, quite complex behaviors can be "shaped" in this way with surprising speed; the human organism is presumably far more sensitive. So important is the principle of programing that it is often regarded as the main contribution of the teaching-machine movement, but the experimental analysis of behavior has much more to contribute to a technology of education.

The direct contact which often exists between teacher and student favors the construction of programed sequences, and the teacher who understands the process can profit from the opportunity to improvise programs as he goes. Programs can be constructed in advance, however, which will successfully shape the behavior of most students without local modifications, and many of them can conveniently be mediated by mechanical devices. Laboratory studies have shown that contingencies emphasizing subtle properties of behavior can often be arranged *only* through instrumentation. There are potentially as many different kinds of teaching machines as there are kinds of contingencies of reinforcement.

Teaching machines which present material to the student and differentially reinforce his responses in well constructed programs differ in several ways from self-testing devices and self-scoring test forms, as well as from the training devices which have long been used by industry and the armed services. As Pressey pointed out many years ago (8), a student will learn while taking a multiple-choice test if he is told immediately whether his answers are right or wrong. He learns not to give wrong answers again, and his right answers are strengthened. But testing has traditionally been distinguished from teaching for good reason. Before using a self-testing device, the student must already have studied the subject and, presumably, learned most of what he is to learn about it. Tests usually occupy only a small part of his time. Their main effect is motivational: A poor score induces him to study harder and possibly more effectively. Materials designed to be used in self-testing devices have recently been programed, but the contingencies which prevail during a test are not favorable to the shaping and maintaining of behavior.

Conventional training devices arrange conditions under which students learn, usually by simulating the conditions under which they eventually perform. Their original purpose was to prevent injury or waste during early stages of learning, but attention has recently been given to programing the actual behaviors they are designed to teach. To the extent that they expedite learning, they are teaching machines. Terminal performances have usually been selected for practical reasons, but a more promising possibility is the analysis and programing of basic motor and perceptual skills—a goal which should have an important place in any statement of educational policy.

In arranging contingencies of reinforcement, machines do many of the things teachers do; in that sense, they teach. The resulting instruction is not impersonal, however. A machine presents a program designed by someone who knew what was to be taught and could prepare an appropriate series of contingencies. It is most effective if used by a teacher who knows the student, has followed his progress, and can adapt available machines and materials to his needs. Instrumentation simply makes it possible for programer and teacher to provide conditions which maximally expedite learning. Instrumentation is thus secondary, but it is nevertheless inevitable if what is now known about behavior is to be used in an effective technology.

THE NEW PEDAGOGY

Any practical application of basic knowledge about teaching and learning is, of course, pedagogy. In the United States at least, the term is now discredited, but by emphasizing an analysis of learning processes, teaching machines and programed instruction have been responsible for some improvement in its status. The significance of the teaching-machine movement can be indicated by noting the astonishing lack of interest which other proposals for the improvement of education show in the teaching process.

Find better teachers.

In his *Talks to Teachers*, William James insisted that there was nothing wrong with the American school system which could not be corrected by "impregnating it with geniuses" (7). It is an old formula: If you cannot solve a problem, find someone who can. If you do not know how to teach, find someone who knows or can find out for himself. But geniuses are in short supply, and good teachers do not come ready-made. Education would no doubt be improved if, as Conant (3) has repeatedly pointed out, good teachers who know and like the subjects they teach could be attracted and retained. But something more is needed. It is not true that "the two essentials of a good teacher are (a) enthusiasm and (b) thorough knowledge of and interest in his subject" (5). A third essential is knowing how to teach.

Emulate model schools.

Rickover's criticism of the present American school system is well-known (9). His only important positive suggestion is to set up model schools, staffed by model teachers. The implication is that we already have, or at least can have for the asking, schools which need no improvement and whose methods can be widely copied. This is a dangerous assumption if it discourages further inquiry into instruction.

Simplify what is to be learned.

Unsuccessful instruction is often blamed on refractory subject matters. Difficulties in teaching the verbal arts are often attributed to the inconsistencies and unnecessary complexities of a language. The pupil is taught manuscript handwriting because it more closely resembles printed forms. He is taught to spell only those words he is likely to use. Phonetic alphabets are devised to help him learn to read. It may be easier to teach such materials, but teaching itself is not thereby improved. Effective teaching would correct these pessimistic estimates of available instructional power.

Reorganize what is to be learned.

The proper structuring of a subject matter is perhaps a part of pedagogy, but it can also serve as a mode of escape. Proposals for improving education by reorganizing what is to be learned usually contain an implicit assumption that students will automatically perceive and remember anything which has "good form"—a doctrine probably traceable to Gestalt psychology. Current revisions of high school curricula often seem to lean heavily on the belief that if what the student is to be taught has been "structured," he cannot help understanding and remembering it (1). Other purposes of such revisions cannot be questioned: materials should be up to date and well organized. But a high school presentation acceptable to a current physicist is no more easily taught or easily remembered than the out-of-date and erroneous material to be found in texts of a decade or more ago. Similarly, the accent of a native speaker encountered in a language laboratory is no more easily learned than a bad accent. No matter how well structured a subject matter may be, it must still be taught.

Improve presentation.

Pedagogy can also be avoided if what is to be learned can be made memorable. Audio-visual devices are often recommended for this purpose. Many of their other purposes are easily defended. It is not always easy to bring the student into contact with the things he is to learn about. Words are easily imported into the classroom, and books, lectures, and discussions are therefore staples of education; but this is often an unfortunate bias. Audio-visual devices can enlarge the student's nonverbal experience. They can also serve to present material clearly and conveniently. Their use in attracting and holding the student's attention and in dramatizing a subject matter in such a way that it is almost automatically remembered must be questioned, however. It is especially tempting to turn to them for these purposes when the teacher does not use punitive methods to "make students study." But the result is not the same. When a student observes or attends to something in order to see it more clearly or remember it more effectively, his behavior must have been shaped and maintained by reinforcement. The temporal order was important. Certain reinforcing events must have occurred *after* the student looked at, read, and perhaps tested himself on the material. But when colored displays, attractive objects, filmed episodes, and other potentially reinforcing materials are used to attract attention, they must occur *before* the student engages in these activities. Nothing can reinforce a student for *paying* attention if it has already been used to *attract* his attention. Material which attracts attention fails to prepare the student to attend to material which is not interesting on its face, and material which is naturally memorable fails to prepare him to study and recall things which are not, in themselves, unforgettable. A well prepared instructional film may appear to be successful in arousing interest in a given subject, and parts of it may be remembered without effort, but it has not taught the student that a subject may *become* interesting when more closely examined or that intensive study of something which is likely to be overlooked may have reinforcing consequences.

Multiply contacts between teacher and students.

Audio-visual devices, particularly when adapted to television, are also used to improve education by bringing one teacher into contact with an indefinitely large number of students. This can be done, of course, without analyzing how the teacher teaches, and it emphasizes a mode of communication which has two serious disadvantages: the teacher cannot see the effect he is having on his students, and large numbers of students must proceed at the same pace. Contributions to pedagogy may be made in designing programs for educational television, but the mere multiplication of contacts is not itself an improvement in teaching.

Expand the educational system.

Inadequate education may be corrected by building more schools and recruiting more teachers so that the total quantity of education is increased, even though there is no change in efficiency.

Raise standards.

Least effective in improving teaching are demands for higher standards. We may agree that students will be better educated when they learn more, but how are they to be induced to do so? Demands for higher standards usually come from critics who have least to offer in improving teaching itself.

The movement symbolized by the teaching machine differs from other proposals in two ways. It emphasizes the direct improvement of teaching on the principle that no enterprise can improve itself to the fullest extent without examining its basic processes. In the second place, it emphasizes the implementation of basic knowledge. If instructional practices violate many basic principles, it is only in part because these principles are not widely known. The teacher cannot put what he knows into practice in the classroom. Teaching machines and programed instruction constitute a direct attack on the problem of implementation. With appropriate administrative changes, they may bridge the gap between an effective pedagogical theory and actual practice.

EDUCATIONAL GOALS

An effective technology of teaching calls for a re-examination of educational objectives. What is the teacher's actual assignment? Educational policy is usually stated in traditional terms: The teacher is to "impart knowledge," "improve skills," "develop rational faculties," and so on. That education is best, says Dr. Hutchins (6), which develops "intellectual power." The task of the teacher is to change certain inner processes or states. He is to improve the mind.

The role of the teacher in fostering mental prowess has a certain prestige. It has always been held superior to the role of the trainer of motor skills. And it has the great advantage of being almost invulnerable to criticism. In reply to the complaint that he has not produced observable results, the teacher of the mind can lay claim to invisible achievements. His students may not be able to read, but he has only been trying to make sure they wanted to learn. They may not be able to solve problems, but he has been teaching them simply to think creatively. They may be ignorant of specific facts, but he has been primarily concerned with their general interest in a field.

Traditional specifications of the goals of education have never told the teacher what to do upon a given occasion. No one knows how to alter a mental process or strengthen a mental power, and no one can be sure that he has done so when he has tried. There have been many good teachers who have supposed themselves to be working on the minds of their students, but their actual practices and the results of those practices can be analyzed in other ways. The well educated student is distinguished by certain characteristics. What are they, and how can they be produced? Perhaps we could answer by redefining traditional goals: instead of imparting knowledge, we could undertake to bring about those changes in behavior which are said to be the conspicuous manifestations of knowledge, or we could set up the behavior which is the mark of a man possessing well developed rational power. But mentalistic formulations are warped by irrelevant historical accidents. The behavior of the educated student is much more effectively analyzed directly as such.

Contrary to frequent assertions, a behavioristic formulation of human behavior is not a crude positivism which rejects mental processes because they are not accessible to the scientific public (12). It does not emphasize the rote learning of verbal responses. It does not neglect the complex systems of verbal behavior which are said to show that a student has had an idea, or developed a concept, or entertained a proposition. It does not ignore the behavior involved in the intellectual and ethical problem solving called "thinking." It does not overlook the value judgments said to be invoked when we decide to teach one thing rather than another or when we defend the time and effort given to education. It is merely an effective formulation of those activities of teacher and student which have always been the concern of educational specialists (11).

Not all behavioristic theories of learning are relevant, however. A distinction is commonly drawn between learning and performance. Learning is said to be a change in some special part of the organism, possibly the nervous system, of which behavior is merely the external and often erratic sign. With modern techniques, however, behavior can be much more successfully studied and manipulated than any such inner system, even when inferences about the latter are drawn from the behavior with the help of sophisticated statistics. An analysis of learning which concentrates on the behavior applies most directly to a technology, for the task of the teacher is to bring about changes in the student's behavior. His methods are equally conspicuous: he makes changes in the environment. A teaching method is simply a way of arranging an environment which expedites learning.

MANAGING CONTINGENCIES

Such a formulation is not easily assimilated to the traditional psychology of learning. The teacher may arrange contingencies of reinforcement to set up new *forms* of response, as in teaching handwriting and speech or nonverbal forms of behavior in the arts, crafts, and sports. He may arrange contingencies to bring responses under new kinds of *stimulus control,* as in teaching the student to read or draw from copy, or to behave effectively upon other kinds of occasions. Current instructional programs designed to fulfill such assignments are mainly verbal, but comparable contingencies generate nonverbal behavior, including perceptual and motor skills and various kinds of intellectual and ethical self-management.

A second kind of programing maintains the student's behavior in strength. The form of the response and the stimulus control may not change; the student is simply more likely to respond. Some relevant methods are traditionally discussed under the heading of motivation. For example, we can strengthen behavior by introducing new reinforcers or making old ones more effective, as in giving the student better reasons for getting an education. The experimental analysis of behavior suggests another important possibility: schedule available reinforcers more effectively. Appropriate terminal schedules of reinforcement will maintain the student's interest, make him industrious and persevering, stimulate his curiosity, and so on; but less demanding schedules, carefully designed to maintain the behavior at every stage, must come first. The programing of schedules of reinforcement is a promising alternative to the aversive control which, in spite of repeated reforms, still prevails in educational practice.

In neglecting programing, teaching methods have merely followed the lead of the experimental psychology of learning, where the almost universal practice has been to submit an organism immediately to terminal contingencies of reinforcement (13). A maze or a discrimination problem, for example, is learned only if the subject acquires appropriate behavior before the behavior he brings to the experiment has extinguished. The intermediate contingencies are largely accidental. The difference in behavior and in rate of learning which appear under these conditions are often attributed to inherited differences in ability.

In maximizing the student's success, programed instruction differs from so-called trial-and-error learning where the student is said to learn from his mistakes. At best, he learns not to make mistakes again. A successful response may survive, but trial-and-error teaching makes little provision for actually strengthening it. The method seems inevitably committed to aversive control. For the same reason, programed instruction does not closely resemble teaching patterned on everyday communication. It is usually not enough simply to tell the student something or induce him to read a book; he must be told or must read and then be questioned. In this "tell-and-test" pattern, the test is not given to measure what he has learned, but to show him what he has not learned and thus induce him to listen and read more carefully in the future. A similar basically aversive pattern is wide-spread at the college level, where the instructor assigns material and then examines on it. The student may learn to read carefully, to make notes, to discover for himself how to study, and so on, because in doing so he avoids aversive consequences, but he has not necessarily been taught. Assigning-and-testing is not teaching. The aversive by-products, familiar to everyone in the field of education, can be avoided through the use of programed positive reinforcement.

Many facts and principles derived from the experimental analysis of behavior are relevant to the construction of effective programs leading to terminal contingencies. The facts and principles are often difficult, but they make up an indispensable armamentarium of the effective teacher and educational specialist. We have long since passed the point at which our basic knowledge of human behavior can be applied to education through the use of a few general principles.

PRINCIPLE AND PRACTICE

The difference between general principles and an effective technology can be seen in certain efforts to assimilate the principles of programed instruction to earlier theories. Programed instruction has, for example, been called "Socratic." It is true that Socrates proceeded by small steps and often led his students through an argument with a series of verbal prompts, but the example often cited to illustrate his method suggests that he was unaware of an important detail—namely, that prompts must eventually be "vanished" in order to put the student on his own. In the famous scene in the *Meno*, Socrates demonstrates his theory that learning is simply recollection by leading an uneducated slave boy through Pythagoras's Golden Theorem. The boy responds with the rather timid compliance to be expected under the circumstances and never without help. Although Socrates himself and some of those among his listeners who were already familiar with the theorem may have understood the proof better at the end of the scene, there is no evidence whatsoever that the boy understood it or could reconstruct it. In this example of Socratic instruction, at least, the student almost certainly learned nothing.[1]

A seventeenth-century anticipation of programed instruction has also been found in the work of Comenius, who advocated teaching in small steps, no step being too great for the student who was about to take it. Programing is sometimes described simply as breaking material into a large number of small pieces, arranged in a plausible genetic order.

[1] The program of the *Meno* episode constructed by Cohen (2) is an improvement in that the student responds with less prompting.

But size of step is not enough. Something must happen to help the student take each step, and something must happen as he takes it. An effective program is usually composed of small steps, but the whole story is not to be found in Comenius's philosophy of education.

Another venerable principle is that the student should not proceed until he has fully understood what he is to learn at a given stage. Several writers have quoted E. L. Thorndike (15) to this effect, who wrote in 1912,

> If, by a miracle of mechanical ingenuity, a book could be so arranged that only to him who had done what was directed on page one would page two become visible, and so on, much that now requires personal instruction could be managed by print.

In commenting on this passage, Finn and Perrin (4) have written, ". . . Here are the insights of a genius. History can very often teach us a lesson in humility—and it does here. The interesting question is: why couldn't we see it then?" We might also ask, why couldn't Thorndike see it then? He remained active in education for at least 30 years, but he turned from this extraordinarily promising principle to another and—as it proved—less profitable approach to educational psychology.

It is always tempting to argue that earlier ideas would have been effective if people had only paid attention to them. But a good idea must be more than right. It must command attention; it must make its own way because of what it does. Education does not need principles which will improve education as soon as people observe them; it needs a technology so powerful that it cannot be ignored. No matter how insightful the anticipation of modern principles in earlier writers may seem to have been, something was lacking or education would be much further advanced. We are on the threshold of a technology which will be not only right but effective (14).

CRITERIA OF RESEARCH

A science of behavior makes its principal contribution to a technology of education through the analysis of useful contingencies of reinforcement. It also suggests a new kind of educational research. Thorndike never realized the potentialities of his early work on learning because he turned to the measurement of mental abilities and to matched-group comparisons of teaching practices. He pioneered in a kind of research which, with the encouragement offered by promising new statistical techniques, was to dominate educational psychology for decades. It led to a serious neglect of the process of instruction.

There are practical reasons why we want to know whether a given method or instruction is successful or whether it is more successful than another. We may want to know what changes it brings about in the student, possibly in addition to those it was designed to effect. The more reliable our answers to such questions, the better. But reliability is not enough. Correlations between test scores and significant differences between group means tell us less about the behavior of the student in the act of learning than results obtained when the investigator can manipulate variables and assess their effects in a manner characteristic of laboratory research. The practices evaluated in studies of groups of students have usually not been suggested by earlier research of a similar nature, but have been drawn from tradition, from the improvisations of skillful teachers, or from suggestions made by theorists working intuitively or with other kinds of facts. No matter how much they may have stimulated the insightful or inventive researcher, the evaluations have seldom led directly to the design of improved practices.

The contrast between statistical evaluation and the experimental analysis of teaching has an illuminating parallel in the field of medicine. Various drugs, regimens, surgical procedures, and so on, must be examined with respect to a very practical question: does the health of the patient improve? But "health" is only a general description of specific physiological processes, and "improvement" is, so to speak, merely a by-product of the changes in these processes induced by a given treatment. Medicine has reached the point where research on specific processes is a much more fertile source of new kinds of therapy than evaluations in terms of improvement in health. Similarly, in education, no matter how important improvement in the student's performance may be, it remains a by-product of specific changes in behavior resulting from the specific changes in the environment wrought by the teacher. Educational research patterned on an experimental analysis of behavior leads to a much better understanding of these basic processes. Research directed toward the behavior of the individual student has, of course, a long history, but it can still profit greatly from the support supplied by an experimental analysis of behavior.

This distinction explains why those concerned with experimental analyses of learning are not likely to take matched-group evaluations of teaching machines and programed instruction very seriously. It is not possible, of course, to evaluate either machines or programs *in general* because only specific instances can be tested, and available examples by no means represent all the possibilities; but even the evaluation of a given machine or program in the traditional manner may not give an accurate account of its effects. For example, those who are concerned with improvement are likely to test the student's capacity to give right answers. Being right has, of course, practical importance, but it is only one result of instruction. It is a doubtful measure of "knowledge" in any useful sense. We say that a student "knows the answer" if he can select it from an array of choices, but this does not mean that he could have given it without help. The right answer to one question does not imply right answers to all questions said to show the "possession of the same fact." Instructional programs are often criticized as repetitious or redundant when they are actually designed to put the student in possession of a number of different responses "expressing the same proposition." Whether such instruction is successful is not shown by any one right answer.

CORRECT OR EDUCATED?

A preoccupation with correct answers has led to a common misunderstanding of programed materials. Since a sentence with a blank to be filled in by the student resembles a test item, it is often supposed that the response demanded by the blank is what is learned. In that case, a student could not be learning much because he may respond correctly in 19 out of 20 frames and must therefore already have known 95 per cent of the answers. The instruction which occurs as he completes an item comes from having responded to other parts of it. The extent of this instruction cannot be estimated from the fact that he is right 19 out of 20 times, either while pursuing a program *or on a subsequent test*. Nor will this statistic tell us whether other conditions are important. Is it most profitable for the student to execute the response by writing it out, by speaking it aloud, by speaking it silently, or by reading it in some other way? These procedures may or may not have different effects on a selected "right-answer" statistic, but no one statistic will cover all their effects.

Research in teaching must not, of course, lose sight of its main objective—to make education more effective. But improvement as such is a questionable dimension of the behavior of either teacher or student. Dimensions which are much more intimately related to the conditions the teacher arranges to expedite learning must be studied even though they do not contribute to it in any way which is not immediately obvious.

The changes in the behavior of the individual student brought about by manipulating the environment are usually immediate and specific. The results of statistical comparisons of group performances usually are not. From his study of the behavior of the individual student, the investigator gains a special kind of confidence. He usually knows what he has done to get some effect and what he must do to get another.

Confidence *in* education is another possible result of an effective technology of teaching. Competition between the various cultures of the world, warlike or friendly, is now an accepted fact, and the role played by education in strengthening and perpetuating a given way of life is clear. No field is in greater need of our most powerful intellectual resources. An effective educational technology based upon an experimental analysis will bring it support commensurate with its importance in the world today.

REFERENCES

1. Bruner, J. S. *The process of education.* Cambridge: Harvard Univ. Press, 1960.
2. Cohen, I. S. Programed learning and the Socratic dialogue. *Amer. Psychologist,* 1962, *17,* 772–775.
3. Conant, J. B. *The education of American teachers.* New York: McGraw-Hill, 1963.
4. Finn, J. D., & Perrin, D. G. *Teaching machines and programmed learning: A survey of the industry, 1962.* Washington, D.C.: US Office of Education, 1962.
5. Helwig, J. Training of college teachers. *Sci.,* 1960, *132,* 845.
6. Hutchins, R. M. *On education.* Santa Barbara: Center for the Study of Democratic Institutions, 1963.
7. James, W. *Talks to teachers.* New York: Holt, 1899.
8. Pressey, S. L. A simple device for teaching, testing, and research in learning. *Sch. & Soc.,* 1926, *23,* 373–376.
9. Rickover, H. G. *Education and freedom.* New York: Dutton, 1959.
10. Skinner, B. F. The science of learning and the art of teaching. *Harvard Educ. Rev.,* 1954, *24,* 86–97.
11. Skinner, B. F. Why we need teaching machines. *Harvard Educ. Rev.,* 1961, *31,* 377–398.
12. Skinner, B. F. Behaviorism at fifty. *Sci.,* 1963, *140,* 951–958.
13. Skinner, B. F. Operant behavior. *Amer. Psychologist,* 1963, *18,* 503–515.
14. Skinner, B. F. *The technology of teaching* (in preparation).
15. Thorndike, E. L. *Education.* New York: Macmillan, 1912.

Chapter 20

What are the conditions which characterize an autotelic responsive environment?

How are the physical and social elements of the environment kept in balance?

What kinds of reactions and experiences have been encountered in using it with children?

How may the human teacher be used effectively in combination with autotelic responsive environments?

AUTOTELIC RESPONSIVE ENVIRONMENTS AND EXCEPTIONAL CHILDREN*

OMAR K. MOORE,
Professor of Social Psychology
University of Pittsburgh

In every society there are those who fail to learn the things which are held to be essential for carrying out the role of a competent adult, or who learn so slowly that they are generally out of phase with the age-graded societal demands imposed upon them. Slow learners are apt to be problems to themselves and to their friends. It is recognized, in scientific circles at least, that there are many and diverse causes for failure to learn at the socially prescribed rate: brain damage, emotional disturbance, social-cultural deprivation, and the like.[1]

What is not perhaps so generally recognized is that prodigies are sometimes out of phase with societal demands also; they tend to make people as uncomfortable as retarded children do. Both retarded children and prodigies unwittingly violate social expectations—they need

*This chapter is reprinted by permission of the author and publisher from *The Special Child in Century 21,* Special Child Publications, Seattle, 1964. Footnotes have been renumbered.

[1] At present there is no way to measure the basic capacities of human beings independently of their experiences. Also, there undoubtedly are interactional effects between CAPACITIES and EXPERIENCES. It is not assumed here that the retarded child is necessarily wanting in "basic capacity." The use here of such terms as "gifted" and "retarded" is simply intended to be consonant with standard usage in the field.

help if they are to reach their full potential. Both the ultrarapid and the ultraslow are *exceptional* children. The main topic of this paper is to describe some methods whereby the acquisition of complex skills can be accelerated, for both ultraslow and ultrarapid learners.

For a number of years my staff and I have been conducting studies of early learning in prenursery, nursery, kindergarten and first grades, where children are in the process of acquiring complex symbolic skills. In the course of this work I formulated the notion of a responsive environment (6) and decided to act on the assumption that an autotelic *responsive environment* is optimal for acquiring such skills. I will now try to make clear just what this assumption means.

I have defined a *responsive environment* as one which satisfies the following conditions:

1. It permits the learner to explore freely.
2. It informs the learner immediately about the consequences of his actions.
3. It is self-pacing, ie., events happen within the environment at a rate determined by the learner.
4. It permits the learner to make full use of his capacity for discovering relations of various kinds.
5. Its structure is such that the learner is likely to make a series of interconnected discoveries about the physical, cultural or social world.

My colleague, Alan Ross Anderson, and I have defined an activity as *autotelic* (1) if engaging in it is done for its own sake rather than for obtaining rewards or avoiding punishments that have no inherent connection with the activity itself. The distinction between autotelic and nonautotelic activities is somewhat vague, but it can be applied in some cases without difficulty.

Consider tennis playing as an example: we cannot play tennis without getting exercise, playing at all is a sufficient condition for exercising—so if we play for this reason, among others, this is an intrinsic reward. However, if we play for money, then the activity is not autotelic, since tennis and money need not go together—witness, amateur players.

In general, setting up a system of extrinsic rewards and punishments for engaging in an activity makes the learning environment more complex. As an illustration, consider a child who is learning to read aloud a list of words such as "fat" and "fate," "mat" and "mate," and "rat" and "rate," etc.; pretend also that an experimenter rewards or punishes the learner depending upon success or failure. Imagine that the reward is candy and that the punishment is mild electric shock.

Under these circumstances, the child not only has the task of learning to read and pronounce these words, but also that of figuring out the relation between candy and electric shock, on the one hand, and his own efforts, on the other. There is no intrinsic relation between the words to be learned or between the letters of the words and the pronunciation, or between candy and the sensation of being shocked. It should be easy to see that learning to read and to pronounce words *and also* to anticipate the candy or the shock introduce irrelevancies which may distract or confuse the learner. It is not irrelevant, however, that after the child masters the words "fat" and "fate," he may be able to generalize to the words "mat" and "mate," or that he may be able to decipher new words not on the list such as "tin" and "tine." Children are pleased, and some become ecstatic, when they make discoveries of this kind. Pleasure thus derived, unlike the pleasure of eating candy, is inherently related to the internal structure of the task (and more broadly to the structure of the spoken and written language) —it is *not* a pleasure arbitrarily associated with the task by the experimenter acting in accord with his own *ad hoc* rule. Of course, sophisticated adults manage to disentangle nonautotelic irrelevancies from the essential features of many tasks—but we hold that this is not an optimal situation for learning difficult things.

The distinction between autotelic and nonautotelic activities is sometimes confounded with the issue as to whether rewards and punishments are either necessary or sufficient for learning to occur at all. Our objection to the use of extrinsic rewards and punishments is that they make learning situations unnecessarily complex—in effect, they add relations to be learned. However, to grant that, generally, there are intrinsic awards and punishments associated with learning is not to prejudge the question as to whether learning could take place without them.

As a theoretical matter it is very difficult to see how a learning experiment could be designed, which would be in any way meaningful to the learner, and which would, at the same time, be devoid of all intrinsic rewards or punishments. In point of fact, we assume (for the sake of conceptual clarity vis-a-vis the making of a distinction between learning and performance, i.e., practicing what has been learned) that rewards and punishments, whether intrinsic or extrinsic, are neither necessary nor sufficient for the occurrence of learning. But of course no one would want to deny that they are highly relevant to the willingness of the learner to continue to learn more and to his desire to practice what he has learned.

From what has been said it is undoubtedly clear that not all responsive environments are autotelic, nor are all autotelic activities carried out within the context of responsive environments. It is the purpose of this paper to describe an environment which is *both* autotelic and responsive. I feel that I have been able to contrive an environment of this kind, which takes the form of a research laboratory, for young children. Some aspects of the autotelic responsive environments laboratory to be described here are novel; for example, the children play with a "talking typewriter." But in order to interpret the behavior of children within this environment, it is well to keep the system as a whole steadily in view—to see it as a social as well as a mechanical system. For this reason, a physical description of the laboratory is followed by a description of the norms under which the laboratory is operated. A cultural characterization of what is to be learned is counterbalanced by a description of equipment and procedures which facilitate the learning. No one aspect of the environment should be thought of as constituting its essence; the laboratory was designed to fulfill all the conditions of an autotelic responsive environment. The techniques of operation are intricate and presuppose careful planning. And since the description of an environment without some reference to the behavior of its denizens is incomplete, at the end of this paper information is given about the background and laboratory behavior of five children: two "educable retardates," one child on the borderline between the "educable retardate" and the "dull normal," one who is on the borderline between the "very bright" and the "gifted," and one "gifted" child (to use standard terminology).

The emphasis in this paper on exceptional children should not be construed as a lack of interest in those who are within the normal range. As a matter of fact, most of my work has been with normal children. However, extreme cases are sometimes illuminating—I hope that this is true here.

To return to the problems of those who do not meet the age-graded demands imposed upon them, the relevance of the research reported here on retarded youngsters is patent—anything which may help them become more competent is of educational interest. On the other hand, it is not at all obvious that accelerating prodigies is a socially useful thing to do—society seems to be organized so as to slow them down, if anything. However, a case can be made for the acceleration of prodigies. Indications will be given as to how prodigies can develop some of their own potentialities while helping other children in the development of theirs.

LABORATORY—PHYSICAL DESCRIPTION[2]

The Responsive Environments Laboratory (see Picture 1) is located at Hamden Hall Country Day School, Hamden, Connecticut, a few

[2] The Responsive Environments Laboratory described here served as the model for four other laboratories.

In order to avoid confusion, everything that is said here pertains to the Hamden Hall Laboratory although the children discussed in the section (p. 442) "Children in a Responsive Environment," did not necessarily come to this laboratory.

Picture 1.

yards from the Hamden Hall preschool classrooms. It consists of two adjoining prefabricated metal sheds, each 20′ x 40′, set on concrete foundations. One shed is windowless and the other has windows only in a small office area; they are centrally heated and air conditioned. The sheds are as simple as modern construction permits; they are made up of one-foot modular sections, have exposed ceiling and wall beams, and so on. In Shed 1 are five portable soundproofed booths, 7′ x 7′ x 7′, lined along two 40′ walls, leaving a middle aisle as well as small aisles between booths for observation through windows with one-way glass. Through a face and by-pass system the booths are separately air conditioned. One booth has camera ports and built-in lighting equipment so that sound motion pictures can be made on a semiautomatic basis (see Picture 2—ordinarily, the booth door is closed). Shed 1 also contains a desk, a conference table and a secretary's desk.

A central two-way communication system permits the staff to speak or listen either at the main console or at the booths themselves.

The interior of Shed 1 gives an impression of psychological warmth despite its spartan construction. Perhaps this is because the booths, which are its most prominent feature, have a natural wood finish. (Booth interiors are finished with off-white, sound-absorbent tiles.)

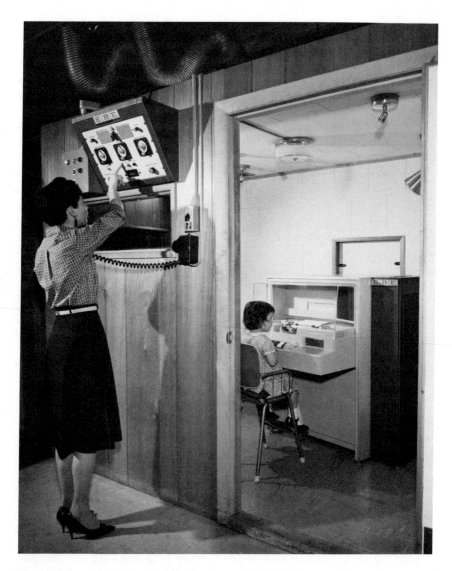

Picture 2.

Shed 2 is divided into three areas separated by natural wood partitions: a small classroom, an office-conference room which also contains a booth for testing, and a bathroom. From the standpoint of construction the 16′ x 20′ classroom is an oversized booth. Like the booths it is soundproofed, air conditioned, equipped with one-way glass, finished in natural wood (exterior) and natural wood and sound-absorbent tile (interior). Again there is provision for the making of motion pictures on a semiautomatic basis. Shed 1 is warm and pleasant in emotional tone; together they form one functional unit.

This laboratory was designed in accord with one overriding objective —that of making it conducive to carrying out autotelic activities by young children: it is simple, distinct, and separate. (a) Simple in the sense that a game board or a playing field is devoid of irrelevancies, (b) distinct in the sense that a playing field has clear-cut boundary lines, and (c) separate in the sense that a grandstand sets barriers between participants and spectators.

The parts of the laboratory used by children are windowless—windows are an open invitation to digress. The absence of windows also increases the children's sense of privacy. Inspection of Picture 2 makes it clear that the booth interiors are free of the attention-grabbing rococo patterns and whirligigs so typical of nursery and elementary classrooms. The soundproofing muffles irrelevant noises and further enhances a sense of privacy. The buildings are air conditioned in order to produce a constant comfortable environment—it makes no difference whether it is raining or snowing, sunny or cloudy, the general laboratory atmosphere is invariant. One-way windows, camera ports, semiautomatic motion-picture controls, and the like, make it possible to observe and document children's behavior without intruding upon them.

It is important to note that children spend only a small fraction of their day in this laboratory. It is not suggested here that gay designs and intriguing novelties are not appropriate in many other contexts.

LABORATORY—AUTOTELIC OPERATIONAL NORMS

Behavioral scientists take it for granted that human organizations function within the context of sets of interlocking social norms; this is certainly true of the Responsive Environments Laboratory as a social organization. By *operational norms* I mean the social rules which govern the relations between laboratory activities, on the one hand, and the school, the parents, and children, on the other.

One problem with which I have been concerned in constructing a new environment is that of being explicit about its normative aspects. A fundamental part of the task of creating a special environment for carrying on activities autotelically is to differentiate these activities from other important aspects of children's lives.

It is worth noting that, in addition to the educational problems mentioned at the outset, all, or nearly all, human societies make provision for engaging in autotelic activities. This is not only a matter of specifying times and places for these activities—the basketball court at game time; the theater at 8:40—but it is also a matter of creating and observing norms which safeguard these activities as autotelic. For example, one is not supposed to bribe a basketball player to shave points—the general public reacts with moral indignation whenever it is discovered that a norm of this kind has been violated. A distinction should be drawn between the norms which surround or protect an activity in its autotelic status and the rules of the activity itself. For example in bridge, onlookers are forbidden to *kibitz,* but this injunction is not a rule of the *game* of bridge. More generally, it is always possible to relax the norms which make an activity autotelic while leaving the rules of the "game" intact. Conversely, autotelic conventions can remain invariant while the rules of the game are changed.

With respect to the Responsive Environments Laboratory, every effort is made to maintain a setting in which "kibitzing" by parents and friends of the children is virtually impossible (there is a rule against their visiting[3] and the physical arrangement ensures privacy vis-a-vis the "significant persons" in the child's life—more technically, the "significant others," in the sense of Mead (3), are excluded.)

The staff seeks to make the laboratory a child-centered milieu. Even the introduction of a child to the laboratory is done by another child rather than an adult. A child guide takes the newcomer through the laboratory (equipment is turned off—the introduction to its operation is made later). Sometimes three introductory visits are needed before a newcomer seems to be at ease—although one visit is sufficient for most children. The guide also explains some of the relevant rules: 1) that he need not come to the laboratory unless he wants to, 2) that he can leave whenever he wishes, 3) that he must leave when his time is up (30 minutes maximum stay), 4) that he need not explain his coming or going, 5) that he go to the booth to which he is assigned for the day, 6) that if he says he wants to leave, or starts to leave, he *can* come back again the next day (but not the same day). Newcomers have the opportunity to explore every nook and corner of the laboratory. The guide watches this activity but does not interfere. After a while newcomers seem to feel satisfied that they have seen everything and are ready to leave.

It should be obvious that the role of the guide requires the ability to communicate clearly and to exercise self-restraint. The task of being a guide is assigned to gifted children; this is but one of many special tasks which they are given.

The laboratory staff is carefully instructed about treating the children. The import of the rules is that we want children to initiate activi-

---

3 As a matter of practice, parents are allowed one visit per school year. The visit is arranged so that they do not see their own child in a booth and the child does not see his parents in the laboratory. However, the laboratory has many visitors — roughly 600 in the past three years. Most visitors are either behavioral scientists or professional educators.

ties. The staff is to respond to them rather than to teach them. Those who are in daily interaction with the children are not permitted to see the background information gathered by the project's professional staff; for example, the operating personnel do not know I.Q. test scores. Operating personnel are randomly assigned to booths every day. (There are two kinds of booths, automated and nonautomated. In nonautomated booths an adult is with the child. Since these adults do not teach, we prefer to call them "booth assistants."[4] The members of the staff who are professional teachers[5] serve as supervisors of the laboratory as a whole, as well as the booths.) No booth assistant should be uniquely associated with any given booth and its equipment, or with any particular child. (Children, as well as booth assistants, are randomly assigned to booths each day.)[6] The conduct of the operating staff is monitored by a supervisor who can talk directly to the booth assistant without interruping a child. This is especially important in training new booth assistants. (The foregoing remarks are applicable to nonautomated booths—at present there is one fully automated booth, which requires no adult in the booth with the child; further details about automation appear below.)

The Hamden Hall children leave their classrooms (nursery, kindergarten and first-grade) to come to the laboratory every school day. When it is a child's turn to come, his classroom teacher[7] lets him know. He then either accepts or rejects his turn for the day. If he decides to come he takes his "pass" and goes by himself the few yards to the laboratory where he is checked in and goes to the booth assistant to whom he has been assigned. One of the most remarkable things about this environment is that, day in and day out, children elect to come

---

4 Booth assistants generally have been the wives of graduate students. (This means we have to train new assistants quite frequently because of husbands' graduating.) One of the qualifications for the job of booth assistant is a strong aesthetic sense — teacher training is not necessary. The importance assigned to aesthetics is perhaps a prejudice on my part. I assume that those who are artistically inclined are likely to find the subtle workings of children's minds to be of continuing interest, and that they are not apt to impose their views on children. This assumption may be unwarranted but it has resulted in the selection of remarkably empathic, nondirective and patient booth assistants.

5 It has been my experience that professional teachers who work out well as laboratory supervisors have both the ability to empathize with children and to organize efficiently. The role of laboratory supervisor is a critical one for the successful employment of the methods we are considering. It is in this role that the teacher, as a professional, can use her training and experience to good advantage. The seasoned professional teacher can draw on her years of experience to do such things as spot the child who is ill and should go home, or to analyze the hitches which arise in the process of performing a task which requires nicely coordinated effort on the part of the staff.

6 Of the 102 children that I have studied there have been a few who, at times, have responded so much better to a particular booth assistant, or to the nonautomated equipment, or to the automated instrumentation than they did to the other conditions, that the laboratory departed from the usual procedure of random assignment until they were able to play with pleasure wherever they found themselves. It will be made clear in the section (p. 442) "Children in a Responsive Environment" that it is important to take individual variability into account.

7 The regular classroom teacher, like the laboratory supervisor, is important to the successful employment of these methods in the context of a school. She must be flexible enough to organize her own classroom activities so that the short individual trips to the laboratory do not unsettle the general routine. Her attitudes toward early learning are also important.

to it—sometimes several months go by without one child of the current group (which numbers 60) refusing his turn. However, it frequently happens that a child does not want to leave when his time is up—in which case he is gently picked up and told that another child is waiting.

From what has been said it should be clear that the adults the child encounters in the laboratory are *not* the significant adults in his life—they are *not* his mother, father, grandmother, etc. Those significant adults who ordinarily are in the best position to reward or punish him have no way of knowing how he spends his time in the laboratory on a day-to-day basis. It is therefore unlike Little League Baseball, with relatives and friends observing from the sidelines; the laboratory time represents 30 minutes *away from* the significant persons in his life.

To "cut off" 30 minutes from the rest of the day in this fashion does not necessarily mean that the experience is without consequences for the remainder of the child's day. Just as most autotelic activities make use of cultural objects (2), (5), (13), (14), which are formally isomorphic with significant features of many serious activities (as Anderson and I (12) have argued before, (a) puzzles, (b) games of chance, (c) games of strategy, and (d) aesthetic objects are formally similar to (a) puzzling situations, (b) the aleatory features of experience, (c) cooperative and competitive undertakings, and (d) the affective side of living) so, too, it is possible to design autotelic responsive environments in which a child can play with cultural objects, which though not ordinarily treated autotelically, are still structurally isomorphic with selected aspects of the world outside the laboratory.

GENERAL DESCRIPTION OF THE CURRICULUM

As remarked above, a responsive environment is so structured that the learner is likely to make a series of interconnected discoveries about the physical, cultural or social world. A responsive environment may occur naturally, or it may be planned; in this paper the main interest is in the latter, i.e., environments that are artificially contrived to achieve certain objectives. Therefore, it is essential to decide what the learners are to be exposed to in the way of a curriculum. It will be explained below in the section, "Procedures and Equipment," that there is a wide range of subjects which can be learned in a responsive environments laboratory.

Recently, and for the past several years, attention has been focused on acquiring languages, especially languages in their written form. From the perspective of a cultural analysis, the topic is a natural language and the children's *task* is to learn how to handle it more effectively. It was taken for granted that the children would already be able to use their native tongue (to date, most of the work has been done with English). My objective, then, was to design an environment (within the microworld of the booths) in which children would learn another form of their language: its written form. This enterprise presupposes that, in the broadest sense, spoken English and written English are isomorphic.

From this standpoint, we can think of written English as visible speech and spoken English as audible writing. It is true that written English is a very imperfect phonetic transcription of speech; nevertheless, in planning this environment, I decided to work on the assumption that the spoken and written forms of English are *sufficiently* isomorphic[8] to enable children to find for themselves some set of rules which would permit them to move back and forth between these two linguistic forms. Certainly, spoken and written English are more nearly isomorphic than are spoken English and written German or spoken Chinese and written Chinese.

One of the obvious differences between spoken and written English is that they are handled through two distinct sensory systems—auditory and visual. There are also social differences between the two linguistic forms in their appropriate occasions of use. But young children do not know this and perhaps by constructing an environment in which writing is on a par with speaking and reading with listening, it might be possible to avoid some of the more unfortunate consequences of our educational system; a system which tends to produce speakers who have difficulty in writing, and tongue-tied writers. There also are avid readers who find it almost impossible to write—and good listeners seem to be in short supply all the way around.

I should like to make it clear (once and for all, I might add) that the Responsive Environments Laboratory is *not* just a place where children learn to read: approximately equal emphasis is given to speaking, writing, listening and reading. The underlying rationale is not only to treat speaking and listening, on the one hand, and writing and reading, on the other, as correlative processes, nor is it only to treat these two pairs of correlatives as elements of a four-cell matrix of linguistic relations. It is also to develop higher-order symbolic skills which are superordinate to these relations.

Speaking and writing are active processes and listening and reading are passive ones. An attempt is made to tie each of these four activities (or passivities) to the others, not only maintaining a balance between

---

[8] By an *isomorphism* I mean something like the vague, usual use of the word in mathematics. Two structures are said to be "isomorphic" if there is a one-to-one correspondence between their elements which "preserves order" in some appropriate sense, i.e., which preserves corresponding relations defined on each structure. In practice we have to define isomorphisms, one at a time, for each structure in which we are interested. But the idea is at least sufficiently clear so that we can usually tell when we have one.

active and passive processes, but also avoiding the pitfalls of under-emphasizing or over-emphasizing any one of them at the expense of the others. The overall objective is to develop higher-order intellectual abilities which may be thought of as ranging over this complex of linguistic processes.

In order to determine whether such overall abilities are developing and, at the same time, to facilitate their development, it is necessary to set some task for the children which involves all four of the processes. There are many jobs which would do the work. The one which was chosen as a part of the laboratory curriculum was publishing a newspaper. The first-grade class publishes its own newspaper (there are also contributions by nursery and kindergarten children) and the four processes (speaking, writing, listening and reading) are subordinate to the superordinate skill of *publishing a newspaper*. A child may begin a newspaper story by speaking into a microphone; later, he will type his own story from dictation—this means that he goes directly from the spoken word to the written word. After he has completed his transcription he may then read it critically before turning it over to one of the other children who is an editor. The editor first proofreads the copy, perhaps reading it aloud to a fellow editor, and then the suggested changes are discussed with the author. Then the children type it on stencils along with other stories. Finally, they mimeograph, collate, staple and distribute the paper. If they wish to discuss the newspaper in their regular classroom, they may do so (with their teacher's permission). It is also permissible to take the newspaper home where it is sometimes subject to further discussion.

It can be seen, then, that publishing a paper, as the children do it, is an achievement which embraces speaking, writing, listening and reading. This activity provides guide lines on the basis of which the children set standards for spelling, punctuation, intelligibility, general relevance and interest. The emergence of such a higher-order skill helps give to reading and writing the same kind of direction and meaning that listening and speaking have by virtue of their ordinary social uses.

Publishing a newspaper is an activity which ordinarily would be beyond the ability of a first-grade class. Permitting the children themselves to set the standards of the newspaper seems like a risky educational practice; however, here again is another vital role for gifted children to play. They are capable of serving as editors and coordinating the efforts of the other children, which allows them to make extensive use of their intellectual abilities within the social context of their peer group.

By the time the laboratory children are able to publish a newspaper the subordinate skills have been learned well enough so that the *learning* problem has been replaced by the *practicing* problem. There are many intrinsic rewards and punishments associated with turning out a newspaper. To be sure, when the proud parents get copies there may be additional extrinsic rewards and punishments—but by this time it is too late for anyone to interfere with the learning of the subordinate skills.

The actual work of turning out the newspaper is done under the supervision of a teacher who introduces the children to the equipment (copy aid, mimeograph, thermofax, etc.) and guides their first efforts. This takes place within the small classroom in the laboratory mentioned in the section "Laboratory—Physical Description." This classroom is called the "transfer room." What this name connotes is the *transfer* of skills acquired individually within the privacy of the booths to social activities. Just as we make explicit provision for the introduction of children to the laboratory with the help of gifted child guides, we also make explicit provision for relating laboratory activities to outside interests through the help of our more precocious children who serve as editors. The children are very proud of their newspaper—everyone contributes in his own way and most importantly it really is *theirs*.

In many schools the curriculum for the first six grades tends to treat reading and writing as separate subjects. Writing in the sense of composing original stories is yet another subject. Spelling and particularly punctuation are handled as special topics; and some punctuation marks (say), the ampersand, asterisk, colon, or semicolon, are entities whose appearance on the printed page remain a mystery to many even beyond the Ph.D. dissertation. The laboratory curriculum represents an attempt to deal with these skills and topics as part of an integrated complex of linguistic processes. In the next section we describe some procedures and equipment by which children can be led to such excellence.

PROCEDURES AND EQUIPMENT

In this section an effort will be made to exploit further the notion of an autotelic responsive environment. Useful as this idea proved to be in constructing my laboratory and in laying down guide lines for its operation, it still did not have a sharp enough cutting edge to be of much help in planning the procedures and equipment to be used by children within the microworld of laboratory booths. I found that it was worthwhile, as an aid to my thinking at least, to make additional assumptions of a psychological kind about personality and human learning processes in order to get a purchase on the problem of designing practical procedures and equipment. Fortunately, I had been working for a number of years on the more general problems of formulating a theory of social interaction. This theory is still in an unsatisfactory state; nonetheless, the procedures and equipment described here are an application of some of its fundamental ideas. It lies beyond the scope of this paper to present even as much of the theory as has been worked out, but for present purposes it probably will be sufficient to say that this theory builds on the work of George Herbert Mead (3), or, more accurately, it builds upon his work as I understand it. It also takes some account of the subject matter of other important psychological and social psychological theories.

Phase 1. Free Exploration.

Let us turn our attention now to the interior of a booth and imagine that a child, already introduced to the laboratory in the manner previously explained, is ready for his first booth session. For convenience of exposition pretend that he is to begin learning in an automated booth. (The reader may find it helpful to re-examine Picture 2 which shows a 2-year 11-month old child sitting at E.R.E.,[9] or what the laboratory children call a "talking typewriter.") The booth assistant helps him get into the elevated chair (because some children do not like to sit in a *high chair,* in the laboratory we call it an "elevated chair"), turns one switch, tells the child to enjoy himself and to raise his hand if he wants anything. Without further comment the assistant leaves the booth, closes the booth door and then goes to a control panel (shown in Picture 2) mounted on the exterior wall of the booth, presses appropriate buttons and begins to watch the child through a one-way window located just below the control panel.

The child is alone in the booth confronted with what may appear to him to be a typewriter with colored keys. (Prior to entering the booth his fingernails have been painted with nontoxic water colors. There is a match between the nail colors and the colored typewriter keys so that striking keys with matching fingers constitutes correct fingering. Also, there is a noticeable difference in pressure between the left-hand and the right-hand keys to help the child orient his hands. Behind the keyboard is a lucite housing which permits him to see everything in front of him, but which keeps his fingers out of the moving parts of the typewriter.) Whether or not he believes that the

[9] E.R.E., the Edison Responsive Environment, is the product of a three-year collaborative effort with an engineering team of the Thomas A. Edison Research Laboratory of West Orange, New Jersey, a division of the McGraw-Edison Company.

Richard Kobler, the head of the engineering team, and I invented E.R.E. and have applied for two key patents in 12 countries. Other members of the team have applied for patents on certain E.R.E. components. (Complete mechanical descriptions of the instrument will be available through patent offices when the patents are issued.)

object in front of him is some kind of a typewriter, as a matter of fact, he is in charge of much more than an electric typewriter—he is at the controls of a computer in-put and read-out device, three distinct memory systems, an audio-recording system, and two visual exhibition systems, all of which are integrated by a central electronic logic and control system. Nevertheless, the operation of this complex instrument is under his management.

Of course, not all of the abilities of the instrument are needed for the child's first session. The booth assistant has set E.R.E. in what is called *Phase 1, Free Exploration,* i.e., the instrument is set so that the child can explore the keyboard freely. Whenever a key is struck, E.R.E. types the letter (the "reaction time" of E.R.E. to a key operation averages $\frac{1}{10}$th of a second.) When a key has been depressed and released no key can be operated for about one second—this gives E.R.E. time to pronounce the name of the character. No two keys can be depressed simultaneously—this makes it impossible to jam keys or to garble pronunciations. The moment any given pronunciation is completed, the keyboard is automatically unlocked so that the child can go on exploring. The keyboard of E.R.E. is, essentially, a full standard one (it has some additional keys which are needed for foreign languages— E.R.E. can be switched to any of six languages and special accent marks are provided—the extra keys are covered when not in use). Because the standard keyboard has both upper and lower cases, and the young child probably does not know this, there are small lights next to the upper- and lower-case keys to show which case is operative. If the child were to play by himself with an ordinary typewriter he might get "stuck" at the end of a line because he does not know about the carriage return. E.R.E. automatically returns the carriage at the end of a line even though there is a carriage return key whose function the child will catch on to sooner or later. His exploration will not be interrupted by using up a sheet of paper—E.R.E. has a fan-folded tape of paper several thousand feet long. It should also be mentioned that E.R.E. is rugged—it withstands the pounding it sometimes receives.

Returning to the hypothetical child, the intriguing question is, what will he do when he is alone at the keyboard of the "talking typewriter"? —until he strikes the first key he does not even know that the typewriter talks. (A motion picture was made of the first few minutes of a normal 2-year 7-month old boy's initial exploration of a keyboard (10). This film shows nonautomated equipment with a booth assistant carrying out the various functions performed by E.R.E. This boy's behavior is typical of many normal children.) One thing we can say with near certainty about our hypothetical child is that he will not sit there for a half an hour simply looking at the instrument. Only one child out of the 102 children whom I have studied sat for as long as 10 minutes before striking a key. Most children begin immediately using fingers, fists, elbows and an occasional nose—if the instrument were not jam-proof, the game would be halted in less than a minute, or if the keyboard were not locked during pronunciations, E.R.E. would babble. There are children who proceed in a very thoughtful way; looking, listening, repeating what the instrument says, reflecting—in brief, they explore systematically. Some notice at once the relation between their colored fingernails and the colored keys and painstakingly match fingers to keys. If, at first, a finger is wayward, they use their other hand to guide it. Some children go on exploring for their full 30 minutes; others raise their hands and want to leave after a few minutes.

In order to guess what our hypothetical child is likely to do, it would be necessary to posit a great deal more about him. I will make one overall comment based on my experience with the laboratory children —he will like his first session and he will want to return to play with this fascinating "toy."

A daily record is kept of each child's performance in the laboratory. Some parts of this cumulative record are quite objective—E.R.E., for example, keeps track of the time the child spends in the booth and his stroke count, i.e., the number of times he depresses keys. Other aspects of the record are less objective—for instance, booth assistants' notes about a child's attitude. There is a daily staff conference at which each child's performance is reviewed. It is the laboratory supervisor's responsibility to decide when a child is beginning to lose interest in any given phase of the curriculum. There are children who will go on happily in Phase 1, Free Exploration, for a number of weeks, whereas others' interest in this phase declines rapidly after as few as two sessions. Sooner or later every child's interest in Phase 1 will wane (at least every child the laboratory has encountered behaved this way) and before his interest completely disappears, he must be shifted to the next phase. If a child were permitted to completely exhaust his interest, he might very well not return to the laboratory. Quite clearly, the decision as to when to shift a child from one phase to another still is a matter of experience and judgment. In the early days of this research I had to make this decision. Later, I trained supervisors who now are fully capable of performing this task. For the most part, the more objective indicators of declining interest are a sufficient basis for judgment—for example, a child's sessions become markedly shorter and his stroke count drops off. Sometimes a child will simply say that he is tired of what he is doing—his opinion counts. As a general rule, it is safer to err on the side of shifting the child too soon. It will be made clear below that explicit provision is made for regressing from advanced phases to more elementary ones, and since no significant persons in his life are there to see this regression, there is little stigma attached to it. All the children whom I have studied have regressed from time to time. The children call Phase 1 (Free Exploration) "plain typing." It is not unusual for even a gifted child to say with a little laugh, "Today I just want to plain type."

Phase 2. Search and Match.

When the laboratory supervisor makes the decision to shift a child from Phase 1 to the next phase, the learner receives no warning—he has to discover for himself that he is playing a new game with new rules. Phase 2 is called "Search and Match." In order to understand what this game involves, let us examine Picture 3.

Picture 3.

This is a close-up view of E.R.E. "opened up"—the lucite housing is raised part way to show how the booth assistant can remove the child's paper. There is a picture of a barn on a rear-view projection screen— the open panel to its right shows where the projector is loaded. To the left of the barn is an illuminated rectangular window—exhibitor cards can be inserted into this space through the open door on top. On the upper right side of E.R.E. is a triangular shaped open panel—this exposes controls for some of E.R.E.'s functions which are set by the booth assistant.

In Phase 2 the exhibitor system on which the picture of a barn is projected is not used. The only new thing about this phase, in terms of visual display, is the use of the rectangular window. In this window characters can be exhibited in four different ways: 1) one character at a time with a red arrow pointing down to it; 2) a cumulative exhibit in which the red arrow points to a newly exposed character while all previously exposed characters on the same line remain visible; 3) all characters on one line are visible with the red arrow pointing to the one to be typed; and 4) all characters on the four lines in the rectangular window are exposed, again with the red arrow pointing to the one to be typed.

In Phase 2, unlike Phase 1, E.R.E. takes the initiative in starting the game. All typewriter characters appear in the rectangular exhibitor window one at a time in random order. When a character appears with the red arrow pointing to it, E.R.E. automatically locks the keyboard with the exception of the appropriate matching key and pronounces the name of the character. If the child wants to get a response from E.R.E., he must find the right key. As soon as he strikes the matching key which causes the character to be typed, E.R.E. repronounces the character and then covers it up before exposing a new one. The game becomes a little more difficult when the new character is in a different case—under this circumstance, E.R.E. first says "upper case" or "lower case" (as the case may be), the appropriate case light flickers, and the keyboard must be changed to the proper case (when this is done it repronounces it) before the matching character is named by E.R.E. and can be struck by the child. It should be mentioned that if a child is fast enough at pressing the appropriate key, he can cause E.R.E. to speed up by omitting redundant pronunciations. If a child's attention has wandered so that he missed the first pronunciation, or if he has forgotten it, there is a repeat cycle which the booth assistant can start, using a delay appropriate for the given child. A dial can be set which will delay E.R.E.'s repronunciation in order to give the child a chance to speak first. E.R.E. is not restricted to pronouncing the names of characters—it also can give phonetic values for them (or, for the linguistic purist, hints as to phonetic values).

What has just been described is the simplest version of Phase 2, Search and Match. As interest wanes in this first version of Phase 2, the booth assistant (following the laboratory supervisor's instructions) can make the game more challenging in many ways. For example, the assistant can cause (by pushing buttons or setting dials) E.R.E. to omit its first pronunciation of characters, or the second, or both. The window display can be changed to show characters cumulatively, one line at a time, or four lines at a time. A blank card can be used in the window so that the match is solely between pronunciation and keys.

I have found that adults, as well as children, like to play with E.R.E. in both Phase 1, Free Exploration, and the various versions of Phase 2, Search and Match. These activities are especially interesting to adults when E.R.E. is switched to a foreign language—one unfamiliar to the players. Of course, for children who are learning to read, the written form of English is a new language. Both children and adults discover that they always can succeed in finding the appropriate key in Search and Match by the simple-minded expedient of trying each key. This is a tedious and boring way to go at it on a continuing basis; both children and adults prefer to learn the characters.

Phase 3. Word Construction.

When a child has eliminated nearly all of the "search" from the Search and Match game, it is time to shift to a new phase of the curriculum. Phase 3 is called "Word Construction"—there are two forms of this game. One form leads to reading, the other to writing, i.e., writing in the sense of composing original stories. We will designate the former as "WC-R" (Word Construction-Reading) and the latter as "WC-W" (Word Construction-Writing). When a child has been shifted to Phase 3 he alternates in his booth sessions between these two forms of the game. Let us take up WC-R first.

Phase 3. WC-R. Up to this point, the child has been dealing exclusively with the building blocks, or primitive elements, of the written language (notice that punctuation marks have not been neglected)—he has been exposed to and can discriminate among the basic set of elements from which all meaningful written expressions are formed. He is in a position to begin to get some sense of the formation rules of the written language. Now other of E.R.E.'s abilities can be brought into play.

Imagine that a child, who has become quick at finding individual characters, is confronted without notice with several of them at a time, isolated either by a margin and a space or by spaces. For instance, the first letters might be *b-a-r-n*. So, the child types *b-a-r-n*. E.R.E. pronounces these letters before and after each is struck and then, following the pronunciation of *n*, it calls for a space. A light flickers just under the space bar, and after the bar is pressed, E.R.E. says, "Space, *b-a-r-n*, barn." E.R.E. may also exhibit a barn on the projector as shown in Picture 3. (As a matter of fact, pictures have been used very sparingly because they can be quite misleading in the early phases of learning to handle written symbols. The referent of many important words such as "if," "then," "either," "or," "some," etc., cannot be pictured in the same way that the referent of the word "barn" can be. Other words which are relational, but not obviously so, as "mother," "father," "sister," etc., are not as easily denoted through pictures as some writers of children's primers seem to think. The use of pictures comes into its own when E.R.E. is "teaching" foreign languages or in Phase 4 where content, e.g., maps for geography, is important.)

From the standpoint of planning the curriculum, WC-R offers an indefinitely large number of choices with respect to the selection of a beginning or basic vocabulary. The question is, What words should come first? There are a great many plausible criteria which have been offered by reading experts, linguists and others who have concerned themselves with this topic. For example, 1) word frequency, 2) letter frequency, 3) pronounceableness, 4) word length, 5) familiarity, 6) stimulus similarity, 7) grapheme-phoneme correspondence, etc. It is apparent that at least some of these are conflicting criteria, for instance, many familiar words are phonetically irregular. A sophisticated analysis could be carried through in which a vocabulary was selected in terms of a multidimensional weighting system based on the contribution various "dimensions" of words make to easy learning. I have no doubt that careful experimental studies would be of value in selecting an optimal basic vocabulary.

For my own part, faced with the problem of selection, I preferred a direct solution, namely, to choose those words which are constituents of interesting stories—that is, stories which have proved to be intriguing to children and adults over a long period of time, for example, Aesop's Fables.[10] Many children can be expected to have lost interest in WC-R long before they have mastered a vocabulary large enough to enable them to read a wide variety of stories. Therefore, it is essential to be able to shift them to at least some stories—they only can do this if they have mastered enough of the words to get started reading them. If the stories are of some intellectual and aesthetic value, it is highly probable that the words out of which they are composed will offer a sufficient basis for making sound inferences about the relations between letters and sets of letters, on the one hand, and appropriate verbalizations, on the other.

The inventor, Samuel Morse, was faced with a similar problem when he was devising his code consisting of spaces, dots and dashes. He wanted, in the interest of efficiency, to have the shorter symbols for the more frequently used letters, and the longer symbols for those less frequently used. If he had been like some contemporary investigators, he might have launched a rather extensive research project sampl-

---

[10] I have also made use of word lists suggested by linguists and at times have combined these lists with those compiled from interesting stories.

ing the distribution of the letters of the alphabet in various writings—but he did nothing of the sort! What he did instead was to count the number of types in the various compartments of a printer's type box. He assumed that printers would have discovered empirically the right proportion of letters to keep on hand in order to set type, and incidentally, this solution to his problem was within 15 percent of an optimal one.[11]

I assume that stories which have stood up over long periods of time use words in ways that are compatible with the intricate sets of relations holding between the spoken and the written forms of the language. I am not quite as sanguine about some of the concocted stories found in contemporary "basal" readers, although children can learn to read using basic vocabularies that are, in all likelihood, far from optimal. One would have to be very unlucky in his selections if he were to happen upon a rare instance of written material in which the author had some fantastic linguistic bias. For example, Gottlob Burmann, a German poet (1737–1805), wrote 130 poems (20,000 words) without once using the letter *e*. In 1641 Alonso Alcalá y Herrera published five stories in which he suppressed a different vowel in each. The 267 page novel *Gadsby*, by Ernest Vincent Wright, published in 1939, was written without any help from the letter *e* (15). This is all good fun, but writings of this sort probably are not satisfactory as basal readers.

Phase 3. WC-W. The form of the Word Construction game explained above is somewhat arbitrary from a child's standpoint. The experimenter has decided, in advance, what is good for him. It is especially important, from the point of view of sustaining children's interest, to let them take the initiative. It is also important to see to it that at times there is an almost perfect correspondence between their verbal skills and the written symbols with which they will be dealing. WC-W serves these purposes. The first step in this activity is to have the child go to the Transfer Room (the small classroom described in *Laboratory— Physical Description*) where he is encouraged to talk—he may talk about anything he pleases—and everything that he says is recorded. Later, an analysis is made of his utterances and a list is compiled consisting of those words which are constituents of coherent statements on some topic in which he was engrossed. Sometimes it has taken weeks with a child to elicit such material. The next step is to program this word list in E.R.E. (E.R.E. is easily programed—it is not necessary to translate material into a machine language, hence, there are no technical difficulties to get in the way.) The child is virtually certain to find some of his own words meaningful.

---

[11] The foregoing information about Morse is found in Pierce's valuable book on information theory (15).

An alternative version of WC-W involves the use of a standard recording-reproducing unit attached to E.R.E. or to an electric typewriter. This version does not require programing. The child simply talks into a microphone and then takes his own dictation, word by word. In this version of the game, he responds to his own voice. Interestingly enough, from a social-psychological perspective, some children reject their own voice, but will type other children's dictation. Some three-year olds have learned to be very skillful in taking dictation. A motion picture (4) was made of a girl 3-years 11-months old doing just this. In this film she first read a story—her voice was recorded —and then she typed the story from listening only; she handled the dictation controls (start, stop, repeat) by herself.

This second version of WC-W eliminates the presentation of written symbols—the child goes directly from verbal utterances to the corresponding written symbols. Visitors who have watched this process are often surprised by children's ability to spell new words that are nonphonetic—or markedly irregular. Indeed, this is extraordinary! I have concluded that there must be some subtle lawfulness holding between the spoken and written forms of English, otherwise young children would not spell as well as they do in this version of WC-W. This should give pause to enthusiasts for spelling reform. In any case, this relation seems worthy of serious study.

Phase 4. Reading and Writing.

Anyone who has followed children's progress from Free Exploration to Search and Match and on through Word Construction easily can see that the shift to Phase 4 comes very naturally. E.R.E. is at its best here. It can read a sentence, a paragraph, or tell a story before or after a child types, while at the same time it can continue to respond to individual characters and words. In sum, it can deal with higher-order units while exercising all of the abilities previously described with reference to the earlier learning sequences.

E.R.E., of course, can ask questions, just as teachers do. The questions may pertain to what is visually exhibited in the rectangular window or on the projection screen—the questions may call for subtle interpretations. Answers can either be typed out or expressed verbally on E.R.E.'s own recording-reproducing unit.

The material programed for E.R.E. can be as banal as the dullest courses in school or it can be as stimulating as the best of new programs, for example, some in modern mathematics or science. (It should be noted that E.R.E. can handle many aspects of mathematics and of science programs—numbers and some arithmetic symbols are on the keyboard.)

Every effort is made to select materials which give children a chance to make imaginative interpretations. As a general principle, it seems advisable to select materials which permit several levels of interpretation. A good case in point is *Alice in Wonderland.* Retarded, normal, and gifted children can all begin reading this story with enjoyment just because it starts off with a little girl and an extraordinary rabbit. Even though gifted children like the manifest content of Alice's adventures, at the same time, they can begin to get glimpses of deeper meanings. A serious objection to many stories found in beginning readers is that they confine children to one interpretation since the manifest content of such stories is all there is to them.

It is in Phase 4[12] that the methodology presented in this paper must come to terms with the traditional school curriculum. The bridging mechanism between the laboratory booths and the school classroom is the Laboratory's Transfer Room. Here, children who have been working alone have an opportunity to engage in cooperative activities, for example, publishing a newspaper, under the guidance of a teacher. Discipline emerges from the interaction of the children with each other.

When children go to first grade, having reached Phase 4 both in reading and composing original stories, a new curriculum is needed. Most of the things which ordinarily are taught in first grade lie far behind them. (This year at the end of first grade, the Hamden Hall Country Day School children who had been in the program at least two years, read, on the average according to the Metropolitan Achievement Test, at the beginning sixth-grade level. For second grade they again will require a totally new curriculum.) The half hour a day the children can spend in the laboratory is certainly not a substitute for the rest of the school day. Fortunately, at Hamden Hall there has been strong administrative support for curriculum revision.[13] However, an adequate curriculum is not the whole answer either—competent teachers are equally necessary. Teachers find that they have independent students on their hands—students who are accustomed to solving problems on their own or in cooperation with their peers.

Handwriting.

One of the five booths is reserved for learning to write by hand. The writing equipment in this booth is primitive—it consists of a lined

---

12 There is a Phase 5, the Dialogue (6), which is not presented here for two reasons: (a) to keep this paper within reasonable bounds, and (b) as yet, I have had no experience with children in this phase. Essentially, the Dialogue has to do with children's interpreting group interaction and taking what is said in dictation, adding the necessary punctuation, and connecting commentary so as to create a plausible reconstruction of on-going social situations in which they were participants. The Dialogue is of theoretical importance because of its connection with the Meadean concept of the "generalized other" (3).

13 It is not within the scope of this paper to present the school curriculum which is still being developed. However, in broad outline, the curriculum is based upon the notion of folk models (1) and their scientific formalizatïon.

blackboard, chalk and eraser. On a random basis children spend about one-tenth of their time in this booth after they have completed Phase 1. I assumed that after children had been exposed to the characters on the typewriter they would begin to reproduce them manually if they had the opportunity. Children begin by scribbling or drawing pictures on the board, but it would appear that some would go on doing this indefinitely if they were not subtly guided by a patient booth assistant. The difficulty lies in the fact that the environment is not sufficiently responsive. (Automated equipment could be devised for facilitating the development of this skill.)

The children are exposed to cursive or manuscript writing, as opposed to printing, through the use of typewriters with cursive type. This serves to familiarize them with this form of writing. Even two- and three-year-olds, including retarded children, can learn to print and write in the cursive style. A motion picture has been made of the printing of a few preschool children in order to show what they can do (9), (10), (11).

      ✿   ✿   ✿   ✿

I promised at the beginning of this section to try to explain the various phases of the learning sequence in terms of the use of automated instrumentation. However, in the development of this program of research, work began with nonautomated equipment—modified electric typewriters, projectors, recording-reproducing units, and so on. The functional specifications for automated equipment were obtained by coding the activities of booth assistants using nonautomated devices.

In the nonautomated form of Phases 1 through 4, the booth assistant sits in a chair beside the child who is at a modified electric typewriter. The booth assistant has a switch which is used to control the typewriter in the same way that E.R.E.'s logic and control circuitry does. The booth assistant is instructed to be passive just as is E.R.E. Of course, not all booth assistants carry out this role perfectly day after day— some have a strong tendency to intrude upon children. It requires constant monitoring by the laboratory supervisor to keep booth assistants from teaching.

At present, four of the five laboratory booths are nonautomated, thus there is a human instructor with the child on an average of four sessions out of five. In time, all booths will be automated, but this does not mean that they always will be operated in a fully automated way— with no human being in the booth with the child. It is not known whether children would continue to come to the laboratory on a daily basis over a long period of time if they were interacting with automated equipment only. Even if they were able to go through all phases on automated equipment this might produce undesirable psychological or social-psychological side effects. No one knows now the optimal mixture of automated and nonautomated equipment. It is reasonably certain, however, that a one to four mix will work—at least it has worked with the children who have come to the laboratory.

One of the interesting consequences of having a fully automated booth has been its effect on assistants. Before such equipment was available, it was difficult to explain to new personnel what was expected of them. Also, some of them apparently did not believe that children would work out problems for themselves—so they tended to be too *helpful*. The automated equipment proved to be a good instructor for new booth asssitants. With reference to this point, there is an illuminating film made of some laboratory children working on a prototype of E.R.E. In one sequence, a little girl (see last sequence (7)), who was in Phase 4, forgot where the lower-case key was. At first she seemed to be nonplused—finally, she regressed to a systematic trial of every key—the right key was almost the last to be tried. Many viewers of this search sequence said that they felt an almost irresistible urge to help her. She, unlike these viewers, was calm about the whole matter—confident in her ability to find her way. Like E.R.E., well-trained booth assistants do not intrude. In my opinion, in too many situations in every day life adults rush to the aid of children, thus depriving them of the opportunity of making discoveries and consequently undermining their confidence in their own resourcefulness.

CHILDREN IN A RESPONSIVE ENVIRONMENT

Before a child enters the Laboratory for his introductory session quite a bit is known about him. Each child is given a general physical examination, and eye examination, and a hearing test. A speech evaluation is made with special attention paid to a child's ability to produce utterances in conformity with the phonemic structure of the language. A clinical psychologist obtains a developmental history from the mother and gives the child an intelligence test as well as projective tests. A sociological analysis is made of the family in terms of socio-economic variables. In sum, an attempt is made to characterize the child's family with reference to its position in the broader society, to see the child within the context of his family, and to understand something about the child himself in the light of this developmental history. The various tests and observations are repeated on a semiannual or annual basis depending upon their nature, for example, I. Q. tests are given annually.

A daily record is kept of each child's behavior in the Laboratory, and the child is examined periodically to determine his level of skill.

Let us now consider children who have gone through the phases presented in the preceding section. Some background information is given with each case. The first two children to be discussed are in the nebulous range between the normal and the exceptional. The last three are clear-cut cases of exceptional children—two are educable retardates, the third is gifted.[14]

Billy.

Bill's mother enrolled him in an integrated public school kindergarten when he was five years old. After a few weeks his teacher reported to her supervisor that he was unable to follow directions and that he disrupted the classroom—for instance, he rolled on tables and stubbornly refused to move. Nothing was done about her complaints until a month later when she delivered a ultimatum—"Either Billy goes or I go." At this point the school psychologist was called in and Billy was given a Stanford-Binet intelligence test with the result that he was classified as an educable retardate with an I.Q. of 65. It was recommended that he be placed in a nursery group for the mentally retarded. The mother, a former special-class student herself, was irate about this recommendation—she caused so much difficulty over it that the school, in self defense, sent Billy to an outside expert who confirmed the prior evaluation. (This second examination was slightly more hopeful in that it placed him on the borderline between the educable retardate and the dull normal.) With great reluctance, Billy's mother acquiesced to his removal from public school at mid-term and to his placement in a nursery group for educable retardates.

When Billy was six years old, he came to the Laboratory under the auspices of a state agency. The Laboratory's initial evaluation of Billy's intelligence (I.Q. 72) agreed with the more promising of the two prior reports. However, it was obvious at once that there were at least two sides to Billy in terms of his ability to get along with adults; for example, the examiner commented, "In the testing situation, Billy was a pleasant child, friendly and responsive and anxious to please." This judgment says something about both Billy and the examiner. This examiner is very skillful in establishing rapport with children and it is a difficult child indeed who does not respond positively to her.

So we have Billy, age six, already out of the mainstream of education. He either could not or would not take directions; what is more, he was willing and able to cause disturbances.

[14] Since it has always been the policy of the Responsive Environments Project to protect the anonymity of children and their families, we have seen to it that there is not a one-to-one correspondence between children shown in pictures (either stills or motion pictures) and case history material. In addition, the children described here are drawn from several responsive environments centers located in five cities and three states. Background and personal data which would be sufficient to identify a particular child and his family have been changed so as to protect their privacy. Although I have personally worked with only 102 subjects on a day-to-day basis, there are over 250 children who have been part of the Project, taken as a whole.

Billy, a light-colored Negro, is always neatly dressed. His appearance is normal but his physical movements are somewhat clumsy although he has an alert manner. He always has been in excellent health; his vision and hearing are normal. However, his speech was very difficult to understand even at six; the speech evaluation showed, for instance, that he omitted most final consonants. Also, there were many repetitions and hesitations in his speech and his mother said that he, unlike her other children, did not talk until he was four. Whatever else, Billy had not done a very good job of mastering his native tongue —he had not developed the requisite verbal skills to express his needs or interests.

The eight members of Billy's family share five rooms in a low-income row house—a reasonably large living room (with a record player and a monstrous T-V set), a large kitchen, and three bedrooms. There are three older boys in their middle teens and Billy and his younger brother and sister, ages 5 and 4. The family is crowded but the apartment is spotless and tastefully decorated. There is a large bookcase nearly full of books topped by a complete set of supermarket encyclopedias. At present, the family is wholly self-supporting, though off and on in the past it has been on welfare. Billy's father, a small, meek, self-effacing person, is an unskilled day laborer who generally works in construction. A social worker, who has known the family for years, classifies the whole family as dull normal.

Billy's mother is the dominant figure around whom everything turns —she is a heavy-handed, strict disciplinarian who can wither her husband and children with a glance. In or out of the family she is a formidable woman who is articulate about her ambitions for her children, but she lacks the knowledge about how to advance them. She had hoped that the older boys would be able to go to college, but their academic records are so poor (she is forcing them to stay in school) that the guidance counselor has told her that college is out of the question. Though the older children are disappointing to her—she still has great hopes for her two youngest children who are developing more rapidly than any of the others did—Billy is the only child who has her worried. He was later than the others in standing, walking, talking and toilet training—toilet training must be a nightmare for Billy, because as she says, "Whenever he goes in his pants, I whack him in front of everybody." (Billy still has accidents quite frequently.) The other members of the family are very fond of Billy, baby him, and try to cover up his many mistakes before they are discovered by his mother. His mother says that Billy is not dumb, he is "stubborn and lazy." When Billy does something that really pleases her, she picks him up and enfolds him in her enormous arms while smothering him with kisses.

Billy's introductory session was calm—he quietly followed the guide around—he could not be drawn into conversation. Once in a while he smiled and in general was wide-eyed. In his second introductory session he explored some on his own but spent most of the time holding the guide's hand. By the end of this session he was becoming curious about the equipment and seemed quite relaxed—and so he was scheduled for the automated booth the following day. The third day he came in—noisy and confident—he permitted the booth assistant to help him into the elevated chair, he watched her leave and then turned his attention immediately to the keyboard. What happened next is best described as an attack upon the instrument. In 30 minutes he typed 1302 characters. The booth assistant had to turn off the instrument and lead him out of the booth when his time was up. For the next nine sessions he continued to "machine gun" the instrument at a gradually slowing pace. In his eleventh session there was a sharp drop in strokes—the booth assistant wrote, "He seems to be getting interested in looking at what he has typed." The laboratory supervisor shifted him from Phase 1, Free Exploration, to Phase 2, Search and Match. Billy was startled and angry—he put up his hand over and over to call the booth assistant in—he evidently thought the instrument was broken and that the assistant would fix it. All previous sessions had lasted 30 minutes but Billy stopped this one after 9 minutes.

He had made five matches by accident (he had not come up with a way of systematically trying all keys). The laboratory supervisor switched him back to Phase 1 for his next session and he was very pleased, although he proceeded more cautiously than he had before—looking, listening, and occasionally repeating what was said. After another five days his time dropped to 15 minutes and the supervisor again switched him to Phase 2 for the following session.

This time he was calmer about the change. After five minutes he was pressing every key with his thumb—he clapped his hands when he made a match. At the end of this 30-minute session he said he wanted to take the 'typewriter' home. For the next 60 days he played Search and Match in its increasingly difficult versions. There seemed to be no diminution in his interest. This was the game for Billy—he made it more complex for himself by shutting his eyes while finding keys, by "dive bombing" the keyboard, by first using one hand and then the other. He was still not using the color coding of fingers to keys, however. The supervisor switched him to Phase 3, Word Construction, R and W, even though his interest had not waned. He could find the characters to make words but he did not want the words—he told the instrument to "shut up." His time dropped down to 3 minutes after five days. He was shifted back to Phase 2. In WC-W he had been nearly mute—he kept mumbling something about "it's not broken." Billy continued in Phase 2 for another 30 days, still eager and interested. His refusal to go on to words was perplexing because by this time he was very expert at finding all characters and was using the color-coding system. Also, he had learned to print all the characters in the handwriting booth (this included the ampersand which most booth assistants have to learn, too).

An interviewer was sent to Billy's home to find out if something unusual was going on there. His mother said that she had caught Billy "playing with himself," and that she had whipped him and told him he would hurt himself. This made it much clearer what Billy was mumbling about. In WC-W the assistant pointed to his penis when he said "it's not broken." She said the word "penis" and spelled it. It was put on the dictation equipment for him in a nonautomated booth. He typed the word "penis" twelve times with manifest enjoyment. In his next WC-W story-telling session he said, among other things, "When my dad took the prayers away, my mother got sick and died"—the constituent words of this story were made into a word list for the next WC-W typing session. Billy liked these words and now was willing to accept word lists in WC-R.

Billy was shifted to Phase 4 in his 130th session. At the end of his laboratory experience (17 sessions) he was reading pre-primer and beginning first-grade stories, he could print nicely, and he could type 5 words a minute with correct fingering on the automated equipment. His typing was comparable to that exhibited by other children classifiable as educable retardates (see documentary film (8)).

When Billy was transferred from public school to the nursery for educable retardates at midyear, he established a satisfactory relation with the skillful teacher in charge of this group. However, he would not accept her assistant—the end-of-the-term report stated, "When he is helped or scolded by the assistant he becomes very belligerent and disrespectful." Billy began his laboratory sessions in late spring while still in this nursery class. Public school officials were invited to watch Billy in his booth sessions. They were so impressed by his good manners and by his ability to concentrate that arrangements were made to re-admit him to public school kindergarten in the fall. Given this second chance he managed to get on with this new teacher, and at the end of the year she passed him to first grade.

Billy entered first grade with 172 laboratory sessions behind him as well as with the benefits of a constructive experience in the nursery group and kindergarten. The Laboratory, of course, was interested in following his progress even though he was no longer in its program.[15]

Billy was placed in a "combined" first grade—that is, a class with a reading readiness group and a first-grade group. He was assigned to the latter section on the basis of a reading-readiness test. His teacher wrote, "When we began our work, Billy was ahead of the other children. He could write and recognize his numbers to 10 and count up to 29. He knows his colors, alphabet, and his knowledge of phonics is very good in that he knows the sounds of each isolated consonant and can tell with what various words begin. What he needs now is to develop his comprehension not only in reading words but in picture interpretation. As you know, to get the idea of a story in the pre-primers and primers, the child should understand the picture. Billy's reasoning and associations are oft times far fetched. I must ask him many questions before he gets the point of the picture. He finds it hard to follow directions, but he will ask many questions in order to get the direction correct. There are now children who have caught up to Billy but he still has an edge on them because he has a better background and the work I am doing now is not completely new to him. The proof of the pudding must wait until I begin to teach in completely new areas, for example, addition and subtraction."

Billy finished first grade successfully and will be in second grade next year—he did have trouble with arithmetic.

Billy was retested by the Laboratory at the end of first grade. His I.Q. score is now 79. The appraisal of his speech placed him in the normal range with respect to the making of phonemic discriminations in speech production—the repetitions and hesitations had disappeared. Billy now can express his needs and interests verbally in a much more adequate way and, as his teacher mentioned, he is able to ask many questions in order to understand directions. One year of first grade did not improve Billy's reading significantly—for all practical purposes, he was held back, though his skill at picture interpretation undoubtedly improved. It is my overall impression that Billy is still a vulnerable dependent child who will rebel if he is not skillfully handled. A second year in the Laboratory would have afforded him a good deal of protection—it would have been especially helpful if his introduction to arithmetic could have been carried out within the context of a responsive environment.

Billy's family is proud of him and now they let him work more things

---

[15] The project, taken as a whole, has conducted a number of pilot studies to determine whether it was feasible to work with various kinds of exceptional children. Billy was part of one such pilot project. There is inevitably a time lag between a pilot study (and an evaluation of its success or failure) and the establishment of long-term programs. Billy, his family and the project would have liked to have had him go on.

out for himself. His mother feels completely vindicated—all the psychologists, social workers and teachers were wrong—Billy is not dumb, he is simply a "stubborn and lazy" child who needs a good whack.

Edward.

Edward's mother was slim, attractive and beautifully groomed. She graduated summa cum laude from a midwestern college at 20 and married immediately. This marriage ended in divorce three years later with the husband keeping their two-year-old daughter. After a year she married Edward's father who was three years her junior and who was working as a tennis instructor at the time—he had completed only two years of college. A year after they were married, she had Edward, went to work part-time in a style shop to help pay for her husband's education (she had an annual income from a trust fund), and voluntarily began what turned out to be 3½ years of psychotherapy.

Edward came to a Project laboratory at four years of age as a referral from a private psychiatric clinic. At 3½ he had developed food allergies and was having difficulty in sleeping through the night (he would wake up screaming). When Edward first came to the laboratory his father was just leaving for another part of the country to take a good position in a large firm (by this time he had gotten his B.A. and M.A. in business administration). Edward's mother did not think it advisable to break off her psychotherapy, so she and Edward did not go with him.

Edward and his mother lived alone, then, in a chic apartment during the time in which he came to the Laboratory. His mother had stopped working and so she was free to make the daily trip to bring Edward.

Up to the age of four, Edward had spent most of his time with "sitters," except for the hours from 5 to 7 in the evening when they had dinner and his mother devoted herself exclusively to him. His father had spent almost no time with the boy. Edward himself was the very opposite of an athlete. He was a thin, frail little boy who was afraid of almost everything physical—cats, dogs, playground equipment—but he was extremely verbal. His mother reported that he began saying words at one year of age, and she had used those daily two-hour devotionals to teach Edward all manner of things. Edward looked and acted like what many people think of as a prodigy. He enjoyed embarrassing children and adults by asking such questions as, "How many planets does Saturn have?" and before an answer could be given he would add, "Stupid! It doesn't have planets, it has rings!" His mother said, "Edward could read at three—he picked it up entirely on his own, but now he will have nothing to do with books." She also said, "I really don't care whether Edward learns to read at the laboratory so long as it is a creative experience for him." His increasingly negative attitude toward learning, his allergies, and his sleeping problem upset her a great deal.

Edward's laboratory experience almost ended before it began when his mother found out about the rule prohibiting parents from watching children. She had seen the film, *Early Reading and Writing* (9), (10), (11), and was looking forward to watching Edward every day. She wanted to know what she could do with herself while he was having his session—it was annoying to her to have time on her hands. Arrangements were made for her to go to a library.

She had purchased a typewriter for Edward to use at home. In her first interview she wanted to know the color coding system so that she could duplicate it. The information was given to her, but as it turned out, Edward would not type at home until much later.

The Laboratory's evaluation of Edward was virtually a duplicate of the private clinic's including the analysis of his responses to projective material. Edward was an extremely tense child, impersonal in outlook, with excellent speech, and his I.Q. placed him on the borderline between very bright and gifted (I.Q. 139). He was difficult to test and free with insulting remarks. He was very much aware of his failures and he categorized difficult test items as "stupid." In fact, everybody was stupid but Edward with the possible exception of his mother. Edward's mother felt that he should spend more time with children his own age, but there were no acceptable children in the apartment house. He played occasionally with a thirteen-year-old girl who sometimes filled in as an emergency sitter.

Edward greeted his child guide, a girl of four, with the statement, "You have an ugly face," followed by, "What are you doing here? I hate it!" The guide shot back, "Don't be ridiculous!" and took him by the hand. He followed meekly. When he went into a booth with a typewriter, he said, "My typewriter at home is better." He did not explore the Laboratory on his own. During his second visit, he was equally prickly and he paced back and forth by himself. In his third introductory visit, he quizzed the guide and was taken aback to find that she knew "bigger" words than he did. He asked if she could type. When she said, "Yes," he said, "Show me!" The guide replied that she did not have to prove it. He shouted derisively, "You can't! You can't! You can't!" The guide laughed and Edward announced that he was going to "learn the typewriter" and that he would be much better than the guide. The supervisor scheduled him for his first booth session the next day.

Edward went willingly into a nonautomated booth. He was extremely serious. He painstakingly matched his fingers to keys, for, as he said "My mother told me to look at my fingers and press the keys with the same colors." Edward did not explore the keyboard. Instead, he searched out the upper-case alphabet—avoiding all punctuation marks and numbers. After a while he was going through the upper-case letters in alphabetic order. After ten minutes of this, he asked for the pictures. He said, "At home my books have colored pictures," and before the booth assistant could say anything, he added, "I hate this stupid thing—I want to go." The assistant immediately turned off the equipment and lifted Edward from the elevated chair. He said, "I want to do it some more." When he was told that he could come back the next day, he cried, "I want to do it now!" Edward left the Laboratory complaining bitterly, but he greeted his mother with the statement, "Their typewriter is better than yours." For the next four sessions, Edward confined himself to the letters with which he was familiar and each day he tried to elicit punitive responses from the booth assistants.

In his 6th, 7th, and 8th sessions, all less than 15 minutes in length, he stopped matching his fingers to keys and tried to get the booth assistants to say how good he was for knowing all the letters. His 9th session marked the first major change in Edward's behavior. Instead of sitting stiffly, he slumped down and began to pick away at the keyboard, spending most of his time on characters new to him. He noted that *period* was the same whether "up or down," he liked the end-of-the-line warning bell and the carriage return. For the first time he stayed 30 minutes and did not insult anyone. Edward's interest grew each day—he repeated aloud nearly every character after they were pronounced by the booth assistants.

The supervisor switched him to Phase 2, Search and Match, for his 15th session. He announced that he was tired of this game during his 21st session—he could match quickly and accurately.

Edward liked WC-R immediately. In free story telling for WC-W he told long complex stories about how he was going to be his father's partner in doubles tennis. He told about not having a ball of his own and that he was spanked for touching his father's tennis racquet—but the balls and racquets were gone now. Edward would not listen to his own voice in dictation. He wanted the little girl's voice (the guide's); he very happily typed her dictated word lists. For the next 30 sessions, Edward stayed in Phase 3. All of his typing was done with one finger of each hand and he became very pleasant to have in the Laboratory.

In Edward's 10th week, his mother asked for a conference about his behavior. She said that at home he had become very "sloppy," for example, he would not put his toys away. More importantly, he had become rude and disrespectful of her. He would not play with the typewriter at home, and, as far as she could see, he had *learned nothing*. He would not look at his books—he had told her that the "Lab" did not have pictures and that pictures were stupid. His allergies were worse, if anything, but he was sleeping a little better. She said she wanted to withdraw him from the program but that he looked forward to the trip every day. What she said she wished to discuss "at a theoretical level" was whether the program tended to make children self-centered.

She was told that it was her privilege to withdraw Edward, but that it would be advisable for her to take him to the referral clinic for a re-evaluation. She accepted this advice. The clinic reported to Edward's mother that he enjoyed his laboratory experience (a representative of the clinic came to the Laboratory to watch Edward for four sessions) and that it was unlikely his sessions were disturbing to him. On the contrary, he seemed to be a little less tense and apprehensive. The question as to whether Edward was learning to read or not was irrelevant from the clinic's standpoint, so long as he found pleasure in this activity. The clinic advised her to put the typewriter at home away until he asked for it. Also, the clinic reiterated the advice it gave her when he was 3½, namely, "Find some children of his own age for Edward to play with." The Laboratory staff reexamined Edward from the standpoint of assessing his emotional stability—the examiner did not find, or expect to find, any marked change, though Edward was friendlier. Edward's mother decided to keep him in the program and she also enrolled him in a nursery school for mornings.

Edward liked the nursery school from the first day on. The experienced teacher slowly and skillfully got him to join in group activities. She also succeeded in getting Edward to play with the group's mascot, a puppy.

In Edward's 53rd session, he was shifted to Phase 4, Reading and Writing. He worked his way rapidly into *Alice's Adventures in Wonderland*—his mother bought the book and record set. He would listen to the records at home, though he would not touch the book.

Edward stayed in Phase 4, without regressing, from then on. At the end of his laboratory experience (93 sessions), he passed a standardized reading test at the second-grade level.[16] His printing was poor, though legible (he never did get along with assistants in the handwriting booth). His typing was rapid but with two fingers only. He came to accept his own voice in dictation. His I.Q. had jumped to 152, his speech continued to be excellent. There were no detectable changes in his personality structure although he had learned more satisfactory ways of dealing with others. His food allergies continued—his mother

16 It should be noted that passing standardized reading tests call for formal academic skills in addition to the ability to read meaningfully. Edward could read and answer questions about, for example, Alice's adventures, yet he passed the test only at the second-grade level.

reported that he was sleeping restfully almost every night. His mother stated that he now liked to go to the library with her to check out books and that he was looking forward to seeing his father.

The referral clinic made a similar assessment of Edward. The clinic's final report stated, in part, "The laboratory and the nursery were positive for Edward. His ability to cope with the demands of his mother is much improved. Edward needs the companionship of his father if he is to keep the gains that he has made."

Although Edward's mother had not planned to leave the area during the school year, she abruptly changed her mind in mid-February. She informed the clinic, the laboratory and the nursery of her decision only one week prior to their departure.

Betty and Jane.

Betty and Jane are physically sturdy, normal-appearing, identical Negro twins. They entered an integrated public school kindergarten at five, and after a month they were referred by their teacher and principal to the school psychologist for examination. During this month they had not spoken to anyone or actively participated in kindergarten activities. For the most part, they sat quietly, smiling irrelevantly from time to time. Children who knew them said that they do not talk but just make noises. When the children in kindergarten stood, Betty and Jane had to be taken by their hands and helped to their feet; when it was time to sit, the twins continued to stand until again they were taken by their hands and shown to their chairs. They constantly sucked their fingers or stuffed their whole hands in their mouths, with saliva flowing freely down their arms and over the fronts of their dresses.

They went willingly with the examiner to take intelligence tests. She reported, "They cannot understand or follow any direction, even when blocks were placed in their hands, they could not put them in tower formation. Their chronological age is 5-years 2-months, but they were unable to pass any test at the 2-year level or beyond." On the basis of the psychological tests and their behavior in kindergarten, it was decided that they were too limited in mental development to profit by kindergarten attendance. They were excluded immediately from school for one year and re-admittance was to be dependent upon the outcome of tests to be given the following year.

The question of re-admittance to public school did not arise the next fall because a social worker, who assisted the family, was able to get the twins into a state agency's class for retarded children. The twins started coming to the Laboratory in late spring after they had attended this special class for eight months. At the same time they came to the Laboratory, according to the psychological examiner for the special class, Betty's I.Q. was 55 and Jane's was 56 as measured by the Stanford-Binet intelligence test. The children still drooled and toilet training had not been completed.

The twins live in a small, three-room apartment in a double-entrance, tumble-down, brownstone complex. The back yard and front side walk are littered with scraps, glass and discarded beer cans. The apartment is cramped and dingy though not filthy. The door to the kitchen balances precariously on one hinge.

The family consists of two younger children, the twins, the mother, and a maternal grandmother. The grandmother seems to be the one who takes the initiative in holding the family together and she is doing her best to raise the children. The twins' mother, who may be thought of as a loving older sister, frequently plays with them on the floor in a child-like unrestrained manner. The grandmother exercises firm, though gentle, control over the twins by confining them, most of the time, to the apartment or back yard. It is her opinion that the twins cannot defend themselves in the streets where the neighborhood children play. The twins thus have had very limited experience with other children or adults. Also, city life is new to the family—only three years before they moved from the South where they had lived in an isolated area. Since coming north the family is totally on welfare—there is no breadwinner.

The eight months the twins had spent in the special class before coming to the Laboratory served to widen their horizons. According to the teacher the children were extremely shy at first and did not speak to anyone. At the end of several months they began to whisper to each other and to the teacher. Within eight months they were able to "shout, scream and talk to the teacher, children, and any other person who enters the classroom." Their teacher reported that in strange situations they were still very shy. The twins enjoyed the class and felt comfortable with the teacher, assistants and other children. In social interaction Jane was the more dominant one; Betty seemed to be stronger in "intellectual" pursuits. However, the twins are so similar in appearance and behavior that even those who know them reasonably well frequently mistake one for the other. At six the twins had not yet learned to exploit, as most identical twins do, the social possibilities inherent in their identity.

The Laboratory's evaluation of the twins concurred with that of the psychologist for the special class with respect to their intellectual abilities—they were definitely in the category *educable retardate*. There was nothing wrong with their general health and eyes. It was not feasible to do initial speech and hearing analyses because of the difficulty of eliciting an adequate number of utterances. The twins were uniformly pleasant but nonresponsive. It was also difficult to determine much about the structure of their personalities—the finger-thumb-hand-sucking, the inane smiling, the extreme shyness and so forth, all would have to be taken into account, of course, in any adequate analysis of their development.

The Laboratory had agreed in advance with the state officials that it would accept a small number of retarded children, free of charge, if the children were·"certified" as retarded by the state's experts. When the twins were sent to the Laboratory, there was no way to have one be a control subject without violating the agreement to accept whatever children were assigned to the Laboratory. It would have been desirable for some scientific purposes to have worked with only one of the twins. Yet, if the laboratory experience proved to be a valuable one, this would have been unfair to the neglected twin and might have had untoward consequences for them in their close relationship to each other. Under these circumstances, I decided to think about the twins from the standpoint of assessing their identicalness. Just how identical are identical twins when each is faced with a new environment?

Betty and Jane were introduced to the Laboratory together for fear that they might be frightened alone. They accepted their guide passively, they asked no questions—in fact, they did not say anything—they drooled and sucked their fingers. Nevertheless, they did not seem to be especially fearful. Their guide was very gracious—she omitted spontaneously the discussion of the Laboratory rules and, instead, assured them over and over that they would like the "Lab." It was decided to have them go separately into nonautomated booths after one introductory visit because they might be passive for weeks.

Betty permitted herself to be seated in the elevated chair without comment. She sat up straight and appeared to be interested in the keyboard. After about one minute she began to rapidly press keys with an odd sort of looping movement of her right hand using her middle finger. She continued to do this for the full period at a nearly constant rate. Her stroke count for the period was 2204. She struck 27 of the 52 keys. However, she concentrated heavily on three keys, the slant, the comma and the period (these keys are located next to each other on the right side of the bottom row.) Forty-nine percent of the keys she struck were these three keys, and of these, the slant was most frequently struck—she produced 815 slants. At the end of her session she was led out of the booth and did not say anything.

Jane permitted herself to be seated in the elevated chair without comment. She sat up straight and appeared to be interested in the keyboard. After about one minute she began to rapidly press keys with an odd sort of looping movement of her right hand using her middle finger. She continued to do this for the full period at a nearly constant rate. Her stroke count for the period was 3189. She struck 35 of the 52 keys. However, she concentrated heavily on three keys, the slant, the comma and the period. Forty-three percent of all the keys she struck were these three keys, and of these, the slant was most frequently struck —she produced 807 slants. At the end of her session she was led out of the booth and did not say anything.

In their 2nd through 5th sessions the twins continued to be very similar in their general approach but they never again were as identical as they were during their first booth session. At the end of five days, Betty's stroke count was 8571 and Jane's was 8724—a difference of 153 strokes. During the 2nd week they began to diverge, Jane became noticeably more active in the booths. Their graphs for stroke counts crossed after three weeks at 14,377 strokes for Betty and 14,202 for Jane. From then on Betty remained slightly more active than her sister. At the completion of 150 sessions, Betty had typed 10,109 more characters than had Jane. On a day-to-day basis, this means behaviorially that Betty did about a line and one half more typing—this is a very small difference but an observable one. The girls were more closely matched in booth time than in stroke count. Each almost always stayed the full period. (Their similarity in time is, in part, an artifact of the methods used in handling them. The girls would stay almost anywhere you put them until told to leave.)

The twins stayed in Phase 1 for 19 sessions. It was decided to shift them to Phase 2 in their 20th session because their stroke count was beginning to fall off rapidly.

They had no difficulty in adjusting to Phase 2, though they were slow in working out a systematic search pattern for finding the correct keys. Neither Betty nor Jane used the color-coding scheme. By their 70th session each was quick to find the appropriate keys. Betty was slightly more accurate.

They were shifted to Phase 3 in their 71st session. They would accept word lists in WC-R; but for five weeks they would not talk in WC-W— also, they would not respond to other children's dictation. Finally, Jane began to make a few disjointed comments during her 97th session in WC-W, Betty during her 100th session.

Leaving aside the WC-W recording sessions, the girls began to talk above a whisper during their 5th week at the Laboratory. They both have deep rich voices—it was hard to guess when they would speak up. Occasionally, they would make rather surprising remarks. For example, the first time Jane encountered the cursive typewriter she shouted, "Dig this crazy typewriter!"

Once the twins were speaking with some regularity in WC-W, it was feasible to do a speech analysis (recall that there were no speech and hearing evaluations because of the difficulty in eliciting utterances). Both were rated as having intelligible speech; Jane's speech was marked by a w/r substitution, Betty made the same w/r substitution and in addition had consonant blend substitutions. Their hearing was checked at this time and it turned out to be normal.

In Betty's 115th session and Jane's 120th, they were shifted to Phase 4. They clearly liked stories, although it was very difficult to tell how much they understood of the stories they typed. It was useless to quiz them about what they had typed because this tended to make them withdraw. Once in a while they would make a fairly incisive comment which indicated some understanding of the material.

The twins completed 150 sessions. By this time they could print all upper- and lower-case letters as well as the punctuation marks and other symbols on the typewriter. On automated equipment they could type four words a minute. There was strong indirect evidence to indicate that they could handle first-grade stories if they would only speak freely. Drooling had almost ceased and they no longer wet their pants in the Laboratory.

With respect to their I.Q., Betty scored 64 on the Stanford-Binet and Jane scored 60. Both were weakest in the verbal language tasks. Betty successfully passed one item at the 6-year-old level—Jane passed none at this level.

Even though the twins had to be dropped from the laboratory program, a follow-up investigation was made one year later. The twins had been re-admitted to public school and assigned to a special class. Their teacher had visited the Laboratory the year before and had seen them at "work." She was favorably disposed toward the girls. She emphasized in her report that they were very different from the rest of the class—in her opinion it was their lack of social experience rather than low I.Q. which was holding them back. Their individual performances in class fluctuated so much that she felt that there was not a sufficient basis for determining which twin performed better. The teacher began to have them read books at the beginning of the spring term (until that time she felt that they were not ready for work at this level). She was uncertain about how much they had retained from their experience at the Laboratory, but she said that at the beginning of school the girls remembered letters and numbers though they apparently had forgotten sounds.

A Laboratory observer, who sat in on the class during a reading session in the second term, reported that the twins read aloud from the Ginn first pre-primer. Each read her own selection both accurately and quickly; the selection was unfamiliar though simple. The twins did not have reading every day. As the Laboratory observer arose from the reading session, Betty, half hiding behind her teacher's skirt, screeched, "Lab, Lab! I wanna go Lab!" The observer's report reads as follows: "I then completed my discussion with the teacher, to speak to the girls. I had hoped that I would be able to talk to each one individually, but I found that impossible because Betty kept hovering over the table mooning at us. Rather than risk Jane 'turning off,' I let them talk with me together. They both recalled many details about the Lab; red building, white chalk, yellow station wagon and colors on their fingers. Jane kept babbling about the yellow station wagon. They both remembered typing, reading books, writing on the table and coloring their nails. Jane recalled they 'played games,' Betty remembered the talking typewriter for the story about the golden chicken. (In all likelihood this is the *Aesop Fable* 'The Goose that Laid the Golden Egg.') They both agreed they had had fun playing at the Lab, and they obviously wanted to come back again. Initially, I was leery about their enthusiasm because the teacher had alerted me to the fact that their grandmother had a record of prompting the girls. Nevertheless, Betty and Jane did recall a lot about the Program that she (the grandmother) could not have known about, and I didn't feel that they were sophisticated enough to show a sustained and artificial enthusiasm, even prompted."

Sandra.

It is the general policy of the Laboratory to obtain children by working with schools, clinics, government agencies, and so forth. In this way the Laboratory gains the benefit of whatever information the relevant organization has about the children in question and the Laboratory's findings can be integrated with those of other organizations which serve children. This policy also obviates the necessity of dealing on an *ad hoc* basis with numerous families. Nevertheless, parents call the Laboratory—most calls are about handicapped children and we suggest that they see their pediatrician or other appropriate specialist.

There is one kind of telephone call which the Laboratory follows up, in an informal way, whenever possible. For instance, a mother may call and say that she has a three-year old who can do extraordinary things—that he is a mathematical prodigy or that he reads like a whiz. Time permitting, an interviewer goes out to see the child in his home, explaining that our concern is to better understand exceptional children.

One of the things that has impressed us about these visits is the lack of information parents have about the achievements of children. Parents are in the unfortunate position of having to judge the possibly unusual achievements (i.e. accomplishments as opposed to the ability to achieve as estimated by some standardized test) of their own child by the standards derived from reading and personal experience. They may conclude that they have a *wunderkind*.

There is also great vagueness about what constitutes reading. We have been in some homes where a child is said to be reading brilliantly when he can only identify a few words. Parents say, almost uniformly, that whatever the child does, he learned all by himself. Yet, even casual inspection of the living room reveals flash cards, slates, or educational toys directly related to the child's accomplishments. Questioning the parents closely is generally sufficient to reveal the method of instruction which the mother, father, grandmother, older sister, or neighbor used. In a few cases, when parents stoutly maintained that the child has had no instruction whatsoever in reading or numbers, we have said to them that if their child, unaided, can discover so much, then perhaps he could help at the University to decipher some heretofore untranslated hieroglyphics—that even the specialists do not know whether to start from the right, left, top or bottom. At this point parents quickly volunteer that of course they answered all of his questions.

I do not wish to impugn the ability of these children to learn, or to minimize their accomplishments in any way, or to make light of the pride their parents take in them, or to discourage such parents. The plain fact is that parents lack comparative information about children's accomplishments—and even if they were to search the relevant scientific literature diligently, they would not receive very much help.[17] Behavioral scientists, including myself, are pretty much in the dark about extraordinary accomplishments. It is for this very reason that we are appreciative of the opportunity to observe children who strike their parents as prodigious.

Sandra's mother called to ask questions about enrolling her 4-year-old daughter in a laboratory program. She said that Sandra, an only child, was beginning to learn to read by herself and that she did many precocious things. A visit to the home was arranged.

Sandra lived with her parents in a rambling winterized beach house which they had rented four years before when they moved to this area. Sandra's father is an engineer and her mother is a painter who occasionally accepts commercial assignments. The house was filled with the accouterments of their work. One room was set aside for the father's extensive files. Sandra was probably the only person who knew where everything was.

Her parents were swimming when the Laboratory interviewer ar-

---

[17] Terman's monumental study (16) is a gold mine of factual information for those who are interested in gifted children.

rived and Sandra introduced herself (she was waiting) and asked if he wanted to see her photographic equipment. Her father had set up a miniature studio for her, with a dark room, three months before. She explained in great detail the complete process of taking pictures and developing them. She also showed some of her work with a running commentary on the quality of each picture. She explained that her current project was to use mirrors in taking pictures. She distinguished clearly between those things which she did by herself and those things which her mother or father helped her with. Also, anything that might be dangerous she would do only when a parent was present. There was no doubt in the interviewer's mind that basically the studio was hers even though she received a great deal of technical assistance.

In about a half an hour her parents came in, wearing their beach robes, and sent Sandra out to play. They reminded her to stay out of the water and to stay within view—the interview took place on the porch where Sandra could be watched. She took a pail, a shovel, a few toys and a camera with her. Her mother apologized for not being there when the interviewer arrived but said that she wanted him to visit with Sandra first.

Sandra's father was 40 and her mother 35. The father received his degree in engineering, the mother went to art school. They wanted to learn about the Laboratory program and also wanted to know whether the interviewer agreed with them that Sandra was some kind of prodigy. Their attitude seemed to be one of concern about what would be best for Sandra. They said that she got along reasonably well with the neighborhood children; nevertheless, most of the time she preferred to pursue her own projects. She would have liked to have played more with some of the older children in the neighborhood, but she could not get them to stay in her studio long enough—besides, they messed things up. The parents had not intended for her to get so wrapped up in photography but once started she had kept after them to tell her more and more about it. She had other hobbies—collecting shells, painting (trying to copy things) and currently she was tying her various hobbies together through photography. She had learned the alphabet while getting things for her father from his files and now she wanted to learn to read so that she could help her parents better and read instructions for herself, especially those related to photography.

Her parents, who were quite relaxed, were somewhat appalled by the thorough, relentless way in which she pursued her interests. They thought that though she was friendly and helpful, even affectionate, she was rapidly becoming more and more exclusive. The only way to get close to her was to become a part of her projects. The parents had great sympathy for the idea of a child pursuing interests independently, but they did not think it was healthy for her to become so absorbed in her own affairs.

The interviewer suggested that Sandra be sent to a clinic for a thorough psychological examination and to see if the clinic felt that it was advisable that the Laboratory accept her. It was pointed out that the clinic probably would recommend that she go to nursery school in conjunction with the laboratory sessions—this recommendation would have to be followed. The parents agreed.

All during this conversation (approximately 45 minutes) Sandra played. When the interviewer was leaving they walked up to see what she was doing—she had made an elaborate sand castle decked out with toys which she was in the process of photographing.

Sandra came to the Laboratory in September and also started nursery school. She was an attractive child, big for her age, in good health, and had normal vision and hearing. Her speech was excellent and her I.Q. tested 160. Her general personality development was sound—she was without marked tensions or anxieties. The examiner commented that she seemed to be somewhat wanting in spontaneity and humor and thought that she needed the companionship of other superior children. The overall assessment was that she was a gifted child in good psychological health. There was no evidence of coaching for the tests or academic pressure at home—she liked the examination and said she wanted to do it again sometime.

Sandra was intrigued by the Laboratory in her introductory visit. She noted the photographic equipment, she said she thought she would like the typing "studio," she got along beautifully with her guide and her main disappointment was that she had to wait till the next day to play with the equipment. The supervisor scheduled her for a nonautomated booth session the next day. When her fingers were painted she wanted to know why—she was told that she would find out. The moment she sat in the elevated chair and looked at the keyboard carefully she remarked that now she knew—from the first she matched fingers to keys. Sandra's search pattern, even in free exploration, was deliberate—she tried every key row by row. When she encountered the lower-case key she started over again, trying each key both ways. She told the booth assistant that it was not necessary to say the letters that she already knew—that she would say them. Sandra stayed 30 minutes and was quite annoyed about having to leave though she controlled her temper. Her stroke count was 410. Her 2nd and 3rd sessions were spent in the same way. At the end of the 3rd session she said that she would like to do something else.

The supervisor switched her to Phase 2, Search and Match, for her 4th session even though she did not know the names of all of the keys. Her first reaction to the new game was to say she understood it. She went quickly through the increasingly difficult forms of the game. At the end of her 13th session she knew the keyboard cold and continued to use correct fingering. She asked when she could have a "really" new game. The supervisor gave her one the next day.

Sandra spent 18 weeks in Phase 3, Word Construction, R and W. In WC-W she talked freely and happily about her projects. She brought material from her studio to copy as well.

In her 103rd session she was shifted to Phase 4 because her stroke count and eager interest were falling off. With her ability to retain whatever she was exposed to, she immediately began reading pre-primers, and two weeks later she was reading first-grade books. Occasionally she asked to go back and do some special word lists. At the end of spring term (170 sessions) the reading test showed she was at the second-grade eighth-month level. She could type 8 words a minute on nonautomated equipment. She printed all typewriter characters with precision.

Sandra's experience in nursery school was not altogether satisfactory to her. She liked her teacher and a few of the children but she complained, in a lady-like way, that it was all too babyish. She attempted to mother the other children and some of the boys said that she was too "bossy." Unfortunately, at the time she came to the Laboratory there was no newspaper project to challenge her, nor was there any other common activity for laboratory children. As things stood, she was a leader sans followers.

A recheck of her I.Q. showed it to be 169. At home she added reading and writing to her other projects. She did very little in the way of creating original stories. Her favorite book, which she had just started to read, was *Tal.*

The personality assessment showed no basic change, however her parents felt that she had changed significantly. She wanted to discuss the stories that she read and it was their opinion that this greater common area of interest was drawing her closer to them again. She continued to pursue her projects independently, but as her father put it, "She is running into ideas that cannot be captured in a photograph."

The family moved to a large city in another state when school was out. Sandra was enrolled in a special class for gifted children. Her parents write occasionally to keep the Laboratory posted. At present, she is in a class with an ungraded program. Thus far, this class has provided a challenge which she enjoys.

CONCLUDING COMMENTS

At the beginning of this paper it was pointed out that slow learners are likely to be out of phase with the age-graded societal demands imposed upon them and that they are apt to be problems to themselves and to their friends. The three slow learners that we have considered, Billy, Betty and Jane, are certainly cases in point. As soon as they appeared in school the duly constituted authorities decided that they were not "ready." In all likelihood, the authorities were correct—these children were not "ready" to be taught by conventional methods. Nevertheless, they could be reached and the procedures through which they learned did not depend upon a rescue by one of those rare marvelous teachers who, through empathy, insight and intelligence, can reach the nearly unreachable.

It also was stated that ultrarapid learners, too, may create problems for themselves and others. Edward and Sandra, in very different ways, made people uncomfortable. Neither Edward nor Sandra had had the opportunity to take part in the full laboratory program where they could have used their intellectual skills within the context of a meaningful group that was heterogeneous in ability.

The vignettes of the background and laboratory behavior of the five children just considered perhaps have served to clarify both the operation of the Laboratory and some of its effects upon exceptional children. It might have been more revealing to have presented some of the children who started coming to the Laboratory at two and three years of age and who are still in the program on a daily basis. Cases of this kind demand a more lengthy and systematic treatment. Also, in my opinion, very early exposure to a responsive environment produces deep personality changes and it would be inappropriate to analyze children thus exposed outside the context of a theoretical interpretation of personality development. Hence, I have focused attention here on children who began their experience at the Laboratory at four, five or six years of age and who remained in the program for only one academic year (or less). These children gained useful skills and attitudes which, with the help of clinicians, nursery school teachers and others, enabled them to deal somewhat more effectively with pressing individual and social demands.

Another reason for selecting these children was that they make manifest some of the subtleties and complexities of the psychodynamics and sociodynamics of learning—this may serve as an antidote to the dangerous notion that a responsive environments laboratory grinds out results in a purely mechanical way. The role of the supervisor was highlighted throughout in order to emphasize that a responsive environments laboratory, though phases of it are automated, does not run by itself. It would be equally foolish to assume that well-designed instruments do not have an important part to play in the daily operation of a laboratory. It was the purpose of this paper to describe an autotelic responsive environment which facilitates the learning of complex symbolic skills. It was suggested initially that no one aspect of the environment should be thought of as constituting its essence. In part, it is a mechanical system, in part it is a social system, and in part, it is a cultural system. All of these parts are constituents of the total system—all of them must be taken into account if the Laboratory is to be understood. The task of designing optimal environments for learning is in its infancy and the theoretical problems of understanding what is going on in the Laboratory are staggering. One would have to be very insensitive to its research possibilities not to imagine quickly a hundred and one experiments that could be carried out within it which might increase our understanding of human beings. For example, the startling similarities between Betty's and Jane's first sessions practically demand further studies of identical twins. The behavior of Bill and Edward may be of special interest to psychoanalytically oriented researchers.

For the present and for an additional year or so I intend to continue to operate my laboratories as a demonstration project rather than as a controlled experiment. I may be mistaken in this policy, but there are hazards connected with focusing sharply on one or another aspect of human behavior before one gets a full sense of its variety in longitudinal perspective. This easily can lead to lop-sided theorizing and debilitating polemics. The Responsive Environments Project is endeavoring to remain open and responsive to whatever changes the continuing observation of children's behavior seems to call for, although it is easy to deceive oneself about such matters.

REFERENCES

1. Anderson, Alan Ross and Moore, Omar Khayyam. *Autotelic Folk-Models.* Technical Report No. 8, Office of Naval Research, Group Psychology Branch, Contract SAR/Nonr-609 (16), New Haven, 1959. Also reprinted in *Sociological Quarterly,* 1: 204–216.
2. Anderson, Alan Ross and Moore, Omar Khayyam. "The Formal Analysis of Normative Concepts." *American Sociological Review,* 22: 9–17.
3. Mead, George Herbert. *Mind, Self and Society.* Chicago, 1934.
4. Moore, Omar Khayyam. *Dictation.* (Motion picture). Will be available through the Responsive Environments Foundation, Inc., 20 Augur Street, Hamden, Connecticut.
5. Moore, Omar Khayyam. "Problem Solving and the Perception of Persons." In *Person Perception and Interpersonal Behavior,* (eds. Renato Tagiuri and Luigi Petrullo), Palo Alto: Stanford University Press, pp. 131–150.
6. Moore, Omar Khayyam. *Orthographic Symbols and the Preschool Child — A New Approach.* Proceedings of the Third Minnesota Conference on Gifted Children. Minneapolis, University of Minnesota Press, pp. 91–101.

7. Moore, Omar Khayyam. *Automated Responsive Environments: Part 1.* (Motion picture), The Responsive Environments Foundation, Inc., Hamden, Conn.
8. Moore, Omar Khayyam. *Automated Responsive Environments: Part 2.* (Motion picture), The Responsive Environments Foundation, Inc., Hamden, Conn.
9. Moore, Omar Khayyam and Anderson, Alan Ross. *Early Reading and Writing, Part 1: Skills.* (Motion picture), Basic Education, Inc., Hamden, Conn.
10. Moore, Omar Khayyam and Anderson, Alan Ross. *Early Reading and Writing, Part 2: Teaching Methods.* (Motion picture), Basic Education, Inc., Hamden, Conn.
11. Moore, Omar Khayyam and Anderson, Alan Ross. *Early Reading and Writing, Part 3: Development.* (Motion picture), Basic Education, Inc., Hamden, Conn.
12. Moore, Omar Khayyam and Anderson, Alan Ross. "Some Puzzling Aspects of Social Interaction." *Mathematical Methods in Small Group Processes,* (eds. J. H. Criswell, H. Solomon, P. Suppes). Stanford University Press, 232–249. Also *Review of Metaphysics,* 15: 409–433, 1962.
13. Moore, Omar Khayyam and Anderson, Alan Ross. "The Structure of Personality" read at the ONR symposium on the "Social self," University of Colorado, October 7–9, 1961. *Review of Metaphysics,* 16: 212–236. *Cognitive Determinants of Motivation and Social Interaction,* (ed. O. J. Harvery), University of Colorado, Ronald Press, 1963.
14. Moore, Omar Khayyam and Lewis, Donald J. "Learning Theory and Culture." *Psychological Review,* 59: 380–388. Also, *Current Perspectives in Social Psychology,* (eds. E. P. Hollander and R. G. Hunt), Oxford University Press, 1963.
15. Pierce, J. R. *Symbols, Signals and Noise: The Nature and Process of Communication.* New York: Harper & Brothers, 1961.
16. Terman, Lewis M. *Genetic Studies of Genius,* volumes 1–5. Stanford University Press, 1925–1959.

Chapter 21

What is meant by computer-assisted instruction, and what is the recent history of development in this new technology?

What theories of learning, information processing or simulation underly student-machine communication in the computer context?

Why do the terms hardware and software take on special connotations in computer-assisted instruction?

What are some of the significant projects or experiments that are current on the national scene, and what is their relationship to future psychological research?

COMPUTER ASSISTANCE
WITH THE EDUCATIONAL PROCESS*

DUNCAN N. HANSEN
Director of Computer Assisted Instruction
Associate Professor of Educational Research
Florida State University

This review will focus primarily on theoretical and experimental developments since 1962 that either employ computer-assisted instruction (CAI) as a research tool or focus on CAI as an educational system. The year 1962 was marked by a number of review articles and books (e.g., Bushnell, 1962; Coulson, 1962; Silberman and Coulson, 1962). Since that date a number of review articles have been published, the most recent being by Coulson (1965) in which he reviewed CAI activities as a follow-up to his book. CAI systems, especially in terms of hardware and software components, were extensively reviewed by Dick (1965), Hickey and

*The work reported here has been supported by the Carnegie Corporation of New York, the National Science Foundation, and, in part, by the U.S. Office of Education. A first draft of this paper was given on May 3, 1965, at a Scientific Computing Symposium in Westchester, New York on Man-Machine Communication, sponsored by IBM. It was later printed as Technical Report #81, Psychology Series, of the Institute for Mathematical Studies in the Social Sciences, dated October 29, 1965. It is reprinted here with permission of the author.

Newton (1966), and Zinn (1966). In addition, the field has the benefit of an abstracting service provided by the *Entelek/CAI Research Abstracts* (Entelek Inc., Newburyport, Mass.). No attempt will be made to show the interrelationship between programed instruction and computer-assisted instruction, as these are provided in earlier reviews (Stolurow and Davis, 1965). In addition, descriptive articles covering the potential uses of CAI in education will not be reviewed inasmuch as they were covered in other articles (Gentile, 1965), nor will coverage be given to learning materials that have been prepared for CAI systems since these were thoroughly indexed by *Entelek/CAI Research Abstracts* and Zinn (1966).

COMPUTER-ASSISTED INSTRUCTION

The first high-speed electronic computers were constructed to do millions of computations in a few instants, and the image of the computer as a very fast desk calculator or adding machine is still strongly held. Educators are just beginning to utilize the full data-processing capabilities of computers with their data banks and records processing. Fewer people, however, have concerned themselves with the computer as an instructional aid and a research tool, probably for the very good reason that existing equipment must be modified and improved to handle increased and diversified demands. The skill and imagination of human beings have had to be modified and improved as well, and it is fortunate that some creative people have been able to begin the task.

The field of computer-assisted instruction is less than a decade old in its creation and evolution. In this short period of time a number of identifiable research trends have evolved. These focus on the theoretical and operational use of CAI in ongoing educational activities and research. Concurrently the development of specialized electronic equipment and accompanying computer languages capable of exercising the electronic hardware has both constrained the level and style of research activities and broadened the prospects for the future.

Theoretical Orientations for CAI

The field of computer-assisted instruction has fostered a number of theoretical stances from which the research activities may be viewed. These stances range from ones that are quite general in terms of the stipulated educational processes to those formulations that are specifically focused on only certain kinds of learning in given educational acts. The most general model was provided by Stolurow (1965a). This cybernetic model of the tutorial process is primarily adaptive in nature and has seven components: (a) learner's characteristics as manifested in aptitude and personality variables; (b) the input facilities or electronic equipment potential and variables representing the nature of the man-machine interaction; (c) output variables relating the kinds of dependent behavior one cares to use in judging the appropriateness of the learning performance; (d) performance standards that are formulated in terms of error standards and levels of improvement as these relate to task objectives; (e) a comparative function by which the learner's output is compared against the standard objectives for the course and a strategy decision is made as to the nature of the next learning sequence; (f) a library of potential instructional information from which the appropriate and optimal selection of learning materials may be made; (g) feedback variables as manifested in reinforcement schedules and motivation variables. The task for the cybernetic system with its associated computer equipment is to relate these seven components in an adaptive process so as to lead to the maximum amount of learning.

A similar type of cybernetic or adaptive model was formulated by Lewis and Pask (1965). This model utilizes analogies from artificial intelligence and teaching-machine processes in order to show how feedback and testing variables should be organized in a closed loop that will make the instructional act more adaptive. The theory stresses not only the nature of the student and the structure of the subject matter, but also the student's particular problem-solving processes and the mechanism by which these processes are brought to bear on the subject matter objectives. There is a very heavy emphasis on hierarchically ordered learning systems. Again, one would characterize this approach as a very general, all-inclusive theory for computer-assisted instruction.

Glaser, Ramage, and Lipson (1964) pointed out the need for a theoretical model that relates learning theory to man-machine relationships in CAI. These man-machine relationships are reflected in the interphase between the learner and the particular CAI terminal equipment. Thus, they proposed that for a given subject matter certain appropriate discrimination learning models should be developed that would specify the optimal kind of equipment and learning material necessary to accomplish the educational goals.

An alternative approach that is more specialized in nature was that of Atkinson and Hansen (1966), Smallwood (1962), and Suppes (1965). This line of theoretical development focused on specific learning situations and attempted to develop quantitative learning models that can be related to optimal instructional sequences so as to maximize the potential learning gains. These quantitative models of optimal instruction will be reviewed in a later section of this paper.

A final class of CAI theories concerns the recent developments in computer simulation or informational processing models developed by Simon and Kotovsky (1963). These models, in essence, would provide a characterization or representation of the learner as he interacts with learning materials. The fruitfulness of these simulation models lies in their explicitness and the fact that the simulation model is within the computer at the same time that one is instructing the learner so that in principle one can utilize the simulation model in the decision-making process that determines the sequencing of the instructional material. Thus, one would use the computer both to control the instruction and to give a theoretical representation of the instructional outcomes.

Hardware

Student-Subject Matter Interface. A persistent question found in the CAI literature deals with the nature and characteristics of the CAI hardware (equipment) as it interrelates with educational tasks and learner characteristics. More simply, how do the learning characteristics of students from preschool through graduate or professional level interrelate with the CAI terminal hardware so that the subject matter will be more effectively acquired and retained? In addition, one must consider the nature of the central processing units of the CAI systems so that important functions like contingent decision making, data recording, time sharing (multiprocessing), and the like can be accomplished.

The most definite study of factors in the student-subject matter interface was performed by Glaser, Ramage, and Lipson (1964). After a thorough task analysis of the subject matter requirements of elementary school mathematics, reading, and science in addition to the learning processes of elementary school children, the authors considered the desired characteristics of both available and future CAI equipment for visual, auditory, and tactile communication. The suggested lines of development for CAI terminal equipment are now an integral part of the University of Pittsburgh Laboratory program for research on man-machine interactions (Ragsdale, 1966).

In the selection and development of hardware equipment for CAI systems, Hansen (1966) proposed these factors as determining the future outcomes and benefits of the equipment: feasibility, adaptability, flexibility, expandability, reliability, availability, and cost. These factors, in essence, relate the desired equipment characteristics and cost factors to the desired educational and research purposes. Heavy stress is given to the reliability factor since each component of a CAI system contributes to the joint probability of overall system reliability.

Existing CAI Systems. This review will not attempt a description of existing CAI systems since these are thoroughly documented in the literature. The general reviews by Gentile (1965), Stolurow and Davis (1965), and Zinn (1966) presented extensive descriptions. The two earliest CAI systems were documented as the IBM 650 Teaching System (Rath, Anderson, and Brainerd, 1959) and the SDC system (Bushnell, 1962). Descriptions of the configuration and use of the IBM 1410 Coursewriter system and its teleprocessing capabilities were given, for example, for Florida State University (Kropp, Hartford, and Stoker, 1965), Michigan (Zinn, 1966), Pennsylvania State (Mitzel, 1966), and Westchester County Schools (Wing, 1964). Two CAI developments are in progress at the University of Illinois—the PLATO system (Bitzer, Braunfeld, and Lichtenberger, 1962) and the SOCRATES system (Stolurow, 1965b). PDP systems are employed at Bolt, Beranek, and Newman, Inc. (Feurzeig, 1964; Swets and others, 1962), Stanford (Suppes, 1964a), and the USAF Decision Science Laboratory (Shuford, 1966). The current Systems Development Corporation system is a multipurpose development called CLASS (Carter and Silberman, 1965).

The University of Pittsburgh CAI Laboratory (Ragsdale, 1966), as noted above, is primarily devoted to investigations and refinements of CAI interface equipment. Using a medium-sized computer (PDP-7), the potentialities of cathode-ray tube devices (CRT), typewriters, random-access audio units, Rand tablets, and a touch-sensitive visual device are under study and further development. The further development of Moore's (1963) "talking typewriter" will undoubtedly continue.

The first integrated CAI system, the 1500 Instructional System, was recently announced by IBM (IBM, 1966a,b). This system was specifically designed for educational activities and provides for time-shared multisensory terminals, CRT's, 16mm film, light pen, keyboard, and audio. The educational plans for the 1500 System were developed by a group at Stanford and included extensive curriculum research in reading and mathematics instruction for elementary school children (Atkinson and Hansen, 1966; Suppes, 1965).

Software

General CAI Language Characteristics. CAI "languages" must be further developed before the full and complete utilization of a CAI hardware system can be gained. CAI languages differ primarily in terms of their intended educational purpose and the given computer system on which they can be employed. The primary evaluations of CAI languages concern efficient computer usage, and that is determined in turn by the power, generality, and reliability of the given software system. Power can be thought of in terms of conceptual efficiency and economic efficiency. Conceptual efficiency is the amount of coding the author must input to perform certain computer tasks such as presenting a line of text, updating a counter, or scanning a list. In addition, conceptual efficiency depends on the programing ease with which one can undertake sophisticated tasks such as contingent decision making based on extensive history records of learners. Economic efficiency is the amount of code that is processed by the central computer unit in unit time (e.g., the amount of code executed by the computer in a given time for such functions as playing an audio message, displaying a line of text, or multiplying an array of numbers). In principle, power is related to the execution speed and capacity of the CAI system.

Generality is the degree to which a language can prove useful in a wide range of instructional and research tasks. The more general the language the more useful it will be for the multipurpose aims of a CAI research group. Thus a CAI language that allows for both the use of conventional mathematical notation plus the use of everyday English would be ideal from a generality point of view. Reliability is the degree to which the language facilitates the detection and prevention of logical and notation errors. The language assembler should detect errors and facilitate communication with the programers so corrections will be efficiently performed.

A second major evaluative focus for CAI languages deals with human factor considerations, i.e., potential programers. An important consideration is the amount of learning time necessary for mastering the language in order to use it efficiently. This is, of course, related to the naturalness of the CAI language in terms of its closeness to English. Of course, the educational background and quantitative sophistication of the programing group will influence this learning time.

Once the language is mastered, the degree to which the language allows easy and efficient editing and debugging procedures will influence its overall rating. This will depend on available terminal equipment, since editing programs are most efficient when using devices such as cathode-ray tubes. All existing CAI languages are capable of providing some useful contributions to future CAI developments. The software section of this review will be more detailed because there has been little or no documentation in this area of the CAI literature.

Existing CAI Languages

CATO is a CAI language developed for the PLATO system at the Co-ordinated Science Laboratory, University of Illinois (Bitzer, Lyman, and Easley, 1966). CATO is a modified Fortran language in which the programer has great flexibility for the preparation of three levels of basic program writing—tutorial, inquiry, and simulation. In the tutorial mode the programer inputs only the learning materials, and the language automatically constructs the decision structure and flow of the instruction according to a fixed logical sequence. In the inquiry mode there is great flexibility which allows for instructional interaction between the text and the learner (e.g., remedial instructional requests and informational aids are available to the user). The third mode, simulation, represents an attempt to provide as near a real-life experience as would be found in a science laboratory or in a political conference. The simulation aspect of the CATO language allows for some of the free flow of information that is associated with these natural situations.

The Coursewriter I language (Maher, 1964) was constructed primarily for the use of subject matter writers rather than for the technical person involved in computer programing. Coursewriter provides a certain amount of power and flexibility for developing various pedagogical logic structures. The most important feature of Coursewriter is the provision for revising instructional material in an easy and rapid manner. The language is designed to present an instructional event consisting of various components such as presentation of information, question posing, evaluation in terms of correct, incorrect, and unanticipated answer sets, and decision making as to the next instructional event. The decision making can be based on the values of numerical counters in which one can record and accumulate learning outcomes. In addition, Coursewriter I has partial answer capabilities in which only part of an answer is in the response set (e.g., initial letters in names or key words in a natural language string).

The Coursewriter II language (IBM, 1966a,b) provides a greater opportunity to record quantitatively the accumulating instructional history of a learner. The most important feature of the language is its provision for MACRO's by which one can formalize the instructional logic and by which one can insert only the informational portions of the subject matter. The language also provides for a much better control over the timing of the instructional events. Like other numerically oriented languages, the 1500 System which uses Coursewriter II also provides for MAT, Mathematical Algorithmic Translater (Iverson, 1962), which allows one to program and solve mathematical equations in a very straightforward manner.

Two languages are in the process of being developed at Bolt, Beranek, and Newman, Inc. The first is Telecomp, a numerically oriented programing language. This language allows high school students to program and solve mathematical problems. The programing codes and techniques are very similar to those of high school algebra. The second language is Mentor, which is imbedded in a more generalized Lisp language (McCarthy and others, 1965). These list processing languages, Lisp and Mentor, provide for great power and versatility in handling natural language statements. For example, one can input a conventional English declarative sentence and a few logical operators connected to it so that one can make contingent decisions depending on the amount of the program through which the user has proceeded.

BASIC is a CAI language developed at Dartmouth College by

Kemeny and Kurtz (1966). BASIC is equivalent to Telecomp and MAT in that mathematical problems may be solved by programing in a simple variable-oriented set of codes. The language is usually learned with less than two hours of instruction. BASIC runs on a 35 terminal time-shared CAI system.

At Systems Development Corporation two languages are in the process of being developed. The first is a time-sharing language which implements the CLASS facility. This language is quite problem oriented and allows one to distinguish between the logic of instructional codes and control statements. The control or decision statements help facilitate the flow of instructional material. A second language, being developed by Feingold and Frye (1966), provides for both instructional activities and numerical analysis for doing computation. The language has five instructional code types: problems, questions, multiple choice, decisions, and copy. The command types allow an author to inset instructional materials into the CAI system quickly and a learner to both calculate and answer problems.

The THOR time-sharing language system developed at Stanford (Brian, 1966) has all of the features found in variable-oriented CAI languages. Simplified subsets of the THOR language have been developed to accomplish specific CAI activities such as mathematical drill problems or tutorial activities. A valuable feature of the THOR language is a real-time debugging aid called RAID (Stygar, 1965). This language aid facilitates editing and course revision work. In the case of arithmetic and spelling drill activities, the THOR language allows for an automated code writer that prepares the program after the subject matter has been specified.

On the SOCRATES system at the University of Illinois, Stolurow and Lippert (1966) developed a language, AUTHOR, that prepares course materials under computer control. AUTHOR allows for natural language text construction. A parallel course preparation language, SYLLOGEN, generates syllogisms and logic problems.

The developments in CAI software are proceeding across a broad range of functions from simplified coding logics such as MACRO's to automated subject matter generators such as AUTHOR. The next few years should produce even more general, yet sophisticated, CAI languages.

THE APPLICATIONS OF COMPUTER-ASSISTED INSTRUCTION

CAI has often been compared with other modes of instruction. Usually the investigators have attempted to automate the instructional process and in most cases make a comparison with conventional classroom procedures. Although this review will refer to only a small number of existing courses of instruction that are available for given CAI systems (Zinn, 1966), the amount of effort it takes to prepare a complete CAI course should be pointed out and acknowledged. The vast majority of the CAI projects have expended tremendous energy in the development of curriculum materials; consequently, this development phase has limited the availability of research findings.

Drill and Practice

One of the natural applications for CAI is the provision of practice and evaluation for a learner who needs extensive training. The CAI system provides the objective learning conditions under which responses receive immediate evaluation and the provision for repeating those items that are presenting difficulty to the learner. In addition, it is now possible to provide a fair amount of individualization in that the difficulty level of the practice material can be adjusted to the competency level of the learner. A case in point is the work of a Stanford University group working in elementary school mathematics and language arts. Suppes, Jerman, and Groen (1966) reported a daily linear mathematics program that reviews and teaches basic number facts to 41 fourth-grade children. Using simple reinforcement procedures that involve indicating incorrect responses and repeating incorrect items immediately, the children showed progressive improvement over a series of arithmetic concepts. An important aspect of this CAI endeavor was the positive reception by the classroom teacher. The teacher was able to receive a detailed item analysis of each child's work. This is one of the first CAI programs to become an integral part of the daily instructional activities of a school. In another experiment carried on during the academic year of 1965–66, the Stanford group provided a daily arithmetic drill to over 300 elementary school children, grades 3 to 6. In addition, 60 intermediate grade children were provided a daily spelling activity. Hansen (1966) reported learning curves for these spelling drills which indicated that this type of CAI activity significantly improved the spelling competency of these elementary school children.

Testing

It has been proposed (Shuford, 1966; Zinn, 1966) that CAI can provide the capability of a type of testing not ordinarily available in more conventional paper-and-pencil procedures. The most important feature of CAI is the concurrent (on-line) analysis and decision making from multiple dependent measures. For example, one can collect and utilize response latency and confidence rating data to determine the exact test items to be presented. Shuford refers to this as cybernetic testing and has presented a number of papers (Shuford, 1966) dealing with the underlying mathematical formulations of this type of activity. As recommended by Mager and Clark (1963) for efficient use of programed instruction, branching a learner systematically through a test can maximize both the desired level of difficulty and the desired coverage of the test content. Moreover, the future will bring the capability to adjust either the number or nature of response alternatives in real time so that even more precise control of the test situation will be possible.

Tutoring

One of the most consistent findings associated with CAI tutorial applications is the marked saving in instructional time with no loss in post-instructional achievement test performance. Grubb and Selfridge (1964) taught descriptive statistics to a small number of college students via CAI. This procedure was compared with college students' taking instruction under conventional lectures and via programed text. Those students working under CAI completed the course material in one-tenth the time and performed almost twice as well on the final achievement test as did the other two groups. Schurdak (1965) taught 48 college students a portion of a course in Fortran programing. After equating for mental ability, the results showed that CAI students saved approximately 10 percent of the work time in completing the course as opposed to students using a standard text or a programed text, and they performed approximately 10 percent better on the final criterion test. Goodman (1964) reported the instruction of 3,000 airline ticket agents via a CAI application used for reservation purposes on airlines. In comparison with a controlled set of ticket agents receiving conventional instruction, CAI reduced the training time by one-half, and final test grades were approximately 5 percent better for the CAI students. In each of these studies a post-test questionnaire revealed that the participants had formed positive views about CAI instruction.

A number of the CAI research projects have collected extensive amounts of CAI-controlled learning data without making comparisons to other pedagogical modes such as lecture or programed text. Braunfeld (1964) reported the teaching of computer programing to a group of college students. The objectives of the course were attained, as measured by the students' test scores and performance through the subject matter. At Florida State University, Lewis (1966) taught 20 elementary school children a unit on geometric concepts using slides under CAI control. The children demonstrated mastery of the geometric concepts. As with the college students, the children reported positive reactions to their CAI experience.

The most extensive CAI tutorial experiments were performed by Wodtke (1965) at Pennsylvania State University. The first experiment focused on the effects of scrambling the implicit sequence of a set of mathematical concepts. Randomizing the sequence of the material led the college students to make more errors in working through the program and to require more instructional time to complete the course. This increase in latencies on individual questions led to a decrease in the efficiency of instruction as indicated by the amount learned per unit time. The scrambling of the material interfered most with the learning of the high-aptitude students. This negative effect on the high-aptitude students was also expressed in the students' self-report on an anxiety scale. In a second study Wodtke (1965) had college students work via CAI through a modern mathematics program and found significant correlations between general intelligence and other aptitude measures with their performance on the CAI course material. This finding is the reverse of that found in many programed instruction experiments. Attitude measures about CAI, although positive, did not vary significantly with any of the CAI achievement outcomes. This series of studies at Pennsylvania State University indicates the uses CAI course materials can have as media by which to investigate instructional variables.

COMPUTER-ASSISTED RESEARCH

Quantitative Instructional Models

The development of quantitative instructional models related to CAI has had its beginning within the last four years. These models attempt to describe the process of optimalizing the sequence of instructional events in a controlled situation like CAI. In the theoretical paper by Groen and Atkinson (1966) these quantitative instructional models were represented as multistage decision processes which determine the efficiency of various orders of presenting learning materials. A distinction was made between response-insensitive decision rules that lead to fixed sequencing strategies as opposed to response-sensitive decision rules that are dynamic in the sense that the accumulating history of a learner influences the precise nature of the decision process. The Groen and Atkinson paper provided a general conception and a formal set of notations for representing the instructional paradigm and for calculating optimal instructional strategies.

Smallwood (1962), in one of the earliest applications of dynamic programing to instructional problems, formulated a simple learning model in which students' performance on a postinstructional test is a function of the number and contributions of blocks of instructional material and the probable time for working through these subject matter blocks. Using a decision rule based on an "acceptable" test score, the model finds the one or more blocks of instruction that will accomplish this goal and then selects the block requiring the least work time. If no block is found that will attain the "acceptable" score, then the block with a maximum expected score value is selected. In the other sections of the monograph Smallwood compared dynamic programing models with various other approaches like regression models as to their ability to determine optimal instructional strategies.

In work growing out of a second-language learning experimentation, Suppes (1964b) and Crothers (1965) developed response-sensitive instructional models for systematically presenting second-language vocabulary items. Suppes (1964b) examined the issue of mass vs. distributed sequencing of items. Assuming a single operator linear process for both the acquisition and the forgetting process, he formulated the following decision model: (a) if the learning parameter is greater than the forgetting parameter for the given list size, then all items should receive a maximum distribution within the sequence of learning events, and (b) if the learning parameter is less than the forgetting parameter, then items should be massed (i.e., maximally repeated) in order to maximize performance on a subsequent test. Under no circumstances does the model predict any intermediate mixing of massed or distributed items. Crothers (1965) generalized these findings for the presentation of examples from contrasting categorical responses when he found that the predicted mean test performance is higher if all members of a category are massed rather than systematically distributed among the exemplars from other categories. This general line of model building represents one selection of the optimality models published in the book *Human Judgments and Optimality* (Shelly and Bryan, 1965).

Dear and Atkinson (1962) introduced the use of simplified Markov learning models for deriving optimal decision strategies. Matheson (1964) investigated via simulation techniques a number of suboptimal strategies for the response-insensitive instructional conditions and found a net reward return of 1 to 7 percent for the optimal strategies.

Karush and Dear (1965) formulated a linear model from which they proved that an optimal strategy existed for any given trial in which the items with the lowest current conditioning probabilities are presented. This line of investigation followed from their earlier work with first-order Markov models in which they were able to show that the optimal strategy is one of presenting the items with the most recent errors if one can assume that the probability of correct response in the conditioning state is less than one. This use of Markov learning models received an experimental test in a paired-associate situation performed by Dear and others (1965). Items in the paired-associate list were presented from one of two sets. The first set of items was presented according to the one-element (first-order Markov) optimization algorithm in which items with the largest current number of errors were presented. Items in the second set were presented with a uniform distribution. This uniform strategy is optimal if a linear model is assumed. It was found that while the acquisition date (e.g., rate of learning) tended to favor items from the one-element optimization algorithm, no significant difference was found in a final test composed of items from the two different presentation sets. Although this work has just begun, it shows great promise for the future in providing a formal basis for theories of instruction and in illustrating one of the most effective properties of a CAI system: real time decisions may be made on accumulating learning histories so that the educational outcome may be maximized.

Computer Simulation Models

Computer simulation models of cognitive processes offer a precise and theoretically rich class of quantitative learning models that are capable of characterizing informational structures, for example, those that result from CAI. Unfortunately, the immediate demands of current problems in computer simulation of human behavior have preoccupied the investigators so that only suggestive starts have been made toward instructionally oriented work.

The basic simulation models and associated problems are collected in the Feigenbaum and Feldman volume, *Computers and Thought* (1963). Reitman recently published *Cognition and Thought* (1965) in which the basic techniques for handling computer simulated learning and memory processes were presented. Reitman (1966) presented techniques for modeling the formulation and usage of conceptual rules such as those of mathematics or grammar. Simon and Kotovsky's (1963) work on the learning of sequential patterns represents an excellent example of a typical educational task common to reading, spelling, and mathematics.

Cognitive simulation research offers great potential to research in that the human cognitive tasks (e.g., playing chess, doing algebraic problems, taking psychological tests, etc.) are on the same level of complexity as instructional activities. The next few years will see a rapid research development in this area.

Processing of Natural Language

The processing of natural language for informational retrieval systems and for machine translation systems will lead to theoretical and applied techniques that may influence CAI especially as to software capability In addition, the use of natural language processing via CAI terminals for other educational tasks such as informational storage systems of the evaluation of essay materials will be part of future developments.

The volume authored by Garvin (1963), *Natural Language and the Computer,* presents most of the early work in the field. Simmons (1964) and Bobrow (1963) have more recent reviews that focus on the syntactical aspects of computer processing, one of the major problem areas. Page (1966) reported the activities of Project Essay Grade in which the essay writing of high school students was evaluated by a computer program. The degree of accuracy and reliability of grading shows great promise for the future, especially if the essay writing takes place at a CAI terminal so that editing behaviors may be studied and the necessity of key-punching the text can be avoided.

Psychological Experimentation

The use of computers in psychological experimentation is growing. The computer facility offers the potentiality for both helping in the construction and sequencing of the stimulus material and providing for highly sophisticated research procedures and data collection. No attempt will be made to review the studies employing computers, but two studies will be mentioned to illustrate the uses of computers in this type of research.

Swets and others (1962) utilized a computer in the random generation of two to five values along five dimensions for the production of non-verbal sounds. These dimensions were frequency, amplitude, interrupt rate, duty cycle, and duration. Four experiments were performed in which the computer allowed the investigators to run exceedingly complex experiments in a simple and ready manner. Brelsford and others (1966) used a computer to investigate immediate memory processes. The computer has also been used to generate random number-letter pairs and to sequence these in pre-defined random orders. The findings from these immediate memory experiments have been most suggestive for investigations of rehearsal hypotheses and of the effect of rehearsal on the storage of information in both short- and long-term memory.

BIBLIOGRAPHY

Atkinson, Richard C., and Hansen, Duncan N. *Computer-Assisted Instruction in Initial Reading: The Stanford Project.* Technical Report No. 93. Stanford, Calif: Institute for Mathematical Studies in the Social Sciences, Stanford University, March 1966. 31 pp. (Offset)

Bitzer, Donald L.; Braunfeld, Paul; and Lichtenberger, W. W. "Plato II: A Multiple-Student, Computer-Controlled, Automatic Teaching Device." *Programmed Learning and Computer-Based Instruction.* (Edited by John E. Coulson.) New York: John Wiley and Sons, 1962. pp. 205–16.

Bitzer, Donald L.; Lyman, Elisabeth R.; and Easley, John A., Jr. "The Uses of PLATO, a Computer-Controlled Teaching System." *Audiovisual Instruction* 11: 16–21; January 1966.

Bobrow, Daniel G. "Syntactic Analysis of English by Computer — A Survey." *AFIPS Conference Proceedings,* Vol. 34. Baltimore: Spartan Books, 1963. pp. 365–87.

Braunfeld, Peter G. "Problems and Prospects of Teaching with a Computer." *Journal of Educational Psychology* 55: 201–11; August, 1964.

Brelsford, J. W., Jr., and others. "Short-Term Recall of Paired-Associates as a Function of the Number of Interpolated Pairs." *Psychonomic Science* 4: 73–74; January 10, 1966.

Brian, Dow. *The THOR Language.* Stanford, Calif.: Institute for Mathematical Studies in the Social Sciences, Stanford University, July 1966. 88 pp. (Offset)

Bushnell, Don. D. "Computer-Based Teaching Machines." *Journal of Educational Research* 55: 528–31; June–July 1962.

Carter, Launor, and Silberman, Harry. *The Systems Approach, Technology and the School.* Professional Paper SP-2025. Santa Monica, Calif.: System Development Corporation, April 1965. 30 pp. (Offset)

Coulson, John E. "A Computer-Based Laboratory for Research and Development in Education." *Programmed Learning and Computer-Based Instruction.* (Edited by John E. Coulson.) New York: John Wiley and Sons. pp. 191–204.

Coulson, John E. *Automation, Cybernetics, and Education.* Professional Paper SP-1966. Santa Monica, Calif.: System Development Corporation, March 1965. 11 pp. (Offset)

Crothers, Edward. "Learning Model Solution to a Problem in Constrained Optimization." *Journal of Mathematical Psychology* 2: 19–25; February 1965.

Dear, Robert E., and Atkinson, Richard C. "Optimal Allocation of Items in a Simple Two-Concept Automated Teaching Model." *Programmed Learning and Computer-Based Instruction.* (Edited by John E. Coulson.) New York: John Wiley and Sons, 1962. pp. 25–45.

Dear, R. E., and others. *An Optimal Strategy for the Presentation of Paired-Associate Items.* Technical Memorandum TM-1935/101/00. Santa Monica, Calif.: System Development Corporation, March 1965. 56 pp. (Offset)

Dick, Walter. "The Development and Current Status of Computer-Based Instruction." *American Educational Research Journal* 2: 41–54; January 1965.

Feigenbaum, Edward A., and Feldman, Julian, editors. *Computers and Thought.* New York: McGraw-Hill Book Co., 1963. 535 pp.

Feingold, S. L., and Frye, C. H. *User's Guide to PLANIT: Programming Language for Interactive Teaching.* Technical Memorandum TM-3055/000/00. Santa Monica, Calif.: System Development Corporation, July 1966. 153 pp. (Offset)

Feurzeig, Wallace. "Conversational Teaching Machine." *Datamation.* 10: 38–42; June 1964.

Garvin, Paul L. *Natural Language and the Computer.* New York: McGraw-Hill Book Co., 1963. 398 pp.

Gentile, J. Ronald. "The First Generation of Computer-Assisted Instructional Systems: An Evaluative Review." *Experimentation with Computer-Assisted Instruction in Technical Education.* (Edited by Harold E. Mitzel and George L. Brandon.) University Park: Computer-Assisted Instruction Laboratory, Pennsylvania State University, December 1965. Appendix, pp. 1–32.

Glaser, Robert; Ramage, William W.; and Lipson, Joseph I. *The Interface Between Student and Subject Matter.* Pittsburgh, Pa.: Learning Research and Development Center, University of Pittsburgh, 1964. 177 pp.

Goodman, Louis S. "Computer-Based Instruction: Today and Tomorrow." *Data Processing for Education* 3: 2–5; April 1964.

Groen, Guy J., and Atkinson, Richard C. "Models for Optimizing the Learning Process." Technical Report No. 92. Stanford, Calif.: Institute for Mathematical Studies in the Social Sciences, Stanford University, February 1966. 34 pp. (Offset)

Grubb, Ralph E., and Selfridge, Lenore D. "Computer Tutoring in Statistics." *Computers and Automation* 13: 20–26; March 1964.

Hansen, Duncan N. *Applications of Computers to Research on Instruction.* Stanford,

Calif.: Institute for Mathematical Studies in the Social Sciences, Stanford, University, 1966. 17 pp. (Mimeo.)

Hickey, Albert E., and Newton, John M. *Computer-Assisted Instruction: A Survey of the Literature.* Newburyport, Mass.: Entelek Inc., January 1966. 31 pp.

International Business Machines Corporation. *IBM 1500 Instructional System, System Summary.* White Plains, N.Y.: the Corporation, 1966. 11 pp. (a)

International Business Machines Corporation. *1500 Operating System Computer-Assisted Instruction Coursewriter II.* White Plains, N.Y.: the Corporation, 1966. 45 pp. (b)

Iverson, Kenneth E. *A Programming Language.* New York: John Wiley and Sons, 1962. 286 pp.

Karush, W., and Dear, R. E. *Optimal Procedure for an N-State Testing and Learning Process — II.* Technical Report SP-1922/001/00. Santa Monica, Calif.: System Development Corporation, October 1965. 18 pp. (Offset)

Kemeny, John G., and Kurtz, Thomas E. *BASIC.* Hanover, N.H.: Computation Center, Dartmouth College, January 1966. 60 pp.

Kropp, R. P.; Hartford, D. L.; and Stoker, H. W. "Quarterly Progress Report." Tallahassee: Computer-Assisted Instruction Center, Florida State University, December 1965. (Unpaged) (Offset)

Lewis, Brian N., and Pask, Gordon. "The Theory and Practice of Adaptive Teaching Systems." *Teaching Machines and Programed Learning, II: Data and Directions.* (Edited by Robert Glaser.) Washington, D.C.: Department of Audiovisual Instruction, National Education Association, 1965. pp. 213–66.

Lewis, Lloyd A., Jr. "A Comparison of Two Modes of Visual Display in a Computer Assisted Instruction Situation." Master's thesis. Tallahassee: Florida State University, 1966. 55 pp.

McCarthy, John, and others. *LISP 1.5 Programmer's Manual.* Cambridge: The Computation Center and Research Laboratory of Electronics, Massachusetts Institute of Technology, February 1965. 97 pp.

Mager, Robert F., and Clark, Cecil. "Explorations in Student-Controlled Instruction." *Psychological Reports* 13: 71-76; August 1963.

Maher, Ann. *Computer-Based Instruction (CBI): Introduction to the IBM Project.* Research Report RC-1114. White Plains, N.Y.: International Business Machines Corporation, 1964. 13 pp.

Matheson, James E. *Optimum Teaching Procedures Derived from Mathematical Learning Models.* Report CCS-2. Stanford, Calif.: Institute in Engineering-Economic Systems, Stanford University, 1964. 70 pp.

Mitzel, Harold E. *The Development and Presentation of Four College Courses by Computer Teleprocessing.* University Park: Computer-Assisted Instruction Laboratory, Pennsylvania State University, 1966. 41 pp. (Offset)

Moore, Omar Khayyam. *Autotelic Responsive Environments and Exceptional Children.* Hamden, Conn.: Responsive Environments Foundation, September 1963. 53 pp. (Offset)

Page, Ellis B. "The Imminence of Grading Essays by Computer." *Phi Delta Kappan* 47: 238–43; January 1966.

Ragsdale, Ronald. "The Learning Research and Development Center's Computer Assisted Laboratory." *DECUS Proceedings, Fall 1965.* Maynard, Mass.: Digital Equipment Computer Users Society, 1966. pp. 65–68.

Rath, Gustave J.; Anderson, Nancy S.; and Brainerd, R. C. "The IBM Research Center Teaching Machine Project." *Automatic Teaching: The State of the Art.* (Edited by Eugene Galanter.) New York: John Wiley and Sons, 1959. Chapter 11, pp. 117–30.

Reitman, Walter R. *Cognition and Thought.* New York: John Wiley and Sons, 1965. 312 pp.

Reitman, Walter R. *Modeling the Formation and Use of Concepts, Percepts and Rules.* Preprint 174. Ann Arbor: Mental Health Research Institute, University of Michigan, January 1966. 29 pp. (Offset)

Schurdak, John J. *An Approach to the Use of Computers in the Instructional Process and an Evaluation.* Research Report RC-1432. Yorktown Heights, N.Y.: IBM Watson Research Center, 1965. 38 pp. (Offset)

Shelly, Maynard W., II, and Bryan, Glenn L., editors. *Human Judgments and Optimality.* New York: John Wiley and Sons, 1965. 436 pp.

Shuford, Emir H. *Cybernetic Testing.* Technical Report ESD-TR-65-467. Bedford, Mass.: Electronic Systems Division, L. G. Hanscomb Field, 1966. 11 pp. (Offset)

Silberman, Harry F., and Coulson, John E. "Automated Teaching." *Computer Applications in the Behavioral Sciences.* (Edited by Harold Borko.) Englewood Cliffs, N.J.: Prentice-Hall, 1962. Chapter 14, pp. 308–35.

Simmons, R. F. *Answering English Questions by Computers: A Survey.* Professional Paper SP-1556. Santa Monica, Calif.: System Development Corporation, April 1964. 63 pp. (Offset)

Simon, Herbert, and Kotovsky, Kenneth. "Human Acquisition of Concepts for Sequential Patterns." *Psychological Review* 70: 534:46; November 1963.

Smallwood, Richard D. "A Decision Structure for Computer-Based Teaching Machines." *Computers and Automation* 11: 9–14; February 1962.

Stolurow, Lawrence M. *Essential Principles of Programmed Instruction.* Technical Report No. 8. Urbana: Training Research Laboratory, University of Illinois, June 1965. 12 pp. (Offset) (a)

Stolurow, Lawrence M. *SOCRATES: System for Organizing Content To Review and Teach Educational Subjects.* Urbana: Training Research Laboratory, University of Illinois, 1965. 6 pp. (Offset) (b)

Stolurow, Lawrence M., and Davis, Daniel. "Teaching Machines and Computer-Based Systems." *Teaching Machines and Programmed Learning, II: Data and Directions.* (Edited by Robert Glaser.) Washington, D.C.: Department of Audio-visual Instruction, National Education Association, 1965. pp. 162–212.

Stolurow, Lawrence M., and Lippert, Henry T. *Automatically Translating Heuristically Organized Routines: AUTHOR I.* Technical Memorandum No. 21. Urbana: Training Research Laboratory, University of Illinois, February 1966. 12 pp. (Offset)

Stygar, Paul. *RAID (Alias TVDDT).* Memorandum No. 37, Stanford Time-Sharing Project. Stanford, Calif.: Stanford University, November 1965. 13 pp. (Offset)

Suppes, Patrick. *Computer-Based Mathematics Instruction: The First Year of the Project.* Stanford, Calif.: Institute for Mathematical Studies in the Social Sciences, Stanford University, 1964. 22 pp. (Offset) (a)

Suppes, Patrick. "Modern Learning Theory and the Elementary-School Curriculum." *American Educational Research Journal* 1: 79–93; March 1964. (b)

Suppes, Patrick. *Computer-Assisted Instruction in the Schools: Potentialities, Problems, Prospects.* Technical Report No. 81. Stanford, Calif.: Institute for Mathematical Studies in the Social Sciences, Stanford University, October 1965. 17 pp. (Offset)

Suppes, Patrick; Jerman, Max; and Groen, Guy. "Arithmetic Drills and Review on a Computer-Based Teletype." *Arithmetic Teacher* 13: 303–309; April 1966.

Swets, John A., and others. "Learning To Identify Nonverbal Sounds: An Application of a Computer as a Teaching Machine." *Journal of the Acoustical Society of America* 34: 928–35; July 1962.

Wing, Richard L. "Computer-Controlled Economics Games for the Elementary School." *Audiovisual Instruction* 9: 681–82; December 1964.

Wodtke, Kenneth H. "Preliminary Research Findings." *Experimentation with Computer-Assisted Instruction in Technical Education.* (Edited by Harold E. Mitzel and George L. Brandon.) University Park: Computer-Assisted Instruction Laboratory, Pennsylvania State University, 1965. pp. 25–41.

Zinn, Karl. *Computer Assistance for Instruction: A Review of Systems and Projects.* CAIS Report 010. Ann Arbor: Center for Research on Learning and Teaching, University of Michigan, 1966. 63 pp. (Ditto)

Chapter 22

What is the concept of a man-machine system, and in such a system how are roles and responsibilities kept proportional?

What are the ramifications of this form of automation in society at large and in education in particular?

What distinction can be drawn between computer-based instruction and instruction about computers?

Assuming that the computer is a sophisticated form of the new media, how will it be used in school situations . . . ranging from instruction to counseling, and other peripheral applications?

THE EMERGING EDUCATIONAL TRIAD: MAN-MACHINES AND INSTRUCTION

MURRAY TONDOW, Director, Educational Data Services
Palo Alto (Calif.) Unified School District

MAN AND MACHINES

Initially this chapter will examine the concept of man-machine systems. This area, in the writer's view, is more important than the area of computers and instruction *per se*. What happens in this broad rubric of man and machine will have a profound effect upon instruction, whether it be related to computers or otherwise.

Briefly stated, the thesis of this paper is that, at the present time and as far into the future as we seem able to project stochastic estimates, we are moving inexorably toward a world which more and more can be described as a man-machine system. It can be stated that we already have man-machine systems. However, this is a misnomer (or, rather, is misleading) and perhaps can best be described in terms of the well known story of the man who advertised his stew as being half rabbit and half buffalo. Upon investigation, the eater would find that this was indeed true—there was one rabbit and one buffalo! At the present state of the art, the buffalo (in terms of size) would tend to be man and the rabbit we can see as machine. However, as we look ahead, we see a much different proportional relationship between man and machine, with more and more productive and problem-solving responsibilities assigned to machines.

The second point is that whether we are accurate in calling systems man-machine systems, or whether we had better call them machine-man systems, is one of the critical concerns that befall us at the present time. This is a particularly critical issue in education, and in the behavioral sciences in general. If machines are to play a larger part in the life of man, then those professions that are primarily committed to the concern of the human condition must begin to play a more active role in understanding and directing man-machine systems. In order to truly assist people, one must have skills—compassion alone is not sufficient. For example, if a man is dying and one does not know how to help him, all one's compassion will be to no avail. It is important, then, that educators and behavioral scientists develop skills relating to man-machine systems; otherwise, we will be abdicating our role and responsibility. It is critical that the behavioral sciences have a major voice in the evolution and development of the newer models of behavior (from individual to the largest social institutions). Problem-solving alone is not sufficient. What is done to people along the way must be paramount. It may not be possible to predefine the ideal behavior for each person or group under all conditions and in all situations. It is possible, however, to assess each act in relation to whether it moves toward or away from an overriding ideal. (7, 9) (While it is not within the realm of this chapter to delve into this point in any depth, let me just state the author's ideal as that of the human worth and dignity of the individual.)

A third concern is that this change, or this intrusion of automation upon our lives, is not something of the future but, rather, is upon us now and is accelerating at an ever increasing rate. A statement of some simple statistics will bear this out. It took man about 500,000 years to reach the first one billion mark on this planet. That was in 1850. At the present time, we are increasing our population at the rate of a billion every twenty years. Between now and the year 2000, the population increase will equal the present world population. One of the characteristics of this statistic is that the percentage of young people is constantly on the rise. In the United States, more than half the population is under twenty-five years of age, and about one-third of the population is under fifteen years of age. This is even more remarkable from a world point of view, in that much of the world has a generally greater percentage of young people than the United States. Along with the population increase there has been an "explosion" of scientists. At the present time, ninety per cent of the scientists of all time are living. There is no reason to believe that their ability is any less than those who came before them. Certainly they have better education, more complete facilities, and greater capabilities of communication than in the past. Thus, we have every reason to expect that the rate of change, insofar as new inventions and generation of new information are concerned, will continue to occur at an ever accelerating rate. At the present time, it is estimated that man's information is doubled every ten years—the equivalent of a 330-volume encyclopedia per day! Yet man's ability to read and assimilate hasn't changed appreciably since 1850. Thus, we have the problem of an ever increasing gap between what an individual knows and what he needs to know. An example of the tremendous change rate that we are now caught up in can be seen from the fact that 13 per cent of the gross national product in the United States in 1965 came from products and services that did not exist in 1964. If this turnover were to be evenly distributed, it would mean that we would have a 100 per cent turnover of all products and services every eight years. Of course, some products and services are much more durable. The point here is merely to emphasize the tremendous change that we are now experiencing.

Perhaps the most dramatic statistics relate to the computer science itself. It is not yet twenty years old. For many of us it did not exist when we went to school. Thus our acquisition of these skills has been sporadic and highly individual, leaving us with many gaps. Of all of man's inventions, the computer remains special, in that it deals with one of the unique qualities of man—the ability for problem-solving. All other inventions relate to relieving man's physical labor. In the sense of problem-solving, then, the computer is not just another tool. It is, indeed, an extension of one of man's unique capabilities, not merely a high-speed calculator. In the short span of twenty years, the computer has been a major factor in making possible the entire aerospace industry, which is itself well on the way to becoming one of the leading worldwide industries. The rate at which this field has developed has surprised even its most ardent supporters (and anguished its detractors!). Ten years ago, it was felt that ten large computers of that era could handle all of the informational needs of the United States. At the present time, there are well over 30,000 computers in the United States, and there is every indication that the sale of computers will continue to increase at an accelerating rate. Within five years, work now going on in micro-miniaturization will give us computers capable of doing work that now takes as many as several thousand computers! It is obvious that the rapid change is beginning to cause some very serious and profound qualitative changes in the world.

While the computer must be viewed as an extension of man, it must not be viewed as a substitute for man. Computers can solve problems, computers can determine problems, computers have the capacity for error, computers can reproduce (e.g., automatically construct other computers) but they have no compassion, no capacity for love, no spiritual or mystical sense, no part of the real essence of man.

ATTITUDE BY EDUCATORS

One of the results of the changes mentioned above concerns a new attitude and behavior on the part of the American people toward education. This change has, in essence, brought the real much closer to the ideal—that is, we have always paid strong lip service to education, but our real behavior often belied this. However, with the increasing complexities of life, people have begun to shift their hope for survival toward education. Numerous communities and states are increasing their economic strength through education; that is, they recognize that good schools are a prerequisite for obtaining the specialized kinds of workers that new industry requires. Workers in the newer industries tend to be young people with growing families. These people expect and demand good education for their children. The quality of education is of critical concern to them. Further, in the long run, an adequate system of higher education assures a continuing source of high-level manpower. As a result, large industry, real estate and other groups (who in the past have often been eloquent in their hostility to educational expenditures) now are in the forefront of supporting greater and greater efforts in these areas.

What we then have is a shift of great expectations toward and a growing dependency upon education. In the 1920s, the great expectation was mass production to bring all the good things to people at a price they could afford. In the middle Sixties, education is expected to handle the insoluble problems. The danger is obvious—the difference between the expectations of people and the capability of education to indeed solve all these problems, many of which we only dimly see and vaguely understand. To give one an idea of the extent to which the society and the economy now have become dependent upon education, note that about half the population (something in excess of 97 million people) can be classified as either part- or full-time students. This includes all programs—from Headstart to the Job Corps. If you now add to this all staff, faculties, and those workers who sell and supply directly to education, you have almost two-thirds of the population.

If you put together the apparent inexorability of this move toward more and more man-machine interaction, the ever accelerating rate of this change, and the increasing expectations upon education, it becomes apparent that we can expect dramatic changes in the structure, form and process of education, in the role of the individual, and, of course, in the entire value system upon which all institutions are based.

Lest the reader think that this is yet to come and is of no immediate concern, let's look at today for a moment. A few years ago, if one were to ask an elementary school principal what age and experience were ideal for a primary teacher, he would probably have said that someone who had graduated from college and who had four or five years of experience (representing a combination of youth and experience—the best of both worlds) was just the kind of new teacher he would prefer to hire. But consider for a moment the problems of today's primary teacher, out of college five years. She is expected to teach the new math— not, for the most part, in any teacher-training curriculum five years ago. She is expected to teach the new science—it just didn't exist five years ago. She is expected to teach some foreign language—very few institutions taught primary teachers how to teach a foreign language. She is expected to teach reading, utilizing all of the newer techniques such as structural linguistics and transformational grammar—very few professors were aware of these terms five years ago. The result is that either these new approaches are not taught by the teacher or she spends a good deal of her free time—evenings during the year and summers— trying to upgrade herself. All this change in education at the primary level; all this in five years. No doubt it is possible for the reader to make even stronger cases for other grade levels, extending through graduate school. As a matter of fact, this writer is convinced that the greatest deterrent to the rate of change at the present time is the education offered at the graduate level. It tends, for the most part, to be geared to today and yesterday, with little relevance to what will be universal tomorrow.

It is important that some attempt be made to gain perspective on what appears to be the direction of education. Obviously, if the roles of teacher, counselor and administrator are changing, then the structure, form and process of education will also be different in the years to come. Let us take the hypothetical situation of how a high school might be operating in 1970. The details here, of course, may be different from school to school, but the overall framework is something we can expect within the next five years. It is possible today. The only reason it is not presently in operation is that funds have not yet been expended to accomplish it. And, of course, we lack sufficient numbers of people skilled in some of the areas that will be described. That is the point made a moment ago—training at the present time does not really prepare people for education as it will manifest itself within even five years. This is a typical secondary school for which we must anticipate and train teachers:

On either side of the main hallway there will be vending machines. The student population will probably be broken into five groups for purposes of load balance of equipment; one-fifth of the students will have their week begin on Monday, one-fifth on Tuesday, etc. As the students enter school, those whose week begins on that day will go to one of these vending machines, take out their ID card (similar to today's credit cards), and insert it into the vending machine. These machines will actually be remote terminals hooked to a remote computer. Immediately, the computer will print out the week's activities for the student, as well as a debriefing, or analysis, of how the student did the previous week. It might, for example, suggest that the student go to the library and check out certain programed materials, use certain study carrels at given times, go to see the counselor at certain hours, meet with particular small groups at given times. As the student performs during the week, much of his activity will be immediately recorded on-line to the computer. Other data will be fed to the computer on an off-line basis (some time after it actually occurs).

Now, while this has the danger of "big brother," it is easy to see that it also has the potential of a much more individualized, much more humanistic, much more flexible, much more meaningful educational experience for students. On this basis, there need not be the lockstep of today. In order for this kind of program to operate, we can literally take today's hardware off the shelves and plug it in. (2, 3, 4, 6, 10) The critical issue as to rate and success of such implementation has to do with openness—openness to new experience—by educators.

Two very important concerns are instructional materials and teacher training. For example, publishing houses, like any institution, tend to hire certain types of individuals with certain attitudes and skills, resulting in a tendency to perpetuate that which exists; an institutional perpetuation. The dependency of American education on materials from the publishers means that the rate of positive change will be directly affected by the capability and willingness of the publisher to retool.

The problems of teacher training have several aspects. There is the need to upgrade today's professor so that he can prepare those studying for the education of tomorrow. It is also necessary to update today's teachers. Institutional perpetuation of the obsolete holds here too. At present, it would appear that school systems are doing more to face this reality than the institutions of higher learning. There is reason to believe that the next several years will see twelve-month contracts for teachers—ten months of teaching, one month of vacation, one month of in-service updating. (This is, of course, a very critical problem today and deserves a great deal of immediate attention.)

A critical aspect of these problems is that no one group (teachers, publishers, etc.) is totally responsible for—nor is any group immune from—the responsibility of facing up to necessary adjustments to allow education to meet its responsibilities. It would seem appropriate to now look at one crucial area of education and discuss how change seems to be developing.

COMPUTERS AND INSTRUCTION

Within the educational community there is no area of more importance than that of instruction. To the extent that computers relate to instruction they will have their greatest impact on education. At the present time, we can break computers and instruction into two broad rubrics.

The computer as the object of instruction. By this we mean concern about the computer and teaching about computers, about computer sciences, and teaching skills relating to the computer sciences, such as computer programing (14).

Computer-based instruction. Here we mean using the computer as the direct mediator between student and information and in this sense it can be called the most sophisticated of the instructional media. This function is often called computer-assisted instruction (CAI), but it would appear that the term computer-based instruction (CBI) is more descriptive. Instruction is used here in its broadest sense; that is, it can relate to any kind of dialogue in which there is an information base, such as what courses a student should choose so that he might be eligible to enter the school of his choice.

Computer as the Object of Instruction

This particular area would seem to have less glamour than that of computer-based instruction. However, we are much further along in using the computer as an object of instruction than in using it as a base for instruction. There are literally hundreds of courses in high schools throughout the United States that now offer programing and related computer skills.

The impact that this can have on education really falls into two categories:

1. The area of skills; that is, teaching people skills relating to the use of the computer. Most commonly this would mean (at the high school level) computer programing and operation of the computer and peripheral equipment. At the college level we would want to include other things, such as systems analysis and design, logic and circuitry.

2. The second area has to do with understanding. In a world

in which machines will play an increasing part in everyone's life, it would seem rather crucial that students, as they go through their educational sequence, learn something about the computer sciences in particular, and technology in general. This might be likened to such courses as music appreciation. Here we are not concerned with learning skills so much as understanding the limitations, the values, the potential and the dangers of technology. After all, one need not be a mechanic to drive an automobile. One need not be completely knowledgeable about the details and the technicalities of the computer sciences to utilize the instrument.

While much is going on in the area of the computer as the object of instruction, we are still not completely clear as to where and how this fits into the curriculum, particularly at the elementary and secondary levels. This answer will probably have to await the evolution of new curricula, or at least the broadening of existing curriculum horizons. (8) At the college level, there has been some sharper articulation, so that now we begin to see graduate departments of computer sciences. However, at the present time there is much fluidity in terms of what is taught, what should be taught and in what sequences. For the most part, departments of computer sciences are made up of "retread" professors from math, engineering, physics and the behavioral sciences. It will take a considerable period of time before that new "breed of cat," the computer scientist, comes upon the scene. However, the direction is clear, and there is definite movement. At present, at the secondary level, computer sciences, in the form of computer programming, can be found most usually in the mathematics department. Some experience can be gained by students in various science courses. It would be hoped that a change in secondary science and math sequences could be developed, resulting in courses in sciences that permit the use of the computer. In other words, some of the limitations we now find in certain science courses, such as physics, chemistry and geology, are due to the amount of computation and/or compilation that is required of the student. It would seem that, should the student have sufficient computer skills, particularly relating to the kinds of problems faced in each of the mentioned science courses, then a much richer science curriculum would be possible. With the computer as a tool, more serious concepts and problems could be dealt with because the actual rote aspects of computations and compilations would be speeded up immeasurably.

More and more, computers and the peripheral equipment, including EAM (electrical accounting machines), are being utilized as the base for updating business machine courses. Experiences in Palo Alto have indicated that such courses have several unexpected salutary effects.

For one thing, the computer still carries a certain mystique, and is perceived as being related to strong intellectual effort. Students who take business education and who have this data processing experience tend to express a much more positive attitude about themselves. We have also noted that upon graduation from high school the business education student's job potential is greatly enhanced when he states that he knows how to run data processing equipment. In this particular kind of program, computer programing is not essential; however, it is highly desirable where time and student ability permit.

Somewhat related to this area is the whole field of vocational or technical training. Since the computer industry is growing so rapidly and has a chronic shortage of personnel at all levels, more and more positions are open to high school graduates. This area seems to be rapidly expanding—particularly at the junior college level.

Adult education is another area where a considerable amount of work appears to be going on. For the most part, these courses can offer upgrading for people who are now employed and offer preparation for those seeking employment.

An area in which more work needs to be done is that of developing a unit for the understanding or appreciation of the impact of the computer sciences. At the present time, the Palo Alto Unified School District has a unit which is part of an eleventh-grade social studies program. The decision to utilize the eleventh grade is one of an a priori nature and, as data is gathered, may prove to be not the best choice. However, it would appear that the most important thing at present is to move ahead, since the kinds of information we need can, at this point, only be gathered from experience.

While computer programing is gaining acceptance as part of the math sequence at the secondary level, further exploration of its curriculum position is needed. For example, a programer need not be a mathematician—indeed, some of the best programers are not. Programing is not mathematics per se. It is logic—but so is any language. Programing is, essentially, communicating between man and machine. For this reason, there appears to be strong justification for programing to be perceived as a second language and offered with other languages in the school curriculum.

We do know that some form of computer programing and some discussion of computers can occur at the elementary level. The author has taught programing to fifth-grade students (5). However, the issue is not whether students can learn such material at this grade level, but whether it belongs in the curriculum at that point—what service it performs, and what must be traded off in order to make room for this experience. From our pilot project we found that the diagramming and flow charting necessary before one starts to actually code is perhaps the most valuable experience. This relates to one way of approaching problem-solving whether it be in social studies, science, mathematics or grammar. The other area that proved to be highly salutary, from both student and teacher point of view, was that of new vocabulary. The earlier that students learn the meaning of some of the words related to the new technology, the more they will gain from the general exposure they receive from newspapers, television and other mass media.

Computer-based Instruction (CBI)

In this area work is really just beginning. Efforts thus far have lacked an orderly, systematic development. The ultimate impact of CBI on education will be profound in the extreme. It will affect the very process and form of education. At the present time, much of the work on CBI moves along a very thin theoretical base. It is hoped that we do not generate expectations more rapidly than we can deliver for, if we do, another disappointment will occur, and another good idea will languish in disrepute unnecessarily. All this will result in actually slowing the rate of implementation in education. For example, we need to know more about the learning situation. We have several theories of learning; however, to this writer's knowledge, we do not agree on a single theory of instruction, and CBI must have some instructional grammar around which it functions. In the interaction between the student (the learner) and the computer (the information base), we must be concerned with a whole host of ecological aspects—such things as the teacher's role, student's attitude, the interaction (or lack thereof) between students, and the scheduling and movement of students.

Much of this, of course, cannot be answered until we gather some actual data. There are a number of projects now going on that should begin to bring us some information which we would hope will allow insights which we now do not have. For the last several years, the Yorktown, N. Y., schools have been experimenting with computer-based instruction. Stanford University has embarked on a large project in reading using first-grade children. The Palo Alto Unified School District has two projects going on: one concerned with computer-based course selection, and one concerned with a fourth-grade ecology unit. Currently in development is a national project, PLAN, the joint effort of 14 school districts, American Institutes for Research, Westinghouse Learning Corporation, and several other organizations. It is developing individualized, modular instruction in the four major disciplines from grades one through twelve, with *every* student's learning profile monitored and diagnosed by computer (12). Other projects are under way at the University of California Medical School, at the University of Illinois, at the Systems

Development Corporation and at the Rand Corporation. These projects are not to be perceived as comprehensive, but are indicators of the stirring that is taking place from elementary school through graduate school. The boldest plan may be the one projected for Columbia City, Md., in which individual homes will be on-line to a central computer, making education available in the living room at any hour convenient to the learner (11). The next few years should bring us some interesting data and, hopefully, help us structure a little more clearly our directions in this particular field.

Within computer-based instruction there are at least three general categories: drill and practice, tutorial approach, and dialogue. The following is an excerpt from an actual dialogue between a ninth-grade student (the name has been changed to protect the innocent!) and a computer: (13)

IS YOUR NAME HOOD, ROBIN   (YES OR NO)

* YES R-S[1]

YOUR LAST REPORT CARD SHOWS THAT YOU WERE TAKING THE FOLLOWING COURSES—

9571	SCHSERV 11	A
7710	METALS 1	C
0217	ENGLISH 1	D
1110	EURHIST 1	D
3097	SCIENCE 1	C
2418	MATH G 1	D
9013	SPORTS	C

DO YOU FIND THAT YOU ARE HAVING ANY PROBLEMS WITH ANY OF THESE COURSES, (YES OR NO)

* NO R-S

EVEN THOUGH YOU INDICATE THAT YOU ARE NOT HAVING ANY PARTICULAR PROBLEMS IN YOUR SUBJECT AREAS, IT WOULD SEEM THAT, ON THE BASIS OF YOUR STANDARD TEST RESULTS, YOU ARE NOT DOING AS WELL AS MIGHT BE EXPECTED IN COURSE

0217
1110
2418

TO HELP YOU DECIDE WHAT CLASSES YOU WANT TO TAKE NEXT YEAR, WE HAVE COLLECTED SOME INFORMATION ABOUT FORMER STUDENTS WHO HAD THE SAME GRADE POINT AVERAGE (GPA) IN 9TH GRADE AS YOU. HERE IS A REVIEW OF HOW YOUR GPA IS CALCULATED. EACH A YOU RECEIVED IS WORTH 4 POINTS, B – 3 POINTS, ETC. ADD ALL THESE POINTS TOGETHER INCLUDING YOUR PREVIOUS SUMMER COURSES TAKEN. FOR YOU THIS WOULD BE 025 GRADE POINTS DIVIDED BY 14 COURSES GIVING A GPA OF 1.79

IT IS IMPORTANT TO REMEMBER THAT THE FOLLOWING STATISTICS ARE

---

[1] One star at the beginning of a line indicates the student response. R-S is the symbol indicating that control has been returned to the computer.

NOT PREDICTIONS OF WHAT YOU CAN DO. ATTENDANCE, INTEREST, ATTITUDE, AND ABILITY ARE SOME OF THE OTHER FACTORS AFFECTING YOUR FUTURE.

FIRST WE WILL EXAMINE THE ENGLISH GRADES

A 1–   B 1–   C+ 1–   C 3   C– 7

NOTICE THE LETTER GRADES A, B, C+, AND C.

C– MEANS ANY GRADE BELOW C.

AFTER EACH GRADE IS A NUMBER. THIS IS THE NUMBER OF STUDENTS OUT OF 10 WHO RECEIVED THAT LETTER GRADE. EACH STUDENT HAD YOUR GPA WHEN HE WAS IN 9TH GRADE.

YOU MAY SEE A 1– WHICH MEANS LESS THAN ONE STUDENT IN TEN RECEIVED THAT GRADE

NOW LET US LOOK AT SOME OTHER SUBJECTS

SPANISH

A 1–   B 1–   C+ 1   C 2   C– 7

FRENCH

A 0   B 0   C+ 1–   C 2   C– 8

OTHER FOREIGN LANGUAGES

A 0   B 1–   C+ 1   C 3   C– 6

BIOLOGY

A 1–   B 1–   C+ 1   C 3   C– 6

CHEMISTRY

A 0   B 1–   C+ 1   C 1   C– 8

PHYSICS

A 0   B 0   C+ 1   C 2   C– 7

MATH – BEYOND ALGEBRA

A 1–   B 1–   C+ 1   C 2   C– 7

FOR YOUR PLANS FOR THE FUTURE YOU MIGHT WANT TO KNOW THE TOTAL HIGH SCHOOL GPA. THE RESULTS ARE

A 0   B 0   C+ 0   C 3   C– 7

HERE IS HOW FORMER STUDENTS DID ACADEMICALLY IN 12TH GRADE–

A 0   B 1–   C+ 1–   C 3   C– 7

YOU CAN SEE IN THIS TABLE THAT YOUR GPA CAN CHANGE – UP OR DOWN DEPENDING ON YOU.

IN THE NEXT PART OF THE INTERVIEW WE WILL TALK ABOUT POST HIGH SCHOOL ACTIVITIES. DO YOU WANT TO CONTINUE NOW (TYPE A) OR LATER (TYPE B)

* A R-S

TO DECIDE WHAT CLASSES YOU WILL TAKE IN HIGH SCHOOL YOU SHOULD HAVE SOME IDEA ABOUT YOUR POST HIGH SCHOOL ACTIVITIES. FIRST, LET US LOOK AT WHAT FORMER STUDENTS DID WHO HAD YOUR 9TH GRADE GPA. HERE ARE THEIR FIRST YEAR ACTIVITIES–

3   COLLEGES OF HIGHEST ENTRANCE REQUIREMENTS

3   COLLEGES OF HIGH ENTRANCE REQUIREMENTS

2   COLLEGES OF MEDIUM ENTRANCE REQUIREMENTS

1   JUNIOR COLLEGES

0   TECHNICAL SCHOOLS

0   MILITARY SERVICE
1— EMPLOYED
1   MARRIED, SEEKING WORK, OR NOT HEARD FROM
NOW LET US SEE WHAT THESE STUDENTS DID IN THEIR SECOND YEAR AFTER
HIGH SCHOOL.
   3 OUT OF EVERY 10 CHANGED THEIR PLANS.
   FOR EVERY 10 STUDENTS WHO ENTERED A FOUR YEAR COLLEGE, 8 OF
   THEM WERE STILL THERE THE SECOND YEAR.
   FOR EVERY 10 STUDENTS WHO ENTERED A JUNIOR COLLEGE, 4 OUT OF
   10 WERE THERE THE SECOND YEAR.
NOW THAT YOU HAVE SEEN WHAT OTHERS DID, DO YOU PLAN TO CONTINUE
YOUR EDUCATION AFTER HIGH SCHOOL
* YES R-S
LOOKING CLOSER AT THE NUMBER OF STUDENTS WHO CONTINUED THEIR
EDUCATION, WE SEE
4 ENTERED COLLEGE GROUP 4
3 ENTERED COLLEGE GROUP 3
2 ENTERED COLLEGE GROUP 2
1 ENTERED COLLEGE GROUP 1
0 ENTERED TECHNICAL SCHOOLS
YOU ARE PROBABLY WONDERING HOW WE HAVE DIVIDED THE COLLEGES
INTO GROUPS. COLLEGES DIFFER IN THEIR SPECIAL UNIT REQUIREMENTS,
SOME DO NOT REQUIRE ANY SPECIAL UNITS AND OTHERS REQUIRE SIX OR
MORE. NOW, WHAT ARE SPECIAL UNITS—
A SPECIAL UNIT IS A YEARS COURSE IN ONE OF THESE AREAS—
FOREIGN LANGUAGES
COLLEGE MATHEMATICS—MATH BEYOND GENERAL MATH
LABORATORY SCIENCE—BIOLOGY, CHEMISTRY, PHYSICS
FOURTH YEAR ENGLISH
A GROUP 1 COLLEGE DOES NOT REQUIRE ANY SPECIAL UNITS. THE REQUIRE-
MENTS FOR OTHER COLLEGES ARE
GROUP 2, 0 TO 2 SPECIAL UNITS
GROUP 3, 2 TO 5 SPECIAL UNITS
GROUP 4, 6 OR MORE SPECIAL UNITS
REMEMBER THAT THIS INFORMATION IS TO BE USED AS A GUIDELINE FOR
SELECTING YOUR CLASSES. IT MAY NOT BE EXACT, AND IT MAY CHANGE
FROM YEAR TO YEAR AS YOU ARE GOING THROUGH HIGH SCHOOL.
YOU MIGHT THINK IT WOULD BE A GOOD IDEA TO TAKE 6 OR MORE SPECIAL
UNITS SO THAT YOU COULD GO TO ANY COLLEGE. THIS IS NOT TRUE. FIRST,
YOU WOULD NOT HAVE TIME TO TAKE MANY ELECTIVES OR COURSES WHICH
ARE NOT ACADEMIC. SOME OF THESE MIGHT BE AS IMPORTANT TO YOUR
FUTURE AS A SPECIAL UNIT COURSE. SECOND, YOU MIGHT NOT BE ABLE TO
KEEP YOUR GRADES UP IF YOU TAKE TOO MANY SPECIAL UNIT COURSES. FOR
YOUR GPA, HERE IS WHAT HAPPENED TO FORMER STUDENTS—FOR EVERY 10
STUDENTS WHO TOOK
   TWO TO FIVE SPECIAL UNITS, 9 PASSED THESE COURSES WITH C OR
   BETTER, AND 9 EARNED B OR BETTER.

SIX OR MORE UNITS, 0+ PASSED WITH C OR BETTER AND 7 EARNED B OR BETTER.

USUALLY STUDENTS DID BETTER TAKING FEWER UNITS.

WOULD YOU LIKE TO SEE HOW WELL STUDENTS DID IN THEIR FIRST YEAR IN COLLEGE (YES OR NO)

* YES R-S

FOOTHILL

NUMBER OF STUDENTS OUT OF TEN

COLLEGE GRADES	HIGH SCHOOL GRADES			
	BELOW C	C	B—	B TO A
B TO A	1—	1—	1	3
B—	1—	1	2	2
C	1	2	3	3
BELOW C	9	7	4	2

YOU CAN SEE FROM THIS CHART THAT OF TEN STUDENTS WHO WENT TO FOOTHILL AND HAD A TOTAL HIGH SCHOOL GPA OF B—, ONE EARNED A B TO A AVERAGE, TWO DID NOT CHANGE, THREE DROPPED TO C AVERAGE, AND FOUR DROPPED BELOW C. HERE ARE FOUR MORE TABLES

OTHER JUNIOR COLLEGES	BELOW C	C	B—	B TO A
B TO A	0	0	2	6
C TO B	4	7	8	4
BELOW C	6	3	1—	0

SAN JOSE STATE	C	C+	B TO A
B TO A	1	1	3
C+	2	1	3
C	1	3	3
BELOW C	6	5	1

UNIVERSITY OF CALIFORNIA– BERKELEY	B	B+	A
B TO A	1	2	3
C+	2	4	6
C	4	3	1
BELOW C	3	1	0

STANFORD	B	B+	A
B TO A	0	3	6
C+	3	3	3
C	4	4	1
BELOW C	3	1—	0

USING THE LIST OF COLLEGES, TYPE IN THE GROUP NUMBER OF THE COLLEGE OF YOUR CHOICE. IF YOU ARE UNDECIDED AT THIS TIME, TYPE 5.

5—UNDECIDED

4—COLLEGES OF HIGHEST ENTRANCE REQUIREMENTS

3—COLLEGES OF HIGH ENTRANCE REQUIREMENTS

2—COLLEGES OF MEDIUM ENTRANCE REQUIREMENTS

1—JUNIOR COLLEGE
0—TECHNICAL AND VOCATIONAL SCHOOLS
* 2 R-S

TYPE IN THE NUMBER OF THE EDUCATIONAL FIELD WHICH APPEALS TO YOU MOST. (PLEASE REFER TO THE BOOKLET FOR EXAMPLES OF JOBS IN EACH FIELD)

11—TEACHING
12—HEALTH SERVICE
13—ENGINEERING
14—PHYSICAL AND EARTH SCIENCES
15—BIOLOGICAL SCIENCES
16—MATHEMATICS
17—SOCIAL SCIENCES
18—LANGUAGE
19—THE CLERGY
20—BUSINESS ADMINISTRATION
21—MUSIC AND ARTS
22—OTHER PROFESSIONAL OCCUPATIONS
23—TECHNICAL OCCUPATIONS
24—OTHER OR UNDECIDED
* 21 R-S

IN THE NEXT PART OF THE INTERVIEW WE WILL TALK ABOUT SELECTING YOUR CLASSES FOR 10TH GRADE.

DO YOU WANT TO CONTINUE NOW (A) OR LATER (B)
* A R-S

NOW WE ARE GOING TO LOOK AT YOUR HIGH SCHOOL COURSE PLANS. THE REQUIRED COURSES FOR THE 10TH GRADE ARE—

ENGLISH 2
CONTEMPORARY WORLD HISTORY AND GEOGRAPHY
PHYSICAL EDUCATION

FOR THE 11TH GRADE YOU MUST TAKE—

UNITED STATES HISTORY
ENGLISH 3
PHYSICAL EDUCATION

AND IN THE 12TH GRADE YOU WILL TAKE—

GOVERNMENT
PHYSICAL EDUCATION

IN ADDITION YOU MUST TAKE THE FOLLOWING IN ORDER TO GRADUATE—

SCIENCE—ONE UNIT IN ANY GRADE BEYOND NINTH
MATH—ONE UNIT IN ANY GRADE INCLUDING NINTH
DRIVER EDUCATION—IN ANY GRADE BEYOND NINTH

ALSO CONSIDER TAKING THESE COURSES IN THE SUMMER.

WE ARE NOW READY TO PLAN YOUR SCHEDULE FOR NEXT YEAR AT PALO ALTO HIGH SCHOOL

ON THE BASIS OF YOUR NINTH GRADE RECORD, YOU ARE QUALIFIED FOR

0228 ENGLISH 2A. AP STUDENTS WILL BE SELECTED LATER FROM THIS GROUP.

ON THE BASIS OF YOUR NINTH GRADE RECORD, YOU ARE QUALIFIED FOR 1210 CONTEMPORARY WORLD 1

TO COMPLETE YOUR 10TH GRADE REQUIREMENTS, YOU WILL ALSO BE ENROLLED IN 9060 Boys PE

DO YOU PLAN TO TAKE MATH (YES OR NO)

* YES R-S

ON THE BASIS OF YOUR NINTH GRADE RECORD, YOU ARE QUALIFIED FOR 2429 MATH AP.

DO YOU PLAN TO TAKE SCIENCE (YES OR NO)

* YES R-S

ON THE BASIS OF YOUR NINTH GRADE RECORD, YOU ARE QUALIFIED FOR ANY OF THE FOLLOWING COURSES —

    3118 BIOLOGY 1 A
    3117 BIOLOGY 1 B
    3300 EARTH SCIENCE 1
    3410 ELECTRONICS 1
    3610 PHOTOGRAPY 1
    3811 LIFE SCIENCE 1

EARTH AND LIFE SCIENCE ARE HALF YEAR COURSES. TYPE IN THE CODE NUMBER OF YOUR CHOICE

* 3117 R-S

DO YOU WANT TO MAKE THE REST OF YOUR COURSE SELECTIONS NOW (YES OR NO)

* YES R-S

PLEASE REFER TO THE COURSE CATALOGUE AND TYPE IN THE CODE NUMBER OF YOUR CHOICE

*4110 R-S

DO YOU WANT TO PICK ANOTHER COURSE (YES OR NO)

* YES R-S

TYPE IN THE CODE NUMBER OF YOUR CHOICE

*5310 R-S

DO YOU WANT TO PICK ANOTHER COURSE (YES OR NO)

* YES R-S

TYPE IN THE CODE NUMBER OF YOUR CHOICE

* 6711 R-S

DO YOU WANT TO PICK ANOTHER COURSE (YES OR NO)

* NO R-S

THAT ABOUT COVERS OUR EXAMINATIONS OF YOUR PROJECTED PLANS. PLEASE CHECK OVER THIS PRINT-OUT OF YOUR COURSES.

NEW COURSES CHOSEN FOR 10TH GRADE—

0228 ENGLISH 2A
1210 CONTWLD 1
9060 Boys PE
2429 MATH G 2AP

3117 BIOLOGY 1 B
4110 FRENCH 1
5310 CERAMIC 1
6711 TYPING 11
HOW DO YOU FEEL ABOUT THIS SCHEDULE
A. I WANT MY COURSE PLANS TO STAY AS THEY ARE
B. I WOULD LIKE TO CONFER WITH A COUNSELOR
* A R-S
I HOPE THIS INTERVIEW HAS PROVIDED YOU WITH SOME INFORMATION TO
THINK ABOUT IN PLANNING YOUR HIGH SCHOOL PROGRAM. PLEASE KEEP IN
MIND THAT THE COURSES YOU HAVE CHOSEN ARE TEMPORARY AND YOU
WILL NOT NECESSARILY BE ENROLLED IN THE SAME ONES NEXT YEAR.
YOUR SCHEDULE IS FLEXIBLE AND IS STILL SUBJECT TO CHANGE.
THE INTERACTION WITH YOU HAS BEEN DELIGHTFUL—THANK YOU. I LOOK
FORWARD TO HAVING ANOTHER DIALOGUE WITH YOU.

In the area of hardware, many problems remain to be solved. There are the difficulties relating to storage and retrieval, communication from remote terminals, problems of queuing and buffering, and the determination of what type of remote devices are best for instructional activities, to list but a few.

In relation to software, we need to concern ourselves with compilers, the value of heuristics, and most certainly utilization of the concepts of dynamic programing which would appear to be most applicable to CBI.

In the substantive area, we know almost nothing about the sequence in which materials should be presented in a given subject. How does it differ subject by subject? There appears to be no one best logic for teaching all things to all people at all times, for all ages and at all ability levels.

CBI opens the question of what kind of educator is needed. An important corollary question is how to upgrade today's educator to meet the requirements of an educational process that includes CBI.

Related to the preparation of curriculum material is the problem of developing curriculum that is appropriate in style and content for CBI. We must also answer the question: What kind of curriculum, for what purpose?

Then there is cost. There is always cost!! Among the problems are the myths which abound concerning this problem. Almost all estimates are a priori figures, and this is especially true of the vendors. Another aspect to be considered is difference in quality between CBI and traditional modes of instruction. Surely quality is worth something! Equipment used for instruction will also be used for information systems and data management activities. As a matter of fact, the interdependency of such data makes this dual use essential. Equipment cost will continue to change downward. In the next five to seven years, micro-miniaturization will certainly bring the cost of equipment down radically, and well within the operating budgets with which schools must function. The computer-based course selection project, described earlier in this chapter, has as one of its goals performance of this activity (CBI) on a small computer, a type now commonly found in schools and colleges. If we can simulate time-sharing and solve communication buffering problems with existing small hardware, we may be able to implement some form of CBI as much as five years earlier than will be possible if we must wait for large-capacity equipment to become financially feasible.

AUGMENTED RECAPITULATION

In writing a chapter (as differentiated from a book), an author fights the frustration of not being able to get in all the points he would like to express. In order to get around this, rather than summarize the material, the writer chooses to recap key points and augment them with additional remarks. It is hoped that these remarks can serve as a focus for further thought and discussion on the part of the reader.

1. Ours is a rapidly changing world where the rate of change itself is one of the major problems. We no longer have the luxury of years and years in which to become accustomed to something new but, rather, are expected to accommodate ourselves to new things at a much more rapid pace than in the past.

2. The direction of change indicates an ever increasing role for technology, with greater and greater interaction between man and machine.

3. We are experiencing an ever accelerating need for, recognition of and expectation from education. The pressures upon education come not only from the burdens of innovation, but from the desires of society for education to help solve some of the major problems that it faces. For better or for worse, education now represents the primary social institution within the United States.

4. There needs to be greater and sharper focus on the future—and it's evident that the demands, the dangers and the potential of the future need to be faced with a greater candidness than now exists. Parenthetically, it might be important to note that there are plenty of each (demands, dangers and potential). For example, we have at one end the danger of the 1984 Big Brother idea engulfing us, and on the other end the potential of much less want and much more freedom of time than ever before. As we look at the future, we come face to face with an apparent contradiction: we, surely, will need more controls so that we may obtain greater freedom. What we must seek out is some delicate balance between control and freedom which optimizes the

human condition. What is meant here is that, with larger and larger data banks of information concerning individuals, we certainly need more legal controls to protect the individual from abuse by other individuals or institutions. If we can develop adequate controls so that we may continue to utilize the value of such data, then indeed there should be greater freedom in the form of behavioral choices than we now have. However, even the most superficial glance at this problem indicates that it is one of great complexity.

5. In the world of more people and bigger machines, we need increasingly to emphasize the individual. This is essential so that the flow of change follows a procedure which offers the greatest hope for a human tomorrow. We must focus on the individual and his behavior model because this relates to and will affect our value system, since values emanate from the individual. If we do this, then we generate change from the individual, through his values, to institutions, rather than the reverse . . . which would have institutions dictating change, forcing behavioral modifications that eventually would result in change of individual values. What is needed is much more concern for the individual in the social process (7), and to work toward creation of a framework (9) that tells us whether we are moving toward or away from that ideal.

6. There needs to be a much stronger commitment on the part of behavioral scientists toward understanding and participating in the technological revolution. If we are to keep the proper balance between man and machine, then those professions that have as their primary concern the human condition must more actively participate in technological development. If we leave it to others, we have abdicated our scientific and social responsibilities, both as individuals and as a group. It is important to understand that to feel compassion or concern is not sufficient. Behavioral scientists must gain skills within a context of technology.

7. There needs to be a great deal more work done toward developing operational definitions of the role and purpose of education at all levels and in all areas, so that we can give sharper focus and meaning to the research and development efforts now going on in computer-based instruction. The reader will note that the word areas was used, rather than disciplines; this is done because we must be open to the possibility that curricula may best be developed relating to skills which cut across existing disciplines (1, 8). The need for this openness is most eloquently stated by Margaret Mead, in the following paraphrase:

> We are now at the point where it is essential that we educate students in what nobody knew yesterday, and prepare them for what no one knows yet, but what people must certainly know tomorrow.

REFERENCES

1. Louis Fein and Murray Tondow. *A Supradisciplinary Curriculum: A Proposal,* 1965.
2. A. Grossman and R. Howe. *Data Processing for Education,* Educational Methods, Inc., 1965.
3. Murray Tondow. "Electronic Data Processing in Education," *Research & Development Bulletin,* Vol. 2, 1961, Chicago Teachers College, North.
4. Murray Tondow. "Expectations in Centers of Student Information," *Journal of Educational Data Processing,* 1962.
5. John Loughary (ed.). *Man-Machine Systems in Education,* Harper & Row, 1966.
6. Murray Tondow. "New Possibilities & Responsibilities: Computer Potential in the Learning Process," *1962 Year Book,* National Council on Measurement in Education.
7. Clyde Arnspiger, *Personality in the Social Process,* Follett Publishing Company, 1961.
8. Murray Tondow. *Social Process Curriculum: A Point of View,* Palo Alto (Monograph), 1966.
9. Murray Tondow, *et al. Social Process Framework: A Programmed Introduction,* Follett Publishing Company, 1962.
10. Murray Tondow (ed.). *Technology in Education: American Association for Advancement of Science Symposium Proceedings,* Monograph 1, 1962, Educational System Corporation.
11. Don Bushnell, Mimeographed speech, Brooks Foundation, Santa Barbara, Calif., 1966
12. John C. Flanagan, "Functional Education for the Seventies," *Phi Delta Kappan,* September 1967.
13. Murray Tondow and Mary Betts, "Computer Based Course Selection," *Journal of Educational Data Processing,* Vol. 4, No. 4, 1967.
14. Judith B. Edwards and Marvin L. Covey, "Oregon's New Computer Instruction Network to Serve High School Students," *Oregon Education Journal,* October 1967.

Part Five

UTILIZATION AND INTEGRATION INTO THE INSTRUCTIONAL PROCESS

Chapter 23

How is the precise statement of objectives related to the selection of an appropriate strategy of instruction?

How does task analysis lead to the development of objectives?

How do teaching objectives relate to students' learning capabilities?

How may forms of behavior be arranged from simple to complex, and how are they related to the essential conditions of learning?

THE IMPLICATIONS OF
INSTRUCTIONAL OBJECTIVES FOR LEARNING*

ROBERT M. GAGNÉ, Professor of Education
University of California

The importance of defining instructional objectives as an initial step in the planning of instruction was emphasized a number of years ago by Tyler (13). There can be little doubt that the activity that was stimulated by this initial formulation has been tremendously productive in the design of achievement tests in many colleges, the conduct of evaluation programs, as well as the broader enterprises of course and curriculum planning. A number of these efforts and their results have been reported in volumes edited by Dressel (4). One can judge from reading these reports that many college and university teachers have derived great benefits from the discipline of thought about teaching and testing that has been generated by their own attempts to define the objectives of instruction.

It should also be mentioned, perhaps, that one can now identify at

*This chapter is a revised version of that which originally appeared in *Report of Regional Commission on Education Coordination and Learning Research,* University of Pittsburgh Press, 1964. It is reprinted with permission of the author and publisher.

least two additional areas of instruction in which the importance of specifying objectives has been explicitly recognized. While it is not clear that these ideas have arisen entirely independently, it is at least noteworthy that such a need has been arrived at via a somewhat different route in each case. The first of these areas is technical training in the military services, in connection with which the terms *task description* and *task analysis* have been employed. Basically, these terms reflected a recognition of the importance of specifying what the outcomes of training needed to be before the training was planned. The necessity for such specification was particularly evident in the case of military training because there is such an immediate relation between the intentions of training itself and the performance of the trained man on the job. Miller (9) was a pioneering thinker in this area, but others also contributed important ideas. There is little formal difference, however, between what is called task description and the definition of instructional objectives.

The second additional source of writing about instructional objectives, a more recent one, comes from the work on programed instruction. Scarcely any writer or systematist in this field has failed to state that the specifying of instructional objectives is an important first step in planning the instructional program as well as the assessment which will follow it. An important chapter in the volume by Taber, Glaser and Schaefer (12) draws out some of the parallels between the approaches suggested by task analysis in military training and the more recently formulated requirements of programed instruction. A delightful book by Mager (7) gives a very clear account of what is meant by preparing objectives for programed instruction, and a description of the implications of this effort for the success of such instruction. Another writer in this field who has dealt explicitly with this problem is Gilbert (5); his mathetics approach is characterized by painstaking attention to the defining of objectives.

Besides these research areas just mentioned, there has been a constantly growing emphasis in educational circles generally upon the essentiality of specifying instructional objectives for planning purposes. Even the modern curriculum builders in science and mathematics have not been able to ignore entirely the voices of those who forcefully insist on the definition of objectives, often in opposition to those scientists who vigorously uphold the point of view that one cannot think about human behavior objectively, at least not in an educational setting.

These recent trends have tended to place increasing emphasis upon the use of specified objectives in drawing inferences about the *tactics of instruction.* This kind of use was recognized by Tyler, and discussed rather briefly in his earlier work. He points out that the task of planning a course, beginning with the definition of objectives, proceeds by inferring from these descriptions the kinds of learning experiences which can be expected best to produce the required outcomes. But this trend of thought has not been developed by those who have followed in this tradition. Bloom's (1) book on a taxonomy of objectives, for example, describes six categories of objectives, which are considered to constitute a hierarchy, in the sense that the later classes of objectives build upon the earlier ones. The categories are: knowledge, comprehension, application, analysis, synthesis and evaluation.

These categories provide a highly informative picture of the variety of kinds of human performances which may reasonably be expected in an educational setting. Yet it cannot be said that they serve clearly to distinguish a similar variety of learning experiences, or a set of tactics for optimal instruction. In particular, some of the members of these categories (as exemplified by test items) are distinct from each other only in terms of their specific content, rather than in terms of formal characteristics which affect their conditions of learning. "Knowledge of terminology," for example, is difficult to distinguish from "knowledge of classifications and categories"; likewise, "knowledge of generalizations" does not appear to be very different from "comprehension," and neither of these from "comprehending the interrelationships of ideas." Beginning with the test items themselves (rather than the names assigned to them) it seems quite possible that a set of inferences might be drawn which would in fact suggest differential training implications. But currently, this task awaits the doing.

Is it in fact possible to divide objectives into categories which differ in their implications for learning? To do this, one has to put together a selected set of learning conditions, on the one hand, and an abstracted set of characteristics of human tasks, on the other. This is the kind of effort which has been called *task analysis*. Its objective is to distinguish, not the tasks themselves (which are infinitely variable), but the *inferred behaviors* which presumably require different conditions of learning. Such behavior categories can be distinguished by means of several different kinds of criteria, which in an ultimate sense should be completely compatible with each other. What I should like to try to do here, however, is to use one particular set of criteria, which pertain to the question of "What is learned?"

In a general sense, what is learned is a *capability*. Furthermore, it is a capability of exhibiting certain performances which could not be exhibited before the learning was undertaken. Is it possible to describe such learned capabilities in terms which will permit distinctions to be made among them? This is the sort of attempt to be made in the following paragraphs.

THE CAPABILITIES ESTABLISHED BY LEARNING

When one sets out to identify capabilities, the suggestion made by the evidence, early in the game, is that these capabilities are arranged in a hierarchy. One depends upon another, in the sense that learning any one capability usually depends upon the previous learning of some other, simpler one. In fact, this may be one of the most important generalizations one can make about human learning.

As a consequence, if one begins at the bottom of such a hierarchy, one must begin with extremely simple forms of behavior. While such simple forms are clearly learned, it is nevertheless difficult to find actual human tasks in which they occur in a pure and uncombined form. In other words, one's credulity would be strained a bit were it to be claimed that these simple forms of behavior often occur, by themselves, as objectives of instruction. They do occur, but rather infrequently. Their importance, however, lies in the fact that they do underlie and support other capabilities which are higher in the hierarchy. For the learning of each of these higher capabilities requires that one or more subordinate capabilities must already have been acquired. The most important condition of learning, it is suggested here, is the specification of what must have been previously learned.

Accordingly, we shall start our description of the varieties of learned capabilities with quite simple forms of behavior, whose usefulness will become fully apparent only when we have proceeded to describe more complex forms.

1. Response learning.

A very basic form of behavior is called response learning, or is sometimes given other names, such as "echoic behavior" (11). The individual learns to respond to a stimulus which is essentially the same as that produced by the response itself. In a child, the mother's spoken word "doll" calls out the response "doll" on the part of the child. Naturally, this kind of learning is particularly evident in instructional objectives applicable to children. In adults, one finds it in the learning of new sounds in a foreign language, as well as in new types of motor acts. Modern language scholars seem to be in pretty good agreement that response learning is basic to other learning in foreign languages.

2. Chains or sequences.

Long chains of responses can most readily be identified in motor acts of various sorts. But there are many kinds of *short* sequences which are very important to the individual's performance. One of the most prominent is a chain of two acts, the first of which is an *observing response.* If one is concerned, for example, with getting someone to "put 17 in the numerator," this act has two main parts: (1) finding the location of the numerator (an observing response), and (2) writing in that place the numeral 17. In establishing such behavior as part of a larger and more complex performance like simplifying fractions, one has to see to it that such a chain is learned. How this is done is a bit more complicated than it seems at first glance. Again, however, the most important consideration is that certain things be *previously learned.* The location of the numerator must previously have been discriminated from other locations, and 17 must have been discriminated from other numerals. Furthermore, the basic responses required must also have been acquired.

3. Verbal associations.

For many years, psychologists appeared to be considering this the most basic form of learning, but such is no longer the case. It is now fairly generally agreed, and supported by a good deal of evidence (6), that the learning of associations involves more than an S-R connection. Instead, an association is perhaps best considered as a three-step chain, containing in order (*a*) an observing response which distinguishes the stimulus, (*b*) a *coding* response which usually is implicit, and (*c*) the response which is to be expected as the outcome of the association. Associations are of course widely prevalent in instruction, and sometimes can be considered important instructional objectives. Learning English equivalents for foreign words has usually been considered the classic example of association learning. There is a great deal of evidence to show that such learning has prerequisites of prior learning as one of its most important conditions. Response learning must have been completed (for optimal results), as the work of Underwood and Schulz (14) emphasizes.

4. Multiple discrimination.

In this form of behavior, the individual acquires the capability of making different responses (or response chains) to a number of different stimuli. Of course, he does this when he identifies colors, or late model cars, or any of a great variety of different stimuli. Multiple discriminations are widespread within the domain of things to be learned in school. Words like *faim* have to be discriminated from *femme* in order that they can really be pronounced differently. Within a given algebraic expression, a coefficient must be distinguished from an exponent, and both from a subscript. Such learning *presupposes* response learning, or in the more usual case, motor or verbal chain learning. To state the matter very simply, if the discriminations learned are to be identified by having the learner construct them on paper, or to say their names, he must already have learned to do these things.

Up to this point, it may be said that I have not talked about the kinds of learned activities that are often very important objectives in instruction. This is quite true, although I have tried to show that sometimes even these simple kinds of behavior may be legitimate objectives. Mainly, though, these kinds of learned capabilities may be considered *subordinate objectives* of instruction. They are the kinds of activities which are only infrequently to be measured by achievement tests. There is no reason why one should expect to find them in Bloom's book, for example. Nevertheless, they are distinguishable kinds of learned capabilities, which appear to depend upon each other for establishment in the order given. But their most important characteristic, by all odds, lies in the fact that they support all the varieties of more complex learning. In attempting to specify the conditions of learning that attend more complex capabilities, one cannot neglect these simpler forms of behavior. This is because the more complex forms depend in a crucial fashion on the simpler forms, in this way: if one tries to establish more complex behavior without the requisite simpler forms having been learned, the learning attempt will be markedly ineffective

But let us now consider these more complex forms which frequently occur in lists of instructional objectives.

CONCEPTS

A concept is acquired when a set of objectives or events *differing* in physical appearance is identified as a class. The class names for common objects, like chairs, houses, hats, are the most familiar examples. Even clearer, however, are such categories as "round," "square," "tall," "middle" and others which are so clearly independent of physical appearance. Concept achievement is observed when the subject becomes capable of responding to different physical objects as if he were placing them in one or more classes, like "round," or "square and large." In other words, the subject is now performing a task which is not defined in terms of specific stimuli. The particular physical characteristics of these objects, pictures, or what not, do not have to remain fixed in physical appearance in order to define the task. They must, however, be capable of being classified by the experimenter into the abstract categories he wants the subject to work with.

In addition, the task of identifying concepts cannot be defined in terms of specific responses. In contrast to paired-associate learning, one does not demand a particular response in order to consider the behavior correct. We may require the subject to *point* to a round object, to *draw* a round object, to *say* the word round, or any of a variety of other things. All that we insist upon is that these responses reliably identify the class "round."

The most important conditions for learning a concept appear to be the pre-learning that must have taken place. If there has not been previous identification of the object, the learner will be unable to acquire the concept. Similarly, he will not be able to learn a concept if he does not have an available response. Suppose a learner is shown an object for which he doesn't have the label "round." Can he then learn the required classification? The prediction is clearly negative. Or suppose, on the other hand, one asks the learner to make a classification the response for which he has not previously learned, like "rhomboid." Can he acquire the concept? Again the prediction is clearly "no." What must be done, if one is interested in concept acquisition *per se*, is to insure that the learner has previously learned all the necessary labels, and has previously acquired all the necessary responses, that he is going to be asked to make. In other words, association learning, stimulus discrimination learning, and response learning are all pre-conditions of concept learning.

If one can assume these more basic forms as having been acquired, then the procedure of concept learning is fairly simple. It consists mainly in establishing associations in which the variety of specific stimuli that make up the class to be acquired are represented. One cannot do this by presenting all of them, of course; accordingly, this is usually done by presenting a suitable variety of objects and seeing to it that they are connected with the desired response. If the concept is *cell,* in biology, obviously one must use a sufficient variety of cells having different physical appearances in order to establish the required classification.

PRINCIPLES

The next more complex form of learning pertains to the acquisition of principles. One can consider these, in their basic form, as a chain of concepts of the form "If A, then B." The learning of principles does not appear to have been studied in an analytic fashion. Yet it is not difficult to imagine an experimental situation in which their acquisition could be observed and measured. Suppose the individual has learned to classify an array of stimuli as "round" or "square," and another array as "the odd one" or "not the odd one." What would be studied in this situation are the conditions leading to the use of the principle "When round, choose the odd one." The stimulus situation would consist of presentations of the two arrays of stimuli (in suitable variety of physical dimensions) simultaneously. Undoubtedly, one could simply present such a situation in repeated trials, and observe the errors made or the number of trials required to attain the rule. But this is not the only kind of learning situation one thinks of, particularly if the question "how could such a principle be most rapidly achieved" is of interest. In a sense, *principle learning* appears to be a simple form of what has been called problem solving.

Let me be as clear as I can about what the task is. It is one in which the individual uses a concept describing one class of objects (or events) to identify another concept describing another class of objects and events. Now whether he can *say* what he is doing is not a necessary criterion of whether he has acquired a principle. But he must have the capability of performing correctly a task of the sort "If A, then B," where A and B are concepts defined by the experimenter.

Of course this is a very important kind of learning. Think how much of what we call knowledge is really this kind of thing! "When a liquid is heated, it changes to a gas"; "if force is increased, acceleration increases"; "if temperature is raised, pressure goes up"; "if the rods are placed in darkness, their sensitivity increases"; and so on. Of course I am not suggesting that all principles are this simple. But I *am* suggesting that most knowledge is principles.

Again it is evident that the important set of conditions necessary for principle learning is previous learning, this time of the concepts which make up the principle. One either assumes that the learner already knows the concepts "liquid," "heating" and "gas," in acquiring the principle, or else they must first be learned. This does not mean, of course, that the attempt cannot be made to undertake everything at once— to teach the concepts and the principle all at one time. But it does mean that the optimal conditions for learning cannot be clearly seen to operate in such a situation. A teacher may find that certain members of his class have not learned the principle "When a liquid is heated, it changes to a gas" because they have never learned to identify the concept "liquid"! But when one can truly assume that concept learning has previously been completed, the conditions for principle learning become clear. The proper chain of events is presented by means of particular objects representing the concepts making up the chain; for example, a container of water may be heated with a flame and the steam collected in another container.

PROBLEM SOLVING

Problem solving is a kind of learning by means of which principles are put together in chains to form what may be called "higher-order principles." Again, this is a form of learning of widespread occurrence in education. Typically, the "higher-order principles" are induced from sets of events presented to the learner in instruction. If carried out properly, these become the generalizations which enable the student to think about an ever-broadening set of new problems.

It may be worthwhile to consider for a moment what the nature of the problem-solving task is, as exhibited by experimental investigations. What can the individual do after he has solved the problem? Suppose it is Maier's Candle Problem (8). We say of the learner that he has achieved problem solution, but what does this mean? It would appear that what Maier and others think it means (without having tested it directly) is this: Having solved the specific problem, the subject is able to solve a whole range of problems similar to it, regardless of variations in the room, the distance involved, the type of candle, the size of tapes, clamps and sticks. The phrase "similar to it" means something in particular, that is, that the subject can achieve correct solutions to an *entire class* of problems which can readily be identified as a class by the experimenter, if not by the subject himself. In this instance, the class of tasks may be roughly described as "using segments of rigid and flexible tubing to construct a long tube capable of conducting air, which can then be made rigid by clamping it to rigid structures like sticks of wood." Notice that it is not necessarily intended that the subject can necessarily *say* a sentence like this when he has solved the problem. But he should be able to *do* it, and it would be helpful if the experimenter were able to say it.

Problem solving begins with the assumption (or the establishment) of pre-available principles. It ends with the demonstration that the individual has acquired a new "higher-order rule," the capability of solving a new kind of problem. A beginning student of algebra is set the problem: "Multiply X^2 and X^3," which he has not seen before at all. First of all, it is clear that he must previously have acquired certain *concepts*, namely, the concepts of variable and exponent (in the sense that he must be able to recognize these stimulus objects as "variables with exponents"). Second, he must previously have acquired some *principles*. One is a rule for multiplication, approximately stated as "multiplying a number by n means adding the number n times." Another is a rule for exponents, roughly, "an exponent r means multiplying the number by itself r times." Can the student solve this problem? Perhaps he will need to be reminded that he knows these subordinate rules. Perhaps he will need some *guidance* or "direction" for his thinking. Whatever may be required to achieve it, what is wanted in solution is the discovery of a new and more inclusive rule to this effect: "Multiplying identical variables with exponents is done by multiplying the variable by itself the number of times represented by the *sum* of the two exponents." The attainment of such a higher-order rule can, under proper circumstances, be inferred by the correct answer X^5, as well as by correct answers to any and all other tasks belonging to the class "multiplying variables with exponents."

STRATEGIES

Are there forms of behavior which are more complex than principles, or than the "higher-order principles" acquired in problem solving? Some authors seem to imply another *form* of learned organization in the strategies with which an individual approaches a problem (3). There can be little doubt as to the existence of such strategies in problem solving (2). It may be that strategies are *mediating principles* which do not appear directly in the performance of the task set to the individual, but which may nevertheless affect the speed or excellence of that performance. Accordingly, one may have to use rather special methods to uncover these strategies, which implies that the job of achievement testing may be a difficult one.

But it is possible to conceive of strategies as being principles in their fundamental nature, and of being made up of chains of concepts. Such strategies as "choose the odd, except when the light is on the right," or "choose the alternate keys in order," are the kind that occur in experimental studies. In education, presumably, there are strategies pertaining to the appreciation of poetry, the understanding of history or the pursuit of scientific inquiry.

If strategies are really a kind of "higher-order" principle, then they obviously can be learned in the same way as other principles. If an individual is going to be able to learn the strategy "first match the internal figures in triangularity," he must already have mastered the concepts "internal figures" and "triangle." If he has previously acquired these concepts, the learning will be fairly easy. If he has not, then it is difficult to say what is happening, since the concepts will have to be learned at the same time as the principle (or strategy). It would appear, therefore, that even in the case of strategies one needs to assume the pre-learning of concepts and principles as a condition of learning of major importance.

BEHAVIOR CATEGORIES AND THE PRE-CONDITIONS OF LEARNING

What has been described in the previous sections are eight major categories of behavior which differ from each other, it is proposed, in terms of the conditions required to make learning occur with optimal effectiveness. Four of these forms of capability are simple ones which occur only rarely as distinct instructional objectives in the higher levels of the educative process. They appear more frequently as objectives in connection with the instruction of young children. Their importance, however, lies in the fact that they underlie the learning of other more complex forms of behavior which are typical of later years. Occasionally, too, it may be necessary to remind ourselves that these simpler forms are really there all the time. If we cannot assume that such learning has occurred, then provisions must be made to make it occur before the more complex varieties can be undertaken with efficacy. An example is the apparent need for response learning of unfamiliar foreign words as a first step in language learning.

These forms of behavior may be arranged in a hierarchy from simple to complex. The major reason for doing this is to indicate that the *learning conditions* for the more complex forms may be described most clearly if the *pre-conditions* are first identified. In fact, these pre-conditions constitute one of the most important things that can be said about the learning of these kinds of behaviors. The hierarchy of behaviors has this appearance:

The Learning of
Problem Solving and *Strategy-Using*
require the pre-learning of:
Principles
which require the pre-learning of:
Concepts
which require the pre-learning of:
Multiple Discriminations
which require the pre-learning of:
Chains, Motor or Verbal
which require the pre-learning of:
Responses

Of course, there are other conditions for learning than the ones implied by this hierarchy. But it is difficult to determine how important they are, mainly because they seem so obvious. *Reinforcement,* for example, as it is defined by Skinner (10) is a condition which one is inclined to assume is present, while admitting that learning cannot occur without it. A new act, we are told, can always be attached by learning to an old act, so long as the latter is the stronger. The implication appears to be, then, that the problem of finding proper conditions of learning reduces to one of finding the right sequences for events in the instructional situation. This is implied by the work of Gilbert (5) in his discussion of the tactics of learning. *Contiguity* is surely an important condition, too, since these sequences of events must occur within certain limited time spans in order for learning to occur. But contiguity is also a fairly obvious condition to the teacher; if the student is to learn the name of an unfamiliar object, the name and his response must somehow be made to occur together within a short time span. The implications of these categories for achievement testing are clear up to a point, but knowledge is limited beyond that point. Certainly the four fundamental categories can be measured, since experimental psychologists have been measuring them for many years. To describe how the more complex forms can be assessed would go beyond the scope of this paper. It is apparent, though, that there are many available techniques in the field of achievement testing for this purpose. The major implication is that these are the categories of objectives to be distinguished, if one approaches the job from the standpoint of differential sets of conditions for optimal learning.

REFERENCES

1. Bloom, B. S. (Ed.) *Taxonomy of Educational Objectives.* New York: Longmans, Green, 1956.
2. Bruner, J. S., Goodnow, J. J., & Austin, G. A. *A Study of Thinking.* New York: Wiley, 1956.
3. Bruner, J. S. "The Art of Discovery," *Harvard Educational Review,* 1961. *31,* 21–32.
4. Dressel, P. L. (Ed.) *Evaluation in General Education.* Dubuque, Iowa: Wm. C. Brown Co., 1954.
5. Gilbert, E. T. "Mathetics: The Technology of Education." *Journal of Mathetics,* 1962. *1,* 7–73.
6. McGuire, W. J. "A Multiprocess Model for Paired-Associate Learning." *Journal of Experimental Psychology,* 1961, 62, 335–347.
7. Mager, R. F. "A Method for Preparing Auto-Instructional Programs." *I.R.E. Trans. on Educ.,* 1961.
8. Maier, N. R. F. "An Aspect of Human Reasoning." *British Journal of Psychology,* 1933, 24, 144–155.
9. Miller, R. B. "A Method for Man-Machine Task Analysis." *Wright Air Development Center Technical Report,* 53–137, 1953.
10. Skinner, B. F. "Are Theories of Learning Necessary"? *Psychol. Review,* 1950, 57, 193–216.
11. Skinner, B. F. *Verbal Behavior.* New York: Appleton-Century-Crofts, 1957.
12. Taber, J. I., Glaser, R., & Schaefer, H. H. *A Guide to the Preparation of Programmed Instructional Material.* Pittsburgh: Department of Psychology, University of Pittsburgh, 1962.
13. Tyler, R. W. "Achievement Testing and Curriculum Construction." In E. G. Williamson (Ed.) *Trends in Student Personnel Work.* Minneapolis: University of Minnesota Press, 1949, 391–407.
14. Underwood, B. J., & Schulz, R. W. *Meaningfulness and Verbal Learning.* Chicago: Lippincott, 1960.

Chapter 24

What sorts of resources and source files should a teacher have access to during the process of planning for instruction?

How does the teacher go about applying criteria for selection of the appropriate resource to meet each objective?

What should be done by way of local production when resources are not readily available?

To what extent does the responsibility of search, selection, production and utilization place demands on the teacher's time?

LOCATING, SELECTING AND PRODUCING
TEACHING AND LEARNING RESOURCES

AMO DE BERNARDIS, President
Portland Community College

There is no question that a variety of teaching and learning resources are needed to carry on effective and efficient programs of instruction. However, if these tools are to be used they must be readily available and the teacher must have a ready reference in order to locate appropriate materials. Many school systems have well integrated materials services for the teachers and, consequently, needed teaching resources are easy to obtain. These schools receive catalogs, bulletins, etc., on new materials as they are added to the collection. Every effort is made to keep teachers and students informed of new materials and services. Nevertheless, the fact remains that many schools do not have access to such effective materials services. It is obviously important for *all* teachers to have information on how to obtain needed teaching and learning resources. Clearly, the problem of locating instructional resources is much more difficult where the school does not have an organized media support service, and in these instances teachers and administrators will need to put forth additional effort to obain the required teaching tools. There are available to any school a variety of sources for all types of instructional materials. Space does not permit a complete listing. This section will indicate some of the sources available.

The School As A Source.

Too often the nearest source for materials—that is, the individual school—is overlooked. Through the years every school has purchased maps, globes, books, exhibits, art prints, models, slides, audiovisual equipment, etc. Often these resources are located in a room or laboratory and their availability is not known to the staff members. Unless there has been a system for cataloging and inventorying these materials, many teachers will not be aware of what is located in the school. Each school should make a periodic inventory of all equipment and materials. Each item should be listed on a separate card and the file made available to all teachers. Usually, an inventory will bring forth a variety of materials and equipment which heretofore remained undiscovered. Keeping such an inventory up-to-date is essential for effective use. If the school is not large enough to have a librarian to do this, the file can be kept by the secretary.

District And County Services.

The increasing number of audiovisual and material service centers maintained by the counties and area district officies brings these services within the reach of most schools. Some of these centers are cooperative—that is, schools pay fees to obtain the services of the center. If such a center exists and a school is not participating, every effort should be made to gain membership. These centers offer a wide variety of materials to meet numerous teaching needs. Perhaps as important as the materials are the media consultants who are available. The consultants are invaluable in assisting the staff in more effective selection and utilization of materials.

College And University Film Libraries.

Many colleges and universities maintain film rental collections. Over the years these collections have grown to include a fine selection of audiovisual materials. As local districts developed their own audiovisual departments some of the colleges and university film departments have become more selective in media acquisition. Even though a school system may have developed a film collection it will be advisable to obtain some of the films which are used only occasionally from regional collections. Information on the materials and services can be obtained by writing to the college or university in your state or region.

State Department Of Education.

In recent years most state departments have added specialists in the area of teaching resources and media. Most of these departments do not distribute material, but they are a rich source of information on the media services available within the state and region. Pamphlets, guides, materials lists and other information are freely given to the teacher. Some departments have field representatives who will assist a school in planning for the use of new media, workshops, in-service classes, etc.

Guides To Sources Of Materials.

Many guides containing annotated listings of all types of materials and their sources can be obtained. The school librarian or audiovisual coordinator should have copies or be able to assist the teacher in obtaining copies. The following are a few of the better known guides. The school or county librarian can assist in locating the many other guides.

Index to 16mm Educational Films, published by McGraw-Hill. This is a new (1967) master listing of films as catalogued by the National Information Center for Educational Media (NICEM). It gives technical information and an annotation for each film.

Guide to Newer Educational Media. Published by the American Library Association. This is a compilation of guides and catalogs concerned with new teaching materials published between 1950 and 1961.

Educators Guide to Free Materials. Published by Educators Progress Service, Randolph, Wisconsin.

George Peabody College for Teachers in Nashville, Tennessee, publishes an annotated list of free and inexpensive learning materials.

H. W. Wilson Company issues a monthly vertical file index which lists inexpensive teaching materials.

Sources of Free and Inexpensive Teaching Aids, by Bruce Miller.

Periodicals.

In each issue professional periodicals list selected materials. Periodicals which deal with specific areas such as social studies, industrial arts, or mathematics are the best source of recent and up-to-date lists for those areas. Periodicals which deal with newer media such as *Audiovisual Instruction,* published by the Department of Audio Visual Instruction, *N.E.A.,* and *Educational Screen and A V Guide* are excellent sources of listing for a variety of audiovisual materials.

Professional Books.

A ready source for locating materials are the professional books which deal with the instructional media field. Although these books do not include extensive lists they do include excellent references to sources for all types of materials. A few of the more comprehensive books in this area are listed below:

Brown, James W., Lewis, Richard B., and Harcleroad, Fred F. *A. V. Instruction: Materials and Methods.* New York: McGraw-Hill Book Company, 1964.

Erickson, Carlton W. H. *Fundamentals of Teaching With Audiovisual Technology.* New York: The Macmillan Company, 1965.

Wittich, Walter A., and Schuller, Charles F. *Audio Visual Materials: Their Nature and Use.* New York: Harper and Row, 1962.

Federal And State Agencies.

Some of the most extensive sources of materials are the many federal and state agencies which produce an increasing variety of information describing the nature of their programs. Teachers will find many valuable teaching and learning aids issued by these agencies.

The many departments which make up the United States Government all issue publications, films, charts and other materials. Space does not permit listing the various departments, but anyone interested in this source should obtain a copy of the *U. S. Government Organization Manual.* This publication gives a complete overview of the federal government agencies and the various departments. It will assist the teacher in narrowing down the alternatives among departments which may have materials in specific teaching areas.

The government printing office has available a most comprehensive list of publications covering a wide range of topics. Information on publications and how to order may be obtained by writing the Superintendent of Documents, Government Printing Office, Washington, D. C.

Each state and local government also makes available many types of informative materials. Schools can get lists by writing the various departments in each of the respective governmental units.

Industrial And Business Sources.

For years business and industry have communicated information to the public about the nature of their business and products. The range of media from this source is extensive—films, filmstrips, pamphlets, books, exhibits, models, etc.—most are free of charge. As with any material used in the schools, these must be selected with great care since the sponsor may be pointing up a special interest of his industry or business. It should also be mentioned that many of the items have been produced for a target audience other than students. However, the fact remains that many good instructional materials are available from business and industry and in some cases may be the only up-to-date versions.

Some school systems have regulations regarding the use of sponsored materials and some do not allow their use. Teachers should check to determine what the policy is regarding this matter.

Sponsored materials will vary with the purpose of the sponsor, from those which try to persuade the viewer or reader to definite conclusions to those which are produced to give information and facts on a particular industry or agency. The latter often are created with the aid of educational consultants and are high quality productions, with school use as an objective. In between these two extremes are many sponsored materials with a variety of motives. It becomes the task of the teacher to evaluate and select from among them those which are appropriate for classroom use. Some basic considerations for the selection of sponsored materials are:[1]

1. Is the authorship clearly identified?
2. Have educators been involved in the production of the material?
3. Has the advertising content been kept to a minimum?
4. Is the material primarily designed for classroom use?
5. Are the facts clearly and accurately presented?

The Community As A Source.

Each community has a gold mine of teaching materials which are readily available to the classroom, if the school is predisposed to locate, classify and use them. It must be remembered that every community can in itself be a laboratory for learning. The people, the factories, the stores, the farms, the businesses, the river, the government can all provide rich and valuable learning experiences. Some schools have found it worthwhile to make an inventory and to catalog these community resources. This list of resources can be limited to field trip possibilities or extended to include resource people, exhibits, films, museums, models, etc. A card file listing these community resources is the most convenient form since it provides an easy method for keeping the list up-to-date. If more than one school is to use the file, duplicate card files can be provided or a printed guide can be issued for each teacher or school.

The preparation of a community resource file can be a most useful project for advanced students in the social studies. A systematic procedure should be adopted for such a study. The plan should include a form for collecting the information. The form should include the facts which will help teachers and students to determine the value of the resource for instruction. Information should be gathered for materials, field trips, resource visits. Sample file cards are shown below:

[1] De Bernardis, Amo, *The Use of Instructional Materials.* New York: © Appleton-Century-Crofts, Inc., 1960. p. 83.

MATERIALS

Subject: _____

Type of Material: _____

Grade Level: _____

Distributor: _____

    Address: _____ Phone: _____

Synopsis: _____

_____

FIELD TRIP

Place: _____

Address: _____

Activities to be observed: _____

_____

Person to contact: _____ Phone: _____

Grade Level: _____

Number of visits per month: _____ Best Time_____

Size of Group: _____

Evaluated by: _____

RESOURCE VISITOR

Subject: _____

Name: _____

    Address: _____ Phone: _____

Time available: _____

Grade Level: _____

Nature of program: _____

Time for presentation: _____

Equipment Needed: _____

_____

Insofar as possible each resource listed should be visited and the material previewed. This procedure will lead to a much more valuable guide. The selection and compilation of this community resource guide results in additional teaching aids for the teacher. If students work in the preparation of the guide they will gain a valuable insight into the make-up of their community.

SELECTING MATERIALS

The abundance of teaching and learning materials available today offers great potential to the classroom. The wise selection of these materials to meet specific needs is an important responsibility of the teacher.

Just as the doctor makes decisions in prescribing drugs so must the teacher use the same professional judgment in selecting the materials for the instructional program.

Preview Or Audition Materials.

Except in rare instances materials to be used in the classroom should be previewed and evaluated before using them with students. Films should be previewed and recordings auditioned so the teacher will be familiar with the content, point of view expressed, ideas which need expansion, etc. Where the opportunity does not exist for a preview, such as a TV program, it is sometimes possible to get insight into the content through the publicity or a guide of the program. If this is not feasible, one should give students some guidelines to assist them in their viewing. The structure of these guidelines should direct their attention to broad generalizations rather than to specific items which may or may not be correct in the presentation.

Select Materials Which Fit The Maturity Level Of The Group.

Because of the wide range of abilities in any instructional group it is difficult to narrow the selection of materials to a specific maturity level. The teacher will need to consider this aspect of selcting materials carefully. The subject matter presented, the ideas, concepts, and vocabulary should all be within the maturity range of the group if the item is to be of greatest value.

Select Materials Which Best Fit The Instructional Objectives.

Many materials are available which will meet the objective of a teaching and learning unit. The teacher should attempt to select the type of material which will *best* fit the specific objective. Careful consideration should be given to the types of media used. A film may be best for one situation while a transparency or chart may be more appropriate for another. No one teaching medium is best suited for all situations. Each must be evaluated in light of the objectives being fulfilled.

Involve The Students In The Selection Of Teaching Materials.

Students can give valuable assistance in locating materials for class utilization. In the process of searching for needed materials, the students gain valuable skills in selection and evaluation of communication media. Also, they become more keenly aware of the variety of learning aids and how they enhance the learning process. In the constantly expanding role of mass media, skills of analyzing communication media are an important aspect of a student's education.

Evaluate And Keep Records Of Materials Used.

Keeping a record and evaluation of the various materials used throughout the year will help the teacher build a valuable personal resource file. This file will make a ready reference for wise selection. A few notes on a card regarding the material, its contents, usefulness in a particular teaching situation, student reaction, etc., will help the teacher make a decision whether to use it at a subsequent time. Unless such a record is kept it is difficult to recall the strengths and weakness of material used in the previous years. A sample of such a card is shown below:

TEACHING MATERIAL USE RECORD

Teaching aid: _____

Type: _____ Date: _____

Source: _____ Cost: _____

Class or Grade: _____ Subject: _____

Strong points: _____

Weak points: _____

Class reaction: _____

Evaluation & Comments: _____

_____

_____

LOCAL PRODUCTION OF TEACHING MATERIALS

Many materials which are needed by the teacher are not available through commercial sources. These must be produced in the school. Flat picture files, displays, single models, and charts have long been produced by the teachers. In recent years simplified photographic and photocopy equipment have made it possible for schools to produce a variety of teaching resources which heretofore could be made only by specialists. Today it is possible for any school to make transparencies for the overhead projector, color slides, copies from printed materials, etc. The equipment cost is reasonable and the skills needed are within the range of the students and the teacher.

The facilities needed for local production need not be extensive. In a small school the office or library workroom will serve as a starter unit. The equipment needed for an initial production unit is:

Hot mounting press—used for mounting photos, and for 'lift' color transfer for transparencies.

Spirit duplicator—used for short runs of printed materials.

Ink duplicator—for making more than one hundred copies of printed materials.

Heat process copy machine—used for making copies from printed materials and for making transparencies for the overhead projector, it also can be used to make spirit masters for the duplicator.

Automatic type color camera—used for making 2″ x 2″ slides.

Polaroid camera—used for "instant" black and white or color photos.

Light table or mimescope—used for making mimeo stencils, transparencies, etc.

Saturn or blue ray printer—used for diazo process of transparency making.

Miscellaneous tools and equipment—paper cutter, scissors, pencils, drawing board, brushes, etc.

The total capital investment for the equipment listed above will be approximately $1500, and this will allow a school to make a significant start towards a materials production unit.

The skills needed to make an acceptable product can be and should be learned by the teachers. However, some schools are hiring instructional material technicians or aides to perform this function. If this is not possible then a clerical person in the school should be trained to assist with this work. Not to be overlooked are the students themselves. Students in junior and senior high school are helpful and interested in production. Their art and mechanical skills can be put to use in creating durable teaching resources.

The potential of a materials production center in a school should not be underestimated. The cost is not prohibitive and the investment will bring significant rewards. With imaginative planning, teaching will be more dynamic because educators can get materials made to fit their own unique instructional needs.

SUMMARY

Modern technology has yielded a wide variety of teaching and learning resources. These aids to teaching and learning have made it possible for the educator to be both more effective and efficient. Today no school can expect to carry out its tasks of education without providing the teachers with these needed resources. Not only should they be accessible but the supporting production hardware should be provided to allow the teacher an opportunity to create materials to fit local learning needs. The teacher needs time to plan, time to think, time to explore, and time to select or produce these modern tools for teaching. Students' needs place upon the teacher a greater responsibility for selection, use and evaluation of media and also place upon the administration the requirement of backing the teachers with sufficient technology to carry on an effective program of instruction.

Chapter 25

Once the media have been utilized, what reasons would there be to justify subsequent classroom activity related to the message just presented?

What possible forms might this follow-up take?

How does follow-up relate to the accomplishment of various kinds of teaching objectives?

Will follow-up techniques vary according to the kind of medium employed?

FOLLOW-UP OF USE
OF AUDIOVISUAL MATERIALS

MARIE McMAHAN, Research Consultant
Title VI B Institute
Instructional Media Center
Michigan State University*

Each experience that a person has changes him in some way. The degree to which an experience with an audiovisual device changes one is dependent largely on how well it serves his purpose and on how skillfully it is used by the teacher and by the learner. Not only should the teaching purpose determine which materials are selected for use, but also the preparation that is made for their use, the manner in which they are presented, and the type of follow-up activities in which the learner engages subsequent to their use. Of these four, follow-up activities tend to give the best indication of how meaningful the experience has been to the learner.

Follow-up activities are many and varied. They vary with the teacher's beliefs about the role of education, the theory of learning to which the teacher subscribes, the nature of the group of learners, the ob-

---

* Miss McMahan was granted a leave from her position as Associate Professor of Education at Western Michigan University.

jective of the specific teaching-learning situation and the type of learning situation.

APPROPRIATE FOLLOW-UP ACTIVITIES ARE DETERMINED IN PART BY THE TEACHER'S CONCEPT OF WHAT EDUCATION IS.

Some teachers feel that education is preparation of the learner to function adequately in the world as it now is; others believe it is to help him not only to live in today's world but also to adapt to and live constructively in a tomorrow that cannot be completely anticipated. The first belief involves teaching pupils information and skills that are currently available, the other helping them to develop the skills of problem-solving and creative thinking that are necessary for life in an unseeable future. In view of the present astonishing rate of proliferation of knowledge, education only for today is highly impractical. Follow-up activities that contribute to problem-solving ability are obviously a necessity.

APPROPRIATE FOLLOW-UP ACTIVITIES ARE DETERMINED IN PART BY THE LEARNING PRINCIPLES TO WHICH THE TEACHER SUBSCRIBES.

Much has been written in recent years about the importance of basing educational practice upon scientific principles of learning, and, to this end, psychologists have been developing various theoretical positions intended to show how people learn. Foremost among these, according to Meierhenry (19), are two major positions, that of the connectionist and that of the cognitive learning theorist. Because these theories have numerous differences which are confusing to the classroom teacher, various educators, including Symonds (24), Meierhenry (19) and others, have attempted to abstract from the several theoretical positions some common elements upon which classroom experience can be based.

Motivation is essential to learning.

People learn only as they are motivated to learn. Different people are motivated by different conditions, depending on their goals; some are motivated by a desire to learn, some by a need to solve a problem or find a logical explanation for an occurrence, some by a wish to win the approval and acceptance of the teacher. Intrinsic motivation, that from within, rather than extrinsic or externally-imposed motivation, appears to be desirable to psychologists. Audiovisual materials, when used with adequate preparation and follow-up, have been shown to kindle a high degree of interest in subjects and topics that might be studied by a group and so have contributed greatly to motivation. (27)

Reward or reinforcement is essential to learning.

Reinforcement and reward appear to have very different meanings for different psychologists. A concept of reinforcement which has many implications for follow-up use of audiovisual materials is that of connectionists: reinforcement is a stimulus which causes an act to be repeated. Used consistently to encourage a pupil through confirming the correctness of a response, this type of reinforcement is one of the most important elements in programed instruction. Other theorists consider achievement of a desired goal by a learner one of the most cogent rewards. As follow-up of audiovisual materials contributes to the achievement of a learner's purpose, it tends to play an important part in rewarding and reinforcing learning.

Participation is essential to learning.

The frequently-quoted educational principle that we 'learn to do by doing' is one that seems to be quite generally accepted by the theorists. Connectionists place great emphasis on the importance of overt behavior and upon objective, scientific evidence that learning has occurred. Other theorists, too, subscribe to the importance of participation, some indicating that people learn the reactions they make, others insisting that people learn only the reactions that are satisfying to them. One of the foremost advantages of audiovisual materials is that, when presented and followed-up in a competent manner, they provide many opportunities for first-hand experience by the learner.

Transfer is essential to learning.

Some years ago Thorndike disproved the faculty theory of transfer of learning, but, according to Snygg (23), he appeared, in doing so, to deny the existence of any kind of transfer. Later, however, it became apparent to psychologists that a theory of transfer is necessary to explain how pupils use knowledge gained in one situation to help in solving problems confronted in other situations. Currently many theorists believe that transfer occurs through the application of general principles, and several studies reported by Snygg (23) indicate not only the importance of allowing pupils to discover basic principles but also the role that a teacher plays in enabling students to apply principles to new situations. It would appear that all of us who are classroom teachers need to become much more sophisticated in the kinds of follow-up activities that we employ, changing our emphasis from regurgitation of factual information to serious efforts to develop meaningful generalizations and to apply basic principles in a variety of situations.

Individual differences must be considered in connection with learning. The mental age of six-year-olds has been shown to vary as much as six years, of nine-year-olds as much as ten years (24). Although the best thinking of many educators has been focused on attempts to devise better organizational schemes for learning, it appears to be impossible to establish classroom groups that are homogeneous in all respects. It becomes obvious, then, that the classroom teacher needs to develop a variety of techniques for dealing effectively with individual differences, among which are methods of using audiovisual materials to assist each student in developing to his greatest capacity.

APPROPRIATE FOLLOW-UP ACTIVITIES ARE DETERMINED IN PART BY THE NATURE OF THE GROUP WITH WHICH AUDIOVISUAL MATERIALS ARE BEING USED.

The fact that groups differ is readily apparent to all classroom teachers. Many of these differences influence the types of follow-up activities that are appropriate for use with various groups. Obviously the age level of the pupils exerts a considerable influence on the sophistication that they display in connection with the various communication, research, and creative skills and abilities that are involved in follow-up. Obviously, too, their out-of-school cultural background and their exposure or lack of exposure to an in-school climate conducive to inquiry and creativity affect kinds of follow-up activities that can be used. Pupils who have never engaged in thoughtful discussion nor attempted to apply principles to new situations, nor used books and other resources to gather additional pertinent data will, of course, begin with these skills in an early formative stage. This is not to say, however, that, because of lack of sophistication in these areas, the teacher disregards them; here, as in all teaching situations, he starts with pupils where they are and attempts to provide a classroom climate and appropriate experience to help them grow in desired directions.

APPROPRIATE FOLLOW-UP ACTIVITIES ARE DETERMINED IN PART BY THE OBJECTIVES OF THE SPECIFIC TEACHING-LEARNING SITUATIONS IN WHICH MATERIALS ARE USED.

Audiovisual materials, like books, are used for a variety of purposes. Printed materials, by and large, are used thoughtfully; sometimes the reader skims a page quickly, sometimes he reads slowly and deliberately, depending on his purpose. So, too, the purpose for which an audiovisual device is being used should be an important factor in determining not only the way in which a group is prepared for viewing the material and the manner in which it is presented but also the type of follow-up in which pupils will engage. Because follow-up varies with purpose, one cannot take a cookbook approach in discussing appropriate techniques, for there is no single prescription that is appropriate to all situations. Disturbing as this statement may be, it is also a challenging one, for it impels the teacher to accept his true role, that of a creative guide to learning who selects children's experiences thoughtfully in terms of the contributions they make to the attainment of objectives.

Despite the fact that it is impossible to identify a standard follow-up procedure which is applicable to all classroom situations, some techniques can be specified which are helpful in terms of follow-up activities when specific teaching purposes are involved. The next section of this chapter will be devoted to attempting to identify some of these techniques.

POSSIBLE FOLLOW-UP ACTIVITIES WHEN USING AUDIOVISUAL MATERIALS TO INTRODUCE A UNIT OR TOPIC.

Research has shown that audiovisual materials are extremely effective in stimulating interest. Used at the beginning of a unit, however, such materials serve the function not only of motivating pupils' desire to study but also of building necessary background to enable them to discuss the topic more intelligently and of helping them identify the aspects of the subject about which they wish to gather additional information. And so, a third grade teacher, taking advantage of an interest that her pupils have expressed in pioneer life, uses a ten-minute film *Pioneer Home* to give them additional background on the early settlers and to encourage them to think about topics that they want to explore during the unit. The film, a short one and by no means comprehensive in content, is well-suited to its purpose. It refers briefly to such aspects of pioneer life as homes, food, clothing, utensils, work, recreation, religion and schooling. Used as a springboard for discussion, it can be accompanied by follow-up activities such as:

discussing the new information gained from the film;

identifying topics (such as pioneer food, pioneer clothing), about which the pupils wish to learn more;

planning how the topics will be studied (all topics by the total group or each one by a committee);

listing appropriate resource materials (filmstrips, books, field trips, and others) and determining how they will be used;

planning how committees will function and on what time schedule they will operate.

A similar approach can be used at the secondary level with a film on a provocative topic about which a group currently has inadequate information on which to base a discussion. A film, for instance, on democracy or communism, labor or management, war or peace can be used effectively in building the background needed for an intelligent discussion of the topic. Out of the showing of such a film grow questions such as:

What are the issues presented in this film?

Is this an unbiased presentation of the issues?

Is it basically an emotional or a factual presentation of the issues?

What evidence do we have that the presentation is biased or unbiased?

What are our reactions to these issues?

Do we, at this point, have adequate information to discuss the issues fairly, or do we need to search for additional information?

To what sources can we go for additional information?

How will we gather information and when will we re-assemble to discuss the issues in greater detail?

POSSIBLE FOLLOW-UP ACTIVITIES WHEN USING AUDIOVISUAL MATERIALS TO CONVEY INFORMATION.

All of us gather information more efficiently if we know before using material what specific information we wish to gain. A teacher utilizing audiovisual materials for purposes of conveying information, therefore, will attempt to orient her group to the kinds of facts available in a specific film, filmstrip, record or tape to be used. This can be accomplished either by listing questions on the chalkboard and calling attention to them before the material is shown or by encouraging pupils to volunteer questions that they have about the topic under consideration. All students can be asked to attempt to discover the answers for all questions, or committees can be asked to react to specific ones. However the preparation for the showing is handled, a logical type of follow-up is to discuss the questions about which the group is concerned. If questions are initially presented by the teacher, answers to all of them should be available from the film. A second showing may be necessary (and indeed research shows it to be desirable) in enabling pupils to answer the more complex questions (27), or pupils may wish to go to other sources to supplement the answers gained from the film. If questions are initially contributed by the students, it is unlikely that answers to all of them will be available in the film. This is not an ineffective teaching situation, however, as it encourages the group to discuss pertinent points such as:

Did all of us find answers to the questions that were of concern to us?

Where might we be able to find answers to those questions not discussed in the film?

How will we proceed with answering these questions?

We as teachers frequently tend, by the questions we ask our students, to restrict them to a rather elementary level of information gathering. Lemler and Bartlett in a pamphlet on how to study pictures (11) list a progression of picture-reading skills that have implications for information gathering from other types of materials as well: enumeration (listing items seen in a picture), description (telling what is occurring), and drawing inferences (formulating hypotheses based on evidence depicted in the picture).

The questions that we ask about a film or other audiovisual material may, in the beginning, be very simple ones:

What (who) did you see in the film? (enumeration)

What were they doing? What was happening? (description)

Later, as pupils gain experience in viewing and reacting to materials, questions may become more thought-provoking:

What evidence did you see that this was a dry (or wet, hot or cold) country? (inferences as to climate)

What did you see that helps you understand the size of mountains? (inferences as to size)

After viewing this film on insects, list as many ways as you can in which honeybees and ants are alike. (comparison)

Contrast the ways in which pioneers obtained their food with the ways in which we procure ours. (contrast)

After studying the time line that we made, can you tell which of these events happened first: the coming of the pioneers to Michigan, the discovery of America by Columbus, the settlement of Plymouth by the Pilgrims? (drawing inferences as to time relationships)

Drawing inferences about materials viewed, begun at elementary school level, can be encouraged by questions involving greater depth of thought at secondary level. Follow-up of use of audiovisual materials, in any case, can be effective only as the teacher adequately assumes responsibility for helping students learn how to use each specific kind of material capably.

POSSIBLE FOLLOW-UP TECHNIQUES WHEN USING AUDIOVISUAL MATERIALS TO DEVELOP CONCEPTS, GENERALIZATIONS, PRINCIPLES.

Bloom (3), in the *Taxonomy of Educational Objectives*, indicates for our consideration a kind of heirarchy of information, ranging from knowledge of specifics at the bottom to knowledge of principles, generalizations, theories and structures at the top. Probably all of us would agree that knowledge in the form of isolated facts is not very useful and that only as bits of information are combined into concepts, generalizations and principles do they become useful to us in solving the many new and different problems with which we are confronted in daily life. Since rich and varied experiencing contributes to the depth of concepts and generalizations that we are able to formulate, audio-visual materials assume an extremely important role in this aspect of learning.

In developing the concept of one half, for instance, many materials are needed: real objects (one half of four apples), a fraction board (two halves make one), flannel board materials (two fourths make one half), etc.

In developing the concept of democracy many experiences contribute to the depth of meaning that it has for our pupils: experiences in functioning democratically in a classroom, a school, a student council, one's community; experiences of using films, filmstrips, records or tapes that document the development of democracy in our country; experiences of viewing materials that explore democracy as it currently exists in various countries around the world.

In developing the generalization that 'topography influences the types of crops grown in an area' various materials play an important part: a relief map with models of crops mounted in appropriate places, a plastic map with topography shown on the base and crops depicted on the overlay, a transparency on which relief features and products are revealed progressively.

How does a teacher determine whether students have adequately developed a concept or generalization? Here, again, the principle of participation becomes important. Since being able to demonstrate the concept for others or being able to apply the principle in other situations provides more accurate evidences of understanding than mere verbalization, the elementary student studying fractions may be asked to indicate half of a group of children or to show relationships between cutout paper fractions that he has made. The junior high student can be asked to prepare a plastic map or transparency showing how topography affects crops grown in another country or how crops in the United States are influenced by other factors such as altitude, rainfall or types of soil. The high school student can be asked to compare the governments of several countries or to operate in a democratic situation in his school.

We, as teachers, too frequently assume that our actions clarify concepts and develop generalizations for children. We use the fraction board at the front of the room, assuming that pupils who have watched us compare two fractions understand the relationship between them. The importance of firsthand discovery of relationships, concepts and generalizations by pupils cannot be overestimated. However, Symonds, in discussing experiments by Craig (24), indicates that the teacher, by organization of materials and by appropriate questions, plays an important role in helping children discover basic principles. His comment that we should not expect children, by themselves, to discover principles that it has taken the great scholars of the world many years to formulate seems very pertinent at this point. This statement has implications for use of audiovisual materials both in group and individual situations.

POSSIBLE FOLLOW-UP ACTIVITIES WHEN USING AUDIOVISUAL MATERIALS TO DEVELOP PROBLEM-SOLVING SKILLS.

In the Taxonomy of Educational Objectives, Bloom (3) also identifies a hierarchy of intellectual skills involving use of knowledge. These start with simpler skills such as comprehension, translation, interpretation and extrapolation of information and extend to more difficult ones such as application, analysis, synthesis and evaluation of knowledge.

Many educators, among them Bode (4) and Dewey (12), have written earnestly about the necessity of developing citizens who have skills in problem-solving, or as Sayers and Madden (22) term them, skills in "inquiry." Snygg (23) emphasizes the fact that, with the world changing at such an astonishing rate, we need to develop skills in solving problems that we ourselves can neither foresee nor solve.

Obviously, then, we are not utilizing materials adequately when we limit our use to gathering information or to forming concepts and generalizations. If we are to develop mature learners, we must ascertain that they gain the skills essential to inquiry, to critical thinking, to problem-solving. They are identified by Bingham (2) as:

1. Identifying the problem and feeling the need to pursue it.
2. Seeking to clarify the problem and understand its nature, scope and subproblems.
3. Collecting data and information related to the problem.
4. Selecting and organizing the data which apply most pertinently to the crux of the problem.
5. Determining the various possible solutions in view of the assembled data and knowledge of the problem.
6. Evaluating the solutions and selecting the best one for the situation.
7. Putting the solution into action.
8. Evaluating the problem-solving process employed.

Thelen (25), in *Education and the Human Quest,* postulates that the most important aspect of problem solving is formulating the key question. Audiovisual materials, as indicated previously in this chapter, are often very helpful during this stage of problem solving since they assist pupils greatly in the identification of questions and problems they wish to pursue. Audiovisual materials can be useful, too, during other stages of problem solving.

One of the basic skills involved is that of locating sources of data pertinent to the problem, and, having located them, of discriminating among them as to the relative merits of the data involved. Various films and filmstrips are now available to help pupils delineate the steps in gathering information about a topic and gain competence in the use of many types of reference tools. An appropriate type of follow-up after use of such a filmstrip is to give students opportunities to practice collecting data pertaining to a specific problem.

Evaluating data on the basis of its relevance, its usefulness, and its authenticity is a crucial skill in problem solving. Younger children, Hoban (15) found, are likely to gather rather general items of information from a film; high school students, on the other hand, gather much more specific information but show a tendency to draw conclusions that cannot be validated on the basis of the evidence in the film. A teacher, using a film thoughtfully with students, can help them not only to identify which of their conclusions about a topic are substantiated by the information presented but also to evaluate the objectivity of the film on the basis of the manner in which evidence is presented and by whom it is presented.

An important aspect of problem solving involves helping pupils determine which solutions or parts of solutions used in previous situations apply to the present one. As previously stated, research indicates the necessity of teachers assisting students in making applications of principles to new situations. This skill can be developed in part by appropriate follow-up activities such as this: asking pupils who have viewed the development of the principle that desert regions tend to occur on the leeward side of high mountains to locate areas on a map that would be likely to be deserts. As with other skills, the ability to apply principles grows as many opportunities are provided for this kind of experience.

POSSIBLE FOLLOW-UP ACTIVITIES WHEN AUDIOVISUAL MATERIALS ARE USED TO BUILD ATTITUDES.

Attitudes, being much less tangible than facts, are less readily measured. Research studies (27) tend to indicate that audiovisual materials do not permanently change attitudes but are instrumental in reinforcing and strengthening ones that already exist. Because an individual's beliefs, values and attitudes are so basic to the way in which he perceives himself, other people and the world in general, and because people's perceptions of reality rather than reality itself determine their actions, it seems imperative that teachers give children every opportunity to re-examine their attitudes and values. One of the ways in which this can be done is by using audiovisual materials—films, filmstrips, role playing, records and tapes—in which problem sequences are depicted and subsequently discussing the implications of these dramatizations of real life situations.

It is obvious to a teacher when his pupils need help with a specific attitude such as courtesy, good sportsmanship or better understanding of other people. Discussion of attitudes in a first-hand situation, as all of us know, is often difficult and not always profitable. A thoughtful teacher can, however, often find appropriate materials involving problem situations in these areas which can be used as a basis for discussion. Following a film on good sportsmanship, a tape recording on being truthful, or a role-playing session on relationships of teen-agers to their parents, a group can discuss such questions as:

What did John do in this situation?

Was this the best solution to the problem, or was Bill's better?

How would you have handled this problem?

Obviously it is much easier for a group to evaluate John's conduct as depicted by the film than its own behavior in the gymnasium. What occurs after such a discussion will depend on the kind of group a teacher has and on his rapport with the group. In some cases, it will be possible for him to say: "What implications does our discussion have for the way in which we work together?" and "Would it be interesting for us to be aware of our actions in the gym during the next few days and evaluate them in terms of our discussion after seeing the film?" With other groups, a teacher may prefer to informally evaluate the conduct of the class in the gymnasium after seeing the film and to use additional materials and techniques for improvement of sportsmanship as group conduct indicates a need for them.

Research studies on use of audiovisual materials in the development of attitudes frequently use pre- and posttests to determine the degree of change. Classroom teachers may wish to experiment with similar techniques.

POSSIBLE FOLLOW-UP TECHNIQUES WHEN USING AUDIOVISUAL MATERIALS TO DEVELOP APPRECIATIONS.

It is said that we appreciate those things in life which we have experienced and enjoyed over a period of time. If this is true, teachers have a tremendous responsibility for exposing their students on as many occasions and in as many ways as possible to all that is good and beautiful in life. Audiovisual materials on the great classics in literature, art and music can be invaluable. So, too, can those materials capable of developing appreciation of our world and of the contributions of other people, past and present, to our culture be invaluable.

Appreciations, like attitudes, are intangible. They do not become a part of us as we are asked to verbalize about them but only as we feel a desire to make them an integral part of ourselves. Therefore, a teacher needs to be extremely subtle in the kinds of follow-up activities that he employs when using audiovisual materials for the purpose of developing appreciations. Discussion, if skillfully done, can be very valuable, but, conversely, if ineffectively used, it can engender dislike rather than appreciation. Let us, then, consider some alternative types of follow-up.

An elementary teacher, using a filmstrip and record on one of the musical classics, said to the children: "I'm going to play a record for you. This record tells a story. Why don't you listen and see whether you can imagine what story it is telling. When we've finished listening, I will give each of you a chance to write your story and share it with the rest of us." Listening thoughtfully and then writing, the children produced some delightful original stories. After all had been read and enjoyed, the teacher said: "The composer of this music had a story in mind when he wrote this beautiful selection. Would you like to know what story he thought the music was telling?" Her follow-up, then, was to use the filmstrip and record simultaneously, letting the children enjoy the composer's story. This technique, obviously, greatly enhanced the group's appreciation of the music.

If material is appropriately introduced and used, various types of follow-up other than discussion can be used to enhance the students' feeling of appreciation. Creative writing, resulting from the skillful use of a film (without commentary), selected slides or pictures, a disk or tape recording can help in developing appreciation. Other creative activities—dramatization, a puppet show, a mural, an illustrated tape recording—provide ways of helping groups share the appreciations they have gained through watching a film or other audiovisual device.

POSSIBLE FOLLOW-UP ACTIVITIES WHEN AUDIOVISUAL MATERIALS ARE USED TO DEVELOP SKILLS.

The number of audiovisual materials available for helping students of all ages become more adept with a variety of basic skills is growing rapidly. These vary from films and filmstrips for teaching the word attack skills in reading, to programed texts for teaching English and mathematics skills, to tape recordings for teaching speaking, listening and foreign language skills.

Which type of material is chosen for which teaching task is again dependent on the purpose that teacher and pupils have in mind. A film may be used to introduce and stimulate interest in the word attack skills, but a filmstrip whose speed of presentation can be regulated to fit the needs of the group will undoubtedly be more desirable for the actual development of the skill. Follow-up of the presentation of such a skill can include a demonstration by the teacher, practice by the pupils of the skill involved, a test or a combination of these. After a discussion by teacher and pupils of the characteristics inherent in a good speech, oral report, vocal or instrumental selection, or group discussion, pupils can, for example, produce a tape of their performance in this area. Listening to the tape, evaluating performance on the basis of the previously described criteria, practicing, making a second tape, and evaluating again, are appropriate kinds of follow-up.

POSSIBLE FOLLOW-UP ACTIVITIES WHEN AUDIOVISUAL MATERIALS ARE USED TO SUMMARIZE AND SHARE LEARNING.

Numerous audiovisual materials are appropriate for assisting students in summarizing and sharing learning. They may include such commercially-produced materials as:

motion pictures (used without sound, with students providing an appropriate commentary),

filmstrips, slides, flat pictures, or transparencies (used with student commentary),

records or tape recordings (used with appropriate student illustrations such as drawings or transparencies).

They may also include such pupil-produced materials as:

objects, models or dioramas;

maps of various kinds, including relief maps;

slides, photographs or transparencies;

demonstration materials such as flannel board or magnetic board sets;

display materials such as bulletin board sets;

dramatized experiences such as plays, role-playing, or puppet or marionette shows;

graphics such as posters, charts or graphs.

If judiciously used, these materials can help students organize and communicate their learning more effectively than would otherwise be possible. However, this use of audiovisual materials also demands a follow-up. Since pupils, like teachers, can grow in their ability to communicate only as they continually evaluate the results of their efforts, sharing learning by means of audiovisual devices should be followed by discussing questions such as the following:

Did you understand the report better because of the visual?

What do you think were the major points made in this presentation?

Were the visuals for this report well chosen?

If pupil-produced, were they well executed?

APPROPRIATE FOLLOW-UP ACTIVITIES ARE DETERMINED BY THE NATURE OF THE LEARNING SITUATION.

It is only recently that new technological developments such as the language laboratory, instructional television and the 8mm cartridge film projector have caused audiovisual specialists to consider the implications of use of materials not only in classroom size groups of thirty but in large groups of a hundred or more and also in individual learning situations. It is only recently, too, that teachers have begun to develop techniques for use of materials which are presented by a specialist outside the classroom but which the classroom member of the team needs to prepare for and follow-up with students. Obviously, all of these special types of learning situations influence the kind of follow-up done by the classroom teacher. It would seem appropriate to explore them, one by one.

Appropriate follow-up activities when using audiovisual materials in a large group situation

Educators are now beginning to consider much more carefully than before the types of activities that are appropriate in groups of varying sizes. Discussion, as we all know from personal experience, grows more easily out of small group situations than large ones. On the other hand, when presentation of information is the basic purpose of a teacher, this can be accomplished as effectively with a large group as a small one, provided, of course, that the teacher is skillful in his technique, that he has adequate tools with which to work, and that appropriate follow-up occurs. And so, for introducing members of several classes to a new unit of study, motivating and inspiring them, and opening up issues that need to be explored, a capable teacher can work simultaneously with more than one group, judiciously selecting and using a film, slides, transparencies or other visuals to help him accomplish his purpose.

Very meaningful follow-up to such a large group demonstration can occur in seminars with either a teacher or student leader and with group members discussing the issues raised, reacting to them, identifying points of agreement and disagreement, and planning areas for further study.

Large group situations can also take advantage of special resources if they are appropriate to the purposes of all the small groups involved and if they are not available to classrooms individually. Such resources include: instructional television programs, well-known speakers made available to the school through the telelecture technique and resource people from the local community. Studies on use of instructional television indicate that teachers need to become more adept at recognizing the important role they play in regard to preparation for and follow-up of such special resources.

Appropriate follow-up activities when using audiovisual materials in individual learning situations

Follow-up procedures for individual use of motion pictures. In situations where the mechanics of allowing individual students to use motion pictures can be worked out, many profitable kinds of learning experiences can occur. Motion pictures with appropriate follow-up tests can be used to help students gather information. Carefully-selected films can be used, with sound, to help individual students gain background for discussion of a topic; others can be used, without sound, to stimulate creative writing. A pupil who is preparing a report may wish to preview a film, parts of which he may decide to share with his class, emphasizing, as he does so, the aspects of the film that relate to his own specific research topic.

Many new 8mm single-concept cartridge films are now available for individual use. Obviously, one advantage of these materials is that a student can use them again and again until he understands the routine that is being depicted. Undoubtedly the most valuable kind of follow-up for such a film is practice of the skill, evaluation of the student's degree of proficiency, and further viewing if necessary.

Cartridge films are being produced which not only add to the pupil's knowledge but stimulate him to try experiments. Science areas can be developed in a corner of the classroom to enable a student to view a film, set up an experiment with the same equipment, and determine whether his results are the same as those depicted in the film. Discovery of and verification of a principle will often lead him to new experiments in which the same principle is involved.

Use of other cartridge films can be followed by answering questions on one's comprehension of the content of the film, outlining the content, or assimilating appropriate portions into a report that the student is preparing.

Follow-up procedures for individual use of filmstrips. There are many filmstrips available for the improvement of skills at both elementary and secondary levels. Such filmstrips include series on use of maps, globes and books, series on procedures in cooking, sewing, producing a school newspaper, preparing reports, and doing mechanical drawing. These filmstrips need not always be viewed by a whole group. Rather, they can be assigned for individual viewing by all members of a group or by those needing additional help. Follow-up for use of such filmstrips might include test exercises or actual application of the skills.

Individual filmstrips can be used, too, for various other purposes: gathering information, solving a problem, or developing a generalization. However they are used, it is important that we, as teachers, give students adequate assistance with the techniques involved in reading pictures before we expect them to use any of the still-picture media effectively in individual learning situations.

Follow-up procedures for individual use of tape recordings. Tape recordings are especially appropriate for individual use in that they can be prepared to fit the needs of specific individuals. For example, pupils who need additional reading experiences can be given practice in reading and comprehending textbook materials, enrichment materials, pictures, maps, globes or graphs. Follow-up activities can include responding to questions asked by the tape and checking to see whether the response is correct. Kinder (17), in *Using Audio-Visual Materials in Education*, gives excellent examples of specific ways of using the tape recorder in individual learning situations.

On a dual-track tape, one track of which can be recorded and erased without changing the master, students can attempt to imitate an excellent model of speech, foreign language or music. If such practice is to be a valuable experience, the practice session will of course be followed by evaluation by the student and the teacher of his progress and the identification of steps needed for further growth.

Language laboratories, at the secondary level, have been shown to be very worthwhile in teaching the speaking-listening skills involved in language. It is hoped that this valuable technological device will, in the future, be conceived more widely as a learning laboratory and used for a much wider variety of speaking, singing and listening skills in a variety of subject matter areas.

Follow-up procedures for individual use of records. It has been said that one of the most-used and least effectively taught communication skills is listening. Teachers who have identified specific listening skills that they wish to develop can use recordings, both in group and individual situations, for achieving this purpose. For example, an English teacher during a unit on biography, assigned both listening and reading experiences designed to help students discover factors that contributed to the lives of great men. After listening to a recording about a famous person, students were asked to answer questions such as:

What obstacles did this person face?

How did he overcome these obstacles?

What character traits did this person have that contributed to his greatness?

Individual listening experiences can be assigned in areas such as music, speech, drama and literature with students being asked to engage in written or oral evaluation as a follow-up.

In the area of shorthand, students can take dictation from a record, checking their transcription at the end of the session by comparing it with a model prepared by the teacher.

Follow-up of individual use of programed materials. It is often assumed that programed materials are prepared primarily for the purpose of teaching skills, and this is frequently true. In such cases the follow-up in the form of testing is built into the program itself.

Individual programs, however, are also produced for the purpose of extending a student's background in a specific area. Programs, then, like books, can assist students in becoming familiar with an area to a degree that they can discuss it intelligently with other students in small seminar groups.

Follow-up of individual use of other audiovisual materials. A creative teacher, sensitive to his students, their interests, their backgrounds and their needs, can discover many types of audiovisual materials that contribute to the growth of individual students. Students who have been strongly motivated in group situations and who have personal goals that lead them on in their search for knowledge will need less teacher-directed follow-up activities. For those who do need more of this kind of help, various means can be found for checking their comprehension of audiovisual materials used in individual learning situations. A file folder, with appropriate matching, completion or true and false statements, can be used following the viewing of a filmstrip. An electric board quiz can be prepared to test a pupil's understanding of a series of pictures, symbols used on a globe, or information presented on a line or bar graph. A programed text can be devised to check a student's learning from a map. As the numbers of students in our schools continue to rise and as groups become more heterogeneous, the importance of tools for individual instruction will become more and more acute, as will the need for effective use of these tools.

IN CONCLUSION

The skill with which pupils use audiovisual materials is dependent, to a large degree, on the competencies that we, as teachers, help them develop. Rich experiences in knowing where to look for appropriate materials, how to gather information from them, how to evaluate the information in terms of learning purposes and how to follow-up use of materials effectively, will carry over into the out-of-school life of our pupils. Again, it is said that every experience a person has changes his life in some way. Good experiences with audiovisual materials, as with books, can make life infinitely richer and more meaningful.

BIBLIOGRAPHY

1. Association for Supervision and Curriculum Development, *Perceiving, Behaving, Becoming*. Washington, D.C.: The Association, 1962.
2. Bingham, Alma I., *Improving Children's Facility in Problem Solving*. New York: Bureau of Publications, Teachers College, Columbia Univ., 1958.
3. Bloom, Benjamin, *Taxonomy of Educational Objectives*. New York: David McKay, 1956.
4. Bode, Boyd H., *Democracy as a Way of Life*. New York: Macmillan, 1936.
5. Brown, James W., Lewis, Richard B., and Harcleroad, Fred F. *A-V Instruction, Materials and Methods*. New York: McGraw-Hill, 1964.
6. Clayton, Thomas E., *Teaching and Learning*. Englewood Cliffs: Prentice-Hall, 1965.
7. Cochran, Lee (ed.), *Summary Report, 9th Annual Lake Okoboji Audiovisual Leadership Conference*. Iowa City: Division of Extension and University Services, State University of Iowa and Department of Audiovisual Instruction, National Education Association, 1963.
8. Costello, Lawrence F., and Gordon, George N. *Teach with Television*. New York: Hastings House, 1961.
9. Cross, A. J. Foy, and Cypher, Irene F. *Audio-Visual Education*. New York: Crowell, 1961.
10. Dale, Edgar, *Audio-Visual Materials in Teaching*. New York: Holt, 1954.
11. Dale, Edgar, Bartlett, Mary M., Lemler, F. L., and Clark, Ella C., *How to Teach with Pictures*. Grand Rapids: Informative Classroom Picture Publishers, 1951.
12. Dewey, John, *Democracy and Education*. New York: Macmillan, 1936.
13. Erickson, Carlton W. H., *Fundamentals of Teaching with Audiovisual Technology*. New York: Macmillan, 1965.
14. Frazier, Alexander (ed.), *Learning More about Learning*. Washington, D.C.: Association for Supervision and Curriculum Development, 1959.
15. Hoban, Charles F., *Focus on Learning*. Washington, D.C.: American Council on Education, 1942.
16. Hoban, Charles F., *Movies That Teach*. New York: Dryden Press, 1946.
17. Kinder, James S., *Using Audio-Visual Materials in Education*. New York: American Book Company, 1965.
18. May, Mark A., *et al.*, *Learning from Films*. New Haven: Yale University Press, 1958.
19. Meierhenry, Wesley C. (ed.), "Learning theory and AV utilization." *Audio Visual Communication Review*, Vol. 9, No. 5. Washington, D.C.: Department of Audiovisual Instruction, National Education Association, September-October, 1961.
20. Miller, Neal E., *et al.*, *Graphic Communication and the Crisis in Education*. (Reprint of *Audio Visual Communication Review*, Vol. 5, No. 3) Washington, D.C.: Department of Audiovisual Instruction, National Education Association, 1957.
21. *New Teaching Aids for the American Classrooms*. Stanford: Institute for Communication Research, Stanford Univ., 1960.
22. Sayers, Ephraim Vern, and Madden, Ward, *Education and the Democratic Faith*. New York: Appleton-Century-Crofts, 1959.

23. Snygg, Donald, "The tortuous path of learning theory." *Audiovisual Instruction,* Vol. 7, No. 1. Washington, D.C.: Department of Audiovisual Instruction, National Education Association, January, 1962.
24. Symonds, Percival M., *What Education Has to Learn from Psychology.* New York: Bureau of Publications, Teachers College, Columbia University.
25. Thelen, Herbert A., *Education and the Human Quest.* New York: Harper and Row, 1960.
26. Trow, William Clark, *What Research Says to the Teacher.* Washington, D.C.: Department of Classroom Teachers and American Educational Research Association, National Education Association, 1963.
27. Wendt, Paul R., *What Research Says to the Teacher.* Washington, D.C.: Department of Classroom Teachers and American Educational Research Association, National Education Association, 1957.
28. Wittich, Walter A., and Schuller, Charles F. *Audiovisual Materials: Their Nature and Use.* New York: Harper and Row, 1967.

Chapter 26

If one accepts the premise that the use of instructional technology requires careful planning and execution, then how does one ascertain the effectiveness of the instruction?

What can achievement tests tell the teacher about the learner?

How can the teacher gain an understanding of the net worth of the separate parts of instructional systems?

In test construction, can the selection and use of test items be so tailored as to distinguish learning outcomes not only between individuals but also between groups?

CRITERION-REFERENCED TESTING FOR THE MEASUREMENT OF EDUCATIONAL OUTCOMES*

ROBERT GLASER and RICHARD C. COX
Learning Research and Development Center
University of Pittsburgh

Modifications of present instructional systems and innovations in instructional technology require consideration of the problems in the assessment of existing levels of competence and achievement. Until recently, test development has been dominated by the particular demands of predictive, correlational aptitude test "theory." Achievement and criterion measurement has attempted frequently to cast itself in his framework. Recent emphasis on programed instruction, teaching machines and other systems for individualizing instruction raises some important questions for achievement test development.

Achievement measurement can be defined as the assessment of ter-

*The research reported herein was supported through the Cooperative Research Program of the Office of Education, U.S. Department of Health, Education and Welfare, Contract Numbers OE 2–10–10–57 and OE 4–10–158. This chapter is a revised version of that which originally appeared in *American Psychologist* in 1963 by Robert Glaser. It is reprinted with permission of the author and publisher, American Psychological Association.

minal or criterion behavior which is the desired outcome of some instructional sequence. Such a definition requires a specification of the characteristics of pupil performance in reference to certain standards. Achievement measurement in this context is distinguished from aptitude measurement in that the instruments used to assess achievement are specifically concerned with the characteristics of present performance, with emphasis on the meaningfulness of its content. In contrast, aptitude measures derive their meaning from a demonstrated relationship between present performance and the future attainment of specified knowledge. In certain circumstances, of course, this contrast is not quite so clear, for example, when achievement measures are used as predictor variables.

The scores obtained from an achievement test provide primarily two kinds of information. One is the relative ordering of individuals with respect to their test performance, for example, whether pupil A can solve his problems more quickly than pupil B. The second type of information that an achievement test score provides is the degree to which the pupil has attained some criterion, for example, whether he can satisfactorily type a certain number of words per minute or solve certain kinds of word problems in arithmetic. The principal difference between these two kinds of information lies in the standard used as a reference. What shall be referred to as norm-referenced measures depend upon a relative standard, while what shall be termed criterion-referenced measures depend upon an absolute standard of quality. Distinctions between these two kinds of measures have been made previously by others. (3, 4)

NORM-REFERENCED MEASURES

One of the basic assumptions from which the theory of achievement measurement derives is the notion of a continuum of knowledge acquisition ranging from no proficiency at all to perfect performance. The achievement test is the measurement device that indicates an individual's proficiency level with respect to other individuals or in reference to certain criterion behaviors specified along the achievement continuum. Achievement tests which convey information about the capability of a pupil compared with the capability of other pupils will be called norm-referenced measures. Grade equivalent or percentile norms, for example, are intended to provide information with which to compare an individual with national or local norm groups. In such cases where a pupil's *relative* standing along the continuum of attainment is the primary purpose of measurement, reference need not be made to criterion behavior. Educational achievement examinations, for example, are administered frequently for the purpose of ordering pupils in a class or school, rather than for assessing their attainment of specified curriculum objectives. When such norm-referenced measures are used, a particular pupil's achievement is evaluated in terms of a comparison between his performance and the performance of other members of the group. Such measures need provide little or no information about the degree of proficiency exhibited by the tested behaviors in terms of what the individual can do. They tell that one pupil is more or less proficient than another, but do not tell how proficient either of them is with respect to the subject-matter tasks involved.

Many of the achievement measures, including both standardized and teacher-made tests, currently employed in education are norm-referenced. This emphasis upon norm-referenced measures has evolved from the preoccupation of test theory with aptitude, and with selection and prediction problems. Norm-referenced measures are useful, perhaps even necessary, for this kind of correlation and regression analyses. The introduction of new instructional technology and measurement of the outcomes of an educational system raises some questions about the purposes, techniques and information to be gained from achievement measurement. The results of the typical correlation-regression analyses are probably not appropriate kinds of information for the evaluation of instructional systems based on the principle of individual differences. There is a need to behaviorally specify minimum levels of achievement that describe the least amount end-of-course competence the pupil is expected to attain, or that he needs in order to go on to the next course in a sequence. Coulson and Cogswell (1) have discussed this need in reference to the use of programed instructional materials utilized in individualized instructional systems. The pressures of such instructional technology is forcing us toward the kind of information made available by the use of criterion-referenced measures.

CRITERION-REFERENCED MEASURES

The degree to which an individual's achievement resembles desired performance at any specified level along the continuum of attainment is assessed by criterion-referenced measures of achievement or proficiency. The standard against which a pupil's performance is compared when measured in this manner is the behavior which defines each point along the achievement continuum. The term criterion, when used in this way, does not necessarily refer to final end-of-course behavior. Criterion levels can be established at any point in instruction where it is necessary to obtain information as to the adequacy of an individual's performance. The point is that the specific behaviors implied at each level of proficiency can be identified and used to describe the specific tasks a pupil must be capable of performing before he achieves one of these knowledge levels. It is in this sense that measures of proficiency can be criterion-referenced.

Along such a continuum of attainment, a pupil's score on a criterion-referenced measure provides explicit information as to what the individual can or cannot do. Criterion-referenced measures indicate the content of the behavioral repertory, and the correspondence between what an individual does and the underlying continuum of achievement. Measures which assess pupil achievement in terms of a criterion standard thus provide information as to the degree of competence attained by a particular pupil which is independent of reference to the performance of others.

IMPLICATIONS FOR ACHIEVEMENT TEST DEVELOPMENT

The distinction between norm-referenced and criterion-referenced measures can be discussed further in the context of test development theory. In the evaluation of instructional systems, achievement tests can be used for two principal purposes. First, performance can be assessed to provide information about the characteristics of an individual's present behavior. Second, achievement can be assessed to provide information about the conditions or instructional treatments which produce that behavior. The primary emphasis of the first use is to discriminate among individuals. Used in the second way, achievement tests are employed to discriminate among treatments, that is, among different instructional procedures by an analysis of *group* differences.

Achievement tests used to provide information about *individual* differences are constructed so as to maximize the discriminations made among people having specified backgrounds and experience. Such tests include items which maximize the likelihood of observing individual differences in performance along various task dimensions; this maximizes the variability of the distribution of scores that are obtained. In practical test construction, the variability of test scores is increased by manipulating the difficulty levels and content of the test items.

On the other hand, achievement tests used primarily to provide information about differences in treatments need to be constructed so as to maximize the discriminations made between *groups* treated differently and to minimize the differences between the individuals in any one group. Such a test will be sensitive to the differences produced by instructional conditions. For example, a test designed to demonstrate the effectiveness of instruction would be constructed so that it was generally difficult for those taking it before training and generally easy after training. The content of the test used to differentiate treatments should be maximally sensitive to the performance changes anticipated from the instructional treatments. In essence, the distinction between achievement tests used to maximize individual differences and tests used to maximize treatment or group differences is established during the selection of test items.

The construction of an achievement test used to assess individual mastery of some specified skill follows the usual procedure suggested by Lindquist (6). The test is planned giving consideration to the subject-matter content and the instructional objectives to be evaluated. Items which measure these objectives are written and administered to a tryout group. Item statistics, typically discrimination and difficulty indices, are computed using the results obtained from the tryout group.

When the test constructor wishes to maximize the differences between *individuals,* he selects items of median difficulty and, subsequently, high discriminating power. Similarly, many statistics used to evaluate reliability or validity require that the spread of scores not be restricted. Those items which are answered by all members of the group or which are answered by none of the group will have 1.00 and 0.00 difficulty levels, respectively, and will not discriminate between individuals. Such items would be eliminated from the final form of the test because their only effect would be to add, or subtract, a constant value to, or from, every score. These techniques of item selection are not appropriate in test construction for the purpose of observing group instead of individual differences.

Instructional systems based upon individualized instruction, while concerned with individual differences, require evaluation instruments that differentiate between groups of individuals who have mastered certain skills and those who have not. Item selection must follow a different course in this situation. For example, where instruction was the treatment variable involved, it would be desirable to retain test items which were responded to correctly by all members of the post-training group, but which were answered incorrectly by pupils who had not yet been trained. In a test constructed for the purpose of differentiating groups, items which indicated substantial variability within either the pre- or posttraining group would be undesirable because of the likelihood that they would cloud the effects which might be attributable to the treatment variable.

A study by Cox and Vargas (2) investigated the effect of employing differential item-selection techniques to identify items which discriminate according to the requirements of norm- and criterion-referenced tests. Two sets of discrimination indices were computed for items on tests which had been administered both as pretests and posttests in an individualized instruction program. The first index was employed on the results of the posttest only and provided information on how well each item discriminated among individuals. The second index was computed by subtracting the percentage of pupils who passed the item on the posttest from the percentage who passed the item on the pretest, thus providing information between pre- and posttest groups. The results indicated that some items which are highly desirable for criterion-referenced tests would be discarded by the typical item-selection techniques because they fail to discriminate among individuals. The conclusion was that the pretest-posttest method of item analysis seemed to produce results sufficiently different from traditional methods to warrant its consideration when criterion-referenced tests are desired.

In brief, items most suitable for measuring individual differences in achievement are those which will differentiate among individuals all exposed to the same treatment variable, while items most suitable for distinguishing between groups are those which are most likely to indicate that a given amount or kind of some instructional treatment was effective. In either case, samples of test items are drawn from a population of items indicating the content of performance; the particular item samples that are drawn, however, are those most useful for the purpose of the kind of measurement being carried out. Hammock (5) has previously discussed such a difference.

To summarize, the points indicated above reflect the achievement measurement concerns that arise as a result of innovations in instructional technology. The purpose for which a test is to be used has implications for the construction of the test. If selection or grading of pupils is desired, norm-referenced measures and traditional item selection procedures suffice. Alternate methods of test construction must be considered when criterion-reference tests are desired.

REFERENCES

1. Coulson, J. E., and Cogswell, J. F., "Effects of individualized instruction on testing," *Journal of Educational Measurement*, 2 No. 1; 59–64, 1965.
2. Cox, R. C. & Vargas, J. S. "A comparison of item selection techniques for norm-referenced and criterion-referenced tests." Paper read at the Annual Meeting of the National Council on Measurement in Education, Chicago, Illinois, February 1966.
3. Ebel, R. L. "Content standard test scores," *Educ. Psychol. Measmt.*, 22: 15–25, 1962.
4. Flanagan, J. C. "Units, scores, and norms," in E. F. Lindquist (ed.), *Educational Measurement*. Washington, D. C.: American Council on Education, 1951. Pp. 695–763.
5. Hammock, J. "Criterion measures: Instruction vs. selection research," *Amer. Psychologist*, 15: 435, 1960. (abstract)
6. Lindquist, E. F. "Preliminary considerations in objective test construction." In E. F. Lindquist (ed.), *Educational Measurement*. Washington, D. C.: American Council on Education, 1951. Pp. 119–158.

Index